INTELLECTUAL PROPERTY: COPYRIGHT, TRADEMARK & PATENT

Statutory Supplement

Professor Ariel Katz
Faculty of Law
University of Toronto

Fall 2017

Table of Contents

Act		Page
Copyright Act		5
Patent Act		193
Trade-marks Act		327
An Act respecting Certain Rights and Liberties of the People		451
Statute of Monopolies		453

This statutory supplement was prepared pursuant to the Reproduction of Federal Law Order SI/97-5, see http://laws-lois.justice.gc.ca/eng/regulations/SI-97-5/

CANADA

CONSOLIDATION

Copyright Act

R.S.C., 1985, c. C-42

CODIFICATION

Loi sur le droit d'auteur

L.R.C. (1985), ch. C-42

Current to August 14, 2017

Last amended on June 19, 2017

À jour au 14 août 2017

Dernière modification le 19 juin 2017

Published by the Minister of Justice at the following address:
http://laws-lois.justice.gc.ca

Publié par le ministre de la Justice à l'adresse suivante :
http://lois-laws.justice.gc.ca

OFFICIAL STATUS OF CONSOLIDATIONS

Subsections 31(1) and (2) of the *Legislation Revision and Consolidation Act*, in force on June 1, 2009, provide as follows:

Published consolidation is evidence
31 (1) Every copy of a consolidated statute or consolidated regulation published by the Minister under this Act in either print or electronic form is evidence of that statute or regulation and of its contents and every copy purporting to be published by the Minister is deemed to be so published, unless the contrary is shown.

Inconsistencies in Acts
(2) In the event of an inconsistency between a consolidated statute published by the Minister under this Act and the original statute or a subsequent amendment as certified by the Clerk of the Parliaments under the *Publication of Statutes Act*, the original statute or amendment prevails to the extent of the inconsistency.

NOTE

This consolidation is current to August 14, 2017. The last amendments came into force on June 19, 2017. Any amendments that were not in force as of August 14, 2017 are set out at the end of this document under the heading "Amendments Not in Force".

CARACTÈRE OFFICIEL DES CODIFICATIONS

Les paragraphes 31(1) et (2) de la *Loi sur la révision et la codification des textes législatifs*, en vigueur le 1er juin 2009, prévoient ce qui suit :

Codifications comme élément de preuve
31 (1) Tout exemplaire d'une loi codifiée ou d'un règlement codifié, publié par le ministre en vertu de la présente loi sur support papier ou sur support électronique, fait foi de cette loi ou de ce règlement et de son contenu. Tout exemplaire donné comme publié par le ministre est réputé avoir été ainsi publié, sauf preuve contraire.

Incompatibilité — lois
(2) Les dispositions de la loi d'origine avec ses modifications subséquentes par le greffier des Parlements en vertu de la *Loi sur la publication des lois* l'emportent sur les dispositions incompatibles de la loi codifiée publiée par le ministre en vertu de la présente loi.

NOTE

Cette codification est à jour au 14 août 2017. Les dernières modifications sont entrées en vigueur le 19 juin 2017. Toutes modifications qui n'étaient pas en vigueur au 14 août 2017 sont énoncées à la fin de ce document sous le titre « Modifications non en vigueur ».

TABLE OF PROVISIONS

An Act respecting copyright

Short Title

1	Short title

Interpretation

2	Definitions
2.1	Compilations
2.11	Definition of maker
2.2	Definition of publication
2.3	Telecommunication
2.4	Communication to the public by telecommunication
2.5	What constitutes rental
2.6	Exclusive distributor
2.7	Exclusive licence

PART I
Copyright and Moral Rights in Works

Copyright

3	Copyright in works

Works in which Copyright may Subsist

5	Conditions for subsistence of copyright

Term of Copyright

6	Term of copyright
6.1	Anonymous and pseudonymous works
6.2	Anonymous and pseudonymous works of joint authorship
7	Term of copyright in posthumous works
9	Cases of joint authorship
11.1	Cinematographic works
12	Where copyright belongs to Her Majesty

Ownership of Copyright

13	Ownership of copyright

TABLE ANALYTIQUE

Loi concernant le droit d'auteur

Titre abrégé

1	Titre abrégé

Définitions et dispositions interprétatives

2	Définitions
2.1	Compilations
2.11	Définition de producteur
2.2	Définition de publication
2.3	Télécommunication
2.4	Communication au public par télécommunication
2.5	Location
2.6	Distributeur exclusif
2.7	Licence exclusive

PARTIE I
Droit d'auteur et droits moraux sur les oeuvres

Droit d'auteur

3	Droit d'auteur sur l'oeuvre

Oeuvres susceptibles de faire l'objet d'un droit d'auteur

5	Conditions d'obtention du droit d'auteur

Durée du droit d'auteur

6	Durée du droit d'auteur
6.1	Oeuvres anonymes et pseudonymes
6.2	Oeuvres anonymes et pseudonymes de collaboration
7	Durée du droit d'auteur sur les oeuvres posthumes
9	Oeuvres créées en collaboration
11.1	Oeuvre cinématographique
12	Quand le droit d'auteur appartient à Sa Majesté

Possession du droit d'auteur

13	Possession du droit d'auteur

14	Limitation where author is first owner of copyright	14	Limitation dans le cas où l'auteur est le premier possesseur du droit d'auteur

Moral Rights / Droits moraux

14.1	Moral rights	14.1	Droits moraux
14.2	Term	14.2	Durée

PART II / PARTIE II

Copyright in Performers' Performances, Sound Recordings and Communication Signals and Moral Rights in Performers' Performances

Droit d'auteur sur les prestations, enregistrements sonores et signaux de communication et droits moraux sur les prestations

Performers' Rights / Droits de l'artiste-interprète

Copyright / Droit d'auteur

15	Copyright in performer's performance	15	Droit d'auteur sur la prestation
16	Contractual arrangements	16	Modalités contractuelles
17	Cinematographic works	17	Oeuvre cinématographique

Moral Rights / Droits moraux

17.1	Moral rights	17.1	Droits moraux
17.2	Application and term	17.2	Application et durée

Rights of Sound Recording Makers / Droits du producteur d'enregistrement sonore

18	Copyright in sound recordings	18	Droit d'auteur sur l'enregistrement sonore

Provisions Applicable to both Performers and Sound Recording Makers / Dispositions communes aux artistes-interprètes et aux producteurs d'enregistrements sonores

19	Right to remuneration — Canada	19	Droit à rémunération : Canada
19.1	Deemed publication — Canada	19.1	Assimilation : Canada
19.2	Deemed publication — WPPT country	19.2	Assimilation : pays partie au traité de l'OIEP
20	Conditions — Canada	20	Conditions : Canada

Rights of Broadcasters / Droits des radiodiffuseurs

21	Copyright in communication signals	21	Droit d'auteur sur le signal de communication

Reciprocity / Réciprocité

22	Reciprocity	22	Réciprocité

Term of Rights / Durée des droits

23	Term of copyright — performer's performance	23	Durée des droits : prestation

Ownership of Copyright / Titularité

24	Ownership of copyright	24	Titularité
25	Assignment of rights	25	Cession

Performers' Rights — WTO Countries / Droits des artistes-interprètes — pays OMC

26	Performer's performance in WTO country	26	Prestation dans un pays membre de l'OMC

PART III

Infringement of Copyright and Moral Rights and Exceptions to Infringement

Infringement of Copyright

General

- 27 Infringement generally

Parallel Importation of Books

- 27.1 Importation of books

Moral Rights Infringement

- 28.1 Infringement generally
- 28.2 Nature of right of integrity

Exceptions

Fair Dealing

- 29 Research, private study, etc.
- 29.1 Criticism or review
- 29.2 News reporting

Non-commercial User-generated Content

- 29.21 Non-commercial user-generated content

Reproduction for Private Purposes

- 29.22 Reproduction for private purposes

Fixing Signals and Recording Programs for Later Listening or Viewing

- 29.23 Reproduction for later listening or viewing

Backup Copies

- 29.24 Backup copies

Acts Undertaken without Motive of Gain

- 29.3 Motive of gain

Educational Institutions

- 29.4 Reproduction for instruction
- 29.5 Performances
- 29.6 News and commentary
- 29.7 Reproduction of broadcast
- 29.8 Unlawful reception
- 29.9 Records and marking
- 30 Literary collections

30.01	Meaning of lesson	30.01	Définition de leçon
30.02	Exception — digital reproduction of works	30.02	Exception : reproduction numérique d'oeuvres
30.03	Royalties — digital reproduction agreement	30.03	Accord de reproduction numérique
30.04	Work available through Internet	30.04	Oeuvre sur Internet

Libraries, Archives and Museums / Bibliothèques, musées ou services d'archives

30.1	Management and maintenance of collection	30.1	Gestion et conservation de collections
30.2	Research or private study	30.2	Étude privée ou recherche
30.21	Copying works deposited in archive	30.21	Copie d'une oeuvre déposée dans un service d'archives

Machines Installed in Educational Institutions, Libraries, Archives and Museums / Disposition commune aux établissements d'enseignement, bibliothèques, musées ou services d'archives

30.3	No infringement by educational institution, etc.	30.3	Reprographie

Libraries, Archives and Museums in Educational Institutions / Bibliothèques, musées ou services d'archives faisant partie d'un établissement d'enseignement

30.4	Application to libraries, etc. within educational institutions	30.4	Précision

Library and Archives of Canada / Bibliothèque et Archives du Canada

30.5	Permitted acts	30.5	Actes licites

Computer Programs / Programmes d'ordinateur

30.6	Permitted acts	30.6	Actes licites
30.61	Interoperability of computer programs	30.61	Interopérabilité

Encryption Research / Recherche sur le chiffrement

30.62	Encryption research	30.62	Recherche sur le chiffrement

Security / Sécurité

30.63	Security	30.63	Sécurité

Incidental Inclusion / Incorporation incidente

30.7	Incidental use	30.7	Incorporation incidente

Temporary Reproductions for Technological Processes / Reproductions temporaires pour processus technologiques

30.71	Temporary reproductions	30.71	Reproductions temporaires

Ephemeral Recordings / Enregistrements éphémères

30.8	Ephemeral recordings	30.8	Enregistrements éphémères : entreprise de programmation
30.9	Ephemeral recordings — broadcasting undertaking	30.9	Enregistrements éphémères : entreprise de radiodiffusion

Retransmission / Retransmission

31	Interpretation	31	Définitions

Network Services / Services réseau

31.1	Network services	31.1	Services réseau

Persons with Perceptual Disabilities

32	Reproduction in alternate format
32.01	Print disability — outside Canada
32.02	Definition of non-profit organization

Statutory Obligations

32.1	No infringement

Miscellaneous

32.2	Permitted acts

Interpretation

32.3	No right to equitable remuneration

Compensation for Acts Done Before Recognition of Copyright of Performers and Broadcasters

32.4	Certain rights and interests protected
32.5	Certain rights and interests protected
32.6	Certain rights and interests protected

Compensation for Acts Done Before Recognition of Copyright or Moral Rights

33	Certain rights and interests protected
33.1	Certain rights and interests protected
33.2	Certain rights and interests protected

PART IV
Remedies

Civil Remedies

Infringement of Copyright and Moral Rights

34	Copyright
34.1	Presumptions respecting copyright and ownership
35	Liability for infringement
38	Recovery of possession of copies, plates
38.1	Statutory damages
38.2	Maximum amount that may be recovered
39	Injunction only remedy when defendant not aware of copyright
39.1	Wide injunction
40	No injunction in case of a building

Technological Protection Measures and Rights Management Information

41	Definitions
41.1	Prohibition
41.11	Law enforcement and national security
41.12	Interoperability of computer programs
41.13	Encryption research
41.14	Personal information
41.15	Security
41.16	Persons with perceptual disabilities
41.17	Broadcasting undertakings
41.18	Radio apparatus
41.19	Reduction of damages
41.2	Injunction only remedy
41.21	Regulations
41.22	Prohibition — rights management information

General Provisions

41.23	Protection of separate rights
41.24	Concurrent jurisdiction of Federal Court

Provisions Respecting Providers of Network Services or Information Location Tools

41.25	Notice of claimed infringement
41.26	Obligations related to notice
41.27	Injunctive relief only — providers of information location tools

Criminal Remedies

42	Offences
43	Infringement in case of dramatic, operatic or musical work

Limitation or Prescription Period

43.1	Limitation or prescription period for civil remedies

Importation and Exportation

Interpretation

44	Definitions

Prohibition and Detention by Customs Officer

Prohibition

44.01	Prohibition on importation or exportation

Request for Assistance

44.02	Request for assistance

	Measures Relating to Detained Copies		Mesures relatives aux exemplaires retenus
44.03	Provision of information by customs officer	44.03	Fourniture de renseignements par l'agent des douanes
44.04	Provision of information to pursue remedy	44.04	Fourniture de renseignements en vue de l'exercice de recours
44.05	Restriction on information use — section 44.03	44.05	Utilisation des renseignements fournis au titre de l'article 44.03
44.06	Inspection	44.06	Inspection
44.07	Liability for charges	44.07	Obligation de payer les frais
	No Liability		Immunité
44.08	No liability	44.08	Immunité
	Powers of Court Relating to Detained Copies		Pouvoirs du tribunal relativement aux exemplaires retenus
44.09	Application to court	44.09	Demande au tribunal
44.1	Damages against copyright owner	44.1	Dommages-intérêts à l'encontre du titulaire du droit d'auteur
	Prohibition Resulting from Notice		Interdiction d'importation sur notification
44.11	Importation of certain copyright works prohibited	44.11	Interdiction : certains exemplaires
	Court-ordered Detention		Ordonnance judiciaire de rétention
44.12	Power of court	44.12	Pouvoir du tribunal
44.2	Importation of books	44.2	Importation de livres
44.3	Limitation	44.3	Restriction
44.4	Importation of other subject-matter	44.4	Application aux autres objets du droit d'auteur
45	Exceptions	45	Importations autorisées

PART V
Administration
Copyright Office

PARTIE V
Administration
Bureau du droit d'auteur

46	Copyright Office	46	Bureau du droit d'auteur
47	Powers of Commissioner and Registrar	47	Pouvoirs du commissaire et du registraire
48	Registrar	48	Registraire
49	Register of Copyrights, certificates and certified copies	49	Inscription, certificat et copie
50	Other duties of Registrar	50	Autres attributions du registraire
52	Control of business and officials	52	Direction des affaires et fonctionnaires
53	Register to be evidence	53	Preuve

Registration
Enregistrement

54	Register of Copyrights	54	Registre des droits d'auteur
55	Copyright in works	55	Oeuvres
56	Copyright in subject-matter other than works	56	Autres objets du droit d'auteur
56.1	Recovery of damages	56.1	Recouvrement
57	Registration of assignment or licence	57	Enregistrement d'une cession ou d'une licence

58	Execution of instruments	58	Exécution de la cession ou de la concession

Fees / Taxes

59	Fees regulations	59	Règlement fixant les taxes

PART VI
Miscellaneous Provisions

PARTIE VI
Divers

Substituted Right / Droits substitués

60	Subsistence of substituted right	60	Droits substitués

Clerical Errors / Erreurs matérielles

61	Clerical errors do not invalidate	61	Les erreurs d'écriture n'entraînent pas l'invalidation

Regulations / Règlements

62	Regulations	62	Règlements

Industrial Designs and Topographies / Dessins industriels et topographies

64	Interpretation	64	Définitions
64.1	Non-infringement re useful article features	64.1	Non-violation : caractéristiques d'objets utilitaires
64.2	Application of Act to topographies	64.2	Application de la loi aux topographies

PART VII
Copyright Board and Collective Administration of Copyright

PARTIE VII
Commission du droit d'auteur et gestion collective

Copyright Board / Commission du droit d'auteur

66	Establishment	66	Constitution
66.1	Duties of chairman	66.1	Rôle du président
66.2	Remuneration and expenses	66.2	Rémunération
66.3	Conflict of interest prohibited	66.3	Conflits d'intérêt
66.4	Staff	66.4	Personnel
66.5	Concluding matters after membership expires	66.5	Prolongation
66.51	Interim decisions	66.51	Décisions provisoires
66.52	Variation of decisions	66.52	Modifications de décisions
66.6	Regulations	66.6	Règlement
66.7	General powers, etc.	66.7	Attributions générales
66.71	Distribution, publication of notices	66.71	Publication d'avis
66.8	Studies	66.8	Études
66.9	Report	66.9	Rapport
66.91	Regulations	66.91	Règlements

Collective Administration of Performing Rights and of Communication Rights / Gestion collective du droit d'exécution et de communication

67	Public access to repertoires	67	Demandes de renseignements
67.1	Filing of proposed tariffs	67.1	Dépôt d'un projet de tarif

68	Board to consider proposed tariffs and objections		68	Examen du projet de tarif
68.1	Special and transitional royalty rates		68.1	Tarifs spéciaux et transitoires
68.2	Effect of fixing royalties		68.2	Portée de l'homologation

Public Performances in Places Other Than Theatres

Collective Administration in Relation to Rights under Sections 3, 15, 18 and 21

Collective Societies

Exécutions en public ailleurs qu'au théâtre

Gestion collective relative aux droits visés aux articles 3, 15, 18 et 21

Sociétés de gestion

70.1	Collective societies		70.1	Sociétés de gestion
70.11	Public information		70.11	Demandes de renseignements
70.12	Tariff or agreement		70.12	Projets de tarif ou ententes

Tariffs

Projets de tarif

70.13	Filing of proposed tariffs		70.13	Dépôt d'un projet de tarif
70.14	Application of certain provisions		70.14	Application de certaines dispositions
70.15	Certification		70.15	Homologation
70.16	Distribution, publication of notices		70.16	Publication d'avis
70.17	Prohibition of enforcement		70.17	Interdiction des recours
70.18	Continuation of rights		70.18	Maintien des droits
70.19	Where agreement exists		70.19	Non-application des articles 70.17 et 70.18
70.191	Agreement		70.191	Entente

Fixing of Royalties in Individual Cases

Fixation des redevances dans des cas particuliers

70.2	Application to fix amount of royalty, etc.		70.2	Demande de fixation de redevances
70.3	Agreement		70.3	Entente préjudicielle
70.4	Effect of Board decision		70.4	Portée de la fixation

Examination of Agreements

Examen des ententes

70.5	Definition of Commissioner		70.5	Définition de commissaire
70.6	Examination and fixing of royalty		70.6	Examen et fixation

Royalties in Particular Cases

Redevances pour les cas particuliers

71	Filing of proposed tariffs		71	Dépôt d'un projet de tarif
72	Publication of proposed tariffs		72	Publication du projet de tarif
73	Certification		73	Mesures à prendre
74	Special case		74	Cas spéciaux
75	Effect of fixing royalties		75	Portée de la fixation
76	Claims by non-members		76	Réclamations des non-membres dans les cas de retransmission

Owners Who Cannot be Located

Titulaires introuvables

77	Circumstances in which licence may be issued by Board		77	Délivrance d'une licence

Compensation for Acts Done Before Recognition of Copyright or Moral Rights

78 Board may determine compensation

PART VIII
Private Copying

Interpretation
79 Definitions

Copying for Private Use
80 Where no infringement of copyright

Right of Remuneration
81 Right of remuneration

Levy on Blank Audio Recording Media
82 Liability to pay levy
83 Filing of proposed tariffs

Distribution of Levies Paid
84 Distribution by collecting body
85 Reciprocity

Exemption from Levy
86 Where no levy payable

Regulations
87 Regulations

Civil Remedies
88 Right of recovery

PART IX
General Provisions

89 No copyright, etc., except by statute
90 Interpretation
91 Adherence to Berne and Rome Conventions
92 Review of Act

SCHEDULE I
Existing Rights

SCHEDULE II

SCHEDULE III

R.S.C., 1985, c. C-42

An Act respecting copyright

Short Title

Short title

1 This Act may be cited as the *Copyright Act*.
R.S., c. C-30, s. 1.

Interpretation

Definitions

2 In this Act,

architectural work means any building or structure or any model of a building or structure; (*œuvre architecturale*)

architectural work of art [Repealed, 1993, c. 44, s. 53]

artistic work includes paintings, drawings, maps, charts, plans, photographs, engravings, sculptures, works of artistic craftsmanship, architectural works, and compilations of artistic works; (*œuvre artistique*)

Berne Convention country means a country that is a party to the Convention for the Protection of Literary and Artistic Works concluded at Berne on September 9, 1886, or any one of its revisions, including the Paris Act of 1971; (*pays partie à la Convention de Berne*)

Board means the Copyright Board established by subsection 66(1); (*Commission*)

book means a volume or a part or division of a volume, in printed form, but does not include

(a) a pamphlet,

(b) a newspaper, review, magazine or other periodical,

L.R.C., 1985, ch. C-42

Loi concernant le droit d'auteur

Titre abrégé

Titre abrégé

1 *Loi sur le droit d'auteur*.
S.R., ch. C-30, art. 1.

Définitions et dispositions interprétatives

Définitions

2 Les définitions qui suivent s'appliquent à la présente loi.

accessible sur le marché S'entend, en ce qui concerne une œuvre ou de tout autre objet du droit d'auteur

a) qu'il est possible de se procurer, au Canada, à un prix et dans un délai raisonnables, et de trouver moyennant des efforts raisonnables;

b) pour lequel il est possible d'obtenir, à un prix et dans un délai raisonnables et moyennant des efforts raisonnables, une licence octroyée par une société de gestion pour la reproduction, l'exécution en public ou la communication au public par télécommunication, selon le cas. (*commercially available*)

appareil récepteur [Abrogée, 1993, ch. 44, art. 79]

artiste interprète [Abrogée, 1997, ch. 24, art. 1]

artiste-interprète Tout artiste-interprète ou exécutant. (*French version only*)

bibliothèque, musée ou service d'archives S'entend :

a) d'un établissement doté ou non de la personnalité morale qui :

(c) a map, chart, plan or sheet music where the map, chart, plan or sheet music is separately published, and

(d) an instruction or repair manual that accompanies a product or that is supplied as an accessory to a service; (*livre*)

broadcaster means a body that, in the course of operating a broadcasting undertaking, broadcasts a communication signal in accordance with the law of the country in which the broadcasting undertaking is carried on, but excludes a body whose primary activity in relation to communication signals is their retransmission; (*radiodiffuseur*)

choreographic work includes any work of choreography, whether or not it has any story line; (*œuvre chorégraphique*)

cinematograph [Repealed, 1997, c. 24, s. 1]

cinematographic work includes any work expressed by any process analogous to cinematography, whether or not accompanied by a soundtrack; (*œuvre cinématographique*)

collective society means a society, association or corporation that carries on the business of collective administration of copyright or of the remuneration right conferred by section 19 or 81 for the benefit of those who, by assignment, grant of licence, appointment of it as their agent or otherwise, authorize it to act on their behalf in relation to that collective administration, and

(a) operates a licensing scheme, applicable in relation to a repertoire of works, performer's performances, sound recordings or communication signals of more than one author, performer, sound recording maker or broadcaster, pursuant to which the society, association or corporation sets out classes of uses that it agrees to authorize under this Act, and the royalties and terms and conditions on which it agrees to authorize those classes of uses, or

(b) carries on the business of collecting and distributing royalties or levies payable pursuant to this Act; (*société de gestion*)

collective work means

(a) an encyclopaedia, dictionary, year book or similar work,

(b) a newspaper, review, magazine or similar periodical, and

(i) d'une part, n'est pas constitué ou administré pour réaliser des profits, ni ne fait partie d'un organisme constitué ou administré pour réaliser des profits, ni n'est administré ou contrôlé directement ou indirectement par un tel organisme,

(ii) d'autre part, rassemble et gère des collections de documents ou d'objets qui sont accessibles au public ou aux chercheurs;

b) de tout autre établissement à but non lucratif visé par règlement. (*library, archive or museum*)

Commission La Commission du droit d'auteur constituée au titre du paragraphe 66(1). (*Board*)

compilation Les œuvres résultant du choix ou de l'arrangement de tout ou partie d'œuvres littéraires, dramatiques, musicales ou artistiques ou de données. (*compilation*)

conférence Sont assimilés à une conférence les allocutions, discours et sermons. (*lecture*)

contrefaçon

a) À l'égard d'une œuvre sur laquelle existe un droit d'auteur, toute reproduction, y compris l'imitation déguisée, qui a été faite contrairement à la présente loi ou qui a fait l'objet d'un acte contraire à la présente loi;

b) à l'égard d'une prestation sur laquelle existe un droit d'auteur, toute fixation ou reproduction de celle-ci qui a été faite contrairement à la présente loi ou qui a fait l'objet d'un acte contraire à la présente loi;

c) à l'égard d'un enregistrement sonore sur lequel existe un droit d'auteur, toute reproduction de celle-ci qui a été faite contrairement à la présente loi ou qui a fait l'objet d'un acte contraire à la présente loi;

d) à l'égard d'un signal de communication sur lequel existe un droit d'auteur, toute fixation ou reproduction de la fixation qui a été faite contrairement à la présente loi ou qui a fait l'objet d'un acte contraire à la présente loi.

La présente définition exclut la reproduction — autre que celle visée par l'alinéa 27(2)e) et l'article 27.1 — faite avec le consentement du titulaire du droit d'auteur dans le pays de production. (*infringing*)

débit [Abrogée, 1997, ch. 24, art. 1]

(c) any work written in distinct parts by different authors, or in which works or parts of works of different authors are incorporated; (*recueil*)

commercially available means, in relation to a work or other subject-matter,

(a) available on the Canadian market within a reasonable time and for a reasonable price and may be located with reasonable effort, or

(b) for which a licence to reproduce, perform in public or communicate to the public by telecommunication is available from a collective society within a reasonable time and for a reasonable price and may be located with reasonable effort; (*accessible sur le marché*)

communication signal means radio waves transmitted through space without any artificial guide, for reception by the public; (*signal de communication*)

compilation means

(a) a work resulting from the selection or arrangement of literary, dramatic, musical or artistic works or of parts thereof, or

(b) a work resulting from the selection or arrangement of data; (*compilation*)

computer program means a set of instructions or statements, expressed, fixed, embodied or stored in any manner, that is to be used directly or indirectly in a computer in order to bring about a specific result; (*programme d'ordinateur*)

copyright means the rights described in

(a) section 3, in the case of a work,

(b) sections 15 and 26, in the case of a performer's performance,

(c) section 18, in the case of a sound recording, or

(d) section 21, in the case of a communication signal; (*droit d'auteur*)

country includes any territory; (*pays*)

defendant includes a respondent to an application; (*Version anglaise seulement*)

delivery [Repealed, 1997, c. 24, s. 1]

dramatic work includes

déficience perceptuelle Déficience qui empêche la lecture ou l'écoute d'une œuvre littéraire, dramatique, musicale ou artistique sur le support original ou la rend difficile, en raison notamment :

a) de la privation en tout ou en grande partie du sens de l'ouïe ou de la vue ou de l'incapacité d'orienter le regard;

b) de l'incapacité de tenir ou de manipuler un livre;

c) d'une insuffisance relative à la compréhension. (*perceptual disability*)

distributeur exclusif S'entend, en ce qui concerne un livre, de toute personne qui remplit les conditions suivantes :

a) le titulaire du droit d'auteur sur le livre au Canada ou le titulaire d'une licence exclusive au Canada s'y rapportant lui a accordé, avant ou après l'entrée en vigueur de la présente définition, par écrit, la qualité d'unique distributeur pour tout ou partie du Canada ou d'unique distributeur pour un secteur du marché pour tout ou partie du Canada;

b) elle répond aux critères fixés par règlement pris en vertu de l'article 2.6.

Il est entendu qu'une personne ne peut être distributeur exclusif au sens de la présente définition si aucun règlement n'est pris en vertu de l'article 2.6. (*exclusive distributor*)

droit d'auteur S'entend du droit visé :

a) dans le cas d'une œuvre, à l'article 3;

b) dans le cas d'une prestation, aux articles 15 et 26;

c) dans le cas d'un enregistrement sonore, à l'article 18;

d) dans le cas d'un signal de communication, à l'article 21. (*copyright*)

droits moraux Les droits visés aux paragraphes 14.1(1) et 17.1(1). (*moral rights*)

enregistrement sonore Enregistrement constitué de sons provenant ou non de l'exécution d'une œuvre et fixés sur un support matériel quelconque; est exclue de la présente définition la bande sonore d'une œuvre cinématographique lorsqu'elle accompagne celle-ci. (*sound recording*)

établissement d'enseignement :

(a) any piece for recitation, choreographic work or mime, the scenic arrangement or acting form of which is fixed in writing or otherwise,

(b) any cinematographic work, and

(c) any compilation of dramatic works; (*œuvre dramatique*)

educational institution means

(a) a non-profit institution licensed or recognized by or under an Act of Parliament or the legislature of a province to provide pre-school, elementary, secondary or post-secondary education,

(b) a non-profit institution that is directed or controlled by a board of education regulated by or under an Act of the legislature of a province and that provides continuing, professional or vocational education or training,

(c) a department or agency of any order of government, or any non-profit body, that controls or supervises education or training referred to in paragraph (a) or (b), or

(d) any other non-profit institution prescribed by regulation; (*établissement d'enseignement*)

engravings includes etchings, lithographs, woodcuts, prints and other similar works, not being photographs; (*gravure*)

every original literary, dramatic, musical and artistic work includes every original production in the literary, scientific or artistic domain, whatever may be the mode or form of its expression, such as compilations, books, pamphlets and other writings, lectures, dramatic or dramatico-musical works, musical works, translations, illustrations, sketches and plastic works relative to geography, topography, architecture or science; (*toute œuvre littéraire, dramatique, musicale ou artistique originale*)

exclusive distributor means, in relation to a book, a person who

(a) has, before or after the coming into force of this definition, been appointed in writing, by the owner or exclusive licensee of the copyright in the book in Canada, as

(i) the only distributor of the book in Canada or any part of Canada, or

a) Établissement sans but lucratif agréé aux termes des lois fédérales ou provinciales pour dispenser de l'enseignement aux niveaux préscolaire, élémentaire, secondaire ou postsecondaire, ou reconnu comme tel;

b) établissement sans but lucratif placé sous l'autorité d'un conseil scolaire régi par une loi provinciale et qui dispense des cours d'éducation ou de formation permanente, technique ou professionnelle;

c) ministère ou organisme, quel que soit l'ordre de gouvernement, ou entité sans but lucratif qui exerce une autorité sur l'enseignement et la formation visés aux alinéas a) et b);

d) tout autre établissement sans but lucratif visé par règlement. (*educational institution*)

gravure Sont assimilées à une gravure les gravures à l'eau-forte, les lithographies, les gravures sur bois, les estampes et autres œuvres similaires, à l'exclusion des photographies. (*engravings*)

livre Tout volume ou toute partie ou division d'un volume présentés sous forme imprimée, à l'exclusion :

a) des brochures;

b) des journaux, revues, magazines et autres périodiques;

c) des feuilles de musique, cartes, graphiques ou plans, s'ils sont publiés séparément;

d) des manuels d'instruction ou d'entretien qui accompagnent un produit ou sont fournis avec des services. (*book*)

locaux S'il s'agit d'un établissement d'enseignement, lieux où celui-ci dispense l'enseignement ou la formation visés à la définition de ce terme ou exerce son autorité sur eux. (*premises*)

membre de l'OMC Membre de l'Organisation mondiale du commerce au sens du paragraphe 2(1) de la *Loi de mise en œuvre de l'Accord sur l'Organisation mondiale du commerce*. (*WTO Member*)

ministre Sauf aux articles 44 à 44.12, le ministre de l'Industrie. (*Minister*)

œuvre Est assimilé à une œuvre le titre de l'œuvre lorsque celui-ci est original et distinctif. (*work*)

œuvre architecturale Tout bâtiment ou édifice ou tout modèle ou maquette de bâtiment ou d'édifice. (*architectural work*)

(ii) the only distributor of the book in Canada or any part of Canada in respect of a particular sector of the market, and

(b) meets the criteria established by regulations made under section 2.6,

and, for greater certainty, if there are no regulations made under section 2.6, then no person qualifies under this definition as an "exclusive distributor"; (*distributeur exclusif*)

Her Majesty's Realms and Territories [Repealed, 1997, c. 24, s. 1]

infringing means

(a) in relation to a work in which copyright subsists, any copy, including any colourable imitation, made or dealt with in contravention of this Act,

(b) in relation to a performer's performance in respect of which copyright subsists, any fixation or copy of a fixation of it made or dealt with in contravention of this Act,

(c) in relation to a sound recording in respect of which copyright subsists, any copy of it made or dealt with in contravention of this Act, or

(d) in relation to a communication signal in respect of which copyright subsists, any fixation or copy of a fixation of it made or dealt with in contravention of this Act.

The definition includes a copy that is imported in the circumstances set out in paragraph 27(2)(e) and section 27.1 but does not otherwise include a copy made with the consent of the owner of the copyright in the country where the copy was made; (*contrefaçon*)

lecture includes address, speech and sermon; (*conférence*)

legal representatives includes heirs, executors, administrators, successors and assigns, or agents or attorneys who are thereunto duly authorized in writing; (*représentants légaux*)

library, archive or museum means

(a) an institution, whether or not incorporated, that is not established or conducted for profit or that does not form a part of, or is not administered or directly or indirectly controlled by, a body that is established or conducted for profit, in which is held and maintained

œuvre artistique Sont compris parmi les œuvres artistiques les peintures, dessins, sculptures, œuvres architecturales, gravures ou photographies, les œuvres artistiques dues à des artisans ainsi que les graphiques, cartes, plans et compilations d'œuvres artistiques. (*artistic work*)

œuvre chorégraphique S'entend de toute chorégraphie, que l'œuvre ait ou non un sujet. (*choreographic work*)

œuvre cinématographique Y est assimilée toute œuvre exprimée par un procédé analogue à la cinématographie, qu'elle soit accompagnée ou non d'une bande sonore. (*cinematographic work*)

œuvre créée en collaboration Œuvre exécutée par la collaboration de deux ou plusieurs auteurs, et dans laquelle la part créée par l'un n'est pas distincte de celle créée par l'autre ou les autres. (*work of joint authorship*)

œuvre d'art architecturale [Abrogée, 1993, ch. 44, art. 53]

œuvre de sculpture [Abrogée, 1997, ch. 24, art. 1]

œuvre dramatique Y sont assimilées les pièces pouvant être récitées, les œuvres chorégraphiques ou les pantomimes dont l'arrangement scénique ou la mise en scène est fixé par écrit ou autrement, les œuvres cinématographiques et les compilations d'œuvres dramatiques. (*dramatic work*)

œuvre littéraire Y sont assimilés les tableaux, les programmes d'ordinateur et les compilations d'œuvres littéraires. (*literary work*)

œuvre musicale Toute œuvre ou toute composition musicale — avec ou sans paroles — et toute compilation de celles-ci. (*musical work*)

pays S'entend notamment d'un territoire. (*country*)

pays partie à la Convention de Berne Pays partie à la Convention pour la protection des œuvres littéraires et artistiques, conclue à Berne le 9 septembre 1886, ou à l'une de ses versions révisées, notamment celle de l'Acte de Paris de 1971. (*Berne Convention country*)

pays partie à la Convention de Rome Pays partie à la Convention internationale sur la protection des artistes interprètes ou exécutants, des producteurs d'enregistrements sonores et des organismes de radiodiffusion, conclue à Rome le 26 octobre 1961. (*Rome Convention country*)

a collection of documents and other materials that is open to the public or to researchers, or

(b) any other non-profit institution prescribed by regulation; (*bibliothèque, musée ou service d'archives*)

literary work includes tables, computer programs, and compilations of literary works; (*œuvre littéraire*)

maker means

(a) in relation to a cinematographic work, the person by whom the arrangements necessary for the making of the work are undertaken, or

(b) in relation to a sound recording, the person by whom the arrangements necessary for the first fixation of the sounds are undertaken; (*producteur*)

Minister, except in sections 44 to 44.12, means the Minister of Industry; (*ministre*)

moral rights means the rights described in subsections 14.1(1) and 17.1(1); (*droits moraux*)

musical work means any work of music or musical composition, with or without words, and includes any compilation thereof; (*œuvre musicale*)

perceptual disability means a disability that prevents or inhibits a person from reading or hearing a literary, musical, dramatic or artistic work in its original format, and includes such a disability resulting from

(a) severe or total impairment of sight or hearing or the inability to focus or move one's eyes,

(b) the inability to hold or manipulate a book, or

(c) an impairment relating to comprehension; (*déficience perceptuelle*)

performance means any acoustic or visual representation of a work, performer's performance, sound recording or communication signal, including a representation made by means of any mechanical instrument, radio receiving set or television receiving set; (*représentation* ou *exécution*)

performer's performance means any of the following when done by a performer:

(a) a performance of an artistic work, dramatic work or musical work, whether or not the work was previously fixed in any material form, and whether or not

pays partie à la Convention universelle Pays partie à la Convention universelle sur le droit d'auteur, adoptée à Genève (Suisse) le 6 septembre 1952, ou dans sa version révisée à Paris (France) le 24 juillet 1971. (*UCC country*)

pays partie au traité de l'ODA Pays partie au Traité de l'OMPI sur le droit d'auteur, adopté à Genève le 20 décembre 1996. (*WCT country*)

pays partie au traité de l'OIEP Pays partie au Traité de l'OMPI sur les interprétations et exécutions et les phonogrammes, adopté à Genève le 20 décembre 1996. (*WPPT country*)

pays signataire Pays partie à la Convention de Berne, à la Convention universelle ou au traité de l'ODA, ou membre de l'OMC. (*treaty country*)

photographie Y sont assimilées les photolithographies et toute œuvre exprimée par un procédé analogue à la photographie. (*photograph*)

planche Sont assimilés à une planche toute planche stéréotypée ou autre, pierre, matrice, transposition et épreuve négative, et tout moule ou cliché, destinés à l'impression ou à la reproduction d'exemplaires d'une œuvre, ainsi que toute matrice ou autre pièce destinées à la fabrication ou à la reproduction d'enregistrements sonores, de prestations ou de signaux de communication, selon le cas. (*plate*)

prestation Selon le cas, que l'œuvre soit encore protégée ou non et qu'elle soit déjà fixée sous une forme matérielle quelconque ou non :

a) l'exécution ou la représentation d'une œuvre artistique, dramatique ou musicale par un artiste-interprète;

b) la récitation ou la lecture d'une œuvre littéraire par celui-ci;

c) une improvisation dramatique, musicale ou littéraire par celui-ci, inspirée ou non d'une œuvre préexistante. (*performer's performance*)

producteur La personne qui effectue les opérations nécessaires à la confection d'une œuvre cinématographique, ou à la première fixation de sons dans le cas d'un enregistrement sonore. (*maker*)

programme d'ordinateur Ensemble d'instructions ou d'énoncés destiné, quelle que soit la façon dont ils sont exprimés, fixés, incorporés ou emmagasinés, à être utilisé directement ou indirectement dans un ordinateur en vue d'un résultat particulier. (*computer program*)

the work's term of copyright protection under this Act has expired,

(b) a recitation or reading of a literary work, whether or not the work's term of copyright protection under this Act has expired, or

(c) an improvisation of a dramatic work, musical work or literary work, whether or not the improvised work is based on a pre-existing work; (*prestation*)

photograph includes photo-lithograph and any work expressed by any process analogous to photography; (*photographie*)

plaintiff includes an applicant; (*Version anglaise seulement*)

plate includes

(a) any stereotype or other plate, stone, block, mould, matrix, transfer or negative used or intended to be used for printing or reproducing copies of any work, and

(b) any matrix or other appliance used or intended to be used for making or reproducing sound recordings, performer's performances or communication signals; (*planche*)

premises means, in relation to an educational institution, a place where education or training referred to in the definition "educational institution" is provided, controlled or supervised by the educational institution; (*locaux*)

receiving device [Repealed, 1993, c. 44, s. 79]

Rome Convention country means a country that is a party to the International Convention for the Protection of Performers, Producers of Phonograms and Broadcasting Organisations, done at Rome on October 26, 1961; (*pays partie à la Convention de Rome*)

sculpture includes a cast or model; (*sculpture*)

sound recording means a recording, fixed in any material form, consisting of sounds, whether or not of a performance of a work, but excludes any soundtrack of a cinematographic work where it accompanies the cinematographic work; (*enregistrement sonore*)

telecommunication means any transmission of signs, signals, writing, images or sounds or intelligence of any nature by wire, radio, visual, optical or other electromagnetic system; (*télécommunication*)

radiodiffuseur Organisme qui, dans le cadre de l'exploitation d'une entreprise de radiodiffusion, émet un signal de communication en conformité avec les lois du pays où il exploite cette entreprise; est exclu de la présente définition l'organisme dont l'activité principale, liée au signal de communication, est la retransmission de celui-ci. (*broadcaster*)

recueil

a) Les encyclopédies, dictionnaires, annuaires ou œuvres analogues;

b) les journaux, revues, magazines ou autres publications périodiques;

c) toute œuvre composée, en parties distinctes, par différents auteurs ou dans laquelle sont incorporées des œuvres ou parties d'œuvres d'auteurs différents. (*collective work*)

représentants légaux Sont compris parmi les représentants légaux les héritiers, exécuteurs testamentaires, administrateurs, successeurs et ayants droit, ou les agents ou fondés de pouvoir régulièrement constitués par mandat écrit. (*legal representatives*)

représentation, ***exécution*** ou ***audition*** [Abrogée, 1997, ch. 24, art. 1]

représentation ou ***exécution*** Toute exécution sonore ou toute représentation visuelle d'une œuvre, d'une prestation, d'un enregistrement sonore ou d'un signal de communication, selon le cas, y compris l'exécution ou la représentation à l'aide d'un instrument mécanique, d'un appareil récepteur de radio ou d'un appareil récepteur de télévision. (*performance*)

royaumes et territoires de Sa Majesté [Abrogée, 1997, ch. 24, art. 1]

sculpture Y sont assimilés les moules et les modèles. (*sculpture*)

signal de communication Ondes radioélectriques diffusées dans l'espace sans guide artificiel, aux fins de réception par le public. (*communication signal*)

société de gestion Association, société ou personne morale autorisée — notamment par voie de cession, licence ou mandat — à se livrer à la gestion collective du droit d'auteur ou du droit à rémunération conféré par les articles 19 ou 81 pour l'exercice des activités suivantes :

a) l'administration d'un système d'octroi de licences portant sur un répertoire d'œuvres, de prestations,

treaty country means a Berne Convention country, UCC country, WCT country or WTO Member; (*pays signataire*)

UCC country means a country that is a party to the Universal Copyright Convention, adopted on September 6, 1952 in Geneva, Switzerland, or to that Convention as revised in Paris, France on July 24, 1971; (*pays partie à la Convention universelle*)

WCT country means a country that is a party to the WIPO Copyright Treaty, adopted in Geneva on December 20, 1996; (*pays partie au traité de l'ODA*)

work includes the title thereof when such title is original and distinctive; (*œuvre*)

work of joint authorship means a work produced by the collaboration of two or more authors in which the contribution of one author is not distinct from the contribution of the other author or authors; (*œuvre créée en collaboration*)

work of sculpture [Repealed, 1997, c. 24, s. 1]

WPPT country means a country that is a party to the WIPO Performances and Phonograms Treaty, adopted in Geneva on December 20, 1996; (*pays partie au traité de l'OIEP*)

WTO Member means a Member of the World Trade Organization as defined in subsection 2(1) of the *World Trade Organization Agreement Implementation Act*. (*membre de l'OMC*)

R.S., 1985, c. C-42, s. 2; R.S., 1985, c. 10 (4th Supp.), s. 1; 1988, c. 65, s. 61; 1992, c. 1, s. 145(F); 1993, c. 23, s. 1, c. 44, ss. 53, 79; 1994, c. 47, s. 56; 1995, c. 1, s. 62; 1997, c. 24, s. 1; 2012, c. 20, s. 2; 2014, c. 32, s. 2.

Compilations

2.1 (1) A compilation containing two or more of the categories of literary, dramatic, musical or artistic works shall be deemed to be a compilation of the category making up the most substantial part of the compilation.

Idem

(2) The mere fact that a work is included in a compilation does not increase, decrease or otherwise affect the protection conferred by this Act in respect of the copyright in the work or the moral rights in respect of the work.

1993, c. 44, s. 54.

Definition of *maker*

2.11 For greater certainty, the arrangements referred to in paragraph (b) of the definition **maker** in section 2, as that term is used in section 19 and in the definition

d'enregistrements sonores ou de signaux de communication de plusieurs auteurs, artistes-interprètes, producteurs d'enregistrements sonores ou radiodiffuseurs et en vertu duquel elle établit les catégories d'utilisation qu'elle autorise au titre de la présente loi ainsi que les redevances et modalités afférentes;

b) la perception et la répartition des redevances payables aux termes de la présente loi. (*collective society*)

télécommunication Vise toute transmission de signes, signaux, écrits, images, sons ou renseignements de toute nature par fil, radio, procédé visuel ou optique, ou autre système électromagnétique. (*telecommunication*)

toute œuvre littéraire, dramatique, musicale ou artistique originale S'entend de toute production originale du domaine littéraire, scientifique ou artistique quels qu'en soient le mode ou la forme d'expression, tels les compilations, livres, brochures et autres écrits, les conférences, les œuvres dramatiques ou dramatico-musicales, les œuvres musicales, les traductions, les illustrations, les croquis et les ouvrages plastiques relatifs à la géographie, à la topographie, à l'architecture ou aux sciences. (*every original literary, dramatic, musical and artistic work*)

L.R. (1985), ch. C-42, art. 2; L.R. (1985), ch. 10 (4e suppl.), art. 1; 1988, ch. 65, art. 61; 1992, ch. 1, art. 145(F); 1993, ch. 23, art. 1, ch. 44, art. 53 et 79; 1994, ch. 47, art. 56; 1995, ch. 1, art. 62; 1997, ch. 24, art. 1; 2012, ch. 20, art. 2; 2014, ch. 32, art. 2.

Compilations

2.1 (1) La compilation d'œuvres de catégories diverses est réputée constituer une compilation de la catégorie représentant la partie la plus importante.

Idem

(2) L'incorporation d'une œuvre dans une compilation ne modifie pas la protection conférée par la présente loi à l'œuvre au titre du droit d'auteur ou des droits moraux.

1993, ch. 44, art. 54.

Définition de *producteur*

2.11 Il est entendu que pour l'application de l'article 19 et de la définition de **producteur admissible** à l'article 79, les opérations nécessaires visées à la définition de

eligible maker in section 79, include arrangements for entering into contracts with performers, financial arrangements and technical arrangements required for the first fixation of the sounds for a sound recording.

1997, c. 24, s. 2.

Definition of *publication*

2.2 (1) For the purposes of this Act, *publication* means

(a) in relation to works,

(i) making copies of a work available to the public,

(ii) the construction of an architectural work, and

(iii) the incorporation of an artistic work into an architectural work, and

(b) in relation to sound recordings, making copies of a sound recording available to the public,

but does not include

(c) the performance in public, or the communication to the public by telecommunication, of a literary, dramatic, musical or artistic work or a sound recording, or

(d) the exhibition in public of an artistic work.

Issue of photographs and engravings

(2) For the purpose of subsection (1), the issue of photographs and engravings of sculptures and architectural works is not deemed to be publication of those works.

Where no consent of copyright owner

(3) For the purposes of this Act, other than in respect of infringement of copyright, a work or other subject-matter is not deemed to be published or performed in public or communicated to the public by telecommunication if that act is done without the consent of the owner of the copyright.

Unpublished works

(4) Where, in the case of an unpublished work, the making of the work is extended over a considerable period, the conditions of this Act conferring copyright are deemed to have been complied with if the author was, during any substantial part of that period, a subject or citizen of, or a person ordinarily resident in, a country to which this Act extends.

1997, c. 24, s. 2.

Telecommunication

2.3 A person who communicates a work or other subject-matter to the public by telecommunication does not by that act alone perform it in public, nor by that act alone is deemed to authorize its performance in public.

1997, c. 24, s. 2.

Communication to the public by telecommunication

2.4 (1) For the purposes of communication to the public by telecommunication,

(a) persons who occupy apartments, hotel rooms or dwelling units situated in the same building are part of the public, and a communication intended to be received exclusively by such persons is a communication to the public;

(b) a person whose only act in respect of the communication of a work or other subject-matter to the public consists of providing the means of telecommunication necessary for another person to so communicate the work or other subject-matter does not communicate that work or other subject-matter to the public; and

(c) where a person, as part of

(i) a network, within the meaning of the *Broadcasting Act*, whose operations result in the communication of works or other subject-matter to the public, or

(ii) any programming undertaking whose operations result in the communication of works or other subject-matter to the public,

transmits by telecommunication a work or other subject-matter that is communicated to the public by another person who is not a retransmitter of a signal within the meaning of subsection 31(1), the transmission and communication of that work or other subject-matter by those persons constitute a single communication to the public for which those persons are jointly and severally liable.

Communication to the public by telecommunication

(1.1) For the purposes of this Act, communication of a work or other subject-matter to the public by telecommunication includes making it available to the public by telecommunication in a way that allows a member of the public to have access to it from a place and at a time individually chosen by that member of the public.

Regulations

(2) The Governor in Council may make regulations defining "programming undertaking" for the purpose of paragraph (1)(c).

Exception

(3) A work is not communicated in the manner described in paragraph (1)(c) or 3(1)(f) where a signal carrying the work is retransmitted to a person who is a retransmitter within the meaning of subsection 31(1).

1997, c. 24, s. 2; 2002, c. 26, s. 1; 2012, c. 20, s. 3.

What constitutes rental

2.5 (1) For the purposes of paragraphs 3(1)(h) and (i), 15(1)(c) and 18(1)(c), an arrangement, whatever its form, constitutes a rental of a computer program or sound recording if, and only if,

(a) it is in substance a rental, having regard to all the circumstances; and

(b) it is entered into with motive of gain in relation to the overall operations of the person who rents out the computer program or sound recording, as the case may be.

Motive of gain

(2) For the purpose of paragraph (1)(b), a person who rents out a computer program or sound recording with the intention of recovering no more than the costs, including overhead, associated with the rental operations does not by that act alone have a motive of gain in relation to the rental operations.

1997, c. 24, s. 2.

Exclusive distributor

2.6 The Governor in Council may make regulations establishing distribution criteria for the purpose of paragraph (b) of the definition "exclusive distributor" in section 2.

1997, c. 24, s. 2.

Exclusive licence

2.7 For the purposes of this Act, an exclusive licence is an authorization to do any act that is subject to copyright to the exclusion of all others including the copyright owner, whether the authorization is granted by the owner or an exclusive licensee claiming under the owner.

1997, c. 24, s. 2.

PART I

Copyright and Moral Rights in Works

Copyright

Copyright in works

3 (1) For the purposes of this Act, **copyright**, in relation to a work, means the sole right to produce or reproduce the work or any substantial part thereof in any material form whatever, to perform the work or any substantial part thereof in public or, if the work is unpublished, to publish the work or any substantial part thereof, and includes the sole right

(a) to produce, reproduce, perform or publish any translation of the work,

(b) in the case of a dramatic work, to convert it into a novel or other non-dramatic work,

(c) in the case of a novel or other non-dramatic work, or of an artistic work, to convert it into a dramatic work, by way of performance in public or otherwise,

(d) in the case of a literary, dramatic or musical work, to make any sound recording, cinematograph film or other contrivance by means of which the work may be mechanically reproduced or performed,

(e) in the case of any literary, dramatic, musical or artistic work, to reproduce, adapt and publicly present the work as a cinematographic work,

(f) in the case of any literary, dramatic, musical or artistic work, to communicate the work to the public by telecommunication,

(g) to present at a public exhibition, for a purpose other than sale or hire, an artistic work created after June 7, 1988, other than a map, chart or plan,

(h) in the case of a computer program that can be reproduced in the ordinary course of its use, other than by a reproduction during its execution in conjunction with a machine, device or computer, to rent out the computer program,

(i) in the case of a musical work, to rent out a sound recording in which the work is embodied, and

(j) in the case of a work that is in the form of a tangible object, to sell or otherwise transfer ownership of the tangible object, as long as that ownership has

PARTIE I

Droit d'auteur et droits moraux sur les œuvres

Droit d'auteur

Droit d'auteur sur l'œuvre

3 (1) Le droit d'auteur sur l'œuvre comporte le droit exclusif de produire ou reproduire la totalité ou une partie importante de l'œuvre, sous une forme matérielle quelconque, d'en exécuter ou d'en représenter la totalité ou une partie importante en public et, si l'œuvre n'est pas publiée, d'en publier la totalité ou une partie importante; ce droit comporte, en outre, le droit exclusif :

a) de produire, reproduire, représenter ou publier une traduction de l'œuvre;

b) s'il s'agit d'une œuvre dramatique, de la transformer en un roman ou en une autre œuvre non dramatique;

c) s'il s'agit d'un roman ou d'une autre œuvre non dramatique, ou d'une œuvre artistique, de transformer cette œuvre en une œuvre dramatique, par voie de représentation publique ou autrement;

d) s'il s'agit d'une œuvre littéraire, dramatique ou musicale, d'en faire un enregistrement sonore, film cinématographique ou autre support, à l'aide desquels l'œuvre peut être reproduite, représentée ou exécutée mécaniquement;

e) s'il s'agit d'une œuvre littéraire, dramatique, musicale ou artistique, de reproduire, d'adapter et de présenter publiquement l'œuvre en tant qu'œuvre cinématographique;

f) de communiquer au public, par télécommunication, une œuvre littéraire, dramatique, musicale ou artistique;

g) de présenter au public lors d'une exposition, à des fins autres que la vente ou la location, une œuvre artistique — autre qu'une carte géographique ou marine, un plan ou un graphique — créée après le 7 juin 1988;

h) de louer un programme d'ordinateur qui peut être reproduit dans le cadre normal de son utilisation, sauf la reproduction effectuée pendant son exécution avec un ordinateur ou autre machine ou appareil;

i) s'il s'agit d'une œuvre musicale, d'en louer tout enregistrement sonore;

never previously been transferred in or outside Canada with the authorization of the copyright owner,

and to authorize any such acts.

Simultaneous fixing

(1.1) A work that is communicated in the manner described in paragraph (1)(f) is fixed even if it is fixed simultaneously with its communication.

(1.2) to (4) [Repealed, 1997, c. 24, s. 3]

R.S., 1985, c. C-42, s. 3; R.S., 1985, c. 10 (4th Supp.), s. 2; 1988, c. 65, s. 62; 1993, c. 23, s. 2; c. 44, s. 55; 1997, c. 24, s. 3; 2012, c. 20, s. 4.

4 [Repealed, 1997, c. 24, s. 4]

Works in which Copyright may Subsist

Conditions for subsistence of copyright

5 (1) Subject to this Act, copyright shall subsist in Canada, for the term hereinafter mentioned, in every original literary, dramatic, musical and artistic work if any one of the following conditions is met:

(a) in the case of any work, whether published or unpublished, including a cinematographic work, the author was, at the date of the making of the work, a citizen or subject of, or a person ordinarily resident in, a treaty country;

(b) in the case of a cinematographic work, whether published or unpublished, the maker, at the date of the making of the cinematographic work,

(i) if a corporation, had its headquarters in a treaty country, or

(ii) if a natural person, was a citizen or subject of, or a person ordinarily resident in, a treaty country; or

(c) in the case of a published work, including a cinematographic work,

(i) in relation to subparagraph 2.2(1)(a)(i), the first publication in such a quantity as to satisfy the reasonable demands of the public, having regard to the nature of the work, occurred in a treaty country, or

j) s'il s'agit d'une œuvre sous forme d'un objet tangible, d'effectuer le transfert de propriété, notamment par vente, de l'objet, dans la mesure où la propriété de celui-ci n'a jamais été transférée au Canada ou à l'étranger avec l'autorisation du titulaire du droit d'auteur.

Est inclus dans la présente définition le droit exclusif d'autoriser ces actes.

Fixation

(1.1) Dans le cadre d'une communication effectuée au titre de l'alinéa (1)f), une œuvre est fixée même si sa fixation se fait au moment de sa communication.

(1.2) à (4) [Abrogés, 1997, ch. 24, art. 3]

L.R. (1985), ch. C-42, art. 3; L.R. (1985), ch. 10 (4ᵉ suppl.), art. 2; 1988, ch. 65, art. 62; 1993, ch. 23, art. 2, ch. 44, art. 55; 1997, ch. 24, art. 3; 2012, ch. 20, art. 4.

4 [Abrogé, 1997, ch. 24, art. 4]

Œuvres susceptibles de faire l'objet d'un droit d'auteur

Conditions d'obtention du droit d'auteur

5 (1) Sous réserve des autres dispositions de la présente loi, le droit d'auteur existe au Canada, pendant la durée mentionnée ci-après, sur toute œuvre littéraire, dramatique, musicale ou artistique originale si l'une des conditions suivantes est réalisée :

a) pour toute œuvre publiée ou non, y compris une œuvre cinématographique, l'auteur était, à la date de sa création, citoyen, sujet ou résident habituel d'un pays signataire;

b) dans le cas d'une œuvre cinématographique — publiée ou non —, à la date de sa création, le producteur était citoyen, sujet ou résident habituel d'un pays signataire ou avait son siège social dans un tel pays;

c) s'il s'agit d'une œuvre publiée, y compris une œuvre cinématographique, selon le cas :

(i) la mise à la disposition du public d'exemplaires de l'œuvre en quantité suffisante pour satisfaire la demande raisonnable du public, compte tenu de la nature de l'œuvre, a eu lieu pour la première fois dans un pays signataire,

(ii) l'édification d'une œuvre architecturale ou l'incorporation d'une œuvre artistique à celle-ci, a eu lieu pour la première fois dans un pays signataire.

(ii) in relation to subparagraph 2.2(1)(a)(ii) or (iii), the first publication occurred in a treaty country.

Protection for older works

(1.01) For the purposes of subsection (1), a country that becomes a Berne Convention country, a WCT country or a WTO Member after the date of the making or publication of a work is deemed to have been a Berne Convention country, a WCT country or a WTO Member, as the case may be, at that date, subject to subsection (1.02) and sections 33 to 33.2.

Limitation

(1.02) Subsection (1.01) does not confer copyright protection in Canada on a work whose term of copyright protection in the country referred to in that subsection had expired before that country became a Berne Convention country, a WCT country or a WTO Member, as the case may be.

Application of subsections (1.01) and (1.02)

(1.03) Subsections (1.01) and (1.02) apply, and are deemed to have applied, regardless of whether the country in question became a Berne Convention country, a WCT country or a WTO Member before or after the coming into force of those subsections.

First publication

(1.1) The first publication described in subparagraph (1)(c)(i) or (ii) is deemed to have occurred in a treaty country notwithstanding that it in fact occurred previously elsewhere, if the interval between those two publications did not exceed thirty days.

Idem

(1.2) Copyright shall not subsist in Canada otherwise than as provided by subsection (1), except in so far as the protection conferred by this Act is extended as hereinafter provided to foreign countries to which this Act does not extend.

Minister may extend copyright to other countries

(2) Where the Minister certifies by notice, published in the *Canada Gazette*, that any country that is not a treaty country grants or has undertaken to grant, either by treaty, convention, agreement or law, to citizens of Canada, the benefit of copyright on substantially the same basis as to its own citizens or copyright protection substantially equal to that conferred by this Act, the country shall, for the purpose of the rights conferred by this Act, be treated as if it were a country to which this Act extends, and the Minister may give a certificate, notwithstanding that the remedies for enforcing the rights, or the restrictions on the importation of copies of works, under the law of such country, differ from those in this Act.

(2.1) [Repealed, 1994, c. 47, s. 57]

(3) to (6) [Repealed, 1997, c. 24, s. 5]

Reciprocity protection preserved

(7) For greater certainty, the protection to which a work is entitled by virtue of a notice published under subsection (2), or under that subsection as it read at any time before the coming into force of this subsection, is not affected by reason only of the country in question becoming a treaty country.

R.S., 1985, c. C-42, s. 5; 1993, c. 15, s. 2, c. 44, s. 57; 1994, c. 47, s. 57; 1997, c. 24, s. 5; 2001, c. 34, s. 34; 2012, c. 20, s. 5.

Term of Copyright

Term of copyright

6 The term for which copyright shall subsist shall, except as otherwise expressly provided by this Act, be the life of the author, the remainder of the calendar year in which the author dies, and a period of fifty years following the end of that calendar year.

R.S., 1985, c. C-42, s. 6; 1993, c. 44, s. 58.

Anonymous and pseudonymous works

6.1 Except as provided in section 6.2, where the identity of the author of a work is unknown, copyright in the work shall subsist for whichever of the following terms ends earlier:

(a) a term consisting of the remainder of the calendar year of the first publication of the work and a period of fifty years following the end of that calendar year, and

(b) a term consisting of the remainder of the calendar year of the making of the work and a period of seventy-five years following the end of that calendar year,

but where, during that term, the author's identity becomes commonly known, the term provided in section 6 applies.

1993, c. 44, s. 58.

Anonymous and pseudonymous works of joint authorship

6.2 Where the identity of all the authors of a work of joint authorship is unknown, copyright in the work shall subsist for whichever of the following terms ends earlier:

(a) a term consisting of the remainder of the calendar year of the first publication of the work and a period of fifty years following the end of that calendar year, and

---

restrictions sur l'importation d'exemplaires des œuvres, aux termes de la loi de ce pays, diffèrent de ceux que prévoit la présente loi.

(2.1) [Abrogé, 1994, ch. 47, art. 57]

(3) à (6) [Abrogés, 1997, ch. 24, art. 5]

Protection du certificat

(7) Il est entendu que le fait, pour le pays visé, de devenir un pays signataire ne modifie en rien la protection conférée par l'avis publié conformément au paragraphe (2), en son état actuel ou en tout état antérieur à l'entrée en vigueur du présent paragraphe.

L.R. (1985), ch. C-42, art. 5; 1993, ch. 15, art. 2, ch. 44, art. 57; 1994, ch. 47, art. 57; 1997, ch. 24, art. 5; 2001, ch. 34, art. 34; 2012, ch. 20, art. 5.

Durée du droit d'auteur

Durée du droit d'auteur

6 Sauf disposition contraire expresse de la présente loi, le droit d'auteur subsiste pendant la vie de l'auteur, puis jusqu'à la fin de la cinquantième année suivant celle de son décès.

L.R. (1985), ch. C-42, art. 6; 1993, ch. 44, art. 58.

Œuvres anonymes et pseudonymes

6.1 Sous réserve de l'article 6.2, lorsque l'identité de l'auteur d'une œuvre n'est pas connue, le droit d'auteur subsiste jusqu'à celle de ces deux dates qui survient en premier :

a) soit la fin de la cinquantième année suivant celle de la première publication de l'œuvre;

b) soit la fin de la soixante-quinzième année suivant celle de la création de l'œuvre.

Toutefois, lorsque, durant cette période, l'identité de l'auteur devient généralement connue, c'est l'article 6 qui s'applique.

1993, ch. 44, art. 58.

Œuvres anonymes et pseudonymes de collaboration

6.2 Lorsque l'identité des coauteurs d'une œuvre créée en collaboration n'est pas connue, le droit d'auteur subsiste jusqu'à celle de ces deux dates qui survient en premier :

a) soit la fin de la cinquantième année suivant celle de la première publication de l'œuvre;

(b) a term consisting of the remainder of the calendar year of the making of the work and a period of seventy-five years following the end of that calendar year,

but where, during that term, the identity of one or more of the authors becomes commonly known, copyright shall subsist for the life of whichever of those authors dies last, the remainder of the calendar year in which that author dies, and a period of fifty years following the end of that calendar year.

1993, c. 44, s. 58.

Term of copyright in posthumous works

7 (1) Subject to subsection (2), in the case of a literary, dramatic or musical work, or an engraving, in which copyright subsists at the date of the death of the author or, in the case of a work of joint authorship, at or immediately before the date of the death of the author who dies last, but which has not been published or, in the case of a lecture or a dramatic or musical work, been performed in public or communicated to the public by telecommunication, before that date, copyright shall subsist until publication, or performance in public or communication to the public by telecommunication, whichever may first happen, for the remainder of the calendar year of the publication or of the performance in public or communication to the public by telecommunication, as the case may be, and for a period of fifty years following the end of that calendar year.

Application of subsection (1)

(2) Subsection (1) applies only where the work in question was published or performed in public or communicated to the public by telecommunication, as the case may be, before the coming into force of this section.

Transitional provision

(3) Where

(a) a work has not, at the coming into force of this section, been published or performed in public or communicated to the public by telecommunication,

(b) subsection (1) would apply to that work if it had been published or performed in public or communicated to the public by telecommunication before the coming into force of this section, and

(c) the relevant death referred to in subsection (1) occurred during the period of fifty years immediately before the coming into force of this section,

copyright shall subsist in the work for the remainder of the calendar year in which this section comes into force and for a period of fifty years following the end of that calendar year, whether or not the work is published or performed in public or communicated to the public by telecommunication after the coming into force of this section.

Transitional provision

(4) Where

(a) a work has not, at the coming into force of this section, been published or performed in public or communicated to the public by telecommunication,

(b) subsection (1) would apply to that work if it had been published or performed in public or communicated to the public by telecommunication before the coming into force of this section, and

(c) the relevant death referred to in subsection (1) occurred more than fifty years before the coming into force of this section,

copyright shall subsist in the work for the remainder of the calendar year in which this section comes into force and for a period of five years following the end of that calendar year, whether or not the work is published or performed in public or communicated to the public by telecommunication after the coming into force of this section.

R.S., 1985, c. C-42, s. 7; 1993, c. 44, s. 58; 1997, c. 24, s. 6.

8 [Repealed, 1993, c. 44, s. 59]

Cases of joint authorship

9 (1) In the case of a work of joint authorship, except as provided in section 6.2, copyright shall subsist during the life of the author who dies last, for the remainder of the calendar year of that author's death, and for a period of fifty years following the end of that calendar year, and references in this Act to the period after the expiration of any specified number of years from the end of the calendar year of the death of the author shall be construed as references to the period after the expiration of the like number of years from the end of the calendar year of the death of the author who dies last.

Nationals of other countries

(2) Authors who are nationals of any country, other than a country that is a party to the North American Free Trade Agreement, that grants a term of protection shorter than that mentioned in subsection (1) are not entitled to claim a longer term of protection in Canada.

R.S., 1985, c. C-42, s. 9; 1993, c. 44, s. 60.

10 [Repealed, 2012, c. 20, s. 6]

11 [Repealed, 1997, c. 24, s. 8]

Disposition transitoire

(4) L'œuvre, qu'elle soit ou non publiée, ou exécutée ou représentée en public ou communiquée au public par télécommunication après la date d'entrée en vigueur du présent article, continue d'être protégée par le droit d'auteur jusqu'à la fin de l'année de l'entrée en vigueur de cet article et pour une période de cinq ans par la suite, dans le cas où :

a) elle n'a pas été publiée, ou exécutée ou représentée en public ou communiquée au public par télécommunication à l'entrée en vigueur du présent article;

b) le paragraphe (1) s'y appliquerait si elle l'avait été;

c) le décès mentionné au paragraphe (1) est survenu plus de cinquante ans avant l'entrée en vigueur du présent article.

L.R. (1985), ch. C-42, art. 7; 1993, ch. 44, art. 58; 1997, ch. 24, art. 6.

8 [Abrogé, 1993, ch. 44, art. 59]

Œuvres créées en collaboration

9 (1) Sous réserve de l'article 6.2, lorsqu'il s'agit d'une œuvre créée en collaboration, le droit d'auteur subsiste pendant la vie du dernier survivant des coauteurs, puis jusqu'à la fin de la cinquantième année suivant celle de son décès. Toute mention dans la présente loi de la période qui suit l'expiration d'un nombre spécifié d'années après l'année de la mort de l'auteur doit s'interpréter comme une mention de la période qui suit l'expiration d'un nombre égal d'années après l'année du décès du dernier survivant des coauteurs.

Auteurs étrangers

(2) Les auteurs ressortissants d'un pays — autre qu'un pays partie à l'Accord de libre-échange nord-américain — qui accorde une durée de protection plus courte que celle qui est indiquée au paragraphe (1) ne sont pas admis à réclamer une plus longue durée de protection au Canada.

L.R. (1985), ch. C-42, art. 9; 1993, ch. 44, art. 60.

10 [Abrogé, 2012, ch. 20, art. 6]

11 [Abrogé, 1997, ch. 24, art. 8]

Cinematographic works

11.1 Except for cinematographic works in which the arrangement or acting form or the combination of incidents represented give the work a dramatic character, copyright in a cinematographic work or a compilation of cinematographic works shall subsist

(a) for the remainder of the calendar year of the first publication of the cinematographic work or of the compilation, and for a period of fifty years following the end of that calendar year; or

(b) if the cinematographic work or compilation is not published before the expiration of fifty years following the end of the calendar year of its making, for the remainder of that calendar year and for a period of fifty years following the end of that calendar year.

1993, c. 44, s. 60; 1997, c. 24, s. 9.

Where copyright belongs to Her Majesty

12 Without prejudice to any rights or privileges of the Crown, where any work is, or has been, prepared or published by or under the direction or control of Her Majesty or any government department, the copyright in the work shall, subject to any agreement with the author, belong to Her Majesty and in that case shall continue for the remainder of the calendar year of the first publication of the work and for a period of fifty years following the end of that calendar year.

R.S., 1985, c. C-42, s. 12; 1993, c. 44, s. 60.

Ownership of Copyright

Ownership of copyright

13 (1) Subject to this Act, the author of a work shall be the first owner of the copyright therein.

(2) [Repealed, 2012, c. 20, s. 7]

Work made in the course of employment

(3) Where the author of a work was in the employment of some other person under a contract of service or apprenticeship and the work was made in the course of his employment by that person, the person by whom the author was employed shall, in the absence of any agreement to the contrary, be the first owner of the copyright, but where the work is an article or other contribution to a newspaper, magazine or similar periodical, there shall, in the absence of any agreement to the contrary, be deemed to be reserved to the author a right to restrain the publication of the work, otherwise than as part of a newspaper, magazine or similar periodical.

Assignments and licences

(4) The owner of the copyright in any work may assign the right, either wholly or partially, and either generally or subject to limitations relating to territory, medium or sector of the market or other limitations relating to the scope of the assignment, and either for the whole term of the copyright or for any other part thereof, and may grant any interest in the right by licence, but no assignment or grant is valid unless it is in writing signed by the owner of the right in respect of which the assignment or grant is made, or by the owner's duly authorized agent.

Ownership in case of partial assignment

(5) Where, under any partial assignment of copyright, the assignee becomes entitled to any right comprised in copyright, the assignee, with respect to the rights so assigned, and the assignor, with respect to the rights not assigned, shall be treated for the purposes of this Act as the owner of the copyright, and this Act has effect accordingly.

Assignment of right of action

(6) For greater certainty, it is deemed always to have been the law that a right of action for infringement of copyright may be assigned in association with the assignment of the copyright or the grant of an interest in the copyright by licence.

Exclusive licence

(7) For greater certainty, it is deemed always to have been the law that a grant of an exclusive licence in a copyright constitutes the grant of an interest in the copyright by licence.

R.S., 1985, c. C-42, s. 13; 1997, c. 24, s. 10; 2012, c. 20, s. 7.

Limitation where author is first owner of copyright

14 (1) Where the author of a work is the first owner of the copyright therein, no assignment of the copyright and no grant of any interest therein, made by him, otherwise than by will, after June 4, 1921, is operative to vest in the assignee or grantee any rights with respect to the copyright in the work beyond the expiration of twenty-five years from the death of the author, and the reversionary interest in the copyright expectant on the termination of that period shall, on the death of the author, notwithstanding any agreement to the contrary, devolve on his legal representatives as part of the estate of the author, and any agreement entered into by the author as to the disposition of such reversionary interest is void.

Restriction

(2) Nothing in subsection (1) shall be construed as applying to the assignment of the copyright in a collective work or a licence to publish a work or part of a work as part of a collective work.

(3) [Repealed, 1997, c. 24, s. 11]

(4) [Repealed, R.S., 1985, c. 10 (4th Supp.), s. 3]

R.S., 1985, c. C-42, s. 14; R.S., 1985, c. 10 (4th Supp.), s. 3; 1997, c. 24, s. 11.

14.01 [Repealed, 1997, c. 24, s. 12]

Moral Rights

Moral rights

14.1 (1) The author of a work has, subject to section 28.2, the right to the integrity of the work and, in connection with an act mentioned in section 3, the right, where reasonable in the circumstances, to be associated with the work as its author by name or under a pseudonym and the right to remain anonymous.

No assignment of moral rights

(2) Moral rights may not be assigned but may be waived in whole or in part.

No waiver by assignment

(3) An assignment of copyright in a work does not by that act alone constitute a waiver of any moral rights.

Effect of waiver

(4) Where a waiver of any moral right is made in favour of an owner or a licensee of copyright, it may be invoked by any person authorized by the owner or licensee to use the work, unless there is an indication to the contrary in the waiver.

R.S., 1985, c. 10 (4th Supp.), s. 4.

Term

14.2 (1) Moral rights in respect of a work subsist for the same term as the copyright in the work.

Succession

(2) The moral rights in respect of a work pass, on the death of its author, to

   (a) the person to whom those rights are specifically bequeathed;

   (b) where there is no specific bequest of those moral rights and the author dies testate in respect of the copyright in the work, the person to whom that copyright is bequeathed; or

(c) where there is no person described in paragraph (a) or (b), the person entitled to any other property in respect of which the author dies intestate.

Subsequent succession

(3) Subsection (2) applies, with such modifications as the circumstances require, on the death of any person who holds moral rights.

R.S., 1985, c. 10 (4th Supp.), s. 4; 1997, c. 24, s. 13.

PART II

Copyright in Performers' Performances, Sound Recordings and Communication Signals and Moral Rights in Performers' Performances

Performers' Rights

Copyright

Copyright in performer's performance

15 (1) Subject to subsection (2), a performer has a copyright in the performer's performance, consisting of the sole right to do the following in relation to the performer's performance or any substantial part thereof:

(a) if it is not fixed,

(i) to communicate it to the public by telecommunication,

(ii) to perform it in public, where it is communicated to the public by telecommunication otherwise than by communication signal, and

(iii) to fix it in any material form,

(b) if it is fixed,

(i) to reproduce any fixation that was made without the performer's authorization,

(ii) where the performer authorized a fixation, to reproduce any reproduction of that fixation, if the reproduction being reproduced was made for a purpose other than that for which the performer's authorization was given, and

(iii) where a fixation was permitted under Part III or VIII, to reproduce any reproduction of that fixation, if the reproduction being reproduced was made for a purpose other than one permitted under Part III or VIII, and

(c) to rent out a sound recording of it,

and to authorize any such acts.

Copyright in performer's performance

(1.1) Subject to subsections (2.1) and (2.2), a performer's copyright in the performer's performance consists of the sole right to do the following acts in relation to the performer's performance or any substantial part of it and to authorize any of those acts:

(a) if it is not fixed,

(i) to communicate it to the public by telecommunication,

(ii) to perform it in public, if it is communicated to the public by telecommunication otherwise than by communication signal, and

(iii) to fix it in any material form;

(b) if it is fixed in a sound recording, to reproduce that fixation;

(c) to rent out a sound recording of it;

(d) to make a sound recording of it available to the public by telecommunication in a way that allows a member of the public to have access to the sound recording from a place and at a time individually chosen by that member of the public and to communicate the sound recording to the public by telecommunication in that way; and

(e) if it is fixed in a sound recording that is in the form of a tangible object, to sell or otherwise transfer ownership of the tangible object, as long as that ownership has never previously been transferred in or outside Canada with the authorization of the owner of the copyright in the performer's performance.

Conditions

(2) Subsection (1) applies only if the performer's performance

(a) takes place in Canada or in a Rome Convention country;

(b) is fixed in

(i) a sound recording whose maker, at the time of the first fixation,

(A) if a natural person, was a Canadian citizen or permanent resident within the meaning of subsection 2(1) of the *Immigration and Refugee Protection Act*, or a citizen or permanent resident of a Rome Convention country, or

(B) if a corporation, had its headquarters in Canada or in a Rome Convention country, or

(ii) a sound recording whose first publication in such a quantity as to satisfy the reasonable demands of the public occurred in Canada or in a Rome Convention country; or

(c) is transmitted at the time of the performer's performance by a communication signal broadcast from Canada or a Rome Convention country by a broadcaster that has its headquarters in the country of broadcast.

Conditions for copyright

(2.1) Subsection (1.1) applies if

(a) the performer's performance takes place in Canada;

(b) the performer's performance is fixed in

(i) a sound recording whose maker, at the time of its first fixation,

(A) was a Canadian citizen or permanent resident as defined in subsection 2(1) of the *Immigration and Refugee Protection Act*, in the case of a natural person, or

(B) had its headquarters in Canada, in the case of a corporation, or

(ii) a sound recording whose first publication in a quantity sufficient to satisfy the reasonable demands of the public occurred in Canada; or

(c) the performer's performance is transmitted at the time of its performance by a communication signal broadcast from Canada by a broadcaster that has its headquarters in Canada.

Conditions for copyright

(2.2) Subsection (1.1) also applies if

(a) the performer's performance takes place in a WPPT country;

(b) the performer's performance is fixed in

　(i) a sound recording whose maker, at the time of its first fixation,

　　(A) was a citizen or permanent resident of a WPPT country, in the case of a natural person, or

　　(B) had its headquarters in a WPPT country, in the case of a corporation, or

　(ii) a sound recording whose first publication in a quantity sufficient to satisfy the reasonable demands of the public occurred in a WPPT country; or

(c) the performer's performance is transmitted at the time of its performance by a communication signal broadcast from a WPPT country by a broadcaster that has its headquarters in that country.

Publication

(3) The first publication is deemed to have occurred in a country referred to in paragraph (2)(b) notwithstanding that it in fact occurred previously elsewhere, if the interval between those two publications does not exceed thirty days.

Publication

(4) The first publication of a sound recording is deemed to have occurred in a WPPT country, despite an earlier publication elsewhere, if the interval between the publication in that WPPT country and the earlier publication does not exceed 30 days.

R.S., 1985, c. C-42, s. 15; 1993, c. 44, s. 61; 1997, c. 24, s. 14; 2001, c. 27, s. 235; 2012, c. 20, s. 9.

Contractual arrangements

16 Nothing in section 15 prevents the performer from entering into a contract governing the use of the performer's performance for the purpose of broadcasting, fixation or retransmission.

R.S., 1985, c. C-42, s. 16; 1994, c. 47, s. 59; 1997, c. 24, s. 14.

Cinematographic works

17 (1) Where the performer authorizes the embodiment of the performer's performance in a cinematographic work, the performer may no longer exercise, in relation to the performance where embodied in that cinematographic work, the copyright referred to in subsection 15(1).

Right to remuneration

(2) Where there is an agreement governing the embodiment referred to in subsection (1) and that agreement provides for a right to remuneration for the reproduction, performance in public or communication to the public by telecommunication of the cinematographic work, the performer may enforce that right against

(a) the other party to the agreement or, if that party assigns the agreement, the assignee, and

(b) any other person who

(i) owns the copyright in the cinematographic work governing the reproduction of the cinematographic work, its performance in public or its communication to the public by telecommunication, and

(ii) reproduces the cinematographic work, performs it in public or communicates it to the public by telecommunication,

and persons referred to in paragraphs (a) and (b) are jointly and severally liable to the performer in respect of the remuneration relating to that copyright.

Application of subsection (2)

(3) Subsection (2) applies only if the performer's performance is embodied in a prescribed cinematographic work.

Exception

(4) If so requested by a country that is a party to the North American Free Trade Agreement, the Minister may, by a statement published in the *Canada Gazette*, grant the benefits conferred by this section, subject to any terms and conditions specified in the statement, to performers who are nationals of that country or another country that is a party to the Agreement or are Canadian citizens or permanent residents within the meaning of subsection 2(1) of the *Immigration and Refugee Protection Act* and whose performer's performances are embodied in works other than the prescribed cinematographic works referred to in subsection (3).

R.S., 1985, c. C-42, s. 17; 1994, c. 47, s. 59; 1997, c. 24, s. 14; 2001, c. 27, s. 236.

Moral Rights

Moral rights

17.1 (1) In the cases referred to in subsections 15(2.1) and (2.2), a performer of a live aural performance or a performance fixed in a sound recording has, subject to subsection 28.2(1), the right to the integrity of the performance, and — in connection with an act mentioned in subsection 15(1.1) or one for which the performer has a right to remuneration under section 19 — the right, if it is reasonable in the circumstances, to be associated with the performance as its performer by name or under a pseudonym and the right to remain anonymous.

No assignment of moral rights

(2) Moral rights may not be assigned but may be waived in whole or in part.

No waiver by assignment

(3) An assignment of copyright in a performer's performance does not by itself constitute a waiver of any moral rights.

Effect of waiver

(4) If a waiver of any moral right is made in favour of an owner or a licensee of a copyright, it may be invoked by any person authorized by the owner or licensee to use the performer's performance, unless there is an indication to the contrary in the waiver.

2012, c. 20, s. 10.

Application and term

17.2 (1) Subsection 17.1(1) applies only in respect of a performer's performance that occurs after the coming into force of that subsection. The moral rights subsist for the same term as the copyright in that performer's performance.

Succession

(2) The moral rights in respect of a performer's performance pass, on the performer's death, to

   (a) the person to whom those rights are specifically bequeathed;

   (b) if there is not a specific bequest of those moral rights and the performer dies testate in respect of the copyright in the performer's performance, the person to whom that copyright is bequeathed; or

   (c) if there is not a person as described in paragraph (a) or (b), the person entitled to any other property in respect of which the performer dies intestate.

Subsequent succession

(3) Subsection (2) applies, with any modifications that the circumstances require, on the death of any person who holds moral rights.

2012, c. 20, s. 10.

Rights of Sound Recording Makers

Copyright in sound recordings

18 (1) Subject to subsection (2), the maker of a sound recording has a copyright in the sound recording, consisting of the sole right to do the following in relation to the sound recording or any substantial part thereof:

(a) to publish it for the first time,

(b) to reproduce it in any material form, and

(c) to rent it out,

and to authorize any such acts.

Copyright in sound recordings

(1.1) Subject to subsections (2.1) and (2.2), a sound recording maker's copyright in the sound recording also includes the sole right to do the following acts in relation to the sound recording or any substantial part of it and to authorize any of those acts:

(a) to make it available to the public by telecommunication in a way that allows a member of the public to have access to it from a place and at a time individually chosen by that member of the public and to communicate it to the public by telecommunication in that way; and

(b) if it is in the form of a tangible object, to sell or otherwise transfer ownership of the tangible object, as long as that ownership has never previously been transferred in or outside Canada with the authorization of the owner of the copyright in the sound recording.

Conditions for copyright

(2) Subsection (1) applies only if

(a) at the time of the first fixation or, if that first fixation was extended over a considerable period, during any substantial part of that period, the maker of the sound recording

(i) was a Canadian citizen or permanent resident as defined in subsection 2(1) of the *Immigration and Refugee Protection Act*,

(ii) was a citizen or permanent resident of a Berne Convention country, a Rome Convention country, a WPPT country or a country that is a WTO Member, or

(iii) had its headquarters in one of those countries, in the case of a corporation; or

(b) the first publication of the sound recording in a quantity sufficient to satisfy the reasonable demands of the public occurred in any country referred to in paragraph (a).

Conditions for copyright

(2.1) Subsection (1.1) applies if

(a) at the time of the first fixation or, if that first fixation was extended over a considerable period, during any substantial part of that period, the maker of the sound recording

(i) was a Canadian citizen or permanent resident as defined in subsection 2(1) of the *Immigration and Refugee Protection Act*, or

(ii) had its headquarters in Canada, in the case of a corporation; or

(b) the first publication of the sound recording in a quantity sufficient to satisfy the reasonable demands of the public occurred in Canada.

Conditions for copyright

(2.2) Subsection (1.1) also applies if

(a) at the time of the first fixation or, if that first fixation was extended over a considerable period, during any substantial part of that period, the maker of the sound recording

(i) was a citizen or permanent resident of a WPPT country, or

(ii) had its headquarters in a WPPT country, in the case of a corporation; or

(b) the first publication of the sound recording in a quantity sufficient to satisfy the reasonable demands of the public occurred in a WPPT country.

à la Convention de Rome ou au traité de l'OIEP, ou membre de l'OMC, soit, s'il s'agit d'une personne morale, a son siège social au Canada ou dans un tel pays, ou, si la première fixation s'étend sur une période considérable, en a été un citoyen ou un résident permanent ou y a eu son siège social pendant une partie importante de cette période;

b) la première publication de l'enregistrement sonore en quantité suffisante pour satisfaire la demande raisonnable du public a eu lieu dans tout pays visé à l'alinéa a).

Autres conditions

(2.1) Le paragraphe (1.1) s'applique lorsque, selon le cas :

a) le producteur, lors de la première fixation, soit est un citoyen canadien ou un résident permanent au sens du paragraphe 2(1) de la *Loi sur l'immigration et la protection des réfugiés*, soit, s'il s'agit d'une personne morale, a son siège social au Canada, ou, si la première fixation s'étend sur une période considérable, en a été un citoyen ou un résident permanent ou y a eu son siège social pendant une partie importante de cette période;

b) la première publication de l'enregistrement sonore en quantité suffisante pour satisfaire la demande raisonnable du public a eu lieu au Canada.

Autres conditions

(2.2) Le paragraphe (1.1) s'applique également lorsque, selon le cas :

a) le producteur, lors de la première fixation, soit est un citoyen ou un résident permanent d'un pays partie au traité de l'OIEP, soit, s'il s'agit d'une personne morale, a son siège social dans un tel pays, ou, si la première fixation s'étend sur une période considérable, en a été un citoyen ou un résident permanent ou y a eu son siège social pendant une partie importante de cette période;

b) la première publication de l'enregistrement sonore en quantité suffisante pour satisfaire la demande raisonnable du public a eu lieu dans un pays partie au traité de l'OIEP.

Publication

(3) The first publication is deemed to have occurred in a country referred to in paragraph (2)(a) notwithstanding that it in fact occurred previously elsewhere, if the interval between those two publications does not exceed thirty days.

Publication

(4) The first publication of a sound recording is deemed to have occurred in a WPPT country, despite an earlier publication elsewhere, if the interval between the publication in that WPPT country and the earlier publication does not exceed 30 days.

<small>R.S., 1985, c. C-42, s. 18; R.S., 1985, c. 10 (4th Supp.), s. 17(F); 1994, c. 47, s. 59; 1997, c. 24, s. 14; 2001, c. 27, s. 237; 2012, c. 20, s. 11.</small>

Provisions Applicable to both Performers and Sound Recording Makers

Right to remuneration — Canada

19 (1) If a sound recording has been published, the performer and maker are entitled, subject to subsection 20(1), to be paid equitable remuneration for its performance in public or its communication to the public by telecommunication, except for a communication in the circumstances referred to in paragraph 15(1.1)(d) or 18(1.1)(a) and any retransmission.

Right to remuneration — Rome Convention country

(1.1) If a sound recording has been published, the performer and maker are entitled, subject to subsections 20(1.1) and (2), to be paid equitable remuneration for its performance in public or its communication to the public by telecommunication, except for

(a) a communication in the circumstances referred to in paragraph 15(1.1)(d) or 18(1.1)(a), if the person entitled to the equitable remuneration is entitled to the right referred to in those paragraphs for that communication; and

(b) any retransmission.

Right to remuneration — WPPT country

(1.2) If a sound recording has been published, the performer and maker are entitled, subject to subsections 20(1.2) and (2.1), to be paid equitable remuneration for its performance in public or its communication to the public by telecommunication, except for a communication in the circumstances referred to in paragraph 15(1.1)(d) or 18(1.1)(a) and any retransmission.

Royalties

(2) For the purpose of providing the remuneration mentioned in this section, a person who performs a published sound recording in public or communicates it to the public by telecommunication is liable to pay royalties

   (a) in the case of a sound recording of a musical work, to the collective society authorized under Part VII to collect them; or

   (b) in the case of a sound recording of a literary work or dramatic work, to either the maker of the sound recording or the performer.

Division of royalties

(3) The royalties, once paid pursuant to paragraph (2)(a) or (b), shall be divided so that

   (a) the performer or performers receive in aggregate fifty per cent; and

   (b) the maker or makers receive in aggregate fifty per cent.

R.S., 1985, c. C-42, s. 19; 1994, c. 47, s. 59; 1997, c. 24, s. 14; 2012, c. 20, s. 12.

Deemed publication — Canada

19.1 Despite subsection 2.2(1), a sound recording that has been made available to the public by telecommunication in a way that allows a member of the public to access it from a place and at a time individually chosen by that member of the public, or that has been communicated to the public by telecommunication in that way, is deemed to have been published for the purposes of subsection 19(1).

2012, c. 20, s. 13.

Deemed publication — WPPT country

19.2 Despite subsection 2.2(1), a sound recording that has been made available to the public by telecommunication in a way that allows a member of the public to access it from a place and at a time individually chosen by that member of the public, or that has been communicated to the public by telecommunication in that way, is deemed to have been published for the purposes of subsection 19(1.2).

2012, c. 20, s. 14.

Conditions — Canada

20 (1) The right to remuneration conferred by subsection 19(1) applies only if

   (a) the maker was, at the date of the first fixation, a Canadian citizen or permanent resident within the meaning of subsection 2(1) of the *Immigration and*

Refugee Protection Act or, if a corporation, had its headquarters in Canada; or

(b) all the fixations done for the sound recording occurred in Canada.

Conditions — Rome Convention country

(1.1) The right to remuneration conferred by subsection 19(1.1) applies only if

(a) the maker was, at the date of the first fixation, a citizen or permanent resident of a Rome Convention country or, if a corporation, had its headquarters in a Rome Convention country; or

(b) all the fixations done for the sound recording occurred in a Rome Convention country.

Conditions — WPPT country

(1.2) The right to remuneration conferred by subsection 19(1.2) applies only if

(a) the maker was, at the date of the first fixation, a citizen or permanent resident of a WPPT country or, if a corporation, had its headquarters in a WPPT country; or

(b) all the fixations done for the sound recording occurred in a WPPT country.

Exception — Rome Convention country

(2) Despite subsection (1.1), if the Minister is of the opinion that a Rome Convention country does not grant a right to remuneration, similar in scope and duration to that provided by subsection 19(1.1), for the performance in public or the communication to the public of a sound recording whose maker, at the date of its first fixation, was a Canadian citizen or permanent resident within the meaning of subsection 2(1) of the *Immigration and Refugee Protection Act* or, if a corporation, had its headquarters in Canada, the Minister may, by a statement published in the *Canada Gazette*, limit the scope and duration of the protection for sound recordings whose first fixation is done by a maker who is a citizen or permanent resident of that country or, if a corporation, has its headquarters in that country.

Exception — WPPT country

(2.1) Despite subsection (1.2), if the Minister is of the opinion that a WPPT country does not grant a right to remuneration, similar in scope and duration to that provided by subsection 19(1.2), for the performance in public or the communication to the public of a sound recording whose maker, at the date of its first fixation, was a Canadian citizen or permanent resident within the meaning of subsection 2(1) of the *Immigration and Refugee Protection Act* or, if a corporation, had its headquarters in Canada, the Minister may, by a statement published in the *Canada Gazette*, limit the scope and duration of the protection for sound recordings whose first fixation is done by a maker who is a citizen or permanent resident of that country or, if a corporation, has its headquarters in that country.

Exception

(3) If so requested by a country that is a party to the North American Free Trade Agreement, the Minister may, by a statement published in the *Canada Gazette*, grant the right to remuneration conferred by subsection 19(1.1) to performers or makers who are nationals of that country and whose sound recordings embody dramatic or literary works.

Application of section 19

(4) Where a statement is published under subsection (3), section 19 applies

 (a) in respect of nationals of a country mentioned in that statement, as if they were citizens of Canada or, in the case of corporations, had their headquarters in Canada; and

 (b) as if the fixations made for the purpose of their sound recordings had been made in Canada.

R.S., 1985, c. C-42, s. 20; 1994, c. 47, s. 59; 1997, c. 24, s. 14; 2001, c. 27, s. 238; 2012, c. 20, s. 15.

Rights of Broadcasters

Copyright in communication signals

21 (1) Subject to subsection (2), a broadcaster has a copyright in the communication signals that it broadcasts, consisting of the sole right to do the following in relation to the communication signal or any substantial part thereof:

 (a) to fix it,

(b) to reproduce any fixation of it that was made without the broadcaster's consent,

(c) to authorize another broadcaster to retransmit it to the public simultaneously with its broadcast, and

(d) in the case of a television communication signal, to perform it in a place open to the public on payment of an entrance fee,

and to authorize any act described in paragraph (a), (b) or (d).

Conditions for copyright

(2) Subsection (1) applies only if the broadcaster

(a) at the time of the broadcast, had its headquarters in Canada, in a country that is a WTO Member or in a Rome Convention country; and

(b) broadcasts the communication signal from that country.

Exception

(3) Notwithstanding subsection (2), if the Minister is of the opinion that a Rome Convention country or a country that is a WTO Member does not grant the right mentioned in paragraph (1)(d), the Minister may, by a statement published in the *Canada Gazette*, declare that broadcasters that have their headquarters in that country are not entitled to that right.

R.S., 1985, c. C-42, s. 21; 1994, c. 47, s. 59; 1997, c. 24, s. 14.

Reciprocity

Reciprocity

22 (1) If the Minister is of the opinion that a country other than a Rome Convention country or a WPPT country grants or has undertaken to grant

(a) to performers and to makers of sound recordings, or

(b) to broadcasters

that are Canadian citizens or permanent residents within the meaning of subsection 2(1) of the *Immigration and Refugee Protection Act* or, if corporations, have their headquarters in Canada, as the case may be, whether by treaty, convention, agreement or law, benefits substantially equivalent to those conferred by this Part, the Minister may, by a statement published in the *Canada Gazette*,

(c) grant the benefits conferred by this Part

(i) to performers and to makers of sound recordings, or

(ii) to broadcasters

as the case may be, that are citizens, subjects or permanent residents of or, if corporations, have their headquarters in that country, and

(d) declare that that country shall, as regards those benefits, be treated as if it were a country to which this Part extends.

Reciprocity

(2) If the Minister is of the opinion that a country other than a Rome Convention country or a WPPT country neither grants nor has undertaken to grant

(a) to performers, and to makers of sound recordings, or

(b) to broadcasters

that are Canadian citizens or permanent residents within the meaning of subsection 2(1) of the *Immigration and Refugee Protection Act* or, if corporations, have their headquarters in Canada, as the case may be, whether by treaty, convention, agreement or law, benefits substantially equivalent to those conferred by this Part, the Minister may, by a statement published in the *Canada Gazette*,

(c) grant the benefits conferred by this Part to performers, makers of sound recordings or broadcasters that are citizens, subjects or permanent residents of or, if corporations, have their headquarters in that country, as the case may be, to the extent that that country grants that those benefits to performers, makers of sound recordings or broadcasters that are Canadian citizens or permanent residents within the meaning of subsection 2(1) of the *Immigration and Refugee Protection Act* or, if corporations, have their headquarters in Canada, and

(d) declare that that country shall, as regards those benefits, be treated as if it were a country to which this Part extends.

Application of Act

(3) Any provision of this Act that the Minister specifies in a statement referred to in subsection (1) or (2)

(a) applies in respect of performers, makers of sound recordings or broadcasters covered by that statement, as if they were citizens of or, if corporations, had their headquarters in Canada; and

Application of Act

(4) Subject to any exceptions that the Minister may specify in a statement referred to in subsection (1) or (2), the other provisions of this Act also apply in the way described in subsection (3).

R.S., 1985, c. C-42, s. 22; 1994, c. 47, s. 59; 1997, c. 24, s. 14; 2001, c. 27, s. 239; 2012, c. 20, s. 16.

Term of Rights

Term of copyright — performer's performance

23 (1) Subject to this Act, copyright in a performer's performance subsists until the end of 50 years after the end of the calendar year in which the performance occurs. However,

   (a) if the performance is fixed in a sound recording before the copyright expires, the copyright continues until the end of 50 years after the end of the calendar year in which the first fixation of the performance in a sound recording occurs; and

   (b) if a sound recording in which the performance is fixed is published before the copyright expires, the copyright continues until the earlier of the end of 70 years after the end of the calendar year in which the first such publication occurs and the end of 100 years after the end of the calendar year in which the first fixation of the performance in a sound recording occurs.

Term of copyright — sound recording

(1.1) Subject to this Act, copyright in a sound recording subsists until the end of 50 years after the end of the calendar year in which the first fixation of the sound recording occurs. However, if the sound recording is published before the copyright expires, the copyright continues until the earlier of the end of 70 years after the end of the calendar year in which the first publication of the sound recording occurs and the end of 100 years after the end of the calendar year in which that first fixation occurs.

Term of copyright — communication signal

(1.2) Subject to this Act, copyright in a communication signal subsists until the end of 50 years after the end of the calendar year in which the communication signal is broadcast.

Term of right to remuneration

(2) The rights to remuneration conferred on performers and makers by section 19 have the same terms, respectively, as those provided by subsections (1) and (1.1).

Application of subsections (1) to (2)

(3) Subsections (1) to (2) apply whether the fixation, performance or broadcast occurred before or after the coming into force of this section.

Berne Convention countries, Rome Convention countries, WTO Members

(4) Where the performer's performance, sound recording or communication signal meets the requirements set out in section 15, 18 or 21, as the case may be, a country that becomes a Berne Convention country, a Rome Convention country or a WTO Member after the date of the fixation, performance or broadcast is, as of becoming a Berne Convention country, Rome Convention country or WTO Member, as the case may be, deemed to have been such at the date of the fixation, performance or broadcast.

Where term of protection expired

(5) Subsection (4) does not confer any protection in Canada where the term of protection in the country referred to in that subsection had expired before that country became a Berne Convention country, Rome Convention country or WTO Member, as the case may be.

R.S., 1985, c. C-42, s. 23; 1994, c. 47, s. 59; 1997, c. 24, s. 14; 2012, c. 20, s. 17; 2015, c. 36, s. 81.

Ownership of Copyright

Ownership of copyright

24 The first owner of the copyright

    (a) in a performer's performance, is the performer;

    (b) in a sound recording, is the maker; or

    (c) in a communication signal, is the broadcaster that broadcasts it.

R.S., 1985, c. C-42, s. 24; 1994, c. 47, s. 59; 1997, c. 24, s. 14.

Assignment of rights

25 Subsections 13(4) to (7) apply, with such modifications as the circumstances require, in respect of the rights conferred by this Part on performers, makers of sound recordings and broadcasters.

R.S., 1985, c. C-42, s. 25; 1993, c. 44, s. 62; 1994, c. 47, s. 59; 1997, c. 24, s. 14.

Performers' Rights — WTO Countries

Performer's performance in WTO country

26 (1) Where a performer's performance takes place on or after January 1, 1996 in a country that is a WTO Member, the performer has, as of the date of the performer's performance, a copyright in the performer's performance, consisting of the sole right to do the following in relation to the performer's performance or any substantial part thereof:

(a) if it is not fixed, to communicate it to the public by telecommunication and to fix it in a sound recording, and

(b) if it has been fixed in a sound recording without the performer's authorization, to reproduce the fixation or any substantial part thereof,

and to authorize any such acts.

Where country joins WTO after Jan. 1, 1996

(2) Where a performer's performance takes place on or after January 1, 1996 in a country that becomes a WTO Member after the date of the performer's performance, the performer has the copyright described in subsection (1) as of the date the country becomes a WTO Member.

Performer's performances before Jan. 1, 1996

(3) Where a performer's performance takes place before January 1, 1996 in a country that is a WTO Member, the performer has, as of January 1, 1996, the sole right to do and to authorize the act described in paragraph (1)(b).

Where country joins WTO after Jan. 1, 1996

(4) Where a performer's performance takes place before January 1, 1996 in a country that becomes a WTO Member on or after January 1, 1996, the performer has the right described in subsection (3) as of the date the country becomes a WTO Member.

Term of performer's rights

(5) The rights conferred by this section subsist for the remainder of the calendar year in which the performer's performance takes place and a period of fifty years following the end of that calendar year.

Assignment of rights

(6) Subsections 13(4) to (7) apply, with such modifications as the circumstances require, in respect of a performer's rights conferred by this section.

Limitation

(7) Notwithstanding an assignment of a performer's right conferred by this section, the performer, as well as the assignee, may

(a) prevent the reproduction of

(i) any fixation of the performer's performance, or

(ii) any substantial part of such a fixation,

where the fixation was made without the performer's consent or the assignee's consent; and

(b) prevent the importation of any fixation of the performer's performance, or any reproduction of such a fixation, that the importer knows or ought to have known was made without the performer's consent or the assignee's consent.

R.S., 1985, c. C-42, s. 26; R.S., 1985, c. 10 (4th Supp.), s. 17(F); 1993, c. 44, s. 63; 1994, c. 47, s. 59; 1997, c. 24, s. 14.

PART III

Infringement of Copyright and Moral Rights and Exceptions to Infringement

Infringement of Copyright

General

Infringement generally

27 (1) It is an infringement of copyright for any person to do, without the consent of the owner of the copyright, anything that by this Act only the owner of the copyright has the right to do.

Secondary infringement

(2) It is an infringement of copyright for any person to

(a) sell or rent out,

(b) distribute to such an extent as to affect prejudicially the owner of the copyright,

(c) by way of trade distribute, expose or offer for sale or rental, or exhibit in public,

(d) possess for the purpose of doing anything referred to in paragraphs (a) to (c), or

(e) import into Canada for the purpose of doing anything referred to in paragraphs (a) to (c),

a copy of a work, sound recording or fixation of a performer's performance or of a communication signal that the person knows or should have known infringes copyright or would infringe copyright if it had been made in Canada by the person who made it.

Clarification

(2.1) For greater certainty, a copy made outside Canada does not infringe copyright under subsection (2) if, had it been made in Canada, it would have been made under a limitation or exception under this Act.

Secondary infringement — exportation

(2.11) It is an infringement of copyright for any person, for the purpose of doing anything referred to in paragraphs (2)(a) to (c), to export or attempt to export a copy — of a work, sound recording or fixation of a performer's performance or of a communication signal — that the person knows or should have known was made without the consent of the owner of the copyright in the country where the copy was made.

Exception

(2.12) Subsection (2.11) does not apply with respect to a copy that was made under a limitation or exception under this Act or, if it was made outside Canada, that would have been made under such a limitation or exception had it been made in Canada.

Secondary infringement related to lesson

(2.2) It is an infringement of copyright for any person to do any of the following acts with respect to anything that the person knows or should have known is a lesson, as defined in subsection 30.01(1), or a fixation of one:

(a) to sell it or to rent it out;

(b) to distribute it to an extent that the owner of the copyright in the work or other subject-matter that is included in the lesson is prejudicially affected;

(c) by way of trade, to distribute it, expose or offer it for sale or rental or exhibit it in public;

(d) to possess it for the purpose of doing anything referred to in any of paragraphs (a) to (c);

(e) to communicate it by telecommunication to any person other than a person referred to in paragraph 30.01(3)(a); or

(f) to circumvent or contravene any measure taken in conformity with paragraph 30.01(6)(b), (c) or (d).

Infringement — provision of services

(2.3) It is an infringement of copyright for a person, by means of the Internet or another digital network, to provide a service primarily for the purpose of enabling acts of copyright infringement if an actual infringement of copyright occurs by means of the Internet or another digital network as a result of the use of that service.

Factors

(2.4) In determining whether a person has infringed copyright under subsection (2.3), the court may consider

(a) whether the person expressly or implicitly marketed or promoted the service as one that could be used to enable acts of copyright infringement;

(b) whether the person had knowledge that the service was used to enable a significant number of acts of copyright infringement;

(c) whether the service has significant uses other than to enable acts of copyright infringement;

(d) the person's ability, as part of providing the service, to limit acts of copyright infringement, and any action taken by the person to do so;

(e) any benefits the person received as a result of enabling the acts of copyright infringement; and

(f) the economic viability of the provision of the service if it were not used to enable acts of copyright infringement.

Knowledge of importer

(3) In determining whether there is an infringement under subsection (2) in the case of an activity referred to in any of paragraphs (2)(a) to (d) in relation to a copy that was imported in the circumstances referred to in paragraph (2)(e), it is irrelevant whether the importer knew or should have known that the importation of the copy infringed copyright.

e) la communication par télécommunication à toute personne qui n'est pas visée à l'alinéa 30.01(3)a);

f) le contournement ou la contravention des mesures prises en conformité avec les alinéas 30.01(6)b), c) ou d).

Violation relative aux fournisseurs de services

(2.3) Constitue une violation du droit d'auteur le fait pour une personne de fournir un service sur Internet ou tout autre réseau numérique principalement en vue de faciliter l'accomplissement d'actes qui constituent une violation du droit d'auteur, si une autre personne commet une telle violation sur Internet ou tout autre réseau numérique en utilisant ce service.

Facteurs

(2.4) Lorsqu'il s'agit de décider si une personne a commis une violation du droit d'auteur prévue au paragraphe (2.3), le tribunal peut prendre en compte les facteurs suivants :

a) le fait que la personne a fait valoir, même implicitement, dans le cadre de la commercialisation du service ou de la publicité relative à celui-ci, qu'il pouvait faciliter l'accomplissement d'actes qui constituent une violation du droit d'auteur;

b) le fait que la personne savait que le service était utilisé pour faciliter l'accomplissement d'un nombre important de ces actes;

c) le fait que le service a des utilisations importantes, autres que celle de faciliter l'accomplissement de ces actes;

d) la capacité de la personne, dans le cadre de la fourniture du service, de limiter la possibilité d'accomplir ces actes et les mesures qu'elle a prises à cette fin;

e) les avantages que la personne a tirés en facilitant l'accomplissement de ces actes;

f) la viabilité économique de la fourniture du service si celui-ci n'était pas utilisé pour faciliter l'accomplissement de ces actes.

Précision

(3) Lorsqu'il s'agit de décider si les actes visés aux alinéas (2)a) à d), dans les cas où ils se rapportent à un exemplaire importé dans les conditions visées à l'alinéa (2)e), constituent des violations du droit d'auteur, le fait que l'importateur savait ou aurait dû savoir que l'importation de l'exemplaire constituait une violation n'est pas pertinent.

Plates

(4) It is an infringement of copyright for any person to make or possess a plate that has been specifically designed or adapted for the purpose of making infringing copies of a work or other subject-matter.

Public performance for profit

(5) It is an infringement of copyright for any person, for profit, to permit a theatre or other place of entertainment to be used for the performance in public of a work or other subject-matter without the consent of the owner of the copyright unless that person was not aware, and had no reasonable ground for suspecting, that the performance would be an infringement of copyright.

R.S., 1985, c. C-42, s. 27; R.S., 1985, c. 1 (3rd Supp.), s. 13, c. 10 (4th Supp.), s. 5; 1993, c. 44, s. 64; 1997, c. 24, s. 15; 2012, c. 20, s. 18; 2014, c. 32, s. 3.

Parallel Importation of Books

Importation of books

27.1 (1) Subject to any regulations made under subsection (6), it is an infringement of copyright in a book for any person to import the book where

(a) copies of the book were made with the consent of the owner of the copyright in the book in the country where the copies were made, but were imported without the consent of the owner of the copyright in the book in Canada; and

(b) the person knows or should have known that the book would infringe copyright if it was made in Canada by the importer.

Secondary infringement

(2) Subject to any regulations made under subsection (6), where the circumstances described in paragraph (1)(a) exist, it is an infringement of copyright in an imported book for any person who knew or should have known that the book would infringe copyright if it was made in Canada by the importer to

(a) sell or rent out the book;

(b) by way of trade, distribute, expose or offer for sale or rental, or exhibit in public, the book; or

(c) possess the book for the purpose of any of the activities referred to in paragraph (a) or (b).

Limitation

(3) Subsections (1) and (2) only apply where there is an exclusive distributor of the book and the acts described in those subsections take place in the part of Canada or in respect of the particular sector of the market for which the person is the exclusive distributor.

Exclusive distributor

(4) An exclusive distributor is deemed, for the purposes of entitlement to any of the remedies under Part IV in relation to an infringement under this section, to derive an interest in the copyright in question by licence.

Notice

(5) No exclusive distributor, copyright owner or exclusive licensee is entitled to a remedy under Part IV in relation to an infringement under this section unless, before the infringement occurred, notice has been given within the prescribed time and in the prescribed manner to the person referred to in subsection (1) or (2), as the case may be, that there is an exclusive distributor of the book.

Regulations

(6) The Governor in Council may, by regulation, establish terms and conditions for the importation of certain categories of books, including remaindered books, books intended solely for re-export and books imported by special order.

1997, c. 24, s. 15.

28 [Repealed, 1997, c. 24, s. 15]

28.01 [Repealed, 1997, c. 24, s. 16]

28.02 and 28.03 [Repealed, 1997, c. 24, s. 17]

Moral Rights Infringement

Infringement generally

28.1 Any act or omission that is contrary to any of the moral rights of the author of a work or of the performer of a performer's performance is, in the absence of the author's or performer's consent, an infringement of those rights.

R.S., 1985, c. 10 (4th Supp.), s. 6; 2012, c. 20, s. 19.

Nature of right of integrity

28.2 (1) The author's or performer's right to the integrity of a work or performer's performance is infringed only if the work or the performance is, to the prejudice of its author's or performer's honour or reputation,

    (a) distorted, mutilated or otherwise modified; or

(b) used in association with a product, service, cause or institution.

Where prejudice deemed

(2) In the case of a painting, sculpture or engraving, the prejudice referred to in subsection (1) shall be deemed to have occurred as a result of any distortion, mutilation or other modification of the work.

When work not distorted, etc.

(3) For the purposes of this section,

(a) a change in the location of a work, the physical means by which a work is exposed or the physical structure containing a work, or

(b) steps taken in good faith to restore or preserve the work

shall not, by that act alone, constitute a distortion, mutilation or other modification of the work.

R.S., 1985, c. 10 (4th Supp.), s. 6; 2012, c. 20, s. 20.

Exceptions

Fair Dealing

Research, private study, etc.

29 Fair dealing for the purpose of research, private study, education, parody or satire does not infringe copyright.

R.S., 1985, c. C-42, s. 29; R.S., 1985, c. 10 (4th Supp.), s. 7; 1994, c. 47, s. 61; 1997, c. 24, s. 18; 2012, c. 20, s. 21.

Criticism or review

29.1 Fair dealing for the purpose of criticism or review does not infringe copyright if the following are mentioned:

(a) the source; and

(b) if given in the source, the name of the

(i) author, in the case of a work,

(ii) performer, in the case of a performer's performance,

(iii) maker, in the case of a sound recording, or

(iv) broadcaster, in the case of a communication signal.

1997, c. 24, s. 18.

News reporting

29.2 Fair dealing for the purpose of news reporting does not infringe copyright if the following are mentioned:

(a) the source; and

(b) if given in the source, the name of the

  (i) author, in the case of a work,

  (ii) performer, in the case of a performer's performance,

  (iii) maker, in the case of a sound recording, or

  (iv) broadcaster, in the case of a communication signal.

1997, c. 24, s. 18.

Non-commercial User-generated Content

Non-commercial user-generated content

29.21 (1) It is not an infringement of copyright for an individual to use an existing work or other subject-matter or copy of one, which has been published or otherwise made available to the public, in the creation of a new work or other subject-matter in which copyright subsists and for the individual — or, with the individual's authorization, a member of their household — to use the new work or other subject-matter or to authorize an intermediary to disseminate it, if

(a) the use of, or the authorization to disseminate, the new work or other subject-matter is done solely for non-commercial purposes;

(b) the source — and, if given in the source, the name of the author, performer, maker or broadcaster — of the existing work or other subject-matter or copy of it are mentioned, if it is reasonable in the circumstances to do so;

(c) the individual had reasonable grounds to believe that the existing work or other subject-matter or copy of it, as the case may be, was not infringing copyright; and

Communication des nouvelles

29.2 L'utilisation équitable d'une œuvre ou de tout autre objet du droit d'auteur pour la communication des nouvelles ne constitue pas une violation du droit d'auteur à la condition que soient mentionnés :

a) d'une part, la source;

b) d'autre part, si ces renseignements figurent dans la source :

  (i) dans le cas d'une œuvre, le nom de l'auteur,

  (ii) dans le cas d'une prestation, le nom de l'artiste-interprète,

  (iii) dans le cas d'un enregistrement sonore, le nom du producteur,

  (iv) dans le cas d'un signal de communication, le nom du radiodiffuseur.

1997, ch. 24, art. 18.

Contenu non commercial généré par l'utilisateur

Contenu non commercial généré par l'utilisateur

29.21 (1) Ne constitue pas une violation du droit d'auteur le fait, pour une personne physique, d'utiliser une œuvre ou tout autre objet du droit d'auteur ou une copie de ceux-ci — déjà publiés ou mis à la disposition du public — pour créer une autre œuvre ou un autre objet du droit d'auteur protégés et, pour cette personne de même que, si elle les y autorise, celles qui résident habituellement avec elle, d'utiliser la nouvelle œuvre ou le nouvel objet ou d'autoriser un intermédiaire à le diffuser, si les conditions suivantes sont réunies :

a) la nouvelle œuvre ou le nouvel objet n'est utilisé qu'à des fins non commerciales, ou l'autorisation de le diffuser n'est donnée qu'à de telles fins;

b) si cela est possible dans les circonstances, la source de l'œuvre ou de l'autre objet ou de la copie de ceux-ci et, si ces renseignements figurent dans la source, les noms de l'auteur, de l'artiste-interprète, du producteur ou du radiodiffuseur sont mentionnés;

c) la personne croit, pour des motifs raisonnables, que l'œuvre ou l'objet ou la copie de ceux-ci, ayant servi à la création n'était pas contrefait;

(d) the use of, or the authorization to disseminate, the new work or other subject-matter does not have a substantial adverse effect, financial or otherwise, on the exploitation or potential exploitation of the existing work or other subject-matter — or copy of it — or on an existing or potential market for it, including that the new work or other subject-matter is not a substitute for the existing one.

Definitions

(2) The following definitions apply in subsection (1).

intermediary means a person or entity who regularly provides space or means for works or other subject-matter to be enjoyed by the public. (*intermédiaire*)

use means to do anything that by this Act the owner of the copyright has the sole right to do, other than the right to authorize anything. (*utiliser*)

2012, c. 20, s. 22.

Reproduction for Private Purposes

Reproduction for private purposes

29.22 (1) It is not an infringement of copyright for an individual to reproduce a work or other subject-matter or any substantial part of a work or other subject-matter if

(a) the copy of the work or other subject-matter from which the reproduction is made is not an infringing copy;

(b) the individual legally obtained the copy of the work or other subject-matter from which the reproduction is made, other than by borrowing it or renting it, and owns or is authorized to use the medium or device on which it is reproduced;

(c) the individual, in order to make the reproduction, did not circumvent, as defined in section 41, a technological protection measure, as defined in that section, or cause one to be circumvented;

(d) the individual does not give the reproduction away; and

(e) the reproduction is used only for the individual's private purposes.

Meaning of *medium or device*

(2) For the purposes of paragraph (1)(b), a ***medium or device*** includes digital memory in which a work or subject-matter may be stored for the purpose of allowing the telecommunication of the work or other subject-matter through the Internet or other digital network.

Limitation — audio recording medium

(3) In the case of a work or other subject-matter that is a musical work embodied in a sound recording, a performer's performance of a musical work embodied in a sound recording or a sound recording in which a musical work or a performer's performance of a musical work is embodied, subsection (1) does not apply if the reproduction is made onto an audio recording medium as defined in section 79.

Limitation — destruction of reproductions

(4) Subsection (1) does not apply if the individual gives away, rents or sells the copy of the work or other subject-matter from which the reproduction is made without first destroying all reproductions of that copy that the individual has made under that subsection.

2012, c. 20, s. 22.

Fixing Signals and Recording Programs for Later Listening or Viewing

Reproduction for later listening or viewing

29.23 (1) It is not an infringement of copyright for an individual to fix a communication signal, to reproduce a work or sound recording that is being broadcast or to fix or reproduce a performer's performance that is being broadcast, in order to record a program for the purpose of listening to or viewing it later, if

(a) the individual receives the program legally;

(b) the individual, in order to record the program, did not circumvent, as defined in section 41, a technological protection measure, as defined in that section, or cause one to be circumvented;

(c) the individual makes no more than one recording of the program;

(d) the individual keeps the recording no longer than is reasonably necessary in order to listen to or view the program at a more convenient time;

(e) the individual does not give the recording away; and

dans laquelle il est possible de stocker une œuvre ou un autre objet du droit d'auteur pour en permettre la communication par télécommunication sur Internet ou tout autre réseau numérique.

Non-application : support audio

(3) Dans le cas où l'œuvre ou l'autre objet est l'enregistrement sonore d'une œuvre musicale ou de la prestation d'une œuvre musicale ou l'œuvre musicale, ou la prestation d'une œuvre musicale fixée au moyen d'un enregistrement sonore, le paragraphe (1) ne s'applique pas si la reproduction est faite sur un support audio, au sens de l'article 79.

Non-application : destruction des reproductions

(4) Le paragraphe (1) ne s'applique pas si la personne donne, loue ou vend la copie reproduite sans en avoir au préalable détruit toutes les reproductions faites au titre de ce paragraphe.

2012, ch. 20, art. 22.

Fixation d'un signal et enregistrement d'une émission pour écoute ou visionnement en différé

Fixation ou reproduction pour écoute ou visionnement en différé

29.23 (1) Ne constitue pas une violation du droit d'auteur le fait, pour une personne physique, de fixer un signal de communication, de reproduire une œuvre ou un enregistrement sonore lorsqu'il est communiqué par radiodiffusion ou de fixer ou de reproduire une prestation lorsqu'elle est ainsi communiquée, afin d'enregistrer une émission pour l'écouter ou la regarder en différé, si les conditions suivantes sont réunies :

a) la personne reçoit l'émission de façon licite;

b) elle ne contourne pas ni ne fait contourner une mesure technique de protection, au sens de ces termes à l'article 41, pour enregistrer l'émission;

c) elle ne fait pas plus d'un enregistrement de l'émission;

d) elle ne conserve l'enregistrement que le temps vraisemblablement nécessaire pour écouter ou regarder l'émission à un moment plus opportun;

e) elle ne donne l'enregistrement à personne;

(f) the recording is used only for the individual's private purposes.

Limitation

(2) Subsection (1) does not apply if the individual receives the work, performer's performance or sound recording under an on-demand service.

Definitions

(3) The following definitions apply in this section.

broadcast means any transmission of a work or other subject-matter by telecommunication for reception by the public, but does not include a transmission that is made solely for performance in public. (*radiodiffusion*)

on-demand service means a service that allows a person to receive works, performer's performances and sound recordings at times of their choosing. (*service sur demande*)

2012, c. 20, s. 22.

Backup Copies

Backup copies

29.24 (1) It is not an infringement of copyright in a work or other subject-matter for a person who owns — or has a licence to use — a copy of the work or subject-matter (in this section referred to as the "source copy") to reproduce the source copy if

(a) the person does so solely for backup purposes in case the source copy is lost, damaged or otherwise rendered unusable;

(b) the source copy is not an infringing copy;

(c) the person, in order to make the reproduction, did not circumvent, as defined in section 41, a technological protection measure, as defined in that section, or cause one to be circumvented; and

(d) the person does not give any of the reproductions away.

Backup copy becomes source copy

(2) If the source copy is lost, damaged or otherwise rendered unusable, one of the reproductions made under subsection (1) becomes the source copy.

Destruction

(3) The person shall immediately destroy all reproductions made under subsection (1) after the person ceases to own, or to have a licence to use, the source copy.

2012, c. 20, s. 22.

Acts Undertaken without Motive of Gain

Motive of gain

29.3 (1) No action referred to in section 29.4, 29.5, 30.2 or 30.21 may be carried out with motive of gain.

Cost recovery

(2) An educational institution, library, archive or museum, or person acting under its authority does not have a motive of gain where it or the person acting under its authority, does anything referred to in section 29.4, 29.5, 30.2 or 30.21 and recovers no more than the costs, including overhead costs, associated with doing that act.

1997, c. 24, s. 18.

Educational Institutions

Reproduction for instruction

29.4 (1) It is not an infringement of copyright for an educational institution or a person acting under its authority for the purposes of education or training on its premises to reproduce a work, or do any other necessary act, in order to display it.

Reproduction for examinations, etc.

(2) It is not an infringement of copyright for an educational institution or a person acting under its authority to

(a) reproduce, translate or perform in public on the premises of the educational institution, or

(b) communicate by telecommunication to the public situated on the premises of the educational institution

a work or other subject-matter as required for a test or examination.

If work commercially available

(3) Except in the case of manual reproduction, the exemption from copyright infringement provided by subsections (1) and (2) does not apply if the work or other subject-matter is commercially available, within the meaning of paragraph (a) of the definition ***commercially available*** in section 2, in a medium that is appropriate for the purposes referred to in those subsections.

1997, c. 24, s. 18; 2012, c. 20, s. 23.

Performances

29.5 It is not an infringement of copyright for an educational institution or a person acting under its authority to do the following acts if they are done on the premises of an educational institution for educational or training purposes and not for profit, before an audience consisting primarily of students of the educational institution, instructors acting under the authority of the educational institution or any person who is directly responsible for setting a curriculum for the educational institution:

(a) the live performance in public, primarily by students of the educational institution, of a work;

(b) the performance in public of a sound recording, or of a work or performer's performance that is embodied in a sound recording, as long as the sound recording is not an infringing copy or the person responsible for the performance has no reasonable grounds to believe that it is an infringing copy;

(c) the performance in public of a work or other subject-matter at the time of its communication to the public by telecommunication; and

(d) the performance in public of a cinematographic work, as long as the work is not an infringing copy or the person responsible for the performance has no reasonable grounds to believe that it is an infringing copy.

1997, c. 24, s. 18; 2012, c. 20, s. 24.

News and commentary

29.6 (1) It is not an infringement of copyright for an educational institution or a person acting under its authority to

(a) make, at the time of its communication to the public by telecommunication, a single copy of a news program or a news commentary program, excluding documentaries, for the purposes of performing the copy for the students of the educational institution for educational or training purposes; and

(b) perform the copy in public before an audience consisting primarily of students of the educational institution on its premises for educational or training purposes.

(2) [Repealed, 2012, c. 20, s. 25]

1997, c. 24, s. 18; 2012, c. 20, s. 25.

Reproduction of broadcast

29.7 (1) Subject to subsection (2) and section 29.9, it is not an infringement of copyright for an educational institution or a person acting under its authority to

(a) make a single copy of a work or other subject-matter at the time that it is communicated to the public by telecommunication; and

(b) keep the copy for up to thirty days to decide whether to perform the copy for educational or training purposes.

Royalties for reproduction

(2) An educational institution that has not destroyed the copy by the expiration of the thirty days infringes copyright in the work or other subject-matter unless it pays any royalties, and complies with any terms and conditions, fixed under this Act for the making of the copy.

Royalties for performance

(3) It is not an infringement of copyright for the educational institution or a person acting under its authority to perform the copy in public for educational or training purposes on the premises of the educational institution before an audience consisting primarily of students of the educational institution if the educational institution pays the royalties and complies with any terms and conditions fixed under this Act for the performance in public.

1997, c. 24, s. 18.

Unlawful reception

29.8 The exceptions to infringement of copyright provided for under sections 29.5 to 29.7 do not apply where the communication to the public by telecommunication was received by unlawful means.

1997, c. 24, s. 18.

Records and marking

29.9 (1) Where an educational institution or person acting under its authority

(a) [Repealed, 2012, c. 20, s. 26]

(b) makes a copy of a work or other subject-matter communicated to the public by telecommunication and performs it pursuant to section 29.7, the educational institution shall keep a record of the information prescribed by regulation in relation to the making of the copy, the destruction of it or any performance in public of it for which royalties are payable under this Act and shall, in addition, mark the copy in the manner prescribed by regulation.

Regulations

(2) The Board may, with the approval of the Governor in Council, make regulations

(a) prescribing the information in relation to the making, destruction, performance and marking of copies that must be kept under subsection (1),

(b) prescribing the manner and form in which records referred to in that subsection must be kept and copies destroyed or marked, and

(c) respecting the sending of information to collective societies referred to in section 71.

1997, c. 24, s. 18; 2012, c. 20, s. 26.

Literary collections

30 The publication in a collection, mainly composed of non-copyright matter, intended for the use of educational institutions, and so described in the title and in any advertisements issued by the publisher, of short passages from published literary works in which copyright subsists and not themselves published for the use of educational institutions, does not infringe copyright in those published literary works if

(a) not more than two passages from works by the same author are published by the same publisher within five years;

(b) the source from which the passages are taken is acknowledged; and

(c) the name of the author, if given in the source, is mentioned.

R.S., 1985, c. C-42, s. 30; R.S., 1985, c. 10 (4th Supp.), s. 7; 1997, c. 24, s. 18.

Meaning of *lesson*

30.01 (1) For the purposes of this section, *lesson* means a lesson, test or examination, or part of one, in which, or during the course of which, an act is done in respect of a work or other subject-matter by an educational institution or a person acting under its authority that would otherwise be an infringement of copyright but is permitted under a limitation or exception under this Act.

Application

(2) This section does not apply so as to permit any act referred to in paragraph (3)(a), (b) or (c) with respect to a work or other subject-matter whose use in the lesson constitutes an infringement of copyright or for whose use in the lesson the consent of the copyright owner is required.

Communication by telecommunication

(3) Subject to subsection (6), it is not an infringement of copyright for an educational institution or a person acting under its authority

(a) to communicate a lesson to the public by telecommunication for educational or training purposes, if that public consists only of students who are enrolled in a course of which the lesson forms a part or of other persons acting under the authority of the educational institution;

(b) to make a fixation of the lesson for the purpose of the act referred to in paragraph (a); or

(c) to do any other act that is necessary for the purpose of the acts referred to in paragraphs (a) and (b).

Participation by telecommunication

(4) A student who is enrolled in a course of which the lesson forms a part is deemed to be a person on the premises of the educational institution when the student participates in or receives the lesson by means of communication by telecommunication under paragraph (3)(a).

Reproducing lessons

(5) It is not an infringement of copyright for a student who has received a lesson by means of communication by telecommunication under paragraph (3)(a) to reproduce the lesson in order to be able to listen to or view it at a more convenient time. However, the student shall destroy the reproduction within 30 days after the day on which the students who are enrolled in the course to which the lesson relates have received their final course evaluations.

Conditions

(6) The educational institution and any person acting under its authority, except a student, shall

(a) destroy any fixation of the lesson within 30 days after the day on which the students who are enrolled in the course to which the lesson relates have received their final course evaluations;

(b) take measures that can reasonably be expected to limit the communication by telecommunication of the lesson to the persons referred to in paragraph (3)(a);

(c) take, in relation to the communication by telecommunication of the lesson in digital form, measures that can reasonably be expected to prevent the students from fixing, reproducing or communicating the lesson other than as they may do under this section; and

(d) take, in relation to a communication by telecommunication in digital form, any measure prescribed by regulation.

2012, c. 20, s. 27.

Exception — digital reproduction of works

30.02 (1) Subject to subsections (3) to (5), it is not an infringement of copyright for an educational institution that has a reprographic reproduction licence under which the institution is authorized to make reprographic reproductions of works in a collective society's repertoire for an educational or training purpose

(a) to make a digital reproduction — of the same general nature and extent as the reprographic reproduction authorized under the licence — of a paper form of any of those works;

(b) to communicate the digital reproduction by telecommunication for an educational or training purpose to persons acting under the authority of the institution; or

(c) to do any other act that is necessary for the purpose of the acts referred to in paragraphs (a) and (b).

Exception

(2) Subject to subsections (3) to (5), it is not an infringement of copyright for a person acting under the authority of the educational institution to whom the work has been communicated under paragraph (1)(b) to print one copy of the work.

Conditions

(3) An educational institution that makes a digital reproduction of a work under paragraph (1)(a) shall

(a) pay to the collective society, with respect to all the persons to whom the digital reproduction is communicated by the institution under paragraph (1)(b), the royalties that would be payable if one reprographic reproduction were distributed by the institution to each of those persons, and comply with the licence terms and conditions applicable to a reprographic reproduction to the extent that they are reasonably applicable to a digital reproduction;

(b) take measures to prevent the digital reproduction from being communicated by telecommunication to any persons who are not acting under the authority of the institution;

(c) take measures to prevent a person to whom the work has been communicated under paragraph (1)(b) from printing more than one copy, and to prevent any other reproduction or communication of the digital reproduction; and

(d) take any measure prescribed by regulation.

Restriction

(4) An educational institution may not make a digital reproduction of a work under paragraph (1)(a) if

(a) the institution has entered into a digital reproduction agreement respecting the work with a collective society under which the institution may make a digital reproduction of the work, may communicate the digital reproduction by telecommunication to persons acting under the authority of the institution and may permit those persons to print at least one copy of the work;

(b) there is a tariff certified under section 70.15 that is applicable to the digital reproduction of the work, to the communication of the digital reproduction by telecommunication to persons acting under the authority of the institution and to the printing by those persons of at least one copy of the work; or

(c) the institution has been informed by the collective society that is authorized to enter into reprographic agreements with respect to the work that the owner of the copyright in the work has informed it, under subsection (5), that the owner refuses to authorize the collective society to enter into a digital reproduction agreement with respect to the work.

Restriction

(5) If the owner of the copyright in a work informs the collective society that is authorized to enter into reprographic agreements with respect to the work that the owner refuses to authorize it to enter into digital reproduction agreements with respect to the work, the collective society shall inform the educational institutions with which it has entered into reprographic reproduction agreements with respect to the work that they are not permitted to make digital reproductions under subsection (1).

de l'œuvre, et respecter les modalités afférentes à la licence autorisant la reprographie qui sont applicables à la reproduction numérique de l'œuvre;

b) prendre des mesures en vue d'empêcher la communication par télécommunication de la reproduction numérique à des personnes autres que celles agissant sous son autorité;

c) prendre des mesures en vue d'empêcher l'impression de la reproduction numérique à plus d'un exemplaire par la personne à qui elle a été communiquée au titre de l'alinéa (1)b), et toute autre reproduction ou communication;

d) prendre toutes les mesures réglementaires.

Restriction

(4) L'établissement d'enseignement n'est pas autorisé à faire une reproduction numérique d'une œuvre au titre de l'alinéa (1)a) si, selon le cas :

a) il a conclu avec une société de gestion un accord de reproduction numérique l'autorisant à faire une reproduction numérique de l'œuvre et à la communiquer par télécommunication aux personnes agissant sous son autorité et autorisant celles-ci à en imprimer un certain nombre d'exemplaires;

b) un tarif homologué en vertu de l'article 70.15 est applicable à la reproduction numérique de l'œuvre, à la communication de celle-ci par télécommunication aux personnes agissant sous son autorité et à l'impression par celles-ci d'un certain nombre d'exemplaires de l'œuvre;

c) la société de gestion autorisée à conclure un accord de reproduction par reprographie de l'œuvre l'a avisé qu'elle a été informée par le titulaire du droit d'auteur sur l'œuvre, au titre du paragraphe (5), que celui-ci lui interdit de conclure un accord de reproduction numérique de celle-ci.

Restriction

(5) Si le titulaire du droit d'auteur sur une œuvre informe la société de gestion autorisée à conclure un accord de reproduction par reprographie de l'œuvre qu'il lui interdit de conclure un accord autorisant la reproduction numérique de celle-ci, la société de gestion informe les établissements d'enseignement avec lesquels elle a conclu un accord de reproduction par reprographie de l'œuvre qu'ils ne sont pas autorisés à faire de reproductions numériques de celle-ci au titre du paragraphe (1).

Deeming provision

(6) The owner of the copyright in a work who, in respect of the work, has authorized a collective society to enter into a reprographic reproduction agreement with an educational institution is deemed to have authorized the society to enter into a digital reproduction agreement with the institution — subject to the same restrictions as a reprographic reproduction agreement — unless the owner has refused to give this authorization under subsection (5) or has authorized another collective society to enter into a digital reproduction agreement with respect to the work.

Maximum amount that may be recovered

(7) In proceedings against an educational institution for making a digital reproduction of a paper form of a work, or for communicating such a reproduction by telecommunication for an educational or training purpose to persons acting under the authority of the institution, the owner of the copyright in the work may not recover an amount more than

(a) in the case where there is a digital reproduction licence that meets the conditions described in paragraph (4)(a) in respect of the work — or, if none exists in respect of the work, in respect of a work of the same category — the amount of royalties that would be payable under that licence in respect of those acts or, if there is more than one applicable licence, the greatest amount of royalties payable under any of those licences; and

(b) in the case where there is no licence described in paragraph (a) but there is a reprographic reproduction licence in respect of the work — or, if none exists in respect of the work, in respect of a work of the same category — the amount of royalties that would be payable under that licence in respect of those acts or, if there is more than one applicable licence, the greatest amount of royalties payable under any of those licences.

No damages

(8) The owner of the copyright in a work may not recover any damages against a person acting under the authority of the educational institution who, in respect of a digital reproduction of the work that is communicated to the person by telecommunication, prints one copy of the work if, at the time of the printing, it was reasonable for the person to believe that the communication was made in accordance with paragraph (1)(b).

2012, c. 20, s. 27.

Royalties — digital reproduction agreement

30.03 (1) If an educational institution has paid royalties to a collective society for the digital reproduction of a work under paragraph 30.02(3)(a) and afterwards the institution enters into a digital reproduction agreement described in paragraph 30.02(4)(a) with any collective society,

(a) in the case where the institution would — under that digital reproduction agreement — pay a greater amount of royalties for the digital reproduction of that work than what was payable under paragraph 30.02(3)(a), the institution shall pay to the collective society to which it paid royalties under that paragraph the difference between

(i) the amount of royalties that the institution would have had to pay for the digital reproduction of that work if the agreement had been entered into on the day on which the institution first made a digital reproduction under paragraph 30.02(1)(a), and

(ii) the amount of royalties that the institution paid to the society under paragraph 30.02(3)(a) for the digital reproduction of that work from the day on which that paragraph comes into force until the day on which they enter into the digital reproduction agreement; and

(b) in the case where the institution would — under that digital reproduction agreement — pay a lesser amount of royalties for the digital reproduction of that work than what was payable under paragraph 30.02(3)(a), the collective society to which the institution paid royalties under that paragraph shall pay to the institution the difference between

(i) the amount of royalties that the institution paid to the society under paragraph 30.02(3)(a) for the digital reproduction of that work from the day on which that paragraph comes into force until the day on which they enter into the digital reproduction agreement, and

(ii) the amount of royalties that the institution would have had to pay for the digital reproduction of that work if the agreement had been entered into on the day on which the institution first made a digital reproduction under paragraph 30.02(1)(a).

Royalties — tariff

(2) If an educational institution has paid royalties to a collective society for the digital reproduction of a work under paragraph 30.02(3)(a) and afterwards a tariff applies to the digital reproduction of that work under paragraph 30.02(4)(b),

Accord de reproduction numérique

30.03 (1) Si l'établissement d'enseignement a versé des redevances à une société de gestion à l'égard de la reproduction numérique d'une œuvre au titre de l'alinéa 30.02(3)a) et qu'il conclut par la suite avec toute société de gestion un accord de reproduction numérique visé à l'alinéa 30.02(4)a) :

a) dans le cas où l'accord prévoit pour la reproduction numérique de l'œuvre des redevances supérieures à celles qui étaient payables au titre de l'alinéa 30.02(3)a), l'établissement d'enseignement doit verser à la première société de gestion la différence entre le montant des redevances qu'il aurait eu à verser si l'accord avait été conclu à la date à laquelle il a fait la première reproduction numérique de l'œuvre au titre de l'alinéa 30.02(1)a) et le montant des redevances qu'il lui a versées au titre de l'alinéa 30.02(3)a) à compter de la date d'entrée en vigueur de cet alinéa jusqu'à la date de conclusion de l'accord;

b) dans le cas où l'accord prévoit pour la reproduction numérique de l'œuvre des redevances inférieures à celles qui étaient payables au titre de l'alinéa 30.02(3)a), la première société de gestion doit verser à l'établissement d'enseignement la différence entre le montant des redevances qu'il lui a versées au titre de cet alinéa à compter de la date d'entrée en vigueur de celui-ci jusqu'à la date de conclusion de l'accord et le montant des redevances qu'il aurait eu à verser si l'accord avait été conclu à la date à laquelle il a fait cette première reproduction numérique au titre de l'alinéa 30.02(1)a).

Tarif pour la reproduction numérique

(2) Si l'établissement d'enseignement a versé des redevances à une société de gestion, au titre de l'alinéa 30.02(3)a), à l'égard de la reproduction numérique d'une œuvre à laquelle s'applique un tarif visé à l'alinéa 30.02(4)b) :

(a) in the case where the institution would — under the tariff — pay a greater amount of royalties for the digital reproduction of that work than what was payable under paragraph 30.02(3)(a), the institution shall pay to the collective society to which it paid royalties under that paragraph the difference between

(i) the amount of royalties that the institution would have had to pay for the digital reproduction of that work if the tariff had been certified on the day on which the institution first made a digital reproduction under paragraph 30.02(1)(a), and

(ii) the amount of royalties that the institution paid to the society under paragraph 30.02(3)(a) for the digital reproduction of that work from the day on which that paragraph comes into force until the day on which the tariff is certified; and

(b) in the case where the institution would — under the tariff — pay a lesser amount of royalties for the digital reproduction of that work than what was payable under paragraph 30.02(3)(a), the collective society to which the institution paid royalties under that paragraph shall pay to the institution the difference between

(i) the amount of royalties that the institution paid to the society under paragraph 30.02(3)(a) for the digital reproduction of that work from the day on which that paragraph comes into force until the day on which the tariff is certified, and

(ii) the amount of royalties that the institution would have had to pay for the digital reproduction of that work if the tariff had been certified on the day on which the institution first made a digital reproduction under paragraph 30.02(1)(a).

2012, c. 20, s. 27.

Work available through Internet

30.04 (1) Subject to subsections (2) to (5), it is not an infringement of copyright for an educational institution, or a person acting under the authority of one, to do any of the following acts for educational or training purposes in respect of a work or other subject-matter that is available through the Internet:

(a) reproduce it;

(b) communicate it to the public by telecommunication, if that public primarily consists of students of the educational institution or other persons acting under its authority;

a) dans le cas où les redevances prévues par le tarif sont supérieures à celles qui étaient payables au titre de l'alinéa 30.02(3)a), l'établissement d'enseignement doit verser à la société de gestion la différence entre le montant des redevances qu'il aurait eu à verser si le tarif avait été homologué à la date à laquelle il a fait la première reproduction numérique de l'œuvre au titre de l'alinéa 30.02(1)a) et le montant des redevances qu'il lui a versées au titre de l'alinéa 30.02(3)a) à compter de la date d'entrée en vigueur de cet alinéa jusqu'à la date de l'homologation;

b) dans le cas où les redevances prévues par le tarif sont inférieures à celles qui étaient payables au titre de l'alinéa 30.02(3)a), la société de gestion doit verser à l'établissement d'enseignement la différence entre le montant des redevances qu'il lui a versées au titre de cet alinéa à compter de la date d'entrée en vigueur de celui-ci jusqu'à la date de l'homologation et le montant des redevances qu'il aurait eu à verser si le tarif avait été homologué à la date à laquelle il a fait cette première reproduction numérique au titre de l'alinéa 30.02(1)a).

2012, ch. 20, art. 27.

Œuvre sur Internet

30.04 (1) Sous réserve des paragraphes (2) à (5), ne constitue pas une violation du droit d'auteur le fait pour un établissement d'enseignement ou une personne agissant sous son autorité d'accomplir les actes ci-après à des fins pédagogiques à l'égard d'une œuvre ou de tout autre objet du droit d'auteur qui sont accessibles sur Internet :

a) les reproduire;

b) les communiquer au public par télécommunication si le public visé est principalement formé d'élèves de l'établissement d'enseignement ou d'autres personnes agissant sous son autorité;

(c) perform it in public, if that public primarily consists of students of the educational institution or other persons acting under its authority; or

(d) do any other act that is necessary for the purpose of the acts referred to in paragraphs (a) to (c).

Conditions

(2) Subsection (1) does not apply unless the educational institution or person acting under its authority, in doing any of the acts described in that subsection in respect of the work or other subject-matter, mentions the following:

(a) the source; and

(b) if given in the source, the name of

(i) the author, in the case of a work,

(ii) the performer, in the case of a performer's performance,

(iii) the maker, in the case of a sound recording, and

(iv) the broadcaster, in the case of a communication signal.

Non-application

(3) Subsection (1) does not apply if the work or other subject-matter — or the Internet site where it is posted — is protected by a technological protection measure that restricts access to the work or other subject-matter or to the Internet site.

Non-application

(4) Subsection (1) does not permit a person to do any act described in that subsection in respect of a work or other subject-matter if

(a) that work or other subject-matter — or the Internet site where it is posted — is protected by a technological protection measure that restricts the doing of that act; or

(b) a clearly visible notice — and not merely the copyright symbol — prohibiting that act is posted at the Internet site where the work or other subject-matter is posted or on the work or other subject-matter itself.

Non-application

(5) Subsection (1) does not apply if the educational institution or person acting under its authority knows or should have known that the work or other subject-matter was made available through the Internet without the consent of the copyright owner.

Regulations

(6) The Governor in Council may make regulations for the purposes of paragraph (4)(b) prescribing what constitutes a clearly visible notice.

2012, c. 20, s. 27.

Libraries, Archives and Museums

Management and maintenance of collection

30.1 (1) It is not an infringement of copyright for a library, archive or museum or a person acting under the authority of a library, archive or museum to make, for the maintenance or management of its permanent collection or the permanent collection of another library, archive or museum, a copy of a work or other subject-matter, whether published or unpublished, in its permanent collection

    (a) if the original is rare or unpublished and is

        (i) deteriorating, damaged or lost, or

        (ii) at risk of deterioration or becoming damaged or lost;

    (b) for the purposes of on-site consultation if the original cannot be viewed, handled or listened to because of its condition or because of the atmospheric conditions in which it must be kept;

    (c) in an alternative format if the library, archive or museum or a person acting under the authority of the library, archive or museum considers that the original is currently in a format that is obsolete or is becoming obsolete, or that the technology required to use the original is unavailable or is becoming unavailable;

    (d) for the purposes of internal record-keeping and cataloguing;

    (e) for insurance purposes or police investigations; or

    (f) if necessary for restoration.

Limitation

(2) Paragraphs (1)(a) to (c) do not apply where an appropriate copy is commercially available in a medium and of a quality that is appropriate for the purposes of subsection (1).

Destruction of intermediate copies

(3) If a person must make an intermediate copy in order to make a copy under subsection (1), the person must destroy the intermediate copy as soon as it is no longer needed.

Regulations

(4) The Governor in Council may make regulations with respect to the procedure for making copies under subsection (1).

1997, c. 24, s. 18; 1999, c. 31, s. 59(E); 2012, c. 20, s. 28.

Research or private study

30.2 (1) It is not an infringement of copyright for a library, archive or museum or a person acting under its authority to do anything on behalf of any person that the person may do personally under section 29 or 29.1.

Copies of articles for research, etc.

(2) It is not an infringement of copyright for a library, archive or museum or a person acting under the authority of a library, archive or museum to make, by reprographic reproduction, for any person requesting to use the copy for research or private study, a copy of a work that is, or that is contained in, an article published in

(a) a scholarly, scientific or technical periodical; or

(b) a newspaper or periodical, other than a scholarly, scientific or technical periodical, if the newspaper or periodical was published more than one year before the copy is made.

Restriction

(3) Paragraph (2)(b) does not apply in respect of a work of fiction or poetry or a dramatic or musical work.

Conditions

(4) A library, archive or museum may provide the person for whom the copy is made under subsection (2) with the copy only on the condition that

(a) the person is provided with a single copy of the work; and

(b) the library, archive or museum informs the person that the copy is to be used solely for research or private study and that any use of the copy for a purpose other than research or private study may require the authorization of the copyright owner of the work in question.

Patrons of other libraries, etc.

(5) Subject to subsection (5.02), a library, archive or museum, or a person acting under the authority of one, may do, on behalf of a patron of another library, archive or museum, anything under subsection (1) or (2) that it is authorized by this section to do on behalf of one of its own patrons.

Deeming

(5.01) For the purpose of subsection (5), the making of a copy of a work other than by reprographic reproduction is deemed to be a making of a copy of the work that may be done under subsection (2).

Limitation regarding copies in digital form

(5.02) A library, archive or museum, or a person acting under the authority of one, may, under subsection (5), provide a copy in digital form to a person who has requested it through another library, archive or museum if the providing library, archive or museum or person takes measures to prevent the person who has requested it from

(a) making any reproduction of the digital copy, including any paper copies, other than printing one copy of it;

(b) communicating the digital copy to any other person; and

(c) using the digital copy for more than five business days from the day on which the person first uses it.

Destruction of intermediate copies

(5.1) Where an intermediate copy is made in order to copy a work referred to in subsection (5), once the copy is given to the patron, the intermediate copy must be destroyed.

Regulations

(6) The Governor in Council may, for the purposes of this section, make regulations

(a) defining "newspaper" and "periodical";

(b) defining scholarly, scientific and technical periodicals;

(c) prescribing the information to be recorded about any action taken under subsection (1) or (5) and the manner and form in which the information is to be kept; and

(d) prescribing the manner and form in which the conditions set out in subsection (4) are to be met.

1997, c. 24, s. 18; 2012, c. 20, s. 29.

Copying works deposited in archive

30.21 (1) Subject to subsections (3) and (3.1), it is not an infringement of copyright for an archive to make, for any person requesting to use the copy for research or private study, a copy of an unpublished work that is deposited in the archive and provide the person with it.

Notice

(2) When a person deposits a work in an archive, the archive must give the person notice that it may copy the work in accordance with this section.

Conditions for copying of works

(3) The archive may copy the work only on the condition that

(a) the person who deposited the work, if a copyright owner, did not, at the time the work was deposited, prohibit its copying; and

(b) copying has not been prohibited by any other owner of copyright in the work.

Condition for providing copy

(3.1) The archive may provide the person for whom a copy is made under subsection (1) with the copy only on the condition that

(a) the person is provided with a single copy of the work; and

(b) the archive informs the person that the copy is to be used solely for research or private study and that any use of the copy for a purpose other than research or private study may require the authorization of the copyright owner of the work in question.

Regulations

(4) The Governor in Council may prescribe by regulation the manner and form in which the conditions set out in subsections (3) and (3.1) may be met.

(5) to (7) [Repealed, 2004, c. 11, s. 21]

1997, c. 24, s. 18; 1999, c. 31, s. 60(E); 2004, c. 11, s. 21; 2012, c. 20, s. 30.

c) préciser les renseignements à obtenir concernant les actes accomplis dans le cadre des paragraphes (1) et (5), ainsi que leur mode de conservation;

d) déterminer la façon dont les conditions visées au paragraphe (4) peuvent être remplies.

1997, ch. 24, art. 18; 2012, ch. 20, art. 29.

Copie d'une œuvre déposée dans un service d'archives

30.21 (1) Sous réserve des paragraphes (3) et (3.1), ne constitue pas une violation du droit d'auteur le fait, pour un service d'archives, de reproduire et de fournir à la personne qui lui en fait la demande à des fins d'étude privée ou de recherche, une œuvre non publiée déposée auprès de lui.

Avis

(2) Au moment du dépôt, le service d'archives doit toutefois aviser le déposant qu'une reproduction de l'œuvre pourrait être faite en vertu du présent article.

Conditions pour la reproduction

(3) Il ne peut faire la reproduction que si :

a) le titulaire du droit d'auteur ne l'a pas interdite au moment où il déposait l'œuvre;

b) aucun autre titulaire du droit d'auteur ne l'a par ailleurs interdite.

Autres conditions applicables au service d'archives

(3.1) Il doit aussi se conformer aux conditions suivantes :

a) ne remettre qu'une seule copie de l'œuvre reproduite au titre du paragraphe (1) à la personne à qui elle est destinée;

b) informer cette personne que la copie ne peut être utilisée qu'à des fins d'étude privée ou de recherche et que tout usage de la copie à d'autres fins peut exiger l'autorisation du titulaire du droit d'auteur sur l'œuvre en cause.

Règlements

(4) Le gouverneur en conseil peut, par règlement, préciser la façon dont le service doit se conformer aux conditions visées aux paragraphes (3) et (3.1).

(5) à (7) [Abrogés, 2004, ch. 11, art. 21]

1997, ch. 24, art. 18; 1999, ch. 31, art. 60(A); 2004, ch. 11, art. 21; 2012, ch. 20, art. 30.

Machines Installed in Educational Institutions, Libraries, Archives and Museums

No infringement by educational institution, etc.

30.3 (1) An educational institution or a library, archive or museum does not infringe copyright where

(a) a copy of a work is made using a machine for the making, by reprographic reproduction, of copies of works in printed form;

(b) the machine is installed by or with the approval of the educational institution, library, archive or museum on its premises for use by students, instructors or staff at the educational institution or by persons using the library, archive or museum; and

(c) there is affixed in the prescribed manner and location a notice warning of infringement of copyright.

Application

(2) Subsection (1) only applies if, in respect of a reprographic reproduction,

(a) the educational institution, library, archive or museum has entered into an agreement with a collective society that is authorized by copyright owners to grant licences on their behalf;

(b) the Board has, in accordance with section 70.2, fixed the royalties and related terms and conditions in respect of a licence;

(c) a tariff has been approved in accordance with section 70.15; or

(d) a collective society has filed a proposed tariff in accordance with section 70.13.

Order

(3) Where a collective society offers to negotiate or has begun to negotiate an agreement referred to in paragraph (2)(a), the Board may, at the request of either party, order that the educational institution, library, archive or museum be treated as an institution to which subsection (1) applies, during the period specified in the order.

Agreement with copyright owner

(4) Where an educational institution, library, archive or museum has entered into an agreement with a copyright owner other than a collective society respecting reprographic reproduction, subsection (1) applies only in respect of the works of the copyright owner that are covered by the agreement.

Regulations

(5) The Governor in Council may, for the purposes of paragraph 1(c), prescribe by regulation the manner of affixing and location of notices and the dimensions, form and contents of notices.

1997, c. 24, s. 18.

Libraries, Archives and Museums in Educational Institutions

Application to libraries, etc. within educational institutions

30.4 For greater certainty, the exceptions to infringement of copyright provided for under sections 29.4 to 30.3 and 45 also apply in respect of a library, archive or museum that forms part of an educational institution.

1997, c. 24, s. 18.

Library and Archives of Canada

Permitted acts

30.5 It is not an infringement of copyright for the Librarian and Archivist of Canada under the *Library and Archives of Canada Act*, to

(a) make a copy of a work or other subject-matter in taking a representative sample for the purpose of preservation under subsection 8(2) of that Act;

(b) effect the fixation of a copy of a publication, as defined in section 2 of that Act, that is provided by telecommunication in accordance with subsection 10(1) of that Act;

(c) make a copy of a recording, as defined in subsection 11(2) of that Act, for the purposes of section 11 of that Act; or

(d) at the time that a broadcasting undertaking, as defined in subsection 2(1) of the *Broadcasting Act*, communicates a work or other subject-matter to the public by telecommunication, make a copy of the work or other subject-matter that is included in that communication.

1997, c. 24, s. 18; 2004, c. 11, s. 25.

Computer Programs

Permitted acts

30.6 It is not an infringement of copyright in a computer program for a person who owns a copy of the computer program that is authorized by the owner of the copyright, or has a licence to use a copy of the computer program, to

(a) reproduce the copy by adapting, modifying or converting it, or translating it into another computer language, if the person proves that the reproduced copy

(i) is essential for the compatibility of the computer program with a particular computer,

(ii) is solely for the person's own use, and

(iii) was destroyed immediately after the person ceased to be the owner of the copy of the computer program or to have a licence to use it; or

(b) reproduce for backup purposes the copy or a reproduced copy referred to in paragraph (a) if the person proves that the reproduction for backup purposes was destroyed immediately after the person ceased to be the owner of the copy of the computer program or to have a licence to use it.

1997, c. 24, s. 18; 2012, c. 20, s. 31.

Interoperability of computer programs

30.61 (1) It is not an infringement of copyright in a computer program for a person who owns a copy of the computer program that is authorized by the owner of the copyright, or has a licence to use a copy of the computer program, to reproduce the copy if

(a) they reproduce the copy for the sole purpose of obtaining information that would allow the person to make the program and another computer program interoperable; and

(b) they do not use or disclose that information, except as necessary to make the program and another computer program interoperable or to assess that interoperability.

No limitation

(2) In the case where that information is used or disclosed as necessary to make another computer program interoperable with the program, subsection (1) applies

Programmes d'ordinateur

Actes licites

30.6 Ne constitue pas une violation du droit d'auteur le fait, pour le propriétaire d'un exemplaire — autorisé par le titulaire du droit d'auteur — d'un programme d'ordinateur, ou pour le titulaire d'une licence permettant l'utilisation d'un exemplaire d'un tel programme :

a) de reproduire l'exemplaire par adaptation, modification ou conversion, ou par traduction en un autre langage informatique, s'il établit que la copie est destinée à assurer la compatibilité du programme avec un ordinateur donné, qu'elle ne sert qu'à son propre usage et qu'elle a été détruite dès qu'il a cessé d'être propriétaire de l'exemplaire ou titulaire de la licence, selon le cas;

b) de reproduire à des fins de sauvegarde l'exemplaire ou la copie visée à l'alinéa a) s'il établit que la reproduction a été détruite dès qu'il a cessé d'être propriétaire de l'exemplaire ou titulaire de la licence, selon le cas.

1997, ch. 24, art. 18; 2012, ch. 20, art. 31.

Interopérabilité

30.61 (1) Ne constitue pas une violation du droit d'auteur le fait, pour le propriétaire d'un exemplaire — autorisé par le titulaire du droit d'auteur — d'un programme d'ordinateur, ou pour le titulaire d'une licence permettant l'utilisation d'un exemplaire d'un tel programme, de le reproduire si les conditions suivantes sont réunies :

a) il reproduit son exemplaire dans le seul but d'obtenir de l'information lui permettant de rendre ce programme et un autre programme d'ordinateur interopérables;

b) toute utilisation ou communication de l'information est nécessaire pour rendre ce programme et un autre programme d'ordinateur interopérables ou pour évaluer leur interopérabilité.

Précision

(2) Lorsque l'utilisation ou la communication de l'information est nécessaire pour permettre de rendre le programme et un autre programme d'ordinateur interopérables, le paragraphe (1) s'applique même si cet autre programme d'ordinateur qui contient cette information

even if the other computer program incorporates the information and is then sold, rented or otherwise distributed.

2012, c. 20, s. 31.

Encryption Research

Encryption research

30.62 (1) Subject to subsections (2) and (3), it is not an infringement of copyright for a person to reproduce a work or other subject-matter for the purposes of encryption research if

(a) it would not be practical to carry out the research without making the copy;

(b) the person has lawfully obtained the work or other subject-matter; and

(c) the person has informed the owner of the copyright in the work or other subject-matter.

Limitation

(2) Subsection (1) does not apply if the person uses or discloses information obtained through the research to commit an act that is an offence under the *Criminal Code*.

Limitation — computer program

(3) Subsection (1) applies with respect to a computer program only if, in the event that the research reveals a vulnerability or a security flaw in the program and the person intends to make the vulnerability or security flaw public, the person gives adequate notice of the vulnerability or security flaw and of their intention to the owner of copyright in the program. However, the person need not give that adequate notice if, in the circumstances, the public interest in having the vulnerability or security flaw made public without adequate notice outweighs the owner's interest in receiving that notice.

2012, c. 20, s. 31.

Security

Security

30.63 (1) Subject to subsections (2) and (3), it is not an infringement of copyright for a person to reproduce a work or other subject-matter for the sole purpose, with the consent of the owner or administrator of a computer, computer system or computer network, of assessing the vulnerability of the computer, system or network or of correcting any security flaws.

est mis en circulation, notamment par la vente ou la location.

2012, ch. 20, art. 31.

Recherche sur le chiffrement

Recherche sur le chiffrement

30.62 (1) Sous réserve des paragraphes (2) et (3), ne constitue pas une violation du droit d'auteur le fait, pour une personne, en vue de faire une recherche sur le chiffrement, de reproduire une œuvre ou tout autre objet du droit d'auteur si les conditions suivantes sont réunies :

a) la recherche est difficilement réalisable autrement;

b) l'œuvre ou autre objet a été obtenu légalement;

c) la personne en a informé le titulaire du droit d'auteur sur l'œuvre ou autre objet.

Réserve

(2) Le paragraphe (1) ne s'applique pas lorsque la personne utilise ou communique de l'information obtenue par l'entremise de la recherche afin de commettre un acte qui constitue une infraction au sens du *Code criminel*.

Réserve — programme d'ordinateur

(3) Lorsqu'une personne découvre, par l'entremise de la recherche, une vulnérabilité ou un défaut de sécurité dans un programme d'ordinateur, le paragraphe (1) s'applique relativement à ce programme si, avant de les rendre publics, elle donne au titulaire du droit d'auteur sur le programme un préavis suffisant faisant état de ceux-ci et de son intention de les rendre publics. Elle peut cependant les rendre publics sans préavis si, compte tenu des circonstances, l'intérêt du public d'être informé à cet égard l'emporte sur l'intérêt du titulaire de recevoir le préavis.

2012, ch. 20, art. 31.

Sécurité

Sécurité

30.63 (1) Sous réserve des paragraphes (2) et (3), ne constitue pas une violation du droit d'auteur le fait, pour une personne, de reproduire une œuvre ou tout autre objet du droit d'auteur dans le seul but d'évaluer la vulnérabilité d'un ordinateur, d'un système informatique ou d'un réseau d'ordinateurs ou de corriger tout défaut de sécurité, dans le cas où l'évaluation ou la correction sont autorisées par le propriétaire ou l'administrateur de ceux-ci.

Limitation

(2) Subsection (1) does not apply if the person uses or discloses information obtained through the assessment or correction to commit an act that is an offence under the *Criminal Code*.

Limitation — computer program

(3) Subsection (1) applies with respect to a computer program only if, in the event that the assessment or correction reveals a vulnerability or a security flaw in the program and the person intends to make the vulnerability or security flaw public, the person gives adequate notice of the vulnerability or security flaw and of their intention to the owner of copyright in the program. However, the person need not give that adequate notice if, in the circumstances, the public interest in having the vulnerability or security flaw made public without adequate notice outweighs the owner's interest in receiving that notice.

2012, c. 20, s. 31.

Incidental Inclusion

Incidental use

30.7 It is not an infringement of copyright to incidentally and not deliberately

(a) include a work or other subject-matter in another work or other subject-matter; or

(b) do any act in relation to a work or other subject-matter that is incidentally and not deliberately included in another work or other subject-matter.

1997, c. 24, s. 18.

Temporary Reproductions for Technological Processes

Temporary reproductions

30.71 It is not an infringement of copyright to make a reproduction of a work or other subject-matter if

(a) the reproduction forms an essential part of a technological process;

(b) the reproduction's only purpose is to facilitate a use that is not an infringement of copyright; and

(c) the reproduction exists only for the duration of the technological process.

2012, c. 20, s. 32.

Ephemeral Recordings

Ephemeral recordings

30.8 (1) It is not an infringement of copyright for a programming undertaking to fix or reproduce in accordance with this section a performer's performance or work, other than a cinematographic work, that is performed live or a sound recording that is performed at the same time as the performer's performance or work, if the undertaking

    (a) is authorized to communicate the performer's performance, work or sound recording to the public by telecommunication;

    (b) makes the fixation or the reproduction itself, for its own broadcasts;

    (c) does not synchronize the fixation or reproduction with all or part of another recording, performer's performance or work; and

    (d) does not cause the fixation or reproduction to be used in an advertisement intended to sell or promote, as the case may be, a product, service, cause or institution.

Record keeping

(2) The programming undertaking must record the dates of the making and destruction of all fixations and reproductions and any other prescribed information about the fixation or reproduction, and keep the record current.

Right of access by copyright owners

(3) The programming undertaking must make the record referred to in subsection (2) available to owners of copyright in the works, sound recordings or performer's performances, or their representatives, within twenty-four hours after receiving a request.

Destruction

(4) The programming undertaking must destroy the fixation or reproduction within thirty days after making it, unless

    (a) the copyright owner authorizes its retention; or

    (b) it is deposited in an archive, in accordance with subsection (6).

Royalties

(5) Where the copyright owner authorizes the fixation or reproduction to be retained after the thirty days, the programming undertaking must pay any applicable royalty.

Archive

(6) Where the programming undertaking considers a fixation or reproduction to be of an exceptional documentary character, the undertaking may, with the consent of an official archive, deposit it in the official archive and must notify the copyright owner, within thirty days, of the deposit of the fixation or reproduction.

Definition of *official archive*

(7) In subsection (6), ***official archive*** means the Library and Archives of Canada or any archive established under the law of a province for the preservation of the official archives of the province.

Application

(8) This section does not apply where a licence is available from a collective society to make the fixation or reproduction of the performer's performance, work or sound recording.

Telecommunications by networks

(9) A broadcasting undertaking, as defined in the *Broadcasting Act*, may make a single reproduction of a fixation or reproduction made by a programming undertaking and communicate it to the public by telecommunication, within the period referred to in subsection (4), if the broadcasting undertaking meets the conditions set out in subsection (1) and is part of a prescribed network that includes the programming undertaking.

Limitations

(10) The reproduction and communication to the public by telecommunication must be made

   (a) in accordance with subsections (2) to (6); and

   (b) within thirty days after the day on which the programming undertaking made the fixation or reproduction.

Definition of *programming undertaking*

(11) In this section, ***programming undertaking*** means

   (a) a programming undertaking as defined in subsection 2(1) of the *Broadcasting Act*;

   (b) a programming undertaking described in paragraph (a) that originates programs within a network, as defined in subsection 2(1) of the *Broadcasting Act*; or

(c) a distribution undertaking as defined in subsection 2(1) of the *Broadcasting Act*, in respect of the programs that it originates.

The undertaking must hold a broadcasting licence issued by the Canadian Radio-television and Telecommunications Commission under the *Broadcasting Act*, or be exempted from this requirement by the Canadian Radio-television and Telecommunications Commission.

1997, c. 24, s. 18; 2004, c. 11, s. 26; 2012, c. 20, s. 33.

Ephemeral recordings — broadcasting undertaking

30.9 (1) It is not an infringement of copyright for a broadcasting undertaking to reproduce in accordance with this section a sound recording, or a performer's performance or work that is embodied in a sound recording, solely for the purpose of their broadcasting, if the undertaking

(a) owns the copy of the sound recording, performer's performance or work and that copy is authorized by the owner of the copyright, or has a licence to use the copy;

(b) is authorized to communicate the sound recording, performer's performance or work to the public by telecommunication;

(c) makes the reproduction itself, for its own broadcasts;

(d) does not synchronize the reproduction with all or part of another recording, performer's performance or work; and

(e) does not cause the reproduction to be used in an advertisement intended to sell or promote, as the case may be, a product, service, cause or institution.

Record keeping

(2) The broadcasting undertaking must record the dates of the making and destruction of all reproductions and any other prescribed information about the reproduction, and keep the record current.

Right of access by copyright owners

(3) The broadcasting undertaking must make the record referred to in subsection (2) available to owners of copyright in the sound recordings, performer's performances or works, or their representatives, within twenty-four hours after receiving a request.

Destruction

(4) The broadcasting undertaking must destroy the reproduction when it no longer possesses the sound recording, or performer's performance or work embodied in the sound recording, or its licence to use the sound recording, performer's performance or work expires, or at the latest within 30 days after making the reproduction, unless the copyright owner authorizes the reproduction to be retained.

Royalty

(5) If the copyright owner authorizes the reproduction to be retained, the broadcasting undertaking must pay any applicable royalty.

(6) [Repealed, 2012, c. 20, s. 34]

Definition of *broadcasting undertaking*

(7) In this section, ***broadcasting undertaking*** means a broadcasting undertaking as defined in subsection 2(1) of the *Broadcasting Act* that holds a broadcasting licence issued by the Canadian Radio-television and Telecommunications Commission under that Act.

1997, c. 24, s. 18; 2012, c. 20, s. 34.

Retransmission

Interpretation

31 (1) In this section,

new media retransmitter means a person whose retransmission is lawful under the *Broadcasting Act* only by reason of the *Exemption Order for New Media Broadcasting Undertakings* issued by the Canadian Radio-television and Telecommunications Commission as Appendix A to Public Notice CRTC 1999-197, as amended from time to time; (*retransmetteur de nouveaux médias*)

retransmitter means a person who performs a function comparable to that of a cable retransmission system, but does not include a new media retransmitter; (*retransmetteur*)

signal means a signal that carries a literary, dramatic, musical or artistic work and is transmitted for free reception by the public by a terrestrial radio or terrestrial television station. (*signal*)

Retransmission of local and distant signals

(2) It is not an infringement of copyright for a retransmitter to communicate to the public by telecommunication any literary, dramatic, musical or artistic work if

(a) the communication is a retransmission of a local or distant signal;

(b) the retransmission is lawful under the *Broadcasting Act*;

(c) the signal is retransmitted simultaneously and without alteration, except as otherwise required or permitted by or under the laws of Canada;

(d) in the case of the retransmission of a distant signal, the retransmitter has paid any royalties, and complied with any terms and conditions, fixed under this Act; and

(e) the retransmitter complies with the applicable conditions, if any, referred to in paragraph (3)(b).

Regulations

(3) The Governor in Council may make regulations

(a) defining "local signal" and "distant signal" for the purposes of subsection (2); and

(b) prescribing conditions for the purposes of paragraph (2)(e), and specifying whether any such condition applies to all retransmitters or only to a class of retransmitter.

R.S., 1985, c. C-42, s. 31; R.S., 1985, c. 10 (4th Suppl.), s. 7; 1988, c. 65, s. 63; 1997, c. 24, ss. 16, 52(F); 2002, c. 26, s. 2.

Network Services

Network services

31.1 (1) A person who, in providing services related to the operation of the Internet or another digital network, provides any means for the telecommunication or the reproduction of a work or other subject-matter through the Internet or that other network does not, solely by reason of providing those means, infringe copyright in that work or other subject-matter.

Incidental acts

(2) Subject to subsection (3), a person referred to in subsection (1) who caches the work or other subject-matter, or does any similar act in relation to it, to make the telecommunication more efficient does not, by virtue of that act alone, infringe copyright in the work or other subject-matter.

Copyright
PART III Infringement of Copyright and Moral Rights and Exceptions to Infringement
Exceptions
Network Services
Section 31.1

Conditions for application

(3) Subsection (2) does not apply unless the person, in respect of the work or other subject-matter,

(a) does not modify it, other than for technical reasons;

(b) ensures that any directions related to its caching or the doing of any similar act, as the case may be, that are specified in a manner consistent with industry practice by whoever made it available for telecommunication through the Internet or another digital network, and that lend themselves to automated reading and execution, are read and executed; and

(c) does not interfere with the use of technology that is lawful and consistent with industry practice in order to obtain data on the use of the work or other subject-matter.

Hosting

(4) Subject to subsection (5), a person who, for the purpose of allowing the telecommunication of a work or other subject-matter through the Internet or another digital network, provides digital memory in which another person stores the work or other subject-matter does not, by virtue of that act alone, infringe copyright in the work or other subject-matter.

Condition for application

(5) Subsection (4) does not apply in respect of a work or other subject-matter if the person providing the digital memory knows of a decision of a court of competent jurisdiction to the effect that the person who has stored the work or other subject-matter in the digital memory infringes copyright by making the copy of the work or other subject-matter that is stored or by the way in which he or she uses the work or other subject-matter.

Exception

(6) Subsections (1), (2) and (4) do not apply in relation to an act that constitutes an infringement of copyright under subsection 27(2.3).

2012, c. 20, s. 35.

Droit d'auteur
PARTIE III Violation du droit d'auteur et des droits moraux, et cas d'exception
Exceptions
Services réseau
Article 31.1

Conditions d'application

(3) Le paragraphe (2) ne s'applique que si la personne respecte les conditions ci-après en ce qui a trait à l'œuvre ou à l'autre objet du droit d'auteur :

a) elle ne les modifie pas, sauf pour des raisons techniques;

b) elle veille à ce que les directives relatives à leur mise en antémémoire ou à l'exécution à leur égard d'une opération similaire, selon le cas, qui ont été formulées, suivant les pratiques de l'industrie, par quiconque les a mis à disposition pour télécommunication par l'intermédiaire d'Internet ou d'un autre réseau numérique soient lues et exécutées automatiquement si elles s'y prêtent;

c) elle n'entrave pas l'usage, à la fois licite et conforme aux pratiques de l'industrie, de la technologie pour l'obtention de données sur leur utilisation.

Stockage

(4) Sous réserve du paragraphe (5), quiconque fournit à une personne une mémoire numérique pour qu'elle y stocke une œuvre ou tout autre objet du droit d'auteur en vue de permettre leur télécommunication par l'intermédiaire d'Internet ou d'un autre réseau numérique ne viole pas le droit d'auteur sur l'œuvre ou l'autre objet du seul fait qu'il fournit cette mémoire.

Conditions d'application

(5) Le paragraphe (4) ne s'applique pas à l'égard d'une œuvre ou de tout autre objet du droit d'auteur si la personne qui fournit la mémoire numérique sait qu'un tribunal compétent a rendu une décision portant que la personne qui y a stocké l'œuvre ou l'autre objet viole le droit d'auteur du fait de leur reproduction ou en raison de la manière dont elle les utilise.

Exception

(6) Les paragraphes (1), (2) et (4) ne s'appliquent pas à l'égard des actes qui constituent une violation du droit d'auteur prévue au paragraphe 27(2.3).

2012, ch. 20, art. 35.

Persons with Perceptual Disabilities

Reproduction in alternate format

32 (1) It is not an infringement of copyright for a person with a perceptual disability, for a person acting at the request of such a person or for a non-profit organization acting for the benefit of such a person to

(a) reproduce a literary, musical, artistic or dramatic work, other than a cinematographic work, in a format specially designed for persons with a perceptual disability;

(a.1) fix a performer's performance of a literary, musical, artistic or dramatic work, other than a cinematographic work, in a format specially designed for persons with a perceptual disability;

(a.2) reproduce a sound recording, or a fixation of a performer's performance referred to in paragraph (a.1), in a format specially designed for persons with a perceptual disability;

(b) translate, adapt or reproduce in sign language a literary or dramatic work, other than a cinematographic work, in a format specially designed for persons with a perceptual disability;

(b.1) provide a person with a perceptual disability with, or provide such a person with access to, a work or other subject-matter to which any of paragraphs (a) to (b) applies, in a format specially designed for persons with a perceptual disability, and do any other act that is necessary for that purpose; or

(c) perform in public a literary or dramatic work, other than a cinematographic work, in sign language, either live or in a format specially designed for persons with a perceptual disability.

Limitation

(2) Subsection (1) does not apply if the work or other subject-matter is commercially available, within the meaning of paragraph (a) of the definition **commercially available** in section 2, in a format specially designed to meet the needs of the person with a perceptual disability referred to in that subsection.

(3) [Repealed, 2016, c. 4, s. 1]

R.S., 1985, c. C-42, s. 32; R.S., 1985, c. 10 (4th Supp.), s. 7; 1997, c. 24, s. 19; 2012, c. 20, s. 36; 2016, c. 4, s. 1.

Print disability — outside Canada

32.01 (1) Subject to this section, it is not an infringement of copyright for a non-profit organization acting for the benefit of persons with a print disability to do any of the following:

   (a) for the purpose of doing any of the acts set out in paragraph (b),

      (i) reproduce a literary, musical, artistic or dramatic work, other than a cinematographic work, in a format specially designed for persons with a print disability,

      (ii) fix a performer's performance of a literary, musical, artistic or dramatic work, other than a cinematographic work, in a format specially designed for persons with a print disability, or

      (iii) reproduce a sound recording, or a fixation of a performer's performance referred to in subparagraph (ii), in a format specially designed for persons with a print disability;

   (b) provide either of the following with, or provide either of the following with access to, a work or other subject-matter to which any of subparagraphs (a)(i) to (iii) applies, in a format specially designed for persons with a print disability, and do any other act that is necessary for that purpose:

      (i) a non-profit organization, in a country other than Canada, acting for the benefit of persons with a print disability in that country, or

      (ii) a person with a print disability, in a country other than Canada, who has made a request to be provided with, or provided with access to, the work or other subject-matter through a non-profit organization acting for the benefit of persons with a print disability in that country.

Available in other country

(2) Paragraph (1)(b) does not apply if the work or other subject-matter, in the format specially designed for persons with a print disability, is available in the other country within a reasonable time and for a reasonable price and may be located in that country with reasonable effort.

Marrakesh Treaty country

(3) An injunction is the only remedy that the owner of the copyright in the work or other subject-matter has against a non-profit organization relying on the exception set out in paragraph (1)(b) if

  (a) the other country referred to in that paragraph is a Marrakesh Treaty country; and

  (b) the non-profit organization infringes copyright by reason only that the work or other subject-matter, in the format described in subsection (2), is available, and may be located, as described in that subsection.

The owner of the copyright bears the burden of demonstrating that the work or other subject-matter, in the format described in subsection (2), is available, and may be located, as described in that subsection.

Not Marrakesh Treaty country

(3.1) An injunction is the only remedy that the owner of the copyright in the work or other subject-matter has against a non-profit organization relying on the exception set out in paragraph (1)(b) if

  (a) the other country referred to in that paragraph is not a Marrakesh Treaty country;

  (b) the non-profit organization infringes copyright by reason only that the work or other subject-matter, in the format described in subsection (2), is available, and may be located, as described in that subsection; and

  (c) the non-profit organization demonstrates that it had reasonable grounds to believe that the work or other subject-matter, in the format described in subsection (2), was not available, and could not be located, as described in that subsection.

Royalty

(4) A non-profit organization relying on the exception set out in subsection (1) shall pay, in accordance with the regulations, any royalty established under the regulations to the copyright owner.

If copyright owner cannot be located

(5) If the organization cannot locate the copyright owner, despite making reasonable efforts to do so, the organization shall pay, in accordance with the regulations, any royalty established under the regulations to a collective society.

Reports

(6) A non-profit organization relying on the exception set out in subsection (1) shall submit reports to an authority, in accordance with the regulations, on the organization's activities under this section.

Regulations

(7) The Governor in Council may make regulations

(a) requiring that, before a non-profit organization provides, or provides access to, a work or other subject-matter under paragraph (1)(b), the organization enter into a contract with respect to the use of the work or other subject-matter with, as the case may be, the recipient non-profit organization or the non-profit organization through which the request was made;

(b) respecting the form and content of such contracts;

(c) respecting any royalties to be paid under subsections (4) and (5);

(d) respecting to which collective society a royalty is payable in relation to works or other subject-matter, or classes of works or other subject-matter, for the purposes of subsection (5);

(e) respecting what constitutes reasonable efforts for the purposes of subsection (5); and

(f) respecting the reports to be made, and the authorities to which the reports are to be submitted, under subsection (6).

Definitions

(8) The following definitions apply in this section.

Marrakesh Treaty country means a country that is a party to the Marrakesh Treaty to Facilitate Access to Published Works for Persons Who Are Blind, Visually Impaired, or Otherwise Print Disabled, done at Marrakesh on June 27, 2013. (*pays partie au Traité de Marrakech*)

print disability means a disability that prevents or inhibits a person from reading a literary, musical, artistic or dramatic work in its original format and includes such a disability resulting from

(a) severe or total impairment of sight or the inability to focus or move one's eyes;

(b) the inability to hold or manipulate a book; or

(c) an impairment relating to comprehension. (*déficience de lecture des imprimés*)

2012, c. 20, s. 37; 2016, c. 4, s. 2.

Definition of *non-profit organization*

32.02 In sections 32 and 32.01, ***non-profit organization*** includes a department, agency or other portion of any order of government, including a municipal or local government, when it is acting on a non-profit basis.

2016, c. 4, s. 3.

Statutory Obligations

No infringement

32.1 (1) It is not an infringement of copyright for any person

(a) to disclose, pursuant to the *Access to Information Act*, a record within the meaning of that Act, or to disclose, pursuant to any like Act of the legislature of a province, like material;

(b) to disclose, pursuant to the *Privacy Act*, personal information within the meaning of that Act, or to disclose, pursuant to any like Act of the legislature of a province, like information;

(c) to make a copy of an object referred to in section 14 of the *Cultural Property Export and Import Act*, for deposit in an institution pursuant to a direction under that section; and

(d) to make a fixation or copy of a work or other subject-matter in order to comply with the *Broadcasting Act* or any rule, regulation or other instrument made under it.

Limitation

(2) Nothing in paragraph (1)(a) or (b) authorizes a person to whom a record or information is disclosed to do anything that, by this Act, only the owner of the copyright in the record, personal information or like information, as the case may be, has a right to do.

Destruction of fixation or copy

(3) Unless the *Broadcasting Act* otherwise provides, a person who makes a fixation or copy under paragraph (1)(d) shall destroy it immediately on the expiration of the period for which it must be kept pursuant to that Act, rule, regulation or other instrument.

1997, c. 24, s. 19.

œuvres publiées, fait à Marrakech le 27 juin 2013. (*Marrakesh Treaty country*)

2012, ch. 20, art. 37; 2016, ch. 4, art. 2.

Définition de *organisme sans but lucratif*

32.02 Aux articles 32 et 32.01, ***organisme sans but lucratif*** s'entend notamment d'un ministère, d'un organisme ou d'un autre secteur de tout ordre de gouvernement — y compris une administration municipale ou locale —, lorsqu'il agit sans but lucratif.

2016, ch. 4, art. 3.

Obligations découlant de la loi

Non-violation

32.1 (1) Ne constituent pas des violations du droit d'auteur :

a) la communication de documents effectuée en vertu de la *Loi sur l'accès à l'information* ou la communication de documents du même genre effectuée en vertu d'une loi provinciale d'objet comparable;

b) la communication de renseignements personnels effectuée en vertu de la *Loi sur la protection des renseignements personnels* ou la communication de renseignements du même genre effectuée en vertu d'une loi provinciale d'objet comparable;

c) la reproduction d'un objet visé à l'article 14 de la *Loi sur l'exportation et l'importation de biens culturels* pour dépôt dans un établissement selon les directives données conformément à cet article;

d) la fixation ou la reproduction d'une œuvre ou de tout autre objet du droit d'auteur destinée à répondre à une exigence de la *Loi sur la radiodiffusion* ou de ses textes d'application.

Restriction s'appliquant aux alinéas (1)a) et b)

(2) Les alinéas (1)a) et b) n'autorisent pas les personnes qui reçoivent communication de documents ou renseignements à exercer les droits que la présente loi ne confère qu'au titulaire d'un droit d'auteur.

Restriction s'appliquant à l'alinéa (1)d)

(3) Sauf disposition contraire de la *Loi sur la radiodiffusion*, la personne qui a produit la fixation ou la reproduction visée à l'alinéa (1)d) doit détruire l'exemplaire à l'expiration de la période de conservation prévue par cette loi ou ses textes d'application.

1997, ch. 24, art. 19.

Miscellaneous

Permitted acts

32.2 (1) It is not an infringement of copyright

(a) for an author of an artistic work who is not the owner of the copyright in the work to use any mould, cast, sketch, plan, model or study made by the author for the purpose of the work, if the author does not thereby repeat or imitate the main design of the work;

(b) for any person to reproduce, in a painting, drawing, engraving, photograph or cinematographic work

  (i) an architectural work, provided the copy is not in the nature of an architectural drawing or plan, or

  (ii) a sculpture or work of artistic craftsmanship or a cast or model of a sculpture or work of artistic craftsmanship, that is permanently situated in a public place or building;

(c) for any person to make or publish, for the purposes of news reporting or news summary, a report of a lecture given in public, unless the report is prohibited by conspicuous written or printed notice affixed before and maintained during the lecture at or about the main entrance of the building in which the lecture is given, and, except while the building is being used for public worship, in a position near the lecturer;

(d) for any person to read or recite in public a reasonable extract from a published work;

(e) for any person to make or publish, for the purposes of news reporting or news summary, a report of an address of a political nature given at a public meeting; or

(f) for an individual to use for private or non-commercial purposes, or permit the use of for those purposes, a photograph or portrait that was commissioned by the individual for personal purposes and made for valuable consideration, unless the individual and the owner of the copyright in the photograph or portrait have agreed otherwise.

Autres cas de non-violation

Actes licites

32.2 (1) Ne constituent pas des violations du droit d'auteur :

a) l'utilisation, par l'auteur d'une œuvre artistique, lequel n'est pas titulaire du droit d'auteur sur cette œuvre, des moules, moulages, esquisses, plans, modèles ou études qu'il a faits en vue de la création de cette œuvre, à la condition de ne pas en répéter ou imiter par là les grandes lignes;

b) la reproduction dans une peinture, un dessin, une gravure, une photographie ou une œuvre cinématographique :

  (i) d'une œuvre architecturale, à la condition de ne pas avoir le caractère de dessins ou plans architecturaux,

  (ii) d'une sculpture ou d'une œuvre artistique due à des artisans, ou d'un moule ou modèle de celles-ci, érigées en permanence sur une place publique ou dans un édifice public;

c) la production ou la publication, pour des comptes rendus d'événements d'actualité ou des revues de presse, du compte rendu d'une conférence faite en public, à moins qu'il n'ait été défendu d'en rendre compte par un avis écrit ou imprimé et visiblement affiché, avant et pendant la conférence, à la porte ou près de la porte d'entrée principale de l'édifice où elle a lieu; l'affiche doit encore être posée près du conférencier, sauf lorsqu'il parle dans un édifice servant, à ce moment, à un culte public;

d) la lecture ou récitation en public, par une personne, d'un extrait, de longueur raisonnable, d'une œuvre publiée;

e) la production ou la publication, pour des comptes rendus d'événements d'actualité ou des revues de presse, du compte rendu d'une allocution de nature politique prononcée lors d'une assemblée publique;

f) le fait pour une personne physique d'utiliser à des fins non commerciales ou privées — ou de permettre d'utiliser à de telles fins — la photographie ou le portrait qu'elle a commandé à des fins personnelles et qui a été confectionné contre rémunération, à moins que la personne physique et le titulaire du droit d'auteur sur la photographie ou le portrait n'aient conclu une entente à l'effet contraire.

Further permitted acts

(2) It is not an infringement of copyright for a person to do any of the following acts without motive of gain at any agricultural or agricultural-industrial exhibition or fair that receives a grant from or is held by its directors under federal, provincial or municipal authority:

(a) the live performance in public of a musical work;

(b) the performance in public of a sound recording embodying a musical work or a performer's performance of a musical work; or

(c) the performance in public of a communication signal carrying

(i) the live performance in public of a musical work, or

(ii) a sound recording embodying a musical work or a performer's performance of a musical work.

Further permitted acts

(3) No religious organization or institution, educational institution and no charitable or fraternal organization shall be held liable to pay any compensation for doing any of the following acts in furtherance of a religious, educational or charitable object:

(a) the live performance in public of a musical work;

(b) the performance in public of a sound recording embodying a musical work or a performer's performance of a musical work; or

(c) the performance in public of a communication signal carrying

(i) the live performance in public of a musical work, or

(ii) a sound recording embodying a musical work or a performer's performance of a musical work.

1997, c. 24, s. 19; 2012, c. 20, s. 38.

Actes licites

(2) Ne constituent pas des violations du droit d'auteur les actes ci-après, s'ils sont accomplis sans intention de gain, à une exposition ou foire agricole ou industrielle et agricole, qui reçoit une subvention fédérale, provinciale ou municipale, ou est tenue par ses administrateurs en vertu d'une autorisation fédérale, provinciale ou municipale :

a) l'exécution, en direct et en public, d'une œuvre musicale;

b) l'exécution en public tant de l'enregistrement sonore que de l'œuvre musicale ou de la prestation de l'œuvre musicale qui le constituent;

c) l'exécution en public du signal de communication porteur :

(i) de l'exécution, en direct et en public, d'une œuvre musicale,

(ii) tant de l'enregistrement sonore que de l'œuvre musicale ou de la prestation d'une œuvre musicale qui le constituent.

Actes licites

(3) Les organisations ou institutions religieuses, les établissements d'enseignement et les organisations charitables ou fraternelles ne sont pas tenus de payer une compensation si les actes suivants sont accomplis dans l'intérêt d'une entreprise religieuse, éducative ou charitable :

a) l'exécution, en direct et en public, d'une œuvre musicale;

b) l'exécution en public tant de l'enregistrement sonore que de l'œuvre musicale ou de la prestation de l'œuvre musicale qui le constituent;

c) l'exécution en public du signal de communication porteur :

(i) de l'exécution, en direct et en public, d'une œuvre musicale,

(ii) tant de l'enregistrement sonore que de l'œuvre musicale ou de la prestation d'une œuvre musicale qui le constituent.

1997, ch. 24, art. 19; 2012, ch. 20, art. 38.

Interpretation

No right to equitable remuneration

32.3 For the purposes of sections 29 to 32.2, an act that does not infringe copyright does not give rise to a right to remuneration conferred by section 19.

1997, c. 24, s. 19.

Compensation for Acts Done Before Recognition of Copyright of Performers and Broadcasters

Certain rights and interests protected

32.4 (1) Notwithstanding section 27, where a person has, before the later of January 1, 1996 and the day on which a country becomes a WTO member, incurred an expenditure or liability in connection with, or in preparation for, the doing of an act that would have infringed copyright under section 26 commencing on the later of those days, had that country been a WTO member, any right or interest of that person that

(a) arises from or in connection with the doing of that act, and

(b) is subsisting and valuable on the later of those days

is not prejudiced or diminished by reason only that that country has become a WTO member, except as provided by an order of the Board made under subsection 78(3).

Compensation

(2) Notwithstanding subsection (1), a person's right or interest that is protected by that subsection terminates if and when the owner of the copyright pays that person such compensation as is agreed to between the parties or, failing agreement, as is determined by the Board in accordance with section 78.

Limitation

(3) Nothing in subsections (1) and (2) affects any right of a performer available in law or equity.

1997, c. 24, s. 19.

Certain rights and interests protected

32.5 (1) Notwithstanding section 27, where a person has, before the later of the coming into force of Part II and the day on which a country becomes a Rome Convention country, incurred an expenditure or liability in

Interprétation

Précision

32.3 Pour l'application des articles 29 à 32.2, un acte qui ne constitue pas une violation du droit d'auteur ne donne pas lieu au droit à rémunération conféré par l'article 19.

1997, ch. 24, art. 19.

Indemnisation pour acte antérieur à la reconnaissance du droit d'auteur des artistes-interprètes et des radiodiffuseurs

Protection de certains droits et intérêts

32.4 (1) Par dérogation à l'article 27, lorsque, avant le 1er janvier 1996 ou, si elle est postérieure, la date où un pays devient membre de l'OMC, une personne a fait des dépenses ou contracté d'autres obligations relatives à l'exécution d'un acte qui, accompli après cette date, violerait le droit d'auteur conféré par l'article 26, le seul fait que ce pays soit devenu membre de l'OMC ne porte pas atteinte aux droits ou intérêts de cette personne, qui, d'une part, sont nés ou résultent de l'exécution de cet acte et, d'autre part, sont appréciables en argent à cette date, sauf dans la mesure prévue par une ordonnance de la Commission rendue en application du paragraphe 78(3).

Indemnisation

(2) Toutefois, les droits ou intérêts protégés en application du paragraphe (1) s'éteignent lorsque le titulaire du droit d'auteur verse à cette personne une indemnité convenue par les deux parties, laquelle, à défaut d'entente, est déterminée par la Commission conformément à l'article 78.

Réserve

(3) Les paragraphes (1) et (2) ne portent pas atteinte aux droits dont dispose l'artiste-interprète en droit ou en equity.

1997, ch. 24, art. 19.

Protection de certains droits et intérêts

32.5 (1) Par dérogation à l'article 27, lorsque, avant la date d'entrée en vigueur de la partie II ou, si elle est postérieure, la date où un pays devient partie à la Convention de Rome, une personne a fait des dépenses ou

connection with, or in preparation for, the doing of an act that would have infringed copyright under section 15 or 21 commencing on the later of those days, had Part II been in force or had that country been a Rome Convention country, any right or interest of that person that

(a) arises from or in connection with the doing of that act, and

(b) is subsisting and valuable on the later of those days

is not prejudiced or diminished by reason only that Part II has come into force or that the country has become a Rome Convention country, except as provided by an order of the Board made under subsection 78(3).

Compensation

(2) Notwithstanding subsection (1), a person's right or interest that is protected by that subsection terminates if and when the owner of the copyright pays that person such compensation as is agreed to between the parties or, failing agreement, as is determined by the Board in accordance with section 78.

Limitation

(3) Nothing in subsections (1) and (2) affects any right of a performer available in law or equity.

1997, c. 24, s. 19.

Certain rights and interests protected

32.6 Despite sections 27, 28.1 and 28.2, if a person has, before the day on which subsection 15(1.1), 17.1(1) or 18(1.1) applies in respect of a particular performers' performance or sound recording, incurred an expenditure or a liability in connection with, or in preparation for, the doing of an act that would, if done after that day, have infringed rights under that subsection, any right or interest of that person that arises from, or in connection with, the doing of that act and that is subsisting and valuable on that day is not, for two years after the day on which this section comes into force, prejudiced or diminished by reason only of the subsequent application of that subsection in respect of the performers' performance or sound recording.

2012, c. 20, s. 39.

contracté d'autres obligations relatives à l'exécution d'un acte qui, s'il était accompli après cette date, violerait le droit d'auteur conféré par les articles 15 ou 21, le seul fait que la partie II soit entrée en vigueur ou que le pays soit devenu partie à la Convention de Rome ne porte pas atteinte aux droits ou intérêts de cette personne, qui, d'une part, sont nés ou résultent de l'exécution de cet acte et, d'autre part, sont appréciables en argent à cette date, sauf dans la mesure prévue par une ordonnance de la Commission rendue en application du paragraphe 78(3).

Indemnisation

(2) Toutefois, les droits ou intérêts protégés en application du paragraphe (1) s'éteignent lorsque le titulaire du droit d'auteur verse à cette personne une indemnité convenue par les deux parties, laquelle, à défaut d'entente, est déterminée par la Commission conformément à l'article 78.

Réserve

(3) Les paragraphes (1) et (2) ne portent pas atteinte aux droits dont dispose l'artiste-interprète en droit ou en equity.

1997, ch. 24, art. 19.

Protection de certains droits et intérêts

32.6 Par dérogation aux articles 27, 28.1 et 28.2, si, avant la date à laquelle les droits visés à l'un des paragraphes 15(1.1), 17.1(1) et 18(1.1) s'appliquent à l'égard d'une prestation ou d'un enregistrement sonore donné, une personne a fait des dépenses ou contracté d'autres obligations relatives à l'exécution d'un acte qui, accompli après cette date, violerait ces droits, le seul fait que l'une de ces dispositions s'applique par la suite à la prestation ou à l'enregistrement sonore ne porte pas atteinte, pendant les deux ans suivant l'entrée en vigueur du présent article, aux droits ou intérêts de cette personne qui, d'une part, sont nés ou résultent de l'exécution de cet acte et, d'autre part, sont appréciables en argent à cette date.

2012, ch. 20, art. 39.

Compensation for Acts Done Before Recognition of Copyright or Moral Rights

Certain rights and interests protected

33 (1) Despite subsections 27(1), (2) and (4) and sections 27.1, 28.1 and 28.2, if a person has, before the later of January 1, 1996 and the day on which a country becomes a treaty country other than a WCT country, incurred an expenditure or liability in connection with, or in preparation for, the doing of an act that, if that country had been such a treaty country, would have infringed copyright in a work or moral rights in respect of a work, any right or interest of that person that arises from, or in connection with, the doing of that act and that is subsisting and valuable on the later of those days is not, except as provided by an order of the Board made under subsection 78(3), prejudiced or diminished by reason only of that country having become such a treaty country.

Compensation

(2) Notwithstanding subsection (1), a person's right or interest that is protected by that subsection terminates, as against the copyright owner or author, if and when that copyright owner or the author, as the case may be, pays that person such compensation as is agreed to between the parties or, failing agreement, as is determined by the Board in accordance with section 78.

R.S., 1985, c. C-42, s. 33; R.S., 1985, c. 10 (4th Supp.), s. 7; 1997, c. 24, s. 19; 2012, c. 20, s. 40.

Certain rights and interests protected

33.1 (1) Despite subsections 27(1), (2) and (4) and sections 27.1, 28.1 and 28.2, if a person has, before the later of the day on which this section comes into force and the day on which a country that is a treaty country but not a WCT country becomes a WCT country, incurred an expenditure or liability in connection with, or in preparation for, the doing of an act that, if that country had been a WCT country, would have infringed a right under paragraph 3(1)(j), any right or interest of that person that arises from, or in connection with, the doing of that act and that is subsisting and valuable on the later of those days is not, except as provided by an order of the Board made under subsection 78(3), prejudiced or diminished by reason only of that country having become a WCT country.

Compensation

(2) Despite subsection (1), a person's right or interest that is protected by that subsection terminates as against the copyright owner if and when the owner pays the person any compensation that is agreed to between the parties or, failing agreement, that is determined by the Board in accordance with section 78.

2012, c. 20, s. 41.

Certain rights and interests protected

33.2 (1) Despite subsections 27(1), (2) and (4) and sections 27.1, 28.1 and 28.2, if a person has, before the later of the day on which this section comes into force and the day on which a country that is not a treaty country becomes a WCT country, incurred an expenditure or a liability in connection with, or in preparation for, the doing of an act that, if that country had been a WCT country, would have infringed copyright in a work or moral rights in respect of a work, any right or interest of that person that arises from, or in connection with, the doing of that act and that is subsisting and valuable on the later of those days is not, except as provided by an order of the Board made under subsection 78(3), prejudiced or diminished by reason only of that country having become a WCT country.

Compensation

(2) Despite subsection (1), a person's right or interest that is protected by that subsection terminates as against the copyright owner if and when that owner pays the person any compensation that is agreed to between the parties or, failing agreement, that is determined by the Board in accordance with section 78.

2012, c. 20, s. 41.

PART IV
Remedies

Civil Remedies

Infringement of Copyright and Moral Rights

Copyright

34 (1) Where copyright has been infringed, the owner of the copyright is, subject to this Act, entitled to all remedies by way of injunction, damages, accounts, delivery up and otherwise that are or may be conferred by law for the infringement of a right.

Moral rights

(2) In any proceedings for an infringement of moral rights, the court may grant to the holder of those rights all remedies by way of injunction, damages, accounts, delivery up and otherwise that are or may be conferred by law for the infringement of a right.

Costs

(3) The costs of all parties in any proceedings in respect of the infringement of a right conferred by this Act shall be in the discretion of the court.

Summary proceedings

(4) The following proceedings may be commenced or proceeded with by way of application or action and shall, in the case of an application, be heard and determined without delay and in a summary way:

   (a) proceedings for infringement of copyright or moral rights;

   (b) proceedings taken under section 44.12, 44.2 or 44.4; and

   (c) proceedings taken in respect of

   (i) a tariff certified by the Board under Part VII or VIII, or

   (ii) agreements referred to in section 70.12.

Practice and procedure

(5) The rules of practice and procedure, in civil matters, of the court in which proceedings are commenced by way of application apply to those proceedings, but where those rules do not provide for the proceedings to be heard and determined without delay and in a summary way, the court may give such directions as it considers necessary in order to so provide.

Actions

(6) The court in which proceedings are instituted by way of application may, where it considers it appropriate, direct that the proceeding be proceeded with as an action.

Meaning of *application*

(7) In this section, ***application*** means a proceeding that is commenced other than by way of a writ or statement of claim.

R.S., 1985, c. C-42, s. 34; R.S., 1985, c. 10 (4th Supp.), s. 8; 1993, c. 15, s. 3(E), c. 44, s. 65; 1994, c. 47, s. 62; 1997, c. 24, s. 20; 2012, c. 20, s. 43; 2014, c. 32, s. 6.

Presumptions respecting copyright and ownership

34.1 (1) In any civil proceedings taken under this Act in which the defendant puts in issue either the existence of the copyright or the title of the plaintiff to it,

ou autrement, et que la loi prévoit ou peut prévoir pour la violation d'un droit.

Frais

(3) Les frais de toutes les parties à des procédures relatives à la violation d'un droit prévu par la présente loi sont à la discrétion du tribunal.

Requête ou action

(4) Les procédures suivantes peuvent être engagées ou continuées par une requête ou une action :

   a) les procédures pour violation du droit d'auteur ou des droits moraux;

   b) les procédures visées aux articles 44.12, 44.2 ou 44.4;

   c) les procédures relatives aux tarifs homologués par la Commission en vertu des parties VII et VIII ou aux ententes visées à l'article 70.12.

Le tribunal statue sur les requêtes sans délai et suivant une procédure sommaire.

Règles applicables

(5) Les requêtes visées au paragraphe (4) sont, en matière civile, régies par les règles de procédure et de pratique du tribunal saisi des requêtes si ces règles ne prévoient pas que les requêtes doivent être jugées sans délai et suivant une procédure sommaire. Le tribunal peut, dans chaque cas, donner les instructions qu'il estime indiquées à cet effet.

Actions

(6) Le tribunal devant lequel les procédures sont engagées par requête peut, s'il l'estime indiqué, ordonner que la requête soit instruite comme s'il s'agissait d'une action.

Définition de *requête*

(7) Au présent article, ***requête*** s'entend d'une procédure engagée autrement que par un bref ou une déclaration.

L.R. (1985), ch. C-42, art. 34; L.R. (1985), ch. 10 (4ᵉ suppl.), art. 8; 1993, ch. 15, art. 3(A), ch. 44, art. 65; 1994, ch. 47, art. 62; 1997, ch. 24, art. 20; 2012, ch. 20, art. 43; 2014, ch. 32, art. 6.

Présomption de propriété

34.1 (1) Dans toute procédure civile engagée en vertu de la présente loi où le défendeur conteste l'existence du droit d'auteur ou la qualité du demandeur :

(a) copyright shall be presumed, unless the contrary is proved, to subsist in the work, performer's performance, sound recording or communication signal, as the case may be; and

(b) the author, performer, maker or broadcaster, as the case may be, shall, unless the contrary is proved, be presumed to be the owner of the copyright.

Where no grant registered

(2) Where any matter referred to in subsection (1) is at issue and no assignment of the copyright, or licence granting an interest in the copyright, has been registered under this Act,

(a) if a name purporting to be that of

(i) the author of the work,

(ii) the performer of the performer's performance,

(iii) the maker of the sound recording, or

(iv) the broadcaster of the communication signal

is printed or otherwise indicated thereon in the usual manner, the person whose name is so printed or indicated shall, unless the contrary is proved, be presumed to be the author, performer, maker or broadcaster;

(b) if

(i) no name is so printed or indicated, or if the name so printed or indicated is not the true name of the author, performer, maker or broadcaster or the name by which that person is commonly known, and

(ii) a name purporting to be that of the publisher or owner of the work, performer's performance, sound recording or communication signal is printed or otherwise indicated thereon in the usual manner,

the person whose name is printed or indicated as described in subparagraph (ii) shall, unless the contrary is proved, be presumed to be the owner of the copyright in question; and

(c) if, on a cinematographic work, a name purporting to be that of the maker of the cinematographic work appears in the usual manner, the person so named shall, unless the contrary is proved, be presumed to be the maker of the cinematographic work.

1997, c. 24, s. 20; 2012, c. 20, s. 44.

a) l'œuvre, la prestation, l'enregistrement sonore ou le signal de communication, selon le cas, est, jusqu'à preuve contraire, présumé être protégé par le droit d'auteur;

b) l'auteur, l'artiste-interprète, le producteur ou le radiodiffuseur, selon le cas, est, jusqu'à preuve contraire, réputé être titulaire de ce droit d'auteur.

Aucun enregistrement

(2) Dans toute contestation de cette nature, lorsque aucun acte de cession du droit d'auteur ni aucune licence concédant un intérêt dans le droit d'auteur n'a été enregistré sous l'autorité de la présente loi :

a) si un nom paraissant être celui de l'auteur de l'œuvre, de l'artiste-interprète de la prestation, du producteur de l'enregistrement sonore ou du radiodiffuseur du signal de communication y est imprimé ou autrement indiqué, de la manière habituelle, la personne dont le nom est ainsi imprimé ou indiqué est, jusqu'à preuve contraire, présumée être l'auteur, l'artiste-interprète, le producteur ou le radiodiffuseur;

b) si aucun nom n'est imprimé ou indiqué de cette façon, ou si le nom ainsi imprimé ou indiqué n'est pas le véritable nom de l'auteur, de l'artiste-interprète, du producteur ou du radiodiffuseur, selon le cas, ou le nom sous lequel il est généralement connu, et si un nom paraissant être celui de l'éditeur ou du titulaire du droit d'auteur y est imprimé ou autrement indiqué de la manière habituelle, la personne dont le nom est ainsi imprimé ou indiqué est, jusqu'à preuve contraire, présumée être le titulaire du droit d'auteur en question;

c) si un nom paraissant être celui du producteur d'une œuvre cinématographique y est indiqué de la manière habituelle, cette personne est présumée, jusqu'à preuve contraire, être le producteur de l'œuvre.

1997, ch. 24, art. 20; 2012, ch. 20, art. 44.

Liability for infringement

35 (1) Where a person infringes copyright, the person is liable to pay such damages to the owner of the copyright as the owner has suffered due to the infringement and, in addition to those damages, such part of the profits that the infringer has made from the infringement and that were not taken into account in calculating the damages as the court considers just.

Proof of profits

(2) In proving profits,

(a) the plaintiff shall be required to prove only receipts or revenues derived from the infringement; and

(b) the defendant shall be required to prove every element of cost that the defendant claims.

R.S., 1985, c. C-42, s. 35; 1997, c. 24, s. 20.

36 [Repealed, 2012, c. 20, s. 45]

37 [Repealed, 2012, c. 20, s. 45]

Recovery of possession of copies, plates

38 (1) Subject to subsection (2), the owner of the copyright in a work or other subject-matter may

(a) recover possession of all infringing copies of that work or other subject-matter, and of all plates used or intended to be used for the production of infringing copies, and

(b) take proceedings for seizure of those copies or plates before judgment if, under the law of Canada or of the province in which those proceedings are taken, a person is entitled to take such proceedings,

as if those copies or plates were the property of the copyright owner.

Powers of court

(2) On application by

(a) a person from whom the copyright owner has recovered possession of copies or plates referred to in subsection (1),

(b) a person against whom proceedings for seizure before judgment of copies or plates referred to in subsection (1) have been taken, or

(c) any other person who has an interest in those copies or plates,

a court may order that those copies or plates be destroyed, or may make any other order that it considers appropriate in the circumstances.

Notice to interested persons

(3) Before making an order under subsection (2), the court shall direct that notice be given to any person who has an interest in the copies or plates in question, unless the court is of the opinion that the interests of justice do not require such notice to be given.

Circumstances court to consider

(4) In making an order under subsection (2), the court shall have regard to all the circumstances, including

(a) the proportion, importance and value of the infringing copy or plate, as compared to the substrate or carrier embodying it; and

(b) the extent to which the infringing copy or plate is severable from, or a distinct part of, the substrate or carrier embodying it.

Limitation

(5) Nothing in this Act entitles the copyright owner to damages in respect of the possession or conversion of the infringing copies or plates.

R.S., 1985, c. C-42, s. 38; 1997, c. 24, s. 20.

Statutory damages

38.1 (1) Subject to this section, a copyright owner may elect, at any time before final judgment is rendered, to recover, instead of damages and profits referred to in subsection 35(1), an award of statutory damages for which any one infringer is liable individually, or for which any two or more infringers are liable jointly and severally,

(a) in a sum of not less than $500 and not more than $20,000 that the court considers just, with respect to all infringements involved in the proceedings for each work or other subject-matter, if the infringements are for commercial purposes; and

(b) in a sum of not less than $100 and not more than $5,000 that the court considers just, with respect to all infringements involved in the proceedings for all works or other subject-matter, if the infringements are for non-commercial purposes.

Autres personnes intéressées

(3) Le tribunal doit, avant de rendre l'ordonnance visée au paragraphe (2), en faire donner préavis aux personnes ayant un intérêt dans les exemplaires ou les planches, sauf s'il estime que l'intérêt de la justice ne l'exige pas.

Facteurs

(4) Le tribunal doit, lorsqu'il rend une ordonnance visée au paragraphe (2), tenir compte notamment des facteurs suivants :

a) la proportion que représente l'exemplaire contrefait ou la planche par rapport au support dans lequel ils sont incorporés, de même que leur valeur et leur importance par rapport à ce support;

b) la mesure dans laquelle cet exemplaire ou cette planche peut être extrait de ce support ou en constitue une partie distincte.

Limite

(5) La présente loi n'a pas pour effet de permettre au titulaire du droit d'auteur de recouvrer des dommages-intérêts en ce qui touche la possession des exemplaires ou des planches visés au paragraphe (1) ou l'usurpation du droit de propriété sur ceux-ci.

L.R. (1985), ch. C-42, art. 38; 1997, ch. 24, art. 20.

Dommages-intérêts préétablis

38.1 (1) Sous réserve des autres dispositions du présent article, le titulaire du droit d'auteur, en sa qualité de demandeur, peut, avant le jugement ou l'ordonnance qui met fin au litige, choisir de recouvrer, au lieu des dommages-intérêts et des profits visés au paragraphe 35(1), les dommages-intérêts préétablis ci-après pour les violations reprochées en l'instance à un même défendeur ou à plusieurs défendeurs solidairement responsables :

a) dans le cas des violations commises à des fins commerciales, pour toutes les violations — relatives à une œuvre donnée ou à un autre objet donné du droit d'auteur —, des dommages-intérêts dont le montant, d'au moins 500 $ et d'au plus 20 000 $, est déterminé selon ce que le tribunal estime équitable en l'occurrence;

b) dans le cas des violations commises à des fins non commerciales, pour toutes les violations — relatives à toutes les œuvres données ou tous les autres objets donnés du droit d'auteur —, des dommages-intérêts, d'au moins 100 $ et d'au plus 5 000 $, dont le montant est déterminé selon ce que le tribunal estime équitable en l'occurrence.

Infringement of subsection 27(2.3)

(1.1) An infringement under subsection 27(2.3) may give rise to an award of statutory damages with respect to a work or other subject-matter only if the copyright in that work or other subject-matter was actually infringed as a result of the use of a service referred to in that subsection.

Deeming — infringement of subsection 27(2.3)

(1.11) For the purpose of subsection (1), an infringement under subsection 27(2.3) is deemed to be for a commercial purpose.

Infringements not involved in proceedings

(1.12) If the copyright owner has made an election under subsection (1) with respect to a defendant's infringements that are for non-commercial purposes, they are barred from recovering statutory damages under this section from that defendant with respect to any other of the defendant's infringements that were done for non-commercial purposes before the institution of the proceedings in which the election was made.

No other statutory damages

(1.2) If a copyright owner has made an election under subsection (1) with respect to a defendant's infringements that are for non-commercial purposes, every other copyright owner is barred from electing to recover statutory damages under this section in respect of that defendant for any of the defendant's infringements that were done for non-commercial purposes before the institution of the proceedings in which the election was made.

If defendant unaware of infringement

(2) If a copyright owner has made an election under subsection (1) and the defendant satisfies the court that the defendant was not aware and had no reasonable grounds to believe that the defendant had infringed copyright, the court may reduce the amount of the award under paragraph (1)(a) to less than $500, but not less than $200.

Special case

(3) In awarding statutory damages under paragraph (1)(a) or subsection (2), the court may award, with respect to each work or other subject-matter, a lower amount than $500 or $200, as the case may be, that the court considers just, if

   (a) either

      (i) there is more than one work or other subject-matter in a single medium, or

(ii) the award relates only to one or more infringements under subsection 27(2.3); and

(b) the awarding of even the minimum amount referred to in that paragraph or that subsection would result in a total award that, in the court's opinion, is grossly out of proportion to the infringement.

Collective societies

(4) Where the defendant has not paid applicable royalties, a collective society referred to in section 67 may only make an election under this section to recover, in lieu of any other remedy of a monetary nature provided by this Act, an award of statutory damages in a sum of not less than three and not more than ten times the amount of the applicable royalties, as the court considers just.

Factors to consider

(5) In exercising its discretion under subsections (1) to (4), the court shall consider all relevant factors, including

(a) the good faith or bad faith of the defendant;

(b) the conduct of the parties before and during the proceedings;

(c) the need to deter other infringements of the copyright in question; and

(d) in the case of infringements for non-commercial purposes, the need for an award to be proportionate to the infringements, in consideration of the hardship the award may cause to the defendant, whether the infringement was for private purposes or not, and the impact of the infringements on the plaintiff.

No award

(6) No statutory damages may be awarded against

(a) an educational institution or a person acting under its authority that has committed an act referred to in section 29.6 or 29.7 and has not paid any royalties or complied with any terms and conditions fixed under this Act in relation to the commission of the act;

(b) an educational institution, library, archive or museum that is sued in the circumstances referred to in section 38.2;

(c) a person who infringes copyright under paragraph 27(2)(e) or section 27.1, where the copy in question

dommages-intérêts serait extrêmement disproportionné à la violation.

Société de gestion

(4) Si le défendeur n'a pas payé les redevances applicables en l'espèce, la société de gestion visée à l'article 67 — au lieu de se prévaloir de tout autre recours en vue d'obtenir un redressement pécuniaire prévu par la présente loi — ne peut, aux termes du présent article, que choisir de recouvrer des dommages-intérêts préétablis dont le montant, de trois à dix fois le montant de ces redevances, est déterminé selon ce que le tribunal estime équitable en l'occurrence.

Facteurs

(5) Lorsqu'il rend une décision relativement aux paragraphes (1) à (4), le tribunal tient compte notamment des facteurs suivants :

a) la bonne ou mauvaise foi du défendeur;

b) le comportement des parties avant l'instance et au cours de celle-ci;

c) la nécessité de créer un effet dissuasif à l'égard de violations éventuelles du droit d'auteur en question;

d) dans le cas d'une violation qui est commise à des fins non commerciales, la nécessité d'octroyer des dommages-intérêts dont le montant soit proportionnel à la violation et tienne compte des difficultés qui en résulteront pour le défendeur, du fait que la violation a été commise à des fins privées ou non et de son effet sur le demandeur.

Cas où les dommages-intérêts préétablis ne peuvent être accordés

(6) Ne peuvent être condamnés aux dommages-intérêts préétablis :

a) l'établissement d'enseignement ou la personne agissant sous l'autorité de celui-ci qui a fait les actes visés aux articles 29.6 ou 29.7 sans acquitter les redevances ou sans observer les modalités afférentes fixées sous le régime de la présente loi;

b) l'établissement d'enseignement, la bibliothèque, le musée ou le service d'archives, selon le cas, qui est poursuivi dans les circonstances prévues à l'article 38.2;

was made with the consent of the copyright owner in the country where the copy was made; or

(d) an educational institution that is sued in the circumstances referred to in subsection 30.02(7) or a person acting under its authority who is sued in the circumstances referred to in subsection 30.02(8).

Exemplary or punitive damages not affected

(7) An election under subsection (1) does not affect any right that the copyright owner may have to exemplary or punitive damages.

1997, c. 24, s. 20; 2012, c. 20, s. 46.

Maximum amount that may be recovered

38.2 (1) An owner of copyright in a work who has not authorized a collective society to authorize its reprographic reproduction may recover, in proceedings against an educational institution, library, archive or museum that has reproduced the work, a maximum amount equal to the amount of royalties that would have been payable to the society in respect of the reprographic reproduction, if it were authorized, either

(a) under any agreement entered into with the collective society; or

(b) under a tariff certified by the Board pursuant to section 70.15.

Agreements with more than one collective society

(2) Where agreements respecting reprographic reproduction have been signed with more than one collective society or where more than one tariff applies or where both agreements and tariffs apply, the maximum amount that the copyright owner may recover is the largest amount of the royalties provided for in any of those agreements or tariffs.

Application

(3) Subsections (1) and (2) apply only where

(a) the collective society is entitled to authorize, or the tariff provides for the payment of royalties in respect of, the reprographic reproduction of that category of work; and

(b) copying of that general nature and extent is covered by the agreement or tariff.

1997, c. 24, s. 20.

Injunction only remedy when defendant not aware of copyright

39 (1) Subject to subsection (2), in any proceedings for infringement of copyright, the plaintiff is not entitled to any remedy other than an injunction in respect of the infringement if the defendant proves that, at the date of the infringement, the defendant was not aware and had no reasonable ground for suspecting that copyright subsisted in the work or other subject-matter in question.

Exception where copyright registered

(2) Subsection (1) does not apply if, at the date of the infringement, the copyright was duly registered under this Act.

R.S., 1985, c. C-42, s. 39; 1997, c. 24, s. 20.

Wide injunction

39.1 (1) When granting an injunction in respect of an infringement of copyright in a work or other subject-matter, the court may further enjoin the defendant from infringing the copyright in any other work or subject-matter if

(a) the plaintiff is the owner of the copyright or the person to whom an interest in the copyright has been granted by licence; and

(b) the plaintiff satisfies the court that the defendant will likely infringe the copyright in those other works or subject-matter unless enjoined by the court from doing so.

Application of injunction

(2) An injunction granted under subsection (1) may extend to works or other subject-matter

(a) in respect of which the plaintiff was not, at the time the proceedings were commenced, the owner of the copyright or the person to whom an interest in the copyright has been granted by licence; or

(b) that did not exist at the time the proceedings were commenced.

1997, c. 24, s. 20.

Cas où le seul recours est l'injonction

39 (1) Sous réserve du paragraphe (2), dans le cas de procédures engagées pour violation du droit d'auteur, le demandeur ne peut obtenir qu'une injonction à l'égard de cette violation si le défendeur prouve que, au moment de la commettre, il ne savait pas et n'avait aucun motif raisonnable de soupçonner que l'œuvre ou tout autre objet du droit d'auteur était protégé par la présente loi.

Exception

(2) Le paragraphe (1) ne s'applique pas si, à la date de la violation, le droit d'auteur était dûment enregistré sous le régime de la présente loi.

L.R. (1985), ch. C-42, art. 39; 1997, ch. 24, art. 20.

Interdiction

39.1 (1) Dans les cas où il accorde une injonction pour violation du droit d'auteur sur une œuvre ou un autre objet, le tribunal peut en outre interdire au défendeur de violer le droit d'auteur sur d'autres œuvres ou d'autres objets dont le demandeur est le titulaire ou sur d'autres œuvres ou d'autres objets dans lesquels il a un intérêt concédé par licence, si le demandeur lui démontre que, en l'absence de cette interdiction, le défendeur violera vraisemblablement le droit d'auteur sur ces autres œuvres ou ces autres objets.

Application de l'injonction

(2) Cette injonction peut viser même les œuvres ou les autres objets sur lesquels le demandeur n'avait pas de droit d'auteur ou à l'égard desquels il n'était pas titulaire d'une licence lui concédant un intérêt sur un droit d'auteur au moment de l'introduction de l'instance, ou qui n'existaient pas à ce moment.

1997, ch. 24, art. 20.

No injunction in case of a building

40 (1) Where the construction of a building or other structure that infringes or that, if completed, would infringe the copyright in some other work has been commenced, the owner of the copyright is not entitled to obtain an injunction in respect of the construction of that building or structure or to order its demolition.

Certain remedies inapplicable

(2) Sections 38 and 42 do not apply in any case in respect of which subsection (1) applies.

R.S., 1985, c. C-42, s. 40; 1997, c. 24, s. 21.

Technological Protection Measures and Rights Management Information

Definitions

41 The following definitions apply in this section and in sections 41.1 to 41.21.

circumvent means,

(a) in respect of a technological protection measure within the meaning of paragraph (a) of the definition *technological protection measure*, to descramble a scrambled work or decrypt an encrypted work or to otherwise avoid, bypass, remove, deactivate or impair the technological protection measure, unless it is done with the authority of the copyright owner; and

(b) in respect of a technological protection measure within the meaning of paragraph (b) of the definition *technological protection measure*, to avoid, bypass, remove, deactivate or impair the technological protection measure. (*contourner*)

technological protection measure means any effective technology, device or component that, in the ordinary course of its operation,

(a) controls access to a work, to a performer's performance fixed in a sound recording or to a sound recording and whose use is authorized by the copyright owner; or

(b) restricts the doing — with respect to a work, to a performer's performance fixed in a sound recording or to a sound recording — of any act referred to in section 3, 15 or 18 and any act for which remuneration is payable under section 19. (*mesure technique de protection*)

R.S., 1985, c. C-42, s. 41; R.S., 1985, c. 10 (4th Supp.), s. 9; 1997, c. 24, s. 22; 2012, c. 20, s. 47.

Prohibition

41.1 (1) No person shall

(a) circumvent a technological protection measure within the meaning of paragraph (a) of the definition **technological protection measure** in section 41;

(b) offer services to the public or provide services if

(i) the services are offered or provided primarily for the purposes of circumventing a technological protection measure,

(ii) the uses or purposes of those services are not commercially significant other than when they are offered or provided for the purposes of circumventing a technological protection measure, or

(iii) the person markets those services as being for the purposes of circumventing a technological protection measure or acts in concert with another person in order to market those services as being for those purposes; or

(c) manufacture, import, distribute, offer for sale or rental or provide — including by selling or renting — any technology, device or component if

(i) the technology, device or component is designed or produced primarily for the purposes of circumventing a technological protection measure,

(ii) the uses or purposes of the technology, device or component are not commercially significant other than when it is used for the purposes of circumventing a technological protection measure, or

(iii) the person markets the technology, device or component as being for the purposes of circumventing a technological protection measure or acts in concert with another person in order to market the technology, device or component as being for those purposes.

Circumvention of technological protection measure

(2) The owner of the copyright in a work, a performer's performance fixed in a sound recording or a sound recording in respect of which paragraph (1)(a) has been contravened is, subject to this Act and any regulations made under section 41.21, entitled to all remedies — by way of injunction, damages, accounts, delivery up and otherwise — that are or may be conferred by law for the infringement of copyright against the person who contravened that paragraph.

No statutory damages

(3) The owner of the copyright in a work, a performer's performance fixed in a sound recording or a sound recording in respect of which paragraph (1)(a) has been contravened may not elect under section 38.1 to recover statutory damages from an individual who contravened that paragraph only for his or her own private purposes.

Services, technology, device or component

(4) Every owner of the copyright in a work, a performer's performance fixed in a sound recording or a sound recording in respect of which a technological protection measure has been or could be circumvented as a result of the contravention of paragraph (1)(b) or (c) is, subject to this Act and any regulations made under section 41.21, entitled to all remedies — by way of injunction, damages, accounts, delivery up and otherwise — that are or may be conferred by law for the infringement of copyright against the person who contravened paragraph (1)(b) or (c).

2012, c. 20, s. 47.

Law enforcement and national security

41.11 (1) Paragraph 41.1(1)(a) does not apply if a technological protection measure is circumvented for the purposes of an investigation related to the enforcement of any Act of Parliament or any Act of the legislature of a province, or for the purposes of activities related to the protection of national security.

Services

(2) Paragraph 41.1(1)(b) does not apply if the services are provided by or for the persons responsible for carrying out such an investigation or such activities.

Technology, device or component

(3) Paragraph 41.1(1)(c) does not apply if the technology, device or component is manufactured, imported or provided by the persons responsible for carrying out such an investigation or such activities, or is manufactured, imported, provided or offered for sale or rental as a service provided to those persons.

2012, c. 20, s. 47.

Interoperability of computer programs

41.12 (1) Paragraph 41.1(1)(a) does not apply to a person who owns a computer program or a copy of one, or

Réserve

(3) Le titulaire du droit d'auteur sur une œuvre, une prestation fixée au moyen d'un enregistrement sonore ou un enregistrement sonore n'est pas admis à recouvrer les dommages-intérêts préétablis visés à l'article 38.1 dans le cas où l'auteur de la contravention à l'alinéa (1)a) est une personne physique et n'a contrevenu à cet alinéa qu'à des fins privées.

Services, technologie, dispositif ou composant

(4) Sous réserve des autres dispositions de la présente loi et des règlements pris en vertu de l'article 41.21, le titulaire du droit d'auteur sur une œuvre, une prestation fixée au moyen d'un enregistrement sonore ou un enregistrement sonore est admis à exercer, contre la personne qui a contrevenu aux alinéas (1)b) ou c), tous les recours — en vue notamment d'une injonction, de dommages-intérêts, d'une reddition de compte ou d'une remise — que la loi prévoit ou peut prévoir pour la violation d'un droit d'auteur, dans le cas où la contravention a entraîné ou pourrait entraîner le contournement de la mesure technique de protection qui protège l'œuvre, la prestation ou l'enregistrement.

2012, ch. 20, art. 47.

Enquêtes

41.11 (1) L'alinéa 41.1(1)a) ne s'applique pas dans le cas où la mesure technique de protection est contournée dans le cadre d'une enquête relative à l'application d'une loi fédérale ou provinciale ou d'activités liées à la sécurité nationale.

Services

(2) L'alinéa 41.1(1)b) ne s'applique pas dans le cas où les services sont fournis par les personnes chargées de mener l'enquête ou les activités ou pour ces personnes.

Technologie, dispositif ou composant

(3) L'alinéa 41.1(1)c) ne s'applique pas dans le cas où la technologie ou le dispositif ou composant est fabriqué, importé ou fourni par les personnes chargées de mener l'enquête ou les activités ou fabriqué, importé, offert en vente ou en location ou fourni dans le cadre de la prestation de services à ces personnes.

2012, ch. 20, art. 47.

Interopérabilité

41.12 (1) L'alinéa 41.1(1)a) ne s'applique pas à la personne qui est le propriétaire d'un programme d'ordinateur ou d'un exemplaire de celui-ci, ou qui est titulaire d'une licence en permettant l'utilisation, et qui contourne la mesure technique de protection dans le seul but d'obtenir de l'information lui permettant de rendre ce

has a licence to use the program or copy, and who circumvents a technological protection measure that protects that program or copy for the sole purpose of obtaining information that would allow the person to make the program and any other computer program interoperable.

Services

(2) Paragraph 41.1(1)(b) does not apply to a person who offers services to the public or provides services for the purposes of circumventing a technological protection measure if the person does so for the purpose of making the computer program and any other computer program interoperable.

Technology, device or component

(3) Paragraph 41.1(1)(c) does not apply to a person who manufactures, imports or provides a technology, device or component for the purposes of circumventing a technological protection measure if the person does so for the purpose of making the computer program and any other computer program interoperable and

  (a) uses that technology, device or component only for that purpose; or

  (b) provides that technology, device or component to another person only for that purpose.

Sharing of information

(4) A person referred to in subsection (1) may communicate the information obtained under that subsection to another person for the purposes of allowing that person to make the computer program and any other computer program interoperable.

Limitation

(5) A person to whom the technology, device or component referred to in subsection (3) is provided or to whom the information referred to in subsection (4) is communicated may use it only for the purpose of making the computer program and any other computer program interoperable.

Non-application

(6) However, a person is not entitled to benefit from the exceptions under subsections (1) to (3) or (5) if, for the purposes of making the computer program and any other computer program interoperable, the person does an act that constitutes an infringement of copyright.

Non-application

(7) Furthermore, a person is not entitled to benefit from the exception under subsection (4) if, for the purposes of making the computer program and any other computer program interoperable, the person does an act that constitutes an infringement of copyright or an act that contravenes any Act of Parliament or any Act of the legislature of a province.

2012, c. 20, s. 47.

Encryption research

41.13 (1) Paragraph 41.1(1)(a) does not apply to a person who, for the purposes of encryption research, circumvents a technological protection measure by means of decryption if

(a) it would not be practical to carry out the research without circumventing the technological protection measure;

(b) the person has lawfully obtained the work, the performer's performance fixed in a sound recording or the sound recording that is protected by the technological protection measure; and

(c) the person has informed the owner of the copyright in the work, the performer's performance fixed in a sound recording or the sound recording who has applied the technological protection measure.

Non-application

(2) However, a person acting in the circumstances referred to in subsection (1) is not entitled to benefit from the exception under that subsection if the person does an act that constitutes an infringement of copyright or an act that contravenes any Act of Parliament or any Act of the legislature of a province.

Technology, device or component

(3) Paragraph 41.1(1)(c) does not apply to a person referred to in subsection (1) who manufactures a technology, device or component for the purposes of circumventing a technological protection measure that is subject to paragraph 41.1(1)(a) if the person does so for the purpose of encryption research and

(a) uses that technology, device or component only for that purpose; or

(b) provides that technology, device or component only for that purpose to another person who is collaborating with the person.

2012, c. 20, s. 47.

Personal information

41.14 (1) Paragraph 41.1(1)(a) does not apply to a person who circumvents a technological protection measure if

(a) the work, performer's performance fixed in a sound recording or sound recording that is protected by the technological protection measure is not accompanied by a notice indicating that its use will permit a third party to collect and communicate personal information relating to the user or, in the case where it is accompanied by such a notice, the user is not provided with the option to prevent the collection and communication of personal information without the user's use of it being restricted; and

(b) the only purpose of circumventing the technological protection measure is to verify whether it permits the collection or communication of personal information and, if it does, to prevent it.

Services, technology, device or component

(2) Paragraphs 41.1(1)(b) and (c) do not apply to a person who offers services to the public or provides services, or manufactures, imports or provides a technology, device or component, for the purposes of circumventing a technological protection measure in accordance with subsection (1), to the extent that the services, technology, device or component do not unduly impair the technological protection measure.

2012, c. 20, s. 47.

Security

41.15 (1) Paragraph 41.1(1)(a) does not apply to a person who circumvents a technological protection measure that is subject to that paragraph for the sole purpose of, with the consent of the owner or administrator of a computer, computer system or computer network, assessing the vulnerability of the computer, system or network or correcting any security flaws.

Services

(2) Paragraph 41.1(1)(b) does not apply if the services are provided to a person described in subsection (1).

Technology, device or component

(3) Paragraph 41.1(1)(c) does not apply if the technology, device or component is manufactured or imported by a person described in subsection (1), or is manufactured, imported, provided — including by selling or renting — offered for sale or rental or distributed as a service provided to that person.

d'une œuvre, d'une prestation fixée au moyen d'un enregistrement sonore ou d'un enregistrement sonore si les conditions suivantes sont réunies :

a) l'œuvre, la prestation ou l'enregistrement n'est pas accompagné d'un avertissement indiquant que son utilisation permet à un tiers de collecter et de communiquer des renseignements personnels sur l'utilisateur ou, s'il l'est, l'utilisateur ne peut empêcher la collecte et la communication de ces renseignements sans que l'utilisation ne soit restreinte;

b) le contournement a uniquement pour objet de vérifier si la mesure technique de protection ou l'œuvre, la prestation ou l'enregistrement permet la collecte ou la communication de renseignements personnels ou, le cas échéant, de les empêcher.

Services, technologie, dispositif ou composant

(2) Les alinéas 41.1(1)b) et c) ne s'appliquent pas à la personne qui offre au public ou fournit des services, ou qui fabrique, importe ou fournit une technologie ou un dispositif ou composant, en vue du contournement d'une mesure technique de protection en conformité avec le paragraphe (1) dans la mesure où les services, la technologie ou le dispositif ou composant ne nuisent pas indûment au fonctionnement de la mesure technique de protection.

2012, ch. 20, art. 47.

Sécurité

41.15 (1) L'alinéa 41.1(1)a) ne s'applique pas à la personne qui contourne la mesure technique de protection visée à cet alinéa dans le seul but d'évaluer la vulnérabilité d'un ordinateur, d'un système informatique ou d'un réseau d'ordinateurs ou de corriger tout défaut de sécurité dans le cas où l'évaluation ou la correction sont autorisées par le propriétaire ou l'administrateur de ceux-ci.

Services

(2) L'alinéa 41.1(1)b) ne s'applique pas dans le cas où les services sont fournis à la personne visée au paragraphe (1).

Technologie, dispositif ou composant

(3) L'alinéa 41.1(1)c) ne s'applique pas dans le cas où la technologie ou le dispositif ou composant est fabriqué ou importé par la personne visée au paragraphe (1), ou est fabriqué, importé, fourni, notamment par vente ou location, offert en vente ou en location ou mis en circulation dans le cadre de services fournis à cette personne.

Non-application

(4) A person acting in the circumstances referred to in subsection (1) is not entitled to benefit from the exception under that subsection if the person does an act that constitutes an infringement of copyright or an act that contravenes any Act of Parliament or any Act of the legislature of a province.

2012, c. 20, s. 47.

Persons with perceptual disabilities

41.16 (1) Paragraph 41.1(1)(a) does not apply to a person with a perceptual disability, to another person acting at their request or to a non-profit organization, as defined in section 32.02, acting for their benefit, if that person or organization circumvents a technological protection measure solely for one or more of the following purposes:

(a) to make a work, a performer's performance fixed in a sound recording or a sound recording perceptible to the person with a perceptual disability;

(b) to permit a person, or a non-profit organization referred to in subsection 32(1), to benefit from the exception set out in section 32;

(c) to permit a non-profit organization referred to in subsection 32.01(1) to benefit from the exception set out in section 32.01.

Services, technology, device or component

(2) Paragraphs 41.1(1)(b) and (c) do not apply to a person who offers or provides services to persons or non-profit organizations referred to in subsection (1) or who manufactures, imports or provides a technology, device or component, for the sole purpose of enabling those persons or non-profit organizations to circumvent a technological protection measure in accordance with that subsection.

2012, c. 20, s. 47; 2016, c. 4, s. 4.

Broadcasting undertakings

41.17 Paragraph 41.1(1)(a) does not apply to a broadcasting undertaking that circumvents a technological protection measure for the sole purpose of making an ephemeral reproduction of a work, a performer's performance fixed in a sound recording or a sound recording in accordance with section 30.9, unless the owner of the copyright in the work, the performer's performance fixed in a sound recording or the sound recording that is protected by the technological protection measure makes available the necessary means to enable the making of such a reproduction in a timely manner in light of the broadcasting undertaking's business requirements.

2012, c. 20, s. 47.

Exclusion

(4) Ne peut toutefois bénéficier de l'application du paragraphe (1) la personne qui, dans les circonstances prévues à ce paragraphe, accomplit un acte qui constitue une violation du droit d'auteur ou qui contrevient à une loi fédérale ou provinciale.

2012, ch. 20, art. 47.

Personnes ayant une déficience perceptuelle

41.16 (1) L'alinéa 41.1(1)a) ne s'applique pas à la personne ayant une déficience perceptuelle — ni à la personne agissant à sa demande ou à l'organisme sans but lucratif, au sens de l'article 32.02, agissant dans son intérêt — qui contourne la mesure technique de protection dans le seul but d'accomplir un ou plusieurs des actes suivants :

a) rendre perceptible l'œuvre, la prestation fixée au moyen d'un enregistrement sonore ou l'enregistrement sonore protégé par la mesure;

b) permettre à une personne, ou à un organisme sans but lucratif visé au paragraphe 32(1), de bénéficier de l'exception prévue à l'article 32;

c) permettre à un organisme sans but lucratif visé au paragraphe 32.01(1) de bénéficier de l'exception prévue à l'article 32.01.

Services, technologie, dispositif ou composant

(2) Les alinéas 41.1(1)b) et c) ne s'appliquent pas à la personne qui offre ou fournit des services, ou qui fabrique, importe ou fournit une technologie ou un dispositif ou composant, dans le seul but de permettre aux personnes ou à l'organisme sans but lucratif visés au paragraphe (1) de contourner une mesure technique de protection en conformité avec ce paragraphe.

2012, ch. 20, art. 47; 2016, ch. 4, art. 4.

Entreprises de radiodiffusion

41.17 L'alinéa 41.1(1)a) ne s'applique pas à l'entreprise de radiodiffusion qui contourne la mesure technique de protection dans le seul but de faire une reproduction éphémère conformément à l'article 30.9 dans le cas où le titulaire du droit d'auteur sur l'œuvre, la prestation fixée au moyen d'un enregistrement sonore ou l'enregistrement sonore protégé par la mesure technique ne lui fournit pas les moyens de faire une telle reproduction en temps utile, compte tenu des exigences des affaires normales de l'entreprise.

2012, ch. 20, art. 47.

Radio apparatus

41.18 (1) Paragraph 41.1(1)(a) does not apply to a person who circumvents a technological protection measure on a radio apparatus for the sole purpose of gaining access to a telecommunications service by means of the radio apparatus.

Services or technology, device or component

(2) Paragraphs 41.1(1)(b) and (c) do not apply to a person who offers the services to the public or provides the services, or manufactures, imports or provides the technology, device or component, for the sole purpose of facilitating access to a telecommunications service by means of a radio apparatus.

Definitions

(3) The following definitions apply in this section.

radio apparatus has the same meaning as in section 2 of the *Radiocommunication Act*. (*appareil radio*)

telecommunications service has the same meaning as in subsection 2(1) of the *Telecommunications Act*. (*service de télécommunication*)

2012, c. 20, s. 47.

Reduction of damages

41.19 A court may reduce or remit the amount of damages it awards in the circumstances described in subsection 41.1(1) if the defendant satisfies the court that the defendant was not aware, and had no reasonable grounds to believe, that the defendant's acts constituted a contravention of that subsection.

2012, c. 20, s. 47.

Injunction only remedy

41.2 If a court finds that a defendant that is a library, archive or museum or an educational institution has contravened subsection 41.1(1) and the defendant satisfies the court that it was not aware, and had no reasonable grounds to believe, that its actions constituted a contravention of that subsection, the plaintiff is not entitled to any remedy other than an injunction.

2012, c. 20, s. 47.

Regulations

41.21 (1) The Governor in Council may make regulations excluding from the application of section 41.1 any technological protection measure that protects a work, a performer's performance fixed in a sound recording or a sound recording, or classes of them, or any class of such technological protection measures, if the Governor in

Appareil radio

41.18 (1) L'alinéa 41.1(1)a) ne s'applique pas à la personne qui contourne la mesure technique de protection d'un appareil radio uniquement afin d'accéder à un service de télécommunication au moyen de celui-ci.

Services

(2) Les alinéas 41.1(1)b) et c) ne s'appliquent pas à la personne qui offre au public ou fournit des services, ou qui fabrique, importe ou fournit une technologie ou un dispositif ou composant visant uniquement à faciliter l'accès à un service de télécommunication au moyen d'un appareil radio.

Définitions

(3) Les définitions qui suivent s'appliquent au présent article.

appareil radio S'entend au sens de l'article 2 de la *Loi sur la radiocommunication*. (*radio apparatus*)

service de télécommunication S'entend au sens du paragraphe 2(1) de la *Loi sur les télécommunications*. (*telecommunications service*)

2012, ch. 20, art. 47.

Annulation ou réduction de dommages-intérêts

41.19 Le tribunal peut annuler ou réduire le montant des dommages-intérêts qu'il accorde, dans les cas visés au paragraphe 41.1(1), si le défendeur le convainc qu'il ne savait pas et n'avait aucun motif raisonnable de croire qu'il avait contrevenu à ce paragraphe.

2012, ch. 20, art. 47.

Cas où le seul recours est l'injonction

41.2 Dans le cas où le défendeur est une bibliothèque, un musée, un service d'archives ou un établissement d'enseignement et où le tribunal est d'avis qu'il a contrevenu au paragraphe 41.1(1), le demandeur ne peut obtenir qu'une injonction à l'égard du défendeur si celui-ci convainc le tribunal qu'il ne savait pas et n'avait aucun motif raisonnable de croire qu'il avait contrevenu à ce paragraphe.

2012, ch. 20, art. 47.

Règlements

41.21 (1) Le gouverneur en conseil peut, par règlement, soustraire à l'application de l'article 41.1 toute mesure technique de protection ou catégorie de mesures techniques de protection de l'œuvre, de la prestation fixée au moyen d'un enregistrement sonore ou de l'enregistrement sonore ou toute catégorie de ceux-ci, s'il estime que

Council considers that the application of that section to the technological protection measure or class of technological protection measures would unduly restrict competition in the aftermarket sector in which the technological protection measure is used.

Regulations

(2) The Governor in Council may make regulations

(a) prescribing additional circumstances in which paragraph 41.1(1)(a) does not apply, having regard to the following factors:

(i) whether not being permitted to circumvent a technological protection measure that is subject to that paragraph could adversely affect the use a person may make of a work, a performer's performance fixed in a sound recording or a sound recording when that use is authorized,

(ii) whether the work, the performer's performance fixed in a sound recording or the sound recording is commercially available,

(iii) whether not being permitted to circumvent a technological protection measure that is subject to that paragraph could adversely affect criticism, review, news reporting, commentary, parody, satire, teaching, scholarship or research that could be made or done in respect of the work, the performer's performance fixed in a sound recording or the sound recording,

(iv) whether being permitted to circumvent a technological protection measure that is subject to that paragraph could adversely affect the market for the work, the performer's performance fixed in a sound recording or the sound recording or its market value,

(v) whether the work, the performer's performance fixed in a sound recording or the sound recording is commercially available in a medium and in a quality that is appropriate for non-profit archival, preservation or educational uses, and

(vi) any other relevant factor; and

(b) requiring the owner of the copyright in a work, a performer's performance fixed in a sound recording or a sound recording that is protected by a technological protection measure to provide access to the work, performer's performance fixed in a sound recording or sound recording to persons who are entitled to the benefit of any of the limitations on the application of paragraph 41.1(1)(a) prescribed under paragraph (a).

l'application de cet article à la mesure diminuerait indûment la concurrence sur le marché secondaire où celle-ci est utilisée.

Règlements

(2) Le gouverneur en conseil peut, par règlement :

a) prévoir d'autres cas dans lesquels l'alinéa 41.1(1)a) ne s'applique pas, compte tenu des critères suivants :

(i) le fait que l'impossibilité de contourner une mesure technique de protection visée à cet alinéa pourrait nuire à une utilisation autorisée qui peut être faite d'une œuvre, d'une prestation fixée au moyen d'un enregistrement sonore ou d'un enregistrement sonore,

(ii) l'accessibilité sur le marché de l'œuvre, de la prestation ou de l'enregistrement,

(iii) le fait que l'impossibilité de contourner une telle mesure technique de protection pourrait nuire à toute critique et à tout compte rendu, nouvelle, commentaire, parodie, satire, enseignement, étude ou recherche dont l'œuvre, la prestation ou l'enregistrement peut faire l'objet,

(iv) le fait que la possibilité de contourner une telle mesure technique de protection pourrait nuire à la valeur marchande, ou à la demande sur le marché, de l'œuvre, de la prestation ou de l'enregistrement,

(v) le fait que l'œuvre, la prestation ou l'enregistrement protégé par une telle mesure technique de protection est accessible sur le marché et est sur un support qui permet l'archivage par une organisation sans but lucratif, la préservation ou l'utilisation à des fins pédagogiques,

(vi) tout autre critère pertinent;

b) prévoir que le titulaire du droit d'auteur sur l'œuvre, la prestation ou l'enregistrement protégé par une telle mesure technique est tenu d'y donner accès à la personne qui jouit d'une exception prévue sous le régime de l'alinéa a) et préciser les modalités — notamment de temps — d'accès ou autres auxquelles le titulaire doit se conformer.

2012, ch. 20, art. 47.

The regulations may prescribe the manner in which, and the time within which, access is to be provided, as well as any conditions that the owner of the copyright is to comply with.

2012, c. 20, s. 47.

Prohibition — rights management information

41.22 (1) No person shall knowingly remove or alter any rights management information in electronic form without the consent of the owner of the copyright in the work, the performer's performance or the sound recording, if the person knows or should have known that the removal or alteration will facilitate or conceal any infringement of the owner's copyright or adversely affect the owner's right to remuneration under section 19.

Removal or alteration of rights management information

(2) The owner of the copyright in a work, a performer's performance fixed in a sound recording or a sound recording is, subject to this Act, entitled to all remedies — by way of injunction, damages, accounts, delivery up and otherwise — that are or may be conferred by law for the infringement of copyright against a person who contravenes subsection (1).

Subsequent acts

(3) The copyright owner referred to in subsection (2) has the same remedies against a person who, without the owner's consent, knowingly does any of the following acts with respect to any material form of the work, the performer's performance fixed in a sound recording or the sound recording and knows or should have known that the rights management information has been removed or altered in a way that would give rise to a remedy under that subsection:

(a) sells it or rents it out;

(b) distributes it to an extent that the copyright owner is prejudicially affected;

(c) by way of trade, distributes it, exposes or offers it for sale or rental or exhibits it in public;

(d) imports it into Canada for the purpose of doing anything referred to in any of paragraphs (a) to (c); or

(e) communicates it to the public by telecommunication.

Interdiction : information sur le régime des droits

41.22 (1) Nul ne peut supprimer ou modifier sciemment, sans l'autorisation du titulaire du droit d'auteur sur l'œuvre, la prestation fixée au moyen d'un enregistrement sonore ou l'enregistrement sonore, l'information sur le régime des droits sous forme électronique, alors qu'il sait ou devrait savoir que cet acte aura pour effet de faciliter ou de cacher toute violation du droit d'auteur du titulaire ou de porter atteinte à son droit d'être rémunéré en vertu de l'article 19.

Suppression ou modification de l'information sur le régime des droits

(2) Le titulaire du droit d'auteur est alors admis, sous réserve des autres dispositions de la présente loi, à exercer contre la personne qui contrevient au paragraphe (1) tous les recours — en vue notamment d'une injonction, de dommages-intérêts, d'une reddition de compte ou d'une remise — que la loi prévoit ou peut prévoir pour la violation d'un droit d'auteur.

Autres actes

(3) Le titulaire du droit d'auteur visé au paragraphe (2) a les mêmes recours contre la personne qui, sans son autorisation, accomplit sciemment tout acte ci-après en ce qui a trait à toute forme matérielle de l'œuvre, de la prestation fixée au moyen d'un enregistrement sonore ou de l'enregistrement sonore, alors qu'elle sait ou devrait savoir que l'information sur le régime des droits a été supprimée ou modifiée de manière à donner lieu à un recours au titre de ce paragraphe :

a) la vente ou la location;

b) la mise en circulation de façon à porter préjudice au titulaire du droit d'auteur;

c) la mise en circulation, la mise ou l'offre en vente ou en location, ou l'exposition en public, dans un but commercial;

d) l'importation au Canada en vue de l'un des actes visés aux alinéas a) à c);

e) la communication au public par télécommunication.

Definition of *rights management information*

(4) In this section, ***rights management information*** means information that

(a) is attached to or embodied in a copy of a work, a performer's performance fixed in a sound recording or a sound recording, or appears in connection with its communication to the public by telecommunication; and

(b) identifies or permits the identification of the work or its author, the performance or its performer, the sound recording or its maker or the holder of any rights in the work, the performance or the sound recording, or concerns the terms or conditions of the work's, performance's or sound recording's use.

2012, c. 20, s. 47.

General Provisions

Protection of separate rights

41.23 (1) Subject to this section, the owner of any copyright, or any person or persons deriving any right, title or interest by assignment or grant in writing from the owner, may individually for himself or herself, as a party to the proceedings in his or her own name, protect and enforce any right that he or she holds, and, to the extent of that right, title and interest, is entitled to the remedies provided by this Act.

Copyright owner to be made party

(2) If proceedings under subsection (1) are taken by a person other than the copyright owner, the copyright owner shall be made a party to those proceedings, except

(a) in the case of proceedings taken under section 44.12, 44.2 or 44.4;

(b) in the case of interlocutory proceedings, unless the court is of the opinion that the interests of justice require the copyright owner to be a party; and

(c) in any other case in which the court is of the opinion that the interests of justice do not require the copyright owner to be a party.

Owner's liability for costs

(3) A copyright owner who is made a party to proceedings under subsection (2) is not liable for any costs unless the copyright owner takes part in the proceedings.

Définition de *information sur le régime des droits*

(4) Au présent article, ***information sur le régime des droits*** s'entend de l'information qui, d'une part, est jointe ou intégrée à un exemplaire d'une œuvre, à une prestation fixée au moyen d'un enregistrement sonore ou à un enregistrement sonore, ou apparaît à l'égard de leur communication au public par télécommunication et qui, d'autre part, les identifie, en identifie l'auteur, l'artiste-interprète ou le producteur, ou identifie tout titulaire d'un droit sur eux, ou permet de le faire. Est également visée par la présente définition l'information sur les conditions et modalités de leur utilisation.

2012, ch. 20, art. 47.

Dispositions générales

Protection des droits distincts

41.23 (1) Sous réserve des autres dispositions du présent article, le titulaire d'un droit d'auteur ou quiconque possède un droit, un titre ou un intérêt acquis par cession ou concession consentie par écrit par le titulaire peut, individuellement pour son propre compte, en son propre nom comme partie à une procédure, soutenir et faire valoir les droits qu'il détient, et il peut exercer les recours prévus par la présente loi dans toute l'étendue de son droit, de son titre et de son intérêt.

Partie à la procédure

(2) Lorsqu'une procédure est engagée au titre du paragraphe (1) par une personne autre que le titulaire du droit d'auteur, ce dernier doit être constitué partie à cette procédure sauf :

a) dans le cas d'une procédure engagée en vertu des articles 44.12, 44.2 ou 44.4;

b) dans le cas d'une procédure interlocutoire, à moins que le tribunal estime qu'il est dans l'intérêt de la justice de constituer le titulaire du droit d'auteur partie à la procédure;

c) dans tous les autres cas où le tribunal estime que l'intérêt de la justice ne l'exige pas.

Frais

(3) Le titulaire du droit d'auteur visé au paragraphe (2) n'est pas tenu de payer les frais à moins d'avoir participé à la procédure.

Apportionment of damages, profits

(4) If a copyright owner is made a party to proceedings under subsection (2), the court, in awarding damages or profits, shall, subject to any agreement between the person who took the proceedings and the copyright owner, apportion the damages or profits referred to in subsection 35(1) between them as the court considers appropriate.

2012, c. 20, s. 47; 2014, c. 32, s. 6.

Concurrent jurisdiction of Federal Court

41.24 The Federal Court has concurrent jurisdiction with provincial courts to hear and determine all proceedings, other than the prosecution of offences under sections 42 and 43, for the enforcement of a provision of this Act or of the civil remedies provided by this Act.

2012, c. 20, s. 47.

Provisions Respecting Providers of Network Services or Information Location Tools

Notice of claimed infringement

41.25 (1) An owner of the copyright in a work or other subject-matter may send a notice of claimed infringement to a person who provides

(a) the means, in the course of providing services related to the operation of the Internet or another digital network, of telecommunication through which the electronic location that is the subject of the claim of infringement is connected to the Internet or another digital network;

(b) for the purpose set out in subsection 31.1(4), the digital memory that is used for the electronic location to which the claim of infringement relates; or

(c) an information location tool as defined in subsection 41.27(5).

Form and content of notice

(2) A notice of claimed infringement shall be in writing in the form, if any, prescribed by regulation and shall

(a) state the claimant's name and address and any other particulars prescribed by regulation that enable communication with the claimant;

(b) identify the work or other subject-matter to which the claimed infringement relates;

Répartition des dommages-intérêts

(4) Le tribunal peut, sous réserve de toute entente entre le demandeur et le titulaire du droit d'auteur visé au paragraphe (2), répartir entre eux, de la manière qu'il estime indiquée, les dommages-intérêts et les profits visés au paragraphe 35(1).

2012, ch. 20, art. 47; 2014, ch. 32, art. 6.

Juridiction concurrente de la Cour fédérale

41.24 La Cour fédérale, concurremment avec les tribunaux provinciaux, connaît de toute procédure liée à l'application de la présente loi, à l'exclusion des poursuites des infractions visées aux articles 42 et 43.

2012, ch. 20, art. 47.

Dispositions concernant les fournisseurs de services réseau et d'outils de repérage

Avis de prétendue violation

41.25 (1) Le titulaire d'un droit d'auteur sur une œuvre ou tout autre objet du droit d'auteur peut envoyer un avis de prétendue violation à la personne qui fournit, selon le cas :

a) dans le cadre de la prestation de services liés à l'exploitation d'Internet ou d'un autre réseau numérique, les moyens de télécommunication par lesquels l'emplacement électronique qui fait l'objet de la prétendue violation est connecté à Internet ou à tout autre réseau numérique;

b) en vue du stockage visé au paragraphe 31.1(4), la mémoire numérique qui est utilisée pour l'emplacement électronique en cause;

c) un outil de repérage au sens du paragraphe 41.27(5).

Forme de l'avis

(2) L'avis de prétendue violation est établi par écrit, en la forme éventuellement prévue par règlement, et, en outre :

a) précise les nom et adresse du demandeur et contient tout autre renseignement prévu par règlement qui permet la communication avec lui;

b) identifie l'œuvre ou l'autre objet du droit d'auteur auquel la prétendue violation se rapporte;

(c) state the claimant's interest or right with respect to the copyright in the work or other subject-matter;

(d) specify the location data for the electronic location to which the claimed infringement relates;

(e) specify the infringement that is claimed;

(f) specify the date and time of the commission of the claimed infringement; and

(g) contain any other information that may be prescribed by regulation.

2012, c. 20, s. 47.

Obligations related to notice

41.26 (1) A person described in paragraph 41.25(1)(a) or (b) who receives a notice of claimed infringement that complies with subsection 41.25(2) shall, on being paid any fee that the person has lawfully charged for doing so,

(a) as soon as feasible forward the notice electronically to the person to whom the electronic location identified by the location data specified in the notice belongs and inform the claimant of its forwarding or, if applicable, of the reason why it was not possible to forward it; and

(b) retain records that will allow the identity of the person to whom the electronic location belongs to be determined, and do so for six months beginning on the day on which the notice of claimed infringement is received or, if the claimant commences proceedings relating to the claimed infringement and so notifies the person before the end of those six months, for one year after the day on which the person receives the notice of claimed infringement.

Fees related to notices

(2) The Minister may, by regulation, fix the maximum fee that a person may charge for performing his or her obligations under subsection (1). If no maximum is fixed by regulation, the person may not charge any amount under that subsection.

Damages related to notices

(3) A claimant's only remedy against a person who fails to perform his or her obligations under subsection (1) is statutory damages in an amount that the court considers just, but not less than $5,000 and not more than $10,000.

c) déclare les intérêts ou droits du demandeur à l'égard de l'œuvre ou de l'autre objet visé;

d) précise les données de localisation de l'emplacement électronique qui fait l'objet de la prétendue violation;

e) précise la prétendue violation;

f) précise la date et l'heure de la commission de la prétendue violation;

g) contient, le cas échéant, tout autre renseignement prévu par règlement.

2012, ch. 20, art. 47.

Obligations

41.26 (1) La personne visée aux alinéas 41.25(1)a) ou b) qui reçoit un avis conforme au paragraphe 41.25(2) a l'obligation d'accomplir les actes ci-après, moyennant paiement des droits qu'elle peut exiger :

a) transmettre dès que possible par voie électronique une copie de l'avis à la personne à qui appartient l'emplacement électronique identifié par les données de localisation qui sont précisées dans l'avis et informer dès que possible le demandeur de cette transmission ou, le cas échéant, des raisons pour lesquelles elle n'a pas pu l'effectuer;

b) conserver, pour une période de six mois à compter de la date de réception de l'avis de prétendue violation, un registre permettant d'identifier la personne à qui appartient l'emplacement électronique et, dans le cas où, avant la fin de cette période, une procédure est engagée par le titulaire du droit d'auteur à l'égard de la prétendue violation et qu'elle en a reçu avis, conserver le registre pour une période d'un an suivant la date de la réception de l'avis de prétendue violation.

Droits

(2) Le ministre peut, par règlement, fixer le montant maximal des droits qui peuvent être exigés pour les actes prévus au paragraphe (1). À défaut de règlement à cet effet, le montant de ces droits est nul.

Dommages-intérêts

(3) Le seul recours dont dispose le demandeur contre la personne qui n'exécute pas les obligations que lui impose le paragraphe (1) est le recouvrement des dommages-intérêts préétablis dont le montant est, selon ce que le tribunal estime équitable en l'occurrence, d'au moins 5 000 $ et d'au plus 10 000 $.

Regulations — change of amounts

(4) The Governor in Council may, by regulation, increase or decrease the minimum or maximum amount of statutory damages set out in subsection (3).

2012, c. 20, s. 47.

Injunctive relief only — providers of information location tools

41.27 (1) In any proceedings for infringement of copyright, the owner of the copyright in a work or other subject-matter is not entitled to any remedy other than an injunction against a provider of an information location tool that is found to have infringed copyright by making a reproduction of the work or other subject-matter or by communicating that reproduction to the public by telecommunication.

Conditions for application

(2) Subsection (1) applies only if the provider, in respect of the work or other subject-matter,

(a) makes and caches, or does any act similar to caching, the reproduction in an automated manner for the purpose of providing the information location tool;

(b) communicates that reproduction to the public by telecommunication for the purpose of providing the information that has been located by the information location tool;

(c) does not modify the reproduction, other than for technical reasons;

(d) complies with any conditions relating to the making or caching, or doing of any act similar to caching, of reproductions of the work or other subject-matter, or to the communication of the reproductions to the public by telecommunication, that were specified in a manner consistent with industry practice by whoever made the work or other subject-matter available through the Internet or another digital network and that lend themselves to automated reading and execution; and

(e) does not interfere with the use of technology that is lawful and consistent with industry practice in order to obtain data on the use of the work or other subject-matter.

Limitation

(3) If the provider receives a notice of claimed infringement, relating to a work or other subject-matter, that complies with subsection 41.25(2) after the work or other subject-matter has been removed from the electronic location set out in the notice, then subsection (1) applies, with respect to reproductions made from that electronic location, only to infringements that occurred before the day that is 30 days — or the period that may be prescribed by regulation — after the day on which the provider receives the notice.

Exception

(4) Subsection (1) does not apply to the provision of the information location tool if the provision of that tool constitutes an infringement of copyright under subsection 27(2.3).

Factors — scope of injunction

(4.1) If it grants an injunction as set out in subsection (1), the court shall, among any other relevant factors, consider the following in establishing the terms of the injunction:

(a) the harm likely to be suffered by the copyright owner if steps are not taken to prevent or restrain the infringement; and

(b) the burden imposed on the provider and on the operation of the information location tool, including

(i) the aggregate effect of the injunction and any injunctions from other proceedings,

(ii) whether implementing the injunction would be technically feasible and effective in addressing the infringement,

(iii) whether implementing the injunction would interfere with the use of the information location tool for non-infringing acts, and

(iv) the availability of less burdensome and comparably effective means of preventing or restraining the infringement.

Limitation

(4.2) A court is not permitted to grant an injunction under section 39.1 against a provider who is the subject of an injunction set out in subsection (1).

Meaning of *information location tool*

(5) In this section, *information location tool* means any tool that makes it possible to locate information that is available through the Internet or another digital network.

2012, c. 20, s. 47.

Exception

(4) Le paragraphe (1) ne s'applique pas à l'égard de la fourniture de l'outil de repérage si celle-ci constitue une violation du droit d'auteur prévue au paragraphe 27(2.3).

Facteurs : portée de l'injonction

(4.1) S'il accorde l'injonction mentionnée au paragraphe (1), le tribunal tient compte lorsqu'il en établit les termes, en plus de tout autre facteur pertinent, de ce qui suit :

a) l'ampleur des dommages que subirait vraisemblablement le titulaire du droit d'auteur si aucune mesure n'était prise pour prévenir ou restreindre la violation;

b) le fardeau imposé au fournisseur de l'outil de repérage ainsi que sur l'exploitation de l'outil de repérage, notamment :

(i) l'effet cumulatif de cette injonction eu égard aux injonctions déjà accordées dans d'autres instances,

(ii) le fait que l'exécution de l'injonction constituerait une solution techniquement réalisable et efficace à l'encontre de la violation,

(iii) la possibilité que l'exécution de l'injonction entrave l'utilisation licite de l'outil de repérage,

(iv) l'existence de moyens aussi efficaces et moins contraignants de prévenir ou restreindre la violation.

Limite

(4.2) Le tribunal ne peut accorder l'injonction visée à l'article 39.1 si le fournisseur est déjà visé par une injonction au titre du paragraphe (1).

Définition de *outil de repérage*

(5) Au présent article, *outil de repérage* s'entend de tout outil permettant de repérer l'information qui est accessible sur l'Internet ou tout autre réseau numérique.

2012, ch. 20, art. 47.

Criminal Remedies

Offences

42 (1) Every person commits an offence who knowingly

(a) makes for sale or rental an infringing copy of a work or other subject-matter in which copyright subsists;

(b) sells or rents out, or by way of trade exposes or offers for sale or rental, an infringing copy of a work or other subject-matter in which copyright subsists;

(c) distributes infringing copies of a work or other subject-matter in which copyright subsists, either for the purpose of trade or to such an extent as to affect prejudicially the owner of the copyright;

(d) by way of trade exhibits in public an infringing copy of a work or other subject-matter in which copyright subsists;

(e) possesses, for sale, rental, distribution for the purpose of trade or exhibition in public by way of trade, an infringing copy of a work or other subject-matter in which copyright subsists;

(f) imports, for sale or rental, into Canada any infringing copy of a work or other subject-matter in which copyright subsists; or

(g) exports or attempts to export, for sale or rental, an infringing copy of a work or other subject-matter in which copyright subsists.

Possession and performance offences

(2) Every person commits an offence who knowingly

(a) makes or possesses any plate that is specifically designed or adapted for the purpose of making infringing copies of any work or other subject-matter in which copyright subsists; or

(b) for private profit causes to be performed in public, without the consent of the owner of the copyright, any work or other subject-matter in which copyright subsists.

Punishment

(2.1) Every person who commits an offence under subsection (1) or (2) is liable

Recours criminels

Infractions et peines

42 (1) Commet une infraction quiconque, sciemment :

a) se livre, en vue de la vente ou de la location, à la contrefaçon d'une œuvre ou d'un autre objet du droit d'auteur protégés;

b) en vend ou en loue, ou commercialement en met ou en offre en vente ou en location un exemplaire contrefait;

c) en met en circulation des exemplaires contrefaits, soit dans un but commercial, soit de façon à porter préjudice au titulaire du droit d'auteur;

d) en expose commercialement en public un exemplaire contrefait;

e) en a un exemplaire contrefait en sa possession, pour le vendre, le louer, le mettre en circulation dans un but commercial ou l'exposer commercialement en public;

f) en importe pour la vente ou la location, au Canada, un exemplaire contrefait;

g) en exporte ou tente d'en exporter, pour la vente ou la location, un exemplaire contrefait.

Possession et infractions découlant d'une action, et peines

(2) Commet une infraction quiconque, sciemment :

a) confectionne ou possède une planche conçue ou adaptée précisément pour la contrefaçon d'une œuvre ou de tout autre objet du droit d'auteur protégés;

b) fait, dans un but de profit, exécuter ou représenter publiquement une œuvre ou un autre objet du droit d'auteur protégés sans le consentement du titulaire du droit d'auteur.

Peine

(2.1) Quiconque commet une infraction visée aux paragraphes (1) ou (2) est passible, sur déclaration de culpabilité :

(a) on conviction on indictment, to a fine of not more than $1,000,000 or to imprisonment for a term of not more than five years or to both; or

(b) on summary conviction, to a fine of not more than $25,000 or to imprisonment for a term of not more than six months or to both.

Power of court to deal with copies or plates

(3) The court before which any proceedings under this section are taken may, on conviction, order that all copies of the work or other subject-matter that appear to it to be infringing copies, or all plates in the possession of the offender predominantly used for making infringing copies, be destroyed or delivered up to the owner of the copyright or otherwise dealt with as the court may think fit.

Notice

(3.01) Before making an order under subsection (3), the court shall require that notice be given to the owner of the copies or plates and to any other person who, in the court's opinion, appears to have a right or interest in them, unless the court is of the opinion that the interests of justice do not require that the notice be given.

Circumvention of technological protection measure

(3.1) Every person, except a person who is acting on behalf of a library, archive or museum or an educational institution, is guilty of an offence who knowingly and for commercial purposes contravenes section 41.1 and is liable

(a) on conviction on indictment, to a fine not exceeding $1,000,000 or to imprisonment for a term not exceeding five years or to both; or

(b) on summary conviction, to a fine not exceeding $25,000 or to imprisonment for a term not exceeding six months or to both.

Limitation period

(4) Proceedings by summary conviction in respect of an offence under this section may be instituted at any time within, but not later than, two years after the time when the offence was committed.

Parallel importation

(5) For the purposes of this section, a copy of a work or other subject-matter is not infringing if the copy was made with the consent of the owner of the copyright in the country where the copy was made.

R.S., 1985, c. C-42, s. 42; R.S., 1985, c. 10 (4th Supp.), s. 10; 1997, c. 24, s. 24; 2012, c. 20, s. 48; 2014, c. 32, s. 4.

Infringement in case of dramatic, operatic or musical work

43 (1) Any person who, without the written consent of the owner of the copyright or of the legal representative of the owner, knowingly performs or causes to be performed in public and for private profit the whole or any part, constituting an infringement, of any dramatic or operatic work or musical composition in which copyright subsists in Canada is guilty of an offence and liable on summary conviction to a fine not exceeding two hundred and fifty dollars and, in the case of a second or subsequent offence, either to that fine or to imprisonment for a term not exceeding two months or to both.

Change or suppression of title or author's name

(2) Any person who makes or causes to be made any change in or suppression of the title, or the name of the author, of any dramatic or operatic work or musical composition in which copyright subsists in Canada, or who makes or causes to be made any change in the work or composition itself without the written consent of the author or of his legal representative, in order that the work or composition may be performed in whole or in part in public for private profit, is guilty of an offence and liable on summary conviction to a fine not exceeding five hundred dollars and, in the case of a second or subsequent offence, either to that fine or to imprisonment for a term not exceeding four months or to both.

R.S., c. C-30, s. 26.

Limitation or Prescription Period

Limitation or prescription period for civil remedies

43.1 (1) Subject to subsection (2), a court may award a remedy for any act or omission that has been done contrary to this Act only if

(a) the proceedings for the act or omission giving rise to a remedy are commenced within three years after it occurred, in the case where the plaintiff knew, or could reasonably have been expected to know, of the act or omission at the time it occurred; or

(b) the proceedings for the act or omission giving rise to a remedy are commenced within three years after the time when the plaintiff first knew of it, or could reasonably have been expected to know of it, in the case where the plaintiff did not know, and could not reasonably have been expected to know, of the act or omission at the time it occurred.

Restriction

(2) The court shall apply the limitation or prescription period set out in paragraph (1)(a) or (b) only in respect of a party who pleads a limitation period.

1994, c. 47, s. 64; 1997, c. 24, s. 25; 2012, c. 20, s. 49.

Importation and Exportation

Interpretation

Definitions

44 The following definitions apply in sections 44.02 to 44.4.

court means the Federal Court or the superior court of a province. (*tribunal*)

customs officer has the meaning assigned by the definition ***officer*** in subsection 2(1) of the *Customs Act*. (*agent des douanes*)

duties has the same meaning as in subsection 2(1) of the *Customs Act*. (*droits*)

Minister means the Minister of Public Safety and Emergency Preparedness. (*ministre*)

release has the same meaning as in subsection 2(1) of the *Customs Act*. (*dédouanement*)

working day means a day other than a Saturday or a holiday. (*jour ouvrable*)

R.S., 1985, c. C-42, s. 44; R.S., 1985, c. 41 (3rd Supp.), s. 116; 1997, c. 36, s. 205; 1999, c. 17, s. 119; 2005, c. 38, s. 139; 2014, c. 32, s. 5.

Prohibition and Detention by Customs Officer

Prohibition

Prohibition on importation or exportation

44.01 (1) Copies of a work or other subject-matter in which copyright subsists shall not be imported or exported if

b) le demandeur engage une procédure dans les trois ans qui suivent le moment où il a pris connaissance du fait visé par le recours ou le moment où il est raisonnable de s'attendre à ce qu'il en ait pris connaissance, s'il n'en avait pas connaissance au moment où il a eu lieu ou s'il n'est pas raisonnable de s'attendre à ce qu'il en ait eu connaissance à ce moment.

Restriction

(2) Le tribunal ne fait jouer la prescription visée aux alinéas (1)a) ou b) qu'à l'égard de la partie qui l'invoque.

1994, ch. 47, art. 64; 1997, ch. 24, art. 25; 2012, ch. 20, art. 49.

Importation et exportation

Définitions

Définitions

44 Les définitions qui suivent s'appliquent aux articles 44.02 à 44.4.

agent des douanes S'entend au sens du paragraphe 2(1) de la *Loi sur les douanes*. (*customs officer*)

dédouanement S'entend au sens du paragraphe 2(1) de la *Loi sur les douanes*. (*release*)

droits S'entend au sens du paragraphe 2(1) de la *Loi sur les douanes*. (*duties*)

jour ouvrable S'entend d'un jour qui n'est ni un samedi, ni un jour férié. (*working day*)

ministre Le ministre de la Sécurité publique et de la Protection civile. (*Minister*)

tribunal La Cour fédérale ou la cour supérieure d'une province. (*court*)

L.R. (1985), ch. C-42, art. 44; L.R. (1985), ch. 41 (3e suppl.), art. 116; 1997, ch. 36, art. 205; 1999, ch. 17, art. 119; 2005, ch. 38, art. 139; 2014, ch. 32, art. 5.

Interdiction et rétention par les agents des douanes

Interdiction

Interdiction d'importation et d'exportation

44.01 (1) Sont interdits d'importation et d'exportation les exemplaires d'une œuvre ou d'un autre objet du droit d'auteur protégés si :

(a) they were made without the consent of the owner of the copyright in the country where they were made; and

(b) they infringe copyright or, if they were not made in Canada, they would infringe copyright had they been made in Canada by the person who made them.

Exception

(2) Subsection (1) does not apply to

(a) copies that are imported or exported by an individual in their possession or baggage if the circumstances, including the number of copies, indicate that the copies are intended only for their personal use; or

(b) copies that, while being shipped from one place outside Canada to another, are in customs transit control or customs transhipment control in Canada.

2014, c. 32, s. 5.

Request for Assistance

Request for assistance

44.02 (1) The owner of copyright in a work or other subject-matter may file with the Minister, in the form and manner specified by the Minister, a request for assistance in pursuing remedies under this Act with respect to copies imported or exported in contravention of section 44.01.

Information in request

(2) The request for assistance shall include the copyright owner's name and address in Canada and any other information that is required by the Minister, including information about the work or other subject-matter in question.

Validity period

(3) A request for assistance is valid for a period of two years beginning on the day on which it is accepted by the Minister. The Minister may, at the request of the copyright owner, extend the period for two years, and may do so more than once.

Security

(4) The Minister may, as a condition of accepting a request for assistance or of extending a request's period of validity, require that the copyright owner furnish security, in an amount and form fixed by the Minister, for the

payment of an amount for which the copyright owner becomes liable under section 44.07.

Update

(5) The copyright owner shall inform the Minister in writing, as soon as practicable, of any changes to

    (a) the subsistence of the copyright that is the subject of the request for assistance; or

    (b) the ownership of that copyright.

2014, c. 32, s. 5.

Measures Relating to Detained Copies

Provision of information by customs officer

44.03 A customs officer who is detaining copies of a work or other subject-matter under section 101 of the *Customs Act* may, in the officer's discretion, to obtain information about whether the importation or exportation of the copies is prohibited under section 44.01, provide the owner of copyright in that work or subject-matter with a sample of the copies and with any information about the copies that the customs officer reasonably believes does not directly or indirectly identify any person.

2014, c. 32, s. 5.

Provision of information to pursue remedy

44.04 (1) A customs officer who is detaining copies of a work or other subject-matter under section 101 of the *Customs Act* and who has reasonable grounds to suspect that the importation or exportation of the copies is prohibited under section 44.01 may, in the officer's discretion, if the Minister has accepted a request for assistance with respect to the work or subject-matter filed by the owner of copyright in it, provide that owner with a sample of the copies and with information about the copies that could assist them in pursuing a remedy under this Act, such as

    (a) a description of the copies and of their characteristics;

    (b) the name and address of their owner, importer, exporter and consignee and of the person who made them;

    (c) their quantity;

    (d) the countries in which they were made and through which they passed in transit; and

d'auteur afin de garantir l'exécution des obligations de ce dernier au titre de l'article 44.07.

Tenue à jour

(5) Le titulaire du droit d'auteur est tenu d'informer par écrit le ministre, dès que possible, de tout changement relatif :

    a) à l'existence du droit d'auteur visé par la demande d'aide;

    b) à la titularité de ce droit d'auteur.

2014, ch. 32, art. 5.

Mesures relatives aux exemplaires retenus

Fourniture de renseignements par l'agent des douanes

44.03 L'agent des douanes qui retient des exemplaires d'une œuvre ou de tout autre objet du droit d'auteur en vertu de l'article 101 de la *Loi sur les douanes* peut, à sa discrétion et en vue d'obtenir des renseignements sur l'éventuelle interdiction, au titre de l'article 44.01, de leur importation ou de leur exportation, fournir au titulaire du droit d'auteur sur l'œuvre ou l'autre objet du droit d'auteur des échantillons des exemplaires et tout renseignement à leur sujet s'il croit, pour des motifs raisonnables, que le renseignement ne peut, même indirectement, identifier quiconque.

2014, ch. 32, art. 5.

Fourniture de renseignements en vue de l'exercice de recours

44.04 (1) L'agent des douanes qui a des motifs raisonnables de soupçonner que des exemplaires d'une œuvre ou d'un autre objet du droit d'auteur qu'il retient en vertu de l'article 101 de la *Loi sur les douanes* sont interdits d'importation ou d'exportation au titre de l'article 44.01 peut, à sa discrétion, fournir au titulaire du droit d'auteur sur l'œuvre ou l'autre objet du droit d'auteur, si celui-ci a présenté une demande d'aide acceptée par le ministre à l'égard de cette œuvre ou de cet autre objet du droit d'auteur, des échantillons des exemplaires ainsi que des renseignements au sujet des exemplaires qui pourraient lui être utiles pour l'exercice de ses recours au titre de la présente loi, tels que :

    a) leur description et celle de leurs caractéristiques;

    b) les nom et adresse de leur propriétaire, importateur, exportateur et consignataire ainsi que de la personne qui les a produits;

    c) leur nombre;

Detention

(2) Subject to subsection (3), the customs officer shall not detain, for the purpose of enforcing section 44.01, the copies for more than 10 working days — or, if the copies are perishable, for more than five days — after the day on which the customs officer first sends or makes available a sample or information to the copyright owner under subsection (1). At the request of the copyright owner made while the copies are detained for the purpose of enforcing section 44.01, the customs officer may, having regard to the circumstances, detain non-perishable copies for one additional period of not more than 10 working days.

Notice of proceedings

(3) If, before the copies are no longer detained for the purpose of enforcing section 44.01, the owner of copyright has provided the Minister, in the manner specified by the Minister, with a copy of a document filed with a court commencing proceedings to obtain a remedy under this Act with respect to the detained copies, the customs officer shall continue to detain them until the Minister is informed in writing that

(a) the proceedings are finally disposed of, settled or abandoned;

(b) a court directs that the copies are no longer to be detained for the purpose of the proceedings; or

(c) the copyright owner consents to the copies no longer being so detained.

Continued detention

(4) The occurrence of any of the events referred to in paragraphs (3)(a) to (c) does not preclude a customs officer from continuing to detain the copies under the *Customs Act* for a purpose other than the proceedings.

2014, c. 32, s. 5.

Restriction on information use — section 44.03

44.05 (1) A person who receives a sample or information that is provided under section 44.03 shall not use the information, or information that is derived from the sample, for any purpose other than to give information to the customs officer about whether the importation or exportation of the copies is prohibited under section 44.01.

Restriction on information use — subsection 44.04(1)

(2) A person who receives a sample or information that is provided under subsection 44.04(1) shall not use the information, or information that is derived from the sample, for any purpose other than to pursue remedies under this Act.

For greater certainty

(3) For greater certainty, subsection (2) does not prevent the confidential communication of information about the copies for the purpose of reaching an out-of-court settlement.

2014, c. 32, s. 5.

Inspection

44.06 After a sample or information has been provided under subsection 44.04(1), a customs officer may, in the officer's discretion, give the owner, importer, exporter and consignee of the detained copies and the owner of copyright an opportunity to inspect the copies.

2014, c. 32, s. 5.

Liability for charges

44.07 (1) The owner of copyright who has received a sample or information under subsection 44.04(1) is liable to Her Majesty in right of Canada for the storage and handling charges for the detained copies — and, if applicable, for the charges for destroying them — for the period beginning on the day after the day on which a customs officer first sends or makes available a sample or information to that owner under that subsection and ending on the first day on which one of the following occurs:

(a) the copies are no longer detained for the purpose of enforcing section 44.01 or, if subsection 44.04(3) applies, for the purpose of the proceedings referred to in that subsection;

(b) the Minister receives written notification in which the owner states that the importation or exportation of the copies does not, with respect to the owner's copyright, contravene section 44.01;

(c) the Minister receives written notification in which the owner states that they will not, while the copies are detained for the purpose of enforcing section 44.01, commence proceedings to obtain a remedy under this Act with respect to them.

Exception — paragraph (1)(a)

(2) Despite paragraph (1)(a), if the copies are forfeited under subsection 39(1) of the *Customs Act* and the Minister did not, before the end of the detention of the copies for the purpose of enforcing section 44.01, receive a copy of a document filed with a court commencing proceedings to obtain a remedy under this Act with respect to the detained copies or the written notification referred to in paragraph (1)(b) or (c), the period ends on the day on which the copies are forfeited.

Exception — paragraph (1)(c)

(3) Despite paragraph (1)(c), if the copies are forfeited under subsection 39(1) of the *Customs Act* after the Minister has received the written notification referred to in that paragraph, the period ends on the day on which the copies are forfeited.

Joint and several or solidary liability

(4) The owner and the importer or exporter of copies that are forfeited in the circumstances set out in subsection (2) or (3) are jointly and severally, or solidarily, liable to the owner of copyright for all the charges under subsection (1) paid by the copyright owner with respect to the period

(a) in the circumstances referred to in subsection (2), beginning on the day on which the copies are no longer detained for the purpose of enforcing section 44.01 and ending on the day on which the copies are forfeited; and

(b) in the circumstances referred to in subsection (3), beginning on the day on which the Minister receives the written notification referred to in paragraph (1)(c) and ending on the day on which the copies are forfeited.

Exception

(5) Subsections (1) to (3) do not apply if

(a) the detention of the copies for the purpose of enforcing section 44.01 ends before the expiry of 10 working days — or, if the copies are perishable, before the expiry of five days — after the day on which the customs officer first sends or makes available a sample or information to the copyright owner under subsection 44.04(1); and

(b) the Minister has not, by the end of the detention, received a copy of a document filed with a court commencing proceedings to obtain a remedy under this Act with respect to the detained copies or the written notification referred to in paragraph (1)(b) or (c).

2014, c. 32, s. 5.

b) d'autre part, sans que le ministre n'ait reçu copie de l'acte introductif d'instance déposé devant un tribunal dans le cadre d'un recours formé au titre de la présente loi à l'égard de ces exemplaires ou l'une des déclarations visées aux alinéas (1)b) ou c).

2014, ch. 32, art. 5.

No Liability / Immunité

No liability / Immunité

44.08 Neither Her Majesty nor a customs officer is liable for any loss or damage suffered in relation to the enforcement or application of sections 44.01 to 44.04 and 44.06 because of

(a) the detention of copies of a work or other subject-matter, except if the detention contravenes subsection 44.04(2);

(b) the failure to detain copies; or

(c) the release or cessation of detention of any copies, except if the release or cessation contravenes subsection 44.04(3).

2014, c. 32, s. 5.

44.08 Ni Sa Majesté ni l'agent des douanes ne peuvent être tenus responsables des dommages ou des pertes liés à l'application ou au contrôle d'application des articles 44.01 à 44.04 et 44.06 qui découlent, selon le cas :

a) de la rétention d'exemplaires d'une œuvre ou de tout autre objet du droit d'auteur, sauf si elle est contraire au paragraphe 44.04(2);

b) de l'omission de retenir des exemplaires;

c) du dédouanement ou de la fin de la rétention d'exemplaires, sauf si l'un ou l'autre est contraire au paragraphe 44.04(3).

2014, ch. 32, art. 5.

Powers of Court Relating to Detained Copies / Pouvoirs du tribunal relativement aux exemplaires retenus

Application to court / Demande au tribunal

44.09 (1) In the course of proceedings referred to in subsection 44.04(3), the court may, on the application of the Minister or a party to the proceedings,

(a) impose conditions on the storage or detention of the copies that are the subject of the proceedings; or

(b) direct that the copies are no longer to be detained for the purpose of the proceedings, on any conditions that the court may impose, if their owner, importer, exporter or consignee furnishes security in an amount fixed by the court.

44.09 (1) Dans le cadre du recours mentionné au paragraphe 44.04(3), le tribunal peut, à la demande du ministre ou d'une partie :

a) assortir de conditions la rétention ou l'entreposage des exemplaires visés;

b) ordonner qu'il soit mis fin, aux conditions qu'il peut préciser, à leur rétention pour l'exercice du recours, si une sûreté, dont il fixe le montant, est fournie par leur propriétaire, importateur, exportateur ou consignataire.

Minister's consent / Consentement du ministre

(2) If a party applies to have the detained copies stored in a place other than a bonded warehouse or a sufferance warehouse, as those terms are defined in subsection 2(1) of the *Customs Act*, the Minister must consent to the storage of the copies in that place before a condition to that effect is imposed under subsection (1).

(2) Si une partie demande que les exemplaires retenus soient entreposés dans un établissement autre qu'un entrepôt d'attente ou un entrepôt de stockage au sens du paragraphe 2(1) de la *Loi sur les douanes*, le ministre doit approuver l'entreposage dans l'établissement avant que le tribunal ne fixe une condition à cet effet.

Customs Act / Loi sur les douanes

(3) The court may impose a condition described in subsection (2) despite section 31 of the *Customs Act*.

(3) Le tribunal peut fixer une condition visée au paragraphe (2) malgré l'article 31 de la *Loi sur les douanes*.

Continued detention

(4) A direction under paragraph (1)(b) that the copies are no longer to be detained for the purpose of the proceedings does not preclude a customs officer from continuing to detain the copies under the *Customs Act* for another purpose.

Security

(5) In the course of proceedings referred to in subsection 44.04(3), the court may, on the application of the Minister or a party to the proceedings, require the owner of copyright to furnish security, in an amount fixed by the court,

(a) to cover duties, storage and handling charges, and any other amount that may become chargeable against the copies; and

(b) to answer any damages that may, because of the detention of the copies, be sustained by the owner, importer, exporter or consignee of the copies.

2014, c. 32, s. 5.

Damages against copyright owner

44.1 (1) The court may award damages against the owner of copyright who commenced proceedings referred to in subsection 44.04(3) to the owner, importer, exporter or consignee of the copies who is a party to the proceedings for losses, costs or prejudice suffered as a result of the detention of the copies if the proceedings are dismissed or discontinued.

Damages awarded to copyright owner

(2) Any damages under subsection 34(1) awarded to the owner of copyright in proceedings referred to in subsection 44.04(3) are to include the charges incurred by the copyright owner as a result of storing, handling or, if applicable, destroying the detained copies.

1993, c. 44, s. 66; 1997, c. 24, s. 27; 2005, c. 38, ss. 142, 145; 2014, c. 32, s. 5.

Prohibition Resulting from Notice

Importation of certain copyright works prohibited

44.11 Copies made outside Canada of any work in which copyright subsists that if made in Canada would infringe copyright and as to which the owner of the copyright gives notice in writing to the Canada Border Services Agency that the owner desires that the copies not be imported into Canada, shall not be so imported and are deemed to be included in tariff item No. 9897.00.00 in the List of Tariff Provisions set out in the schedule to the *Customs Tariff*, with section 136 of that Act applying accordingly.

2014, c. 32, s. 5.

Court-ordered Detention

Power of court

44.12 (1) A court may make an order described in subsection (3) if the court is satisfied that

(a) copies of the work are about to be imported into Canada, or have been imported into Canada but have not been released;

(b) the copies were either

(i) made without the consent of the person who is owner of the copyright in the country where they were made, or

(ii) made elsewhere than in a country to which this Act extends; and

(c) the copies would infringe copyright if they were made in Canada by the importer and the importer knows or should have known this.

Who may apply

(2) A court may make an order described in subsection (3) on application by the owner of the copyright in a work in Canada.

Order of court

(3) In an order made under subsection (1), the court may

(a) direct the Minister

(i) to take reasonable measures, on the basis of information reasonably required by the Minister and provided by the applicant, to detain the copies of the work, and

(ii) to notify the applicant and the importer, immediately after detaining the copies of the work, of the detention and the reasons for the detention; and

(b) provide for any other matters that the court considers appropriate.

How application made

(4) An application for an order under subsection (1) may be made in an action or otherwise, and either on notice or *ex parte*, except that it must always be made on notice to the Minister.

Security

(5) Before making an order under subsection (1), the court may require the applicant to furnish security, in an amount fixed by the court,

> **(a)** to cover duties, storage and handling charges and any other amount that may become chargeable against the copies of the work; and
>
> **(b)** to answer any damages that may by reason of the order be incurred by the owner, importer or consignee of the work.

Application for directions

(6) The Minister may apply to the court for directions in implementing an order made under subsection (1).

Minister may allow inspection

(7) The Minister may give the applicant or the importer an opportunity to inspect the detained copies of the work for the purpose of substantiating or refuting, as the case may be, the applicant's claim.

If applicant fails to commence action

(8) Unless an order made under subsection (1) provides otherwise, the Minister shall, subject to the *Customs Act* and to any other Act of Parliament that prohibits, controls or regulates the importation or exportation of goods, release the copies of the work without further notice to the applicant if, within 10 working days after the applicant has been notified under subparagraph (3)(a)(ii), the applicant has not notified the Minister that they have commenced a proceeding for a final determination by the court of the issues referred to in paragraphs (1)(b) and (c).

If court finds in plaintiff's favour

(9) If, in a proceeding commenced under this section, the court is satisfied that the circumstances referred to in paragraphs (1)(b) and (c) existed, the court may make any order that it considers appropriate in the circumstances, including an order that the copies of the work be destroyed, or that they be delivered up to the plaintiff as the plaintiff's property absolutely.

Other remedies not affected

(10) For greater certainty, nothing in this section affects any remedy available under any other provision of this Act or any other Act of Parliament.

2014, c. 32, s. 5.

Importation of books

44.2 (1) A court may, subject to this section, make an order described in subsection 44.12(3) in relation to a book where the court is satisfied that

(a) copies of the book are about to be imported into Canada, or have been imported into Canada but have not yet been released;

(b) copies of the book were made with the consent of the owner of the copyright in the book in the country where the copies were made, but were imported without the consent of the owner in Canada of the copyright in the book; and

(c) the copies would infringe copyright if they were made in Canada by the importer and the importer knows or should have known this.

Who may apply

(2) A court may make an order described in subsection 44.12(3) in relation to a book on application by

(a) the owner of the copyright in the book in Canada;

(b) the exclusive licensee of the copyright in the book in Canada; or

(c) the exclusive distributor of the book.

Limitation

(3) Subsections (1) and (2) only apply where there is an exclusive distributor of the book and the acts described in those subsections take place in the part of Canada or in respect of the particular sector of the market for which the person is the exclusive distributor.

Application of certain provisions

(4) Subsections 44.12(3) to (10) apply, with such modifications as the circumstances require, in respect of an order made under subsection (1).

1994, c. 47, s. 66; 1997, c. 24, s. 28; 2014, c. 32, s. 6.

Limitation

44.3 No exclusive licensee of the copyright in a book in Canada, and no exclusive distributor of a book, may obtain an order under section 44.2 against another exclusive licensee of the copyright in that book in Canada or against another exclusive distributor of that book.

1997, c. 24, s. 28.

Importation of other subject-matter

44.4 Section 44.12 applies, with such modifications as the circumstances require, in respect of a sound recording, performer's performance or communication signal, where a fixation or a reproduction of a fixation of it

(a) is about to be imported into Canada, or has been imported into Canada but has not yet been released;

(b) either

(i) was made without the consent of the person who then owned the copyright in the sound recording, performer's performance or communication signal, as the case may be, in the country where the fixation or reproduction was made, or

(ii) was made elsewhere than in a country to which Part II extends; and

(c) would infringe the right of the owner of copyright in the sound recording, performer's performance or communication signal if it was made in Canada by the importer and the importer knows or should have known this.

1997, c. 24, s. 28; 2014, c. 32, s. 6.

Exceptions

45 (1) Notwithstanding anything in this Act, it is lawful for a person

(a) to import for their own use not more than two copies of a work or other subject-matter made with the consent of the owner of the copyright in the country where it was made;

(b) to import for use by a department of the Government of Canada or a province copies of a work or other subject-matter made with the consent of the owner of the copyright in the country where it was made;

(c) at any time before copies of a work or other subject-matter are made in Canada, to import any copies, except copies of a book, made with the consent of the owner of the copyright in the country where the copies were made, that are required for the use of a library, archive, museum or educational institution;

(d) to import, for the use of a library, archive, museum or educational institution, not more than one copy of a book that is made with the consent of the owner of

Application aux autres objets du droit d'auteur

44.4 L'article 44.12 s'applique, avec les adaptations nécessaires, à la prestation de l'artiste-interprète, à l'enregistrement sonore ou au signal de communication lorsque, dans le cas d'une fixation de ceux-ci ou d'une reproduction d'une telle fixation, les conditions suivantes sont réunies :

a) la fixation ou la reproduction de la fixation est importée au Canada — ou sur le point de l'être — sans être dédouanée;

b) elle a été faite soit sans le consentement du titulaire du droit d'auteur dans le pays de la fixation ou de la reproduction, soit ailleurs que dans un pays visé par la partie II;

c) l'importateur sait ou aurait dû savoir que la fixation ou la reproduction violerait les droits du titulaire du droit d'auteur concerné s'il l'avait faite au Canada.

1997, ch. 24, art. 28; 2014, ch. 32, art. 6.

Importations autorisées

45 (1) Malgré les autres dispositions de la présente loi, il est loisible à toute personne :

a) d'importer pour son propre usage deux exemplaires au plus d'une œuvre ou d'un autre objet du droit d'auteur produits avec le consentement du titulaire du droit d'auteur dans le pays de production;

b) d'importer, pour l'usage d'un ministère du gouvernement du Canada ou de l'une des provinces, des exemplaires — produits avec le consentement du titulaire du droit d'auteur dans le pays de production — d'une œuvre ou d'un autre objet du droit d'auteur;

c) en tout temps avant la production au Canada d'exemplaires d'une œuvre ou d'un autre objet du droit d'auteur, d'importer les exemplaires, sauf ceux d'un livre, — produits avec le consentement du titulaire du droit d'auteur dans le pays de production — requis pour l'usage d'un établissement d'enseignement, d'une bibliothèque, d'un service d'archives ou d'un musée;

the copyright in the country where the book was made; and

(e) to import copies, made with the consent of the owner of the copyright in the country where they were made, of any used books, except textbooks of a scientific, technical or scholarly nature for use within an educational institution in a course of instruction.

Satisfactory evidence

(2) An officer of customs may, in the officer's discretion, require a person seeking to import a copy of a work or other subject-matter under this section to produce satisfactory evidence of the facts necessary to establish the person's right to import the copy.

R.S., 1985, c. C-42, s. 45; R.S., 1985, c. 41 (3rd Supp.), s. 117; 1993, c. 44, s. 67; 1994, c. 47, s. 67; 1997, c. 24, s. 28.

PART V

Administration

Copyright Office

Copyright Office

46 The Copyright Office shall be attached to the Patent Office.

R.S., c. C-30, s. 29.

Powers of Commissioner and Registrar

47 The Commissioner of Patents shall exercise the powers conferred and perform the duties imposed on him by this Act under the direction of the Minister, and, in the absence of the Commissioner of Patents or if the Commissioner is unable to act, the Registrar of Copyrights or other officer temporarily appointed by the Minister may, as Acting Commissioner, exercise those powers and perform those duties under the direction of the Minister.

R.S., c. C-30, s. 30.

Registrar

48 There shall be a Registrar of Copyrights.

R.S., c. C-30, s. 31.

Register of Copyrights, certificates and certified copies

49 The Commissioner of Patents, the Registrar of Copyrights or an officer, clerk or employee of the Copyright

Office may sign certificates and certified copies of the Register of Copyrights.

R.S., 1985, c. C-42, s. 49; 1992, c. 1, s. 47; 1993, c. 15, s. 4.

Other duties of Registrar

50 The Registrar of Copyrights shall perform such other duties in connection with the administration of this Act as may be assigned to him by the Commissioner of Patents.

R.S., c. C-30, s. 33.

51 [Repealed, 1992, c. 1, s. 48]

Control of business and officials

52 The Commissioner of Patents shall, subject to the Minister, oversee and direct the officers, clerks and employees of the Copyright Office, have general control of the business thereof and perform such other duties as are assigned to him by the Governor in Council.

R.S., c. C-30, s. 35.

Register to be evidence

53 (1) The Register of Copyrights is evidence of the particulars entered in it, and a copy of an entry in the Register is evidence of the particulars of the entry if it is certified by the Commissioner of Patents, the Registrar of Copyrights or an officer, clerk or employee of the Copyright Office as a true copy.

Owner of copyright

(2) A certificate of registration of copyright is evidence that the copyright subsists and that the person registered is the owner of the copyright.

Assignee

(2.1) A certificate of registration of an assignment of copyright is evidence that the right recorded on the certificate has been assigned and that the assignee registered is the owner of that right.

Licensee

(2.2) A certificate of registration of a licence granting an interest in a copyright is evidence that the interest recorded on the certificate has been granted and that the licensee registered is the holder of that interest.

Admissibility

(3) A certified copy or certificate appearing to have been issued under this section is admissible in all courts without proof of the signature or official character of the person appearing to have signed it.

R.S., 1985, c. C-42, s. 53; 1992, c. 1, s. 49; 1993, c. 15, s. 5; 1997, c. 24, s. 30.

Registration

Register of Copyrights

54 (1) The Minister shall cause to be kept at the Copyright Office a register to be called the Register of Copyrights in which may be entered

(a) the names or titles of works and of other subject-matter in which copyright subsists;

(b) the names and addresses of authors, performers, makers of sound recordings, broadcasters, owners of copyright, assignees of copyright, and persons to whom an interest in copyright has been granted by licence; and

(c) such other particulars as may be prescribed by regulation.

(2) [Repealed, 1997, c. 24, s. 31]

Single entry sufficient

(3) In the case of an encyclopaedia, newspaper, review, magazine or other periodical work, or work published in a series of books or parts, it is not necessary to make a separate entry for each number or part, but a single entry for the whole work is sufficient.

Indices

(4) There shall also be kept at the Copyright Office such indices of the Register established under this section as may be prescribed by regulation.

Inspection and extracts

(5) The Register and indices established under this section shall at all reasonable times be open to inspection, and any person is entitled to make copies of or take extracts from the Register.

Former registration effective

(6) Any registration made under the *Copyright Act*, chapter 70 of the Revised Statutes of Canada, 1906, has the same force and effect as if made under this Act.

Subsisting copyright

(7) Any work in which copyright, operative in Canada, subsisted immediately before January 1, 1924 is registrable under this Act.

R.S., 1985, c. C-42, s. 54; 1992, c. 1, s. 50; 1997, c. 24, s. 31.

Copyright in works

55 (1) Application for the registration of a copyright in a work may be made by or on behalf of the author of the work, the owner of the copyright in the work, an assignee of the copyright, or a person to whom an interest in the copyright has been granted by licence.

Application for registration

(2) An application under subsection (1) must be filed with the Copyright Office, be accompanied by the fee prescribed by or determined under the regulations, and contain the following information:

(a) the name and address of the owner of the copyright in the work;

(b) a declaration that the applicant is the author of the work, the owner of the copyright in the work, an assignee of the copyright, or a person to whom an interest in the copyright has been granted by licence;

(c) the category of the work;

(d) the title of the work;

(e) the name of the author and, if the author is dead, the date of the author's death, if known;

(f) in the case of a published work, the date and place of the first publication; and

(g) any additional information prescribed by regulation.

R.S., 1985, c. C-42, s. 55; 1997, c. 24, s. 32.

Copyright in subject-matter other than works

56 (1) Application for the registration of a copyright in subject-matter other than a work may be made by or on behalf of the owner of the copyright in the subject-matter, an assignee of the copyright, or a person to whom an interest in the copyright has been granted by licence.

Application for registration

(2) An application under subsection (1) must be filed with the Copyright Office, be accompanied by the fee prescribed by or determined under the regulations, and contain the following information:

(a) the name and address of the owner of the copyright in the subject-matter;

(b) a declaration that the applicant is the owner of the copyright in the subject-matter, an assignee of the copyright, or a person to whom an interest in the copyright has been granted by licence;

(c) whether the subject-matter is a performer's performance, a sound recording or a communication signal;

(d) the title, if any, of the subject-matter;

(e) the date of

(i) in the case of a performer's performance, its first fixation in a sound recording or, if it is not fixed in a sound recording, its first performance,

(ii) in the case of a sound recording, the first fixation, or

(iii) in the case of a communication signal, its broadcast; and

(f) any additional information prescribed by regulation.

R.S., 1985, c. C-42, s. 56; 1993, c. 15, s. 6; 1997, c. 24, s. 32.

b) une déclaration précisant que le demandeur est le titulaire ou le cessionnaire de ce droit, ou le titulaire d'une licence accordant un intérêt dans celui-ci;

c) l'objet du droit d'auteur;

d) son titre, s'il y a lieu;

e) la date de la première fixation d'une prestation au moyen d'un enregistrement sonore, ou de sa première exécution si elle n'est pas ainsi fixée, la date de la première fixation dans le cas de l'enregistrement sonore et la date de l'émission dans le cas du signal de communication;

f) tout renseignement supplémentaire prévu par règlement.

L.R. (1985), ch. C-42, art. 56; 1993, ch. 15, art. 6; 1997, ch. 24, art. 32.

Recovery of damages

56.1 Where a person purports to have the authority to apply for the registration of a copyright under section 55 or 56 on behalf of another person, any damage caused by a fraudulent or erroneous assumption of such authority is recoverable in any court of competent jurisdiction.

1997, c. 24, s. 32.

Recouvrement

56.1 Tout dommage causé par erreur ou par l'action frauduleuse d'une personne qui prétend pouvoir au nom de l'une des personnes visées aux articles 55 ou 56 faire une demande d'enregistrement peut être recouvré devant un tribunal compétent.

1997, ch. 24, art. 32.

Registration of assignment or licence

57 (1) The Registrar of Copyrights shall register an assignment of copyright, or a licence granting an interest in a copyright, on being furnished with

(a) the original instrument or a certified copy of it, or other evidence satisfactory to the Registrar of the assignment or licence; and

(b) the fee prescribed by or determined under the regulations.

(2) [Repealed, 1992, c. 1, s. 51]

Enregistrement d'une cession ou d'une licence

57 (1) Le registraire des droits d'auteur enregistre, sur production du document original ou d'une copie certifiée conforme ou de toute autre preuve qu'il estime satisfaisante et sur paiement de la taxe dont le montant est fixé par les règlements ou déterminé conformément à ceux-ci, l'acte de cession d'un droit d'auteur ou la licence accordant un intérêt dans ce droit.

(2) [Abrogé, 1992, ch. 1, art. 51]

When assignment or licence is void

(3) Any assignment of copyright, or any licence granting an interest in a copyright, shall be adjudged void against any subsequent assignee or licensee for valuable

Annulation de la cession ou de la concession

(3) Tout acte de cession d'un droit d'auteur ou toute licence concédant un intérêt dans un droit d'auteur doit être déclaré nul à l'encontre de tout cessionnaire du droit

consideration without actual notice, unless the prior assignment or licence is registered in the manner prescribed by this Act before the registering of the instrument under which the subsequent assignee or licensee claims.

Rectification of Register by the Court

(4) The Federal Court may, on application of the Registrar of Copyrights or of any interested person, order the rectification of the Register of Copyrights by

> **(a)** the making of any entry wrongly omitted to be made in the Register,
>
> **(b)** the expunging of any entry wrongly made in or remaining on the Register, or
>
> **(c)** the correction of any error or defect in the Register,

and any rectification of the Register under this subsection shall be retroactive from such date as the Court may order.

R.S., 1985, c. C-42, s. 57; 1992, c. 1, s. 51; 1993, c. 15, s. 7; 1997, c. 24, s. 33.

Execution of instruments

58 (1) Any assignment of a copyright, or any licence granting an interest in a copyright, may be executed, subscribed or acknowledged at any place in a treaty country, a Rome Convention country or a WPPT country by the assignor, licensor or secured or hypothecary debtor, before any notary public, commissioner or other official, or the judge of any court, who is authorized by law to administer oaths or certify documents in that place and who also subscribes their signature and affixes to, or impresses on, the assignment or licence their official seal or the seal of the court of which they are a judge.

Execution of instruments

(2) Any assignment of copyright, or any licence granting an interest in a copyright, may be executed, subscribed or acknowledged by the assignor, licensor or mortgagor, in any other foreign country before any notary public, commissioner or other official or the judge of any court of the foreign country, who is authorized to administer oaths or perform notarial acts in that foreign country and whose authority shall be proved by the certificate of a diplomatic or consular officer of Canada performing their functions in that foreign country.

Seals to be evidence

(3) The official seal or seal of the court or the certificate of a diplomatic or consular officer is evidence of the execution of the instrument, and the instrument with the

Other testimony

(4) The provisions of subsections (1) and (2) shall be deemed to be permissive only, and the execution of any assignment of copyright, or any licence granting an interest in a copyright, may in any case be proved in accordance with the applicable rules of evidence.

R.S., 1985, c. C-42, s. 58; 1997, c. 24, s. 34; 2012, c. 20, s. 50.

Fees

Fees regulations

59 The Governor in Council may make regulations

(a) prescribing fees, or the manner of determining fees, to be paid for anything required or authorized to be done in the administration of this Act; and

(b) prescribing the time and manner in which the fees must be paid.

R.S., 1985, c. C-42, s. 59; 1993, c. 15, s. 8.

PART VI
Miscellaneous Provisions

Substituted Right

Subsistence of substituted right

60 (1) Where any person is immediately before January 1, 1924 entitled to any right in any work that is set out in column I of Schedule I, or to any interest in such a right, he is, as from that date, entitled to the substituted right set out in column II of that Schedule, or to the same interest in the substituted right, and to no other right or interest, and the substituted right shall subsist for the term for which it would have subsisted if this Act had been in force at the date when the work was made, and the work had been one entitled to copyright thereunder.

Where author has assigned the right

(2) Where the author of any work in which any right that is set out in column I of Schedule I subsists on January 1, 1924 has, before that date, assigned the right or granted any interest therein for the whole term of the right, then at the date when, but for the passing of this Act, the right would have expired, the substituted right conferred by this section shall, in the absence of express agreement, pass to the author of the work, and any interest therein created before January 1, 1924 and then subsisting shall determine, but the person who immediately before the date at which the right would have expired was the owner of the right or interest is entitled at his option either

(a) on giving such notice as is hereinafter mentioned, to an assignment of the right or the grant of a similar interest therein for the remainder of the term of the right for such consideration as, failing agreement, may be determined by arbitration, or

(b) without any assignment or grant, to continue to reproduce or perform the work in like manner as theretofore subject to the payment, if demanded by the author within three years after the date at which the right would have expired, of such royalties to the author as, failing agreement, may be determined by arbitration, or, where the work is incorporated in a collective work and the owner of the right or interest is the proprietor of that collective work, without any payment,

and the notice referred to in paragraph (a) must be given not more than one year or less than six months before the date at which the right would have expired, and must be sent by registered post to the author, or, if he cannot with reasonable diligence be found, advertised in the *Canada Gazette*.

Definition of *author*

(3) For the purposes of this section, ***author*** includes the legal representatives of a deceased author.

Works made before this Act in force

(4) Subject to this Act, copyright shall not subsist in any work made before January 1, 1924 otherwise than under and in accordance with the provisions of this section.

R.S., 1985, c. C-42, s. 60; R.S., 1985, c. 10 (4th Supp.), s. 17(F); 1997, c. 24, s. 52(F).

Clerical Errors

Clerical errors do not invalidate

61 Clerical errors in any instrument of record in the Copyright Office do not invalidate the instrument, but they may be corrected under the authority of the Registrar of Copyrights.

R.S., 1985, c. C-42, s. 61; 1992, c. 1, s. 52; 1993, c. 15, s. 10.

Regulations

Regulations

62 (1) The Governor in Council may make regulations

(a) for the purposes of paragraph 30.01(6)(d), respecting measures, which may vary according to circumstances specified in the regulations;

(b) for the purposes of paragraph 30.02(3)(d), respecting measures, which may vary according to circumstances specified in the regulations;

(c) prescribing the form of a notice of claimed infringement referred to in subsection 41.25(2) and prescribing information to be contained in it;

(d) prescribing anything that by this Act is to be prescribed by regulation; and

(e) generally for carrying out the purposes and provisions of this Act.

Rights saved

(2) The Governor in Council may make orders for altering, revoking or varying any order in council made under this Act, but any order made under this section does not affect prejudicially any rights or interests acquired or accrued at the date when the order comes into operation, and shall provide for the protection of those rights and interests.

R.S., 1985, c. C-42, s. 62; 1997, c. 24, s. 37; 2012, c. 20, s. 51.

Industrial Designs and Topographies

63 [Repealed, 1997, c. 24, s. 38]

Interpretation

64 (1) In this section and section 64.1,

article means any thing that is made by hand, tool or machine; (*objet*)

design means features of shape, configuration, pattern or ornament and any combination of those features that, in a finished article, appeal to and are judged solely by the eye; (*dessin*)

useful article means an article that has a utilitarian function and includes a model of any such article; (*objet utilitaire*)

utilitarian function, in respect of an article, means a function other than merely serving as a substrate or carrier for artistic or literary matter. (*fonction utilitaire*)

Non-infringement re certain designs

(2) Where copyright subsists in a design applied to a useful article or in an artistic work from which the design is derived and, by or under the authority of any person who owns the copyright in Canada or who owns the copyright elsewhere,

(a) the article is reproduced in a quantity of more than fifty, or

(b) where the article is a plate, engraving or cast, the article is used for producing more than fifty useful articles,

it shall not thereafter be an infringement of the copyright or the moral rights for anyone

(c) to reproduce the design of the article or a design not differing substantially from the design of the article by

(i) making the article, or

(ii) making a drawing or other reproduction in any material form of the article, or

(d) to do with an article, drawing or reproduction that is made as described in paragraph (c) anything that the owner of the copyright has the sole right to do with the design or artistic work in which the copyright subsists.

Exception

(3) Subsection (2) does not apply in respect of the copyright or the moral rights in an artistic work in so far as the work is used as or for

(a) a graphic or photographic representation that is applied to the face of an article;

(b) a trade-mark or a representation thereof or a label;

(c) material that has a woven or knitted pattern or that is suitable for piece goods or surface coverings or for making wearing apparel;

(d) an architectural work that is a building or a model of a building;

(e) a representation of a real or fictitious being, event or place that is applied to an article as a feature of shape, configuration, pattern or ornament;

objet utilitaire Objet remplissant une fonction utilitaire, y compris tout modèle ou toute maquette de celui-ci. (*useful article*)

Non-violation : cas de certains dessins

(2) Ne constitue pas une violation du droit d'auteur ou des droits moraux sur un dessin appliqué à un objet utilitaire, ou sur une œuvre artistique dont le dessin est tiré, ni le fait de reproduire ce dessin, ou un dessin qui n'en diffère pas sensiblement, en réalisant l'objet ou toute reproduction graphique ou matérielle de celui-ci, ni le fait d'accomplir avec un objet ainsi réalisé, ou sa reproduction, un acte réservé exclusivement au titulaire du droit, pourvu que l'objet, de par l'autorisation du titulaire — au Canada ou à l'étranger — remplisse l'une des conditions suivantes :

a) être reproduit à plus de cinquante exemplaires;

b) s'agissant d'une planche, d'une gravure ou d'un moule, servir à la production de plus de cinquante objets utilitaires.

Exception

(3) Le paragraphe (2) ne s'applique pas au droit d'auteur ou aux droits moraux sur une œuvre artistique dans la mesure où elle est utilisée à l'une ou l'autre des fins suivantes :

a) représentations graphiques ou photographiques appliquées sur un objet;

b) marques de commerce, ou leurs représentations, ou étiquettes;

c) matériel dont le motif est tissé ou tricoté ou utilisable à la pièce ou comme revêtement ou vêtement;

d) œuvres architecturales qui sont des bâtiments ou des modèles ou maquettes de bâtiments;

e) représentations d'êtres, de lieux ou de scènes réels ou imaginaires pour donner une configuration, un motif ou un élément décoratif à un objet;

(f) articles that are sold as a set, unless more than fifty sets are made; or

(g) such other work or article as may be prescribed by regulation.

Idem

(4) Subsections (2) and (3) apply only in respect of designs created after the coming into force of this subsection, and section 64 of this Act and the *Industrial Design Act*, as they read immediately before the coming into force of this subsection, as well as the rules made under them, continue to apply in respect of designs created before that coming into force.

R.S., 1985, c. C-42, s. 64; R.S., 1985, c. 10 (4th Supp.), s. 11; 1993, c. 44, s. 68; 1997, c. 24, s. 39.

Non-infringement re useful article features

64.1 (1) The following acts do not constitute an infringement of the copyright or moral rights in a work:

(a) applying to a useful article features that are dictated solely by a utilitarian function of the article;

(b) by reference solely to a useful article, making a drawing or other reproduction in any material form of any features of the article that are dictated solely by a utilitarian function of the article;

(c) doing with a useful article having only features described in paragraph (a), or with a drawing or reproduction made as described in paragraph (b), anything that the owner of the copyright has the sole right to do with the work; and

(d) using any method or principle of manufacture or construction.

Exception

(2) Nothing in subsection (1) affects

(a) the copyright, or

(b) the moral rights, if any,

in any sound recording, cinematograph film or other contrivance by means of which a work may be mechanically reproduced or performed.

R.S., 1985, c. 10 (4th Supp.), s. 11; 1997, c. 24, s. 40.

Application of Act to topographies

64.2 (1) This Act does not apply, and shall be deemed never to have applied, to any topography or to any design, however expressed, that is intended to generate all or part of a topography.

f) objets vendus par ensembles, pourvu qu'il n'y ait pas plus de cinquante ensembles;

g) autres œuvres ou objets désignés par règlement.

Idem

(4) Les paragraphes (2) et (3) ne s'appliquent qu'aux dessins créés après leur entrée en vigueur. L'article 64 de la présente loi et la *Loi sur les dessins industriels*, dans leur version antérieure à l'entrée en vigueur du présent article, et leurs règles d'application, continuent de s'appliquer aux dessins créés avant celle-ci.

L.R. (1985), ch. C-42, art. 64; L.R. (1985), ch. 10 (4ᵉ suppl.), art. 11; 1993, ch. 44, art. 68; 1997, ch. 24, art. 39.

Non-violation : caractéristiques d'objets utilitaires

64.1 (1) Ne constitue pas une violation du droit d'auteur ou des droits moraux sur une œuvre le fait :

a) de conférer à un objet utilitaire des caractéristiques de celui-ci résultant uniquement de sa fonction utilitaire;

b) de faire, à partir seulement d'un objet utilitaire, une reproduction graphique ou matérielle des caractéristiques de celui-ci qui résultent uniquement de sa fonction utilitaire;

c) d'accomplir, avec un objet visé à l'alinéa a) ou avec une reproduction visée à l'alinéa b), un acte réservé exclusivement au titulaire du droit;

d) d'utiliser tout principe ou toute méthode de réalisation de l'œuvre.

Exception

(2) Le paragraphe (1) ne vise pas le droit d'auteur ou, le cas échéant, les droits moraux sur tout enregistrement sonore, film cinématographique ou autre support, à l'aide desquels l'œuvre peut être reproduite, représentée ou exécutée mécaniquement.

L.R. (1985), ch. 10 (4ᵉ suppl.), art. 11; 1997, ch. 24, art. 40.

Application de la loi aux topographies

64.2 (1) La présente loi ne s'applique pas et est réputée ne s'être jamais appliquée aux topographies ou aux schémas, sous quelque forme qu'ils soient, destinés à produire tout ou partie d'une topographie.

Computer programs

(2) For greater certainty, the incorporation of a computer program into an integrated circuit product or the incorporation of a work into such a computer program may constitute an infringement of the copyright or moral rights in a work.

Definitions

(3) In this section, "topography" and "integrated circuit product" have the same meaning as in the *Integrated Circuit Topography Act*.

1990, c. 37, s. 33.

65 [Repealed, 1993, c. 44, s. 69]

PART VII

Copyright Board and Collective Administration of Copyright

Copyright Board

Establishment

66 (1) There is hereby established a Board, to be known as the Copyright Board, consisting of not more than five members, including a chairman and a vice-chairman, to be appointed by the Governor in Council.

Service

(2) The members of the Board shall be appointed to serve either full-time or part-time.

Chairman

(3) The chairman must be a judge, either sitting or retired, of a superior, county or district court.

Tenure

(4) Each member of the Board shall hold office during good behaviour for a term not exceeding five years, but may be removed at any time by the Governor in Council for cause.

Re-appointment

(5) A member of the Board is eligible to be re-appointed once only.

Prohibition

(6) A member of the Board shall not be employed in the public service within the meaning of the *Federal Public*

Sector Labour Relations Act during the member's term of office.

Members deemed public service employees

(7) A full-time member of the Board, other than the chairman, shall be deemed to be employed in

(a) the public service for the purposes of the *Public Service Superannuation Act*; and

(b) the federal public administration for the purposes of any regulations made pursuant to section 9 of the *Aeronautics Act*.

R.S., 1985, c. C-42, s. 66; R.S., 1985, c. 10 (1st Supp.), s. 1, c. 10 (4th Supp.), s. 12; 2003, c. 22, s. 154(E), 224(E), 225(E); 2017, c. 9, s. 55.

Duties of chairman

66.1 (1) The chairman shall direct the work of the Board and apportion its work among the members of the Board.

Absence or incapacity of chairman

(2) If the chairman is absent or incapacitated or if the office of chairman is vacant, the vice-chairman has all the powers and functions of the chairman during the absence, incapacity or vacancy.

Duties of vice-chairman

(3) The vice-chairman is the chief executive officer of the Board and has supervision over and direction of the Board and its staff.

R.S., 1985, c. 10 (4th Supp.), s. 12.

Remuneration and expenses

66.2 The members of the Board shall be paid such remuneration as may be fixed by the Governor in Council and are entitled to be paid reasonable travel and living expenses incurred by them in the course of their duties under this Act while absent from their ordinary place of residence.

R.S., 1985, c. 10 (4th Supp.), s. 12.

Conflict of interest prohibited

66.3 (1) A member of the Board shall not, directly or indirectly, engage in any activity, have any interest in a business or accept or engage in any office or employment that is inconsistent with the member's duties.

Termination of conflict of interest

(2) Where a member of the Board becomes aware that he is in a conflict of interest contrary to subsection (1), the member shall, within one hundred and twenty days, terminate the conflict or resign.

R.S., 1985, c. 10 (4th Supp.), s. 12.

Staff

66.4 (1) Such officers and employees as are necessary for the proper conduct of the work of the Board shall be appointed in accordance with the *Public Service Employment Act*.

Idem

(2) The officers and employees referred to in subsection (1) shall be deemed to be employed in the public service for the purposes of the *Public Service Superannuation Act*.

Technical assistance

(3) The Board may engage on a temporary basis the services of persons having technical or specialized knowledge to advise and assist in the performance of its duties and the Board may, in accordance with Treasury Board directives, fix and pay the remuneration and expenses of those persons.

R.S., 1985, c. 10 (4th Supp.), s. 12; 2003, c. 22, s. 225(E).

Concluding matters after membership expires

66.5 (1) A member of the Board whose term expires may conclude the matters that the member has begun to consider.

Decisions

(2) Matters before the Board shall be decided by a majority of the members of the Board and the presiding member shall have a second vote in the case of a tie.

R.S., 1985, c. 10 (4th Supp.), s. 12.

Interim decisions

66.51 The Board may, on application, make an interim decision.

R.S., 1985, c. 10 (4th Supp.), s. 12.

Variation of decisions

66.52 A decision of the Board respecting royalties or their related terms and conditions that is made under subsection 68(3), sections 68.1 or 70.15 or subsections 70.2(2), 70.6(1), 73(1) or 83(8) may, on application, be varied by the Board if, in its opinion, there has been a material change in circumstances since the decision was made.

R.S., 1985, c. 10 (4th Supp.), s. 12; 1988, c. 65, s. 64; 1997, c. 24, s. 42.

Regulations

66.6 (1) The Board may, with the approval of the Governor in Council, make regulations governing

(a) the practice and procedure in respect of the Board's hearings, including the number of members of the Board that constitutes a quorum;

(b) the time and manner in which applications and notices must be made or given;

(c) the establishment of forms for the making or giving of applications and notices; and

(d) the carrying out of the work of the Board, the management of its internal affairs and the duties of its officers and employees.

Publication of proposed regulations

(2) A copy of each regulation that the Board proposes to make under subsection (1) shall be published in the *Canada Gazette* at least sixty days before the proposed effective date thereof and a reasonable opportunity shall be given to interested persons to make representations with respect thereto.

Exception

(3) No proposed regulation that has been published pursuant to subsection (2) need again be published under that subsection, whether or not it has been altered as a result of representations made with respect thereto.

R.S., 1985, c. 10 (4th Supp.), s. 12.

General powers, etc.

66.7 (1) The Board has, with respect to the attendance, swearing and examination of witnesses, the production and inspection of documents, the enforcement of its decisions and other matters necessary or proper for the due exercise of its jurisdiction, all such powers, rights and privileges as are vested in a superior court of record.

Enforcement of decisions

(2) Any decision of the Board may, for the purposes of its enforcement, be made an order of the Federal Court or of any superior court and is enforceable in the same manner as an order thereof.

Procedure

(3) To make a decision of the Board an order of a court, the usual practice and procedure of the court in such matters may be followed or a certified copy of the decision may be filed with the registrar of the court and thereupon the decision becomes an order of the court.

Effect of variation of decision

(4) Where a decision of the Board that has been made an order of a court is varied by a subsequent decision of the Board, the order of the court shall be deemed to have

a) la pratique et la procédure des audiences, ainsi que le quorum;

b) les modalités, y compris les délais, d'établissement des demandes et les avis à donner;

c) l'établissement de formules pour les demandes et les avis;

d) de façon générale, l'exercice de ses activités, la gestion de ses affaires et les fonctions de son personnel.

Publication des projets de règlement

(2) Les projets de règlements d'application du paragraphe (1) sont publiés dans la *Gazette du Canada* au moins soixante jours avant la date prévue pour leur entrée en vigueur, les intéressés se voyant accorder la possibilité de présenter à la Commission leurs observations à cet égard.

Exception

(3) Ne sont pas visés les projets de règlement déjà publiés dans les conditions prévues au paragraphe (2), même s'ils ont été modifiés à la suite des observations.

L.R. (1985), ch. 10 (4ᵉ suppl.), art. 12.

Attributions générales

66.7 (1) La Commission a, pour la comparution, la prestation de serments, l'assignation et l'interrogatoire des témoins, ainsi que pour la production d'éléments de preuve, l'exécution de ses décisions et toutes autres questions relevant de sa compétence, les attributions d'une cour supérieure d'archives.

Assimilation

(2) Les décisions de la Commission peuvent, en vue de leur exécution, être assimilées à des actes de la Cour fédérale ou de toute cour supérieure; le cas échéant, leur exécution s'effectue selon les mêmes modalités.

Procédure

(3) L'assimilation se fait selon la pratique et la procédure suivies par le tribunal saisi ou par la production au greffe du tribunal d'une copie certifiée conforme de la décision. La décision devient dès lors un acte du tribunal.

Décisions modificatives

(4) Les décisions qui modifient les décisions déjà assimilées à des actes d'un tribunal sont réputées modifier

been varied accordingly and the subsequent decision may, in the same manner, be made an order of the court.

R.S., 1985, c. 10 (4th Supp.), s. 12; 2002, c. 8, s. 131(F).

Distribution, publication of notices

66.71 Independently of any other provision of this Act relating to the distribution or publication of information or documents by the Board, the Board may at any time cause to be distributed or published, in any manner and on any terms and conditions that it sees fit, any notice that it sees fit to be distributed or published.

1997, c. 24, s. 43.

Studies

66.8 The Board shall conduct such studies with respect to the exercise of its powers as are requested by the Minister.

R.S., 1985, c. 10 (4th Supp.), s. 12.

Report

66.9 (1) The Board shall, not later than August 31 in each year, submit to the Governor in Council through the Minister an annual report on the Board's activities for the preceding year describing briefly the applications made to the Board, the Board's decisions and any other matter that the Board considers relevant.

Tabling

(2) The Minister shall cause a copy of each annual report to be laid before each House of Parliament on any of the first fifteen days on which that House is sitting after the Minister receives the report.

R.S., 1985, c. 10 (4th Supp.), s. 12.

Regulations

66.91 The Governor in Council may make regulations issuing policy directions to the Board and establishing general criteria to be applied by the Board or to which the Board must have regard

(a) in establishing fair and equitable royalties to be paid pursuant to this Act; and

(b) in rendering its decisions in any matter within its jurisdiction.

1997, c. 24, s. 44.

Publication d'avis

66.71 La Commission peut en tout temps ordonner l'envoi ou la publication de tout avis qu'elle estime nécessaire, indépendamment de toute autre disposition de la présente loi relative à l'envoi ou à la publication de renseignements ou de documents, ou y procéder elle-même, et ce de la manière et aux conditions qu'elle estime indiquées.

1997, ch. 24, art. 43.

Études

66.8 À la demande du ministre, la Commission effectue toute étude touchant ses attributions.

L.R. (1985), ch. 10 (4ᵉ suppl.), art. 12.

Rapport

66.9 (1) Au plus tard le 31 août, la Commission présente au gouverneur en conseil, par l'intermédiaire du ministre, un rapport annuel de ses activités résumant les demandes qui lui ont été présentées et les conclusions auxquelles elle est arrivée et toute autre question qu'elle estime pertinente.

Dépôt

(2) Le ministre fait déposer le rapport devant chaque chambre du Parlement dans les quinze premiers jours de séance de celle-ci suivant sa réception.

L.R. (1985), ch. 10 (4ᵉ suppl.), art. 12.

Règlements

66.91 Le gouverneur en conseil peut, par règlement, donner des instructions sur des questions d'orientation à la Commission et établir les critères de nature générale à suivre par celle-ci, ou à prendre en compte par celle-ci, dans les domaines suivants :

a) la fixation des redevances justes et équitables à verser aux termes de la présente loi;

b) le prononcé des décisions de la Commission dans les cas qui relèvent de la compétence de celle-ci.

1997, ch. 24, art. 44.

Collective Administration of Performing Rights and of Communication Rights

Public access to repertoires

67 Each collective society that carries on

(a) the business of granting licences or collecting royalties for the performance in public of musical works, dramatico-musical works, performer's performances of such works, or sound recordings embodying such works, or

(b) the business of granting licences or collecting royalties for the communication to the public by telecommunication of musical works, dramatico-musical works, performer's performances of such works, or sound recordings embodying such works, other than the communication of musical works or dramatico-musical works in a manner described in subsection 31(2),

must answer within a reasonable time all reasonable requests from the public for information about its repertoire of works, performer's performances or sound recordings, that are in current use.

R.S., 1985, c. C-42, s. 67; R.S., 1985, c. 10 (1st Supp.), s. 1, c. 10 (4th Supp.), s. 12; 1993, c. 23, s. 3; 1997, c. 24, s. 45.

Filing of proposed tariffs

67.1 (1) Each collective society referred to in section 67 shall, on or before the March 31 immediately before the date when its last tariff approved pursuant to subsection 68(3) expires, file with the Board a proposed tariff, in both official languages, of all royalties to be collected by the collective society.

Where no previous tariff

(2) A collective society referred to in subsection (1) in respect of which no tariff has been approved pursuant to subsection 68(3) shall file with the Board its proposed tariff, in both official languages, of all royalties to be collected by it, on or before the March 31 immediately before its proposed effective date.

Effective period of tariffs

(3) A proposed tariff must provide that the royalties are to be effective for periods of one or more calendar years.

Prohibition of enforcement

(4) If a proposed tariff is not filed with respect to the work, performer's performance or sound recording in question, no action may be commenced, without the written consent of the Minister, for

(a) the infringement of the rights, referred to in section 3, to perform a work in public or to communicate it to the public by telecommunication;

(b) the infringement of the rights referred to in paragraph 15(1.1)(d) or 18(1.1)(a); or

(c) the recovery of royalties referred to in section 19.

Publication of proposed tariffs

(5) As soon as practicable after the receipt of a proposed tariff filed pursuant to subsection (1), the Board shall publish it in the *Canada Gazette* and shall give notice that, within sixty days after the publication of the tariff, prospective users or their representatives may file written objections to the tariff with the Board.

R.S., 1985, c. 10 (4th Supp.), s. 12; 1997, c. 24, s. 45; 2001, c. 34, s. 35(E); 2012, c. 20, s. 52.

67.2 and 67.3 [Repealed, 1997, c. 24, s. 45]

Board to consider proposed tariffs and objections

68 (1) The Board shall, as soon as practicable, consider a proposed tariff and any objections thereto referred to in subsection 67.1(5) or raised by the Board, and

(a) send to the collective society concerned a copy of the objections so as to permit it to reply; and

(b) send to the persons who filed the objections a copy of any reply thereto.

Criteria and factors

(2) In examining a proposed tariff for the performance in public or the communication to the public by telecommunication of performer's performances of musical works, or of sound recordings embodying such performer's performances, the Board

(a) shall ensure that

(i) the tariff applies in respect of performer's performances and sound recordings only in the situations referred to in the provisions of section 20 other than subsections 20(3) and (4),

(ii) the tariff does not, because of linguistic and content requirements of Canada's broadcasting policy set out in section 3 of the *Broadcasting Act*, place some users that are subject to that Act at a greater financial disadvantage than others, and

(iii) the payment of royalties by users pursuant to section 19 will be made in a single payment; and

(b) may take into account any factor that it considers appropriate.

Certification

(3) The Board shall certify the tariffs as approved, with such alterations to the royalties and to the terms and conditions related thereto as the Board considers necessary, having regard to

(a) any objections to the tariffs under subsection 67.1(5); and

(b) the matters referred to in subsection (2).

Publication of approved tariffs

(4) The Board shall

(a) publish the approved tariffs in the *Canada Gazette* as soon as practicable; and

(b) send a copy of each approved tariff, together with the reasons for the Board's decision, to each collective society that filed a proposed tariff and to any person who filed an objection.

R.S., 1985, c. C-42, s. 68; R.S., 1985, c. 10 (4th Supp.), s. 13; 1993, c. 23, s. 5; 1997, c. 24, s. 45; 2012, c. 20, s. 53.

Special and transitional royalty rates

68.1 (1) Notwithstanding the tariffs approved by the Board under subsection 68(3) for the performance in public or the communication to the public by telecommunication of performer's performances of musical works, or of sound recordings embodying such performer's performances,

(a) wireless transmission systems, except community systems and public transmission systems, shall pay royalties as follows:

(i) in respect of each year, $100 on the first 1.25 million dollars of annual advertising revenues, and

(ii) on any portion of annual advertising revenues exceeding 1.25 million dollars,

(A) for the first year following the coming into force of this section, thirty-three and one third per cent of the royalties set out in the approved tariff for that year,

(B) for the second year following the coming into force of this section, sixty-six and two thirds per cent of the royalties set out in the approved tariff for that year, and

(C) for the third year following the coming into force of this section, one hundred per cent of the royalties set out in the approved tariff for that year;

(b) community systems shall pay royalties of $100 in respect of each year; and

(c) public transmission systems shall pay royalties, in respect of each of the first three years following the coming into force of this section, as follows:

(i) for the first year following the coming into force of this section, thirty-three and one third per cent of the royalties set out in the approved tariff for that year,

(ii) for the second year following the coming into force of this section, sixty-six and two thirds per cent of the royalties set out in the approved tariff for that year, and

(iii) for the third year following the coming into force of this section, one hundred per cent of the royalties set out in the approved tariff for that year.

Effect of paying royalties

(2) The payment of the royalties set out in subsection (1) fully discharges all liabilities of the system in question in respect of the approved tariffs.

Definition of *advertising revenues*

(3) The Board may, by regulation, define ***advertising revenues*** for the purposes of subsection (1).

Preferential royalty rates

(4) The Board shall, in certifying a tariff as approved under subsection 68(3), ensure that there is a preferential royalty rate for small cable transmission systems.

Regulations

(5) The Governor in Council may make regulations defining "small cable transmission system", "community system", "public transmission system" and "wireless transmission system" for the purposes of this section.

1997, c. 24, s. 45.

Effect of fixing royalties

68.2 (1) Without prejudice to any other remedies available to it, a collective society may, for the period specified in its approved tariff, collect the royalties specified in the tariff and, in default of their payment, recover them in a court of competent jurisdiction.

Proceedings barred if royalties tendered or paid

(2) No proceedings may be brought against a person who has paid or offered to pay the royalties specified in an approved tariff for

(a) the infringement of the right to perform in public or the right to communicate to the public by telecommunication, referred to in section 3;

(b) the infringement of the rights referred to in paragraph 15(1.1)(d) or 18(1.1)(a); or

(c) the recovery of royalties referred to in section 19.

Continuation of rights

(3) Where a collective society files a proposed tariff in accordance with subsection 67.1(1),

(a) any person entitled to perform in public or communicate to the public by telecommunication those works, performer's performances or sound recordings pursuant to the previous tariff may do so, even though the royalties set out therein have ceased to be in effect, and

(b) the collective society may collect the royalties in accordance with the previous tariff,

until the proposed tariff is approved.

1997, c. 24, s. 45; 2012, c. 20, s. 54.

Public Performances in Places Other Than Theatres

69 (1) [Repealed, R.S., 1985, c. 10 (4th Supp.), s. 14]

Radio performances in places other than theatres

(2) In respect of public performances by means of any radio receiving set in any place other than a theatre that is ordinarily and regularly used for entertainments to which an admission charge is made, no royalties shall be collectable from the owner or user of the radio receiving set, but the Board shall, in so far as possible, provide for the collection in advance from radio broadcasting stations of royalties appropriate to the conditions produced by the provisions of this subsection and shall fix the amount of the same.

Expenses to be taken into account

(3) In fixing royalties pursuant to subsection (2), the Board shall take into account all expenses of collection and other outlays, if any, saved or savable by, for or on behalf of the owner of the copyright or performing right concerned or his agents, in consequence of subsection (2).

(4) [Repealed, R.S., 1985, c. 10 (4th Supp.), s. 14]

R.S., 1985, c. C-42, s. 69; R.S., 1985, c. 10 (4th Supp.), s. 14; 1993, c. 44, s. 73; 1997, c. 24, s. 52(F).

70 [Repealed, R.S., 1985, c. 10 (4th Supp.), s. 15]

Collective Administration in Relation to Rights under Sections 3, 15, 18 and 21

Collective Societies

Collective societies

70.1 Sections 70.11 to 70.6 apply in respect of a collective society that operates

(a) a licensing scheme, applicable in relation to a repertoire of works of more than one author, pursuant to which the society sets out the classes of uses for which and the royalties and terms and conditions on which it agrees to authorize the doing of an act mentioned in section 3 in respect of those works;

(a.1) a licensing scheme, applicable in relation to a repertoire of performer's performances of more than one performer, pursuant to which the society sets out the classes of uses for which and the royalties and terms and conditions on which it agrees to authorize the doing of an act mentioned in section 15 in respect of those performer's performances;

(b) a licensing scheme, applicable in relation to a repertoire of sound recordings of more than one maker, pursuant to which the society sets out the classes of uses for which and the royalties and terms and conditions on which it agrees to authorize the doing of an act mentioned in section 18 in respect of those sound recordings; or

(c) a licensing scheme, applicable in relation to a repertoire of communication signals of more than one broadcaster, pursuant to which the society sets out the classes of uses for which and the royalties and terms and conditions on which it agrees to authorize the doing of an act mentioned in section 21 in respect of those communication signals.

R.S., 1985, c. 10 (4th Supp.), s. 16; 1997, c. 24, s. 46.

Public information

70.11 A collective society referred to in section 70.1 must answer within a reasonable time all reasonable requests from the public for information about its repertoire of works, performer's performances, sound recordings or communication signals.

1997, c. 24, s. 46.

Tariff or agreement

70.12 A collective society may, for the purpose of setting out by licence the royalties and terms and conditions relating to classes of uses,

(a) file a proposed tariff with the Board; or

(b) enter into agreements with users.

1997, c. 24, s. 46.

Tariffs

Filing of proposed tariffs

70.13 (1) Each collective society referred to in section 70.1 may, on or before the March 31 immediately before the date when its last tariff approved pursuant to subsection 70.15(1) expires, file with the Board a proposed tariff, in both official languages, of royalties to be collected by the collective society for issuing licences.

Where no previous tariff

(2) A collective society referred to in subsection (1) in respect of which no tariff has been approved pursuant to subsection 70.15(1) shall file with the Board its proposed tariff, in both official languages, of all royalties to be collected by it for issuing licences, on or before the March 31 immediately before its proposed effective date.

1997, c. 24, s. 46.

Application of certain provisions

70.14 Where a proposed tariff is filed under section 70.13, subsections 67.1(3) and (5) and subsection 68(1) apply, with such modifications as the circumstances require.

1997, c. 24, s. 46.

Certification

70.15 (1) The Board shall certify the tariffs as approved, with such alterations to the royalties and to the terms and conditions related thereto as the Board considers necessary, having regard to any objections to the tariffs.

Projets de tarif ou ententes

70.12 Les sociétés de gestion peuvent, en vue d'établir par licence les redevances à verser et les modalités à respecter relativement aux catégories d'utilisation :

a) soit déposer auprès de la Commission un projet de tarif;

b) soit conclure des ententes avec les utilisateurs.

1997, ch. 24, art. 46.

Projets de tarif

Dépôt d'un projet de tarif

70.13 (1) Les sociétés de gestion peuvent déposer auprès de la Commission, au plus tard le 31 mars précédant la cessation d'effet d'un tarif homologué au titre du paragraphe 70.15(1), un projet de tarif, dans les deux langues officielles, des redevances à percevoir pour l'octroi de licences.

Sociétés non régies par un tarif homologué

(2) Lorsque les sociétés de gestion ne sont pas régies par un tarif homologué au titre du paragraphe 70.15(1), le dépôt du projet de tarif auprès de la Commission doit s'effectuer au plus tard le 31 mars précédant la date prévue pour sa prise d'effet.

1997, ch. 24, art. 46.

Application de certaines dispositions

70.14 Dans le cas du dépôt, conformément à l'article 70.13, d'un projet de tarif, les paragraphes 67.1(3) et (5) et 68(1) s'appliquent avec les adaptations nécessaires.

1997, ch. 24, art. 46.

Homologation

70.15 (1) La Commission homologue les projets de tarifs après avoir apporté aux redevances et aux modalités afférentes les modifications qu'elle estime nécessaires compte tenu, le cas échéant, des oppositions.

Application of certain provisions

(2) Where a tariff is approved under subsection (1), subsections 68(4) and 68.2(1) apply, with such modifications as the circumstances require.

1997, c. 24, s. 46.

Distribution, publication of notices

70.16 Independently of any other provision of this Act relating to the distribution or publication of information or documents by the Board, the Board shall notify persons affected by a proposed tariff, by

(a) distributing or publishing a notice, or

(b) directing another person or body to distribute or publish a notice,

in such manner and on such terms and conditions as the Board sees fit.

1997, c. 24, s. 46.

Prohibition of enforcement

70.17 Subject to section 70.19, no proceedings may be brought for the infringement of a right referred to in section 3, 15, 18 or 21 against a person who has paid or offered to pay the royalties specified in an approved tariff.

1997, c. 24, s. 46.

Continuation of rights

70.18 Subject to section 70.19, where a collective society files a proposed tariff in accordance with section 70.13,

(a) any person authorized by the collective society to do an act referred to in section 3, 15, 18 or 21, as the case may be, pursuant to the previous tariff may do so, even though the royalties set out therein have ceased to be in effect, and

(b) the collective society may collect the royalties in accordance with the previous tariff,

until the proposed tariff is approved.

1997, c. 24, s. 46.

Where agreement exists

70.19 If there is an agreement mentioned in paragraph 70.12(b), sections 70.17 and 70.18 do not apply in respect of the matters covered by the agreement.

1997, c. 24, s. 46.

Agreement

70.191 An approved tariff does not apply where there is an agreement between a collective society and a person authorized to do an act mentioned in section 3, 15, 18 or

Application de certaines dispositions

(2) Dans le cas d'un tarif homologué, les paragraphes 68(4) et 68.2(1) s'appliquent avec les adaptations nécessaires.

1997, ch. 24, art. 46.

Publication d'avis

70.16 La Commission doit ordonner l'envoi ou la publication d'un avis à l'intention des personnes visées par le projet de tarif, indépendamment de toute autre disposition de la présente loi relative à l'envoi ou à la publication de renseignements ou de documents, ou y procéder elle-même, et ce de la manière et aux conditions qu'elle estime indiquées.

1997, ch. 24, art. 46.

Interdiction des recours

70.17 Sous réserve de l'article 70.19, il ne peut être intenté aucun recours pour violation d'un droit prévu aux articles 3, 15, 18 ou 21 contre quiconque a payé ou offert de payer les redevances figurant au tarif homologué.

1997, ch. 24, art. 46.

Maintien des droits

70.18 Sous réserve de l'article 70.19 et malgré la cessation d'effet du tarif, toute personne autorisée par la société de gestion à accomplir tel des actes visés aux articles 3, 15, 18 ou 21, selon le cas, a le droit, dès lors qu'un projet de tarif est déposé conformément à l'article 70.13, d'accomplir cet acte et ce jusqu'à l'homologation d'un nouveau tarif. Par ailleurs, la société de gestion intéressée peut percevoir les redevances prévues par le tarif antérieur jusqu'à cette homologation.

1997, ch. 24, art. 46.

Non-application des articles 70.17 et 70.18

70.19 Les articles 70.17 et 70.18 ne s'appliquent pas aux questions réglées par toute entente visée à l'alinéa 70.12b).

1997, ch. 24, art. 46.

Entente

70.191 Le tarif homologué ne s'applique pas en cas de conclusion d'une entente entre une société de gestion et une personne autorisée à accomplir tel des actes visés aux articles 3, 15, 18 ou 21, selon le cas, si cette entente

21, as the case may be, if the agreement is in effect during the period covered by the approved tariff.

1997, c. 24, s. 46.

Fixing of Royalties in Individual Cases

Application to fix amount of royalty, etc.

70.2 (1) Where a collective society and any person not otherwise authorized to do an act mentioned in section 3, 15, 18 or 21, as the case may be, in respect of the works, sound recordings or communication signals included in the collective society's repertoire are unable to agree on the royalties to be paid for the right to do the act or on their related terms and conditions, either of them or a representative of either may, after giving notice to the other, apply to the Board to fix the royalties and their related terms and conditions.

Fixing royalties, etc.

(2) The Board may fix the royalties and their related terms and conditions in respect of a licence during such period of not less than one year as the Board may specify and, as soon as practicable after rendering its decision, the Board shall send a copy thereof, together with the reasons therefor, to the collective society and the person concerned or that person's representative.

R.S., 1985, c. 10 (4th Supp.), s. 16; 1997, c. 24, s. 46.

Agreement

70.3 (1) The Board shall not proceed with an application under section 70.2 where a notice is filed with the Board that an agreement touching the matters in issue has been reached.

Idem

(2) An agreement referred to in subsection (1) is effective during the year following the expiration of the previous agreement, if any, or of the last period specified under subsection 70.2(2).

R.S., 1985, c. 10 (4th Supp.), s. 16.

Effect of Board decision

70.4 Where any royalties are fixed for a period pursuant to subsection 70.2(2), the person concerned may, during the period, subject to the related terms and conditions fixed by the Board and to the terms and conditions set out in the scheme and on paying or offering to pay the royalties, do the act with respect to which the royalties and their related terms and conditions are fixed and the collective society may, without prejudice to any other remedies available to it, collect the royalties or, in default

est exécutoire pendant la période d'application du tarif homologué.

1997, ch. 24, art. 46.

Fixation des redevances dans des cas particuliers

Demande de fixation de redevances

70.2 (1) À défaut d'une entente sur les redevances, ou les modalités afférentes, relatives à une licence autorisant l'intéressé à accomplir tel des actes mentionnés aux articles 3, 15, 18 ou 21, selon le cas, la société de gestion ou l'intéressé, ou leurs représentants, peuvent, après en avoir avisé l'autre partie, demander à la Commission de fixer ces redevances ou modalités.

Modalités de la fixation

(2) La Commission peut, selon les modalités, mais pour une période minimale d'un an, qu'elle arrête, fixer les redevances et les modalités afférentes relatives à la licence. Dès que possible après la fixation, elle en communique un double, accompagné des motifs de sa décision, à la société de gestion et à l'intéressé, ou au représentant de celui-ci.

L.R. (1985), ch. 10 (4ᵉ suppl.), art. 16; 1997, ch. 24, art. 46.

Entente préjudicielle

70.3 (1) Le dépôt auprès de la Commission d'un avis faisant état d'une entente conclue avant la fixation opère dessaisissement.

Durée de l'entente

(2) L'entente visée au paragraphe (1) vaut, sauf stipulation d'une durée plus longue, pour un an à compter de la date d'expiration de l'entente précédente ou de la période visée au paragraphe 70.2(2).

L.R. (1985), ch. 10 (4ᵉ suppl.), art. 16.

Portée de la fixation

70.4 L'intéressé peut, pour la période arrêtée par la Commission, accomplir les actes à l'égard desquels des redevances ont été fixées, moyennant paiement ou offre de paiement de ces redevances et conformément aux modalités afférentes fixées par la Commission et à celles établies par la société de gestion au titre de son système d'octroi de licences. La société de gestion peut, pour la même période, percevoir les redevances ainsi fixées et,

of their payment, recover them in a court of competent jurisdiction.

R.S., 1985, c. 10 (4th Supp.), s. 16; 1997, c. 24, s. 47.

Examination of Agreements

Definition of *Commissioner*

70.5 (1) For the purposes of this section and section 70.6, ***Commissioner*** means the Commissioner of Competition appointed under the *Competition Act*.

Filing agreement with the Board

(2) Where a collective society concludes an agreement to grant a licence authorizing a person to do an act mentioned in section 3, 15, 18 or 21, as the case may be, the collective society or the person may file a copy of the agreement with the Board within fifteen days after it is concluded.

Idem

(3) Section 45 of the *Competition Act* does not apply in respect of any royalties or related terms and conditions arising under an agreement filed in accordance with subsection (2).

Access by Commissioner

(4) The Commissioner may have access to the copy of an agreement filed in accordance with subsection (2).

Request for examination

(5) Where the Commissioner considers that an agreement filed in accordance with subsection (2) is contrary to the public interest, the Commissioner may, after advising the parties concerned, request the Board to examine the agreement.

R.S., 1985, c. 10 (4th Supp.), s. 16; 1997, c. 24, s. 48; 1999, c. 2, ss. 45, 46.

Examination and fixing of royalty

70.6 (1) The Board shall, as soon as practicable, consider a request by the Commissioner to examine an agreement and the Board may, after giving the Commissioner and the parties concerned an opportunity to present their arguments, alter the royalties and any related terms and conditions arising under the agreement, in which case section 70.4 applies with such modifications as the circumstances require.

Idem

(2) As soon as practicable after rendering its decision, the Board shall send a copy thereof, together with the reasons therefor, to the parties concerned and to the Commissioner.

R.S., 1985, c. 10 (4th Supp.), s. 16; 1997, c. 24, s. 49(F); 1999, c. 2, s. 46.

70.61 to 70.8 [Repealed, 1997, c. 24, s. 50]

Royalties in Particular Cases

Filing of proposed tariffs

71 (1) Each collective society that carries on the business of collecting royalties referred to in subsection 29.7(2) or (3) or paragraph 31(2)(d) shall file with the Board a proposed tariff, but no other person may file such a tariff.

Times for filing

(2) A proposed tariff must be

    (a) in both official languages; and

    (b) filed on or before the March 31 immediately before the date that the approved tariff ceases to be effective.

Where no previous tariff

(3) A collective society in respect of which no proposed tariff has been certified pursuant to paragraph 73(1)(d) shall file its proposed tariff on or before the March 31 immediately before its proposed effective date.

Effective period of tariffs

(4) A proposed tariff must provide that the royalties are to be effective for periods of one or more calendar years.

R.S., 1985, c. C-42, s. 71; 1997, c. 24, s. 50; 2012, c. 20, s. 55.

Publication of proposed tariffs

72 (1) As soon as practicable after the receipt of a proposed tariff filed pursuant to section 71, the Board shall publish it in the *Canada Gazette* and shall give notice that, within sixty days after the publication of the tariff, educational institutions or prospective retransmitters within the meaning of subsection 31(1), or their representatives, may file written objections to the tariff with the Board.

Board to consider proposed tariffs and objections

(2) The Board shall, as soon as practicable, consider a proposed tariff and any objections thereto referred to in subsection (1) or raised by the Board, and

    (a) send to the collective society concerned a copy of the objections so as to permit it to reply; and

    (b) send to the persons who filed the objections a copy of any reply thereto.

1997, c. 24, s. 50; 1999, c. 31, s. 61; 2002, c. 26, s. 3.

Certification

73 (1) On the conclusion of its consideration of proposed tariffs, the Board shall

(a) establish

(i) a manner of determining the royalties to be paid by educational institutions and by retransmitters within the meaning of subsection 31(1), and

(ii) such terms and conditions related to those royalties as the Board considers appropriate;

(b) determine the portion of the royalties referred to in paragraph (a) that is to be paid to each collective society;

(c) vary the tariffs accordingly; and

(d) certify the tariffs as the approved tariffs, whereupon the tariffs become for the purposes of this Act the approved tariffs.

No discrimination

(2) For greater certainty, the Board, in establishing a manner of determining royalties under paragraph (1)(a) or in apportioning them under paragraph (1)(b), may not discriminate between owners of copyright on the ground of their nationality or residence.

Publication of approved tariffs

(3) The Board shall publish the approved tariffs in the *Canada Gazette* as soon as practicable and send a copy of each approved tariff, together with the reasons for the Board's decision, to each collective society that filed a proposed tariff and to any person who filed an objection.

1997, c. 24, s. 50; 1999, c. 31, s. 62; 2002, c. 26, s. 4.

Special case

74 (1) The Board shall, in establishing a manner of determining royalties under paragraph 73(1)(a), ensure that there is a preferential rate for small retransmission systems.

Regulations

(2) The Governor in Council may make regulations defining "small retransmission systems" for the purpose of subsection (1).

1997, c. 24, s. 50.

Effect of fixing royalties

75 Without prejudice to any other remedies available to it, a collective society may, for the period specified in its approved tariff, collect the royalties specified in the tariff and, in default of their payment, recover them in a court of competent jurisdiction.

1997, c. 24, s. 50.

Claims by non-members

76 (1) An owner of copyright who does not authorize a collective society to collect, for that person's benefit, royalties referred to in paragraph 31(2)(d) is, if the work is communicated to the public by telecommunication during a period when an approved tariff that is applicable to that kind of work is effective, entitled to be paid those royalties by the collective society that is designated by the Board, of its own motion or on application, subject to the same conditions as those to which a person who has so authorized that collective society is subject.

Royalties that may be recovered

(2) An owner of copyright who does not authorize a collective society to collect, for that person's benefit, royalties referred to in subsection 29.7(2) or (3) is, if such royalties are payable during a period when an approved tariff that is applicable to that kind of work or other subject-matter is effective, entitled to be paid those royalties by the collective society that is designated by the Board, of its own motion or on application, subject to the same conditions as those to which a person who has so authorized that collective society is subject.

Exclusion of remedies

(3) The entitlement referred to in subsections (1) and (2) is the only remedy of the owner of the copyright for the payment of royalties for the communication, making of the copy or sound recording or performance in public, as the case may be.

Regulations

(4) The Board may, for the purposes of this section,

(a) require a collective society to file with the Board information relating to payments of royalties collected by it to the persons who have authorized it to collect those royalties; and

(b) by regulation, establish periods of not less than twelve months within which the entitlements referred to in subsections (1) and (2) must be exercised, in the case of royalties referred to in

(i) and (ii) [Repealed, 2012, c. 20, s. 56]

Portée de la fixation

75 La société de gestion peut, pour la période mentionnée au tarif homologué, percevoir les redevances qui y figurent et, indépendamment de tout autre recours, le cas échéant, en poursuivre le recouvrement en justice.

1997, ch. 24, art. 50.

Réclamations des non-membres dans les cas de retransmission

76 (1) Tout titulaire d'un droit d'auteur qui n'a pas habilité une société de gestion à agir à son profit peut, si son œuvre a été communiquée dans le cadre du paragraphe 31(2) alors qu'un tarif homologué s'appliquait en l'occurrence à ce type d'œuvres, réclamer auprès de la société de gestion désignée, d'office ou sur demande, par la Commission le paiement de ces redevances aux mêmes conditions qu'une personne qui a habilité la société de gestion à cette fin.

Réclamation des non-membres dans les autres cas

(2) Tout titulaire d'un droit d'auteur qui n'a habilité aucune société de gestion à agir à son profit pour la perception des redevances visées aux paragraphes 29.7(2) et (3) peut, si ces redevances sont exigibles lorsqu'un tarif homologué s'applique en l'occurrence à ce type d'œuvres ou d'objets du droit d'auteur, réclamer auprès de la société de gestion désignée, d'office ou sur demande, par la Commission le paiement de ces redevances aux mêmes conditions qu'une personne qui a habilité la société de gestion à cette fin.

Exclusion des autres recours

(3) Les recours visés aux paragraphes (1) et (2) sont les seuls dont dispose le titulaire pour obtenir le paiement des redevances relatives à la communication, à la reproduction, à la production de l'enregistrement sonore ou à l'exécution en public, selon le cas.

Mesures d'application

(4) Pour l'application du présent article, la Commission peut :

a) exiger des sociétés de gestion le dépôt de tout renseignement relatif aux versements des redevances aux personnes qui les ont habilitées à cette fin;

b) fixer par règlement les délais de déchéance pour les réclamations, qui ne sauraient être de moins de douze mois à compter :

(i) et (ii) [Abrogés, 2012, ch. 20, art. 56]

(iii) subsection 29.7(2), beginning on the making of the copy,

(iv) subsection 29.7(3), beginning on the performance in public, or

(v) paragraph 31(2)(d), beginning on the communication to the public by telecommunication.

1997, c. 24, s. 50; 2012, c. 20, s. 56.

Owners Who Cannot be Located

Circumstances in which licence may be issued by Board

77 (1) Where, on application to the Board by a person who wishes to obtain a licence to use

(a) a published work,

(b) a fixation of a performer's performance,

(c) a published sound recording, or

(d) a fixation of a communication signal

in which copyright subsists, the Board is satisfied that the applicant has made reasonable efforts to locate the owner of the copyright and that the owner cannot be located, the Board may issue to the applicant a licence to do an act mentioned in section 3, 15, 18 or 21, as the case may be.

Conditions of licence

(2) A licence issued under subsection (1) is non-exclusive and is subject to such terms and conditions as the Board may establish.

Payment to owner

(3) The owner of a copyright may, not later than five years after the expiration of a licence issued pursuant to subsection (1) in respect of the copyright, collect the royalties fixed in the licence or, in default of their payment, commence an action to recover them in a court of competent jurisdiction.

Regulations

(4) The Copyright Board may make regulations governing the issuance of licences under subsection (1).

1997, c. 24, s. 50.

Compensation for Acts Done Before Recognition of Copyright or Moral Rights

Board may determine compensation

78 (1) Subject to subsection (2), for the purposes of subsections 32.4(2), 32.5(2), 33(2), 33.1(2) and 33.2(2), the Board may, on application by any of the parties referred to in one of those provisions, determine the amount of the compensation referred to in that provision that the Board considers reasonable, having regard to all the circumstances, including any judgment of a court in an action between the parties for the enforcement of a right mentioned in subsection 32.4(3) or 32.5(3).

Limitation

(2) The Board shall not

(a) proceed with an application under subsection (1) where a notice is filed with the Board that an agreement regarding the matters in issue has been reached; or

(b) where a court action between the parties for enforcement of a right referred to in subsection 32.4(3) or 32.5(3), as the case may be, has been commenced, continue with an application under subsection (1) until the court action is finally concluded.

Interim orders

(3) Where the Board proceeds with an application under subsection (1), it may, for the purpose of avoiding serious prejudice to any party, make an interim order requiring a party to refrain from doing any act described in the order until the determination of compensation is made under subsection (1).

1997, c. 24, s. 50; 2012, c. 20, s. 57.

PART VIII

Private Copying

Interpretation

Definitions

79 In this Part,

audio recording medium means a recording medium, regardless of its material form, onto which a sound recording may be reproduced and that is of a kind ordinarily used by individual consumers for that purpose, excluding any prescribed kind of recording medium; (*support audio*)

blank audio recording medium means

(a) an audio recording medium onto which no sounds have ever been fixed, and

(b) any other prescribed audio recording medium; (*support audio vierge*)

collecting body means the collective society, or other society, association or corporation, that is designated as the collecting body under subsection 83(8); (*organisme de perception*)

eligible author means an author of a musical work, whether created before or after the coming into force of this Part, that is embodied in a sound recording, whether made before or after the coming into force of this Part, if copyright subsists in Canada in that musical work; (*auteur admissible*)

eligible maker means a maker of a sound recording that embodies a musical work, whether the first fixation of the sound recording occurred before or after the coming into force of this Part, if

(a) both the following two conditions are met:

(i) the maker, at the date of that first fixation, if a corporation, had its headquarters in Canada or, if a natural person, was a Canadian citizen or permanent resident within the meaning of subsection 2(1) of the *Immigration and Refugee Protection Act*, and

(ii) copyright subsists in Canada in the sound recording, or

(b) the maker, at the date of that first fixation, if a corporation, had its headquarters in a country referred to in a statement published under section 85 or, if a natural person, was a citizen, subject or permanent resident of such a country; (*producteur admissible*)

eligible performer means the performer of a performer's performance of a musical work, whether it took place before or after the coming into force of this Part, if the performer's performance is embodied in a sound recording and

(a) both the following two conditions are met:

(i) the performer was, at the date of the first fixation of the sound recording, a Canadian citizen or permanent resident within the meaning of

a) soit est protégée par le droit d'auteur au Canada et a été fixée pour la première fois au moyen d'un enregistrement sonore alors que l'artiste-interprète était un citoyen canadien ou un résident permanent au sens du paragraphe 2(1) de la *Loi sur l'immigration et la protection des réfugiés*;

b) soit a été fixée pour la première fois au moyen d'un enregistrement sonore alors que l'artiste-interprète était sujet, citoyen ou résident permanent d'un pays visé par la déclaration publiée en vertu de l'article 85. (*eligible performer*)

auteur admissible Auteur d'une œuvre musicale fixée au moyen d'un enregistrement sonore et protégée par le droit d'auteur au Canada, que l'œuvre ou l'enregistrement sonore ait été respectivement créée ou confectionné avant ou après l'entrée en vigueur de la présente partie. (*eligible author*)

organisme de perception Société de gestion ou autre société, association ou personne morale désignée aux termes du paragraphe 83(8). (*collecting body*)

producteur admissible Le producteur de l'enregistrement sonore d'une œuvre musicale, que la première fixation ait eu lieu avant ou après l'entrée en vigueur de la présente partie :

a) soit si l'enregistrement sonore est protégé par le droit d'auteur au Canada et qu'à la date de la première fixation, le producteur était un citoyen canadien ou un résident permanent au sens du paragraphe 2(1) de la *Loi sur l'immigration et la protection des réfugiés* ou, s'il s'agit d'une personne morale, avait son siège social au Canada;

b) soit si le producteur était, à la date de la première fixation, sujet, citoyen ou résident permanent d'un pays visé dans la déclaration publiée en vertu de l'article 85 ou, s'il s'agit d'une personne morale, avait son siège social dans un tel pays. (*eligible maker*)

support audio Tout support audio habituellement utilisé par les consommateurs pour reproduire des enregistrements sonores, à l'exception toutefois de ceux exclus par règlement. (*audio recording medium*)

support audio vierge Tout support audio sur lequel aucun son n'a encore été fixé et tout autre support audio précisé par règlement. (*blank audio recording medium*)

1997, ch. 24, art. 50; 2001, ch. 27, art. 240.

subsection 2(1) of the *Immigration and Refugee Protection Act*, and

(ii) copyright subsists in Canada in the performer's performance, or

(b) the performer was, at the date of the first fixation of the sound recording, a citizen, subject or permanent resident of a country referred to in a statement published under section 85; (*artiste-interprète admissible*)

prescribed means prescribed by regulations made under this Part. (*Version anglaise seulement*)

1997, c. 24, s. 50; 2001, c. 27, s. 240.

Copying for Private Use

Where no infringement of copyright

80 (1) Subject to subsection (2), the act of reproducing all or any substantial part of

(a) a musical work embodied in a sound recording,

(b) a performer's performance of a musical work embodied in a sound recording, or

(c) a sound recording in which a musical work, or a performer's performance of a musical work, is embodied

onto an audio recording medium for the private use of the person who makes the copy does not constitute an infringement of the copyright in the musical work, the performer's performance or the sound recording.

Limitation

(2) Subsection (1) does not apply if the act described in that subsection is done for the purpose of doing any of the following in relation to any of the things referred to in paragraphs (1)(a) to (c):

(a) selling or renting out, or by way of trade exposing or offering for sale or rental;

(b) distributing, whether or not for the purpose of trade;

(c) communicating to the public by telecommunication; or

(d) performing, or causing to be performed, in public.

1997, c. 24, s. 50.

Copie pour usage privé

Non-violation du droit d'auteur

80 (1) Sous réserve du paragraphe (2), ne constitue pas une violation du droit d'auteur protégeant tant l'enregistrement sonore que l'œuvre musicale ou la prestation d'une œuvre musicale qui le constituent, le fait de reproduire pour usage privé l'intégralité ou toute partie importante de cet enregistrement sonore, de cette œuvre ou de cette prestation sur un support audio.

Limite

(2) Le paragraphe (1) ne s'applique pas à la reproduction de l'intégralité ou de toute partie importante d'un enregistrement sonore, ou de l'œuvre musicale ou de la prestation d'une œuvre musicale qui le constituent, sur un support audio pour les usages suivants :

a) vente ou location, ou exposition commerciale;

b) distribution dans un but commercial ou non;

c) communication au public par télécommunication;

d) exécution ou représentation en public.

1997, ch. 24, art. 50.

Right of Remuneration

Right of remuneration

81 (1) Subject to and in accordance with this Part, eligible authors, eligible performers and eligible makers have a right to receive remuneration from manufacturers and importers of blank audio recording media in respect of the reproduction for private use of

(a) a musical work embodied in a sound recording;

(b) a performer's performance of a musical work embodied in a sound recording; or

(c) a sound recording in which a musical work, or a performer's performance of a musical work, is embodied.

Assignment of rights

(2) Subsections 13(4) to (7) apply, with such modifications as the circumstances require, in respect of the rights conferred by subsection (1) on eligible authors, performers and makers.

1997, c. 24, s. 50.

Levy on Blank Audio Recording Media

Liability to pay levy

82 (1) Every person who, for the purpose of trade, manufactures a blank audio recording medium in Canada or imports a blank audio recording medium into Canada

(a) is liable, subject to subsection (2) and section 86, to pay a levy to the collecting body on selling or otherwise disposing of those blank audio recording media in Canada; and

(b) shall, in accordance with subsection 83(8), keep statements of account of the activities referred to in paragraph (a), as well as of exports of those blank audio recording media, and shall furnish those statements to the collecting body.

No levy for exports

(2) No levy is payable where it is a term of the sale or other disposition of the blank audio recording medium that the medium is to be exported from Canada, and it is exported from Canada.

1997, c. 24, s. 50.

Filing of proposed tariffs

83 (1) Subject to subsection (14), each collective society may file with the Board a proposed tariff for the benefit of those eligible authors, eligible performers and eligible makers who, by assignment, grant of licence, appointment of the society as their agent or otherwise, authorize it to act on their behalf for that purpose, but no person other than a collective society may file any such tariff.

Collecting body

(2) Without limiting the generality of what may be included in a proposed tariff, the tariff may include a suggestion as to whom the Board should designate under paragraph (8)(d) as the collecting body.

Times for filing

(3) Proposed tariffs must be in both official languages and must be filed on or before the March 31 immediately before the date when the approved tariffs cease to be effective.

Where no previous tariff

(4) A collective society in respect of which no proposed tariff has been certified pursuant to paragraph (8)(c) shall file its proposed tariff on or before the March 31 immediately before its proposed effective date.

Effective period of levies

(5) A proposed tariff must provide that the levies are to be effective for periods of one or more calendar years.

Publication of proposed tariffs

(6) As soon as practicable after the receipt of a proposed tariff filed pursuant to subsection (1), the Board shall publish it in the *Canada Gazette* and shall give notice that, within sixty days after the publication of the tariff, any person may file written objections to the tariff with the Board.

Board to consider proposed tariffs and objections

(7) The Board shall, as soon as practicable, consider a proposed tariff and any objections thereto referred to in subsection (6) or raised by the Board, and

    (a) send to the collective society concerned a copy of the objections so as to permit it to reply; and

    (b) send to the persons who filed the objections a copy of any reply thereto.

Duties of Board

(8) On the conclusion of its consideration of the proposed tariff, the Board shall

    (a) establish, in accordance with subsection (9),

        (i) the manner of determining the levies, and

cette fin par voie de cession, licence, mandat ou autrement peuvent déposer auprès de la Commission un projet de tarif des redevances à percevoir.

Organisme de perception

(2) Le projet de tarif peut notamment proposer un organisme de perception en vue de la désignation prévue à l'alinéa (8)d).

Délai de dépôt

(3) Il est à déposer, dans les deux langues officielles, au plus tard le 31 mars précédant la cessation d'effet du tarif homologué.

Société non régie par un tarif homologué

(4) Lorsqu'elle n'est pas régie par un tarif homologué au titre de l'alinéa (8)c), la société de gestion doit déposer son projet de tarif auprès de la Commission au plus tard le 31 mars précédant la date prévue pour sa prise d'effet.

Durée de validité

(5) Le projet de tarif prévoit des périodes d'effet d'une ou de plusieurs années civiles.

Publication

(6) Dès que possible, la Commission le fait publier dans la *Gazette du Canada* et donne un avis indiquant que quiconque peut y faire opposition en déposant auprès d'elle une déclaration en ce sens dans les soixante jours suivant la publication.

Examen du projet de tarif

(7) Elle procède dans les meilleurs délais à l'examen du projet de tarif et, le cas échéant, des oppositions; elle peut également faire opposition au projet. Elle communique à la société de gestion en cause copie des oppositions et aux opposants les réponses éventuelles de celle-ci.

Mesures à prendre

(8) Au terme de son examen, la Commission :

    a) établit conformément au paragraphe (9) :

        (i) la formule tarifaire qui permet de déterminer les redevances,

(ii) such terms and conditions related to those levies as the Board considers appropriate, including, without limiting the generality of the foregoing, the form, content and frequency of the statements of account mentioned in subsection 82(1), measures for the protection of confidential information contained in those statements, and the times at which the levies are payable,

(b) vary the tariff accordingly,

(c) certify the tariff as the approved tariff, whereupon that tariff becomes for the purposes of this Part the approved tariff, and

(d) designate as the collecting body the collective society or other society, association or corporation that, in the Board's opinion, will best fulfil the objects of sections 82, 84 and 86,

but the Board is not obligated to exercise its power under paragraph (d) if it has previously done so, and a designation under that paragraph remains in effect until the Board makes another designation, which it may do at any time whatsoever, on application.

Factors Board to consider

(9) In exercising its power under paragraph (8)(a), the Board shall satisfy itself that the levies are fair and equitable, having regard to any prescribed criteria.

Publication of approved tariffs

(10) The Board shall publish the approved tariffs in the *Canada Gazette* as soon as practicable and shall send a copy of each approved tariff, together with the reasons for the Board's decision, to the collecting body, to each collective society that filed a proposed tariff, and to any person who filed an objection.

Authors, etc., not represented by collective society

(11) An eligible author, eligible performer or eligible maker who does not authorize a collective society to file a proposed tariff under subsection (1) is entitled, in relation to

(a) a musical work,

(b) a performer's performance of a musical work, or

(c) a sound recording in which a musical work, or a performer's performance of a musical work, is embodied,

as the case may be, to be paid by the collective society that is designated by the Board, of the Board's own motion or on application, the remuneration referred to in

(ii) à son appréciation, les modalités afférentes à celles-ci, notamment en ce qui concerne leurs dates de versement, la forme, la teneur et la fréquence des états de compte visés au paragraphe 82(1) et les mesures de protection des renseignements confidentiels qui y figurent;

b) modifie le projet de tarif en conséquence;

c) le certifie, celui-ci devenant dès lors le tarif homologué pour la société de gestion en cause;

d) désigne, à titre d'organisme de perception, la société de gestion ou autre société, association ou personne morale la mieux en mesure, à son avis, de s'acquitter des responsabilités ou fonctions découlant des articles 82, 84 et 86.

La Commission n'est pas tenue de faire une désignation en vertu de l'alinéa d) si une telle désignation a déjà été faite. Celle-ci demeure en vigueur jusqu'à ce que la Commission procède à une nouvelle désignation, ce qu'elle peut faire sur demande en tout temps.

Critères particuliers

(9) Pour l'exercice de l'attribution prévue à l'alinéa (8)a), la Commission doit s'assurer que les redevances sont justes et équitables compte tenu, le cas échéant, des critères réglementaires.

Publication

(10) Elle publie dès que possible dans la *Gazette du Canada* les tarifs homologués; elle en envoie copie, accompagnée des motifs de sa décision, à l'organisme de perception, à chaque société de gestion ayant déposé un projet de tarif et à toutes les personnes ayant déposé une opposition.

Auteurs, artistes-interprètes non représentés

(11) Les auteurs, artistes-interprètes et producteurs admissibles qui ne sont pas représentés par une société de gestion peuvent, aux mêmes conditions que ceux qui le sont, réclamer la rémunération visée à l'article 81 auprès de la société de gestion désignée par la Commission, d'office ou sur demande, si pendant la période où une telle rémunération est payable, un tarif homologué s'applique à leur type d'œuvre musicale, de prestation d'une œuvre musicale ou d'enregistrement sonore constitué d'une œuvre musicale ou d'une prestation d'une œuvre musicale, selon le cas.

section 81 if such remuneration is payable during a period when an approved tariff that is applicable to that kind of work, performer's performance or sound recording is effective, subject to the same conditions as those to which a person who has so authorized that collective society is subject.

Exclusion of other remedies

(12) The entitlement referred to in subsection (11) is the only remedy of the eligible author, eligible performer or eligible maker referred to in that subsection in respect of the reproducing of sound recordings for private use.

Powers of Board

(13) The Board may, for the purposes of subsections (11) and (12),

(a) require a collective society to file with the Board information relating to payments of moneys received by the society pursuant to section 84 to the persons who have authorized it to file a tariff under subsection (1); and

(b) by regulation, establish the periods, which shall not be less than twelve months, beginning when the applicable approved tariff ceases to be effective, within which the entitlement referred to in subsection (11) must be exercised.

Single proposed tariff

(14) Where all the collective societies that intend to file a proposed tariff authorize a particular person or body to file a single proposed tariff on their behalf, that person or body may do so, and in that case this section applies, with such modifications as the circumstances require, in respect of that proposed tariff.

1997, c. 24, s. 50.

Distribution of Levies Paid

Distribution by collecting body

84 As soon as practicable after receiving the levies paid to it, the collecting body shall distribute the levies to the collective societies representing eligible authors, eligible performers and eligible makers, in the proportions fixed by the Board.

1997, c. 24, s. 50.

Reciprocity

85 (1) Where the Minister is of the opinion that another country grants or has undertaken to grant to performers and makers of sound recordings that are Canadian citizens or permanent residents within the meaning of subsection 2(1) of the *Immigration and Refugee Protection*

Act or, if corporations, have their headquarters in Canada, as the case may be, whether by treaty, convention, agreement or law, benefits substantially equivalent to those conferred by this Part, the Minister may, by a statement published in the *Canada Gazette*,

(a) grant the benefits conferred by this Part to performers or makers of sound recordings that are citizens, subjects or permanent residents of or, if corporations, have their headquarters in that country; and

(b) declare that that country shall, as regards those benefits, be treated as if it were a country to which this Part extends.

Reciprocity

(2) Where the Minister is of the opinion that another country neither grants nor has undertaken to grant to performers or makers of sound recordings that are Canadian citizens or permanent residents within the meaning of subsection 2(1) of the *Immigration and Refugee Protection Act* or, if corporations, have their headquarters in Canada, as the case may be, whether by treaty, convention, agreement or law, benefits substantially equivalent to those conferred by this Part, the Minister may, by a statement published in the *Canada Gazette*,

(a) grant the benefits conferred by this Part to performers or makers of sound recordings that are citizens, subjects or permanent residents of or, if corporations, have their headquarters in that country, as the case may be, to the extent that that country grants those benefits to performers or makers of sound recordings that are Canadian citizens or permanent residents within the meaning of subsection 2(1) of the *Immigration and Refugee Protection Act* or, if corporations, have their headquarters in Canada; and

(b) declare that that country shall, as regards those benefits, be treated as if it were a country to which this Part extends.

Application of Act

(3) Any provision of this Act that the Minister specifies in a statement referred to in subsection (1) or (2)

(a) applies in respect of performers or makers of sound recordings covered by that statement, as if they were citizens of or, if corporations, had their headquarters in Canada; and

(b) applies in respect of a country covered by that statement, as if that country were Canada.

Application of Act

(4) Subject to any exceptions that the Minister may specify in a statement referred to in subsection (1) or (2), the other provisions of this Act also apply in the way described in subsection (3).

1997, c. 24, s. 50; 2001, c. 27, s. 241.

Exemption from Levy

Where no levy payable

86 (1) No levy is payable under this Part where the manufacturer or importer of a blank audio recording medium sells or otherwise disposes of it to a society, association or corporation that represents persons with a perceptual disability.

Refunds

(2) Where a society, association or corporation referred to in subsection (1)

(a) purchases a blank audio recording medium in Canada from a person other than the manufacturer or importer, and

(b) provides the collecting body with proof of that purchase, on or before June 30 in the calendar year following the calendar year in which the purchase was made,

the collecting body is liable to pay forthwith to the society, association or corporation an amount equal to the amount of the levy paid in respect of the blank audio recording medium purchased.

If registration system exists

(3) If regulations made under paragraph 87(a) provide for the registration of societies, associations or corporations that represent persons with a perceptual disability, subsections (1) and (2) shall be read as referring to societies, associations or corporations that are so registered.

1997, c. 24, s. 50.

Regulations

Regulations

87 The Governor in Council may make regulations

(a) respecting the exemptions and refunds provided for in section 86, including, without limiting the generality of the foregoing,

(i) regulations respecting procedures governing those exemptions and refunds,

(ii) regulations respecting applications for those exemptions and refunds, and

(iii) regulations for the registration of societies, associations or corporations that represent persons with a perceptual disability;

(b) prescribing anything that by this Part is to be prescribed; and

(c) generally for carrying out the purposes and provisions of this Part.

1997, c. 24, s. 50.

Civil Remedies

Right of recovery

88 (1) Without prejudice to any other remedies available to it, the collecting body may, for the period specified in an approved tariff, collect the levies due to it under the tariff and, in default of their payment, recover them in a court of competent jurisdiction.

Failure to pay royalties

(2) The court may order a person who fails to pay any levy due under this Part to pay an amount not exceeding five times the amount of the levy to the collecting body. The collecting body must distribute the payment in the manner set out in section 84.

Order directing compliance

(3) Where any obligation imposed by this Part is not complied with, the collecting body may, in addition to any other remedy available, apply to a court of competent jurisdiction for an order directing compliance with that obligation.

Factors to consider

(4) Before making an order under subsection (2), the court must take into account

(a) whether the person who failed to pay the levy acted in good faith or bad faith;

(b) the conduct of the parties before and during the proceedings; and

(c) the need to deter persons from failing to pay levies.

1997, c. 24, s. 50.

PART IX

General Provisions

No copyright, etc., except by statute

89 No person is entitled to copyright otherwise than under and in accordance with this Act or any other Act of Parliament, but nothing in this section shall be construed as abrogating any right or jurisdiction in respect of a breach of trust or confidence.

1997, c. 24, s. 50.

Interpretation

90 No provision of this Act relating to

(a) copyright in performer's performances, sound recordings or communication signals, or

(b) the right of performers or makers to remuneration

shall be construed as prejudicing any rights conferred by Part I or, in and of itself, as prejudicing the amount of royalties that the Board may fix in respect of those rights.

1997, c. 24, s. 50.

Adherence to Berne and Rome Conventions

91 The Governor in Council shall take such measures as are necessary to secure the adherence of Canada to

(a) the Convention for the Protection of Literary and Artistic Works concluded at Berne on September 9, 1886, as revised by the Paris Act of 1971; and

(b) the International Convention for the Protection of Performers, Producers of Phonograms and Broadcasting Organisations, done at Rome on October 26, 1961.

1997, c. 24, s. 50.

Review of Act

92 Five years after the day on which this section comes into force and at the end of each subsequent period of five years, a committee of the Senate, of the House of Commons or of both Houses of Parliament is to be designated or established for the purpose of reviewing this Act.

1997, c. 24, s. 50; 2012, c. 20, s. 58.

SCHEDULE I

(Section 60)

Existing Rights

Column I Existing Right	Column II Substituted Right
Works other than Dramatic and Musical Works	
Copyright	Copyright as defined by this Act[1].
Musical and Dramatic Works	
Both copyright and performing right	Copyright as defined by this Act.
Copyright, but not performing right	Copyright as defined by this Act, except the sole right to perform the work or any substantial part thereof in public.
Performing right, but not copyright	The sole right to perform the work in public, but none of the other rights comprised in copyright as defined by this Act.

[1] In the case of an essay, article or portion forming part of and first published in a review, magazine or other periodical or work of a like nature, the right shall be subject to any right of publishing the essay, article or portion in a separate form to which the author is entitled on January 1, 1924 or would if this Act had not been passed have become entitled under section 18 of *An Act to amend the Law of Copyright*, being chapter 45 of the Statutes of the United Kingdom, 1842.

For the purposes of this Schedule the following expressions, where used in column I thereof, have the following meanings:

Copyright in the case of a work that according to the law in force immediately before January 1, 1924 has not been published before that date and statutory copyright wherein depends on publication, includes the right at common law, if any, to restrain publication or other dealing with the work;

Performing right, in the case of a work that has not been performed in public before January 1, 1924, includes the right at common law, if any, to restrain the performance thereof in public.

R.S., c. C-30, Sch. I; 1976-77, c. 28, s. 10.

ANNEXE I

(article 60)

Droits existants

Colonne I Droit actuel	Colonne II Droit substitué
Œuvres autres que les œuvres dramatiques et musicales	
Droit d'auteur	Droit d'auteur tel qu'il est défini par la présente loi[1].
Œuvres dramatiques et musicales	
Droit de reproduction aussi bien que droit d'exécution et de représentation	Droit d'auteur tel qu'il est défini par la présente loi.
Droit de reproduction, sans le droit d'exécution ou de représentation	Droit d'auteur tel qu'il est défini par la présente loi, à l'exception du seul droit d'exécuter ou de représenter en public l'œuvre ou une de ses parties importantes.
Droit d'exécution ou de représentation, mais sans le droit de reproduction	Le seul droit d'exécuter ou de représenter l'œuvre en public, à l'exception de toute autre faculté comprise dans le droit d'auteur, tel qu'il est défini par la présente loi.

[1] Lorsqu'il s'agit d'un essai, d'un article ou d'une contribution, insérés et publiés pour la première fois dans une revue, un magazine ou un autre périodique ou ouvrage de même nature, le droit d'auteur est assujetti à celui de publier séparément l'essai, l'article ou la contribution, auquel l'auteur est admis le 1er janvier 1924, ou l'aurait été en vertu de l'article 18 de la loi intitulée *An Act to amend the Law of Copyright*, chapitre 45 des Statuts du Royaume-Uni de 1842, n'eût été l'adoption de la présente loi.

Pour l'application de la présente annexe, les expressions ci-après, employées dans la colonne I, ont la signification suivante :

L'expression **droit d'auteur** ou **droit de reproduction**, lorsqu'il s'agit d'une œuvre qui, selon la loi en vigueur immédiatement avant le 1er janvier 1924, n'a pas été publiée avant cette date, et à l'égard de laquelle le droit d'auteur prévu par une loi dépend de la publication, comprend la faculté d'après la *common law*, si elle existe sur ce point, d'empêcher la publication de l'œuvre ou toute autre action à son égard.

L'expression **droit d'exécution ou de représentation**, lorsqu'il s'agit d'une œuvre qui n'a pas encore été exécutée ou représentée en public avant le 1er janvier 1924, comprend la faculté d'après la *common law*, si elle existe sur ce point, d'empêcher l'exécution ou la représentation publique de l'œuvre.

S.R., ch. C-30, ann. I; 1976-77, ch. 28, art. 10.

SCHEDULE II
[Repealed, 1993, c. 44, s. 74]

ANNEXE II
[Abrogée, 1993, ch. 44, art. 74]

SCHEDULE III
[Repealed, 1997, c. 24, s. 51]

ANNEXE III
[Abrogée, 1997, ch. 24, art. 51]

RELATED PROVISIONS

— R.S., 1985, c. 10 (4th Supp.), ss. 23 to 27

Application re moral rights

23 (1) The rights referred to in section 14.1 of the *Copyright Act*, as enacted by section 4, subsist in respect of a work even if the work was created before the coming into force of section 4.

Restriction

(2) A remedy referred to in subsection 34(1.1) of the *Copyright Act*, as enacted by section 8, may only be obtained where the infringement of the moral rights of the author occurs after the coming into force of section 8.

Idem

(3) Notwithstanding subsection (1) and the repeal by section 3 of subsection 14(4) of the *Copyright Act*, the rights referred to in section 14.1 of that Act, as enacted by section 4, are not enforceable against

(a) a person who, on the coming into force of this section, is the owner of the copyright in, or holds a licence in relation to, a work, or

(b) a person authorized by a person described in paragraph (a) to do an act mentioned in section 3 of that Act,

in respect of any thing done during the period for which the person described in paragraph (a) is the owner or for which the licence is in force, and the rights referred to in subsection 14(4) of that Act continue to be enforceable against a person described in paragraph (a) or (b) during that period as if subsection 14(4) of that Act were not repealed.

— R.S., 1985, c. 10 (4th Supp.), ss. 23 to 27

Application re computer programs

24 Subsection 1(2), the definition *computer program* in subsection 1(3) and section 5 apply in respect of a computer program that was made prior to the day on which those provisions come into force but where, by virtue only of subsections 1(2) and (3) and this section, copyright subsists in a computer program that was made prior to May 27, 1987, nothing done in respect of the computer program before May 27, 1987 shall be construed to constitute an infringement of the copyright.

— R.S., 1985, c. 10 (4th Supp.), ss. 23 to 27

Making of records, perforated rolls, etc.

25 It shall be deemed not to be an infringement of copyright in any musical, literary or dramatic work for any person to make within Canada during the six months following the coming into force of section 7 records, perforated rolls or other contrivances by means of which sounds may be reproduced and by means of which the work may be mechanically performed, if the person proves

(a) that before the coming into force of section 7, the person made such contrivances in respect of that work in accordance with section 29 or 30 of the *Copyright Act* and any regulation made under section 33 of that Act, as they read immediately before the coming into force of section 7; and

(b) that the making would, had it occurred before the coming into force of section 7, have been deemed not to have been an infringement of copyright by section 29 or 30 of the *Copyright Act*, as it read immediately before the coming into force of section 7.

— R.S., 1985, c. 10 (4th Supp.), ss. 23 to 27

Infringements before coming into force

26 Subsection 64(1) and section 64.1 of the *Copyright Act*, as enacted by section 11, apply in respect of any alleged infringement of copyright occurring prior to, on or after the day on which section 11 comes into force.

— R.S., 1985, c. 10 (4th Supp.), ss. 23 to 27

Continuation in office

27 Notwithstanding any other provision of this Act, the members of the Copyright Appeal Board appointed pursuant to section 68 of the *Copyright Act*, as it read immediately before the coming into force of section 13, continue in office and may continue to perform their duties and exercise their powers to the extent necessary to consider and deal with any matter before it pursuant to section 69 of that Act before the coming into force of section 14.

— 1988, c. 65, s. 149

First certified statements of royalties

149 For greater certainty, the royalties in the first statements certified under paragraph 70.63(1)(d) of the *Copyright Act* become effective on January 1, 1990 regardless of when the statements are so certified.

— 1993, c. 23, ss. 6, 7

Transitional: Statements of royalties

6 (1) Notwithstanding section 67 of the *Copyright Act*, a statement filed with the Copyright Board pursuant to subsection 67(2) or (3) of that Act on or before September 1, 1992

dramatique le fait de confectionner, au Canada, dans les six mois suivant l'entrée en vigueur de l'article 7 de la présente loi, des empreintes, rouleaux perforés ou autres dispositifs au moyen desquels des sons peuvent être reproduits et l'œuvre, soit exécutée, soit représentée mécaniquement, lorsque celui qui les confectionne prouve :

a) qu'il en avait déjà fabriqué en conformité avec les dispositions des articles 29 ou 30 de la *Loi sur le droit d'auteur*, abrogés par l'entrée en vigueur de l'article 7 de la présente loi, et des règlements d'application de l'article 33;

b) qu'il s'est conformé, en ce qui a trait aux dispositifs fabriqués dans les six mois suivant l'entrée en vigueur de l'article 7 de la présente loi, aux articles 29 ou 30 de la *Loi sur le droit d'auteur*, dans leur version antérieure à l'entrée en vigueur de cet article 7.

— L.R. (1985), ch. 10 (4e suppl.), art. 23 à 27

Violations antérieures

26 Le paragraphe 64(1) et l'article 64.1 de la *Loi sur le droit d'auteur*, édictés par l'article 11, s'appliquent à toute prétendue violation du droit d'auteur, même quand elle survient avant l'entrée en vigueur de cet article.

— L.R. (1985), ch. 10 (4e suppl.), art. 23 à 27

Maintien en poste

27 Indépendamment des autres dispositions de la présente loi, les membres de la Commission d'appel du droit d'auteur, nommés en application de la version de l'article 68 de la *Loi sur le droit d'auteur* antérieure à l'entrée en vigueur de l'article 13 de la présente loi, sont maintenus en poste et peuvent continuer d'exercer leurs attributions dans la mesure uniquement où il leur faut donner suite aux examens, et aux mesures en découlant, commencés en application de l'article 69 de la même loi avant l'entrée en vigueur de l'article 14 de la présente loi.

— 1988, ch. 65, art. 149

Disposition transitoire

149 Il demeure entendu que, peu importe la date à laquelle la Commission certifie pour la première fois un tarif au titre de l'alinéa 70.63(1)d) de la *Loi sur le droit d'auteur*, la prise d'effet de celui-ci est le 1er janvier 1990.

— 1993, ch. 23, art. 6 et 7

Projets de tarif

6 (1) Malgré l'article 67 de la *Loi sur le droit d'auteur*, un projet de tarif déposé en vertu des paragraphes 67(2) ou (3) de cette loi à la Commission du droit d'auteur au plus tard le 1er septembre 1992 peut prévoir ou, avec

(a) may provide, or

(b) may be amended with leave of the Board, if application therefor is made to the Board within twenty-eight days after the coming into force of this Act, to provide

for the payment of royalties, for the period beginning on the coming into force of this Act and ending at the end of 1993, in respect of the communication of dramatico-musical or musical works to the public by telecommunication, and a statement so filed or amended is effective for that period to the extent that the Board certifies it as approved pursuant to subsection 67.2(1) of the *Copyright Act*.

No duplication of royalties

(2) Where a statement referred to in subsection (1) is certified as approved, the Board shall not certify as approved any other statement filed by the same applicant, to the extent that it provides for royalties in respect of the same act and for the same period as set out in the statement previously certified as approved.

— 1993, c. 23, ss. 6, 7

Where this Act does not apply

7 This Act does not apply in respect of statements filed with the Board pursuant to subsection 67(2) or (3) of the *Copyright Act* on or before September 1, 1991 that relate to any year before 1993.

— 1993, c. 44, ss. 60(2), (3)

Application of amendments to s. 10

(2) Subject to subsection 75(2) of this Act, section 10 of the *Copyright Act*, as enacted by subsection (1) of this section, applies to all photographs, whether made before or after the coming into force of this section.

— 1993, c. 44, ss. 60(2), (3)

Application of amendments to s. 11

(3) Except as provided by section 75 of this Act,

(a) section 11 of the *Copyright Act*, as enacted by subsection (1) of this section, applies only in respect of contrivances made after the coming into force of this section; and

(b) section 11 of the *Copyright Act*, as it read immediately before the coming into force of this section, continues to apply in respect of contrivances made before the coming into force of this section.

l'agrément de la Commission, être modifié, sur demande présentée dans les vingt-huit jours suivant l'entrée en vigueur de la présente loi, de façon à prévoir, à compter de la date d'entrée en vigueur de la présente loi jusqu'au 31 décembre 1993, les droits à percevoir pour la communication au public par télécommunication d'œuvres musicales ou dramatico-musicales. Une fois le projet certifié par la Commission, en vertu du paragraphe 67.2(1) de la *Loi sur le droit d'auteur*, le tarif est homologué.

Chevauchement des droits

(2) Lorsque le projet de tarif visé au paragraphe (1) est homologué, la Commission ne peut homologuer un autre projet dans la mesure où celui-ci prévoit des droits pour l'activité et la période visées par le tarif déjà homologué à l'égard de la même association, société ou personne morale.

— 1993, ch. 23, art. 6 et 7

Exclusion

7 La présente loi ne s'applique pas aux projets de tarif déposés en vertu des paragraphes 67(2) ou (3) de la *Loi sur le droit d'auteur* à la Commission au plus tard le 1er septembre 1991 et visant toute année antérieure à 1993.

— 1993, ch. 44, par. 60(2) et (3)

Application de l'article 10

(2) Sous réserve du paragraphe 75(2) de la présente loi, l'article 10 de la *Loi sur le droit d'auteur*, dans sa version édictée par le paragraphe (1), s'applique à toutes les photographies, qu'elles aient été créées avant ou après l'entrée en vigueur du présent article.

— 1993, ch. 44, par. 60(2) et (3)

Application de l'article 11

(3) Sous réserve de l'article 75 de la présente loi, l'article 11 de la *Loi sur le droit d'auteur*, dans sa version édictée par le paragraphe (1), ne s'applique qu'aux organes fabriqués après l'entrée en vigueur du présent article, et l'article 11 de cette loi, en son état à l'entrée en vigueur du présent article, s'applique aux organes fabriqués avant l'entrée en vigueur du présent article.

— 1993, c. 44, ss. 75 to 77

Application of certain amendments

75 (1) Subject to subsection (2), amendments to the *Copyright Act* made by this Act relating to the term of copyright apply in respect of all works, whether made before or after the coming into force of this section.

Idem

(2) Where the term of the copyright in a work expires before the coming into force of this section, nothing in this Act shall be construed as extending or reviving that term.

— 1993, c. 44, ss. 75 to 77

Cinematographs

76 (1) Except as provided by subsection (2) of this section, the *Copyright Act*, as amended by this Act, applies in respect of all cinematographs, whether made before or after the coming into force of this section, subject to subsection 75(2) of this Act.

Idem

(2) Section 10 of the *Copyright Act*, as that section read immediately before the coming into force of this section and in so far as it governs who is the author of a photograph, continues to apply in respect of all cinematographs made before the coming into force of this section that were, before the coming into force of this section, protected as photographs.

— 1993, c. 44, ss. 75 to 77

Application of section 5

77 Nothing in section 5 of the *Copyright Act*, as amended by this Act, confers copyright on works made before the coming into force of this section that did not qualify for copyright under section 5 of the *Copyright Act* as it read immediately before the coming into force of this section.

— 1997, c. 24, s. 18(2)

(2) Section 30 of the Act, as enacted by subsection (1) of this section, does not apply in respect of collections referred to in section 30 that are published before the coming into force of section 30. Such collections continue to be governed by paragraph 27(2)(d) of the Act as it read before the coming into force of section 15 of this Act.

— 1997, c. 24, ss. 20(3), (4)

(3) Section 38.1 of the *Copyright Act*, as enacted by subsection (1) of this section, only applies

(a) to proceedings commenced after the date of the coming into force of that subsection; and

(b) where the infringement to which those proceedings relate occurred after that date.

— 1997, c. 24, ss. 20(3), (4)

(4) Section 39.1 of the *Copyright Act*, as enacted by subsection (1) of this section, applies in respect of

(a) proceedings commenced but not concluded before the coming into force of subsection (1) of this section; and

(b) proceedings commenced after the coming into force of subsection (1) of this section.

— 1997, c. 24, s. 22(2)

(2) Subsection (1) applies in respect of

(a) proceedings commenced but not concluded before this section comes into force; and

(b) proceedings commenced after this section comes into force.

— 1997, c. 24, ss. 53 to 58.1

53 The levies in the first tariffs certified under paragraph 83(8)(c) of the *Copyright Act*, as enacted by section 50 of this Act, become effective at the beginning of the first calendar year following the coming into force of that paragraph, regardless of when the tariffs are so certified, and are effective for a period of two calendar years.

— 1997, c. 24, ss. 53 to 58.1

53.1 Notwithstanding subsection 67.1(2) and section 70.13 of the *Copyright Act*, as enacted by sections 45 and 46 of this Act, the date for the filing of the first proposed tariffs under those sections shall be on or before September 1 of the year of the coming into force of this section.

— 1997, c. 24, ss. 53 to 58.1

54 For greater certainty, all notices published under subsection 5(2) of the *Copyright Act* before the coming into force of this section are deemed to have been validly made and to have had force and effect in accordance with their terms.

— 1997, c. 24, ss. 53 to 58.1

54.1 Section 6 of the *Copyright Act* applies to a photograph in which copyright subsists on the date of the coming into force of this section, if the author is

(a) a natural person who is the author of the photograph referred to in subsection 10(2) of the *Copyright Act*, as enacted by section 7 of this Act; or

(b) the natural person referred to in subsection 10(1.1) of the *Copyright Act*, as enacted by section 7 of this Act.

— 1997, c. 24, ss. 53 to 58.1

55 (1) Part II of the *Copyright Act*, as enacted by section 14 of this Act, shall be construed as a replacement for subsections 5(3) to (6) and section 11 of the *Copyright Act* as those provisions read immediately before the coming into force of subsection 5(3) and section 8, respectively, of this Act.

(2) The rights conferred by Part II of the *Copyright Act*, as enacted by section 14 of this Act, shall not be construed as diminishing the rights conferred by subsections 5(3) to (6) and section 11 of the *Copyright Act* as those provisions read immediately before the coming into force of subsection 5(3) and section 8, respectively, of this Act, in relation to records, perforated rolls and other contrivances by means of which sounds may be mechanically reproduced that were made before the coming into force of subsection 5(3) and section 8, respectively, of this Act.

(3) Where an assignment of copyright or a grant of any interest therein

(a) was made before the coming into force of Part II of the *Copyright Act*, as enacted by section 14 of this Act, and

(b) was made by the maker of a sound recording who was a natural person,

subsections 14(1) and (2) of the *Copyright Act* continue to apply in respect of that assignment or grant, with such modifications as the circumstances require, as if the sound recording was the work referred to in those subsections and the maker of the sound recording was its author.

— 1997, c. 24, ss. 53 to 58.1

56 Nothing in this Act shall be construed as diminishing the right conferred by section 14.01 of the *Copyright Act* as that section read immediately before the coming into force of section 12 of this Act.

— 1997, c. 24, ss. 53 to 58.1

57 For greater certainty, the amendments to the *Copyright Act* that eliminate references to "British subject" and "Her Majesty's Realms and Territories" do not affect any copyright or moral rights that subsisted in Canada

a) une personne physique auteur de la photographie au sens du paragraphe 10(2) de la *Loi sur le droit d'auteur*, édicté par l'article 7 de la présente loi;

b) une personne physique visée au paragraphe 10(1.1) de la *Loi sur le droit d'auteur*, édicté par l'article 7 de la présente loi.

— 1997, ch. 24, art. 53 à 58.1

55 (1) La partie II de la *Loi sur le droit d'auteur*, édictée par l'article 14 de la présente loi, a pour effet de remplacer les paragraphes 5(3) à (6) et l'article 11 de cette loi dans leur version antérieure à la date d'entrée en vigueur du paragraphe 5(3) et de l'article 8, respectivement, de la présente loi.

(2) Les droits conférés par la partie II de la *Loi sur le droit d'auteur*, édictée par l'article 14 de la présente loi, n'ont pas pour effet de restreindre les droits conférés, en vertu des paragraphes 5(3) à (6) et de l'article 11 de cette loi dans leur version antérieure à la date d'entrée en vigueur du paragraphe 5(3) et de l'article 8, respectivement, de la présente loi, relativement aux empreintes, rouleaux perforés et autres organes au moyen desquels des sons peuvent être reproduits mécaniquement et qui ont été confectionnés avant l'entrée en vigueur du paragraphe 5(3) et de l'article 8, respectivement, de la présente loi.

(3) Les paragraphes 14(1) et (2) de la *Loi sur le droit d'auteur* continuent de s'appliquer, avec les adaptations nécessaires, à la cession du droit d'auteur ou à la concession d'un intérêt dans ce droit effectuées, avant l'entrée en vigueur de la partie II de la *Loi sur le droit d'auteur*, édictée par l'article 14 de la présente loi, par le producteur d'un enregistrement sonore qui est une personne physique comme si l'enregistrement sonore était l'œuvre et le producteur, l'auteur de celle-ci.

— 1997, ch. 24, art. 53 à 58.1

56 La présente loi n'a pas pour effet de restreindre le droit conféré en vertu de l'article 14.01 de la *Loi sur le droit d'auteur* dans sa version antérieure à la date d'entrée en vigueur de l'article 12 de la présente loi.

— 1997, ch. 24, art. 53 à 58.1

57 Il est entendu que l'abrogation dans la *Loi sur le droit d'auteur* des mentions « sujet britannique » et « royaumes et territoires de Sa Majesté » ne porte pas atteinte au droit d'auteur ou aux droits moraux qui

immediately before the coming into force of those amendments.

— 1997, c. 24, ss. 53 to 58.1

58 Nothing in this Act shall be construed as reviving a copyright that expired before the coming into force of this section.

— 1997, c. 24, ss. 53 to 58.1

58.1 No agreement concluded before April 25, 1996 that assigns a right or grants an interest by licence in a right that would be a copyright or a right to remuneration under this Act shall be construed as assigning or granting any rights conferred for the first time by this Act, unless the agreement specifically provides for the assignment or grant.

— 1997, c. 24, ss. 62, 63

Coming into force

62 (1) The following provisions come into force or are deemed to have come into force on June 30, 1996:

(a) the definitions *exclusive distributor*, *educational institution* and *library, archive or museum* in section 2 of the *Copyright Act*, as enacted by subsection 1(5) of this Act;

(b) section 2.6 of the *Copyright Act*, as enacted by section 2 of this Act;

(c) section 27.1 of the *Copyright Act*, as enacted by section 15 of this Act; and

(d) section 45 of the *Copyright Act*, as enacted by section 28 of this Act.

(2) Notwithstanding subsection (1), the definition *exclusive distributor* referred to in paragraph (1)(a) shall be read as follows during the period beginning on June 30, 1996 and ending on the day that is sixty days after the day on which this Act is assented to:

exclusive distributor means, in relation to a book, a person who has, before or after the coming into force of this definition, been appointed in writing, by the owner or exclusive licensee of the copyright in the book in Canada, as

(a) the only distributor of the book in Canada or any part of Canada, or

(b) the only distributor of the book in Canada or any part of Canada in respect of a particular sector of the market. (*distributeur exclusif*)

existaient au Canada avant l'entrée en vigueur de ces modifications.

— 1997, ch. 24, art. 53 à 58.1

58 La présente loi n'a pas pour effet de réactiver le droit d'auteur éteint avant l'entrée en vigueur du présent article.

— 1997, ch. 24, art. 53 à 58.1

58.1 Les ententes en matière de cession d'un droit qui, en vertu de la présente loi, constitue un droit d'auteur ou à rémunération, ou en matière de licence concédant un intérêt dans un tel droit, conclues avant le 25 avril 1996 ne valent pas cession ou concession d'un droit conféré à l'origine par la présente loi, sauf mention expresse du droit à cet effet.

— 1997, ch. 24, art. 62 et 63

Entrée en vigueur

62 (1) Les dispositions suivantes entrent en vigueur ou sont réputées être entrées en vigueur le 30 juin 1996 :

a) les définitions de *bibliothèque, musée ou service d'archives*, *distributeur exclusif* et *établissement d'enseignement*, à l'article 2 de la *Loi sur le droit d'auteur*, édictées par le paragraphe 1(5) de la présente loi;

b) l'article 2.6 de la *Loi sur le droit d'auteur*, édicté par l'article 2 de la présente loi;

c) l'article 27.1 de la *Loi sur le droit d'auteur*, édicté par l'article 15 de la présente loi;

d) l'article 45 de la *Loi sur le droit d'auteur*, édicté par l'article 28 de la présente loi.

(2) Toutefois, la définition de *distributeur exclusif* visée à l'alinéa (1)a) est réputée rédigée comme suit pour la période qui commence le 30 juin 1996 et se termine soixante jours après la date de sanction de la présente loi :

distributeur exclusif S'entend, en ce qui concerne un livre, de toute personne à qui le titulaire du droit d'auteur sur le livre au Canada ou le titulaire d'une licence exclusive au Canada s'y rapportant a accordé, avant ou après l'entrée en vigueur de la présente définition, par écrit, la qualité d'unique distributeur pour tout ou partie du Canada ou d'unique distributeur pour un secteur du marché pour tout ou partie du Canada; (*exclusive distributor*)

(3) Notwithstanding paragraph (1)(d), paragraph 45(1)(e) of the *Copyright Act*, as enacted by section 28 of this Act, shall be read as follows for the period beginning on June 30, 1996 and ending on the day that is sixty days after the day on which this Act is assented to:

(e) to import copies, made with the consent of the owner of the copyright in the country where they were made, of any used books.

— 1997, c. 24, ss. 62, 63

63 (1) No exclusive distributor, within the meaning assigned to that expression by subsection 62(2) of this Act, copyright owner or exclusive licensee is entitled to a remedy referred to in the *Copyright Act* in relation to an infringement referred to in subsection 27.1(1) or (2) of that Act, as enacted by section 15 of this Act, during the period beginning on June 30, 1996 and ending on the day on which this Act is assented to, unless

(a) before the infringement occurred, notice in writing has been given to the person referred to in subsection 27.1(1) or (2) of that Act, as enacted by section 15 of this Act, as the case may be, that

(i) there is an exclusive distributor of the book in Canada, and

(ii) section 27.1 of that Act came into force or was deemed to have come into force on June 30, 1996; and

(b) in the case of an infringement referred to in section 27.1 of that Act, as enacted by section 15 of this Act, the remedy is only in relation to a book that was imported during that period and forms part of the inventory of the person referred to in section 27.1 of that Act on the day on which this Act is assented to.

(2) No exclusive distributor, copyright owner or exclusive licensee is entitled to a remedy referred to in subsection (1) against an educational institution, library, archive or museum.

(3) For greater certainty, the expiration of the period referred to in subsection 62(2) of this Act does not affect the right of an exclusive distributor to continue, after the expiration of that period, legal proceedings validly commenced during that period.

— 2004, c. 11, s. 21(4)

Application

21 (4) Subsection (1) applies in respect of unpublished works deposited in an archive on or before September 1, 1999 or at any time after that date.

— 2012, c. 20, s. 59

No revival of copyright in photograph

59 (1) The repeal of section 10 of the *Copyright Act* by section 6 does not have the effect of reviving copyright in any photograph in which, on the coming into force of that section 6, copyright had expired.

Cases where corporations were deemed to be authors

(2) In any case in which, immediately before the coming into force of section 6, a corporation is deemed, by virtue of subsection 10(2) of the *Copyright Act* as it read before the coming into force of that section 6, to be the author of a photograph in which copyright subsists at that time, the copyright in that photograph continues to subsist for the term determined in accordance with sections 6, 6.1, 6.2, 9, 11.1 or 12 of the *Copyright Act* as if its author were the individual who would have been considered the author of the photograph apart from that subsection 10(2).

Cases where individuals were deemed to be authors

(3) In any case in which an individual is deemed to be the author of a photograph, by virtue of subsection 10(2) of the *Copyright Act* as it read before the coming into force of section 6, the individual continues, after the coming into force of that section 6, to be the author of that photograph for the purposes of the *Copyright Act*.

— 2012, c. 20, s. 60

Engraving, photograph or portrait

60 Subsection 13(2) of the *Copyright Act*, as it read immediately before the coming into force of section 7, continues to apply with respect to any engraving, photograph or portrait the plate or original of which was commissioned before the coming into force of that section 7.

— 2012, c. 20, s. 61

No revival of copyright

61 Subsections 23(1) to (2) of the *Copyright Act*, as enacted by section 17, do not have the effect of reviving the copyright, or a right to remuneration, in any performer's performance or sound recording in which the copyright or the right to remuneration had expired on the coming into force of those subsections.

— 2012, ch. 20, art. 59

Droit d'auteur sur une photographie

59 (1) L'abrogation de l'article 10 de la *Loi sur le droit d'auteur* par l'article 6 n'a pas pour effet de réactiver le droit d'auteur sur une photographie éteint à la date d'entrée en vigueur de cet article 6.

Photographie dont une personne morale est réputée être l'auteur

(2) Si une personne morale est, en vertu du paragraphe 10(2) de la *Loi sur le droit d'auteur* dans sa version antérieure à l'entrée en vigueur de l'article 6, considérée comme l'auteur d'une photographie sur laquelle existe un droit d'auteur à l'entrée en vigueur de cet article 6, le droit d'auteur sur la photographie subsiste pour la période déterminée en conformité avec les articles 6, 6.1, 6.2, 9, 11.1 et 12 de la *Loi sur le droit d'auteur* comme si l'auteur était la personne physique qui aurait été considérée comme l'auteur de la photographie n'eût été ce paragraphe 10(2).

Photographie dont une personne physique est réputée être l'auteur

(3) Si une personne physique est, en vertu du paragraphe 10(2) de la *Loi sur le droit d'auteur* dans sa version antérieure à l'entrée en vigueur de l'article 6, considérée comme l'auteur d'une photographie, elle continue de l'être pour l'application de la *Loi sur le droit d'auteur* à l'entrée en vigueur de cet article 6.

— 2012, ch. 20, art. 60

Gravure, photographie, portrait

60 Le paragraphe 13(2) de la *Loi sur le droit d'auteur*, dans sa version antérieure à l'entrée en vigueur de l'article 7, continue de s'appliquer à l'égard des gravures, photographies et portraits dont la planche ou toute autre production originale a été commandée avant l'entrée en vigueur de cet article 7.

— 2012, ch. 20, art. 61

Droit d'auteur éteint

61 Les paragraphes 23(1) à (2) de la *Loi sur le droit d'auteur*, édictés par l'article 17, n'ont pas pour effet de réactiver le droit d'auteur ou le droit à rémunération, selon le cas, sur une prestation ou un enregistrement sonore éteint à la date d'entrée en vigueur de ces paragraphes.

— 2012, c. 20, s. 62

Limitation or prescription period

62 (1) Subsection 43.1(1) of the *Copyright Act*, as enacted by section 49, applies only to proceedings with respect to an act or omission that occurred after the coming into force of that section.

Former limitation or prescription period continued

(2) Subsection 41(1) of the *Copyright Act*, as it read immediately before the coming into force of section 47, applies to proceedings with respect to an infringement that occurred before the coming into force of that section.

— 2015, c. 36, s. 82

No revival of copyright

82 Paragraph 23(1)(b) and subsection 23(1.1) of the *Copyright Act*, as enacted by section 81, do not have the effect of reviving the copyright, or a right to remuneration, in a sound recording or performer's performance fixed in a sound recording in which the copyright or the right to remuneration had expired on the coming into force of those provisions.

CANADA

CONSOLIDATION

Patent Act

R.S.C., 1985, c. P-4

CODIFICATION

Loi sur les brevets

L.R.C. (1985), ch. P-4

Current to August 14, 2017

Last amended on June 24, 2016

À jour au 14 août 2017

Dernière modification le 24 juin 2016

Published by the Minister of Justice at the following address:
http://laws-lois.justice.gc.ca

Publié par le ministre de la Justice à l'adresse suivante :
http://lois-laws.justice.gc.ca

OFFICIAL STATUS OF CONSOLIDATIONS

Subsections 31(1) and (2) of the *Legislation Revision and Consolidation Act*, in force on June 1, 2009, provide as follows:

Published consolidation is evidence

31 (1) Every copy of a consolidated statute or consolidated regulation published by the Minister under this Act in either print or electronic form is evidence of that statute or regulation and of its contents and every copy purporting to be published by the Minister is deemed to be so published, unless the contrary is shown.

Inconsistencies in Acts

(2) In the event of an inconsistency between a consolidated statute published by the Minister under this Act and the original statute or a subsequent amendment as certified by the Clerk of the Parliaments under the *Publication of Statutes Act*, the original statute or amendment prevails to the extent of the inconsistency.

NOTE

This consolidation is current to August 14, 2017. The last amendments came into force on June 24, 2016. Any amendments that were not in force as of August 14, 2017 are set out at the end of this document under the heading "Amendments Not in Force".

CARACTÈRE OFFICIEL DES CODIFICATIONS

Les paragraphes 31(1) et (2) de la *Loi sur la révision et la codification des textes législatifs*, en vigueur le 1er juin 2009, prévoient ce qui suit :

Codifications comme élément de preuve

31 (1) Tout exemplaire d'une loi codifiée ou d'un règlement codifié, publié par le ministre en vertu de la présente loi sur support papier ou sur support électronique, fait foi de cette loi ou de ce règlement et de son contenu. Tout exemplaire donné comme publié par le ministre est réputé avoir été ainsi publié, sauf preuve contraire.

Incompatibilité — lois

(2) Les dispositions de la loi d'origine avec ses modifications subséquentes par le greffier des Parlements en vertu de la *Loi sur la publication des lois* l'emportent sur les dispositions incompatibles de la loi codifiée publiée par le ministre en vertu de la présente loi.

NOTE

Cette codification est à jour au 14 août 2017. Les dernières modifications sont entrées en vigueur le 24 juin 2016. Toutes modifications qui n'étaient pas en vigueur au 14 août 2017 sont énoncées à la fin de ce document sous le titre « Modifications non en vigueur ».

TABLE OF PROVISIONS

An Act respecting patents of invention

Short Title

1 Short title

Interpretation

2 Definitions

Her Majesty

2.1 Binding on Her Majesty

Patent Office and Officers

3 Patent Office
4 Commissioner of Patents
5 Assistant Commissioner
6 Staff
7 Officers of Patent Office not to deal in patents
8 Clerical errors
8.1 Electronic or other submission of documents, information or fees
8.2 Storage of documents or information in electronic or other form
9 Destroyed or lost patents
10 Inspection by the public
11 Patents issued out of Canada

Rules and Regulations

12 Rules and regulations

Seal

13 Seal of office

Proof of Patents

14 Certified copies of patents as evidence

Patent Agents

15 Register of patent agents

16	Misconduct	16	Inconduite
16.1	Privileged communication	16.1	Communication protégée

Appeals

Appels

17	Practice on appeals	17	Pratique d'appel
18	Notice on appeal	18	Avis d'appel

Use of Patents by Government

Usages de brevets par le gouvernement

19	Government may apply to use patented invention	19	Demande d'usage d'une invention brevetée par le gouvernement
19.1	Conditions for authorizing use	19.1	Conditions préalables
19.2	Appeal	19.2	Appel
19.3	Regulations	19.3	Règlements

Government Owned Patents

Brevets appartenant au gouvernement

20	Assignment to Minister of National Defence	20	Cession au ministre de la Défense nationale
21	Agreement between Canada and other government	21	Accord entre le Canada et un autre gouvernement

Use of Patents for International Humanitarian Purposes to Address Public Health Problems

Usage de brevets à des fins humanitaires internationales en vue de remédier aux problèmes de santé publique

21.01	Purpose	21.01	Objet
21.02	Definitions	21.02	Définitions
21.03	Amending Schedules	21.03	Modification des annexes
21.04	Authorization	21.04	Autorisation
21.05	Form and content of authorization	21.05	Forme et contenu de l'autorisation
21.06	Disclosure of information on website	21.06	Affichage sur site Internet
21.07	Export notice	21.07	Avis d'exportation
21.08	Royalty	21.08	Redevances
21.09	Duration	21.09	Durée de l'autorisation
21.1	Use is non-exclusive	21.1	Usage non exclusif
21.11	Authorization is non-transferable	21.11	Autorisation incessible
21.12	Renewal	21.12	Renouvellement de l'autorisation
21.13	Termination	21.13	Expiration de l'autorisation
21.14	Termination by Federal Court	21.14	Cour fédérale
21.15	Notice to patentee	21.15	Avis
21.16	Obligation to provide copy of agreement	21.16	Obligation de fournir une copie de l'accord
21.17	Application when agreement is commercial in nature	21.17	Demande – accord de nature commerciale

21.18	Advisory committee	21.18	Comité consultatif
21.19	Website for notices to Canada	21.19	Établissement d'un site Internet
21.2	Review	21.2	Examen

Patents Relating to Nuclear Energy

Brevets liés à l'énergie nucléaire

22	Communication to Canadian Nuclear Safety Commission	22	Communication à la Commission canadienne de sûreté nucléaire

General

Dispositions générales

23	Patented invention in vessels, aircraft, etc., of any country	23	Usage d'une invention brevetée, sur navires, aéronefs, etc. d'un pays
25	Cost of proceedings before the court	25	Frais de procédure devant le tribunal
26	Annual report	26	Rapport annuel
26.1	Publication of list of patents	26.1	Liste des brevets

Application for Patents

Demandes de brevets

27	Commissioner may grant patents	27	Délivrance de brevet
27.1	Maintenance fees	27.1	Taxes périodiques
28	Filing date	28	Date de dépôt
28.1	Claim date	28.1	Date de la revendication
28.2	Subject-matter of claim must not be previously disclosed	28.2	Objet non divulgué
28.3	Invention must not be obvious	28.3	Objet non évident
28.4	Request for priority	28.4	Demande de priorité
29	Non-resident applicants	29	Demandeur non-résident

Joint Applications

Demandes collectives

31	Effect of refusal of a joint inventor to proceed	31	Effet du refus par un inventeur conjoint de poursuivre la demande

Improvements

Perfectionnement

32	Improvements	32	Perfectionnement

Filing of Prior Art

Dossier d'antériorité

34.1	Filing	34.1	Dépôt

Examination

Examen

35	Request for examination	35	Requête d'examen

Divisional Applications

Demandes complémentaires

36	Patent for one invention only	36	Brevet pour une seule invention

Drawings, Models and Biological Materials

37	Drawings
38	Models and specimens
38.1	Biological material may be deposited

Amendments to Specifications and Drawings

38.2	Amendments to specifications and drawings

Refusal of Patents

40	Refusal by Commissioner
41	Appeal to Federal Court

Grant of Patents

42	Contents of patent

Form and Term of Patents

43	Form and duration of patents
44	Term of patents based on applications filed on or after October 1, 1989
45	Term of patents based on applications filed before October 1, 1989
46	Maintenance fees

Reissue of Patents

47	Issue of new or amended patents

Disclaimers

48	Patentee may disclaim anything included in patent by mistake

Re-examination

48.1	Request for re-examination
48.2	Establishment of re-examination board
48.3	Re-examination proceeding
48.4	Certificate of board
48.5	Appeals

Assignments and Devolutions

49	Assignee or personal representatives
50	Patents to be assignable

Dessins, modèles et matières biologiques

37	Dessins
38	Modèles et échantillons
38.1	Matières biologiques

Modification du mémoire descriptif et des dessins

38.2	Modification du mémoire descriptif et des dessins

Rejet des demandes de brevets

40	Le commissaire peut refuser le brevet
41	Appel à la Cour fédérale

Octroi des brevets

42	Contenu du brevet

Forme et durée des brevets

43	Délivrance
44	Durée du brevet
45	Durée de dix-sept ans
46	Taxes périodiques

Redélivrance de brevets

47	Délivrance de brevets nouveaux ou rectifiés

Renonciations

48	Cas de renonciation

Réexamen

48.1	Demande
48.2	Constitution d'un conseil de réexamen
48.3	Procédure de réexamen
48.4	Constat
48.5	Appel

Cessions et dévolutions

49	Cessionnaire ou représentants personnels
50	Les brevets sont cessibles

51	When assignment void	51	Nullité de la cession, à défaut d'enregistrement
52	Jurisdiction of Federal Court	52	Juridiction de la Cour fédérale

Legal Proceedings in Respect of Patents

Procédures judiciaires relatives aux brevets

53	Void in certain cases, or valid only for parts	53	Nul en certains cas, ou valide en partie seulement

Infringement

Contrefaçon

54	Jurisdiction of courts	54	Juridiction des tribunaux
55	Liability for patent infringement	55	Contrefaçon et recours
55.01	Limitation	55.01	Prescription
55.1	Burden of proof for patented process	55.1	Nouveau produit
55.2	Exception	55.2	Exception
56	Patent not to affect previous purchaser	56	Droit de l'acquéreur antérieur
57	Injunction may issue	57	Interdiction
58	Invalid claims not to affect valid claims	58	Revendications invalides
59	Defence	59	Défense

Impeachment

Invalidation

60	Impeachment of patents or claims	60	Invalidation de brevets ou de revendications

Judgments

Jugements

62	Judgment voiding patent	62	Jugement qui annule un brevet
63	Appeal	63	Appel

Conditions

Conditions

65	Abuse of rights under patents	65	Abus des droits de brevets
66	Powers of Commissioner in cases of abuse	66	Pouvoirs du commissaire en cas d'abus
68	Contents of applications	68	Teneur des requêtes
69	Opposition and counter statement	69	Opposition et contre-mémoire
70	Licence deemed to be by deed	70	La licence considérée comme un acte
71	Appeal to Federal Court	71	Appel à la Cour fédérale

Abandonment and Reinstatement of Applications

Abandon et rétablissement des demandes

73	Deemed abandonment of applications	73	Abandon

Offences and Punishment

Infractions et peines

75	Offences	75	Infractions et peines
76	False representations, false entries, etc.	76	Exposé faux, fausses inscriptions, etc.
76.1	Offence respecting patented medicines	76.1	Infractions relatives aux médicaments brevetés

Miscellaneous Matters

78 Time limit deemed extended

Transitional Provisions

78.1 Patent applications filed before October 1, 1989
78.2 Patents issued before October 1, 1989
78.3 Previous version of section 43 applies
78.4 Patent applications filed on or after October 1, 1989
78.5 Patents issued on or after October 1, 1989
78.6 Payment of prescribed fees

Patented Medicines

Interpretation

79 Definitions

Pricing Information

80 Pricing information, etc., required by regulations
81 Pricing information, etc. required by Board
82 Notice of introductory price

Excessive Prices

83 Order re excessive prices
84 Compliance
85 Factors to be considered
86 Hearings to be public
87 Information, etc., privileged

Sales and Expense Information

88 Sales and expense information, etc., to be provided
89 Report

Inquiries

90 Inquiries

Patented Medicine Prices Review Board

91 Establishment
92 Advisory panel
93 Chairperson and Vice-chairperson
94 Staff
95 Principal office

Dispositions diverses

78 Le délai est réputé prorogé

Dispositions transitoires

78.1 Régime applicable aux demandes déposées avant le 1er octobre 1989
78.2 Régime applicable aux brevets délivrés avant le 1er octobre 1989
78.3 Version antérieure de l'article 43
78.4 Régime applicable au traitement de certaines demandes
78.5 Régime applicable aux affaires relatives à certains brevets
78.6 Paiement de taxes réglementaires

Médicaments brevetés

Définitions

79 Définitions

Renseignements sur les prix

80 Renseignements réglementaires à fournir sur les prix
81 Renseignements sur les prix exigés par le Conseil
82 Avis du prix de lancement

Prix excessifs

83 Ordonnance relative aux prix excessifs
84 Exécution
85 Facteurs de fixation du prix
86 Audiences publiques
87 Protection des renseignements

Renseignements sur les recettes et dépenses

88 Obligations des brevetés
89 Rapport

Enquêtes

90 Enquêtes

Conseil d'examen du prix des médicaments brevetés

91 Constitution
92 Comité consultatif
93 Président et vice-président
94 Personnel
95 Siège

96	General powers, etc.		96	Attributions générales du Conseil
97	Proceedings		97	Procédures
98	Orders		98	Entrée en vigueur des ordonnances
99	Enforcement of orders		99	Assimilation
100	Report of Board		100	Rapport

Regulations / Règlements

101	Regulations		101	Règlements

Meetings with Minister / Réunions ministérielles

102	Meetings with Minister		102	Réunions ministérielles

Agreements with Provinces / Ententes avec les provinces

103	Agreements with provinces		103	Ententes avec les provinces

SCHEDULE 1 — **ANNEXE 1**

SCHEDULE 2 — **ANNEXE 2**

SCHEDULE 3 — **ANNEXE 3**

SCHEDULE 4 — **ANNEXE 4**

R.S.C., 1985, c. P-4

An Act respecting patents of invention

Short Title

Short title

1 This Act may be cited as the *Patent Act*.
R.S., c. P-4, s. 1.

Interpretation

Definitions

2 In this Act, except as otherwise provided,

applicant includes an inventor and the legal representatives of an applicant or inventor; (*demandeur*)

claim date means the date of a claim in an application for a patent in Canada, as determined in accordance with section 28.1;

Commissioner means the Commissioner of Patents; (*commissaire*)

country includes a Member of the World Trade Organization, as defined in subsection 2(1) of the *World Trade Organization Agreement Implementation Act*; (*pays*)

filing date means, in relation to an application for a patent in Canada, the date on which the application is filed, as determined in accordance with section 28; (*date de dépôt*)

invention means any new and useful art, process, machine, manufacture or composition of matter, or any new and useful improvement in any art, process, machine, manufacture or composition of matter; (*invention*)

legal representatives includes heirs, executors, administrators, guardians, curators, tutors, assigns and all other persons claiming through or under applicants for patents and patentees of inventions; (*représentants légaux*)

L.R.C., 1985, ch. P-4

Loi concernant les brevets d'invention

Titre abrégé

Titre abrégé

1 *Loi sur les brevets*.
S.R., ch. P-4, art. 1.

Définitions

Définitions

2 Sauf disposition contraire, les définitions qui suivent s'appliquent à la présente loi.

brevet Lettres patentes couvrant une invention. (*patent*)

breveté ou ***titulaire d'un brevet*** Le titulaire ayant pour le moment droit à l'avantage d'un brevet. (*patentee*)

commissaire Le commissaire aux brevets. (*Commissioner*)

date de dépôt La date du dépôt d'une demande de brevet, déterminée conformément à l'article 28. (*filing date*)

date de priorité [Abrogée, 1993, ch. 15, art. 26]

demande de priorité La demande visée à l'article 28.4. (*request for priority*)

demandeur Sont assimilés à un demandeur un inventeur et les représentants légaux d'un demandeur ou d'un inventeur. (*applicant*)

exploitation sur une échelle commerciale [Abrogée, 1993, ch. 44, art. 189]

invention Toute réalisation, tout procédé, toute machine, fabrication ou composition de matières, ainsi que tout perfectionnement de l'un d'eux, présentant le caractère de la nouveauté et de l'utilité. (*invention*)

Minister means the Minister of Industry or such other member of the Queen's Privy Council for Canada as is designated by the Governor in Council as the Minister for the purposes of this Act; (*ministre*)

patent means letters patent for an invention; (*brevet*)

patentee means the person for the time being entitled to the benefit of a patent; (*breveté* ou *titulaire d'un brevet*)

predecessor in title includes any person through whom an applicant for a patent in Canada claims the right to the patent; (*prédécesseur en droit*)

prescribed means prescribed by rules or regulations of the Governor in Council and, in the case of a fee, includes a fee determined in the manner prescribed; (*réglementaire*)

prescribed fee [Repealed, R.S., 1985, c. 33 (3rd Supp.), s. 1]

priority date [Repealed, 1993, c. 15, s. 26]

regulation and **rule** include rule, regulation and form; (*règlement* et *règle*)

request for priority means a request under section 28.4. (*demande de priorité*)

work on a commercial scale [Repealed, 1993, c. 44, s. 189]

R.S., 1985, c. P-4, s. 2; R.S., 1985, c. 33 (3rd Supp.), s. 1; 1992, c. 1, s. 145(F); 1993, c. 2, s. 2, c. 15, s. 26, c. 44, s. 189; 1994, c. 47, s. 141; 1995, c. 1, s. 62.

Her Majesty

Binding on Her Majesty

2.1 This Act is binding on Her Majesty in right of Canada or a province.

1993, c. 44, s. 190.

Patent Office and Officers

Patent Office

3 There shall be attached to the Department of Industry, or to such other department of the Government of Canada as may be determined by the Governor in Council, an office called the Patent Office.

R.S., 1985, c. P-4, s. 3; 1992, c. 1, s. 145(F); 1995, c. 1, s. 63.

Commissioner of Patents

4 (1) The Governor in Council may appoint a Commissioner of Patents who shall, under the direction of the Minister, exercise the powers and perform the duties conferred and imposed on that officer by or pursuant to this Act.

Duties of Commissioner

(2) The Commissioner shall receive all applications, fees, papers, documents and models for patents, shall perform and do all acts and things requisite for the granting and issuing of patents of invention, shall have the charge and custody of the books, records, papers, models, machines and other things belonging to the Patent Office and shall have, for the purposes of this Act, all the powers that are or may be given by the *Inquiries Act* to a commissioner appointed under Part II of that Act.

Tenure of office and salary

(3) The Commissioner holds office during pleasure and shall be paid such annual salary as may be determined by the Governor in Council.

Delegation

(4) The Commissioner may, after consultation with the Minister, delegate to any person he deems qualified any of his powers, duties and functions under this Act, except the power to delegate under this subsection.

Appeal

(5) Any decision under this Act of a person authorized to make the decision pursuant to subsection (4) may be appealed in the like manner and subject to the like conditions as a decision of the Commissioner under this Act.

R.S., c. P-4, s. 4; 1984, c. 40, s. 57.

Assistant Commissioner

5 (1) An Assistant Commissioner of Patents may be appointed in the manner authorized by law and shall be a technical officer experienced in the administration of the Patent Office.

Absence or inability to act

(2) When the Commissioner is absent or unable to act, the Assistant Commissioner, or, if he also is at the same time absent or unable to act, another officer designated by the Minister, may exercise the powers and shall perform the duties of the Commissioner.

R.S., c. P-4, s. 5.

Staff

6 There may be appointed in the manner authorized by law such principal examiners, examiners, associate examiners and assistant examiners, clerks, stenographers and other assistants as are necessary for the administration of this Act.

R.S., c. P-4, s. 6.

Officers of Patent Office not to deal in patents

7 (1) No officer or employee of the Patent Office shall buy, sell, acquire or traffic in any invention, patent or right to a patent, or any interest therein, and every purchase, sale, assignment, acquisition or transfer of any invention, patent or right to a patent, or any interest therein, made by or to any officer or employee is void.

Restriction

(2) Subsection (1) does not apply to a sale by an original inventor or to an acquisition under the last will, or by the intestacy, of a deceased person.

R.S., c. P-4, s. 7.

Clerical errors

8 Clerical errors in any instrument of record in the Patent Office do not invalidate the instrument, but they may be corrected under the authority of the Commissioner.

R.S., 1985, c. P-4, s. 8; 1993, c. 15, s. 27.

Electronic or other submission of documents, information or fees

8.1 (1) Subject to the regulations, any document, information or fee that is authorized or required to be submitted to the Commissioner under this Act may be submitted in electronic or other form in any manner specified by the Commissioner.

Time of receipt

(2) For the purposes of this Act, any document, information or fee submitted in accordance with subsection (1) is deemed to be received by the Commissioner at the time provided by the regulations.

1993, c. 15, s. 27.

Storage of documents or information in electronic or other form

8.2 Subject to the regulations, any document or information received by the Commissioner under this Act in electronic or other form may be entered or recorded by any information storage device, including any system of mechanical or electronic data processing, that is capable

Personnel

6 Sont nommés, de la manière autorisée par la loi, les examinateurs principaux, les examinateurs, les examinateurs associés, les examinateurs adjoints et les autres personnes nécessaires à l'application de la présente loi.

S.R., ch. P-4, art. 6.

Le personnel du Bureau ne peut acheter ou vendre des brevets

7 (1) Il est interdit au personnel du Bureau des brevets d'acheter, de vendre ou d'acquérir une invention, un brevet ou un droit à un brevet, ou tout intérêt y afférent, ou d'en faire le commerce. Est nul tout achat, vente, cession, acquisition ou transport d'une invention, d'un brevet, d'un droit à un brevet, ou de tout intérêt y afférent, auquel est partie un membre du personnel du Bureau.

Restriction

(2) Le paragraphe (1) ne s'applique pas à une vente effectuée par l'auteur original d'une invention, ni à une acquisition par dernier testament ou par succession ab intestat d'une personne décédée.

S.R., ch. P-4, art. 7.

Erreurs d'écriture

8 Un document en dépôt au Bureau des brevets n'est pas invalide en raison d'erreurs d'écriture; elles peuvent être corrigées sous l'autorité du commissaire.

L.R. (1985), ch. P-4, art. 8; 1993, ch. 15, art. 27.

Transmission électronique

8.1 (1) Sous réserve des règlements, les documents, renseignements ou taxes dont la présente loi exige ou autorise la remise au commissaire peuvent lui être transmis sous forme électronique ou autre, de la manière qu'il précise.

Date de réception

(2) Pour l'application de la présente loi, les documents, renseignements ou taxes ainsi transmis sont réputés avoir été reçus par le commissaire au moment déterminé par règlement.

1993, ch. 15, art. 27.

Mise en mémoire

8.2 Sous réserve des règlements, les documents ou renseignements reçus par le commissaire, en application de la présente loi, sous forme électronique ou autre, peuvent

Destroyed or lost patents

9 If any patent is destroyed or lost, a certified copy may be issued in lieu thereof on payment of the prescribed fee.

R.S., c. P-4, s. 9.

Inspection by the public

10 (1) Subject to subsections (2) to (6) and section 20, all patents, applications for patents and documents filed in connection with patents or applications for patents shall be open to public inspection at the Patent Office, under such conditions as may be prescribed.

Confidentiality period

(2) Except with the approval of the applicant, an application for a patent, or a document filed in connection with the application, shall not be open to public inspection before a confidentiality period of eighteen months has expired.

Beginning of confidentiality period

(3) The confidentiality period begins on the filing date of the application or, where a request for priority has been made in respect of the application, it begins on the earliest filing date of any previously regularly filed application on which the request is based.

Withdrawal of request

(4) Where a request for priority is withdrawn on or before the prescribed date, it shall, for the purposes of subsection (3) and to the extent that it is withdrawn, be considered never to have been made.

Withdrawn applications

(5) An application shall not be open to public inspection if it is withdrawn in accordance with the regulations on or before the prescribed date.

Prescribed date

(6) A prescribed date referred to in subsection (4) or (5) must be no later than the date on which the confidentiality period expires.

R.S., 1985, c. P-4, s. 10; R.S., 1985, c. 33 (3rd Supp.), s. 2; 1993, c. 15, s. 28.

Patents issued out of Canada

11 Notwithstanding the exception in section 10, the Commissioner, on the request of any person who states

of reproducing stored documents or information in intelligible form within a reasonable time.

1993, c. 15, s. 27.

in writing the name of the inventor, if available, the title of the invention and the number and date of a patent said to have been granted in a named country other than Canada, and who pays or tenders the prescribed fee, shall inform that person whether an application for a patent of the same invention is or is not pending in Canada.

R.S., c. P-4, s. 11.

Rules and Regulations

Rules and regulations

12 (1) The Governor in Council may make rules or regulations

(a) respecting the form and contents of applications for patents;

(b) respecting the form of the Register of Patents and of the indexes thereto;

(c) respecting the registration of assignments, transmissions, disclaimers, judgments or other documents relating to any patent;

(d) respecting the form and contents of any certificate issued pursuant to this Act;

(e) prescribing the fees or the manner of determining the fees that may be charged in respect of the filing of applications for patents or the taking of other proceedings under this Act or under any rule or regulation made pursuant to this Act, or in respect of any services or the use of any facilities provided thereunder by the Commissioner or any person employed in the Patent Office;

(f) prescribing the fees or the manner of determining the fees that shall be paid to maintain in effect an application for a patent or to maintain the rights accorded by a patent;

(g) respecting the payment of any prescribed fees including the time when and the manner in which such fees shall be paid, the additional fees that may be charged for the late payment of such fees and the circumstances in which any fees previously paid may be refunded in whole or in part;

(h) for carrying into effect the terms of any treaty, convention, arrangement or engagement that subsists between Canada and any other country;

(i) for carrying into effect, notwithstanding anything in this Act, the Patent Cooperation Treaty done at

Washington on June 19, 1970, including any amendments, modifications and revisions made from time to time to which Canada is a party;

(j) respecting the entry on, the maintenance of and the removal from the register of patent agents of the names of persons and firms, including the qualifications that must be met and the conditions that must be fulfilled by a person or firm before the name of the person or firm is entered thereon and to maintain the name of the person or firm on the register;

(j.1) respecting the submission of documents, information or fees under section 8.1, including

    (i) the documents, information or fees that may be submitted in electronic or other form under that section,

    (ii) the persons or classes of persons by whom they may be submitted, and

    (iii) the time at which they are deemed to be received by the Commissioner;

(j.2) respecting the entering or recording of any document or information under section 8.2;

(j.3) prescribing the manner in which an application for a patent may be withdrawn and, for the purposes of subsections 10(4) and (5), prescribing the date, or the manner of determining the date, on or before which a request for priority or an application for a patent must be withdrawn;

(j.4) respecting requests for priority, including

    (i) the period within which priority must be requested,

    (ii) the manner in which and period within which the Commissioner must be informed of the matters referred to in subsection 28.4(2),

    (iii) the documentation that must be filed in support of requests for priority, and

    (iv) the withdrawal of requests for priority;

(j.5) respecting the time within which requests for examination must be made and prescribed fees must be paid under subsection 35(1);

(j.6) respecting the deposit of biological material for the purposes of section 38.1;

j) prévoir l'inscription, le maintien et la suppression des noms de personne et d'entreprise dans le registre des agents de brevets, et notamment les conditions que doit remplir toute personne ou entreprise pour que son nom soit ainsi inscrit et maintenu;

j.1) régir la transmission des documents, renseignements et taxes visés à l'article 8.1, notamment en déterminant ceux qui peuvent être remis au titre du paragraphe 8.1(1), les personnes ou catégories de personnes habilitées à cet effet et les règles d'application du paragraphe 8.1(2);

j.2) régir la mise en mémoire des renseignements et documents visés à l'article 8.2;

j.3) déterminer les modalités de retrait des demandes de brevet et, pour l'application des paragraphes 10(4) et (5), préciser les dates, ou leur mode de détermination, de retrait des demandes de priorité et des demandes de brevet;

j.4) régir les demandes de priorité, notamment en ce qui a trait à leur délai de présentation, aux renseignements et documents à fournir à l'appui de celles-ci, au délai de transmission au commissaire de ces renseignements et documents ainsi qu'au retrait de ces demandes;

j.5) déterminer le délai de présentation des requêtes d'examen et fixer les taxes à payer aux termes du paragraphe 35(1);

j.6) régir le dépôt de matières biologiques visé à l'article 38.1;

j.7) déterminer les modalités de modification des mémoires descriptifs et des dessins faisant partie de la demande de brevet;

j.8) autoriser le commissaire, si celui-ci estime que les circonstances le justifient, à proroger, aux conditions réglementaires, tout délai fixé par la présente loi ou en vertu de celle-ci pour l'accomplissement d'un acte;

k) prendre toute autre mesure d'ordre réglementaire prévue par la présente loi;

l) prendre toute autre mesure d'application de la présente loi ou pour en assurer la mise en œuvre par le commissaire et le personnel du Bureau des brevets.

(j.7) respecting the manner in which amendments may be made to specifications or drawings furnished as part of an application for a patent;

(j.8) authorizing the Commissioner to extend, subject to any prescribed terms and conditions, the time fixed by or under this Act for doing anything where the Commissioner is satisfied that the circumstances justify the extension;

(k) prescribing any other matter that by any provision of this Act is to be prescribed; and

(l) generally, for carrying into effect the objects and purposes of this Act or for ensuring the due administration thereof by the Commissioner and other officers and employees of the Patent Office.

Effect

(2) Any rule or regulation made by the Governor in Council has the same force and effect as if it had been enacted herein.

R.S., 1985, c. P-4, s. 12; R.S., 1985, c. 33 (3rd Supp.), s. 3; 1993, c. 15, s. 29.

Seal

Seal of office

13 (1) The Commissioner shall cause a seal to be made for the purposes of this Act and may cause to be sealed therewith every patent and other instrument and copy thereof issuing from the Patent Office.

Seal to be evidence

(2) Every court, judge and person shall take notice of the seal of the Patent Office, shall admit the impressions thereof in evidence in like manner as the impressions of the Great Seal are admitted in evidence and shall take notice of and admit in evidence, without further proof and without production of the originals, all copies or extracts certified under the seal of the Patent Office to be copies of or extracts from documents deposited in that Office.

R.S., c. P-4, s. 13.

Proof of Patents

Certified copies of patents as evidence

14 In any action or proceeding respecting a patent authorized to be had or taken in Canada under this Act, a copy of any patent granted in any other country, or any official document connected therewith, purporting to be certified under the hand of the proper officer of the government of the country in which the patent has been obtained, may be produced before the court or a judge thereof, and the copy of the patent or document purporting to be so certified may be admitted in evidence without production of the original and without proof of the signature or official character of the person appearing to have signed it.

R.S., c. P-4, s. 14.

Patent Agents

Register of patent agents

15 A register of patent agents shall be kept in the Patent Office on which shall be entered the names of all persons and firms entitled to represent applicants in the presentation and prosecution of applications for patents or in other business before the Patent Office.

R.S., 1985, c. P-4, s. 15; R.S., 1985, c. 33 (3rd Supp.), s. 4.

Misconduct

16 For gross misconduct or any other cause that he may deem sufficient, the Commissioner may refuse to recognize any person as a patent agent or attorney either generally or in any particular case.

R.S., c. P-4, s. 16.

Privileged communication

16.1 (1) A communication that meets the following conditions is privileged in the same way as a communication that is subject to solicitor-client privilege or, in civil law, to professional secrecy of advocates and notaries and no person shall be required to disclose, or give testimony on, the communication in a civil, criminal or administrative action or proceeding:

(a) it is between an individual whose name is entered on the register of patent agents and that individual's client;

(b) it is intended to be confidential; and

(c) it is made for the purpose of seeking or giving advice with respect to any matter relating to the protection of an invention.

Waiver

(2) Subsection (1) does not apply if the client expressly or implicitly waives the privilege.

Exceptions

(3) Exceptions to solicitor-client privilege or, in civil law, to professional secrecy of advocates and notaries apply to a communication that meets the conditions set out in paragraphs (1)(a) to (c).

Patent agents — country other than Canada

(4) A communication between an individual who is authorized to act as a patent agent under the law of a country other than Canada and that individual's client that is privileged under the law of that other country and that would be privileged under subsection (1) had it been made between an individual whose name is entered on the register of patent agents and that individual's client is deemed to be a communication that meets the conditions set out in paragraphs (1)(a) to (c).

Individual acting on behalf of patent agent or client

(5) For the purposes of this section, an individual whose name is entered on the register of patent agents or an individual who is authorized to act as a patent agent under the law of a country other than Canada includes an individual acting on their behalf and a client includes an individual acting on the client's behalf.

Application

(6) This section applies to communications that are made before the day on which this section comes into force if they are still confidential on that day and to communications that are made after that day. However, this section does not apply in respect of an action or proceeding commenced before that day.

2015, c. 36, s. 54.

Appeals

Practice on appeals

17 In all cases where an appeal is provided from the decision of the Commissioner to the Federal Court under this Act, the appeal shall be had and taken pursuant to the *Federal Courts Act* and the rules and practice of that Court.

R.S., 1985, c. P-4, s. 17; 2002, c. 8, s. 182.

Notice on appeal

18 (1) Whenever an appeal to the Federal Court from the decision of the Commissioner is permitted under this Act, notice of the decision shall be mailed by the Commissioner by registered letter addressed to the interested parties or their respective agents.

Time for taking appeal

(2) The appeal shall be taken within three months after the date of mailing of the notice, unless otherwise provided by or under this Act.

R.S., 1985, c. P-4, s. 18; 1993, c. 15, s. 30.

Use of Patents by Government

Government may apply to use patented invention

19 (1) Subject to section 19.1, the Commissioner may, on application by the Government of Canada or the government of a province, authorize the use of a patented invention by that government.

Terms of use

(2) Subject to section 19.1, the use of the patented invention may be authorized for such purpose, for such period and on such other terms as the Commissioner considers expedient but the Commissioner shall settle those terms in accordance with the following principles:

(a) the scope and duration of the use shall be limited to the purpose for which the use is authorized;

(b) the use authorized shall be non-exclusive; and

(c) any use shall be authorized predominantly to supply the domestic market.

Notice

(3) The Commissioner shall notify the patentee of any use of the patented invention that is authorized under this section.

Payment of remuneration

(4) Where the use of the patented invention is authorized, the authorized user shall pay to the patentee such amount as the Commissioner considers to be adequate remuneration in the circumstances, taking into account the economic value of the authorization.

Termination of authorization

(5) The Commissioner may, on application by the patentee and after giving all concerned parties an opportunity to be heard, terminate the authorization if the Commissioner is satisfied that the circumstances that led to the granting of the authorization have ceased to exist and are unlikely to recur, subject to such conditions as the Commissioner deems appropriate to protect the legitimate interests of the authorized user.

Délai

(2) L'appel doit être interjeté dans un délai de trois mois à compter de la date de l'envoi de cet avis, à moins qu'un autre délai ne soit fixé sous le régime de la présente loi.

L.R. (1985), ch. P-4, art. 18; 1993, ch. 15, art. 30.

Usages de brevets par le gouvernement

Demande d'usage d'une invention brevetée par le gouvernement

19 (1) Sous réserve de l'article 19.1, le commissaire peut, sur demande du gouvernement du Canada ou d'une province, autoriser celui-ci à faire usage d'une invention brevetée.

Modalités

(2) Sous réserve de l'article 19.1, l'usage de l'invention brevetée peut être autorisé aux fins, pour la durée et selon les autres modalités que le commissaire estime convenables. Celui-ci fixe ces modalités en tenant compte des principes suivants :

a) la portée et la durée de l'usage doivent être limitées aux fins auxquelles celui-ci a été autorisé;

b) l'usage ne peut être exclusif;

c) l'usage doit être avant tout autorisé pour l'approvisionnement du marché intérieur.

Avis

(3) Le commissaire avise le breveté des usages de l'invention brevetée qui sont autorisés sous le régime du présent article.

Paiement d'une rémunération

(4) L'usager de l'invention brevetée paie au breveté la rémunération que le commissaire estime adéquate en l'espèce, compte tenu de la valeur économique de l'autorisation.

Fin de l'autorisation

(5) Le commissaire peut, sur demande du breveté et après avoir donné aux intéressés la possibilité de se faire entendre, mettre fin à l'autorisation s'il est convaincu que les circonstances qui y ont conduit ont cessé d'exister et ne se reproduiront vraisemblablement pas. Le cas échéant, il doit toutefois veiller à ce que les intérêts légitimes des personnes autorisées soient protégés de façon adéquate.

Authorization not transferable

(6) An authorization granted under this section is not transferable.

R.S., 1985, c. P-4, s. 19; 1993, c. 44, s. 191.

Conditions for authorizing use

19.1 (1) The Commissioner may not authorize the use of a patented invention under section 19 unless the applicant establishes that

(a) it has made efforts to obtain from the patentee on reasonable commercial terms and conditions the authority to use the patented invention; and

(b) its efforts have not been successful within a reasonable period.

Exception

(2) Subsection (1) does not apply in cases of national emergency or extreme urgency or where the use for which the authorization is sought is a public non-commercial use.

Prescribed uses

(3) The Commissioner may not, under section 19, authorize any use that is a prescribed use unless the proposed user complies with the prescribed conditions.

Limitation on use of semi-conductor technology

(4) The Commissioner may not, under section 19, authorize any use of semi-conductor technology other than a public non-commercial use.

1993, c. 44, s. 191; 1994, c. 47, s. 142.

Appeal

19.2 Any decision made by the Commissioner under section 19 or 19.1 is subject to appeal to the Federal Court.

1993, c. 44, s. 191.

Regulations

19.3 (1) The Governor in Council may make regulations for the purpose of implementing, in relation to patents, Article 1720 of the Agreement.

Definition of *Agreement*

(2) In subsection (1), ***Agreement*** has the same meaning as in subsection 2(1) of the *North American Free Trade Agreement Implementation Act*.

1993, c. 44, s. 191.

Government Owned Patents

Assignment to Minister of National Defence

20 (1) Any officer, servant or employee of the Crown or of a corporation that is an agent or servant of the Crown, who, acting within the scope of his duties and employment, invents any invention in instruments or munitions of war shall, if so required by the Minister of National Defence, assign to that Minister on behalf of Her Majesty all the benefits of the invention and of any patent obtained or to be obtained for the invention.

Idem

(2) Any person other than a person described in subsection (1) who invents an invention described in that subsection may assign to the Minister of National Defence on behalf of Her Majesty all the benefits of the invention and of any patent obtained or to be obtained for the invention.

Inventor entitled to compensation

(3) An inventor described in subsection (2) is entitled to compensation for an assignment to the Minister of National Defence under this Act and in the event that the consideration to be paid for the assignment is not agreed on, it is the duty of the Commissioner to determine the amount of the consideration, which decision is subject to appeal to the Federal Court.

Proceedings before Federal Court

(4) Proceedings before the Federal Court under subsection (3) shall be held in camera on request made to the court by any party to the proceedings.

Vesting on assignment

(5) An assignment to the Minister of National Defence under this Act effectually vests the benefits of the invention and patent in the Minister of National Defence on behalf of Her Majesty, and all covenants and agreements therein contained for keeping the invention secret and otherwise are valid and effectual, notwithstanding any want of valuable consideration, and may be enforced accordingly by the Minister of National Defence.

Person making assignment and person having knowledge thereof

(6) Any person who has made an assignment to the Minister of National Defence under this section, in respect of any covenants and agreements contained in such assignment for keeping the invention secret and otherwise in respect of all matters relating to that invention, and any other person who has knowledge of such assignment and of such covenants and agreements, shall be, for the purposes of the *Security of Information Act*, deemed to be persons having in their possession or control information respecting those matters that has been entrusted to them in confidence by any person holding office under Her Majesty, and the communication of any of that information by the first mentioned persons to any person other than one to whom they are authorized to communicate with, by or on behalf of the Minister of National Defence, is an offence under section 4 of the *Security of Information Act*.

Minister may submit application for patent

(7) Where any agreement for an assignment to the Minister of National Defence under this Act has been made, the Minister of National Defence may submit an application for patent for the invention to the Commissioner, with the request that it be examined for patentability, and if the application is found allowable may, before the grant of any patent thereon, certify to the Commissioner that, in the public interest, the particulars of the invention and of the manner in which it is to be worked are to be kept secret.

Secret application

(8) If the Minister of National Defence so certifies, the application and specification, with the drawing, if any, and any amendment of the application, and any copies of those documents and the drawing and the patent granted thereon shall be placed in a packet sealed by the Commissioner under authority of the Minister of National Defence.

Custody of secret application

(9) The packet described in subsection (8) shall, until the expiration of the term during which a patent for the invention may be in force, be kept sealed by the Commissioner, and shall not be opened except under the authority of an order of the Minister of National Defence.

Delivery of secret application

(10) The packet described in subsection (8) shall be delivered at any time during the continuance of the patent to any person authorized by the Minister of National Defence to receive it, and shall, if returned to the Commissioner, be kept sealed by him.

Delivery to Minister

(11) On the expiration of the term of the patent, the packet described in subsection (8) shall be delivered to the Minister of National Defence.

l'invention en question, et toute autre personne qui est au courant d'une telle cession et de ces engagements et conventions sont, pour l'application de la *Loi sur la protection de l'information*, réputées des personnes ayant en leur possession ou sous leur contrôle des renseignements sur ces matières qui leur ont été commis en toute confiance par une personne détenant un poste qui relève de Sa Majesté. La communication de l'un de ces renseignements par les personnes mentionnées en premier lieu à une personne autre que celle avec laquelle elles sont autorisées à communiquer par le ministre de la Défense nationale ou en son nom, constitue une infraction à l'article 4 de la *Loi sur la protection de l'information*.

Le ministre peut présenter une demande de brevet

(7) Lorsqu'une convention a été conclue pour une telle cession, le ministre de la Défense nationale peut présenter au commissaire une demande de brevet pour l'invention, accompagnée d'une requête pour étude en vue de déterminer si elle est brevetable, et si cette demande est jugée recevable, il peut, avant que soit accordé tout brevet en l'espèce, certifier au commissaire que, dans l'intérêt public, les détails de l'invention et de la manière dont elle sera exploitée doivent être tenus secrets.

Demande secrète

(8) Si le ministre de la Défense nationale le certifie, la demande et le mémoire descriptif, avec le dessin, le cas échéant, ainsi que toute modification de la demande et toutes copies de ces documents et dessin, de même que le brevet accordé en l'espèce, sont placés dans un paquet scellé par le commissaire sous l'autorité du ministre de la Défense nationale.

Garde de la demande secrète

(9) Jusqu'à l'expiration de la période durant laquelle un brevet pour l'invention peut être en vigueur, le paquet est gardé scellé par le commissaire, et il ne peut être ouvert que sous l'autorité d'un arrêté du ministre de la Défense nationale.

Transmission de la demande secrète

(10) Le paquet est remis pendant la durée du brevet à toute personne autorisée par le ministre de la Défense nationale à le recevoir, et, s'il est retourné au commissaire, ce dernier le garde scellé.

Transmission au ministre

(11) À l'expiration de la durée du brevet, le paquet est transmis au ministre de la Défense nationale.

Revocation

(12) No proceeding by petition or otherwise lies to have declared invalid or void a patent granted for an invention in relation to which a certificate has been given by the Minister of National Defence under subsection (7), except by permission of the Minister.

Prohibition of publication and inspection

(13) No copy of any specification or other document or drawing in respect of an invention and patent, by this section required to be placed in a sealed packet, shall in any manner whatever be published or open to the inspection of the public, but, except as otherwise provided in this section, this Act shall apply in respect of the invention and patent.

Waiver by Minister

(14) The Minister of National Defence may at any time waive the benefit of this section with respect to any particular invention, and the specification, documents and drawing relating thereto shall thereafter be kept and dealt with in the regular way.

Rights protected

(15) No claim shall be allowed in respect of any infringement of a patent that occurred in good faith during the time that the patent was kept secret under this section, and any person who, before the publication of the patent, had in good faith done any act that, but for this subsection would have given rise to a claim, is entitled, after the publication, to obtain a licence to manufacture, use and sell the patented invention on such terms as may, in the absence of agreement between the parties, be settled by the Commissioner or by the Federal Court on appeal from the Commissioner.

Communication to Minister

(16) The communication of any invention for any improvement in munitions of war to the Minister of National Defence, or to any person or persons authorized by the Minister of National Defence to investigate the invention or the merits thereof, shall not, nor shall anything done for the purposes of the investigation, be deemed use or publication of the invention so as to prejudice the grant or validity of any patent for the invention.

Order to keep non-assigned application secret

(17) The Governor in Council, if satisfied that an invention relating to any instrument or munition of war, described in any specified application for patent not assigned to the Minister of National Defence, is vital to the defence of Canada and that the publication of a patent therefor should be prevented in order to preserve the safety of the State, may order that the invention and application and all the documents relating thereto shall be treated for all purposes of this section as if the invention had been assigned or agreed to be assigned to the Minister of National Defence.

Rules

(18) The Governor in Council may make rules for the purpose of ensuring secrecy with respect to applications and patents to which this section applies and generally to give effect to the purpose and intent thereof.

R.S., 1985, c. P-4, s. 20; 2001, c. 41, s. 36.

Agreement between Canada and other government

21 Where by any agreement between the Government of Canada and any other government it is provided that the Government of Canada will apply section 20 to inventions disclosed in any application for a patent assigned or agreed to be assigned by the inventor to that other government, and the Commissioner is notified by any minister of the Crown that the agreement extends to an invention in a specified application, the application and all the documents relating thereto shall be dealt with as provided in section 20, except subsections (3) and (4), as if the invention had been assigned or agreed to be assigned to the Minister of National Defence.

R.S., c. P-4, s. 21.

Use of Patents for International Humanitarian Purposes to Address Public Health Problems

Purpose

21.01 The purpose of sections 21.02 to 21.2 is to give effect to Canada's and Jean Chrétien's pledge to Africa by facilitating access to pharmaceutical products to address public health problems afflicting many developing and least-developed countries, especially those resulting from HIV/AIDS, tuberculosis, malaria and other epidemics.

2004, c. 23, s. 1.

Definitions

21.02 The definitions in this section apply in this section and in sections 21.03 to 21.19.

authorization means an authorization granted under subsection 21.04(1), and includes an authorization renewed under subsection 21.12(1). (*autorisation*)

General Council means the General Council of the WTO established by paragraph 2 of Article IV of the Agreement Establishing the World Trade Organization, signed at Marrakesh on April 15, 1994. (*Conseil général*)

General Council Decision means the decision of the General Council of August 30, 2003 respecting Article 31 of the TRIPS Agreement, including the interpretation of that decision in the General Council Chairperson's statement of that date. (*décision du Conseil général*)

patented product means a product the making, constructing, using or selling of which in Canada would infringe a patent in the absence of the consent of the patentee. (*produit breveté*)

pharmaceutical product means any patented product listed in Schedule 1 in, if applicable, the dosage form, the strength and the route of administration specified in that Schedule in relation to the product. (*produit pharmaceutique*)

TRIPS Agreement means the Agreement on Trade-Related Aspects of Intellectual Property Rights, being Annex 1C of the Agreement Establishing the World Trade Organization, signed at Marrakesh on April 15, 1994. (*Accord sur les ADPIC*)

TRIPS Council means the council referred to in the TRIPS Agreement. (*Conseil des ADPIC*)

WTO means the World Trade Organization established by Article I of the Agreement Establishing the World Trade Organization, signed at Marrakesh on April 15, 1994. (*OMC*)

2004, c. 23, s. 1.

Amending Schedules

21.03 (1) The Governor in Council may, by order,

(a) on the recommendation of the Minister and the Minister of Health, amend Schedule 1

(i) by adding the name of any patented product that may be used to address public health problems afflicting many developing and least-developed countries, especially those resulting from HIV/AIDS, tuberculosis, malaria and other epidemics and, if the Governor in Council considers it appropriate to do so, by adding one or more of the following in respect of the patented product, namely, a dosage form, a strength and a route of administration, and

(ii) by removing any entry listed in it;

(b) on the recommendation of the Minister of Foreign Affairs, the Minister for International Trade and the Minister for International Development, amend Schedule 2 by adding the name of any country recognized by the United Nations as being a least-developed country that has,

(i) if it is a WTO Member, provided the TRIPS Council with a notice in writing stating that the country intends to import, in accordance with the General Council Decision, pharmaceutical products, as defined in paragraph 1(a) of that decision, and

(ii) if it is not a WTO Member, provided the Government of Canada with a notice in writing through diplomatic channels stating that the country intends to import pharmaceutical products, as defined in paragraph 1(a) of the General Council Decision, that it agrees that those products will not be used for commercial purposes and that it undertakes to adopt the measures referred to in Article 4 of that decision;

(c) on the recommendation of the Minister of Foreign Affairs, the Minister for International Trade and the Minister for International Development, amend Schedule 3 by adding the name of any WTO Member not listed in Schedule 2 that has provided the TRIPS Council with a notice in writing stating that the WTO Member intends to import, in accordance with the General Council Decision, pharmaceutical products, as defined in paragraph 1(a) of that decision; and

(d) on the recommendation of the Minister of Foreign Affairs, the Minister for International Trade and the Minister for International Development, amend Schedule 4 by adding the name of

(i) any WTO Member not listed in Schedule 2 or 3 that has provided the TRIPS Council with a notice in writing stating that the WTO Member intends to import, in accordance with the General Council Decision, pharmaceutical products, as defined in paragraph 1(a) of that decision, or

(ii) any country that is not a WTO Member and that is named on the Organization for Economic Co-operation and Development's list of countries that are eligible for official development assistance and that has provided the Government of Canada

(ii) par suppression du nom d'un produit breveté ou d'une mention y figurant;

b) sur recommandation du ministre des Affaires étrangères, du ministre du Commerce international et du ministre du Développement international, modifier l'annexe 2, par adjonction du nom de tout pays qui, étant un pays moins avancé selon les Nations Unies, a transmis :

(i) s'il est membre de l'OMC, au Conseil des ADPIC un avis écrit de son intention d'importer, conformément à la décision du Conseil général, des produits pharmaceutiques au sens de l'alinéa 1a) de cette décision,

(ii) s'il n'est pas membre de l'OMC, au gouvernement du Canada, par la voie diplomatique, un avis écrit de son intention d'importer des produits pharmaceutiques au sens de l'alinéa 1a) de la décision du Conseil général, dans lequel il s'engage à ne pas utiliser les produits à des fins commerciales et à prendre les mesures visées à l'article 4 de cette décision;

c) sur recommandation du ministre des Affaires étrangères, du ministre du Commerce international et du ministre du Développement international, modifier l'annexe 3, par adjonction du nom de tout membre de l'OMC ne figurant pas à l'annexe 2 qui a transmis au Conseil des ADPIC un avis écrit de son intention d'importer, conformément à la décision du Conseil général, des produits pharmaceutiques au sens de l'alinéa 1a) de cette décision;

d) sur recommandation du ministre des Affaires étrangères, du ministre du Commerce international et du ministre du Développement international, modifier l'annexe 4, par adjonction :

(i) du nom de tout membre de l'OMC ne figurant pas à l'annexe 2 ou 3 qui a transmis au Conseil des ADPIC un avis écrit de son intention d'importer, conformément à la décision du Conseil général, des produits pharmaceutiques au sens de l'alinéa 1a) de cette décision,

(ii) du nom de tout pays non-membre de l'OMC qui figure sur la liste des pays admissibles à l'aide publique au développement établie par l'Organisation de coopération et de développement économiques, à la condition qu'il ait transmis au gouvernement du Canada, par la voie diplomatique, un avis écrit dans lequel il :

with a notice in writing through diplomatic channels

(A) stating that it is faced with a national emergency or other circumstances of extreme urgency,

(B) specifying the name of the pharmaceutical product, as defined in paragraph 1(a) of the General Council Decision, and the quantity of that product, needed by the country to deal with the emergency or other urgency,

(C) stating that it has no, or insufficient, pharmaceutical capacity to manufacture that product, and

(D) stating that it agrees that that product will not be used for commercial purposes and that it undertakes to adopt the measures referred to in Article 4 of the General Council Decision.

Restriction - Schedule 3

(2) The Governor in Council may not add to Schedule 3 the name of any WTO Member that has notified the TRIPS Council that it will import, in accordance with the General Council Decision, pharmaceutical products, as defined in paragraph 1(a) of that decision, only if faced with a national emergency or other circumstances of extreme urgency.

Removal from Schedules 2 to 4

(3) The Governor in Council may, by order, on the recommendation of the Minister of Foreign Affairs, the Minister for International Trade and the Minister for International Development, amend any of Schedules 2 to 4 to remove the name of any country or WTO Member if

(a) in the case of a country or WTO Member listed in Schedule 2, the country or WTO Member has ceased to be recognized by the United Nations as being a least-developed country or, in the case of a country that is not a WTO Member, the country has permitted any product imported into that country under an authorization to be used for commercial purposes or has failed to adopt the measures referred to in Article 4 of the General Council Decision;

(b) in the case of a WTO Member listed in Schedule 3, the WTO Member has notified the TRIPS Council that it will import, in accordance with the General Council Decision, pharmaceutical products, as defined in paragraph 1(a) of that decision, only if faced with a national emergency or other circumstances of extreme urgency;

(c) in the case of a WTO Member listed in Schedule 4, the WTO Member has revoked any notification it has given to the TRIPS Council that it will import pharmaceutical products, as defined in paragraph 1(a) of the General Council Decision, only if faced with a national emergency or other circumstances of extreme urgency;

(d) in the case of a country listed in Schedule 4 that is not a WTO Member,

(i) the name of the country is no longer on the Organization for Economic Co-operation and Development's list of countries that are eligible for official development assistance,

(ii) the country no longer faces a national emergency or other circumstances of extreme urgency,

(iii) the country has permitted any product imported into that country under an authorization to be used for commercial purposes, or

(iv) the country has failed to adopt the measures referred to in Article 4 of the General Council Decision;

(e) in the case of any country or WTO Member listed in Schedule 3 or 4, the country or WTO Member has become recognized by the United Nations as a least-developed country; and

(f) in the case of any country or WTO Member listed in any of Schedules 2 to 4, the country has notified the Government of Canada, or the WTO Member has notified the TRIPS Council, that it will not import pharmaceutical products, as defined in paragraph 1(a) of the General Council Decision.

Timeliness of orders

(4) An order under this section shall be made in a timely manner.
2004, c. 23, s. 1; 2013, c. 33, s. 196.

Authorization

21.04 (1) Subject to subsection (3), the Commissioner shall, on the application of any person and on the payment of the prescribed fee, authorize the person to make, construct and use a patented invention solely for purposes directly related to the manufacture of the pharmaceutical product named in the application and to sell it for export to a country or WTO Member that is listed in any of Schedules 2 to 4 and that is named in the application.

Contents of application

(2) The application must be in the prescribed form and set out

(a) the name of the pharmaceutical product to be manufactured and sold for export under the authorization;

(b) prescribed information in respect of the version of the pharmaceutical product to be manufactured and sold for export under the authorization;

(c) the maximum quantity of the pharmaceutical product to be manufactured and sold for export under the authorization;

(d) for each patented invention to which the application relates, the name of the patentee of the invention and the number, as recorded in the Patent Office, of the patent issued in respect of that invention;

(e) the name of the country or WTO Member to which the pharmaceutical product is to be exported;

(f) the name of the governmental person or entity, or the person or entity permitted by the government of the importing country, to which the product is to be sold, and prescribed information, if any, concerning that person or entity; and

(g) any other information that may be prescribed.

Conditions for granting of authorization

(3) The Commissioner shall authorize the use of the patented invention only if

(a) the applicant has complied with the prescribed requirements, if any;

(b) the Minister of Health has notified the Commissioner that the version of the pharmaceutical product that is named in the application meets the requirements of the *Food and Drugs Act* and its regulations, including the requirements under those regulations relating to the marking, embossing, labelling and packaging that identify that version of the product as having been manufactured

   (i) in Canada as permitted by the General Council Decision, and

   (ii) in a manner that distinguishes it from the version of the pharmaceutical product sold in Canada by, or with the consent of, the patentee or patentees, as the case may be;

(c) the applicant provides the Commissioner with a solemn or statutory declaration in the prescribed form stating that the applicant had, at least thirty days before filing the application,

(i) sought from the patentee or, if there is more than one, from each of the patentees, by certified or registered mail, a licence to manufacture and sell the pharmaceutical product for export to the country or WTO Member named in the application on reasonable terms and conditions and that such efforts have not been successful, and

(ii) provided the patentee, or each of the patentees, as the case may be, by certified or registered mail, in the written request for a licence, with the information that is in all material respects identical to the information referred to in paragraphs (2)(a) to (g); and

(d) the applicant also provides the Commissioner with

(i) if the application relates to a WTO Member listed in Schedule 2, a certified copy of the notice in writing that the WTO Member has provided to the TRIPS Council specifying the name of the pharmaceutical product, as defined in paragraph 1(a) of the General Council Decision, and the quantity of that product, needed by the WTO Member, and

(A) a solemn or statutory declaration in the prescribed form by the person filing the application stating that the product to which the application relates is the product specified in the notice and that the product is not patented in that WTO Member, or

(B) a solemn or statutory declaration in the prescribed form by the person filing the application stating that the product to which the application relates is the product specified in the notice and a certified copy of the notice in writing that the WTO Member has provided to the TRIPS Council confirming that the WTO Member has, in accordance with Article 31 of the TRIPS Agreement and the provisions of the General Council Decision, granted or intends to grant a compulsory licence to use the invention pertaining to the product,

(ii) if the application relates to a country listed in Schedule 2 that is not a WTO Member, a certified copy of the notice in writing that the country has provided to the Government of Canada through diplomatic channels specifying the name of the pharmaceutical product, as defined in paragraph

c) le demandeur a fourni au commissaire une déclaration solennelle, en la forme réglementaire, selon laquelle, au moins trente jours avant le dépôt de la demande, il a :

(i) tenté d'obtenir une licence du breveté - ou de chacun des brevetés - par courrier certifié ou recommandé en vue de fabriquer et de vendre aux fins d'exportation le produit au pays ou au membre de l'OMC mentionné dans la demande, et ce à des conditions raisonnables et sans succès,

(ii) fourni au breveté - ou à chacun des brevetés - par courrier certifié ou recommandé, dans cette demande de licence, des renseignements qui sont, à tous égards importants, identiques à ceux énumérés aux alinéas (2)a) à g);

d) le demandeur a également fourni au commissaire :

(i) dans le cas d'une demande concernant un membre de l'OMC visé à l'annexe 2, d'une part, une copie certifiée de l'avis écrit transmis au Conseil des ADPIC dans lequel le membre précise le nom et la quantité du produit pharmaceutique, au sens de l'alinéa 1a) de la décision du Conseil général, dont il a besoin et, d'autre part :

(A) soit une déclaration solennelle, en la forme réglementaire, dans laquelle lui-même affirme que le produit mentionné dans sa demande est le produit précisé dans l'avis et n'est pas un produit breveté sur le territoire du membre,

(B) soit, d'une part, une déclaration solennelle, en la forme réglementaire, dans laquelle lui-même affirme que le produit mentionné dans sa demande est le produit précisé dans l'avis et, d'autre part, une copie certifiée de l'avis écrit transmis au Conseil des ADPIC dans lequel le membre confirme qu'il a accordé ou accordera, conformément à l'article 31 de l'Accord sur les ADPIC et aux dispositions de la décision du Conseil général, la licence obligatoire nécessaire à l'utilisation de l'invention relative au produit,

(ii) dans le cas d'une demande concernant un pays visé à l'annexe 2 qui n'est pas membre de l'OMC, d'une part, une copie certifiée de l'avis écrit transmis au gouvernement du Canada, par la voie diplomatique, dans lequel le pays précise le nom et la quantité du produit pharmaceutique, au sens de l'alinéa 1a) de la décision du Conseil général, dont il a besoin, et, d'autre part :

(A) soit une déclaration solennelle, en la forme réglementaire, dans laquelle lui-même affirme

1(a) of the General Council Decision, and the quantity of that product, needed by the country, and

(A) a solemn or statutory declaration in the prescribed form by the person filing the application stating that the product to which the application relates is the product specified in the notice and that the product is not patented in that country, or

(B) a solemn or statutory declaration in the prescribed form by the person filing the application stating that the product to which the application relates is the product specified in the notice and a certified copy of the notice in writing that the country has provided to the Government of Canada through diplomatic channels confirming that the country has granted or intends to grant a compulsory licence to use the invention pertaining to the product,

(iii) if the application relates to a WTO Member listed in Schedule 3, a certified copy of the notice in writing that the WTO Member has provided to the TRIPS Council specifying the name of the pharmaceutical product, as defined in paragraph 1(a) of the General Council Decision, and the quantity of that product, needed by the WTO Member, and stating that the WTO Member has insufficient or no pharmaceutical manufacturing capacity for the production of the product to which the application relates, and

(A) a solemn or statutory declaration in the prescribed form by the person filing the application stating that the product to which the application relates is not patented in that WTO Member, or

(B) a certified copy of the notice in writing that the WTO Member has provided to the TRIPS Council confirming that the WTO Member has, in accordance with Article 31 of the TRIPS Agreement and the provisions of the General Council Decision, granted or intends to grant a compulsory licence to use the invention pertaining to the product,

(iv) if the application relates to a WTO Member listed in Schedule 4, a certified copy of the notice in writing that the WTO Member has provided to the TRIPS Council specifying the name of the pharmaceutical product, as defined in paragraph 1(a) of the General Council Decision, and the quantity of that product, needed by the WTO Member, and stating that the WTO Member is faced with a national emergency or other circumstances of extreme

que le produit mentionné dans sa demande est le produit précisé dans l'avis et n'est pas un produit breveté sur le territoire du pays,

(B) soit, d'une part, une déclaration solennelle, en la forme réglementaire, dans laquelle lui-même affirme que le produit mentionné dans sa demande est le produit précisé dans l'avis et, d'autre part, une copie certifiée de l'avis écrit transmis au gouvernement du Canada, par la voie diplomatique, dans lequel le pays confirme qu'il a accordé ou accordera la licence obligatoire nécessaire à l'utilisation de l'invention relative au produit,

(iii) dans le cas d'une demande concernant un membre de l'OMC visé à l'annexe 3, d'une part, une copie certifiée de l'avis écrit transmis au Conseil des ADPIC dans lequel le membre précise le nom et la quantité du produit pharmaceutique, au sens de l'alinéa 1a) de la décision du Conseil général, dont il a besoin et confirme qu'il n'a pas la capacité de fabrication du produit visé par la demande ou que cette capacité est insuffisante, et, d'autre part :

(A) soit une déclaration solennelle, en la forme réglementaire, dans laquelle lui-même affirme que le produit mentionné dans sa demande n'est pas un produit breveté sur le territoire du membre,

(B) soit une copie certifiée de l'avis écrit transmis au Conseil des ADPIC dans lequel le membre confirme qu'il a accordé ou accordera, conformément à l'article 31 de l'Accord sur les ADPIC et aux dispositions de la décision du Conseil général, la licence obligatoire nécessaire à l'utilisation de l'invention relative au produit,

(iv) dans le cas d'une demande concernant un membre de l'OMC visé à l'annexe 4, d'une part, une copie certifiée de l'avis écrit transmis au Conseil des ADPIC dans lequel le membre précise le nom et la quantité du produit pharmaceutique, au sens de l'alinéa 1a) de la décision du Conseil général, dont il a besoin et confirme qu'il fait face à une situation d'urgence nationale ou à d'autres circonstances d'extrême urgence et qu'il n'a pas la capacité de fabrication du produit visé par la demande ou que cette capacité est insuffisante, et, d'autre part :

(A) soit une déclaration solennelle, en la forme réglementaire, dans laquelle lui-même affirme que le produit mentionné dans sa demande n'est pas un produit breveté sur le territoire du membre,

urgency and that it has insufficient or no pharmaceutical manufacturing capacity for the production of the product to which the application relates, and

(A) a solemn or statutory declaration in the prescribed form by the person filing the application stating that the product to which the application relates is not patented in that WTO Member, or

(B) a certified copy of the notice in writing that the WTO Member has provided to the TRIPS Council confirming that the WTO Member has, in accordance with Article 31 of the TRIPS Agreement and the provisions of the General Council Decision, granted or intends to grant a compulsory licence to use the invention pertaining to the product, or

(v) if the application relates to a country listed in Schedule 4 that is not a WTO Member, a certified copy of the notice in writing that the country has provided to the Government of Canada through diplomatic channels specifying the name of the pharmaceutical product, as defined in paragraph 1(a) of the General Council Decision, and the quantity of that product, needed by the country, and stating that it is faced with a national emergency or other circumstances of extreme urgency, that it has insufficient or no pharmaceutical manufacturing capacity for the production of the product to which the application relates, that it agrees that product will not be used for commercial purposes and that it undertakes to adopt the measures referred to in Article 4 of the General Council Decision, and

(A) a solemn or statutory declaration in the prescribed form by the person filing the application stating that the product to which the application relates is not patented in that country, or

(B) a certified copy of the notice in writing that the country has provided to the Government of Canada through diplomatic channels confirming that the country has granted or intends to grant a compulsory licence to use the invention pertaining to the product.

2004, c. 23, s. 1.

Form and content of authorization

21.05 (1) The authorization must be in the prescribed form and, subject to subsection (2), contain the prescribed information.

Quantity

(2) The quantity of the product authorized to be manufactured by an authorization may not be more than the lesser of

(a) the maximum quantity set out in the application for the authorization, and

(b) the quantity set out in the notice referred to in any of subparagraphs 21.04(3)(d)(i) to (v), whichever is applicable.

2004, c. 23, s. 1.

Disclosure of information on website

21.06 (1) Before exporting a product manufactured under an authorization, the holder of the authorization must establish a website on which is disclosed the prescribed information respecting the name of the product, the name of the country or WTO Member to which it is to be exported, the quantity that is authorized to be manufactured and sold for export and the distinguishing features of the product, and of its label and packaging, as required by regulations made under the *Food and Drugs Act*, as well as information identifying every known party that will be handling the product while it is in transit from Canada to the country or WTO Member to which it is to be exported.

Obligation to maintain

(2) The holder must maintain the website during the entire period during which the authorization is valid.

Links to other websites

(3) The Commissioner shall post and maintain on the website of the Canadian Intellectual Property Office a link to each website required to be maintained by the holder of an authorization under subsection (1).

Posting on the website

(4) The Commissioner shall, within seven days of receipt, post on the website of the Canadian Intellectual Property Office each application for authorization filed under subsection 21.04(1).

2004, c. 23, s. 1.

Export notice

21.07 Before each shipment of any quantity of a product manufactured under an authorization, the holder of the authorization must, within fifteen days before the product is exported, provide to each of the following a notice, by certified or registered mail, specifying the quantity to be exported, as well as every known party that will be handling the product while it is in transit from Canada to the country or WTO Member to which it is to be exported:

(a) the patentee or each of the patentees, as the case may be;

(b) the country or WTO Member named in the authorization; and

(c) the person or entity that purchased the product to which the authorization relates.

2004, c. 23, s. 1.

Royalty

21.08 (1) Subject to subsections (3) and (4), on the occurrence of a prescribed event, the holder of an authorization is required to pay to the patentee or each patentee, as the case may be, a royalty determined in the prescribed manner.

Factors to consider when making regulations

(2) In making regulations for the purposes of subsection (1), the Governor in Council must consider the humanitarian and non-commercial reasons underlying the issuance of authorizations under subsection 21.04(1).

Time for payment

(3) The royalties payable under this section must be paid within the prescribed time.

Federal Court may determine royalty

(4) The Federal Court may, in relation to any authorization, make an order providing for the payment of a royalty that is greater than the royalty that would otherwise be required to be paid under subsection (1).

Application and notice

(5) An order may be made only on the application of the patentee, or one of the patentees, as the case may be, and on notice of the application being given by the applicant to the holder of the authorization.

Contents of order

(6) An order may provide for a royalty of a fixed amount or for a royalty to be determined as specified in the order, and the order may be subject to any terms that the Federal Court considers appropriate.

a) au breveté ou à chacun des brevetés, selon le cas;

b) au pays ou au membre de l'OMC mentionné dans l'autorisation;

c) à la personne ou à l'entité qui a acheté le produit visé par celle-ci.

2004, ch. 23, art. 1.

Redevances

21.08 (1) Sous réserve des paragraphes (3) et (4), le titulaire de l'autorisation est tenu de verser, à la survenance de tout événement visé par règlement, au breveté – ou à chacun des brevetés – la redevance déterminée de la manière réglementaire.

Critère - règlements

(2) Pour la prise de tout règlement au titre du paragraphe (1), le gouverneur en conseil prend en considération le fait que l'octroi d'autorisations au titre du paragraphe 21.04(1) est fondé sur des motifs humanitaires et non commerciaux.

Modalités de temps

(3) Le titulaire est tenu de verser les redevances dans le délai réglementaire.

Fixation de la redevance par la Cour fédérale

(4) La Cour fédérale peut, par ordonnance, prévoir le versement d'une redevance dont le montant dépasse celui établi au titre du paragraphe (1).

Demande et avis

(5) L'ordonnance ne peut être rendue que sur demande présentée par le breveté, ou l'un des brevetés, et qu'après signification de celle-ci au titulaire de l'autorisation.

Contenu de l'ordonnance

(6) L'ordonnance peut soit préciser le montant de la redevance, soit en prévoir les modalités de détermination, et être assortie des conditions que le tribunal juge indiquées.

Conditions for making of order

(7) The Federal Court may make an order only if it is satisfied that the royalty otherwise required to be paid is not adequate remuneration for the use of the invention or inventions to which the authorization relates, taking into account

(a) the humanitarian and non-commercial reasons underlying the issuance of the authorization; and

(b) the economic value of the use of the invention or inventions to the country or WTO Member.

2004, c. 23, s. 1.

Duration

21.09 An authorization granted under subsection 21.04(1) is valid for a period of two years beginning on the day on which the authorization is granted.

2004, c. 23, s. 1.

Use is non-exclusive

21.1 The use of a patented invention under an authorization is non-exclusive.

2004, c. 23, s. 1.

Authorization is non-transferable

21.11 An authorization is non-transferable, other than where the authorization is an asset of a corporation or enterprise and the part of the corporation or enterprise that enjoys the use of the authorization is sold, assigned or otherwise transferred.

2004, c. 23, s. 1.

Renewal

21.12 (1) The Commissioner shall, on the application of the person to whom an authorization was granted and on the payment of the prescribed fee, renew the authorization if the person certifies under oath in the renewal application that the quantities of the pharmaceutical product authorized to be exported were not exported before the authorization ceases to be valid and that the person has complied with the terms of the authorization and the requirements of sections 21.06 to 21.08.

One renewal

(2) An authorization may be renewed only once.

When application must be made

(3) The application for renewal must be made within the 30 days immediately before the authorization ceases to be valid.

Duration

(4) An authorization that is renewed is valid for a period of two years beginning on the day immediately following the day of the expiry of the period referred to in section 21.09 in respect of the authorization.

Prescribed form

(5) Applications for renewal and renewed authorizations issued under subsection (1) must be in the prescribed form.

2004, c. 23, s. 1.

Termination

21.13 Subject to section 21.14, an authorization ceases to be valid on the earliest of

(a) the expiry of the period referred to in section 21.09 in respect of the authorization, or the expiry of the period referred to in subsection 21.12(4) if the authorization has been renewed, as the case may be,

(b) the day on which the Commissioner sends, by registered mail, to the holder of the authorization a copy of a notice sent by the Minister of Health notifying the Commissioner that the Minister of Health is of the opinion that the pharmaceutical product referred to in paragraph 21.04(3)(b) has ceased to meet the requirements of the *Food and Drugs Act* and its regulations,

(c) the day on which the last of the pharmaceutical product authorized by the authorization to be exported is actually exported,

(d) thirty days after the day on which

(i) the name of the pharmaceutical product authorized to be exported by the authorization is removed from Schedule 1, or

(ii) the name of the country or WTO Member to which the pharmaceutical product was, or is to be, exported is removed from Schedule 2, 3 or 4, as the case may be, and not added to any other of those Schedules, and

(e) on any other day that is prescribed.

2004, c. 23, s. 1.

Termination by Federal Court

21.14 On the application of a patentee, and on notice given by the patentee to the person to whom an authorization was granted, the Federal Court may make an order, on any terms that it considers appropriate, terminating the authorization if the patentee establishes that

(a) the application for the authorization or any of the documents provided to the Commissioner in relation to the application contained any material information that is inaccurate;

(b) the holder of the authorization has failed to establish a website as required by section 21.06, has failed to disclose on that website the information required to be disclosed by that section or has failed to maintain the website as required by that section;

(c) the holder of the authorization has failed to provide a notice required to be given under section 21.07;

(d) the holder of the authorization has failed to pay, within the required time, any royalty required to be paid as a result of the authorization;

(e) the holder of the authorization has failed to comply with subsection 21.16(2);

(f) the product exported to the country or WTO Member, as the case may be, under the authorization has been, with the knowledge of the holder of the authorization, re-exported in a manner that is contrary to the General Council Decision;

(g) the product was exported, other than in the normal course of transit, to a country or WTO Member other than the country or WTO Member named in the authorization;

(h) the product was exported in a quantity greater than the quantity authorized to be manufactured; or

(i) if the product was exported to a country that is not a WTO Member, the country has permitted the product to be used for commercial purposes or has failed to adopt the measures referred to in Article 4 of the General Council Decision.

2004, c. 23, s. 1.

Notice to patentee

21.15 The Commissioner shall, without delay, notify the patentee, or each of the patentees, as the case may be, in writing of any authorization granted in respect of the patentee's invention.

2004, c. 23, s. 1.

Obligation to provide copy of agreement

21.16 (1) Within fifteen days after the later of the day on which the authorization was granted and the day on which the agreement for the sale of the product to which the authorization relates was entered into, the holder of an authorization must provide by certified or registered mail, the Commissioner and the patentee, or each patentee, as the case may be, with

(a) a copy of the agreement it has reached with the person or entity referred to in paragraph 21.04(2)(f) for the supply of the product authorized to be manufactured and sold, which agreement must incorporate information that is in all material respects identical to the information referred to in paragraphs 21.04(2)(a), (b), (e) and (f); and

(b) a solemn or statutory declaration in the prescribed form setting out

(i) the total monetary value of the agreement as it relates to the product authorized to be manufactured and sold, expressed in Canadian currency, and

(ii) the number of units of the product to be sold under the terms of the agreement.

Prohibition

(2) The holder of an authorization may not export any product to which the authorization relates until after the holder has complied with subsection (1).

2004, c. 23, s. 1.

Application when agreement is commercial in nature

21.17 (1) If the average price of the product to be manufactured under an authorization is equal to or greater than 25 per cent of the average price in Canada of the equivalent product sold by or with the consent of the patentee, the patentee may, on notice given by the patentee to the person to whom an authorization was granted, apply to the Federal Court for an order under subsection (3) on the grounds that the essence of the agreement under which the product is to be sold is commercial in nature.

Factors for determining whether agreement is commercial in nature

(2) In determining whether the agreement is commercial in nature, the Federal Court must take into account

(a) the need for the holder of the authorization to make a reasonable return sufficient to sustain a continued participation in humanitarian initiatives;

(b) the ordinary levels of profitability, in Canada, of commercial agreements involving pharmaceutical products, as defined in paragraph 1(a) of the General Council Decision; and

a) une copie de l'accord qu'il a conclu avec la personne ou l'entité visée à l'alinéa 21.04(2)f) pour fournir le produit dont la fabrication et la vente sont autorisées, lequel accord inclut des renseignements qui sont, à tous égards importants, identiques à ceux énumérés aux alinéas 21.04(2)a), b), e) et f);

b) une déclaration solennelle, en la forme réglementaire, précisant :

(i) la valeur pécuniaire de l'accord, relativement au produit dont la fabrication et la vente sont autorisées, exprimée en monnaie canadienne,

(ii) le nombre d'unités du produit à vendre aux termes de l'accord.

Interdiction

(2) Le titulaire ne peut exporter le produit visé par l'autorisation tant qu'il ne s'est pas conformé au paragraphe (1).

2004, ch. 23, art. 1.

Demande – accord de nature commerciale

21.17 (1) Dans le cas où le prix moyen du produit à fabriquer au titre de l'autorisation est égal ou supérieur à vingt-cinq pour cent du prix moyen au Canada du produit équivalent vendu par le breveté ou avec son consentement, celui-ci peut, après avis donné au titulaire de l'autorisation, demander à la Cour fédérale de rendre une ordonnance au titre du paragraphe (3) au motif que l'accord aux termes duquel le produit sera vendu est par essence de nature commerciale.

Nature commerciale de l'accord – facteurs

(2) Pour décider de la nature commerciale d'un accord, le tribunal tient compte :

a) du fait que le titulaire de l'autorisation doit obtenir un juste rendement pour pouvoir continuer à participer aux initiatives humanitaires;

b) des niveaux de rentabilité au Canada des accords commerciaux relatifs aux produits pharmaceutiques, au sens de l'alinéa 1a) de la décision du Conseil général;

(c) international trends in prices as reported by the United Nations for the supply of such products for humanitarian purposes.

Order

(3) If the Federal Court determines that the agreement is commercial in nature, it may make an order, on any terms that it considers appropriate,

(a) terminating the authorization; or

(b) requiring the holder to pay, in addition to the royalty otherwise required to be paid, an amount that the Federal Court considers adequate to compensate the patentee for the commercial use of the patent.

Additional order

(4) If the Federal Court makes an order terminating the authorization, the Federal Court may also, if it considers it appropriate to do so, make an order, on any terms that it considers appropriate,

(a) requiring the holder to deliver to the patentee any of the product to which the authorization relates remaining in the holder's possession as though the holder had been determined to have been infringing a patent; or

(b) with the consent of the patentee, requiring the holder to export any of the product to which the authorization relates remaining in the holder's possession to the country or WTO Member named in the authorization.

Restriction

(5) The Federal Court may not make an order under subsection (3) if, under the protection of a confidentiality order made by the Court, the holder of the authorization submits to a Court-supervised audit and that audit establishes that the average price of the product manufactured under the authorization does not exceed an amount equal to the direct supply cost of the product plus 15 per cent of that direct supply cost.

Definitions

(6) The following definitions apply in this section.

average price means

(a) in relation to a product to be manufactured under an authorization, the total monetary value of the agreement under which the product is to be sold, expressed in Canadian currency, divided by the number of units of the product to be sold under the terms of the agreement; and

(b) in relation to an equivalent product sold by or with the consent of the patentee, the average of the prices in Canada of that product as those prices are reported in prescribed publications on the day on which the application for the authorization was filed. (*prix moyen*)

direct supply cost, in relation to a product to be manufactured under an authorization, means the cost of the materials and of the labour, and any other manufacturing costs, directly related to the production of the quantity of the product that is to be manufactured under the authorization. (*coût direct de fourniture*)

unit, in relation to any product, means a single tablet, capsule or other individual dosage form of the product, and if applicable, in a particular strength. (*unité*)

2004, c. 23, s. 1.

Advisory committee

21.18 (1) The Minister and the Minister of Health shall establish, within three years after the day this section comes into force, an advisory committee to advise them on the recommendations that they may make to the Governor in Council respecting the amendment of Schedule 1.

Standing committee

(2) The standing committee of each House of Parliament that normally considers matters related to industry shall assess all candidates for appointment to the advisory committee and make recommendations to the Minister and the Minister of Health on the eligibility and qualifications of those candidates.

2004, c. 23, s. 1; 2005, c. 18, s. 1.

Website for notices to Canada

21.19 The person designated by the Governor in Council for the purpose of this section must maintain a website on which is set out a copy of every notice referred to in subparagraphs 21.04(3)(d)(ii) and (v) that is provided to the Government of Canada through diplomatic channels by a country that is not a WTO Member. The copy must be added to the website as soon as possible after the notice has been provided to the Government of Canada.

2004, c. 23, s. 1.

Review

21.2 (1) A review of sections 21.01 to 21.19 and their application must be completed by the Minister two years after this section comes into force.

Tabling of report

(2) The Minister must cause a report of the results of the review to be laid before each House of Parliament on any of the first fifteen days on which that House is sitting after the report has been completed.

2004, c. 23, s. 1.

Patents Relating to Nuclear Energy

Communication to Canadian Nuclear Safety Commission

22 Any application for a patent for an invention that, in the opinion of the Commissioner, relates to the production, application or use of nuclear energy shall, before it is dealt with by an examiner appointed pursuant to section 6 or is open to inspection by the public under section 10, be communicated by the Commissioner to the Canadian Nuclear Safety Commission.

R.S., 1985, c. P-4, s. 22; R.S., 1985, c. 33 (3rd Supp.), s. 5; 1997, c. 9, s. 111.

General

Patented invention in vessels, aircraft, etc., of any country

23 No patent shall extend to prevent the use of any invention in any ship, vessel, aircraft or land vehicle of any country entering Canada temporarily or accidentally, if the invention is employed exclusively for the needs of the ship, vessel, aircraft or land vehicle, and not so used for the manufacture of any goods to be sold within or exported from Canada.

R.S., c. P-4, s. 23.

24 [Repealed, R.S., 1985, c. 33 (3rd Supp.), s. 6]

Cost of proceedings before the court

25 In all proceedings before any court under this Act, the costs of the Commissioner are in the discretion of the court, but the Commissioner shall not be ordered to pay the costs of any other of the parties.

R.S., c. P-4, s. 25.

Annual report

26 The Commissioner shall, in each year, cause to be prepared and laid before Parliament a report of the proceedings under this Act.

R.S., 1985, c. P-4, s. 26; R.S., 1985, c. 33 (3rd Supp.), s. 7.

Dépôt du rapport

(2) Le ministre fait déposer le rapport devant chaque chambre du Parlement dans les quinze jours de séance de celle-ci suivant l'établissement du rapport.

2004, ch. 23, art. 1.

Brevets liés à l'énergie nucléaire

Communication à la Commission canadienne de sûreté nucléaire

22 Le commissaire est tenu de communiquer à la Commission canadienne de sûreté nucléaire toute demande de brevet qui, selon lui, concerne la production, les applications ou les usages de l'énergie nucléaire avant que ne l'étudie un examinateur nommé conformément à l'article 6 ou qu'elle ne soit accessible sous le régime de l'article 10.

L.R. (1985), ch. P-4, art. 22; L.R. (1985), ch. 33 (3ᵉ suppl.), art. 5; 1997, ch. 9, art. 111.

Dispositions générales

Usage d'une invention brevetée, sur navires, aéronefs, etc. d'un pays

23 Aucun brevet ne peut aller jusqu'à empêcher l'usage d'une invention sur un vaisseau, navire, aéronef ou véhicule terrestre de tout pays, qui entre temporairement ou accidentellement au Canada, pourvu que cette invention serve exclusivement aux besoins du vaisseau, navire, aéronef ou véhicule terrestre, et qu'elle ne soit pas ainsi utilisée à fabriquer des objets destinés à être vendus au Canada ou à en être exportés.

S.R., ch. P-4, art. 23.

24 [Abrogé, L.R. (1985), ch. 33 (3ᵉ suppl.), art. 6]

Frais de procédure devant le tribunal

25 Les frais du commissaire, dans toutes procédures devant un tribunal en vertu de la présente loi, sont à la discrétion du tribunal, mais il ne peut être ordonné au commissaire de payer les frais de toute autre partie.

S.R., ch. P-4, art. 25.

Rapport annuel

26 Le commissaire fait, chaque année, établir et déposer un rapport d'exercice devant le Parlement.

L.R. (1985), ch. P-4, art. 26; L.R. (1985), ch. 33 (3ᵉ suppl.), art. 7.

Publication of list of patents

26.1 (1) The Commissioner shall, at least once in each year, publish a list of all patents issued in the year.

Publication and printing of documents

(2) The Commissioner may publish any document open to the inspection of the public under section 10 and may print or cause to be printed, for distribution or sale, any such document.

R.S., 1985, c. 33 (3rd Supp.), s. 7.

Application for Patents

Commissioner may grant patents

27 (1) The Commissioner shall grant a patent for an invention to the inventor or the inventor's legal representative if an application for the patent in Canada is filed in accordance with this Act and all other requirements for the issuance of a patent under this Act are met.

Application requirements

(2) The prescribed application fee must be paid and the application must be filed in accordance with the regulations by the inventor or the inventor's legal representative and the application must contain a petition and a specification of the invention.

Specification

(3) The specification of an invention must

(a) correctly and fully describe the invention and its operation or use as contemplated by the inventor;

(b) set out clearly the various steps in a process, or the method of constructing, making, compounding or using a machine, manufacture or composition of matter, in such full, clear, concise and exact terms as to enable any person skilled in the art or science to which it pertains, or with which it is most closely connected, to make, construct, compound or use it;

(c) in the case of a machine, explain the principle of the machine and the best mode in which the inventor has contemplated the application of that principle; and

(d) in the case of a process, explain the necessary sequence, if any, of the various steps, so as to distinguish the invention from other inventions.

Claims

(4) The specification must end with a claim or claims defining distinctly and in explicit terms the subject-matter of the invention for which an exclusive privilege or property is claimed.

Alternative definition of subject-matter

(5) For greater certainty, where a claim defines the subject-matter of an invention in the alternative, each alternative is a separate claim for the purposes of sections 2, 28.1 to 28.3 and 78.3.

When application to be completed

(6) Where an application does not completely meet the requirements of subsection (2) on its filing date, the Commissioner shall, by notice to the applicant, require the application to be completed on or before the date specified in the notice.

Specified period

(7) The specified date must be at least three months after the date of the notice and at least twelve months after the filing date of the application.

What may not be patented

(8) No patent shall be granted for any mere scientific principle or abstract theorem.

R.S., 1985, c. P-4, s. 27; R.S., 1985, c. 33 (3rd Supp.), s. 8; 1993, c. 15, s. 31, c. 44, s. 192.

Maintenance fees

27.1 (1) An applicant for a patent shall, to maintain the application in effect, pay to the Commissioner such fees, in respect of such periods, as may be prescribed.

(2) and (3) [Repealed, 1993, c. 15, s. 32]

R.S., 1985, c. 33 (3rd Supp.), s. 9; 1993, c. 15, s. 32.

Filing date

28 (1) The filing date of an application for a patent in Canada is the date on which the Commissioner receives the documents, information and fees prescribed for the purposes of this section or, if they are received on different dates, the last date.

Deemed date of receipt of fees

(2) The Commissioner may, for the purposes of this section, deem prescribed fees to have been received on a date earlier than the date of their receipt if the Commissioner considers it just to do so.

R.S., 1985, c. P-4, s. 28; R.S., 1985, c. 33 (3rd Supp.), s. 10; 1993, c. 15, s. 33.

Revendications

(4) Le mémoire descriptif se termine par une ou plusieurs revendications définissant distinctement et en des termes explicites l'objet de l'invention dont le demandeur revendique la propriété ou le privilège exclusif.

Variantes

(5) Il est entendu que, pour l'application des articles 2, 28.1 à 28.3 et 78.3, si une revendication définit, par variantes, l'objet de l'invention, chacune d'elles constitue une revendication distincte.

Demande incomplète

(6) Si, à la date de dépôt, la demande ne remplit pas les conditions prévues au paragraphe (2), le commissaire doit, par avis, requérir le demandeur de la compléter au plus tard à la date qui y est mentionnée.

Délai

(7) Ce délai est d'au moins trois mois à compter de l'avis et d'au moins douze mois à compter de la date de dépôt de la demande.

Ce qui n'est pas brevetable

(8) Il ne peut être octroyé de brevet pour de simples principes scientifiques ou conceptions théoriques.

L.R. (1985), ch. P-4, art. 27; L.R. (1985), ch. 33 (3ᵉ suppl.), art. 8; 1993, ch. 15, art. 31, ch. 44, art. 192.

Taxes périodiques

27.1 (1) Le demandeur est tenu de payer au commissaire, afin de maintenir sa demande en état, les taxes réglementaires pour chaque période réglementaire.

(2) et (3) [Abrogés, 1993, ch. 15, art. 32]

L.R. (1985), ch. 33 (3ᵉ suppl.), art. 9; 1993, ch. 15, art. 32.

Date de dépôt

28 (1) La date de dépôt d'une demande de brevet est la date à laquelle le commissaire reçoit les documents, renseignements et taxes réglementaires prévus pour l'application du présent article. S'ils sont reçus à des dates différentes, il s'agit de la dernière d'entre elles.

Taxes réglementaires

(2) Pour l'application du paragraphe (1), le commissaire peut, s'il estime que cela est équitable, fixer une date de réception des taxes antérieure à celle à laquelle elles ont été reçues.

L.R. (1985), ch. P-4, art. 28; L.R. (1985), ch. 33 (3ᵉ suppl.), art. 10; 1993, ch. 15, art. 33.

Claim date

28.1 (1) The date of a claim in an application for a patent in Canada (the "pending application") is the filing date of the application, unless

(a) the pending application is filed by

(i) a person who has, or whose agent, legal representative or predecessor in title has, previously regularly filed in or for Canada an application for a patent disclosing the subject-matter defined by the claim, or

(ii) a person who is entitled to protection under the terms of any treaty or convention relating to patents to which Canada is a party and who has, or whose agent, legal representative or predecessor in title has, previously regularly filed in or for any other country that by treaty, convention or law affords similar protection to citizens of Canada an application for a patent disclosing the subject-matter defined by the claim;

(b) the filing date of the pending application is within twelve months after the filing date of the previously regularly filed application; and

(c) the applicant has made a request for priority on the basis of the previously regularly filed application.

Claims based on previously regularly filed applications

(2) In the circumstances described in paragraphs (1)(a) to (c), the claim date is the filing date of the previously regularly filed application.

1993, c. 15, s. 33.

Subject-matter of claim must not be previously disclosed

28.2 (1) The subject-matter defined by a claim in an application for a patent in Canada (the "pending application") must not have been disclosed

(a) more than one year before the filing date by the applicant, or by a person who obtained knowledge, directly or indirectly, from the applicant, in such a manner that the subject-matter became available to the public in Canada or elsewhere;

(b) before the claim date by a person not mentioned in paragraph (a) in such a manner that the subject-matter became available to the public in Canada or elsewhere;

Date de la revendication

28.1 (1) La date de la revendication d'une demande de brevet est la date de dépôt de celle-ci, sauf si :

a) la demande est déposée, selon le cas :

(i) par une personne qui a antérieurement déposé de façon régulière, au Canada ou pour le Canada, ou dont l'agent, le représentant légal ou le prédécesseur en droit l'a fait, une demande de brevet divulguant l'objet que définit la revendication,

(ii) par une personne qui a antérieurement déposé de façon régulière, dans un autre pays ou pour un autre pays, ou dont l'agent, le représentant légal ou le prédécesseur en droit l'a fait, une demande de brevet divulguant l'objet que définit la revendication, dans le cas où ce pays protège les droits de cette personne par traité ou convention, relatif aux brevets, auquel le Canada est partie, et accorde par traité, convention ou loi une protection similaire aux citoyens du Canada;

b) elle est déposée dans les douze mois de la date de dépôt de la demande déposée antérieurement;

c) le demandeur a présenté, à l'égard de sa demande, une demande de priorité fondée sur la demande déposée antérieurement.

Date de dépôt de la demande antérieure

(2) Dans le cas où les alinéas (1)a) à c) s'appliquent, la date de la revendication est la date de dépôt de la demande antérieurement déposée de façon régulière.

1993, ch. 15, art. 33.

Objet non divulgué

28.2 (1) L'objet que définit la revendication d'une demande de brevet ne doit pas :

a) plus d'un an avant la date de dépôt de celle-ci, avoir fait, de la part du demandeur ou d'un tiers ayant obtenu de lui l'information à cet égard de façon directe ou autrement, l'objet d'une communication qui l'a rendu accessible au public au Canada ou ailleurs;

b) avant la date de la revendication, avoir fait, de la part d'une autre personne, l'objet d'une communication qui l'a rendu accessible au public au Canada ou ailleurs;

c) avoir été divulgué dans une demande de brevet qui a été déposée au Canada par une personne autre que le demandeur et dont la date de dépôt est antérieure à

(c) in an application for a patent that is filed in Canada by a person other than the applicant, and has a filing date that is before the claim date; or

(d) in an application (the "co-pending application") for a patent that is filed in Canada by a person other than the applicant and has a filing date that is on or after the claim date if

(i) the co-pending application is filed by

(A) a person who has, or whose agent, legal representative or predecessor in title has, previously regularly filed in or for Canada an application for a patent disclosing the subject-matter defined by the claim, or

(B) a person who is entitled to protection under the terms of any treaty or convention relating to patents to which Canada is a party and who has, or whose agent, legal representative or predecessor in title has, previously regularly filed in or for any other country that by treaty, convention or law affords similar protection to citizens of Canada an application for a patent disclosing the subject-matter defined by the claim,

(ii) the filing date of the previously regularly filed application is before the claim date of the pending application,

(iii) the filing date of the co-pending application is within twelve months after the filing date of the previously regularly filed application, and

(iv) the applicant has, in respect of the co-pending application, made a request for priority on the basis of the previously regularly filed application.

Withdrawal of application

(2) An application mentioned in paragraph (1)(c) or a co-pending application mentioned in paragraph (1)(d) that is withdrawn before it is open to public inspection shall, for the purposes of this section, be considered never to have been filed.

1993, c. 15, s. 33.

Invention must not be obvious

28.3 The subject-matter defined by a claim in an application for a patent in Canada must be subject-matter that would not have been obvious on the claim date to a person skilled in the art or science to which it pertains, having regard to

(a) information disclosed more than one year before the filing date by the applicant, or by a person who obtained knowledge, directly or indirectly, from the applicant in such a manner that the information became available to the public in Canada or elsewhere; and

(b) information disclosed before the claim date by a person not mentioned in paragraph (a) in such a manner that the information became available to the public in Canada or elsewhere.

1993, c. 15, s. 33.

Request for priority

28.4 (1) For the purposes of sections 28.1, 28.2 and 78.3, an applicant for a patent in Canada may request priority in respect of the application on the basis of one or more previously regularly filed applications.

Requirements governing request

(2) The request for priority must be made in accordance with the regulations and the applicant must inform the Commissioner of the filing date, country or office of filing and number of each previously regularly filed application on which the request is based.

Withdrawal of request

(3) An applicant may, in accordance with the regulations, withdraw a request for priority, either entirely or with respect to one or more previously regularly filed applications.

Multiple previously regularly filed applications

(4) Where two or more applications have been previously regularly filed as described in paragraph 28.1(1)(a), subparagraph 28.2(1)(d)(i) or paragraph 78.3(1)(a) or (2)(a), either in the same country or in different countries,

(a) paragraph 28.1(1)(b), subparagraph 28.2(1)(d)(iii) or paragraph 78.3(1)(b) or (2)(b), as the case may be, shall be applied using the earliest filing date of the previously regularly filed applications; and

(b) subsection 28.1(2), subparagraph 28.2(1)(d)(ii) or paragraph 78.3(1)(d) or (2)(d), as the case may be, shall be applied using the earliest filing date of the previously regularly filed applications on the basis of which a request for priority is made.

Withdrawal, etc., of previously regularly filed applications

(5) A previously regularly filed application mentioned in section 28.1 or 28.2 or subsection 78.3(1) or (2) shall, for

ou autrement, de manière telle qu'elle est devenue accessible au public au Canada ou ailleurs;

b) qui a été faite par toute autre personne avant la date de la revendication de manière telle qu'elle est devenue accessible au public au Canada ou ailleurs.

1993, ch. 15, art. 33.

Demande de priorité

28.4 (1) Pour l'application des articles 28.1, 28.2 et 78.3, le demandeur de brevet peut présenter une demande de priorité fondée sur une ou plusieurs demandes de brevet antérieurement déposées de façon régulière.

Conditions

(2) Le demandeur la présente selon les modalités réglementaires; il doit aussi informer le commissaire du nom du pays ou du bureau où a été déposée toute demande de brevet sur laquelle la demande de priorité est fondée, ainsi que de la date de dépôt et du numéro de cette demande de brevet.

Retrait de la demande

(3) Il peut, selon les modalités réglementaires, la retirer à l'égard de la demande déposée antérieurement; dans les cas où la demande de priorité est fondée sur plusieurs demandes, il peut la retirer à l'égard de toutes celles-ci ou d'une ou de plusieurs d'entre elles.

Plusieurs demandes

(4) Dans le cas où plusieurs demandes de brevet ont été déposées antérieurement dans le même pays ou non :

a) la date de dépôt de la première demande est retenue pour l'application de l'alinéa 28.1(1)b), du sous-alinéa 28.2(1)d)(iii) et des alinéas 78.3(1)b) et (2)b), selon le cas;

b) la date de dépôt de la première des demandes sur lesquelles la demande de priorité est fondée est retenue pour l'application du paragraphe 28.1(2), du sous-alinéa 28.2(1)d)(ii) et des alinéas 78.3(1)d) et (2)d), selon le cas.

Retrait de demandes déposées antérieurement

(5) Pour l'application des articles 28.1 et 28.2 et des paragraphes 78.3(1) et (2), une demande de brevet déposée

the purposes of that section or subsection, be considered never to have been filed if

(a) it was filed more than twelve months before the filing date of

(i) the pending application, in the case of section 28.1,

(ii) the co-pending application, in the case of section 28.2,

(iii) the later application, in the case of subsection 78.3(1), or

(iv) the earlier application, in the case of subsection 78.3(2);

(b) before the filing date referred to in paragraph (a), another application

(i) is filed by the person who filed the previously regularly filed application or by the agent, legal representative or predecessor in title of that person,

(ii) is filed in or for the country where the previously regularly filed application was filed, and

(iii) discloses the subject-matter defined by the claim in the application mentioned in paragraph (a); and

(c) on the filing date of the other application mentioned in paragraph (b) or, if there is more than one such application, on the earliest of their filing dates, the previously regularly filed application

(i) has been withdrawn, abandoned or refused without having been opened to public inspection and without leaving any rights outstanding, and

(ii) has not served as a basis for a request for priority in any country, including Canada.

1993, c. 15, s. 33; 2001, c. 34, s. 63.

Non-resident applicants

29 (1) An applicant for a patent who does not appear to reside or carry on business at a specified address in Canada shall, on the filing date of the application, appoint as a representative a person or firm residing or carrying on business at a specified address in Canada.

Nominee deemed representative

(2) Subject to this section, a nominee of an applicant shall be deemed to be the representative for all purposes of this Act, including the service of any proceedings taken

antérieurement est réputée ne pas l'avoir été si les conditions suivantes sont réunies :

a) la demande a été déposée plus de douze mois avant la date de dépôt de la demande à l'égard de laquelle une demande de priorité a été présentée;

b) avant la date de dépôt de la demande à l'égard de laquelle une demande de priorité a été présentée, une autre demande de brevet divulguant l'objet que définit la revendication de celle-ci a été déposée :

(i) par la personne qui a déposé la demande antérieurement déposée, ou par l'agent, le représentant légal ou le prédécesseur en droit de celle-ci,

(ii) dans le pays ou pour le pays où l'a été la demande antérieurement déposée;

c) à la date de dépôt de cette autre demande — ou s'il y en a plusieurs, à la date de dépôt de la première demande —, la demande antérieurement déposée a été retirée, abandonnée ou refusée, sans avoir été accessible pour consultation et sans laisser subsister de droits, et n'a pas été invoquée pour réclamer une priorité au Canada ou ailleurs.

1993, ch. 15, art. 33; 2001, ch. 34, art. 63.

Demandeur non-résident

29 (1) Le demandeur de brevet qui ne semble pas résider ou faire des opérations à une adresse spécifiée au Canada désigne, à la date de dépôt de sa demande, une personne ou une maison d'affaires résidant ou faisant des opérations à une adresse spécifiée au Canada pour le représenter.

Personne désignée censée représenter

(2) Sous réserve des autres dispositions du présent article, cette personne ou maison désignée est réputée, pour toutes les fins de la présente loi, y compris la

under it, of the applicant and of any patentee of a patent issued on his application who does not appear to reside or carry on business at a specified address in Canada, and shall be recorded as such by the Commissioner.

New representatives

(3) An applicant for a patent or a patentee

(a) may, by giving notice to the Commissioner, appoint a new representative in place of the latest recorded representative, or may give notice to the Commissioner of a change in the address of the latest recorded representative; and

(b) shall so appoint a new representative or supply a new and correct address of the latest recorded representative on receipt of a request of the Commissioner stating that the latest recorded representative has died or that a letter addressed to the latest recorded representative at the latest recorded address and sent by ordinary mail has been returned undelivered.

Where no new appointment is made or no new address supplied

(4) Where the Commissioner makes a request under paragraph (3)(b) and no new appointment is made or no new and correct address is supplied by the applicant or patentee within three months, the Federal Court or the Commissioner may dispose of any proceedings under this Act without requiring service on the applicant or patentee of any process in the proceedings.

When fee payable

(5) No fee is payable on the appointment of a new representative or the supply of a new and correct address, unless that appointment or supply follows a request by the Commissioner under subsection (3), in which case the prescribed fee is payable.

R.S., 1985, c. P-4, s. 29; 1993, c. 15, s. 34.

30 [Repealed, 1993, c. 15, s. 35]

Joint Applications

Effect of refusal of a joint inventor to proceed

31 (1) Where an invention is made by two or more inventors and one of them refuses to make application for a patent or his whereabouts cannot be ascertained after diligent inquiry, the other inventors or their legal representatives may make application, and a patent may be granted in the name of the inventors who make the application, on satisfying the Commissioner that the joint inventor has refused to make application or that his whereabouts cannot be ascertained after diligent inquiry.

Powers of Commissioner

(2) In any case where

(a) an applicant has agreed in writing to assign a patent, when granted, to another person or to a joint applicant and refuses to proceed with the application, or

(b) disputes arise between joint applicants with respect to proceeding with an application,

the Commissioner, on proof of the agreement to his satisfaction, or if satisfied that one or more of the joint applicants ought to be allowed to proceed alone, may allow that other person or joint applicant to proceed with the application, and may grant a patent to him in such manner that all persons interested are entitled to be heard before the Commissioner after such notice as he may deem requisite and sufficient.

Procedure when one joint applicant retires

(3) Where an application is filed by joint applicants and it subsequently appears that one or more of them has had no part in the invention, the prosecution of the application may be carried on by the remaining applicant or applicants on satisfying the Commissioner by affidavit that the remaining applicant or applicants is or are the sole inventor or inventors.

Joining applicants

(4) Where an application is filed by one or more applicants and it subsequently appears that one or more further applicants should have been joined, the further applicant or applicants may be joined on satisfying the Commissioner that he or they should be so joined, and that the omission of the further applicant or applicants had been by inadvertence or mistake and was not for the purpose of delay.

To whom granted

(5) Subject to this section, in cases of joint applications, the patent shall be granted in the names of all the applicants.

Appeal

(6) An appeal lies to the Federal Court from the decision of the Commissioner under this section.

R.S., c. P-4, s. 33; R.S., c. 10(2nd Supp.), s. 64.

convaincu que l'inventeur conjoint a refusé de soumettre une demande ou que le lieu où il se trouve ne peut être déterminé après une enquête diligente.

Pouvoirs du commissaire

(2) Lorsque, selon le cas :

a) un demandeur a consenti par écrit à céder un brevet, une fois concédé, à une autre personne ou à un codemandeur, et refuse de poursuivre la demande;

b) un différend survient entre des codemandeurs quant à la poursuite d'une demande,

le commissaire peut, si cette convention est établie à sa satisfaction, ou s'il est convaincu qu'il devrait être permis à un ou plusieurs de ces codemandeurs de procéder isolément, permettre à cette autre personne ou à ce codemandeur de poursuivre la demande, et il peut lui accorder un brevet, de telle manière cependant que toutes les personnes intéressées aient droit d'être entendues devant le commissaire, après l'avis qu'il juge nécessaire et suffisant.

Procédure quand un codemandeur se retire

(3) Lorsqu'une demande est déposée par des codemandeurs et qu'il apparaît par la suite que l'un ou plusieurs d'entre eux n'ont pas participé à l'invention, la poursuite de cette demande peut être conduite par le ou les demandeurs qui restent, à la condition de démontrer par affidavit au commissaire que le ou les derniers demandeurs sont les seuls inventeurs.

Codemandeurs

(4) Lorsque la demande est déposée par un ou plusieurs demandeurs et qu'il apparaît par la suite qu'un autre ou plusieurs autres demandeurs auraient dû se joindre à la demande, cet autre ou ces autres demandeurs peuvent se joindre à la demande, à la condition de démontrer au commissaire qu'ils doivent y être joints, et que leur omission s'est produite par inadvertance ou par erreur, et non pas dans le dessein de causer un délai.

Brevet accordé à tous

(5) Sous réserve des autres dispositions du présent article, dans le cas de demandes collectives, le brevet est accordé nommément à tous les demandeurs.

Appel

(6) Appel de la décision rendue par le commissaire en vertu du présent article peut être interjeté à la Cour fédérale.

S.R., ch. P-4, art. 33; S.R., ch. 10(2ᵉ suppl.), art. 64.

Improvements

Improvements

32 Any person who has invented any improvement on any patented invention may obtain a patent for the improvement, but he does not thereby obtain the right of making, vending or using the original invention, nor does the patent for the original invention confer the right of making, vending or using the patented improvement.

R.S., c. P-4, s. 34.

33 and 34 [Repealed, 1993, c. 15, s. 36]

Filing of Prior Art

Filing

34.1 (1) Any person may file with the Commissioner prior art, consisting of patents, applications for patents open to public inspection and printed publications, that the person believes has a bearing on the patentability of any claim in an application for a patent.

Pertinency

(2) A person who files prior art with the Commissioner under subsection (1) shall explain the pertinency of the prior art.

R.S., 1985, c. 33 (3rd Supp.), s. 11; 1993, c. 15, s. 37.

Examination

Request for examination

35 (1) The Commissioner shall, on the request of any person made in such manner as may be prescribed and on payment of a prescribed fee, cause an application for a patent to be examined by competent examiners to be employed in the Patent Office for that purpose.

Required examination

(2) The Commissioner may by notice require an applicant for a patent to make a request for examination pursuant to subsection (1) or to pay the prescribed fee within the time specified in the notice, but the specified time may not exceed the time provided by the regulations for making the request and paying the fee.

(3) and (4) [Repealed, 1993, c. 15, s. 38]

R.S., 1985, c. P-4, s. 35; R.S., 1985, c. 33 (3rd Supp.), s. 12; 1993, c. 15, s. 38.

Divisional Applications

Patent for one invention only

36 (1) A patent shall be granted for one invention only but in an action or other proceeding a patent shall not be deemed to be invalid by reason only that it has been granted for more than one invention.

Limitation of claims by applicant

(2) Where an application (the "original application") describes more than one invention, the applicant may limit the claims to one invention only, and any other invention disclosed may be made the subject of a divisional application, if the divisional application is filed before the issue of a patent on the original application.

Limitation of claims on direction of Commissioner

(2.1) Where an application (the "original application") describes and claims more than one invention, the applicant shall, on the direction of the Commissioner, limit the claims to one invention only, and any other invention disclosed may be made the subject of a divisional application, if the divisional application is filed before the issue of a patent on the original application.

Original application abandoned

(3) If an original application mentioned in subsection (2) or (2.1) becomes abandoned, the time for filing a divisional application terminates with the expiration of the time for reinstating the original application under this Act.

Separate applications

(4) A divisional application shall be deemed to be a separate and distinct application under this Act, to which its provisions apply as fully as may be, and separate fees shall be paid on the divisional application and it shall have the same filing date as the original application.

R.S., 1985, c. P-4, s. 36; 1993, c. 15, s. 39.

Drawings, Models and Biological Materials

Drawings

37 (1) In the case of a machine, or in any other case in which an invention admits of illustration by means of drawings, the applicant shall, as part of the application, furnish drawings of the invention that clearly show all parts of the invention.

Particulars

(2) Each drawing must include references corresponding with the specification, and the Commissioner may require further drawings or dispense with any of them as the Commissioner sees fit.

R.S., 1985, c. P-4, s. 37; 1993, c. 15, s. 40.

Models and specimens

38 (1) In all cases in which an invention admits of representation by model, the applicant, if required by the Commissioner, shall furnish a model of convenient size exhibiting its several parts in due proportion, and when an invention is a composition of matter, the applicant, if required by the Commissioner, shall furnish specimens of the ingredients, and of the composition, sufficient in quantity for the purpose of experiment.

Dangerous substances

(2) If the ingredients or composition referred to in subsection (1) are of an explosive or dangerous character, they shall be furnished with such precautions as are specified in the requisition therefor.

R.S., 1985, c. P-4, s. 38; R.S., 1985, c. 33 (3rd Supp.), s. 13.

Biological material may be deposited

38.1 (1) Where a specification refers to a deposit of biological material and the deposit is in accordance with the regulations, the deposit shall be considered part of the specification and, to the extent that subsection 27(3) cannot otherwise reasonably be complied with, the deposit shall be taken into consideration in determining whether the specification complies with that subsection.

Deposit not required

(2) For greater certainty, a reference to a deposit of biological material in a specification does not create a presumption that the deposit is required for the purpose of complying with subsection 27(3).

1993, c. 15, s. 41.

Amendments to Specifications and Drawings

Amendments to specifications and drawings

38.2 (1) Subject to subsections (2) and (3) and the regulations, the specification and any drawings furnished as part of an application for a patent in Canada may be amended before the patent is issued.

Restriction on amendments to specifications

(2) The specification may not be amended to describe matter not reasonably to be inferred from the specification or drawings as originally filed, except in so far as it is admitted in the specification that the matter is prior art with respect to the application.

Restriction on amendments to drawings

(3) Drawings may not be amended to add matter not reasonably to be inferred from the specification or drawings as originally filed, except in so far as it is admitted in the specification that the matter is prior art with respect to the application.

1993, c. 15, s. 41.

39 to 39.26 [Repealed, 1993, c. 2, s. 3]

Refusal of Patents

Refusal by Commissioner

40 Whenever the Commissioner is satisfied that an applicant is not by law entitled to be granted a patent, he shall refuse the application and, by registered letter addressed to the applicant or his registered agent, notify the applicant of the refusal and of the ground or reason therefor.

R.S., c. P-4, s. 42.

Appeal to Federal Court

41 Every person who has failed to obtain a patent by reason of a refusal of the Commissioner to grant it may, at any time within six months after notice as provided for in section 40 has been mailed, appeal from the decision of the Commissioner to the Federal Court and that Court has exclusive jurisdiction to hear and determine the appeal.

R.S., 1985, c. P-4, s. 41; R.S., 1985, c. 33 (3rd Supp.), s. 16.

Grant of Patents

Contents of patent

42 Every patent granted under this Act shall contain the title or name of the invention, with a reference to the specification, and shall, subject to this Act, grant to the patentee and the patentee's legal representatives for the term of the patent, from the granting of the patent, the exclusive right, privilege and liberty of making, constructing and using the invention and selling it to others to be used, subject to adjudication in respect thereof before any court of competent jurisdiction.

R.S., 1985, c. P-4, s. 42; R.S., 1985, c. 33 (3rd Supp.), s. 16.

Limite

(2) Le mémoire descriptif ne peut être modifié pour décrire des éléments qui ne peuvent raisonnablement s'inférer de celui-ci ou des dessins faisant partie de la demande, sauf dans la mesure où il est mentionné dans le mémoire qu'il s'agit d'une invention ou découverte antérieure.

Idem

(3) Les dessins ne peuvent être modifiés pour y ajouter des éléments qui ne peuvent raisonnablement s'inférer de ceux-ci ou du mémoire descriptif faisant partie de la demande, sauf dans la mesure où il est mentionné dans le mémoire qu'il s'agit d'une invention ou découverte antérieure.

1993, ch. 15, art. 41.

39 à 39.26 [Abrogés, 1993, ch. 2, art. 3]

Rejet des demandes de brevets

Le commissaire peut refuser le brevet

40 Chaque fois que le commissaire s'est assuré que le demandeur n'est pas fondé en droit à obtenir la concession d'un brevet, il rejette la demande et, par courrier recommandé adressé au demandeur ou à son agent enregistré, notifie à ce demandeur le rejet de la demande, ainsi que les motifs ou raisons du rejet.

S.R., ch. P-4, art. 42.

Appel à la Cour fédérale

41 Dans les six mois suivant la mise à la poste de l'avis, celui qui n'a pas réussi à obtenir un brevet en raison du refus ou de l'opposition du commissaire peut interjeter appel de la décision du commissaire à la Cour fédérale qui, à l'exclusion de toute autre juridiction, peut s'en saisir et en décider.

L.R. (1985), ch. P-4, art. 41; L.R. (1985), ch. 33 (3ᵉ suppl.), art. 16.

Octroi des brevets

Contenu du brevet

42 Tout brevet accordé en vertu de la présente loi contient le titre ou le nom de l'invention avec renvoi au mémoire descriptif et accorde, sous réserve des autres dispositions de la présente loi, au breveté et à ses représentants légaux, pour la durée du brevet à compter de la date où il a été accordé, le droit, la faculté et le privilège exclusif de fabriquer, construire, exploiter et vendre à d'autres, pour qu'ils l'exploitent, l'objet de l'invention, sauf jugement en l'espèce par un tribunal compétent.

L.R. (1985), ch. P-4, art. 42; L.R. (1985), ch. 33 (3ᵉ suppl.), art. 16.

Form and Term of Patents

Form and duration of patents

43 (1) Subject to section 46, every patent granted under this Act shall be issued under the seal of the Patent Office, and shall bear on its face the filing date of the application for the patent, the date on which the application became open to public inspection under section 10, the date on which the patent is granted and issued and any prescribed information.

Validity of patent

(2) After the patent is issued, it shall, in the absence of any evidence to the contrary, be valid and avail the patentee and the legal representatives of the patentee for the term mentioned in section 44 or 45, whichever is applicable.

R.S., 1985, c. P-4, s. 43; R.S., 1985, c. 33 (3rd Supp.), s. 16; 1993, c. 15, s. 42.

Term of patents based on applications filed on or after October 1, 1989

44 Subject to section 46, where an application for a patent is filed under this Act on or after October 1, 1989, the term limited for the duration of the patent is twenty years from the filing date.

R.S., 1985, c. P-4, s. 44; R.S., 1985, c. 33 (3rd Supp.), s. 16; 1993, c. 15, s. 42.

Term of patents based on applications filed before October 1, 1989

45 (1) Subject to section 46, where an application for a patent is filed under this Act before October 1, 1989, the term limited for the duration of the patent is seventeen years from the date on which the patent is issued.

Term from date of issue or filing

(2) Where the term limited for the duration of a patent referred to in subsection (1) had not expired before the day on which this section came into force, the term is seventeen years from the date on which the patent is issued or twenty years from the filing date, whichever term expires later.

R.S., 1985, c. P-4, s. 45; R.S., 1985, c. 33 (3rd Supp.), s. 16; 1993, c. 15, s. 42; 2001, c. 10, s. 1.

Maintenance fees

46 (1) A patentee of a patent issued by the Patent Office under this Act after the coming into force of this section shall, to maintain the rights accorded by the patent, pay to the Commissioner such fees, in respect of such periods, as may be prescribed.

Forme et durée des brevets

Délivrance

43 (1) Sous réserve de l'article 46, le brevet accordé sous le régime de la présente loi est délivré sous le sceau du Bureau des brevets. Il mentionne la date de dépôt de la demande, celle à laquelle elle est devenue accessible au public sous le régime de l'article 10, celle à laquelle il a été accordé et délivré ainsi que tout renseignement réglementaire.

Validité

(2) Une fois délivré, le brevet est, sauf preuve contraire, valide et acquis au breveté ou à ses représentants légaux pour la période mentionnée aux articles 44 ou 45.

L.R. (1985), ch. P-4, art. 43; L.R. (1985), ch. 33 (3ᵉ suppl.), art. 16; 1993, ch. 15, art. 42.

Durée du brevet

44 Sous réserve de l'article 46, la durée du brevet délivré sur une demande déposée le 1ᵉʳ octobre 1989 ou par la suite est limitée à vingt ans à compter de la date de dépôt de cette demande.

L.R. (1985), ch. P-4, art. 44; L.R. (1985), ch. 33 (3ᵉ suppl.), art. 16; 1993, ch. 15, art. 42.

Durée de dix-sept ans

45 (1) Sous réserve de l'article 46, la durée du brevet délivré au titre d'une demande déposée avant le 1ᵉʳ octobre 1989 est limitée à dix-sept ans à compter de la date à laquelle il est délivré.

La date d'expiration la plus tardive s'applique

(2) Si le brevet visé au paragraphe (1) n'est pas périmé à la date de l'entrée en vigueur du présent article, sa durée est limitée à dix-sept ans à compter de la date à laquelle il a été délivré ou à vingt ans à compter de la date de dépôt de la demande, la date d'expiration la plus tardive prévalant.

L.R. (1985), ch. P-4, art. 45; L.R. (1985), ch. 33 (3ᵉ suppl.), art. 16; 1993, ch. 15, art. 42; 2001, ch. 10, art. 1.

Taxes périodiques

46 (1) Le titulaire d'un brevet délivré par le Bureau des brevets conformément à la présente loi après l'entrée en vigueur du présent article est tenu de payer au commissaire, afin de maintenir les droits conférés par le brevet en état, les taxes réglementaires pour chaque période réglementaire.

Lapse of term if maintenance fees not paid

(2) Where the fees payable under subsection (1) are not paid within the time provided by the regulations, the term limited for the duration of the patent shall be deemed to have expired at the end of that time.

R.S., 1985, c. P-4, s. 46; R.S., 1985, c. 33 (3rd Supp.), s. 16; 1993, c. 15, s. 43.

Reissue of Patents

Issue of new or amended patents

47 (1) Whenever any patent is deemed defective or inoperative by reason of insufficient description and specification, or by reason of the patentee's claiming more or less than he had a right to claim as new, but at the same time it appears that the error arose from inadvertence, accident or mistake, without any fraudulent or deceptive intention, the Commissioner may, on the surrender of the patent within four years from its date and the payment of a further prescribed fee, cause a new patent, in accordance with an amended description and specification made by the patentee, to be issued to him for the same invention for the then unexpired term for which the original patent was granted.

Effect of new patent

(2) The surrender referred to in subsection (1) takes effect only on the issue of the new patent, and the new patent and the amended description and specification have the same effect in law, on the trial of any action thereafter commenced for any cause subsequently accruing, as if the amended description and specification had been originally filed in their corrected form before the issue of the original patent, but, in so far as the claims of the original and reissued patents are identical, the surrender does not affect any action pending at the time of reissue or abate any cause of action then existing, and the reissued patent to the extent that its claims are identical with the original patent constitutes a continuation thereof and has effect continuously from the date of the original patent.

Separate patents for separate parts

(3) The Commissioner may entertain separate applications and cause patents to be issued for distinct and separate parts of the invention patented, on payment of the fee for a reissue for each of the reissued patents.

R.S., c. P-4, s. 50.

Disclaimers

Patentee may disclaim anything included in patent by mistake

48 (1) Whenever, by any mistake, accident or inadvertence, and without any wilful intent to defraud or mislead the public, a patentee has

(a) made a specification too broad, claiming more than that of which the patentee or the person through whom the patentee claims was the inventor, or

(b) in the specification, claimed that the patentee or the person through whom the patentee claims was the inventor of any material or substantial part of the invention patented of which the patentee was not the inventor, and to which the patentee had no lawful right,

the patentee may, on payment of a prescribed fee, make a disclaimer of such parts as the patentee does not claim to hold by virtue of the patent or the assignment thereof.

Form and attestation of disclaimer

(2) A disclaimer shall be filed in the prescribed form and manner.

(3) [Repealed, 1993, c. 15, s. 44]

Pending suits not affected

(4) No disclaimer affects any action pending at the time when it is made, unless there is unreasonable neglect or delay in making it.

Death of patentee

(5) In case of the death of an original patentee or of his having assigned the patent, a like right to disclaim vests in his legal representatives, any of whom may exercise it.

Effect of disclaimer

(6) A patent shall, after disclaimer as provided in this section, be deemed to be valid for such material and substantial part of the invention, definitely distinguished from other parts thereof claimed without right, as is not disclaimed and is truly the invention of the disclaimant, and the disclaimant is entitled to maintain an action or suit in respect of that part accordingly.

R.S., 1985, c. P-4, s. 48; R.S., 1985, c. 33 (3rd Supp.), s. 17; 1993, c. 15, s. 44.

Renonciations

Cas de renonciation

48 (1) Le breveté peut, en acquittant la taxe réglementaire, renoncer à tel des éléments qu'il ne prétend pas retenir au titre du brevet, ou d'une cession de celui-ci, si, par erreur, accident ou inadvertance, et sans intention de frauder ou tromper le public, dans l'un ou l'autre des cas suivants :

a) il a donné trop d'étendue à son mémoire descriptif, en revendiquant plus que la chose dont lui-même, ou son mandataire, est l'inventeur;

b) il s'est représenté dans le mémoire descriptif, ou a représenté son mandataire, comme étant l'inventeur d'un élément matériel ou substantiel de l'invention brevetée, alors qu'il n'en était pas l'inventeur et qu'il n'y avait aucun droit.

Forme et attestation de la renonciation

(2) L'acte de renonciation est déposé selon les modalités réglementaires, notamment de forme.

(3) [Abrogé, 1993, ch. 15, art. 44]

Sans effet sur les actions pendantes

(4) Dans toute action pendante au moment où elle est faite, aucune renonciation n'a d'effet, sauf à l'égard de la négligence ou du retard inexcusable à la faire.

Décès du breveté

(5) Si le breveté original meurt, ou s'il cède son brevet, la faculté qu'il avait de faire une renonciation passe à ses représentants légaux, et chacun d'eux peut exercer cette faculté.

Effet de la renonciation

(6) Après la renonciation, le brevet est considéré comme valide quant à tel élément matériel et substantiel de l'invention, nettement distinct des autres éléments de l'invention qui avaient été indûment revendiqués, auquel il n'a pas été renoncé et qui constitue véritablement l'invention de l'auteur de la renonciation, et celui-ci est admis à soutenir en conséquence une action ou poursuite à l'égard de cet élément.

L.R. (1985), ch. P-4, art. 48; L.R. (1985), ch. 33 (3ᵉ suppl.), art. 17; 1993, ch. 15, art. 44.

Re-examination

Request for re-examination

48.1 (1) Any person may request a re-examination of any claim of a patent by filing with the Commissioner prior art, consisting of patents, applications for patents open to public inspection and printed publications, and by paying a prescribed fee.

Pertinency of request

(2) A request for re-examination under subsection (1) shall set forth the pertinency of the prior art and the manner of applying the prior art to the claim for which re-examination is requested.

Notice to patentee

(3) Forthwith after receipt of a request for re-examination under subsection (1), the Commissioner shall send a copy of the request to the patentee of the patent in respect of which the request is made, unless the patentee is the person who made the request.

R.S., 1985, c. 33 (3rd Supp.), s. 18; 1993, c. 15, s. 45.

Establishment of re-examination board

48.2 (1) Forthwith after receipt of a request for re-examination under subsection 48.1(1), the Commissioner shall establish a re-examination board consisting of not fewer than three persons, at least two of whom shall be employees of the Patent Office, to which the request shall be referred for determination.

Determination to be made by board

(2) A re-examination board shall, within three months following its establishment, determine whether a substantial new question of patentability affecting any claim of the patent concerned is raised by the request for re-examination.

Notice

(3) Where a re-examination board has determined that a request for re-examination does not raise a substantial new question affecting the patentability of a claim of the patent concerned, the board shall so notify the person who filed the request and the decision of the board is final for all purposes and is not subject to appeal or to review by any court.

Idem

(4) Where a re-examination board has determined that a request for re-examination raises a substantial new question affecting the patentability of a claim of the patent concerned, the board shall notify the patentee of the determination and the reasons therefor.

Filing of reply

(5) A patentee who receives notice under subsection (4) may, within three months of the date of the notice, submit to the re-examination board a reply to the notice setting out submissions on the question of the patentability of the claim of the patent in respect of which the notice was given.

R.S., 1985, c. 33 (3rd Supp.), s. 18; 1993, c. 15, s. 46(F).

Re-examination proceeding

48.3 (1) On receipt of a reply under subsection 48.2(5) or in the absence of any reply within three months after notice is given under subsection 48.2(4), a re-examination board shall forthwith cause a re-examination to be made of the claim of the patent in respect of which the request for re-examination was submitted.

Patentee may submit amendments

(2) In any re-examination proceeding under subsection (1), the patentee may propose any amendment to the patent or any new claims in relation thereto but no proposed amendment or new claim enlarging the scope of a claim of the patent shall be permitted.

Time limitation

(3) A re-examination proceeding in respect of a claim of a patent shall be completed within twelve months of the commencement of the proceedings under subsection (1).

R.S., 1985, c. 33 (3rd Supp.), s. 18.

Certificate of board

48.4 (1) On conclusion of a re-examination proceeding in respect of a claim of a patent, the re-examination board shall issue a certificate

(a) cancelling any claim of the patent determined to be unpatentable;

(b) confirming any claim of the patent determined to be patentable; or

(c) incorporating in the patent any proposed amended or new claim determined to be patentable.

Certificate attached to patent

(2) A certificate issued in respect of a patent under subsection (1) shall be attached to the patent and made part thereof by reference, and a copy of the certificate shall be sent by registered mail to the patentee.

Effect of certificate

(3) For the purposes of this Act, where a certificate issued in respect of a patent under subsection (1)

Réponse

(5) Dans les trois mois suivant la date de l'avis, le titulaire en cause peut expédier au conseil une réponse exposant ses observations sur la brevetabilité des revendications du brevet visé par l'avis.

L.R. (1985), ch. 33 (3ᵉ suppl.), art. 18; 1993, ch. 15, art. 46(F).

Procédure de réexamen

48.3 (1) Sur réception de la réponse ou au plus tard trois mois après l'avis mentionné au paragraphe 48.2(4), le conseil se saisit du réexamen des revendications du brevet en cause.

Dépôt de modifications

(2) Le titulaire peut proposer des modifications au brevet ou toute nouvelle revendication à cet égard qui n'ont pas pour effet d'élargir la portée des revendications du brevet original.

Durée

(3) Le réexamen doit être terminé dans les douze mois suivant le début de la procédure.

L.R. (1985), ch. 33 (3ᵉ suppl.), art. 18.

Constat

48.4 (1) À l'issue du réexamen, le conseil délivre un constat portant rejet ou confirmation des revendications du brevet attaqué ou, le cas échéant, versant au brevet toute modification ou nouvelle revendication jugée brevetable.

Annexe

(2) Le constat est annexé au brevet, dont il fait partie intégrante. Un double en est expédié, par courrier recommandé, au titulaire du brevet.

Effet du constat

(3) Pour l'application de la présente loi, lorsqu'un constat :

(a) cancels any claim but not all claims of the patent, the patent shall be deemed to have been issued, from the date of grant, in the corrected form;

(b) cancels all claims of the patent, the patent shall be deemed never to have been issued; or

(c) amends any claim of the patent or incorporates a new claim in the patent, the amended claim or new claim shall be effective, from the date of the certificate, for the unexpired term of the patent.

Appeals

(4) Subsection (3) does not apply until the time for taking an appeal has expired under subsection 48.5(2) and, if an appeal is taken, subsection (3) applies only to the extent provided in the final judgment on the appeal.

R.S., 1985, c. 33 (3rd Supp.), s. 18; 1993, c. 15, s. 47.

Appeals

48.5 (1) Any decision of a re-examination board set out in a certificate issued under subsection 48.4(1) is subject to appeal by the patentee to the Federal Court.

Limitation

(2) No appeal may be taken under subsection (1) after three months from the date a copy of the certificate is sent by registered mail to the patentee.

R.S., 1985, c. 33 (3rd Supp.), s. 18.

Assignments and Devolutions

Assignee or personal representatives

49 (1) A patent may be granted to any person to whom an inventor, entitled under this Act to obtain a patent, has assigned in writing or bequeathed by his last will his right to obtain it, and, in the absence of an assignment or bequest, the patent may be granted to the personal representatives of the estate of the deceased inventor.

Assignees may object

(2) Where an applicant for a patent has, after filing the application, assigned his right to obtain the patent, or where the applicant has either before or after filing the application assigned in writing the whole or part of his property or interest in the invention, the assignee may register the assignment in the Patent Office in such manner as may be determined by the Commissioner, and no application for a patent may be withdrawn without the consent in writing of every such registered assignee.

Attestation

(3) No assignment shall be registered in the Patent Office unless it is accompanied by the affidavit of a subscribing witness or established by other proof to the satisfaction of the Commissioner that the assignment has been signed and executed by the assignor.

R.S., 1985, c. P-4, s. 49; R.S., 1985, c. 33 (3rd Supp.), s. 19.

Patents to be assignable

50 (1) Every patent issued for an invention is assignable in law, either as to the whole interest or as to any part thereof, by an instrument in writing.

Registration

(2) Every assignment of a patent, and every grant and conveyance of any exclusive right to make and use and to grant to others the right to make and use the invention patented, within and throughout Canada or any part thereof, shall be registered in the Patent Office in the manner determined by the Commissioner.

Attestation

(3) No assignment, grant or conveyance shall be registered in the Patent Office unless it is accompanied by the affidavit of a subscribing witness or established by other proof to the satisfaction of the Commissioner that the assignment, grant or conveyance has been signed and executed by the assignor and by every other party thereto.

R.S., 1985, c. P-4, s. 50; R.S., 1985, c. 33 (3rd Supp.), s. 20.

When assignment void

51 Every assignment affecting a patent for invention, whether it is one referred to in section 49 or 50, is void against any subsequent assignee, unless the assignment is registered as prescribed by those sections, before the registration of the instrument under which the subsequent assignee claims.

R.S., c. P-4, s. 53.

Jurisdiction of Federal Court

52 The Federal Court has jurisdiction, on the application of the Commissioner or of any person interested, to order that any entry in the records of the Patent Office relating to the title to a patent be varied or expunged.

R.S., c. P-4, s. 54; R.S., c. 10(2nd Supp.), s. 64.

Legal Proceedings in Respect of Patents

Void in certain cases, or valid only for parts

53 (1) A patent is void if any material allegation in the petition of the applicant in respect of the patent is untrue, or if the specification and drawings contain more or less than is necessary for obtaining the end for which they purport to be made, and the omission or addition is wilfully made for the purpose of misleading.

Exception

(2) Where it appears to a court that the omission or addition referred to in subsection (1) was an involuntary error and it is proved that the patentee is entitled to the remainder of his patent, the court shall render a judgment in accordance with the facts, and shall determine the costs, and the patent shall be held valid for that part of the invention described to which the patentee is so found to be entitled.

Copies of judgment

(3) Two office copies of the judgment rendered under subsection (1) shall be furnished to the Patent Office by the patentee, one of which shall be registered and remain of record in the Office and the other attached to the patent and made a part of it by a reference thereto.

R.S., c. P-4, s. 55.

Infringement

Jurisdiction of courts

54 (1) An action for the infringement of a patent may be brought in that court of record that, in the province in which the infringement is said to have occurred, has jurisdiction, pecuniarily, to the amount of the damages claimed and that, with relation to the other courts of the province, holds its sittings nearest to the place of residence or of business of the defendant, and that court shall decide the case and determine the costs, and assumption of jurisdiction by the court is of itself sufficient proof of jurisdiction.

Jurisdiction of Federal Court

(2) Nothing in this section impairs the jurisdiction of the Federal Court under section 20 of the *Federal Courts Act* or otherwise.

R.S., 1985, c. P-4, s. 54; 2002, c. 8, s. 182.

Liability for patent infringement

55 (1) A person who infringes a patent is liable to the patentee and to all persons claiming under the patentee for all damage sustained by the patentee or by any such person, after the grant of the patent, by reason of the infringement.

Liability damage before patent is granted

(2) A person is liable to pay reasonable compensation to a patentee and to all persons claiming under the patentee for any damage sustained by the patentee or by any of those persons by reason of any act on the part of that person, after the application for the patent became open to public inspection under section 10 and before the grant of the patent, that would have constituted an infringement of the patent if the patent had been granted on the day the application became open to public inspection under that section.

Patentee to be a party

(3) Unless otherwise expressly provided, the patentee shall be or be made a party to any proceeding under subsection (1) or (2).

Deemed action for infringement

(4) For the purposes of this section and sections 54 and 55.01 to 59, any proceeding under subsection (2) is deemed to be an action for the infringement of a patent and the act on which that proceeding is based is deemed to be an act of infringement of the patent.

R.S., 1985, c. P-4, s. 55; R.S., 1985, c. 33 (3rd Supp.), s. 21; 1993, c. 15, s. 48.

Limitation

55.01 No remedy may be awarded for an act of infringement committed more than six years before the commencement of the action for infringement.

1993, c. 15, s. 48.

Burden of proof for patented process

55.1 In an action for infringement of a patent granted for a process for obtaining a new product, any product that is the same as the new product shall, in the absence of proof to the contrary, be considered to have been produced by the patented process.

1993, c. 2, s. 4, c. 44, s. 193.

Exception

55.2 (1) It is not an infringement of a patent for any person to make, construct, use or sell the patented invention solely for uses reasonably related to the development and submission of information required under any law of Canada, a province or a country other than Canada that regulates the manufacture, construction, use or sale of any product.

(2) and (3) [Repealed, 2001, c. 10, s. 2]

Regulations

(4) The Governor in Council may make such regulations as the Governor in Council considers necessary for preventing the infringement of a patent by any person who makes, constructs, uses or sells a patented invention in accordance with subsection (1), including, without limiting the generality of the foregoing, regulations

(a) respecting the conditions that must be fulfilled before a notice, certificate, permit or other document concerning any product to which a patent may relate may be issued to a patentee or other person under any Act of Parliament that regulates the manufacture, construction, use or sale of that product, in addition to any conditions provided for by or under that Act;

(b) respecting the earliest date on which a notice, certificate, permit or other document referred to in paragraph (a) that is issued or to be issued to a person other than the patentee may take effect and respecting the manner in which that date is to be determined;

(c) governing the resolution of disputes between a patentee or former patentee and any person who applies for a notice, certificate, permit or other document referred to in paragraph (a) as to the date on which that notice, certificate, permit or other document may be issued or take effect;

(d) conferring rights of action in any court of competent jurisdiction with respect to any disputes referred to in paragraph (c) and respecting the remedies that may be sought in the court, the procedure of the court in the matter and the decisions and orders it may make; and

(e) generally governing the issue of a notice, certificate, permit or other document referred to in paragraph (a) in circumstances where the issue of that notice, certificate, permit or other document might result directly or indirectly in the infringement of a patent.

Inconsistency or conflict

(5) In the event of any inconsistency or conflict between

(a) this section or any regulations made under this section, and

(b) any Act of Parliament or any regulations made thereunder,

Règlements

(4) Afin d'empêcher la contrefaçon d'un brevet d'invention par l'utilisateur, le fabricant, le constructeur ou le vendeur d'une invention brevetée au sens du paragraphe (1), le gouverneur en conseil peut prendre des règlements, notamment :

a) fixant des conditions complémentaires nécessaires à la délivrance, en vertu de lois fédérales régissant l'exploitation, la fabrication, la construction ou la vente de produits sur lesquels porte un brevet, d'avis, de certificats, de permis ou de tout autre titre à quiconque n'est pas le breveté;

b) concernant la première date, et la manière de la fixer, à laquelle un titre visé à l'alinéa a) peut être délivré à quelqu'un qui n'est pas le breveté et à laquelle elle peut prendre effet;

c) concernant le règlement des litiges entre le breveté, ou l'ancien titulaire du brevet, et le demandeur d'un titre visé à l'alinéa a), quant à la date à laquelle le titre en question peut être délivré ou prendre effet;

d) conférant des droits d'action devant tout tribunal compétent concernant les litiges visés à l'alinéa c), les conclusions qui peuvent être recherchées, la procédure devant ce tribunal et les décisions qui peuvent être rendues;

e) sur toute autre mesure concernant la délivrance d'un titre visé à l'alinéa a) lorsque celle-ci peut avoir pour effet la contrefaçon de brevet.

Divergences

(5) Une disposition réglementaire prise sous le régime du présent article prévaut sur toute disposition législative ou réglementaire fédérale divergente.

For greater certainty

(6) For greater certainty, subsection (1) does not affect any exception to the exclusive property or privilege granted by a patent that exists at law in respect of acts done privately and on a non-commercial scale or for a non-commercial purpose or in respect of any use, manufacture, construction or sale of the patented invention solely for the purpose of experiments that relate to the subject-matter of the patent.

1993, c. 2, s. 4; 2001, c. 10, s. 2.

Patent not to affect previous purchaser

56 (1) Every person who, before the claim date of a claim in a patent has purchased, constructed or acquired the subject matter defined by the claim, has the right to use and sell to others the specific article, machine, manufacture or composition of matter patented and so purchased, constructed or acquired without being liable to the patentee or the legal representatives of the patentee for so doing.

Non-application

(2) Subsection (1) does not apply in respect of a purchase, construction or acquisition referred to in subsection (3) or (4).

Special case

(3) Section 56 of the *Patent Act*, as it read immediately before the day on which subsection (1) came into force, applies in respect of a purchase, construction or acquisition made before that day of an invention for which a patent is issued on the basis of an application filed after October 1, 1989 and before the day on which subsection (1) came into force.

Idem

(4) Section 56 of the *Patent Act*, as it read immediately before October 1, 1989, applies in respect of a purchase, construction or acquisition made before the day on which subsection (1) came into force of an invention for which a patent is issued before October 1, 1989 or is issued after October 1, 1989 on the basis of an application filed before October 1, 1989.

R.S., 1985, c. P-4, s. 56; R.S., 1985, c. 33 (3rd Supp.), s. 22; 1993, c. 44, ss. 194, 199.

Injunction may issue

57 (1) In any action for infringement of a patent, the court, or any judge thereof, may, on the application of the plaintiff or defendant, make such order as the court or judge sees fit,

(a) restraining or enjoining the opposite party from further use, manufacture or sale of the subject-matter of the patent, and for his punishment in the event of disobedience of that order, or

(b) for and respecting inspection or account,

and generally, respecting the proceedings in the action.

Appeal

(2) An appeal lies from any order made under subsection (1) in the same circumstances and to the same court as from other judgments or orders of the court in which the order is made.

R.S., c. P-4, s. 59.

Invalid claims not to affect valid claims

58 When, in any action or proceeding respecting a patent that contains two or more claims, one or more of those claims is or are held to be valid but another or others is or are held to be invalid or void, effect shall be given to the patent as if it contained only the valid claim or claims.

R.S., c. P-4, s. 60.

Defence

59 The defendant, in any action for infringement of a patent may plead as matter of defence any fact or default which by this Act or by law renders the patent void, and the court shall take cognizance of that pleading and of the relevant facts and decide accordingly.

R.S., c. P-4, s. 61.

Impeachment

Impeachment of patents or claims

60 (1) A patent or any claim in a patent may be declared invalid or void by the Federal Court at the instance of the Attorney General of Canada or at the instance of any interested person.

Declaration as to infringement

(2) Where any person has reasonable cause to believe that any process used or proposed to be used or any article made, used or sold or proposed to be made, used or sold by him might be alleged by any patentee to constitute an infringement of an exclusive property or privilege granted thereby, he may bring an action in the Federal Court against the patentee for a declaration that the process or article does not or would not constitute an infringement of the exclusive property or privilege.

Security for costs

(3) With the exception of the Attorney General of Canada or the attorney general of a province, the plaintiff in any action under this section shall, before proceeding therein, give security for the costs of the patentee in such sum as the Federal Court may direct, but a defendant in any action for the infringement of a patent is entitled to obtain a declaration under this section without being required to furnish any security.

R.S., c. P-4, s. 62; R.S., c. 10(2nd Supp.), s. 64.

61 [Repealed, R.S., 1985, c. 33 (3rd Supp.), s. 23]

Judgments

Judgment voiding patent

62 A certificate of a judgment voiding in whole or in part any patent shall, at the request of any person filing it to make it a record in the Patent Office, be registered in the Patent Office, and the patent, or such part as is voided, shall thereupon be and be held to have been void and of no effect, unless the judgment is reversed on appeal as provided in section 63.

R.S., 1985, c. P-4, s. 62; 1993, c. 15, s. 49.

Appeal

63 Every judgment voiding in whole or in part or refusing to void in whole or in part any patent is subject to appeal to any court having appellate jurisdiction in other cases decided by the court by which the judgment was rendered.

R.S., c. P-4, s. 65.

Conditions

64 [Repealed, 1993, c. 44, s. 195]

Abuse of rights under patents

65 (1) The Attorney General of Canada or any person interested may, at any time after the expiration of three years from the date of the grant of a patent, apply to the Commissioner alleging in the case of that patent that there has been an abuse of the exclusive rights thereunder and asking for relief under this Act.

What amounts to abuse

(2) The exclusive rights under a patent shall be deemed to have been abused in any of the following circumstances:

(a) and (b) [Repealed, 1993, c. 44, s. 196]

(c) if the demand for the patented article in Canada is not being met to an adequate extent and on reasonable terms;

(d) if, by reason of the refusal of the patentee to grant a licence or licences on reasonable terms, the trade or industry of Canada or the trade of any person or class of persons trading in Canada, or the establishment of any new trade or industry in Canada, is prejudiced, and it is in the public interest that a licence or licences should be granted;

(e) if any trade or industry in Canada, or any person or class of persons engaged therein, is unfairly prejudiced by the conditions attached by the patentee, whether before or after the passing of this Act, to the purchase, hire, licence or use of the patented article or to the using or working of the patented process; or

(f) if it is shown that the existence of the patent, being a patent for an invention relating to a process involving the use of materials not protected by the patent or for an invention relating to a substance produced by such a process, has been utilized by the patentee so as unfairly to prejudice in Canada the manufacture, use or sale of any materials.

(3) and (4) [Repealed, 1993, c. 44, s. 196]

Definition of *patented article*

(5) For the purposes of this section, the expression **patented article** includes articles made by a patented process.

R.S., 1985, c. P-4, s. 65; 1993, c. 2, s. 5, c. 15, s. 51, c. 44, s. 196.

Powers of Commissioner in cases of abuse

66 (1) On being satisfied that a case of abuse of the exclusive rights under a patent has been established, the Commissioner may exercise any of the following powers as he may deem expedient in the circumstances:

(a) he may order the grant to the applicant of a licence on such terms as the Commissioner may think expedient, including a term precluding the licensee from importing into Canada any goods the importation of which, if made by persons other than the patentee or persons claiming under him, would be an infringement of the patent, and in that case the patentee and all licensees for the time being shall be deemed to have mutually covenanted against that importation;

(b) [Repealed, 1993, c. 44, s. 197]

(c) if the Commissioner is satisfied that the exclusive rights have been abused in the circumstances specified in paragraph 65(2)(f), he may order the grant of licences to the applicant and to such of his customers, and containing such terms, as the Commissioner may think expedient;

(d) if the Commissioner is satisfied that the objects of this section and section 65 cannot be attained by the exercise of any of the foregoing powers, the Commissioner shall order the patent to be revoked, either forthwith or after such reasonable interval as may be specified in the order, unless in the meantime such conditions as may be specified in the order with a view to attaining the objects of this section and section 65 are fulfilled, and the Commissioner may, on reasonable cause shown in any case, by subsequent order extend the interval so specified, but the Commissioner shall not make an order for revocation which is at variance with any treaty, convention, arrangement, or engagement with any other country to which Canada is a party; or

(e) if the Commissioner is of opinion that the objects of this section and section 65 will be best attained by not making an order under the provisions of this section, he may make an order refusing the application and dispose of any question as to costs thereon as he thinks just.

Proceedings to prevent infringement

(2) A licensee under paragraph (1)(a) is entitled to call on the patentee to take proceedings to prevent infringement of the patent, and if the patentee refuses or neglects to do so within two months after being so called on, the licensee may institute proceedings for infringement in his own name as though he were the patentee, making the patentee a defendant, but a patentee added as defendant is not liable for any costs unless he enters an appearance and takes part in the proceedings.

convenables et qui contiennent une clause interdisant au porteur de licence d'importer au Canada des marchandises dont l'importation, si elle était pratiquée par d'autres personnes que le breveté ou des personnes se réclamant de lui, constituerait une violation du brevet; en pareil cas, le breveté et toutes les personnes détenant alors une licence sont réputés être mutuellement convenus d'empêcher une telle importation;

b) [Abrogé, 1993, ch. 44, art. 197]

c) s'il est convaincu que les droits exclusifs ont donné lieu à des abus dans les circonstances spécifiées à l'alinéa 65(2)f), il peut ordonner la concession de licences au demandeur et à tels de ses clients, à telles conditions, que le commissaire juge convenables;

d) s'il est convaincu que l'exercice de l'un des pouvoirs prévus au présent article ne peut en réaliser les objets et ceux de l'article 65, il ordonne la déchéance du brevet, soit immédiatement, soit à l'expiration d'un délai raisonnable que spécifie l'ordonnance, à moins que dans l'intervalle n'aient été remplies les conditions que fixe l'ordonnance en vue de réaliser les objets du présent article et de l'article 65; il peut, pour des motifs raisonnables et démontrés en chaque cas, prolonger par ordonnance subséquente le délai ainsi spécifié, mais il ne peut rendre aucune ordonnance de déchéance qui contrarie un traité, une convention, un accord ou un engagement avec un autre pays, auquel le Canada est partie;

e) s'il est d'avis que les objets du présent article et de l'article 65 seront plus efficacement réalisés en ne rendant aucune ordonnance aux termes des dispositions du présent article, il peut rendre une ordonnance qui rejette la requête, et décider comme il l'estime juste toute question de frais.

Procédures en vue de prévenir la violation du brevet

(2) Un porteur de licence aux termes de l'alinéa (1)a) a le droit d'exiger du breveté qu'il intente des procédures en vue de prévenir la violation du brevet; si le breveté refuse ou néglige d'intenter des procédures dans un délai de deux mois après en avoir été ainsi requis, le porteur de licence peut, en son propre nom, comme s'il était lui-même le breveté, intenter une action en contrefaçon et mettre le breveté en cause comme défendeur. Un breveté ainsi mis en cause comme défendeur n'encourt aucuns frais, à moins qu'il ne produise une comparution et ne prenne part à l'instance.

Service on patentee

(3) Service on a patentee added as a defendant may be effected by leaving the writ at his address or at the address of his representative for service as appearing in the records of the Patent Office.

Considerations by which Commissioner to be guided

(4) In settling the terms of a licence under paragraph (1)(a), the Commissioner shall be guided as far as possible by the following considerations:

(a) he shall endeavour to secure the widest possible use of the invention in Canada consistent with the patentee deriving a reasonable advantage from his patent rights;

(b) he shall endeavour to secure to the patentee the maximum advantage consistent with the invention being worked by the licensee at a reasonable profit in Canada; and

(c) he shall endeavour to secure equality of advantage among the several licensees, and for this purpose may, on due cause being shown, reduce the royalties or other payments accruing to the patentee under any licence previously granted.

R.S., 1985, c. P-4, s. 66; R.S., 1985, c. 33 (3rd Supp.), s. 24; 1993, c. 44, s. 197.

67 [Repealed, 1993, c. 44, s. 198]

Contents of applications

68 (1) Every application presented to the Commissioner under section 65 or 66 shall

(a) set out fully the nature of the applicant's interest, the facts on which the applicant bases his case and the relief that he seeks; and

(b) be accompanied by statutory declarations verifying the applicant's interest and the facts set out in the application.

Service

(2) The Commissioner shall consider the matters alleged in the application and declarations referred to in subsection (1), and, if satisfied that the applicant has a *bona fide* interest and that a case for relief has been made, he shall direct the applicant to serve copies of the application and declarations on the patentee or his representative for service and on any other persons appearing from the records of the Patent Office to be interested in the patent, and the applicant shall advertise the application in the *Canada Gazette* and the *Canadian Patent Office Record*.

R.S., c. P-4, s. 70.

Opposition and counter statement

69 (1) If the patentee or any person is desirous of opposing the granting of any relief under sections 65 to 70, he shall, within such time as may be prescribed or within such extended time as the Commissioner may on application further allow, deliver to the Commissioner a counter statement verified by a statutory declaration fully setting out the grounds on which the application is to be opposed.

Attendance for cross-examination

(2) The Commissioner shall consider the counter statement and declaration referred to in subsection (1) and may thereupon dismiss the application if satisfied that the allegations in the application have been adequately answered, unless any of the parties demands a hearing or unless the Commissioner himself appoints a hearing, and in any case the Commissioner may require the attendance before him of any of the declarants to be cross-examined or further examined on matters relevant to the issues raised in the application and counter statement, and he may, subject to due precautions against disclosure of information to rivals in trade, require the production before him of books and documents relating to the matter in issue.

Reference to Federal Court

(3) In any case where the Commissioner does not dismiss an application as provided in subsection (2), and

   (a) if the parties interested consent, or

   (b) if the proceedings require any prolonged examination of documents or any scientific or local investigation that cannot in the opinion of the Commissioner conveniently be made before him,

the Commissioner, with the approval in writing of the Minister, may order the whole proceedings or any issue of fact arising thereunder to be referred to the Federal Court, which has jurisdiction in the premises.

Idem

(4) Where the whole proceedings are referred under subsection (1), the judgment, decision or order of the Federal Court is final, and where a question or issue of fact is referred under that subsection, the Court shall report its findings to the Commissioner.

R.S., c. P-4, s. 71; R.S., c. 10(2nd Supp.), s. 64.

Licence deemed to be by deed

70 Any order for the grant of a licence under this Act, without prejudice to any other method of enforcement, operates as if it were embodied in a deed granting a licence executed by the patentee and all other necessary parties.

R.S., c. P-4, s. 72.

Appeal to Federal Court

71 All orders and decisions of the Commissioner under sections 65 to 70 are subject to appeal to the Federal Court, and on any such appeal the Attorney General of Canada or such counsel as he may appoint is entitled to appear and be heard.

R.S., c. P-4, s. 73; R.S., c. 10(2nd Supp.), s. 64.

72 [Repealed, R.S., 1985, c. 33 (3rd Supp.), s. 25]

Abandonment and Reinstatement of Applications

Deemed abandonment of applications

73 (1) An application for a patent in Canada shall be deemed to be abandoned if the applicant does not

(a) reply in good faith to any requisition made by an examiner in connection with an examination, within six months after the requisition is made or within any shorter period established by the Commissioner;

(b) comply with a notice given pursuant to subsection 27(6);

(c) pay the fees payable under section 27.1, within the time provided by the regulations;

(d) make a request for examination or pay the prescribed fee under subsection 35(1) within the time provided by the regulations;

(e) comply with a notice given under subsection 35(2); or

(f) pay the prescribed fees stated to be payable in a notice of allowance of patent within six months after the date of the notice.

Deemed abandonment in prescribed circumstances

(2) An application shall also be deemed to be abandoned in any other circumstances that are prescribed.

Reinstatement

(3) An application deemed to be abandoned under this section shall be reinstated if the applicant

(a) makes a request for reinstatement to the Commissioner within the prescribed period;

incorporée dans un acte de concession d'une licence souscrit par le breveté et par les autres parties nécessaires.

S.R., ch. P-4, art. 72.

Appel à la Cour fédérale

71 Toutes les ordonnances et décisions rendues par le commissaire sous l'autorité des articles 65 à 70 sont sujettes à appel à la Cour fédérale, et en tel cas, le procureur général du Canada ou un avocat qu'il peut désigner a le droit de comparaître et d'être entendu.

S.R., ch. P-4, art. 73; S.R., ch. 10(2ᵉ suppl.), art. 64.

72 [Abrogé, L.R. (1985), ch. 33 (3ᵉ suppl.), art. 25]

Abandon et rétablissement des demandes

Abandon

73 (1) La demande de brevet est considérée comme abandonnée si le demandeur omet, selon le cas :

a) de répondre de bonne foi, dans le cadre d'un examen, à toute demande de l'examinateur, dans les six mois suivant cette demande ou dans le délai plus court déterminé par le commissaire;

b) de se conformer à l'avis mentionné au paragraphe 27(6);

c) de payer, dans le délai réglementaire, les taxes visées à l'article 27.1;

d) de présenter la requête visée au paragraphe 35(1) ou de payer la taxe réglementaire dans le délai réglementaire;

e) de se conformer à l'avis mentionné au paragraphe 35(2);

f) de payer les taxes réglementaires mentionnées dans l'avis d'acceptation de la demande de brevet dans les six mois suivant celui-ci.

Idem

(2) Elle est aussi considérée comme abandonnée dans les circonstances réglementaires.

Rétablissement

(3) Elle est rétablie si le demandeur :

a) présente au commissaire, dans le délai réglementaire, une requête à cet effet;

(b) takes the action that should have been taken in order to avoid the abandonment; and

(c) pays the prescribed fee before the expiration of the prescribed period.

Amendment and re-examination

(4) An application that has been abandoned pursuant to paragraph (1)(f) and reinstated is subject to amendment and further examination.

Original filing date

(5) An application that is reinstated retains its original filing date.

R.S., 1985, c. P-4, s. 73; 1993, c. 15, s. 52; 2015, c. 3, s. 138(F).

Offences and Punishment

74 [Repealed, R.S., 1985, c. 33 (3rd Supp.), s. 26]

Offences

75 Every person who

(a) without the consent of the patentee, writes, paints, prints, moulds, casts, carves, engraves, stamps or otherwise marks on anything made or sold by him, and for the sole making or selling of which he is not the patentee, the name or any imitation of the name of any patentee for the sole making or selling of that thing,

(b) without the consent of the patentee, writes, paints, prints, moulds, casts, carves, engraves, stamps or otherwise marks on anything not purchased from the patentee, the words "Patent", "Letters Patent", "Queen's (or King's) Patent", "Patented" or any word or words of like import, with the intent of counterfeiting or imitating the stamp, mark or device of the patentee, or of deceiving the public and inducing them to believe that the thing in question was made or sold by or with the consent of the patentee, or

(c) with intent to deceive the public offers for sale as patented in Canada any article not patented in Canada,

is guilty of an indictable offence and liable to a fine not exceeding two hundred dollars or to imprisonment for a term not exceeding three months or to both.

R.S., c. P-4, s. 78.

False representations, false entries, etc.

76 Every person who, in relation to the purposes of this Act and knowing it to be false,

(a) makes any false representation,

(b) makes or causes to be made any false entry in any register or book,

(b.1) submits or causes to be submitted, in an electronic form, any false document, false information or document containing false information,

(c) makes or causes to be made any false document or alters the form of a copy of any document, or

(d) produces or tenders any document containing false information,

is guilty of an indictable offence and liable on conviction to a fine not exceeding five hundred dollars or to imprisonment for a term not exceeding six months or to both.

R.S., 1985, c. P-4, s. 76; 1993, c. 15, s. 53.

Offence respecting patented medicines

76.1 (1) Every person who contravenes or fails to comply with section 80, 81, 82 or 88 or any order made thereunder is guilty of an offence punishable on summary conviction and liable

(a) in the case of an individual, to a fine not exceeding five thousand dollars or to imprisonment for a term not exceeding six months or to both; and

(b) in the case of a corporation, to a fine not exceeding twenty-five thousand dollars.

Idem

(2) Every person who contravenes or fails to comply with section 84 or any order made under section 83 is guilty of an offence punishable on summary conviction and liable

(a) in the case of an individual, to a fine not exceeding twenty-five thousand dollars or to imprisonment for a term not exceeding one year or to both; and

(b) in the case of a corporation, to a fine not exceeding one hundred thousand dollars.

Limitation period

(3) Proceedings for an offence under subsection (1) or (2) may be commenced within, but not later than, two years after the time when the subject-matter of the proceedings arose.

a) fait un exposé faux;

b) effectue ou fait effectuer une fausse inscription dans un registre ou livre;

b.1) remet ou fait remettre, sous forme électronique, de faux documents ou renseignements ou des documents renfermant des renseignements faux;

c) fait ou fait faire un faux document ou altère la forme d'une copie de document;

d) produit ou présente un document renfermant des renseignements faux,

commet un acte criminel et encourt, sur déclaration de culpabilité, une amende maximale de cinq cents dollars et un emprisonnement maximal de six mois, ou l'une de ces peines.

L.R. (1985), ch. P-4, art. 76; 1993, ch. 15, art. 53.

Infractions relatives aux médicaments brevetés

76.1 (1) Quiconque contrevient aux articles 80, 81, 82 ou 88 ou à une ordonnance prise sous le régime de l'un ou l'autre de ces articles commet une infraction et encourt, sur déclaration de culpabilité par procédure sommaire :

a) une amende maximale de cinq mille dollars et un emprisonnement maximal de six mois, ou l'une de ces peines, s'il s'agit d'une personne physique;

b) une amende maximale de vingt-cinq mille dollars, s'il s'agit d'une personne morale.

Idem

(2) Quiconque contrevient à l'article 84 ou à une ordonnance prise sous le régime de l'article 83 commet une infraction et encourt, sur déclaration de culpabilité par procédure sommaire :

a) une amende maximale de vingt-cinq mille dollars et un emprisonnement maximal d'un an, ou l'une de ces peines, s'il s'agit d'une personne physique;

b) une amende maximale de cent mille dollars, s'il s'agit d'une personne morale.

Prescription

(3) La poursuite d'une infraction visée aux paragraphes (1) ou (2) se prescrit par deux ans à compter de sa perpétration.

Continuing offence

(4) Where an offence under subsection (1) or (2) is committed or continued on more than one day, the person who committed the offence is liable to be convicted for a separate offence for each day on which the offence is committed or continued.

1993, c. 2, s. 6.

Miscellaneous Matters

77 [Repealed, 1993, c. 15, s. 54]

Time limit deemed extended

78 (1) Where any time limit or period of limitation specified under or pursuant to this Act expires on a day when the Patent Office is closed for business, that time limit or period of limitation shall be deemed to be extended to the next day when the Patent Office is open for business.

When Patent Office closed for business

(2) The Patent Office shall be closed for business on Saturdays and holidays and on such other days as the Minister by order declares that it shall be closed for business.

Publication

(3) Every order made by the Minister under subsection (2) shall be published in the *Canadian Patent Office Record* as soon as possible after it is made.

R.S., c. P-4, s. 81.

Transitional Provisions

Patent applications filed before October 1, 1989

78.1 Applications for patents in Canada filed before October 1, 1989 shall be dealt with and disposed of in accordance with section 38.1 and with the provisions of this Act as they read immediately before October 1, 1989.

1993, c. 15, s. 55; 2001, c. 10, s. 3.

Patents issued before October 1, 1989

78.2 (1) Subject to subsection (3), any matter arising on or after October 1, 1989 in respect of a patent issued before that date shall be dealt with and disposed of in accordance with sections 38.1 and 45 and with the provisions of this Act, other than section 46, as they read immediately before October 1, 1989.

Patents issued on or after October 1, 1989 on the basis of previously filed applications

(2) Subject to subsection (3), any matter arising on or after October 1, 1989 in respect of a patent issued on or after that date on the basis of an application filed before that date shall be dealt with and disposed of in accordance with sections 38.1, 45, 46 and 48.1 to 48.5 and with the provisions of this Act, other than section 46, as they read immediately before October 1, 1989.

Application

(3) The provisions of this Act that apply as provided in subsections (1) and (2) shall be read subject to any amendments to this Act, other than the amendments that came into force on October 1, 1989 or October 1, 1996.

1993, c. 15, s. 55; 2001, c. 10, s. 3.

Previous version of section 43 applies

78.3 (1) Where a conflict, as defined in section 43 as it read immediately before October 1, 1989, exists between an application for a patent in Canada filed before October 1, 1989 (the "earlier application") and an application for a patent in Canada filed on or after that date (the "later application") and

(a) the later application is filed by a person who is entitled to protection under the terms of any treaty or convention relating to patents to which Canada is a party and who has previously regularly filed in or for any other country that by treaty, convention or law affords similar protection to citizens of Canada an application for a patent describing the same invention,

(b) the later application is filed within twelve months after the filing of the previously regularly filed application,

(c) the applicant in the later application has made a request for priority in respect of that application on the basis of the previously regularly filed application, and

(d) the earlier application is filed after the filing of the previously regularly filed application,

the applicant having the earlier date of invention shall be entitled to a patent and the applications shall be dealt with and disposed of in accordance with section 43, as it read immediately before October 1, 1989.

Exception

(2) Subsection (1) does not apply if

(a) the earlier application is filed by a person who is entitled to protection under the terms of any treaty or convention relating to patents to which Canada is a party and who has previously regularly filed in or for any other country that by treaty, convention or law affords similar protection to citizens of Canada an application for a patent describing the same invention;

(b) the earlier application is filed within twelve months after the filing of the previously regularly filed application mentioned in paragraph (a);

(c) the applicant in the earlier application has made a request for priority in respect of that application on the basis of the previously regularly filed application mentioned in paragraph (a); and

(d) the previously regularly filed application mentioned in paragraph (a) was filed before the filing of the previously regularly filed application mentioned in subsection (1).

1993, c. 15, s. 55.

Patent applications filed on or after October 1, 1989

78.4 Applications for patents in Canada filed on or after October 1, 1989, but before October 1, 1996, shall be dealt with and disposed of in accordance with subsection 27(2) as it read immediately before October 1, 1996 and with the provisions of this Act as they read on October 1, 1996.

1993, c. 15, s. 55; 2001, c. 10, s. 4.

Patents issued on or after October 1, 1989

78.5 Any matter arising in respect of a patent issued on the basis of an application filed on or after October 1, 1989, but before October 1, 1996, shall be dealt with and disposed of in accordance with the provisions of this Act and with subsection 27(2) as it read immediately before October 1, 1996.

1993, c. 15, s. 55; 2001, c. 10, s. 4.

Payment of prescribed fees

78.6 (1) If, before the day on which this section comes into force, a person has paid a prescribed fee applicable to a small entity, within the meaning of the *Patent Rules* as they read at the time of payment, but should have paid the prescribed fee applicable to an entity other than a small entity and a payment equivalent to the difference between the two amounts is submitted to the Commissioner in accordance with subsection (2) either before or no later than twelve months after that day, the payment is deemed to have been paid on the day on which the prescribed fee was paid, regardless of whether an action or other proceeding relating to the patent or patent

Information to be provided

(2) Any person who submits a payment to the Commissioner in accordance with subsection (1) is required to provide information with respect to the service or proceeding in respect of which the fee was paid and the patent or application in respect of which the fee was paid.

No refund

(3) A payment submitted in accordance with subsection (1) shall not be refunded.

Action and proceedings barred

(4) No action or proceeding for any compensation or damages lies against Her Majesty in right of Canada in respect of any direct or indirect consequence resulting from the application of this section.

Application

(5) For greater certainty, this section also applies to applications for patents mentioned in sections 78.1 and 78.4.

2005, c. 18, s. 2.

Patented Medicines

Interpretation

Definitions

79 (1) In this section and in sections 80 to 103,

Board means the Patented Medicine Prices Review Board continued by section 91; (*Conseil*)

Consumer Price Index means the Consumer Price Index published by Statistics Canada under the authority of the *Statistics Act*; (*indice des prix à la consommation*)

Minister means the Minister of Health or such other Member of the Queen's Privy Council for Canada as is designated by the Governor in Council as the Minister for the purposes of this section and sections 80 to 103; (*ministre*)

patentee, in respect of an invention pertaining to a medicine, means the person for the time being entitled to the benefit of the patent for that invention and includes, where any other person is entitled to exercise any rights in relation to that patent other than under a licence continued by subsection 11(1) of the *Patent Act Amendment*

Act, 1992, that other person in respect of those rights; (*breveté* ou *titulaire d'un brevet*)

regulations means regulations made under section 101. (*règlement*)

Invention pertaining to a medicine

(2) For the purposes of subsection (1) and sections 80 to 101, an invention pertains to a medicine if the invention is intended or capable of being used for medicine or for the preparation or production of medicine.

1993, c. 2, s. 7; 1996, c. 8, s. 32.

Pricing Information

Pricing information, etc., required by regulations

80 (1) A patentee of an invention pertaining to a medicine shall, as required by and in accordance with the regulations, provide the Board with such information and documents as the regulations may specify respecting

(a) the identity of the medicine;

(b) the price at which the medicine is being or has been sold in any market in Canada and elsewhere;

(c) the costs of making and marketing the medicine, where that information is available to the patentee in Canada or is within the knowledge or control of the patentee;

(d) the factors referred to in section 85; and

(e) any other related matters.

Idem

(2) Subject to subsection (3), a person who is a former patentee of an invention pertaining to a medicine shall, as required by and in accordance with the regulations, provide the Board with such information and documents as the regulations may specify respecting

(a) the identity of the medicine;

(b) the price at which the medicine was sold in any market in Canada and elsewhere during the period in which the person was a patentee of the invention;

(c) the costs of making and marketing the medicine produced during that period, whether incurred before or after the patent was issued, where that information is available to the person in Canada or is within the knowledge or control of the person;

gouverneur en conseil de l'application du présent article et des articles 80 à 103. (*Minister*)

règlement Les règlements pris au titre de l'article 101. (*regulations*)

Définition de *invention liée à un médicament*

(2) Pour l'application du paragraphe (1) et des articles 80 à 101, une invention est liée à un médicament si elle est destinée à des médicaments ou à la préparation ou la production de médicaments, ou susceptible d'être utilisée à de telles fins.

1993, ch. 2, art. 7; 1996, ch. 8, art. 32.

Renseignements sur les prix

Renseignements réglementaires à fournir sur les prix

80 (1) Le breveté est tenu de fournir au Conseil, conformément aux règlements, les renseignements et documents sur les points suivants :

a) l'identification du médicament en cause;

b) le prix de vente — antérieur ou actuel — du médicament sur les marchés canadien et étranger;

c) les coûts de réalisation et de mise en marché du médicament s'il dispose de ces derniers renseignements au Canada ou s'il en a connaissance ou le contrôle;

d) les facteurs énumérés à l'article 85;

e) tout autre point afférent précisé par règlement.

Idem

(2) Sous réserve du paragraphe (3), l'ancien titulaire d'un brevet est tenu de fournir au Conseil, conformément aux règlements, les renseignements et les documents sur les points suivants :

a) l'identification du médicament en cause;

b) le prix de vente du médicament sur les marchés canadien et étranger pendant la période où il était titulaire du brevet;

c) les coûts de réalisation et de mise en marché du médicament pendant cette période, qu'ils aient été assumés avant ou après la délivrance du brevet, s'il dispose de ces derniers renseignements au Canada ou s'il en a connaissance ou le contrôle;

d) les facteurs énumérés à l'article 85;

(d) the factors referred to in section 85; and

(e) any other related matters.

Limitation

(3) Subsection (2) does not apply to a person who has not been entitled to the benefit of the patent or to exercise any rights in relation to the patent for a period of three or more years.

1993, c. 2, s. 7.

Pricing information, etc. required by Board

81 (1) The Board may, by order, require a patentee or former patentee of an invention pertaining to a medicine to provide the Board with information and documents respecting

(a) in the case of a patentee, any of the matters referred to in paragraphs 80(1)(a) to (e);

(b) in the case of a former patentee, any of the matters referred to in paragraphs 80(2)(a) to (e); and

(c) such other related matters as the Board may require.

Compliance with order

(2) A patentee or former patentee in respect of whom an order is made under subsection (1) shall comply with the order within such time as is specified in the order or as the Board may allow.

Limitation

(3) No order may be made under subsection (1) in respect of a former patentee who, more than three years before the day on which the order is proposed to be made, ceased to be entitled to the benefit of the patent or to exercise any rights in relation to the patent.

1993, c. 2, s. 7.

Notice of introductory price

82 (1) A patentee of an invention pertaining to a medicine who intends to sell the medicine in a market in Canada in which it has not previously been sold shall, as soon as practicable after determining the date on which the medicine will be first offered for sale in that market, notify the Board of its intention and of that date.

Pricing information and documents

(2) Where the Board receives a notice under subsection (1) from a patentee or otherwise has reason to believe that a patentee of an invention pertaining to a medicine intends to sell the medicine in a market in Canada in which the medicine has not previously been sold, the

e) tout autre point afférent précisé par règlement.

Prescription

(3) Le paragraphe (2) ne vise pas celui qui, pendant une période d'au moins trois ans, a cessé d'avoir droit à l'avantage du brevet ou d'exercer les droits du titulaire.

1993, ch. 2, art. 7.

Renseignements sur les prix exigés par le Conseil

81 (1) Le Conseil peut, par ordonnance, enjoindre le breveté ou l'ancien titulaire du brevet de lui fournir les renseignements et les documents sur les points visés aux alinéas 80(1)a) à e), dans le cas du breveté, ou, dans le cas de l'ancien breveté, aux alinéas 80(2)a) à e) ainsi que sur tout autre point qu'il précise.

Respect

(2) L'ordonnance est à exécuter dans le délai précisé ou que peut fixer le Conseil.

Prescription

(3) Il ne peut être pris d'ordonnances en vertu du paragraphe (1) plus de trois ans après qu'une personne ait cessé d'avoir droit aux avantages du brevet ou d'exercer les droits du titulaire.

1993, ch. 2, art. 7.

Avis du prix de lancement

82 (1) Tout breveté doit, dès que possible après avoir fixé la date à laquelle il compte mettre en vente sur un marché canadien un médicament qui n'y a jamais été vendu, notifier le Conseil de son intention et de la date à laquelle il compte le faire.

Renseignements sur les prix

(2) Sur réception de l'avis visé au paragraphe (1) ou lorsqu'il a des motifs de croire qu'un breveté se propose de vendre sur un marché canadien un médicament qui n'y a

Board may, by order, require the patentee to provide the Board with information and documents respecting the price at which the medicine is intended to be sold in that market.

Compliance with order

(3) Subject to subsection (4), a patentee in respect of whom an order is made under subsection (2) shall comply with the order within such time as is specified in the order or as the Board may allow.

Limitation

(4) No patentee shall be required to comply with an order made under subsection (2) prior to the sixtieth day preceding the date on which the patentee intends to first offer the medicine for sale in the relevant market.

1993, c. 2, s. 7.

Excessive Prices

Order re excessive prices

83 (1) Where the Board finds that a patentee of an invention pertaining to a medicine is selling the medicine in any market in Canada at a price that, in the Board's opinion, is excessive, the Board may, by order, direct the patentee to cause the maximum price at which the patentee sells the medicine in that market to be reduced to such level as the Board considers not to be excessive and as is specified in the order.

Idem

(2) Subject to subsection (4), where the Board finds that a patentee of an invention pertaining to a medicine has, while a patentee, sold the medicine in any market in Canada at a price that, in the Board's opinion, was excessive, the Board may, by order, direct the patentee to do any one or more of the following things as will, in the Board's opinion, offset the amount of the excess revenues estimated by it to have been derived by the patentee from the sale of the medicine at an excessive price:

(a) reduce the price at which the patentee sells the medicine in any market in Canada, to such extent and for such period as is specified in the order;

(b) reduce the price at which the patentee sells one other medicine to which a patented invention of the patentee pertains in any market in Canada, to such extent and for such period as is specified in the order; or

(c) pay to Her Majesty in right of Canada an amount specified in the order.

jamais été vendu, le Conseil peut, par ordonnance, demander au breveté de lui fournir les renseignements et les documents concernant le prix proposé sur ce marché.

Respect

(3) Sous réserve du paragraphe (4), l'ordonnance est à exécuter dans le délai précisé ou que peut fixer le Conseil.

Prescription

(4) Une ordonnance prise en vertu du paragraphe (2) n'oblige pas le breveté avant le soixantième jour de la date prévue pour la mise en vente du médicament sur le marché proposé.

1993, ch. 2, art. 7.

Prix excessifs

Ordonnance relative aux prix excessifs

83 (1) Lorsqu'il estime que le breveté vend sur un marché canadien le médicament à un prix qu'il juge être excessif, le Conseil peut, par ordonnance, lui enjoindre de baisser le prix de vente maximal du médicament dans ce marché au niveau précisé dans l'ordonnance et de façon qu'il ne puisse pas être excessif.

Idem

(2) Sous réserve du paragraphe (4), lorsqu'il estime que le breveté a vendu, alors qu'il était titulaire du brevet, le médicament sur un marché canadien à un prix qu'il juge avoir été excessif, le Conseil peut, par ordonnance, lui enjoindre de prendre l'une ou plusieurs des mesures suivantes pour compenser, selon lui, l'excédent qu'aurait procuré au breveté la vente du médicament au prix excessif :

a) baisser, dans un marché canadien, le prix de vente du médicament dans la mesure et pour la période prévue par l'ordonnance;

b) baisser, dans un marché canadien, le prix de vente de tout autre médicament lié à une invention brevetée du titulaire dans la mesure et pour la période prévue par l'ordonnance;

c) payer à Sa Majesté du chef du Canada le montant précisé dans l'ordonnance.

Idem

(3) Subject to subsection (4), where the Board finds that a former patentee of an invention pertaining to a medicine had, while a patentee, sold the medicine in any market in Canada at a price that, in the Board's opinion, was excessive, the Board may, by order, direct the former patentee to do any one or more of the following things as will, in the Board's opinion, offset the amount of the excess revenues estimated by it to have been derived by the former patentee from the sale of the medicine at an excessive price:

(a) reduce the price at which the former patentee sells a medicine to which a patented invention of the former patentee pertains in any market in Canada, to such extent and for such period as is specified in the order; or

(b) pay to Her Majesty in right of Canada an amount specified in the order.

Where policy to sell at excessive price

(4) Where the Board, having regard to the extent and duration of the sales of the medicine at an excessive price, is of the opinion that the patentee or former patentee has engaged in a policy of selling the medicine at an excessive price, the Board may, by order, in lieu of any order it may make under subsection (2) or (3), as the case may be, direct the patentee or former patentee to do any one or more of the things referred to in that subsection as will, in the Board's opinion, offset not more than twice the amount of the excess revenues estimated by it to have been derived by the patentee or former patentee from the sale of the medicine at an excessive price.

Excess revenues

(5) In estimating the amount of excess revenues under subsection (2), (3) or (4), the Board shall not consider any revenues derived by a patentee or former patentee before December 20, 1991 or any revenues derived by a former patentee after the former patentee ceased to be entitled to the benefit of the patent or to exercise any rights in relation to the patent.

Right to hearing

(6) Before the Board makes an order under this section, it shall provide the patentee or former patentee with a reasonable opportunity to be heard.

Limitation period

(7) No order may be made under this section in respect of a former patentee who, more than three years before

Idem

(3) Sous réserve du paragraphe (4), lorsqu'il estime que l'ancien breveté a vendu, alors qu'il était titulaire du brevet, le médicament à un prix qu'il juge avoir été excessif, le Conseil peut, par ordonnance, lui enjoindre de prendre l'une ou plusieurs des mesures suivantes pour compenser, selon lui, l'excédent qu'aurait procuré à l'ancien breveté la vente du médicament au prix excessif :

a) baisser, dans un marché canadien, le prix de vente de tout autre médicament lié à une invention dont il est titulaire du brevet dans la mesure et pour la période prévue par l'ordonnance;

b) payer à Sa Majesté du chef du Canada le montant précisé dans l'ordonnance.

Cas de politique de vente à prix excessif

(4) S'il estime que le breveté ou l'ancien breveté s'est livré à une politique de vente du médicament à un prix excessif, compte tenu de l'envergure et de la durée des ventes à un tel prix, le Conseil peut, par ordonnance, au lieu de celles qu'il peut prendre en application, selon le cas, des paragraphes (2) ou (3), lui enjoindre de prendre l'une ou plusieurs des mesures visées par ce paragraphe de façon à réduire suffisamment les recettes pour compenser, selon lui, au plus le double de l'excédent procuré par la vente au prix excessif.

Excédent

(5) Aux fins des paragraphes (2), (3) ou (4), il n'est pas tenu compte, dans le calcul de l'excédent, des recettes antérieures au 20 décembre 1991 ni, dans le cas de l'ancien breveté, des recettes faites après qu'il a cessé d'avoir droit aux avantages du brevet ou d'exercer les droits du titulaire.

Droit à l'audition

(6) Avant de prendre une ordonnance en vertu du présent article, le Conseil doit donner au breveté ou à l'ancien breveté la possibilité de présenter ses observations.

Prescription

(7) Le présent article ne permet pas de prendre une ordonnance à l'encontre des anciens brevetés qui, plus de trois ans avant le début des procédures, ont cessé d'avoir

the day on which the proceedings in the matter commenced, ceased to be entitled to the benefit of the patent or to exercise any rights in relation to the patent.

1993, c. 2, s. 7; 1994, c. 26, s. 54(F).

Compliance

84 (1) A patentee or former patentee who is required by any order made under section 83 to reduce the price of a medicine shall commence compliance with the order within one month after the date of the order or within such greater period after that date as the Board determines is practical and reasonable, having regard to the circumstances of the patentee or former patentee.

Idem

(2) A patentee or former patentee who is directed by any order made under section 83 to pay an amount to Her Majesty shall pay that amount within one month after the date of the order or within such greater period after that date as the Board determines is practical and reasonable, having regard to the circumstances of the patentee or former patentee.

Debt due to Her Majesty

(3) An amount payable by a patentee or former patentee to Her Majesty under any order made under section 83 constitutes a debt due to Her Majesty and may be recovered in any court of competent jurisdiction.

1993, c. 2, s. 7.

Factors to be considered

85 (1) In determining under section 83 whether a medicine is being or has been sold at an excessive price in any market in Canada, the Board shall take into consideration the following factors, to the extent that information on the factors is available to the Board:

(a) the prices at which the medicine has been sold in the relevant market;

(b) the prices at which other medicines in the same therapeutic class have been sold in the relevant market;

(c) the prices at which the medicine and other medicines in the same therapeutic class have been sold in countries other than Canada;

(d) changes in the Consumer Price Index; and

(e) such other factors as may be specified in any regulations made for the purposes of this subsection.

droit aux avantages du brevet ou d'exercer les droits du titulaire.

1993, ch. 2, art. 7; 1994, ch. 26, art. 54(F).

Exécution

84 (1) Le breveté ou l'ancien breveté est tenu de commencer l'exécution de l'ordonnance de réduction des prix dans le mois suivant sa prise ou dans le délai supérieur que le Conseil estime pratique et raisonnable compte tenu de sa situation.

Idem

(2) Le breveté ou l'ancien breveté est tenu d'exécuter l'ordonnance de paiement à Sa Majesté dans le mois suivant sa prise ou dans le délai supérieur que le Conseil estime pratique et raisonnable, compte tenu de sa situation.

Recouvrement des créances

(3) Les sommes payables en application d'une ordonnance prise en vertu du présent article constituent des créances de Sa Majesté, dont le recouvrement peut être poursuivi à ce titre devant toute juridiction compétente.

1993, ch. 2, art. 7.

Facteurs de fixation du prix

85 (1) Pour décider si le prix d'un médicament vendu sur un marché canadien est excessif, le Conseil tient compte des facteurs suivants, dans la mesure où des renseignements sur ces facteurs lui sont disponibles :

a) le prix de vente du médicament sur un tel marché;

b) le prix de vente de médicaments de la même catégorie thérapeutique sur un tel marché;

c) le prix de vente du médicament et d'autres médicaments de la même catégorie thérapeutique à l'étranger;

d) les variations de l'indice des prix à la consommation;

e) tous les autres facteurs précisés par les règlements d'application du présent paragraphe.

Additional factors

(2) Where, after taking into consideration the factors referred to in subsection (1), the Board is unable to determine whether the medicine is being or has been sold in any market in Canada at an excessive price, the Board may take into consideration the following factors:

(a) the costs of making and marketing the medicine; and

(b) such other factors as may be specified in any regulations made for the purposes of this subsection or as are, in the opinion of the Board, relevant in the circumstances.

Research costs

(3) In determining under section 83 whether a medicine is being or has been sold in any market in Canada at an excessive price, the Board shall not take into consideration research costs other than the Canadian portion of the world costs related to the research that led to the invention pertaining to that medicine or to the development and commercialization of that invention, calculated in proportion to the ratio of sales by the patentee in Canada of that medicine to total world sales.

1993, c. 2, s. 7.

Hearings to be public

86 (1) A hearing under section 83 shall be held in public unless the Board is satisfied on representations made by the person to whom the hearing relates that specific, direct and substantial harm would be caused to the person by the disclosure of information or documents at a public hearing, in which case the hearing or any part thereof may, at the discretion of the Board, be held in private.

Notice of hearing to certain persons

(2) The Board shall give notice to the Minister of Industry or such other Minister as may be designated by the regulations and to provincial ministers of the Crown responsible for health of any hearing under section 83, and each of them is entitled to appear and make representations to the Board with respect to the matter being heard.

1993, c. 2, s. 7; 1995, c. 1, s. 62.

Information, etc., privileged

87 (1) Subject to subsection (2), any information or document provided to the Board under section 80, 81 or 82 or in any proceeding under section 83 is privileged, and no person who has obtained the information or document pursuant to this Act shall, without the authorization of the person who provided the information or document, knowingly disclose the information or document

Facteurs complémentaires

(2) Si, après avoir tenu compte de ces facteurs, il est incapable de décider si le prix d'un médicament vendu sur un marché canadien est excessif, le Conseil peut tenir compte des facteurs suivants :

a) les coûts de réalisation et de mise en marché;

b) tous les autres facteurs précisés par les règlements d'application du présent paragraphe ou qu'il estime pertinents.

Coûts de recherche

(3) Pour l'application de l'article 83, le Conseil ne tient compte, dans les coûts de recherche, que de la part canadienne des coûts mondiaux directement liée à la recherche qui a abouti soit à l'invention du médicament, soit à sa mise au point et à sa mise en marché, calculée proportionnellement au rapport entre les ventes canadiennes du médicament par le breveté et le total des ventes mondiales.

1993, ch. 2, art. 7.

Audiences publiques

86 (1) Les audiences tenues dans le cadre de l'article 83 sont publiques, sauf si le Conseil est convaincu, à la suite d'observations faites par l'intéressé, que la divulgation des renseignements ou documents en cause causerait directement à celui-ci un préjudice réel et sérieux; le cas échéant, l'audience peut, selon ce que décide le Conseil, se tenir à huis clos en tout ou en partie.

Avis

(2) Le Conseil avise le ministre de l'Industrie, ou tout autre ministre désigné par règlement, et les ministres provinciaux responsables de la santé de toute audience tenue aux termes de l'article 83 et leur donne la possibilité de présenter leurs observations.

1993, ch. 2, art. 7; 1995, ch. 1, art. 62.

Protection des renseignements

87 (1) Sous réserve du paragraphe (2), les renseignements ou documents fournis au Conseil en application des articles 80, 81, 82 ou 83 sont protégés; nul ne peut, après les avoir obtenus en conformité avec la présente loi, sciemment les communiquer ou en permettre la communication sans l'autorisation de la personne qui les a fournis, sauf s'ils ont été divulgués dans le cadre d'une audience publique tenue en vertu de l'article 83.

or allow it to be disclosed unless it has been disclosed at a public hearing under section 83.

Disclosure, etc.

(2) Any information or document referred to in subsection (1)

(a) may be disclosed by the Board to any person engaged in the administration of this Act under the direction of the Board, to the Minister of Industry or such other Minister as may be designated by the regulations and to the provincial ministers of the Crown responsible for health and their officials for use only for the purpose of making representations referred to in subsection 86(2); and

(b) may be used by the Board for the purpose of the report referred to in section 100.

1993, c. 2, s. 7; 1995, c. 1, s. 62.

Sales and Expense Information

Sales and expense information, etc., to be provided

88 (1) A patentee of an invention pertaining to a medicine shall, as required by and in accordance with the regulations, or as the Board may, by order, require, provide the Board with such information and documents as the regulations or the order may specify respecting

(a) the identity of the licensees in Canada of the patentee;

(b) the revenue of the patentee, and details of the source of the revenue, whether direct or indirect, from sales of medicine in Canada; and

(c) the expenditures made by the patentee in Canada on research and development relating to medicine.

Additional information, etc.

(2) Where the Board believes on reasonable grounds that any person has information or documents pertaining to the value of sales of medicine in Canada by a patentee or the expenditures made by a patentee in Canada on research and development relating to medicine, the Board may, by order, require the person to provide the Board with any of the information or documents that are specified in the order, or with copies thereof.

Compliance with order

(3) A person in respect of whom an order is made under subsection (1) or (2) shall comply with the order within

Communication

(2) Le Conseil peut communiquer les renseignements ou documents qui lui sont confiés à quiconque est chargé, sous sa responsabilité, de l'application de la présente loi, ainsi qu'au ministre de l'Industrie, ou tout autre ministre désigné par règlement, ou à un ministre provincial responsable de la santé, ou à tel de leurs fonctionnaires, à seule fin de leur permettre de présenter leurs observations au titre du paragraphe 86(2); il peut aussi s'en servir pour établir le rapport visé à l'article 100.

1993, ch. 2, art. 7; 1995, ch. 1, art. 62.

Renseignements sur les recettes et dépenses

Obligations des brevetés

88 (1) Le breveté est tenu, conformément aux règlements ou aux ordonnances du Conseil, de fournir à celui-ci des renseignements et documents sur les points suivants :

a) l'identité des titulaires des licences découlant du brevet au Canada;

b) les recettes directes ou indirectes qu'il a tirées de la vente au Canada du médicament, ainsi que la source de ces recettes;

c) les dépenses de recherche et développement faites au Canada relativement au médicament.

Renseignements complémentaires

(2) S'il estime pour des motifs raisonnables qu'une personne a des renseignements ou documents sur le montant des ventes au Canada de tout médicament ou sur les dépenses de recherche et développement supportées à cet égard au Canada par un titulaire de brevet, le Conseil peut, par ordonnance, l'obliger à les lui fournir — ou une copie de ceux-ci — selon ce que précise l'ordonnance.

Délai

(3) L'ordonnance est à exécuter dans le délai précisé ou que peut fixer le Conseil.

Information, etc., privileged

(4) Subject to section 89, any information or document provided to the Board under subsection (1) or (2) is privileged, and no person who has obtained the information or document pursuant to this Act shall, without the authorization of the person who provided the information or document, knowingly disclose the information or allow it to be disclosed, except for the purposes of the administration of this Act.

1993, c. 2, s. 7.

Report

89 (1) The Board shall in each year submit to the Minister a report setting out

(a) the Board's estimate of the proportion, as a percentage, that the expenditures of each patentee in Canada in the preceding year on research and development relating to medicine is of the revenues of those patentees from sales of medicine in Canada in that year; and

(b) the Board's estimate of the proportion, as a percentage, that the total of the expenditures of patentees in Canada in the preceding year on research and development relating to medicine is of the total of the revenues of those patentees from sales of medicine in Canada in that year.

Basis of report

(2) The report shall be based on an analysis of information and documents provided to the Board under subsections 88(1) and (2) and of such other information and documents relating to the revenues and expenditures referred to in subsection 88(1) as the Board considers relevant but, subject to subsection (3), shall not be set out in a manner that would make it possible to identify a person who provided any information or document under subsection 88(1) or (2).

Exception

(3) The Board shall, in the report, identify the patentees in respect of whom an estimate referred to in subsection (1) is given in the report, and may, in the report, identify any person who has failed to comply with subsection 88(1) or (2) at any time in the year in respect of which the report is made.

Tabling of report

(4) The Minister shall cause a copy of the report to be laid before each House of Parliament on any of the first thirty days on which that House is sitting after the report is submitted to the Minister.

1993, c. 2, s. 7.

Inquiries

Inquiries

90 The Board shall inquire into any matter that the Minister refers to the Board for inquiry and shall report to the Minister at the time and in accordance with the terms of reference established by the Minister.

1993, c. 2, s. 7.

Patented Medicine Prices Review Board

Establishment

91 (1) The Patented Medicine Prices Review Board is hereby continued, and shall consist of not more than five members to be appointed by the Governor in Council.

Tenure

(2) Each member of the Board shall hold office during good behaviour for a period of five years, but may be removed at any time by the Governor in Council for cause.

Reappointment

(3) A member of the Board, on the expiration of a first term of office, is eligible to be reappointed for one further term.

Acting after expiration of appointment

(4) A person may continue to act as a member of the Board after the expiration of the person's term of appointment in respect of any matter in which the person became engaged during the term of appointment.

Remuneration and expenses

(5) The members of the Board shall be paid such remuneration as may be fixed by the Governor in Council and are entitled to be paid reasonable travel and living expenses incurred by them in the course of their duties under this Act while absent from their ordinary place of residence.

1993, c. 2, s. 7.

Dépôt au Parlement

(4) Le ministre fait déposer le rapport devant chaque chambre du Parlement dans les trente premiers jours de séance de celle-ci suivant sa remise.

1993, ch. 2, art. 7.

Enquêtes

Enquêtes

90 Le Conseil fait enquête sur toute question que lui défère le ministre et lui fait rapport dans le délai prescrit et dans le cadre strict du mandat dont il est investi par le ministre.

1993, ch. 2, art. 7.

Conseil d'examen du prix des médicaments brevetés

Constitution

91 (1) Le Conseil d'examen du prix des médicaments brevetés est prorogé; il se compose d'au plus cinq conseillers nommés par le gouverneur en conseil.

Mandat

(2) Les conseillers sont nommés à titre inamovible pour un mandat de cinq ans, sous réserve de révocation motivée que prononce le gouverneur en conseil.

Nouveau mandat

(3) Les mandats des conseillers sont renouvelables une seule fois.

Prolongation

(4) Le conseiller dont le mandat est échu peut terminer les affaires dont il est saisi.

Rémunération

(5) Les conseillers reçoivent la rémunération fixée par le gouverneur en conseil et ont droit aux frais de déplacement et autres entraînés par l'accomplissement de leurs fonctions hors du lieu de leur résidence habituelle.

1993, ch. 2, art. 7.

Advisory panel

92 (1) The Minister may establish an advisory panel to advise the Minister on the appointment of persons to the Board, which panel shall include representatives of the provincial ministers of the Crown responsible for health, representatives of consumer groups, representatives of the pharmaceutical industry and such other persons as the Minister considers appropriate to appoint.

Consultation

(2) The Minister shall consult with an advisory panel established under subsection (1) for the purpose of making a recommendation to the Governor in Council with respect to the appointment of a person to the Board.

1993, c. 2, s. 7.

Chairperson and Vice-chairperson

93 (1) The Governor in Council shall designate one of the members of the Board to be Chairperson of the Board and one of the members to be Vice-chairperson of the Board.

Duties of Chairperson

(2) The Chairperson is the chief executive officer of the Board and has supervision over and direction of the work of the Board, including

   (a) the apportionment of the work among the members thereof and the assignment of members to deal with matters before the Board and to sit at hearings of the Board and to preside at hearings or other proceedings; and

   (b) generally, the conduct of the work of the Board, the management of its internal affairs and the duties of its staff.

Duties of Vice-chairperson

(3) If the Chairperson is absent or incapacitated or if the office of Chairperson is vacant, the Vice-chairperson has all the powers and functions of the Chairperson during the absence, incapacity or vacancy.

1993, c. 2, s. 7.

Staff

94 (1) Such officers and employees as are necessary for the proper conduct of the work of the Board shall be appointed in accordance with the *Public Service Employment Act*.

Idem

(2) Persons appointed under subsection (1) shall be deemed to be employed in the public service for the purposes of the *Public Service Superannuation Act*.

Comité consultatif

92 (1) Le ministre peut constituer un comité consultatif chargé de le conseiller sur la nomination des conseillers au Conseil. Le comité est formé de représentants des ministres provinciaux responsables de la santé, de représentants des groupes de consommateurs, de représentants de l'industrie pharmaceutique et de toute autre personne que le ministre estime indiqué d'y nommer.

Consultation

(2) Le ministre doit consulter le comité avant de faire ses recommandations au gouverneur en conseil sur la nomination d'un conseiller au Conseil.

1993, ch. 2, art. 7.

Président et vice-président

93 (1) Le gouverneur en conseil désigne, parmi les conseillers, un président et un vice-président.

Attributions du président

(2) Le président est le premier dirigeant du Conseil et, à ce titre, il en assure la direction. Il est notamment chargé de la répartition des affaires entre les conseillers, de la constitution et de la présidence des audiences et des autres procédures, ainsi que de la conduite des travaux du Conseil et de la gestion de son personnel.

Attributions du vice-président

(3) En cas d'absence ou d'empêchement du président, ou de vacance de son poste, la présidence est assumée par le vice-président.

1993, ch. 2, art. 7.

Personnel

94 (1) Le personnel nécessaire à l'exercice des activités du Conseil est nommé conformément à la *Loi sur l'emploi dans la fonction publique*.

Idem

(2) Ce personnel est réputé faire partie de la fonction publique pour l'application de la *Loi sur la pension de la fonction publique*.

Technical assistance

(3) The Board may engage on a temporary basis the services of persons having technical or specialized knowledge to advise and assist in the performance of its duties and, with the approval of the Treasury Board, the Board may fix and pay the remuneration and expenses of those persons.

1993, c. 2, s. 7; 2003, c. 22, s. 225(E).

Principal office

95 (1) The principal office of the Board shall be in the National Capital Region described in the schedule to the *National Capital Act*.

Meetings

(2) The Board may meet at such times and places in Canada as the Chairperson deems advisable.

1993, c. 2, s. 7.

General powers, etc.

96 (1) The Board has, with respect to the attendance, swearing and examination of witnesses, the production and inspection of documents, the enforcement of its orders and other matters necessary or proper for the due exercise of its jurisdiction, all such powers, rights and privileges as are vested in a superior court.

Rules

(2) The Board may, with the approval of the Governor in Council, make general rules

(a) specifying the number of members of the Board that constitutes a quorum in respect of any matter; and

(b) for regulating the practice and procedure of the Board.

By-laws

(3) The Board may make by-laws for carrying out the work of the Board, the management of its internal affairs and the duties of its staff.

Guidelines

(4) Subject to subsection (5), the Board may issue guidelines with respect to any matter within its jurisdiction but such guidelines are not binding on the Board or any patentee.

Consultation

(5) Before the Board issues any guidelines, it shall consult with the Minister, the provincial ministers of the Crown responsible for health and such representatives of consumer groups and representatives of the pharmaceutical industry as the Minister may designate for the purpose.

Non-application of *Statutory Instruments Act*

(6) The *Statutory Instruments Act* does not apply to guidelines issued under subsection (4).

1993, c. 2, s. 7.

Proceedings

97 (1) All proceedings before the Board shall be dealt with as informally and expeditiously as the circumstances and considerations of fairness permit.

Differences of opinion among members

(2) In any proceedings before the Board,

(a) in the event of a difference of opinion among the members determining any question, the opinion of the majority shall prevail; and

(b) in the event of an equally divided opinion among the members determining any question, the presiding member may determine the question.

1993, c. 2, s. 7.

Orders

98 (1) The Board may, in any order, direct

(a) that the order or any portion thereof shall come into force at a future time, on the happening of a contingency, event or condition specified in the order or on the performance to the satisfaction of the Board, or a person named by it, of any terms specified in the order; and

(b) that the whole or any portion of the order shall have effect for a limited time or until the happening of a specified event.

Interim orders, etc.

(2) The Board may make interim orders or reserve further directions for an adjourned hearing of a matter.

Rescission and variation

(3) The Board may vary or rescind any order made by it and may re-hear any matter.

Certificates

(4) Where any person satisfies the Board that the Board would not have sufficient grounds to make an order under section 83 in respect of the person, the Board may, after the person pays any fees required to be paid by the regulations, issue to the person a certificate to that effect, but no certificate is binding on the Board.

1993, c. 2, s. 7.

Enforcement of orders

99 (1) Any order of the Board may be made an order of the Federal Court or any superior court of a province and is enforceable in the same manner as an order of the court.

Procedure

(2) To make an order of the Board an order of a court, the usual practice and procedure of the court in such matters may be followed or, in lieu thereof, the Board may file with the registrar of the court a certified copy of the Board's order, and thereupon the order becomes an order of the court.

Effect of variation or rescission

(3) Where an order of the Board that has been made an order of a court is varied or rescinded by a subsequent order of the Board, the subsequent order of the Board shall be made an order of the court in the manner described in subsection (1), and the order of the court shall be deemed to have been varied or rescinded accordingly.

Option to enforce

(4) Nothing in this section prevents the Board from exercising any of its powers under this Act.

1993, c. 2, s. 7.

Report of Board

100 (1) The Board shall in each year submit to the Minister a report on its activities during the preceding year.

Idem

(2) The report shall contain

(a) a summary of pricing trends in the pharmaceutical industry; and

(b) the name of each patentee in respect of whom an order was made under subsection 80(2) during the year and a statement as to the status of the matter in respect of which the order was made.

Report summary

(3) The summary referred to in paragraph (2)(a) may be based on information and documents provided to the Board by any patentee under section 80, 81 or 82 or in any proceeding under section 83, but shall not be set out

des droits réglementaires, délivrer à l'intéressé un certificat en ce sens, sans toutefois être lié par celui-ci.

1993, ch. 2, art. 7.

Assimilation

99 (1) Les ordonnances du Conseil peuvent être assimilées à des ordonnances de la Cour fédérale ou d'une cour supérieure; le cas échéant, leur exécution s'effectue selon les mêmes modalités.

Procédure

(2) L'assimilation se fait selon la pratique et la procédure suivies par le tribunal saisi ou par la production au greffe du tribunal d'une copie certifiée conforme de l'ordonnance. L'ordonnance est dès lors une ordonnance de la cour.

Modification ou annulation

(3) Les ordonnances du Conseil qui modifient ou annulent des ordonnances déjà assimilées doivent, selon les mêmes modalités, faire l'objet d'une assimilation; l'ordonnance est alors réputée les modifier ou les annuler, selon le cas.

Faculté d'exécution

(4) Le présent article n'a pas pour effet de limiter l'exercice par le Conseil des compétences conférées par la présente loi.

1993, ch. 2, art. 7.

Rapport

100 (1) Le Conseil remet au ministre un rapport d'activité pour l'année précédente.

Idem

(2) Ce rapport comporte, outre un résumé des tendances des prix dans le secteur pharmaceutique, le nom de tous les brevetés ayant fait l'objet d'une ordonnance dans le cadre du paragraphe 80(2) et l'exposé de la situation dans chacun de ces cas.

Résumé

(3) Le résumé peut se fonder sur les renseignements ou documents confiés au Conseil en application des articles 80, 81, 82 ou 83, mais sans permettre l'identification du breveté.

in a manner that would make it possible to identify that patentee.

Tabling of report

(4) The Minister shall cause a copy of the report to be laid before each House of Parliament on any of the first thirty days on which that House is sitting after the report is submitted to the Minister.

1993, c. 2, s. 7.

Regulations

Regulations

101 (1) Subject to subsection (2), the Governor in Council may make regulations

(a) specifying the information and documents that shall be provided to the Board under subsection 80(1) or (2) or 88(1);

(b) respecting the form and manner in which and times at which such information and documents shall be provided to the Board and imposing conditions respecting the provision of such information and documents;

(c) specifying a period for the purposes of subsection 80(2);

(d) specifying factors for the purposes of subsection 85(1) or (2), including factors relating to the introductory price of any medicine to which a patented invention pertains;

(e) designating a Minister for the purposes of subsection 86(2) or paragraph 87(2)(a);

(f) defining, for the purposes of sections 88 and 89, the expression *research and development*;

(g) requiring fees to be paid before the issue of any certificate referred to in subsection 98(4) and specifying those fees or the manner of determining those fees;

(h) requiring or authorizing the Board to perform such duties, in addition to those provided for in this Act, as are specified in the regulations, including duties to be performed by the Board in relation to the introductory price of any medicine to which a patented invention pertains; and

(i) conferring on the Board such powers, in addition to those provided for in this Act, as will, in the opinion of the Governor in Council, enable the Board to perform any duties required or authorized to be performed by it by any regulations made under paragraph (h).

Recommendation

(2) No regulations may be made under paragraph (1)(d), (f), (h) or (i) except on the recommendation of the Minister, made after the Minister has consulted with the provincial ministers of the Crown responsible for health and with such representatives of consumer groups and representatives of the pharmaceutical industry as the Minister considers appropriate.

1993, c. 2, s. 7.

Meetings with Minister

Meetings with Minister

102 (1) The Minister may at any time convene a meeting of the following persons:

(a) the Chairperson and such members of the Board as the Chairperson may designate;

(b) the provincial ministers of the Crown responsible for health or such representatives as they may designate;

(c) such representatives of consumer groups and representatives of the pharmaceutical industry as the Minister may designate; and

(d) such other persons as the Minister considers appropriate.

Agenda

(2) The participants at a meeting convened under subsection (1) shall consider such matters in relation to the administration or operation of sections 79 to 101 as the Minister may determine.

1993, c. 2, s. 7.

Agreements with Provinces

Agreements with provinces

103 The Minister may enter into agreements with any province respecting the distribution of, and may pay to that province out of the Consolidated Revenue Fund, amounts received or collected by the Receiver General under section 83 or 84 or in respect of an undertaking given by a patentee or former patentee that is accepted by the Board in lieu of holding a hearing or making an order under section 83, less any costs incurred in relation to the collection and distribution of those amounts.

1993, c. 2, s. 7; 1994, c. 26, s. 55(F); 1999, c. 26, s. 50.

verser en partage à la province sont payables sur le Trésor.

1993, ch. 2, art. 7; 1994, ch. 26, art. 55(F); 1999, ch. 26, art. 50.

SCHEDULE 1

(Definition "pharmaceutical product" in section 21.02 and paragraph 21.03(1)(a))

abacavir (ABC)	tablet, 300 mg (as sulfate); oral solution, 100 mg (as sulfate)/5 mL
abacavir + lamivudine + zidovudine	tablet, 300 mg (as sulfate) + 150 mg + 300 mg
aciclovir	tablet, 200 mg; powder for injection, 250 mg (as sodium salt) in vial
amphotericin B	powder for injection, 50 mg in vial
amprenavir	tablet, 150 mg; capsule, 50 mg or 150 mg; oral solution, 15 mg/mL
azithromycin	capsule, 250 mg or 500 mg; suspension, 200 mg/5 mL
beclometasone	inhalation (aerosol), 50 micrograms per dose (dipropionate) or 250 micrograms (dipropionate) per dose
ceftazidime	powder for injection, 250 mg (as pentahydrate) in vial
ceftriaxone	injection, 500 mg (as sodium); powder for injection, 250 mg (as sodium salt) in vial
ciclosporin	capsule, 25 mg; concentrate for injection, 50 mg/mL in 1-mL ampoule (for organ transplantation)
ciprofloxacin	tablet, 250 mg (as hydrochloride)
ciprofloxacin	tablet, 250 mg or 500 mg
daunorubicin	powder for injection, 50 mg (as hydrochloride) in vial
delavirdine	capsule or tablet, 100 mg (as mesylate)
didanosine (ddl)	buffered chewable, dispersible tablet, 25 mg, 50 mg, 100 mg, 150 mg, 200 mg; buffered powder for oral solution, 100 mg, 167 mg, 250 mg, packets; unbuffered enteric coated capsule, 125 mg, 200 mg, 250 mg, 400 mg
diphtheria antitoxin	injection, 10 000 IU or 20 000 IU in vial
diphtheria vaccine	
doxorubicin	powder for injection, 10 mg or 50 mg (hydrochloride) in vial
efavirenz (EFV or EFZ)	capsule, 50 mg, 100 mg or 200 mg; oral solution, 150 mg/5 mL
efavirenz + emtricitabine + tenofovir disoproxil	tablet, 600 mg + 200 mg + 300 mg
eflornithine	injection, 200 mg (hydrochloride)/mL in 100-mL bottles
emtricitabine + tenofovir disoproxil	tablet, 200 mg + 300 mg
enalapril	tablet, 2.5 mg
erythromycin	capsule or tablet, 250 mg (as stearate or ethyl succinate); powder for oral suspension, 125 mg (as stearate or ethyl succinate); powder for injection, 500 mg (as lactobionate) in vial
etoposide	capsule, 100 mg; injection, 20 mg/mL in 5-mL ampoule
factor IX (complex coagulation factors II, VII, IX, X) concentrate	dried
hepatitis B vaccine	
ibuprofen	tablet, 200 mg or 400 mg
indinavir (IDV)	capsule, 200 mg, 333 mg or 400 mg (as sulfate)
insulin injection (soluble)	injection, 40 IU/mL in 10-mL vial or 100 IU/mL in 10-mL vial
intermediate-acting insulin	injection, 40 IU/mL in 10-mL vial; 100 IU/mL in 10-mL vial (as compound insulin zinc suspension or isophane insulin)
isoniazid + pyrazinamide + rifampin	tablet, 50 mg + 300 mg + 120 mg
ivermectin	scored tablet, 3 mg or 6 mg
lamivudine (3TC)	capsule or tablet, 150 mg; oral solution 50 mg/5 mL
lamivudine + nevirapine + zidovudine	tablet, 150 mg + 200 mg + 300 mg
lamivudine + zidovudine	tablet, 150 mg + 300 mg
levodopa + carbidopa	tablet, 100 mg + 10 mg or 250 mg + 25 mg
levofloxacin	tablet, 250 mg or 500 mg
lithium carbonate	capsule or tablet, 300 mg
lopinavir + ritonavir (LPV/r)	capsule, 133.3 mg + 33.3 mg; oral solution, 400 mg + 100 mg/5 mL
metoclopramide	tablet, 10 mg (hydrochloride); injection, 5 mg (hydrochloride)/mL in 2-mL ampoule
metronidazole	tablet, 250 mg or 500 mg; injection, 500 mg in 100-mL vial; suppository, 500 mg or 1 g; oral suspension, 200 mg (as benzoate)/5 mL
morphine	injection, 10 mg in 1-mL ampoule (sulfate or hydrochloride); oral solution, 10 mg (hydrochloride or sulfate)/5 mL; tablet, 10 mg (sulfate)
nelfinavir (NFV)	tablet, 250 mg (as mesilate); oral powder, 50 mg/g
nevirapine (NVP)	tablet, 200 mg; oral suspension, 50 mg/5 mL
nifedipine	sustained release formulations, tablet, 10 mg
nitrofurantoin	tablet, 100 mg
ofloxacin	tablet, 200 mg or 400 mg
oseltamivir phosphate	capsule, 75 mg; powder for oral suspension, 12 mg/mL
potassium chloride	powder for solution
ranitidine	tablet, 150 mg (as hydrochloride); oral solution, 75 mg/5 mL; injection, 25 mg/mL in 2-mL ampoule
ritonavir	capsule, 100 mg; oral solution, 400 mg/5 mL
salbutamol	tablet, 2 mg or 4 mg (as sulfate); inhalation (aerosol), 100 micrograms (as sulfate) per dose; syrup, 2 mg/5 mL; injection, 50 micrograms (as sulfate)/mL in 5-mL ampoule; respirator solution for use in nebulizers, 5 mg (as sulfate)/mL

saquinavir (SQV)	capsule, 200 mg
stavudine (d4T)	capsule, 15 mg, 20 mg, 30 mg or 40 mg; powder for oral solution, 5 mg/5 mL
tenofovir disoproxil	tablet, 300 mg
testosterone	injection, 200 mg (enantate) in 1-mL ampoule
timolol	solution (eye drops), 0.25% or 0.5% (as maleate)
verapamil	tablet, 40 mg or 80 mg (hydrochloride); injection, 2.5 mg (hydrochloride)/mL in 2-mL ampoule
zalcitabine	capsule or tablet, 0.375 mg or 0.750 mg
zidovudine (ZDV or AZT)	tablet, 300 mg; capsule, 100 mg or 250 mg; oral solution or syrup, 50 mg/5 mL; solution for IV infusion injection, 10 mg/mL in 20-mL vial

2004, c. 23, Sch. 1; SOR/2005-276; SOR/2006-204; SOR/2015-154.

ANNEXE 1

(définition de « produit pharmaceutique » à l'article 21.02 et alinéa 21.03(1)a))

abacavir (ABC)	comprimé, 300 mg (sous forme de sulfate); solution buvable, 100 mg (sous forme de sulfate)/5 ml
abacavir + lamivudine + zidovudine	comprimé, 300 mg (sous forme de sulfate) + 150 mg + 300 mg
aciclovir	comprimé, 200 mg; poudre pour préparations injectables, 250 mg (sous forme de sel de sodium) en flacon
amphotéricine B	poudre pour préparations injectables, 50 mg en flacon
amprenavir	comprimé, 150 mg; gélule, 50 mg ou 150 mg; solution buvable, 15 mg/ml
antitoxine diphtérique	solution injectable, 10 000 UI ou 20 000 UI en flacon
azithromycine	gélules, 250 mg ou 500 mg; suspension, 200 mg/5 ml
béclométasone	solution pour inhalation (aérosol), 50 microgrammes par dose (dipropionate) ou 250 microgrammes (dipropionate) par dose
carbonate de lithium	gélule ou comprimé, 300 mg
ceftazidime	poudre pour préparations injectables, 250 mg (sous forme de pentahydrate) en flacon
ceftriaxone	solution injectable, 500 mg (sous forme de sodium); poudre pour préparations injectables, 250 mg (sous forme de sel de sodium) en flacon
chlorure de potassium	poudre pour solution
ciclosporine	gélule, 25 mg; concentré pour solution injectable, 50 mg/ml en ampoule de 1 ml (pour les transplantations d'organes)
ciprofloxacine	comprimé, 250 mg (sous forme de chlorhydrate)
ciprofloxacine	comprimé, 250 mg ou 500 mg
complexe de facteur IX (concentré des facteurs de coagulation II, VII, IX, X)	desséché
daunorubicine	poudre pour préparations injectables, 50 mg (sous forme de chlorhydrate) en flacon
delavirdine	gélule ou comprimé, 100 mg (sous forme de mésilate)
didanosine (ddl)	comprimé à croquer, dispersible tamponné, 25 mg, 50 mg, 100 mg, 150 mg, 200 mg; poudre tamponnée pour solution buvable, 100 mg, 167 mg, 250 mg en sachets; gélule gastro-résistante non tamponnée, 125 mg, 200 mg, 250 mg, 400 mg
doxorubicine	poudre pour préparations injectables, 10 mg ou 50 mg (chlorhydrate) en flacon
efavirenz (EFV ou EFZ)	gélule, 50 mg, 100 mg ou 200 mg; solution buvable, 150 mg/5 ml
efavirenz + emtricitabine + ténofovir disoproxil	comprimé, 600 mg + 200 mg + 300 mg
éflornithine	solution injectable, 200 mg (chlorhydrate)/ml en flacon de 100 ml
emtricitabine + ténofovir disoproxil	comprimé, 200 mg + 300 mg
énalapril	comprimé, 2,5 mg
érythromycine	gélule ou comprimé, 250 mg (sous forme de stéarate ou d'éthylsuccinate); poudre pour suspension buvable, 125 mg (sous forme de stéarate ou d'éthylsuccinate); poudre pour préparations injectables, 500 mg (sous forme de lactobionate) en flacon
étoposide	gélule, 100 mg; solution injectable, 20 mg/ml en ampoule de 5 ml
ibuprofène	comprimé, 200 mg ou 400 mg
indinavir (IDV)	gélule, 200 mg, 333 mg ou 400 mg (sous forme de sulfate)
insuline d'action intermédiaire	solution injectable, 40 UI/ml en flacon de 10 ml ou 100 UI/ml en flacon de 10 ml (sous forme d'un complexe d'insuline zinc en suspension ou d'insuline isophane)
insuline injectable (soluble)	solution injectable, 40 UI/ml en flacon de 10 ml ou 100 UI/ml en flacon de 10 ml
isoniazide + pyrazinamide + rifampine	comprimé, 50 mg + 300 mg + 120 mg
ivermectine	comprimé sécable, 3 mg ou 6 mg
lamivudine (3TC)	gélule ou comprimé, 150 mg; solution buvable, 50 mg/5 ml
lamivudine + névirapine + zidovudine	comprimé, 150 mg + 200 mg + 300 mg
lamivudine + zidovudine	comprimé, 150 mg + 300 mg
lévodopa + carbidopa	comprimé, 100 mg + 10 mg ou 250 mg + 25 mg
lévofloxacine	comprimé, 250 mg ou 500 mg
lopinavir + ritonavir (LPV/r)	gélule, 133,3 mg + 33,3 mg; solution buvable, 400 mg + 100 mg/5 ml
métoclopramide	comprimé, 10 mg (chlorhydrate); solution injectable, 5 mg (chlorhydrate)/ml en ampoule de 2 ml
métronidazole	comprimé, 250 mg ou 500 mg; solution injectable, 500 mg en flacon de 100 ml; suppositoire, 500 mg ou 1 g; suspension buvable, 200 mg (sous forme de benzoate)/5 ml
morphine	solution injectable, 10 mg (sulfate ou chlorhydrate) en ampoule de 1 ml; solution buvable, 10 mg (chlorhydrate ou sulfate)/5 ml; comprimé, 10 mg (sulfate)
nelfinavir (NFV)	comprimé, 250 mg (sous forme de mésilate); poudre pour administration orale, 50 mg/g
névirapine (NVP)	comprimé, 200 mg; suspension buvable, 50 mg/5 ml
nifédipine	formulations à libération prolongée, comprimé à 10 mg
nitrofurantoïne	comprimé, 100 mg
ofloxacine	comprimé, 200 mg ou 400 mg
phosphate d'oseltamivir	gélule, 75 mg; poudre pour suspension buvable, 12 mg/ml

ranitidine	comprimé, 150 mg (sous forme de chlorhydrate); solution buvable, 75 mg/5 ml; solution injectable, 25 mg/ml en ampoule de 2 ml
ritonavir	gélule, 100 mg; solution buvable, 400 mg/5 ml
salbutamol	comprimé, 2 mg ou 4 mg (sous forme de sulfate); solution pour inhalation (aérosol), 100 microgrammes (sous forme de sulfate) par dose; sirop, 2 mg (sous forme de sulfate)/5 ml; solution injectable, 50 microgrammes (sous forme de sulfate)/ml en ampoule de 5 ml; solution pour nébuliseur, 5 mg (sous forme de sulfate)/ml
saquinavir (SQV)	gélule, 200 mg
stavudine (d4T)	gélule, 15 mg, 20 mg, 30 mg ou 40 mg; poudre pour solution buvable, 5 mg/5 ml
ténofovir disoproxil	comprimé, 300 mg
testostérone	solution injectable, 200 mg (énantate) en ampoule de 1 ml
timolol	solution (collyre), 0,25 % ou 0,5 % (sous forme de maléate)
vaccin antidiphtérique	
vaccin antihépatite B	
vérapamil	comprimé, 40 mg ou 80 mg (chlorhydrate); solution injectable, 2,5 mg (chlorhydrate)/ml en ampoule de 2 ml
zalcitabine	gélule ou comprimé, 0,375 mg ou 0,750 mg
zidovudine (ZDV ou AZT)	comprimé, 300 mg; gélule, 100 mg ou 250 mg; solution buvable ou sirop, 50 mg/5 ml; solution pour perfusion intraveineuse, 10 mg/ml en flacon de 20 ml

2004, ch. 23, ann. 1; DORS/2005-276; DORS/2006-204; DORS/2015-154.

SCHEDULE 2

(Paragraph 21.03(1)(b))

Afghanistan
Afghanistan
Angola
Angola
Bangladesh
Bangladesh
Benin
Bénin
Bhutan
Bhoutan
Burkina Faso
Burkina Faso
Burundi
Burundi
Cambodia
Cambodge
Cape Verde
Cap-Vert
Central African Republic
République centrafricaine
Chad
Tchad
Comoros
Comores
Democratic Republic of the Congo
République démocratique du Congo
Djibouti
Djibouti
Equatorial Guinea
Guinée équatoriale
Eritrea
Érythrée
Ethiopia
Éthiopie
Gambia
Gambie
Guinea
Guinée
Guinea-Bissau
Guinée-Bissau
Haiti
Haïti
Kiribati
Kiribati
Lao People's Democratic Republic
République démocratique populaire lao
Lesotho
Lesotho
Liberia
Libéria
Madagascar
Madagascar

ANNEXE 2

(alinéa 21.03(1)b))

Afghanistan
Afghanistan
Angola
Angola
Bangladesh
Bangladesh
Bénin
Benin
Bhoutan
Bhutan
Burkina Faso
Burkina Faso
Burundi
Burundi
Cambodge
Cambodia
Cap-Vert
Cape Verde
Comores
Comoros
Djibouti
Djibouti
Érythrée
Eritrea
Éthiopie
Ethiopia
Gambie
Gambia
Guinée
Guinea
Guinée-Bissau
Guinea-Bissau
Guinée équatoriale
Equatorial Guinea
Haïti
Haiti
Îles Salomon
Solomon Islands
Kiribati
Kiribati
Lesotho
Lesotho
Libéria
Liberia
Madagascar
Madagascar
Malawi
Malawi
Maldives
Maldives
Mali
Mali

Patent
SCHEDULE 2

Brevets
ANNEXE 2

Malawi
Malawi

Maldives
Maldives

Mali
Mali

Mauritania
Mauritanie

Mozambique
Mozambique

Myanmar
Myanmar

Nepal
Népal

Niger
Niger

Rwanda
Rwanda

Samoa
Samoa

Sao Tome and Principe
Sao Tomé-et-Principe

Senegal
Sénégal

Sierra Leone
Sierra Leone

Solomon Islands
Îles Salomon

Somalia
Somalie

Sudan
Soudan

Timor-Leste
Timor-Leste

Togo
Togo

Tuvalu
Tuvalu

Uganda
Ouganda

United Republic of Tanzania
République-Unie de Tanzanie

Vanuatu
Vanuatu

Yemen
Yémen

Zambia
Zambie

2004, c. 23, Sch. 2.

Mauritanie
Mauritania

Mozambique
Mozambique

Myanmar
Myanmar

Népal
Nepal

Niger
Niger

Ouganda
Uganda

République centrafricaine
Central African Republic

République démocratique du Congo
Democratic Republic of the Congo

République démocratique populaire lao
Lao People's Democratic Republic

République-Unie de Tanzanie
United Republic of Tanzania

Rwanda
Rwanda

Samoa
Samoa

Sao Tomé-et-Principe
Sao Tome and Principe

Sénégal
Senegal

Sierra Leone
Sierra Leone

Somalie
Somalia

Soudan
Sudan

Tchad
Chad

Timor-Leste
Timor-Leste

Togo
Togo

Tuvalu
Tuvalu

Vanuatu
Vanuatu

Yémen
Yemen

Zambie
Zambia

2004, ch. 23, ann. 2.

SCHEDULE 3
(Paragraph 21.03(1)(c))

Albania
Albanie
Antigua and Barbuda
Antigua-et-Barbuda
Argentina
Argentine
Armenia
Arménie
Bahrain, Kingdom of
Bahreïn, Royaume de
Barbados
Barbade
Belize
Belize
Bolivia
Bolivie
Botswana
Botswana
Brazil
Brésil
Brunei Darussalam
Brunéi Darussalam
Bulgaria
Bulgarie
Cameroon
Cameroun
Chile
Chili
China
Chine
Colombia
Colombie
Congo
Congo
Costa Rica
Costa Rica
Côte d'Ivoire
Côte d'Ivoire
Croatia
Croatie
Cuba
Cuba
Dominica
Dominique
Dominican Republic
République dominicaine
Ecuador
Équateur
Egypt
Égypte
El Salvador
El Salvador

ANNEXE 3
(alinéa 21.03(1)c))

Afrique du Sud
South Africa
Albanie
Albania
Antigua-et-Barbuda
Antigua and Barbuda
Argentine
Argentina
Arménie
Armenia
Bahreïn, Royaume de
Bahrain, Kingdom of
Barbade
Barbados
Belize
Belize
Bolivie
Bolivia
Botswana
Botswana
Brésil
Brazil
Brunéi Darussalam
Brunei Darussalam
Bulgarie
Bulgaria
Cameroun
Cameroon
Chili
Chile
Chine
China
Colombie
Colombia
Congo
Congo
Costa Rica
Costa Rica
Côte d'Ivoire
Côte d'Ivoire
Croatie
Croatia
Cuba
Cuba
Dominique
Dominica
Égypte
Egypt
El Salvador
El Salvador
Équateur
Ecuador

Patent
SCHEDULE 3

Brevets
ANNEXE 3

Fiji
Fidji

Former Yugoslav Republic of Macedonia
Ex-République yougoslave de Macédoine

Gabon
Gabon

Georgia
Géorgie

Ghana
Ghana

Grenada
Grenade

Guatemala
Guatemala

Guyana
Guyana

Honduras
Honduras

India
Inde

Indonesia
Indonésie

Jamaica
Jamaïque

Jordan
Jordanie

Kenya
Kenya

Kyrgyz Republic
République kirghize

Liechtenstein
Liechtenstein

Malaysia
Malaisie

Mauritius
Maurice

Moldova
Moldova

Mongolia
Mongolie

Morocco
Maroc

Namibia
Namibie

Nicaragua
Nicaragua

Nigeria
Nigéria

Oman
Oman

Pakistan
Pakistan

Panama
Panama

Papua New Guinea
Papouasie-Nouvelle-Guinée

Ex-République yougoslave de Macédoine
Former Yugoslav Republic of Macedonia

Fidji
Fiji

Gabon
Gabon

Géorgie
Georgia

Ghana
Ghana

Grenade
Grenada

Guatemala
Guatemala

Guyana
Guyana

Honduras
Honduras

Inde
India

Indonésie
Indonesia

Jamaïque
Jamaica

Jordanie
Jordan

Kenya
Kenya

Liechtenstein
Liechtenstein

Malaisie
Malaysia

Maroc
Morocco

Maurice
Mauritius

Moldova
Moldova

Mongolie
Mongolia

Namibie
Namibia

Nicaragua
Nicaragua

Nigéria
Nigeria

Oman
Oman

Pakistan
Pakistan

Panama
Panama

Papouasie-Nouvelle-Guinée
Papua New Guinea

Paraguay
Paraguay

Patent
SCHEDULE 3

Brevets
ANNEXE 3

Paraguay *Paraguay*	Pérou *Peru*
Peru *Pérou*	Philippines *Philippines*
Philippines *Philippines*	République dominicaine *Dominican Republic*
Romania *Roumanie*	République kirghize *Kyrgyz Republic*
Saint Kitts and Nevis *Saint-Kitts-et-Nevis*	Roumanie *Romania*
Saint Lucia *Sainte-Lucie*	Sainte-Lucie *Saint Lucia*
Saint Vincent and the Grenadines *Saint-Vincent-et-les-Grenadines*	Saint-Kitts-et-Nevis *Saint Kitts and Nevis*
South Africa *Afrique du Sud*	Saint-Vincent-et-les-Grenadines *Saint Vincent and the Grenadines*
Sri Lanka *Sri Lanka*	Sri Lanka *Sri Lanka*
Suriname *Suriname*	Suriname *Suriname*
Swaziland *Swaziland*	Swaziland *Swaziland*
Thailand *Thaïlande*	Thaïlande *Thailand*
Trinidad and Tobago *Trinité-et-Tobago*	Trinité-et-Tobago *Trinidad and Tobago*
Tunisia *Tunisie*	Tunisie *Tunisia*
Uruguay *Uruguay*	Uruguay *Uruguay*
Venezuela *Venezuela*	Venezuela *Venezuela*
Zimbabwe *Zimbabwe*	Zimbabwe *Zimbabwe*
2004, c. 23, Sch. 3.	2004, ch. 23, ann. 3.

SCHEDULE 4

(Paragraph 21.03(1)(d))

Cyprus
Chypre

Czech Republic
République tchèque

Estonia
Estonie

Hong Kong, China
Hong Kong, Chine

Hungary
Hongrie

Israel
Israël

Korea
Corée

Kuwait
Koweït

Latvia
Lettonie

Lithuania
Lituanie

Macao, China
Macao, Chine

Malta
Malte

Mexico
Mexique

Poland
Pologne

Qatar
Qatar

Singapore
Singapour

Slovak Republic
République slovaque

Slovenia
Slovénie

Chinese Taipei
Taipei chinois

Turkey
Turquie

United Arab Emirates
Émirats arabes unis

2004, c. 23, Sch. 4.

ANNEXE 4

(alinéa 21.03(1)d))

Chypre
Cyprus

Corée
Korea

Émirats arabes unis
United Arab Emirates

Estonie
Estonia

Hong Kong, Chine
Hong Kong, China

Hongrie
Hungary

Israël
Israel

Koweït
Kuwait

Lettonie
Latvia

Lituanie
Lithuania

Macao, Chine
Macao, China

Malte
Malta

Mexique
Mexico

Pologne
Poland

Qatar
Qatar

République slovaque
Slovak Republic

République tchèque
Czech Republic

Singapour
Singapore

Slovénie
Slovenia

Taipei chinois
Chinese Taipei

Turquie
Turkey

2004, ch. 23, ann. 4.

RELATED PROVISIONS

— R.S., 1985, c. 33 (3rd Supp.), s. 31, as amended by 1992, c. 1, s. 145(F) (Sch. VIII, item 22)

Payments to provinces

31 (1) The Minister of Consumer and Corporate Affairs shall pay to each province for each of the fiscal years commencing in the period April 1, 1987 to March 31, 1991, for the purpose of research and development relating to medicine, an amount equal to the product obtained by multiplying

  (a) the quotient obtained by dividing

   (i) twenty-five million dollars

  by

   (ii) the total population of all provinces for the fiscal year in respect of which the payment is made,

by

  (b) the population of the province for the fiscal year in respect of which the payment is made.

Time and manner of payment

(2) Payment of any amount under this section shall be made out of the Consolidated Revenue Fund at such times and in such manner as the Governor in Council may, by regulation, prescribe.

Determination of population

(3) For the purposes of this section, the population of a province for a fiscal year shall be the population of that province on June 1 of that year as determined and published by the Chief Statistician of Canada.

— R.S., 1985, c. 33 (3rd Supp.), s. 32, as amended by 1992, c. 1, s. 145(F) (Sch. VIII, item 22)

Prohibition

32 (1) Notwithstanding anything in section 39 of the *Patent Act* or in any licence granted under that section, no person shall, under a licence granted prior to March 28, 1989 under that section in respect of a patent pertaining to the medicine Diltiazem hydrochloride, have or exercise any right to

  (a) import Diltiazem hydrochloride, if it is to be sold for consumption in Canada; or

  (b) make Diltiazem hydrochloride for sale for consumption in Canada.

Duration of prohibition

(2) The prohibition under subsection (1) expires on March 28, 1989.

Actions and proceedings barred

(3) No action or proceedings for any compensation or damages lie against Her Majesty in right of Canada as a result of the application of subsection (1) to a licence referred to in that subsection.

— 1993, c. 2, s. 9

Definitions

9 In this section and sections 10 to 13,

commencement day means the day on which section 3 of this Act comes into force; (*date d'entrée en vigueur*)

former Act means the *Patent Act*, as it read immediately before the commencement day. (*loi antérieure*)

— 1993, c. 2, s. 10

Pending proceedings

10 Any proceeding pending before the Patented Medicine Prices Review Board immediately before the commencement day shall be taken up and continued under and in accordance with sections 79 to 101 of the *Patent Act*, as enacted by section 7 of this Act, as if the proceeding had been commenced on or after that day.

— 1993, c. 2, s. 11

Licences continued

11 (1) A licence that has been granted under section 39 of the former Act before December 20, 1991 and that has not been terminated before the commencement day shall continue in effect according to its terms and, subject to subsection (2), sections 39 to 39.14 of the former Act shall continue to apply in respect of that licence as if they had not been repealed by section 3 of this Act.

Exception

(2) For the purposes of applying sections 39 to 39.14 of the former Act in respect of a licence continued by subsection (1), the prohibitions set out in subsections 39.11(1) and 39.14(1) of the former Act do not apply in respect of any medicine or medicines in respect of which an order has been made under paragraph 39.15(3)(d) of the former Act, if that order is in force immediately before the commencement day.

Durée de l'interdiction

(2) L'interdiction est levée le 28 mars 1989.

Interdiction des actions

(3) Il ne peut être intenté d'action, ou autre procédure, en dommages-intérêts contre Sa Majesté du chef du Canada pour l'application du paragraphe (1) à une licence qui y est visée.

— 1993, ch. 2, art. 9

Définitions

9 Les définitions qui suivent s'appliquent au présent article et aux articles 10 à 13.

date d'entrée en vigueur La date d'entrée en vigueur de l'article 3 de la présente loi. (*commencement day*)

loi antérieure La *Loi sur les brevets* dans sa version à la date d'entrée en vigueur. (*former Act*)

— 1993, ch. 2, art. 10

Procédures pendantes

10 Toutes les procédures qui, à la date d'entrée en vigueur, sont en cours devant le Conseil d'examen du prix des médicaments brevetés se poursuivent conformément aux articles 79 à 101 de la *Loi sur les brevets*, édictés par l'article 7 de la présente loi, comme si elles avaient été entamées à cette date.

— 1993, ch. 2, art. 11

Validité d'une licence au titre de la loi antérieure

11 (1) Toute licence accordée au titre de l'article 39 de la loi antérieure avant le 20 décembre 1991 et en cours de validité à la date d'entrée en vigueur reste valide dans les limites de ses conditions. Les articles 39 à 39.14 de la loi antérieure s'appliquent à elle comme s'ils n'avaient pas été abrogés par l'article 3 de la présente loi.

Exception

(2) Pour l'application des articles 39 à 39.14 de la loi antérieure aux licences prorogées au titre du paragraphe (1), les interdictions prévues aux paragraphes 39.11(1) et 39.14(1) de la loi antérieure ne s'appliquent pas aux médicaments visés par une ordonnance prise au titre de l'alinéa 39.15(3)d) de la loi antérieure si cette ordonnance est en vigueur avant la date d'entrée en vigueur.

— 1993, c. 2, s. 12

Licences ceasing to have effect

12 (1) Every licence granted under section 39 of the former Act on or after December 20, 1991 shall cease to have effect on the expiration of the day preceding the commencement day, and all rights or privileges acquired or accrued under that licence or under the former Act in relation to that licence shall thereupon be extinguished.

Actions for infringement barred

(2) For greater certainty, no action for infringement of a patent lies under the *Patent Act* in respect of any act that is done before the commencement day under a licence referred to in subsection (1) in accordance with the terms of that licence and sections 39 to 39.17 of the former Act.

— 1993, c. 2, s. 13

Actions and proceedings barred

13 No action or proceeding for any compensation or damages lies against Her Majesty in right of Canada in respect of any direct or indirect consequence resulting from the application of section 11 or 12 or the repeal of sections 39 to 39.17 of the former Act.

— 1993, c. 2, s. 14

Review of certain sections

14 (1) On the expiration of four years after this Act is assented to, the provisions of the *Patent Act* enacted by this Act shall be referred to such committee of the House of Commons, of the Senate or of both Houses of Parliament as may be designated or established for the purpose of the review referred to in subsection (2).

Idem

(2) The committee shall undertake a comprehensive review of the provisions of the *Patent Act* enacted by this Act and shall, within one year after the review is undertaken or within such further time as the House or Houses that designated or established the committee may authorize, submit a report thereon, including such recommendations as the committee may wish to make pertaining to those provisions.

— 1993, c. 44, s. 191(2)

No liability

191 (2) Her Majesty in right of Canada or a province is not, by reason only of the enactment of subsection (1), liable for any use of a patented invention before the day on which subsection (1) comes into force.

AMENDMENTS NOT IN FORCE

— 2014, c. 39, s. 114

1993, c. 15, s. 26(2)

114 The definitions *filing date* and *legal representatives* in section 2 of the *Patent Act* are replaced by the following:

filing date means the date on which an application for a patent in Canada is filed, as determined in accordance with section 28 or subsection 28.01(2) or 36(4); (*date de dépôt*)

legal representatives includes heirs, executors or administrators of the estate, liquidators of the succession, guardians, curators, tutors, transferees and all other persons claiming through applicants for patents and patentees of inventions; (*représentants légaux*)

— 2014, c. 39, s. 115

115 Subsection 4(2) of the Act is replaced by the following:

Duties of Commissioner
(2) The Commissioner shall receive all applications, fees, and documents relating to patents, shall perform and do all acts and things requisite for the granting and issuing of patents, shall have the charge and custody of the books, records and other things belonging to the Patent Office and shall have, for the purposes of this Act, all the powers that are or may be given by the *Inquiries Act* to a commissioner appointed under Part II of that Act.

— 2014, c. 39, s. 116

116 Subsection 7(1) of the Act is replaced by the following:

Officers and employees of Patent Office not to deal in patents
7 (1) No officer or employee of the Patent Office shall buy, sell, acquire or traffic in any invention, patent or right to a patent, or any interest in an invention, patent or right to a patent, and every purchase, sale, acquisition or transfer of any invention, patent or right to a patent, or any interest in an invention, patent or right to a patent, made by or to any officer or employee is void, or in Quebec, null.

— 2014, c. 39, s. 117

1993, c. 15, s. 27

117 Sections 8.1 and 8.2 of the Act are replaced by the following:

Electronic form and means

8.1 (1) Subject to the regulations, any document, information or fee that is submitted to the Commissioner or the Patent Office under this Act may be submitted in any electronic form, and by any electronic means, that is specified by the Commissioner.

Collection, storage, etc.

(2) Subject to the regulations, the Commissioner and the Patent Office may use electronic means to create, collect, receive, store, transfer, distribute, publish, certify or otherwise deal with documents or information or to seal a patent or other document.

Definition of *electronic*

(3) In this section, *electronic*, in reference to a form or means, includes optical, magnetic and other similar forms or means.

— 2014, c. 39, s. 118

118 (1) Subsection 12(1) of the Act is amended by adding the following after paragraph (a):

(**a.1**) defining *drawing* for the purposes of this Act and respecting the circumstances in which certain drawings may be furnished as part of applications for patents;

(**a.2**) respecting abstracts in applications for patents, including authorizing the Commissioner to amend or replace abstracts;

(**a.3**) respecting the consequences of a failure to comply with a notice given under subsection 27(7);

(**a.4**) respecting the processing and examination of applications for patents;

R.S., c. 33 (3rd Supp.), s. 3

(2) Paragraph 12(1)(c) of the Act is replaced by the following:

(**c**) respecting the registration of transmissions, disclaimers, judgments or other documents relating to a patent or an application for a patent;

(c.1) respecting the recording of transfers of patents or applications for patents;

(3) Subsection 12(1) of the Act is amended by adding the following after paragraph (i):

(i.1) for carrying into effect the Patent Law Treaty, done at Geneva on June 1, 2000, including any amendments and revisions made from time to time to which Canada is a party;

1993, c. 15, s. 29(2)

(4) Paragraphs 12(1)(j.1) to (j.5) of the Act are replaced by the following:

(j.01) respecting the circumstances in which an applicant, patentee or other person may or must be represented by a patent agent or other person in business before the Patent Office;

(j.1) respecting the submission, including in electronic form and by electronic means, of documents and information to the Commissioner or the Patent Office, including the time at which they are deemed to be received by the Commissioner or the Patent Office;

(j.2) respecting the use of electronic means for the purposes of subsection 8.1(2);

(j.3) respecting the withdrawal of an application for a patent and, for the purposes of subsections 10(4) and (5), prescribing the date, or the manner of determining the date, on or before which a request for priority or an application for a patent is to be withdrawn;

(j.31) respecting additions to the specification and additions of drawings for the purposes of subsection 28.01(1);

(j.4) respecting requests for priority, including

(i) the period within which priority is to be requested,

(ii) the information and documents that are to be submitted in support of requests for priority,

(iii) the period within which that information and those documents are to be submitted,

(iv) the withdrawal of requests for priority, and

(v) the correction of requests for priority or of information or documents submitted in support of them and the effect of corrections on the duration of the confidentiality period referred to in subsection 10(3);

(j.41) respecting the application of subsection 28.4(6);

(j.5) for the purposes of section 36,

    (i) defining *one invention*, and

    (ii) respecting requirements for divisional applications;

1993, c. 15, s. 29(2)

(5) Paragraph 12(1)(j.8) of the Act is replaced by the following:

(j.71) respecting amendments to the specification or drawings for the purposes of subsection 38.2(1);

(j.72) respecting the replacement of all or part of the text matter of a specification or drawing contained in an application for a patent that is in a language other than English or French with a translation into English or French, for the purposes of paragraph 38.2(3)(b);

(j.73) respecting the conditions set out in subsection 46(5), including the circumstances in which subparagraph 46(5)(a)(ii) and paragraph 46(5)(b) do not apply;

(j.74) establishing a period for the purposes of subsection 55.11(2);

(j.75) establishing a period for the purposes of subsection 55.11(3);

(j.76) respecting the reinstatement of applications for patents under subsection 73(3), including the circumstances in which subparagraph 73(3)(a)(ii) and paragraph 73(3)(b) do not apply;

(j.77) respecting communications between the Commissioner and any other person;

(j.8) authorizing the Commissioner to, during or after the end of the time period fixed under this Act for doing anything, extend that time period, subject to any prescribed terms and conditions, if the Commissioner considers that the circumstances justify the extension;

— 2014, c. 39, s. 119

R.S., c. 33 (3rd Supp.), s. 4

119 Section 15 of the Act is replaced by the following:

Register of patent agents

15 A register shall be kept in the Patent Office, on which shall be entered the names of all persons and firms that may act as patent agents.

(i) définir l'expression « une seule invention »,

(ii) régir les exigences relatives aux demandes complémentaires;

1993, ch. 15, par. 29(2)

(5) L'alinéa 12(1)j.8) de la même loi est remplacé par ce qui suit :

j.71) régir la modification des dessins et du mémoire descriptif pour l'application du paragraphe 38.2(1);

j.72) régir, pour l'application de l'alinéa 38.2(3)b), le remplacement de tout ou partie du texte des dessins ou du mémoire descriptif compris dans une demande de brevet qui est dans une langue autre que le français ou l'anglais par une traduction en français ou en anglais;

j.73) régir les conditions prévues au paragraphe 46(5), notamment les circonstances dans lesquelles le sous-alinéa 46(5)a)(ii) et l'alinéa 46(5)b) ne s'appliquent pas;

j.74) prévoir une période pour l'application du paragraphe 55.11(2);

j.75) prévoir une période pour l'application du paragraphe 55.11(3);

j.76) régir le rétablissement des demandes de brevet au titre du paragraphe 73(3), notamment les circonstances dans lesquelles le sous-alinéa 73(3)a)(ii) et l'alinéa 73(3)b) ne s'appliquent pas;

j.77) régir les communications entre le commissaire et toute autre personne;

j.8) autoriser le commissaire à proroger, si celui-ci estime que les circonstances le justifient, aux conditions réglementaires et même après son expiration, tout délai fixé sous le régime de la présente loi pour l'accomplissement d'un acte;

— 2014, ch. 39, art. 119

L.R., ch. 33 (3ᵉ suppl.), art. 4

119 L'article 15 de la même loi est remplacé par ce qui suit :

Registre des agents de brevets

15 Au Bureau des brevets est tenu un registre des personnes et entreprises pouvant agir à titre d'agents de brevets.

Representation by patent agents

15.1 In the prescribed circumstances, an applicant, patentee or other person shall be represented by a patent agent in all business before the Patent Office.

— 2014, c. 39, s. 120

1993, c. 15, s. 31

120 (1) Subsection 27(2) of the French version of the Act is replaced by the following:

Dépôt de la demande

(2) L'inventeur ou son représentant légal doit, conformément aux règlements, déposer une demande qui comprend une pétition et un mémoire descriptif de l'invention et payer la taxe réglementaire.

1993, c. 15, s. 31

(2) Subsections 27(6) and (7) of the Act are replaced by the following:

Drawings

(5.1) In the case of a machine, or in any other case in which an invention admits of illustration by means of drawings, the applicant shall, as part of the application, furnish drawings of the invention that clearly show all parts of the invention.

Particulars

(5.2) Each drawing is to include references corresponding with the specification. The Commissioner may, as the Commissioner sees fit, require further drawings or dispense with the requirement to furnish any drawing.

Requirements not met

(6) If, on its filing date, an application does not meet the requirements of subsection (2), other than the payment of the application fee, the Commissioner shall, by notice, require the applicant to meet those requirements on or before the prescribed date.

Application fee not paid

(7) If, on the filing date of the application, the application fee is not paid, the Commissioner shall, by notice, require the applicant to pay the application fee and the prescribed late fee on or before the prescribed date.

— 2014, c. 39, s. 121

R.S., c. 33 (3rd Supp.), s. 9; 1993, c. 15, ss. 32 and 33

121 Sections 27.1 and 28 of the Act are replaced by the following:

Représentation par un agent de brevets

15.1 Dans les circonstances réglementaires, une personne — demandeur de brevet, breveté ou autre — est tenue d'être représentée par un agent de brevets dans toute affaire devant le Bureau des brevets.

— 2014, ch. 39, art. 120

1993, ch. 15, art. 31

120 (1) Le paragraphe 27(2) de la version française de la même loi est remplacé par ce qui suit :

Dépôt de la demande

(2) L'inventeur ou son représentant légal doit, conformément aux règlements, déposer une demande qui comprend une pétition et un mémoire descriptif de l'invention et payer la taxe réglementaire.

1993, ch. 15, art. 31

(2) Les paragraphes 27(6) et (7) de la même loi sont remplacés par ce qui suit :

Dessins

(5.1) Dans le cas d'une machine ou dans tout autre cas où, pour l'intelligence de l'invention, il peut être fait usage de dessins, le demandeur fournit, dans sa demande, des dessins représentant clairement toutes les parties de l'invention.

Précisions

(5.2) Chaque dessin comporte les renvois correspondant au mémoire descriptif. Le commissaire peut, à son appréciation, exiger de nouveaux dessins ou dispenser de l'obligation de fournir tout dessin.

Conditions non remplies

(6) Si, à la date de dépôt, la demande ne remplit pas les conditions prévues au paragraphe (2) autres que le paiement de la taxe réglementaire, le commissaire doit, par avis, requérir le demandeur de les remplir au plus tard à la date réglementaire.

Non-paiement de la taxe réglementaire

(7) Si, à la date de dépôt, la taxe réglementaire visée au paragraphe (2) n'a pas été payée, le commissaire doit, par avis, requérir le demandeur de la payer et de payer la surtaxe réglementaire au plus tard à la date réglementaire.

— 2014, ch. 39, art. 121

L.R., ch. 33 (3ᵉ suppl.), art. 9; 1993, ch. 15, art. 32 et 33

121 Les articles 27.1 et 28 de la même loi sont remplacés par ce qui suit :

Patent
AMENDMENTS NOT IN FORCE

Brevets
MODIFICATIONS NON EN VIGUEUR

Reference to previously filed application

27.01 (1) Subject to the prescribed requirements and within the prescribed period, an applicant may submit to the Commissioner a statement to the effect that a reference to a specified previously filed application for a patent is being submitted instead of all or part of the specification contained in or a drawing that is required to be contained in the application. The prescribed period shall not end later than six months after the earliest date on which the Commissioner receives any document or information under subsection 28(1).

Specification or drawing deemed in application

(2) If the applicant submits the statement within the prescribed period and meets the prescribed requirements, the specification or drawing in the previously filed application is deemed to have been contained in the application on the date on which the Commissioner receives the statement.

Maintenance fees

27.1 (1) To maintain an application for a patent in effect, the prescribed fees shall be paid on or before the prescribed dates.

Late fee and notice

(2) If a prescribed fee is not paid on or before the applicable prescribed date,

   (a) the prescribed late fee shall be paid, in addition to the prescribed fee; and

   (b) the Commissioner shall send a notice to the applicant stating that the application will be deemed to be abandoned if the prescribed fee and late fee are not paid before the later of the end of six months after the applicable prescribed date and the end of two months after the date of the notice.

Prescribed fee deemed paid on prescribed date

(3) If the prescribed fee and late fee are paid before a notice is sent or, if a notice is sent, the prescribed fee and late fee are paid before the later of the end of six months after the applicable prescribed date and the end of two months after the date of the notice, the prescribed fee shall be deemed to have been paid on the applicable prescribed date.

Patent not invalid

(4) A patent shall not be declared invalid by reason only that the application on the basis of which the patent was granted was not maintained in effect.

Renvoi à une demande déposée antérieurement

27.01 (1) Sous réserve des exigences réglementaires, le demandeur peut, dans le délai réglementaire, fournir au commissaire une déclaration énonçant que le renvoi à la demande de brevet antérieurement déposée qu'il précise tient lieu de tout ou partie des dessins ou du mémoire descriptif qui doivent être compris dans sa demande de brevet. Le délai réglementaire se termine au plus tard six mois après la première date où le commissaire reçoit des documents ou renseignements visés au paragraphe 28(1).

Dessins et mémoire descriptif réputés faire partie de la demande

(2) Si le demandeur fournit la déclaration dans le délai imparti et satisfait aux exigences réglementaires, les dessins et le mémoire descriptif qui sont compris dans la demande antérieurement déposée sont réputés faire partie de la demande de brevet du demandeur à la date où le commissaire reçoit la déclaration.

Taxes pour maintenir une demande en état

27.1 (1) Afin de maintenir une demande de brevet en état, les taxes réglementaires doivent être payées au plus tard aux dates réglementaires.

Surtaxe et avis

(2) Si une taxe réglementaire n'est pas payée au plus tard à la date réglementaire applicable :

   a) la surtaxe réglementaire doit être payée en plus de la taxe réglementaire;

   b) le commissaire envoie au demandeur un avis l'informant que sa demande sera réputée abandonnée si la taxe et la surtaxe ne sont pas payées dans les six mois qui suivent la date réglementaire applicable ou, s'ils se terminent plus tard, dans les deux mois qui suivent la date de l'avis.

Taxe réglementaire réputée payée à la date réglementaire

(3) Si la taxe et la surtaxe sont payées soit avant l'envoi de l'avis, soit, dans le cas où celui-ci a été envoyé, dans les six mois qui suivent la date réglementaire applicable ou, s'ils se terminent plus tard, dans les deux mois qui suivent la date de l'avis, la taxe réglementaire est réputée avoir été payée à la date réglementaire applicable.

Brevet non invalide

(4) Un brevet ne peut être déclaré invalide du seul fait qu'il a été accordé au titre d'une demande qui n'a pas été maintenue en état.

Filing date

28 (1) Subject to subsections 28.01(2) and 36(4), the filing date of an application for a patent in Canada is the date on which the Commissioner receives the prescribed documents and information or, if they are received on different dates, the latest of those dates.

Outstanding documents and information

(2) The Commissioner shall notify an applicant whose application does not contain all of the documents and information referred to in subsection (1) of the documents and information that are outstanding and require that the applicant submit them within two months after the date of the notice.

Application deemed never filed

(3) If the Commissioner does not receive the outstanding documents and information within that two-month period, the application is deemed never to have been filed. However, any fees paid in respect of the application shall not be refunded to the applicant.

Addition to specification or addition of drawing to application

28.01 (1) Subject to the regulations, an applicant may, within the prescribed period, add to the specification that is contained in their application or add a drawing to their application for a patent by submitting the addition to the Commissioner along with a statement by the applicant indicating that the addition is being made under this section. The prescribed period shall not end later than six months after the earliest date on which the Commissioner receives any document or information under subsection 28(1).

Filing date

(2) If an applicant submits an addition to the Commissioner under subsection (1) and the addition is not withdrawn within the prescribed period, the filing date of the application is the later of the date on which the Commissioner receives the addition and the filing date referred to in subsection 28(1), unless

(a) the applicant has, on the earliest date on which the Commissioner receives any document or information under subsection 28(1), made a request for priority in respect of the application under section 28.4;

(b) the addition is completely contained in a previously regularly filed application on which the request for priority is based;

(c) the applicant requests, in accordance with the regulations, that the filing date be the filing date referred to in subsection 28(1); and

(d) the applicant complies with any prescribed requirements.

Addition deemed in application

(3) In the circumstances set out in paragraphs (2)(a) to (d), the addition is deemed to have been contained in the application on its filing date for the purposes of subsections 38.2(2) and (3).

— 2014, c. 39, s. 122

1993, c. 15, s. 33

122 Paragraph 28.1(1)(b) of the French version of the Act is replaced by the following:

b) à cette date, il s'est écoulé, depuis la date de dépôt de la demande déposée antérieurement, au plus douze mois;

— 2014, c. 39, s. 123

1993, c. 15, s. 33

123 Paragraph 28.2(1)(a) of the Act is replaced by the following:

(a) before the one-year period immediately preceding the filing date or, if the claim date is before that period, before the claim date by the applicant, or by a person who obtained knowledge, directly or indirectly, from the applicant, in such a manner that the subject-matter became available to the public in Canada or elsewhere;

— 2014, c. 39, s. 124

1993, c. 15, s. 33

124 Paragraph 28.3(a) of the Act is replaced by the following:

(a) information disclosed before the one-year period immediately preceding the filing date or, if the claim date is before that period, before the claim date by the applicant, or by a person who obtained knowledge, directly or indirectly, from the applicant in such a manner that the information became available to the public in Canada or elsewhere; and

— 2014, c. 39, s. 125

2001, c. 34, s. 63

125 (1) Subsection 28.4(2) of the Act is replaced by the following:

Requirements for request

(2) The request for priority shall be made in accordance with the regulations and the applicant shall submit to the Commissioner the filing date, the name of the country or

d) le demandeur satisfait aux exigences réglementaires.

Éléments ou dessin réputés avoir été compris dans la demande

(3) Dans les cas où les alinéas (2)a) à d) s'appliquent, pour l'application des paragraphes 38.2(2) et (3), les éléments ou le dessin sont réputés avoir été compris dans la demande à sa date de dépôt.

— 2014, ch. 39, art. 122

1993, ch. 15, art. 33

122 L'alinéa 28.1(1)b) de la version française de la même loi est remplacé par ce qui suit :

b) à cette date, il s'est écoulé, depuis la date de dépôt de la demande déposée antérieurement, au plus douze mois;

— 2014, ch. 39, art. 123

1993, ch. 15, art. 33

123 L'alinéa 28.2(1)a) de la même loi est remplacé par ce qui suit :

a) soit plus d'un an avant la date de dépôt de celle-ci, soit, si la date de la revendication est antérieure au début de cet an, avant la date de la revendication, avoir fait, de la part du demandeur ou d'un tiers ayant obtenu de lui l'information à cet égard de façon directe ou autrement, l'objet d'une communication qui l'a rendu accessible au public au Canada ou ailleurs;

— 2014, ch. 39, art. 124

1993, ch. 15, art. 33

124 L'alinéa 28.3a) de la même loi est remplacé par ce qui suit :

a) qui a été faite, soit plus d'un an avant la date de dépôt de la demande, soit, si la date de la revendication est antérieure au début de cet an, avant la date de la revendication, par le demandeur ou un tiers ayant obtenu de lui l'information à cet égard de façon directe ou autrement, de manière telle qu'elle est devenue accessible au public au Canada ou ailleurs;

— 2014, ch. 39, art. 125

2001, ch. 34, art. 63

125 (1) Le paragraphe 28.4(2) de la même loi est remplacé par ce qui suit :

Conditions

(2) Le demandeur la présente selon les modalités réglementaires; il doit aussi fournir au commissaire le nom du pays ou du bureau où a été déposée toute demande de

office of filing and the number of each previously regularly filed application on which the request is based.

Request deemed never filed

(2.1) A request for priority is deemed never to have been made if the request is not made in accordance with the regulations or if the applicant does not submit the information, other than the number of each previously regularly filed application, required under subsection (2).

1993, c. 15, s. 33

(2) Subsection 28.4(3) of the French version of the Act is replaced by the following:

Retrait de la demande

(3) Le demandeur peut, selon les modalités réglementaires, retirer la demande de priorité à l'égard de la demande déposée antérieurement; si elle est fondée sur plusieurs demandes, il peut la retirer à l'égard de toutes celles-ci ou d'une ou de plusieurs d'entre elles.

1993, c. 15, s. 33

(3) The portion of paragraph 28.4(5)(a) of the Act before subparagraph (i) is replaced by the following:

(a) on the filing date of one of the following applications, as the case may be, more than 12 months have elapsed since the filing date of the previously regularly filed application:

1993, c. 15, s. 33

(4) The portion of paragraph 28.4(5)(b) of the English version of the Act before subparagraph (i) is replaced by the following:

(b) before the filing date of the application referred to in one of subparagraphs (a)(i) to (iv), as the case may be, another application

(5) Section 28.4 of the Act is amended by adding the following after subsection (5):

Filing date deemed to be within 12 months

(6) Subject to the regulations, for the purposes of paragraph 28.1(1)(b) and subparagraphs 28.2(1)(d)(iii) and 28.4(5)(a)(i) and (ii), the filing date of the pending application or the co-pending application, as the case may be, shall be deemed to be within 12 months after the filing date of the previously regularly filed application if

(a) the filing date of the pending application or the co-pending application, as the case may be, is more than 12 months after the filing date of the previously regularly filed application but within two months after the end of those 12 months; and

brevet sur laquelle la demande de priorité est fondée, ainsi que la date de dépôt et le numéro de cette demande de brevet.

Demande réputée n'avoir jamais été présentée

(2.1) La demande de priorité est réputée n'avoir jamais été présentée si le demandeur ne la présente pas selon les modalités réglementaires ou ne fournit pas les renseignements — autres que le numéro — exigés au paragraphe (2).

1993, ch. 15, art. 33

(2) Le paragraphe 28.4(3) de la version française de la même loi est remplacé par ce qui suit :

Retrait de la demande

(3) Le demandeur peut, selon les modalités réglementaires, retirer la demande de priorité à l'égard de la demande déposée antérieurement; si elle est fondée sur plusieurs demandes, il peut la retirer à l'égard de toutes celles-ci ou d'une ou de plusieurs d'entre elles.

1993, ch. 15, art. 33

(3) L'alinéa 28.4(5)a) de la même loi est remplacé par ce qui suit :

a) à la date de dépôt de la demande à l'égard de laquelle une demande de priorité a été présentée, il s'est écoulé, depuis la date de dépôt de la demande antérieurement déposée, plus de douze mois;

1993, ch. 15, art. 33

(4) Le passage de l'alinéa 28.4(5)b) de la version anglaise de la même loi précédant le sous-alinéa (i) est remplacé par ce qui suit :

(b) before the filing date of the application referred to in one of subparagraphs (a)(i) to (iv), as the case may be, another application

(5) L'article 28.4 de la même loi est modifié par adjonction, après le paragraphe (5), de ce qui suit :

Délai d'au plus douze mois réputé écoulé

(6) Sous réserve des règlements, pour l'application de l'alinéa 28.1(1)b), du sous-alinéa 28.2(1)d)(iii) et, dans la mesure où il s'applique aux articles 28.1 et 28.2, de l'alinéa 28.4(5)a), il est réputé, à la date de dépôt de la demande à l'égard de laquelle une demande de priorité a été présentée ou pourrait l'être, s'être écoulé au plus douze mois depuis la date de dépôt de la demande déposée antérieurement, si :

a) à cette première date de dépôt, il s'est écoulé plus de douze mois depuis cette deuxième date de dépôt

(b) the applicant, within the prescribed time,

(i) makes a request to the Commissioner for this subsection to apply,

(ii) states, in the request, that the failure to file the pending application or the co-pending application, as the case may be, within 12 months after the filing date of the previously regularly filed application was unintentional, and

(iii) complies with any prescribed requirements.

Powers of the Federal Court

(7) If subsection (6) applies, the Federal Court may, by order, declare that subsection never to have produced its effects if the Federal Court determines that the failure referred to in subparagraph (6)(b)(ii) was intentional.

— 2014, c. 39, s. 126

1993, c. 15, s. 34

126 Section 29 of the Act is repealed.

— 2014, c. 39, s. 127

127 Paragraph 31(2)(a) of the Act is replaced by the following:

(a) an applicant has agreed in writing to transfer a patent, when granted, to another person or to a joint applicant and refuses to proceed with the application, or

— 2014, c. 39, s. 128

1993, c. 15, s. 38

128 Subsection 35(2) of the Act is replaced by the following:

Prescribed time

(2) The request shall be made within the prescribed time and the prescribed fee shall be paid within that time.

Late fee and notice

(3) If the request is not made or the prescribed fee is not paid within the prescribed time,

(a) the prescribed late fee shall be paid, in addition to the prescribed fee; and

(b) the Commissioner shall send a notice to the applicant stating that the application will be deemed to be abandoned if the request is not made and the prescribed fee and late fee are not paid before the end of two months after the date of the notice.

Request deemed made and prescribed fee deemed paid within prescribed time

(4) If the request is made and the prescribed fee and late fee are paid before a notice is sent or, if a notice has been sent, the request is made and the prescribed fee and late fee are paid before the end of two months after the date of the notice, the request shall be deemed to have been made and the prescribed fee shall be deemed to have been paid within the prescribed time.

Required examination

(5) The Commissioner may by a notice sent to the applicant, require that the request be made and the prescribed fee be paid within the prescribed time. However, the Commissioner is not authorized to send the notice if the prescribed time would end after the prescribed time referred to in subsection (2).

Non-application

(6) If a notice is sent under subsection (5), subsections (2) to (4) do not apply.

— 2014, c. 39, s. 129

1993, c. 15, s. 39

129 Subsection 36(3) of the Act is replaced by the following:

Original application abandoned

(3) If an original application mentioned in subsection (2) or (2.1) is deemed to be abandoned and is not reinstated, the time for filing a divisional application ends on the later of the day on which the original application is deemed to be abandoned and the end of the prescribed time referred to in subsection 73(3).

— 2014, c. 39, s. 130

R.S., c. 33 (3rd Supp.), s. 13; 1993, c. 15, s. 40

130 The heading before section 37 and sections 37 and 38 of the Act are replaced by the following:

Biological Materials

— 2014, c. 39, s. 131

1993, c. 15, s. 41

131 (1) Subsection 38.2(1) of the French version of the Act is replaced by the following:

Modification du mémoire descriptif et des dessins

38.2 (1) Sous réserve des paragraphes (2) et (3) et des règlements, les dessins et le mémoire descriptif qui sont compris dans la demande de brevet peuvent être modifiés avant la délivrance du brevet.

1993, c. 15, s. 41

(2) Subsections 38.2(2) and (3) of the Act are replaced by the following:

Restriction

(2) The specification and drawings may not be amended to add matter not reasonably to be inferred from the specification or drawings contained in the application on its filing date.

Language other than English or French

(3) However, if all or part of the text matter of the specification or drawings contained in the application on its filing date is in a language other than English or French, the specification and drawings may not be amended to add matter not reasonably to be inferred from both

(a) the specification or drawings contained in the application on its filing date, and

(b) the specification or drawings contained in the application immediately after the text matter is replaced by an English or French translation, in accordance with the regulations.

Non-application of subsections (2) and (3)

(4) Subsections (2) and (3) do not apply if it is admitted in the specification that the matter is prior art with respect to the application.

— 2014, c. 39, s. 132

R.S., c. 33 (3rd Supp.), s. 16; 1993, c. 15, s. 43

132 Section 46 of the Act is replaced by the following:

Maintenance fees

46 (1) To maintain the rights accorded by a patent issued under this Act in effect, the prescribed fees shall be paid on or before the prescribed dates.

Late fee and notice

(2) If a prescribed fee is not paid on or before the applicable prescribed date,

(a) the prescribed late fee shall be paid, in addition to the prescribed fee; and

---

compris dans la demande de brevet peuvent être modifiés avant la délivrance du brevet.

1993, ch. 15, art. 41

(2) Les paragraphes 38.2(2) et (3) de la même loi sont remplacés par ce qui suit :

Limite

(2) Les dessins et le mémoire descriptif ne peuvent être modifiés pour y ajouter des éléments qui ne peuvent raisonnablement s'inférer des dessins ou du mémoire descriptif qui sont compris dans la demande à sa date de dépôt.

Texte dans une langue autre que le français ou l'anglais

(3) Toutefois, si tout ou partie du texte des dessins ou du mémoire descriptif qui sont compris dans la demande à sa date de dépôt est dans une langue autre que le français ou l'anglais, les dessins et le mémoire descriptif ne peuvent être modifiés pour y ajouter des éléments qui ne peuvent raisonnablement s'inférer à la fois :

a) des dessins ou du mémoire descriptif qui sont compris dans la demande à sa date de dépôt;

b) des dessins ou du mémoire descriptif qui sont compris dans la demande immédiatement après que le texte dans la langue autre que le français ou l'anglais a été remplacé, conformément aux règlements, par une traduction en français ou en anglais.

Non-application des paragraphes (2) et (3)

(4) La mention dans le mémoire descriptif que les éléments en cause sont des inventions ou découvertes antérieures rend inapplicables les paragraphes (2) et (3).

— 2014, ch. 39, art. 132

L.R., ch. 33 (3ᵉ suppl.), art. 16; 1993, ch. 15, art. 43

132 L'article 46 de la même loi est remplacé par ce qui suit :

Taxes pour maintenir des droits en état

46 (1) Afin de maintenir en état les droits conférés par un brevet délivré sous le régime de la présente loi, les taxes réglementaires doivent être payées au plus tard aux dates réglementaires.

Surtaxe et avis

(2) Si une taxe réglementaire n'est pas payée au plus tard à la date réglementaire applicable :

a) la surtaxe réglementaire doit être payée en plus de la taxe réglementaire;

(b) the Commissioner shall send a notice to the patentee stating that the term limited for the duration of the patent will be deemed to have expired if the prescribed fee and late fee are not paid before the later of the end of six months after the applicable prescribed date and the end of two months after the date of the notice.

Prescribed fee deemed paid on prescribed date

(3) If the prescribed fee and late fee are paid before a notice is sent or, if a notice is sent, the prescribed fee and late fee are paid before the later of the end of six months after the applicable prescribed date and the end of two months after the date of the notice, the prescribed fee shall be deemed to have been paid on the applicable prescribed date.

Term limited deemed expired on prescribed date

(4) If the prescribed fee and late fee are not paid before the later of the end of six months after the applicable prescribed date and the end of two months after the date of the notice, the term limited for the duration of the patent shall be deemed to have expired on the applicable prescribed date.

Subsection (4) deemed never to have produced its effects

(5) Subject to the regulations, if the term limited for the duration of a patent is deemed to have expired under subsection (4), that subsection is deemed never to have produced its effects if

(a) the patentee, within the prescribed time,

(i) makes a request to the Commissioner for the term limited for the duration of the patent to never have been deemed to have expired,

(ii) states, in the request, the reasons for the failure to pay the prescribed fee and late fee before the later of the end of six months after the applicable prescribed date and the end of two months after the date of the notice, and

(iii) pays the prescribed fee, the late fee and any additional prescribed fee; and

(b) the Commissioner determines that the failure occurred in spite of the due care required by the circumstances having been taken and informs the patentee of this determination.

Powers of the Federal Court

(6) If subsection (5) applies, the Federal Court may, by order, declare the term limited for the duration of the patent to have expired on the applicable prescribed date if the Federal Court determines either

(a) that the statement of the reasons referred to in subparagraph (5)(a)(ii) contains a material allegation that is untrue, or

(b) that, if paragraph (5)(b) applies, the failure referred to in subparagraph (5)(a)(ii) did not occur in spite of the due care required by the circumstances having been taken.

— 2014, c. 39, s. 133

R.S., c. 33 (3rd Supp.), s. 17

133 (1) The portion of subsection 48(1) of the Act after paragraph (b) is replaced by the following:

the patentee may, on payment of a prescribed fee, make a disclaimer of the parts that the patentee does not claim to hold by virtue of the patent or a transfer of the patent.

(2) Subsection 48(5) of the Act is repealed.

— 2014, c. 39, s. 134

R.S., c. 33 (3rd Supp.), ss. 19 and 20

134 The heading before section 49 and sections 49 to 51 of the Act are replaced by the following:

Transfers

Patent, application and right or interest in invention

49 (1) A patent, an application for a patent, and the right or interest in an invention are transferable, in whole or in part.

Recording of transfer of application

(2) The Commissioner shall, subject to the regulations, record the transfer of an application for a patent on the request of the applicant or, upon receipt of evidence satisfactory to the Commissioner of the transfer, on the request of a transferee of the application.

Recording of transfer of patent

(3) The Commissioner shall, subject to the regulations, record the transfer of a patent on the request of the patentee or, upon receipt of evidence satisfactory to the Commissioner of the transfer, on the request of a transferee of the patent.

a) l'exposé des raisons visé au sous-alinéa (5)a)(ii) comprend quelque allégation importante qui n'est pas conforme à la vérité;

b) en cas d'application de l'alinéa (5)b), l'omission visée à ce sous-alinéa n'a pas été commise bien que la diligence requise en l'espèce ait été exercée.

— 2014, ch. 39, art. 133

L.R., ch. 33 (3ᵉ suppl.), art. 17

133 (1) Le passage du paragraphe 48(1) de la même loi précédant l'alinéa a) est remplacé par ce qui suit :

Cas de renonciation

48 (1) Le breveté peut, en acquittant la taxe réglementaire, renoncer à tel des éléments qu'il ne prétend pas retenir au titre du brevet, ou d'un transfert de celui-ci, si, par erreur, accident ou inadvertance, et sans intention de frauder ou de tromper le public, dans l'un ou l'autre des cas suivants :

(2) Le paragraphe 48(5) de la même loi est abrogé.

— 2014, ch. 39, art. 134

L.R., ch. 33 (3ᵉ suppl.), art. 19 et 20

134 L'intertitre précédant l'article 49 et les articles 49 à 51 de la même loi sont remplacés par ce qui suit :

Transferts

Droits ou intérêts dans une invention, demandes de brevets et brevets

49 (1) Tout droit ou intérêt dans une invention, toute demande de brevet et tout brevet est transférable en tout ou en partie.

Inscription du transfert — demande de brevet

(2) Sous réserve des règlements, le commissaire inscrit le transfert de toute demande de brevet sur demande du demandeur ou, à la réception d'une preuve du transfert qu'il juge satisfaisante, d'un cessionnaire de la demande.

Inscription du transfert — brevet

(3) Sous réserve des règlements, le commissaire inscrit le transfert de tout brevet sur demande du titulaire du brevet ou, à la réception d'une preuve du transfert qu'il juge satisfaisante, d'un cessionnaire du brevet.

Transfer void

(4) A transfer of a patent that has not been recorded is void against a subsequent transferee if the transfer to the subsequent transferee has been recorded.

Removal of recording

(5) The Commissioner shall remove the recording of the transfer of an application for a patent or the transfer of a patent on receipt of evidence satisfactory to the Commissioner that the transfer should not have been recorded.

Limitation

(6) The Commissioner is not authorized to remove the recording of a transfer of a patent for the reason only that the transferor had previously transferred the patent to another person.

— 2014, c. 39, s. 135

1993, c. 15, s. 48

135 Subsection 55(2) of the Act is replaced by the following:

Liability damage before patent is granted

(2) A person is liable to pay reasonable compensation to a patentee and to all persons claiming under the patentee for any damage sustained by the patentee or by any of those persons by reason of any act on the part of that person, after the specification contained in the application for the patent became open to public inspection, in English or French, under section 10 and before the grant of the patent, that would have constituted an infringement of the patent if the patent had been granted on the day the specification became open to public inspection, in English or French, under that section.

— 2014, c. 39, s. 136

136 The Act is amended by adding the following after section 55.1:

Exception — third party rights

55.11 (1) This section applies only in respect of the following patents:

(a) a patent that was granted on the basis of an application

(i) in respect of which the prescribed fee referred to in subsection 27.1(2) was not paid on or before the applicable prescribed date referred to in that subsection, without taking into account subsection 27.1(3),

(ii) in respect of which a request referred to in subsection 35(2) was not made and the prescribed fee referred to in that subsection was not paid within the prescribed time referred to in that subsection, without taking into account subsection 35(4), or

(iii) that was deemed abandoned under paragraph 73(1)(a), (b), (e) or (f) or subsection 73(2);

(b) a patent that was granted on the basis of a divisional application that

(i) results, under subsection 36(2) or (2.1), from the division of an original application that is an application referred to in this paragraph or paragraph (a), and

(ii) was filed after the beginning of the period referred to in subsection (2) or, if it is earlier, the period referred to in subsection (3), that applies to the patent granted on the basis of the original application or that would apply to that patent if it were granted; and

(c) a patent in respect of which the prescribed fee referred to in subsection 46(2) was not paid on or before the applicable prescribed date referred to in that subsection, without taking into account subsection 46(3).

Act committed during period

(2) No action for infringement of a patent lies against a person in respect of an act that would otherwise constitute an infringement of the patent if that act is committed in good faith by the person during a period that is established by regulations made under paragraph 12(1)(j.74).

Act committed after period or transfer

(3) If, during a period established by regulations made under paragraph 12(1)(j.75), a person, in good faith, committed an act that would otherwise constitute an infringement of a patent or made serious and effective preparations to commit that act,

(a) no action for infringement of the patent lies against the person in respect of that act if the person commits it after that period but before the person transfers the business or the part of the business in the course of which the act was committed or the preparations were made; and

(b) no action for infringement of the patent lies, if the business or the part of the business in the course of which the act was committed or the preparations were made is transferred, against the transferee in respect of that act if the transferee commits it after the transfer but before the transferee subsequently transfers the business or the part of the business.

(ii) pour laquelle la requête visée au paragraphe 35(2) n'a pas été faite — et la taxe réglementaire visée à celui-ci n'a pas été payée — dans le délai réglementaire visé à ce paragraphe, compte non tenu du paragraphe 35(4),

(iii) qui a été réputée abandonnée par application des alinéas 73(1)a), b), e) ou f) ou du paragraphe 73(2);

b) le brevet qui a été accordé au titre d'une demande complémentaire qui, à la fois :

(i) résulte, au titre des paragraphes 36(2) ou (2.1), de la division d'une demande originale qui est une demande visée au présent alinéa ou à l'alinéa a),

(ii) a été déposée après le début d'une période — celle visée au paragraphe (2) ou, si elle est antérieure, celle visée au paragraphe (3) — qui s'applique au brevet accordé au titre de la demande originale ou qui s'appliquerait à un tel brevet s'il était accordé;

c) le brevet à l'égard duquel la taxe réglementaire visée au paragraphe 46(2) n'a pas été payée au plus tard à la date réglementaire applicable visée à ce paragraphe, compte non tenu du paragraphe 46(3).

Actes commis pendant la période

(2) Il ne peut être intenté d'action en contrefaçon d'un brevet contre une personne à l'égard d'un acte — qui par ailleurs constituerait un acte de contrefaçon du brevet — qu'elle a commis de bonne foi pendant une période prévue par règlement pris en vertu de l'alinéa 12(1)j.74).

Actes commis après la période ou après un transfert

(3) Si, pendant une période prévue par règlement pris en vertu de l'alinéa 12(1)j.75), une personne a commis de bonne foi un acte qui par ailleurs constituerait un acte de contrefaçon d'un brevet ou a fait de bonne foi des préparatifs effectifs et sérieux en vue de le commettre :

a) il ne peut être intenté d'action en contrefaçon du brevet contre elle à l'égard de cet acte qu'elle commet après cette période mais avant qu'elle ne transfère tout ou partie de l'entreprise dans le cadre de laquelle l'acte a été commis ou les préparatifs ont été faits;

b) en cas de transfert de tout ou partie de l'entreprise dans le cadre de laquelle l'acte a été commis ou les préparatifs ont été faits, il ne peut être intenté d'action en contrefaçon du brevet contre le cessionnaire à l'égard de cet acte qu'il commet après le transfert mais avant qu'il ne transfère lui-même tout ou partie de l'entreprise.

Subsequent acquisition

(4) No action for infringement of a patent lies against a person in respect of the use or sale of a specific article, machine, manufacture or composition of matter if the person acquired the specific article, machine, manufacture or composition of matter, directly or indirectly, from a person who made it and against whom no action for infringement of the patent lies under subsection (2) or (3) for making that specific article, machine, manufacture or composition of matter.

— 2014, c. 39, s. 137

1993, c. 15, s. 52

137 (1) Subsection 73(1) of the Act is replaced by the following:

Deemed abandonment of applications

73 (1) An application for a patent in Canada shall be deemed to be abandoned if

(a) the applicant does not reply in good faith, within the prescribed time, to any requisition made by an examiner in connection with an examination;

(b) the applicant does not comply with a notice given under subsection 27(6);

(c) the prescribed fee and late fee referred to in a notice sent under paragraph 27.1(2)(b) are not paid before the later of the end of six months after the applicable prescribed date and the end of two months after the date of the notice;

(d) the request referred to in a notice sent under paragraph 35(3)(b) is not made and the prescribed fee and late fee referred to in that notice are not paid before the end of two months after the date of the notice;

(e) the request referred to in a notice sent under subsection 35(5) is not made and the prescribed fee referred to in that notice is not paid within the prescribed time; or

(f) the applicant does not pay the prescribed fees stated to be payable in a notice of allowance of patent within six months after the date of the notice.

1993, c. 15, s. 52

(2) Subsection 73(2) of the French version of the Act is replaced by the following:

Abandon

(2) Elle est aussi réputée abandonnée dans les circonstances réglementaires.

1993, c. 15, s. 52

(3) Subsection 73(3) of the Act is replaced by the following:

Reinstatement

(3) Subject to the regulations, an application that is deemed to be abandoned is reinstated if

   (a) the applicant, within the prescribed time,

   (i) makes a request for reinstatement to the Commissioner,

   (ii) states, in the request, the reasons for the failure to take the action that should have been taken in order to avoid the abandonment,

   (iii) takes the action that should have been taken in order to avoid the abandonment, and

   (iv) pays the prescribed fee; and

   (b) the Commissioner determines that the failure occurred in spite of the due care required by the circumstances having been taken and informs the applicant of this determination.

Powers of the Federal Court

(3.1) The Federal Court may, by order, declare an application that is reinstated under subsection (3) to never have been reinstated if the Federal Court determines either

   (a) that the statement of the reasons referred to in subparagraph (3)(a)(ii) contains a material allegation that is untrue, or

   (b) that, if paragraph (3)(b) applies, the failure referred to in subparagraph (3)(a)(ii) did not occur in spite of the due care required by the circumstances having been taken.

— 2014, c. 39, s. 138

138 The Act is amended by adding the following after section 73:

Patent not invalid

73.1 (1) A patent shall not be declared invalid by reason only that the application on the basis of which the patent was granted was deemed to be abandoned and was not reinstated.

Exception

(2) Subsection (1) does not apply if the Federal Court makes an order under subsection 73(3.1) in respect of the application on the basis of which the patent was granted.

1993, ch. 15, art. 52

(3) Le paragraphe 73(3) de la même loi est remplacé par ce qui suit :

Rétablissement

(3) Sous réserve des règlements, la demande de brevet est rétablie si :

   a) le demandeur, dans le délai réglementaire :

   (i) présente au commissaire une requête à cet effet,

   (ii) expose dans la requête les raisons pour lesquelles il a omis de prendre les mesures qui s'imposaient pour éviter l'abandon,

   (iii) prend ces mesures,

   (iv) paie la taxe réglementaire;

   b) le commissaire décide que l'omission a été commise bien que la diligence requise en l'espèce ait été exercée et avise le demandeur de sa décision.

Pouvoir de la Cour fédérale

(3.1) La Cour fédérale peut, par ordonnance, déclarer que la demande de brevet rétablie au titre du paragraphe (3) n'a jamais été ainsi rétablie si elle conclut que, selon le cas :

   a) l'exposé des raisons visé au sous-alinéa (3)a)(ii) comprend quelque allégation importante qui n'est pas conforme à la vérité;

   b) en cas d'application de l'alinéa (3)b), l'omission visée à ce sous-alinéa n'a pas été commise bien que la diligence requise en l'espèce ait été exercée.

— 2014, ch. 39, art. 138

138 La même loi est modifiée par adjonction, après l'article 73, de ce qui suit :

Brevet non invalide

73.1 (1) Un brevet ne peut être déclaré invalide du seul fait qu'il a été accordé au titre d'une demande qui a été réputée abandonnée mais qui n'a pas été rétablie.

Exception

(2) Le paragraphe (1) ne s'applique pas si la Cour fédérale rend une ordonnance en vertu du paragraphe 73(3.1) relativement à la demande au titre de laquelle le brevet a été accordé.

— 2014, c. 39, s. 139

2001, c. 10, s. 3

139 Sections 78.1 and 78.2 of the Act are replaced by the following:

Definition of *coming-into-force date*

78.1 (1) In sections 78.2, 78.21 and 78.5 to 78.56, *coming-into-force date* means the day on which section 121 of the *Economic Action Plan 2014 Act, No. 2* comes into force.

Definition of *filing date*

(2) In sections 78.21, 78.22, 78.4, 78.5, 78.53 and 78.54, *filing date* means the date on which an application for a patent in Canada is filed, as determined in accordance with section 78.2.

Filing date

78.2 The filing date of an application for a patent is

 (a) with respect to an original application,

  (i) if all of the following elements were received by the Commissioner before October 1, 1989, the date on which they were received or, if they were received on different dates, the latest of those different dates:

   (A) a statement that the granting of a patent is sought, executed by the applicant or by a patent agent on the applicant's behalf,

   (B) a specification, including claims,

   (C) any drawing referred to in the specification,

   (D) an abstract of the part of the specification other than the claims,

   (E) the fee set out in item 1 of Schedule II to the *Patent Rules* as that item read on the day on which the fee was received,

  (ii) if subparagraph (i) does not apply, one or more of the following elements were received by the Commissioner on or after October 1, 1989 and all of the following elements were received by the Commissioner before October 1, 1996, the date on which they were received or, if they were received on different dates, the latest of those different dates:

   (A) a petition executed by the applicant or by a patent agent on the applicant's behalf,

   (B) a specification, including claims,

   (C) any drawing referred to in the specification,

— 2014, ch. 39, art. 139

2001, ch. 10, art. 3

139 Les articles 78.1 et 78.2 de la même loi sont remplacés par ce qui suit :

Définition de *date d'entrée en vigueur*

78.1 (1) Aux articles 78.2, 78.21 et 78.5 à 78.56, *date d'entrée en vigueur* s'entend de la date d'entrée en vigueur de l'article 121 de la *Loi n° 2 sur le plan d'action économique de 2014*.

Définition de *date de dépôt*

(2) Aux articles 78.21, 78.22, 78.4, 78.5, 78.53 et 78.54, *date de dépôt* s'entend de la date du dépôt d'une demande de brevet déposée au Canada, déterminée conformément à l'article 78.2.

Date de dépôt

78.2 La date de dépôt d'une demande de brevet est la suivante :

 a) s'agissant d'une demande originale :

  (i) si le commissaire a reçu tous les éléments ci-après avant le 1er octobre 1989, la date où il les a reçus ou, s'il les a reçus à des dates différentes, la dernière d'entre elles :

   (A) une attestation portant que l'octroi d'un brevet est demandé, signée par le demandeur ou par un agent de brevets en son nom,

   (B) un mémoire descriptif, comprenant les revendications,

   (C) tout dessin auquel renvoie le mémoire descriptif,

   (D) un abrégé de la partie du mémoire descriptif distincte des revendications,

   (E) la taxe prévue à l'article 1 de l'annexe II des *Règles sur les brevets*, dans la version de cet article à la date de la réception de la taxe,

  (ii) si le sous-alinéa (i) ne s'applique pas, si le commissaire a reçu au moins un des éléments ci-après le 1er octobre 1989 ou après cette date et s'il les a tous reçus avant le 1er octobre 1996, la date où il les a reçus ou, s'il les a reçus à des dates différentes, la dernière d'entre elles :

   (A) une pétition signée par le demandeur ou par un agent de brevets en son nom,

   (B) un mémoire descriptif, comprenant les revendications,

(D) an abstract of the part of the specification other than the claims,

(E) the fee set out in item 1 of Schedule II to the *Patent Rules* as that item read on the day on which the fee was received,

(iii) if subparagraphs (i) and (ii) do not apply, one or more of the following elements were received by the Commissioner on or after October 1, 1996 and all of the following elements were received by the Commissioner before June 2, 2007, the date on which they were received or, if they were received on different dates, the latest of those different dates:

(A) an indication, in English or French, that the granting of a Canadian patent is sought,

(B) the applicant's name,

(C) the address of the applicant or of their patent agent,

(D) a document, in English or French, that on its face appears to describe an invention,

(E) the fee set out in item 1 of Schedule II to the *Patent Rules* as that item read on the day on which the fee was received, and

(iv) if subparagraphs (i) to (iii) do not apply, one or more of the following elements were received by the Commissioner on or after June 2, 2007 and all of the following elements were received by the Commissioner before the coming-into-force date, the date on which they were received or, if they were received on different dates, the latest of those different dates:

(A) an indication, in English or French, that the granting of a Canadian patent is sought,

(B) the applicant's name,

(C) the address of the applicant or of their patent agent,

(D) a document, in English or French, that on its face appears to describe an invention,

(E) either a small entity declaration, in accordance with section 3.01 of the *Patent Rules* as it read on the day on which the declaration was received, and the small entity fee set out in item 1 of Schedule II to those Rules as that item read on the day on which that fee was received or the standard fee set out in item 1 of that Schedule, as that item read on the day on which that standard fee was received; or

(C) tout dessin auquel renvoie le mémoire descriptif,

(D) un abrégé de la partie du mémoire descriptif distincte des revendications,

(E) la taxe prévue à l'article 1 de l'annexe II des *Règles sur les brevets*, dans la version de cet article à la date de la réception de la taxe,

(iii) si les sous-alinéas (i) et (ii) ne s'appliquent pas, si le commissaire a reçu au moins un des éléments ci-après le 1er octobre 1996 ou après cette date et s'il les a tous reçus avant le 2 juin 2007, la date où il les a reçus ou, s'il les a reçus à des dates différentes, la dernière d'entre elles :

(A) une indication en français ou en anglais selon laquelle l'octroi d'un brevet canadien est demandé,

(B) le nom du demandeur,

(C) l'adresse du demandeur ou de son agent de brevets,

(D) un document rédigé en français ou en anglais qui, à première vue, semble décrire une invention,

(E) la taxe prévue à l'article 1 de l'annexe II des *Règles sur les brevets*, dans la version de cet article à la date de la réception de la taxe,

(iv) si les sous-alinéas (i) à (iii) ne s'appliquent pas, si le commissaire a reçu au moins un des éléments ci-après le 2 juin 2007 ou après cette date et s'il les a tous reçus avant la date d'entrée en vigueur, la date où il les a reçus ou, s'il les a reçus à des dates différentes, la dernière d'entre elles :

(A) une indication en français ou en anglais selon laquelle l'octroi d'un brevet canadien est demandé,

(B) le nom du demandeur,

(C) l'adresse du demandeur ou de son agent de brevets,

(D) un document rédigé en français ou en anglais qui, à première vue, semble décrire une invention,

(E) soit la déclaration du statut de petite entité conforme à l'article 3.01 des *Règles sur les brevets*, dans sa version à la date de réception de la déclaration, et la taxe applicable aux petites entités prévue à l'article 1 de l'annexe II de ces *Règles*, dans la version de cet article à la date de

(b) with respect to a divisional application, the filing date of the original application from which the divisional application results, determined in accordance with this section.

Applications — no filing date

78.21 An application for a patent that is filed before the coming-into-force date and that does not have a filing date on the coming-into-force date shall be deemed never to have been filed.

Applications — filing date before October 1, 1989

78.22 An application for a patent whose filing date is before October 1, 1989 shall be dealt with and disposed of in accordance with

(a) the provisions of this Act as they read immediately before October 1, 1989, other than the definition *legal representatives* in section 2, subsections 4(2) and 7(1), sections 15 and 29, paragraph 31(2)(a) and sections 49 to 51; and

(b) the definition *legal representatives* in section 2, subsections 4(2) and 7(1), sections 8.1, 15 and 15.1, paragraph 31(2)(a) and sections 38.1, 49 and 78.2.

— 2014, c. 39, s. 140

2001, c. 10, s. 4

140 Sections 78.4 and 78.5 of the Act are replaced by the following:

Applications — filing date October 1, 1989 to before October 1, 1996

78.4 Subject to sections 78.51 and 78.52, an application for a patent whose filing date is on or after October 1, 1989 but before October 1, 1996 shall be dealt with and disposed of in accordance with

(a) the provisions of this Act, other than the definition *filing date* in section 2, subsection 27(7), sections 27.01, 28 and 28.01 and subsection 28.4(6); and

(b) subsection 27(2) as it read immediately before October 1, 1996.

Applications — filing date October 1, 1996 to before coming-into-force date

78.5 Subject to sections 78.51 and 78.52, an application for a patent whose filing date is on or after October 1, 1996 but before the coming-into-force date shall be dealt with and disposed of in accordance with the provisions of this Act, other than the definition *filing date* in section 2, subsection 27(7), sections 27.01, 28 and 28.01 and subsection 28.4(6).

Abandonment before coming-into-force date

78.51 If an application for a patent was deemed to be abandoned under section 73 as it read immediately before the coming-into-force date, that section 73 applies in respect of that abandonment.

Abandonment — requisition or notice before coming-into-force date

78.52 (1) If, on or after the coming-into-force date, an applicant fails to do any act described in paragraph 73(1)(a), (b), (e) or (f), as those paragraphs read immediately before that date, in respect of a requisition made or notice given, as the case may be, before that date, section 73 as it read immediately before that date applies in respect of any abandonment resulting from the failure.

Abandonment — section 97 of the *Patent Rules*

(2) If, on or after the coming-into-force date, an applicant fails to do any act described in section 97 of the *Patent Rules*, as that section read immediately before that date, in respect of a requisition of the Commissioner that was given before that date, section 73 as it read immediately before that date applies in respect of any abandonment resulting from the failure.

Patents filing date before October 1, 1989

78.53 Subject to subsection 78.55(2), any matter arising on or after the coming-into-force date, in respect of a patent granted on the basis of an application whose filing date is before October 1, 1989, shall be dealt with and disposed of in accordance with

(a) the provisions of this Act, other than the definitions *claim date*, *filing date* and *request for priority* in section 2, sections 10, 27 to 28.4, 34.1 to 36, 38.2 and 55 and paragraphs 55.11(1)(a) and (b); and

(b) sections 10 and 55 and subsections 61(1) and (3), as they read immediately before October 1, 1989.

Patents — filing date October 1, 1989 to before coming-into-force date

78.54 Subject to subsection 78.55(1) and section 78.56, any matter arising on or after the coming-into-force date in respect of a patent granted on the basis of an application whose filing date is on or after October 1, 1989 but before the coming-into-force date shall be dealt with and disposed of in accordance with the provisions of this Act, other than the definition *filing date* in section 2 and section 28.

Application of section 46 — item 31 of Schedule II to *Patent Rules*

78.55 (1) If the time, not including a period of grace, set out in item 31 of Schedule II to the *Patent Rules* to pay the applicable fee to maintain the rights accorded by a patent in effect ends before the coming-into-force date, section 46 as it read immediately before the coming-into-force date applies in respect of that fee.

Application of section 46 — item 32 of Schedule II to *Patent Rules*

(2) If the time, not including a period of grace, set out in item 32 of Schedule II to the *Patent Rules* to pay the applicable fee to maintain the rights accorded by a patent in effect ends before the coming-into-force date, section 46 as it read immediately before the coming-into-force date applies in respect of that fee.

Non-application of subsection 27.1(4) and section 73.1

78.56 Subsection 27.1(4) and section 73.1 do not apply to a patent that was granted before the coming-into-force date or to a reissued patent if the original patent was granted before that date.

Reissued patents

78.57 For greater certainty, for the purposes of sections 78.53 and 78.54, a reissued patent is considered to be issued on the basis of the original application.

Regulations

78.58 For greater certainty, a regulation made under subsection 12(1) applies to an application for a patent referred to in section 78.22, unless the regulation provides otherwise.

— 2014, c. 39, s. 141

2005, c. 18, s. 2

141 Subsection 78.6(5) of the Act is replaced by the following:

Application

(5) For greater certainty, this section also applies to applications for patents mentioned in section 78.22.

— 2015, c. 36, s. 50

50 Subsection 5(2) of the *Patent Act* is replaced by the following:

Absence, inability to act or vacancy

(2) If the Commissioner is absent or unable to act or the office of Commissioner is vacant, the Assistant Commissioner or, if at the same time the Assistant Commissioner is absent or unable to act or the office of Assistant

Commissioner is vacant, another officer designated by the Minister may exercise the powers and shall perform the duties of the Commissioner.

— 2015, c. 36, s. 51

51 Section 8 of the Act is repealed.

— 2015, c. 36, s. 52

52 Section 11 of the Act is repealed.

— 2015, c. 36, s. 53

53 (1) Subsection 12(1) of the Act is amended by adding the following after paragraph (g):

(g.1) authorizing the Commissioner to waive, subject to any prescribed terms and conditions, the payment of a fee if the Commissioner is satisfied that the circumstances justify it;

(2) Paragraph 12(1)(j.5) of the Act is replaced by the following:

(j.5) respecting divisional applications, including the time period within which divisional applications may be filed and the persons who may file divisional applications;

(j.51) defining *one invention* for the purposes of section 36;

(3) Subsection 12(1) of the Act is amended by adding the following after paragraph (j.8):

(j.81) respecting the correction of obvious errors in documents submitted to the Commissioner or the Patent Office or in patents or other documents issued under this Act, including

(i) the determination of what constitutes an obvious error, and

(ii) the effect of the correction;

— 2015, c. 36, s. 55

55 Section 26 of the Act is replaced by the following:

Annual report

26 The Commissioner shall, in each year, cause to be prepared and laid before Parliament a report of the Commissioner's activities under this Act.

cas d'absence ou d'empêchement de celui-ci ou de vacance de son poste, un autre fonctionnaire désigné par le ministre exerce les pouvoirs et fonctions du commissaire.

— 2015, ch. 36, art. 51

51 L'article 8 de la même loi est abrogé.

— 2015, ch. 36, art. 52

52 L'article 11 de la même loi est abrogé.

— 2015, ch. 36, art. 53

53 (1) Le paragraphe 12(1) de la même loi est modifié par adjonction, après l'alinéa g), de ce qui suit :

g.1) autoriser le commissaire à renoncer, si celui-ci est convaincu que les circonstances le justifient et aux conditions réglementaires, au versement de taxes;

(2) L'alinéa 12(1)j.5) de la même loi est remplacé par ce qui suit :

j.5) régir les demandes divisionnaires, notamment en ce qui a trait à leur délai de présentation et aux personnes qui peuvent les déposer;

j.51) définir l'expression *une seule invention* pour l'application de l'article 36;

(3) Le paragraphe 12(1) de la même loi est modifié par adjonction, après l'alinéa j.8), de ce qui suit :

j.81) régir la correction d'erreurs évidentes dans les documents transmis au commissaire ou au Bureau des brevets ou dans les brevets ou autres documents délivrés sous le régime de la présente loi, notamment en ce qui a trait :

(i) à ce qui constitue une erreur évidente,

(ii) aux effets de la correction;

— 2015, ch. 36, art. 55

55 L'article 26 de la même loi est remplacé par ce qui suit :

Rapport annuel

26 Le commissaire fait, chaque année, établir et déposer devant le Parlement un rapport sur les activités qu'il a exercées au titre de la présente loi.

— 2015, c. 36, s. 56

56 Subsection 26.1(1) of the Act is repealed.

— 2015, c. 36, s. 57

57 The portion of subsection 28.4(4) of the Act before paragraph (a) is replaced by the following:

Multiple previously regularly filed applications

(4) If two or more applications have been previously regularly filed as described in paragraph 28.1(1)(a), subparagraph 28.2(1)(d)(i) or paragraph 78.3(1)(a) or (2)(a), either in or for the same country or in or for different countries,

— 2015, c. 36, s. 58

58 (1) Subsections 38.2(1) and (2) of the Act are replaced by the following:

Amendments to specifications and drawings

38.2 (1) Subject to subsections (2) to (3.1) and the regulations, the specification and drawings contained in an application for a patent in Canada may be amended before the patent is issued.

Restriction

(2) The specification and drawings contained in an application, other than a divisional application, may not be amended to add matter that cannot reasonably be inferred from the specification or drawings contained in the application on its filing date.

(2) Subsection 38.2(4) of the Act is replaced by the following:

Divisional application

(3.1) The specification and drawings contained in a divisional application may not be amended to add matter

(a) that may not be or could not have been added, under subsection (2) or (3) or this subsection, to the specification and drawings contained in the application for a patent from which the divisional application results; or

(b) that cannot reasonably be inferred from the specification or drawings contained in the divisional application on the date on which the Commissioner, in respect of that application, receives the prescribed documents and information or, if they are received on different dates, on the latest of those dates.

— 2015, ch. 36, art. 56

56 Le paragraphe 26.1(1) de la même loi est abrogé.

— 2015, ch. 36, art. 57

57 Le passage du paragraphe 28.4(4) de la même loi précédant l'alinéa a) est remplacé par ce qui suit :

Plusieurs demandes

(4) Dans le cas où plusieurs demandes de brevet ont été déposées antérieurement dans le même pays ou non ou pour le même pays ou non :

— 2015, ch. 36, art. 58

58 (1) Les paragraphes 38.2(1) et (2) de la même loi sont remplacés par ce qui suit :

Modification du mémoire descriptif et des dessins

38.2 (1) Sous réserve des paragraphes (2) à (3.1) et des règlements, les dessins et le mémoire descriptif qui sont compris dans la demande de brevet peuvent être modifiés avant la délivrance du brevet.

Limite

(2) Les dessins et le mémoire descriptif qui sont compris dans une demande autre qu'une demande divisionnaire ne peuvent être modifiés pour y ajouter des éléments qui ne peuvent raisonnablement s'inférer des dessins ou du mémoire descriptif qui sont compris dans la demande à sa date de dépôt.

(2) Le paragraphe 38.2(4) de la même loi est remplacé par ce qui suit :

Demande divisionnaire

(3.1) Les dessins et le mémoire descriptif qui sont compris dans une demande divisionnaire ne peuvent être modifiés pour y ajouter les éléments suivants :

a) ceux qui ne pourraient ou n'auraient pas pu être ajoutés, en application des paragraphes (2) ou (3) ou du présent paragraphe, aux dessins et au mémoire descriptif qui sont compris dans la demande de brevet dont résulte la demande divisionnaire;

b) ceux qui ne peuvent raisonnablement s'inférer des dessins ou du mémoire descriptif qui sont compris dans la demande divisionnaire à la date à laquelle le commissaire reçoit, relativement à cette demande, les documents et renseignements réglementaires ou, s'il les reçoit à des dates différentes, à la dernière d'entre elles.

Non-application of subsections (2) to (3.1)

(4) Subsections (2) to (3.1) do not apply if it is admitted in the specification that the matter is prior art with respect to the application.

Application subject to regulations

(5) Subsections (2) to (3.1) apply subject to any regulations made under paragraph 12(1)(j.81).

— 2015, c. 36, s. 59

59 Subparagraph 55.11(1)(a)(iii) of the Act is replaced by the following:

> **(iii)** that was deemed abandoned under paragraph 73(1)(a), (b) or (e), under paragraph 73(1)(f) as it read at any time before the coming into force of this subparagraph or under subsection 73(2);

— 2015, c. 36, s. 60

60 Section 62 of the Act is repealed.

— 2015, c. 36, s. 61

61 (1) The portion of subsection 68(1) of the Act before paragraph (a) is replaced by the following:

Contents of applications

68 (1) Every application presented to the Commissioner under section 65 shall

(2) Subsection 68(2) of the Act is replaced by the following:

Service

(2) The Commissioner shall consider the matters alleged in the application and declarations referred to in subsection (1) and, if satisfied that the applicant has a *bona fide* interest and that a case for relief has been made, the Commissioner shall direct the applicant to serve copies of the application and declarations on the patentee or the patentee's representative for service and on any other persons appearing from the records of the Patent Office to be interested in the patent, and the applicant shall advertise the application both

> **(a)** in the *Canada Gazette*, and

> **(b)** on the website of the Canadian Intellectual Property Office or in any other prescribed location.

— 2015, c. 36, s. 62

62 (1) Subsection 73(1) of the Act is amended by adding "or" at the end of paragraph (d), by striking out "or" at the end of paragraph (e) and by repealing paragraph (f).

(2) Subsections 73(4) and (5) of the Act are replaced by the following:

Filing date

(5) An application that is reinstated retains its filing date.

— 2015, c. 36, s. 63

63 Section 78 of the Act is replaced by the following:

Time period extended

78 (1) If a time period fixed under this Act for doing anything ends on a prescribed day or a day that is designated by the Commissioner, that time period is extended to the next day that is not a prescribed day or a designated day.

Power to designate day

(2) The Commissioner may, on account of unforeseen circumstances and if the Commissioner is satisfied that it is in the public interest to do so, designate any day for the purposes of subsection (1). If a day is designated, the Commissioner shall inform the public of that fact on the website of the Canadian Intellectual Property Office.

— 2015, c. 36, s. 64

64 Paragraphs 78.22(a) and (b) of the Act are replaced by the following:

(a) the provisions of this Act as they read immediately before October 1, 1989, other than the definition **legal representatives** in section 2, subsections 4(2), 5(2) and 7(1), sections 8, 15 and 29, paragraph 31(2)(a) and sections 49 to 51 and 78; and

(b) the definition **legal representatives** in section 2, subsections 4(2), 5(2) and 7(1), sections 8.1, 15 and 15.1, paragraph 31(2)(a) and sections 38.1, 49, 78 and 78.2.

— 2015, ch. 36, art. 62

62 (1) L'alinéa 73(1)f) de la même loi est abrogé.

(2) Les paragraphes 73(4) et (5) de la même loi sont remplacés par ce qui suit :

Date de dépôt

(5) La demande rétablie conserve sa date de dépôt.

— 2015, ch. 36, art. 63

63 L'article 78 de la même loi est remplacé par ce qui suit :

Délai prorogé

78 (1) Le délai fixé sous le régime de la présente loi pour l'accomplissement d'un acte qui expire un jour réglementaire ou un jour désigné par le commissaire est prorogé jusqu'au premier jour suivant qui n'est ni réglementaire ni désigné par le commissaire.

Pouvoir de désigner un jour

(2) Le commissaire peut, en raison de circonstances imprévues et s'il est convaincu qu'il est dans l'intérêt public de le faire, désigner un jour pour l'application du paragraphe (1) et, le cas échéant, il en informe le public sur le site Web de l'Office de la propriété intellectuelle du Canada.

— 2015, ch. 36, art. 64

64 Les alinéas 78.22a) et b) de la même loi sont remplacés par ce qui suit :

a) par les dispositions de la présente loi, dans leur version antérieure au 1er octobre 1989, à l'exception de la définition de **représentants légaux** à l'article 2, des paragraphes 4(2), 5(2) et 7(1), des articles 8, 15 et 29, de l'alinéa 31(2)a) et des articles 49 à 51 et 78;

b) par la définition de **représentants légaux** à l'article 2, les paragraphes 4(2), 5(2) et 7(1), les articles 8.1, 15 et 15.1, l'alinéa 31(2)a) et les articles 38.1, 49, 78 et 78.2.

CANADA

CONSOLIDATION

Trade-marks Act

R.S.C., 1985, c. T-13

CODIFICATION

Loi sur les marques de commerce

L.R.C. (1985), ch. T-13

Current to August 14, 2017

Last amended on June 24, 2016

À jour au 14 août 2017

Dernière modification le 24 juin 2016

Published by the Minister of Justice at the following address:
http://laws-lois.justice.gc.ca

Publié par le ministre de la Justice à l'adresse suivante :
http://lois-laws.justice.gc.ca

OFFICIAL STATUS OF CONSOLIDATIONS

Subsections 31(1) and (2) of the *Legislation Revision and Consolidation Act*, in force on June 1, 2009, provide as follows:

Published consolidation is evidence

31 (1) Every copy of a consolidated statute or consolidated regulation published by the Minister under this Act in either print or electronic form is evidence of that statute or regulation and of its contents and every copy purporting to be published by the Minister is deemed to be so published, unless the contrary is shown.

Inconsistencies in Acts

(2) In the event of an inconsistency between a consolidated statute published by the Minister under this Act and the original statute or a subsequent amendment as certified by the Clerk of the Parliaments under the *Publication of Statutes Act*, the original statute or amendment prevails to the extent of the inconsistency.

NOTE

This consolidation is current to August 14, 2017. The last amendments came into force on June 24, 2016. Any amendments that were not in force as of August 14, 2017 are set out at the end of this document under the heading "Amendments Not in Force".

CARACTÈRE OFFICIEL DES CODIFICATIONS

Les paragraphes 31(1) et (2) de la *Loi sur la révision et la codification des textes législatifs*, en vigueur le 1er juin 2009, prévoient ce qui suit :

Codifications comme élément de preuve

31 (1) Tout exemplaire d'une loi codifiée ou d'un règlement codifié, publié par le ministre en vertu de la présente loi sur support papier ou sur support électronique, fait foi de cette loi ou de ce règlement et de son contenu. Tout exemplaire donné comme publié par le ministre est réputé avoir été ainsi publié, sauf preuve contraire.

Incompatibilité — lois

(2) Les dispositions de la loi d'origine avec ses modifications subséquentes par le greffier des Parlements en vertu de la *Loi sur la publication des lois* l'emportent sur les dispositions incompatibles de la loi codifiée publiée par le ministre en vertu de la présente loi.

NOTE

Cette codification est à jour au 14 août 2017. Les dernières modifications sont entrées en vigueur le 24 juin 2016. Toutes modifications qui n'étaient pas en vigueur au 14 août 2017 sont énoncées à la fin de ce document sous le titre « Modifications non en vigueur ».

TABLE OF PROVISIONS

An Act relating to trade-marks and unfair competition

Short Title

1 Short title

Interpretation

2 Definitions
3 When deemed to be adopted
4 When deemed to be used
5 When deemed to be made known
6 When mark or name confusing

Unfair Competition and Prohibited Marks

7 Prohibitions
8 Warranty of lawful use
9 Prohibited marks
10 Further prohibitions
10.1 Further prohibitions
11 Further prohibitions
11.1 Further prohibitions
11.11 Definitions
11.12 List
11.13 Statement of objection
11.14 Prohibited adoption of indication for wines
11.15 Prohibited adoption of indication for spirits
11.16 Exception for personal names
11.17 Continued use
11.18 Exception for disuse
11.19 Exception for failure to take proceedings
11.2 Transitional

Registrable Trade-marks

12 When trade-mark registrable
13 When distinguishing guises registrable

14	Registration of marks registered abroad	14	Enregistrement de marques déposées à l'étranger
15	Registration of confusing marks	15	Enregistrement de marques créant de la confusion

Persons Entitled to Registration of Trade-marks

Personnes admises à l'enregistrement des marques de commerce

16	Registration of marks used or made known in Canada	16	Enregistrement des marques employées ou révélées au Canada

Validity and Effect of Registration

Validité et effet de l'enregistrement

17	Effect of registration in relation to previous use, etc.	17	Effet de l'enregistrement relativement à l'emploi antérieur, etc.
18	When registration invalid	18	Quand l'enregistrement est invalide
19	Rights conferred by registration	19	Droits conférés par l'enregistrement
20	Infringement	20	Violation
21	Concurrent use of confusing marks	21	Emploi simultané de marques créant de la confusion
22	Depreciation of goodwill	22	Dépréciation de l'achalandage

Certification Marks

Marques de certification

23	Registration of certification marks	23	Enregistrement de marques de certification
24	Registration of trade-mark confusing with certification mark	24	Enregistrement d'une marque de commerce créant de la confusion avec la marque de certification
25	Descriptive certification mark	25	Marque de certification descriptive

Register of Trade-marks

Registre des marques de commerce

26	Register	26	Registre
27	Register under Unfair Competition Act	27	Registre prévu par la Loi sur la concurrence déloyale
28	Indexes	28	Index
29	Inspection	29	Inspection

Applications for Registration of Trade-marks

Demandes d'enregistrement de marques de commerce

30	Contents of application	30	Contenu d'une demande
31	Applications based on registration abroad	31	Demandes fondées sur l'enregistrement à l'étranger
32	Further information in certain cases	32	Autres renseignements dans certains cas
33	Applications by trade unions, etc.	33	Demandes de la part de syndicats ouvriers, etc.
34	Date of application abroad deemed date of application in Canada	34	La date de demande à l'étranger est réputée être la date de demande au Canada
35	Disclaimer	35	Désistement
36	Abandonment	36	Abandon
37	When applications to be refused	37	Demandes rejetées
38	Statement of opposition	38	Déclaration d'opposition

39	When application to be allowed	39	Quand la demande est admise

Registration of Trade-marks

Enregistrement des marques de commerce

40	Registration of trade-marks	40	Enregistrement des marques de commerce

Amendment of the Register

Modification du registre

41	Amendments to register	41	Modifications au registre
42	Representative for service	42	Représentant pour signification
43	Additional representations	43	Représentations supplémentaires
44	Notice for information	44	Demande de renseignements
45	Registrar may request evidence of user	45	Le registraire peut exiger une preuve d'emploi

Renewal of Registrations

Renouvellement des enregistrements

46	Renewal	46	Renouvellement

Extensions of Time

Prolongation de délai

47	Extensions of time	47	Prorogations

Transfer

Transfert

48	Trade-mark transferable	48	Une marque de commerce est transférable

Change of Purpose in Use of Mark

Changement apporté aux fins de l'emploi d'une marque

49	Change of purpose	49	Autres fins

Licences

Licences

50	Licence to use trade-mark	50	Licence d'emploi d'une marque de commerce
51	Use of trade-mark by related companies	51	Utilisation d'une marque de commerce par des compagnies connexes

Offences and Punishment

Infractions et peines

51.01	Sale, etc., of goods	51.01	Vente de produits

Importation and Exportation

Importation et exportation

Interpretation

Définitions

51.02	Definitions	51.02	Définitions

Prohibition

Interdiction

51.03	No importation or exportation	51.03	Importation et exportation

Request for Assistance

Demande d'aide

51.04	Request for assistance	51.04	Demande d'aide

Measures Relating to Detained Goods

51.05 Provision of information by customs officer
51.06 Provision of information to pursue remedy
51.07 Restriction on information use — section 51.05
51.08 Inspection
51.09 Liability for charges

No Liability

51.1 No liability

Powers of Court Relating to Detained Goods

51.11 Application to court
51.12 Damages against trade-mark owner

Trade-mark Agents

51.13 Privileged communication

Legal Proceedings

52 Definitions
53 Proceedings for interim custody
53.1 Proceedings for detention by Minister
53.2 Power of court to grant relief
53.3 Unaltered state — exportation, sale or distribution
54 Evidence
55 Jurisdiction of Federal Court
56 Appeal
57 Exclusive jurisdiction of Federal Court
58 How proceedings instituted
59 Notice to set out grounds
60 Registrar to transmit documents
61 Judgments to be filed

General

62 Administration
63 Registrar
64 Publication of registrations
65 Regulations

Mesures relatives aux produits retenus

51.05 Fourniture de renseignements par l'agent des douanes
51.06 Fourniture de renseignements en vue de l'exercice de recours
51.07 Utilisation des renseignements fournis au titre de l'article 51.05
51.08 Inspection
51.09 Obligation de payer les frais

Immunité

51.1 Immunité

Pouvoirs du tribunal relativement aux produits retenus

51.11 Demande au tribunal
51.12 Dommages-intérêts à l'encontre du propriétaire de la marque de commerce

Agents de marques de commerce

51.13 Communication protégée

Procédures judiciaires

52 Définitions
53 Rétention provisoire de produits faisant l'objet de contraventions
53.1 Ordonnance visant le ministre
53.2 Pouvoir du tribunal d'accorder une réparation
53.3 Exportation, vente ou distribution des produits non modifiés
54 Preuve
55 Compétence de la Cour fédérale
56 Appel
57 Juridiction exclusive de la Cour fédérale
58 Comment sont intentées les procédures
59 L'avis indique les motifs
60 Le registraire transmet les documents
61 Production des jugements

Dispositions générales

62 Application
63 Registraire
64 Publication des enregistrements
65 Règlements

66	Time limit deemed extended	66	Le délai est réputé prorogé

Newfoundland

Terre-Neuve

67	Registration of trade-mark before April 1, 1949	67	Enregistrement d'une marque de commerce — Terre-Neuve
68	Use of trade-mark or trade-name before April 1, 1949	68	Emploi d'une marque de commerce — Terre-Neuve

Transitional Provision

Disposition transitoire

69	Prior applications for registration	69	Demande d'enregistrement

SCHEDULE 6

ANNEXE 6

R.S.C., 1985, c. T-13

An Act relating to trade-marks and unfair competition

Short Title

Short title

1 This Act may be cited as the *Trade-marks Act*.
R.S., c. T-10, s. 1.

Interpretation

Definitions

2 In this Act,

certification mark means a mark that is used for the purpose of distinguishing or so as to distinguish goods or services that are of a defined standard with respect to

(a) the character or quality of the goods or services,

(b) the working conditions under which the goods have been produced or the services performed,

(c) the class of persons by whom the goods have been produced or the services performed, or

(d) the area within which the goods have been produced or the services performed,

from goods or services that are not of that defined standard; (*marque de certification*)

confusing, when applied as an adjective to a trade-mark or trade-name, means a trade-mark or trade-name the use of which would cause confusion in the manner and circumstances described in section 6; (*créant de la confusion*)

Convention means the Convention of the Union of Paris made on March 20, 1883 and any amendments and revisions thereof made before or after July 1, 1954 to which Canada is party; (*Convention*)

L.R.C., 1985, ch. T-13

Loi concernant les marques de commerce et la concurrence déloyale

Titre abrégé

Titre abrégé

1 *Loi sur les marques de commerce.*
S.R., ch. T-10, art. 1.

Définitions et interprétation

Définitions

2 Les définitions qui suivent s'appliquent à la présente loi.

Accord sur l'OMC S'entend de l'Accord au sens du paragraphe 2(1) de la *Loi de mise en œuvre de l'Accord sur l'Organisation mondiale du commerce*. (*WTO Agreement*)

compagnies connexes Compagnies qui sont membres d'un groupe de deux ou plusieurs compagnies dont l'une, directement ou indirectement, a la propriété ou le contrôle d'une majorité des actions émises, à droit de vote, des autres compagnies. (*related companies*)

Convention La Convention d'Union de Paris, intervenue le 20 mars 1883, et toutes ses modifications et révisions, adoptées indépendamment de la date du 1ᵉʳ juillet 1954, auxquelles le Canada est partie. (*Convention*)

créant de la confusion Relativement à une marque de commerce ou un nom commercial, s'entend au sens de l'article 6. (*confusing*)

dédouanement S'entend au sens du paragraphe 2(1) de la *Loi sur les douanes*. (*release*)

distinctive Relativement à une marque de commerce, celle qui distingue véritablement les produits ou services

country of origin means

(a) the country of the Union in which the applicant for registration of a trade-mark had at the date of the application a real and effective industrial or commercial establishment, or

(b) if the applicant for registration of a trade-mark did not at the date of the application have in a country of the Union an establishment as described in paragraph (a), the country of the Union where he on that date had his domicile, or

(c) if the applicant for registration of a trade-mark did not at the date of the application have in a country of the Union an establishment as described in paragraph (a) or a domicile as described in paragraph (b), the country of the Union of which he was on that date a citizen or national; (*pays d'origine*)

country of the Union means

(a) any country that is a member of the Union for the Protection of Industrial Property constituted under the Convention, or

(b) any WTO Member; (*pays de l'Union*)

distinctive, in relation to a trade-mark, means a trade-mark that actually distinguishes the goods or services in association with which it is used by its owner from the goods or services of others or is adapted so to distinguish them; (*distinctive*)

distinguishing guise means

(a) a shaping of goods or their containers, or

(b) a mode of wrapping or packaging goods

the appearance of which is used by a person for the purpose of distinguishing or so as to distinguish goods or services manufactured, sold, leased, hired or performed by him from those manufactured, sold, leased, hired or performed by others; (*signe distinctif*)

geographical indication means, in respect of a wine or spirit, an indication that

(a) identifies the wine or spirit as originating in the territory of a WTO Member, or a region or locality of that territory, where a quality, reputation or other characteristic of the wine or spirit is essentially attributable to its geographical origin, and

(b) except in the case of an indication identifying a wine or spirit originating in Canada, is protected by

en liaison avec lesquels elle est employée par son propriétaire, des produits ou services d'autres propriétaires, ou qui est adaptée à les distinguer ainsi. (*distinctive*)

emploi ou *usage* À l'égard d'une marque de commerce, tout emploi qui, selon l'article 4, est réputé un emploi en liaison avec des produits ou services. (*use*)

indication géographique Désignation d'un vin ou spiritueux par la dénomination de son lieu d'origine — territoire d'un membre de l'OMC, ou région ou localité de ce territoire — dans les cas où sa réputation ou une autre de ses qualités ou caractéristiques peuvent être essentiellement attribuées à cette origine géographique; cette désignation doit être protégée par le droit applicable à ce membre, sauf si le lieu d'origine est le Canada. (*geographical indication*)

indication géographique protégée Indication géographique figurant sur la liste prévue au paragraphe 11.12(1). (*protected geographical indication*)

marchandises [Abrogée, 2014, ch. 32, art. 7]

marque de certification Marque employée pour distinguer, ou de façon à distinguer, les produits ou services qui sont d'une norme définie par rapport à ceux qui ne le sont pas, en ce qui concerne :

a) soit la nature ou la qualité des produits ou services;

b) soit les conditions de travail dans lesquelles ont eu lieu leur production ou leur exécution;

c) soit la catégorie de personnes qui les a produits ou exécutés;

d) soit la région dans laquelle ont eu lieu leur production ou leur exécution. (*certification mark*)

marque de commerce Selon le cas :

a) marque employée par une personne pour distinguer, ou de façon à distinguer, les produits fabriqués, vendus, donnés à bail ou loués ou les services loués ou exécutés, par elle, des produits fabriqués, vendus, donnés à bail ou loués ou des services loués ou exécutés, par d'autres;

b) marque de certification;

c) signe distinctif;

d) marque de commerce projetée. (*trade-mark*)

marque de commerce déposée Marque de commerce qui se trouve au registre. (*registered trade-mark*)

the laws applicable to that WTO Member; (*indication géographique*)

owner, in relation to a certification mark, means the person by whom the defined standard has been established; (*propriétaire*)

package [Repealed, 2014, c. 32, s. 7]

person includes any lawful trade union and any lawful association engaged in trade or business or the promotion thereof, and the administrative authority of any country, state, province, municipality or other organized administrative area; (*personne*)

person interested includes any person who is affected or reasonably apprehends that he may be affected by any entry in the register, or by any act or omission or contemplated act or omission under or contrary to this Act, and includes the Attorney General of Canada; (*personne intéressée*)

prescribed means prescribed by or under the regulations; (*prescrit*)

proposed trade-mark means a mark that is proposed to be used by a person for the purpose of distinguishing or so as to distinguish goods or services manufactured, sold, leased, hired or performed by him from those manufactured, sold, leased, hired or performed by others; (*marque de commerce projetée*)

protected geographical indication means a geographical indication that is on the list kept pursuant to subsection 11.12(1); (*indication géographique protégée*)

register means the register kept under section 26; (*registre*)

registered trade-mark means a trade-mark that is on the register; (*marque de commerce déposée*)

registered user [Repealed, 1993, c. 15, s. 57]

Registrar means the Registrar of Trade-marks who is described in subsection 63(1); (*registraire*)

related companies means companies that are members of a group of two or more companies one of which, directly or indirectly, owns or controls a majority of the issued voting stock of the others; (*compagnies connexes*)

release has the same meaning as in subsection 2(1) of the *Customs Act*; (*dédouanement*)

marque de commerce projetée Marque qu'une personne projette d'employer pour distinguer, ou de façon à distinguer, les produits fabriqués, vendus, donnés à bail ou loués ou les services loués ou exécutés, par elle, des produits fabriqués, vendus, donnés à bail ou loués ou des services loués ou exécutés, par d'autres. (*proposed trade-mark*)

membre de l'OMC Membre de l'Organisation mondiale du commerce instituée par l'article I de l'Accord sur l'OMC. (*WTO Member*)

nom commercial Nom sous lequel une entreprise est exercée, qu'il s'agisse ou non d'une personne morale, d'une société de personnes ou d'un particulier. (*trade-name*)

paquet ou **colis** [Abrogée, 2014, ch. 32, art. 7]

pays de l'Union Tout pays qui est membre de l'Union pour la protection de la propriété industrielle, constituée en vertu de la Convention, ou tout membre de l'OMC. (*country of the Union*)

pays d'origine

a) Le pays de l'Union où l'auteur d'une demande d'enregistrement d'une marque de commerce avait, à la date de la demande, un établissement industriel ou commercial réel et effectif;

b) si l'auteur de la demande, à la date de la demande, n'avait aucun établissement décrit à l'alinéa a) dans un pays de l'Union, le pays de celle-ci où il avait son domicile à la date en question;

c) si l'auteur de la demande, à la date de la demande, n'avait aucun établissement décrit à l'alinéa a) ni aucun domicile décrit à l'alinéa b) dans un pays de l'Union, le pays de celle-ci dont il était alors citoyen ou ressortissant. (*country of origin*)

personne Sont assimilés à une personne tout syndicat ouvrier légitime et toute association légitime se livrant à un commerce ou à une entreprise, ou au développement de ce commerce ou de cette entreprise, ainsi que l'autorité administrative de tout pays ou État, de toute province, municipalité ou autre région administrative organisée. (*person*)

personne intéressée Sont assimilés à une personne intéressée le procureur général du Canada et quiconque est atteint ou a des motifs valables d'appréhender qu'il sera atteint par une inscription dans le registre, ou par tout acte ou omission, ou tout acte ou omission projeté, sous

representative for service means the person or firm named under paragraph 30(g), subsection 38(3), paragraph 41(1)(a) or subsection 42(1); (*représentant pour signification*)

trade-mark means

(a) a mark that is used by a person for the purpose of distinguishing or so as to distinguish goods or services manufactured, sold, leased, hired or performed by him from those manufactured, sold, leased, hired or performed by others,

(b) a certification mark,

(c) a distinguishing guise, or

(d) a proposed trade-mark; (*marque de commerce*)

trade-name means the name under which any business is carried on, whether or not it is the name of a corporation, a partnership or an individual; (*nom commercial*)

use, in relation to a trade-mark, means any use that by section 4 is deemed to be a use in association with goods or services; (*emploi* ou *usage*)

wares [Repealed, 2014, c. 32, s. 7]

WTO Agreement has the meaning given to the word "Agreement" by subsection 2(1) of the *World Trade Organization Agreement Implementation Act*; (*Accord sur l'OMC*)

WTO Member means a Member of the World Trade Organization established by Article I of the WTO Agreement. (*membre de l'OMC*)

R.S., 1985, c. T-13, s. 2; 1993, c. 15, s. 57; 1994, c. 47, s. 190; 2014, c. 20, s. 369, c. 32, ss. 7, 53.

When deemed to be adopted

3 A trade-mark is deemed to have been adopted by a person when that person or his predecessor in title commenced to use it in Canada or to make it known in Canada or, if that person or his predecessor had not previously so used it or made it known, when that person or his predecessor filed an application for its registration in Canada.

R.S., c. T-10, s. 3.

When deemed to be used

4 (1) A trade-mark is deemed to be used in association with goods if, at the time of the transfer of the property in or possession of the goods, in the normal course of trade, it is marked on the goods themselves or on the packages

le régime ou à l'encontre de la présente loi. (*person interested*)

prescrit Prescrit par les règlements ou sous leur régime. (*prescribed*)

propriétaire Relativement à une marque de certification, la personne qui a établi la norme définie. (*owner*)

registraire Le titulaire du poste de registraire des marques de commerce institué par le paragraphe 63(1). (*Registrar*)

registre Le registre tenu selon l'article 26. (*register*)

représentant pour signification La personne ou firme nommée en vertu de l'alinéa 30g), du paragraphe 38(3), de l'alinéa 41(1)a) ou du paragraphe 42(1). (*representative for service*)

signe distinctif Selon le cas :

a) façonnement de produits ou de leurs contenants;

b) mode d'envelopper ou empaqueter des produits,

dont la présentation est employée par une personne afin de distinguer, ou de façon à distinguer, les produits fabriqués, vendus, donnés à bail ou loués ou les services loués ou exécutés, par elle, des produits fabriqués, vendus, donnés à bail ou loués ou des services loués ou exécutés, par d'autres. (*distinguishing guise*)

usager inscrit [Abrogée, 1993, ch. 15, art. 57]

L.R. (1985), ch. T-13, art. 2; 1993, ch. 15, art. 57; 1994, ch. 47, art. 190; 2014, ch. 20, art. 369, ch. 32, art. 7 et 53.

Quand une marque de commerce est réputée adoptée

3 Une marque de commerce est réputée avoir été adoptée par une personne, lorsque cette personne ou son prédécesseur en titre a commencé à l'employer au Canada ou à l'y faire connaître, ou, si la personne ou le prédécesseur en question ne l'avait pas antérieurement ainsi employée ou fait connaître, lorsque l'un d'eux a produit une demande d'enregistrement de cette marque au Canada.

S.R., ch. T-10, art. 3.

Quand une marque de commerce est réputée employée

4 (1) Une marque de commerce est réputée employée en liaison avec des produits si, lors du transfert de la propriété ou de la possession de ces produits, dans la pratique normale du commerce, elle est apposée sur les

in which they are distributed or it is in any other manner so associated with the goods that notice of the association is then given to the person to whom the property or possession is transferred.

Idem

(2) A trade-mark is deemed to be used in association with services if it is used or displayed in the performance or advertising of those services.

Use by export

(3) A trade-mark that is marked in Canada on goods or on the packages in which they are contained is, when the goods are exported from Canada, deemed to be used in Canada in association with those goods.

R.S., 1985, c. T-13, s. 4; 2014, c. 32, ss. 53, 54(F).

When deemed to be made known

5 A trade-mark is deemed to be made known in Canada by a person only if it is used by that person in a country of the Union, other than Canada, in association with goods or services, and

(a) the goods are distributed in association with it in Canada, or

(b) the goods or services are advertised in association with it in

(i) any printed publication circulated in Canada in the ordinary course of commerce among potential dealers in or users of the goods or services, or

(ii) radio broadcasts ordinarily received in Canada by potential dealers in or users of the goods or services,

and it has become well known in Canada by reason of the distribution or advertising.

R.S., 1985, c. T-13, s. 5; 2014, c. 32, s. 53.

When mark or name confusing

6 (1) For the purposes of this Act, a trade-mark or trade-name is confusing with another trade-mark or trade-name if the use of the first mentioned trade-mark or trade-name would cause confusion with the last mentioned trade-mark or trade-name in the manner and circumstances described in this section.

Idem

(2) The use of a trade-mark causes confusion with another trade-mark if the use of both trade-marks in the same area would be likely to lead to the inference that the goods or services associated with those trade-marks are manufactured, sold, leased, hired or performed by the same person, whether or not the goods or services are of the same general class.

Idem

(3) The use of a trade-mark causes confusion with a trade-name if the use of both the trade-mark and trade-name in the same area would be likely to lead to the inference that the goods or services associated with the trade-mark and those associated with the business carried on under the trade-name are manufactured, sold, leased, hired or performed by the same person, whether or not the goods or services are of the same general class.

Idem

(4) The use of a trade-name causes confusion with a trade-mark if the use of both the trade-name and trade-mark in the same area would be likely to lead to the inference that the goods or services associated with the business carried on under the trade-name and those associated with the trade-mark are manufactured, sold, leased, hired or performed by the same person, whether or not the goods or services are of the same general class.

What to be considered

(5) In determining whether trade-marks or trade-names are confusing, the court or the Registrar, as the case may be, shall have regard to all the surrounding circumstances including

(a) the inherent distinctiveness of the trade-marks or trade-names and the extent to which they have become known;

(b) the length of time the trade-marks or trade-names have been in use;

(c) the nature of the goods, services or business;

(d) the nature of the trade; and

(e) the degree of resemblance between the trade-marks or trade-names in appearance or sound or in the ideas suggested by them.

R.S., 1985, c. T-13, s. 6; 2014, c. 32, s. 53.

Unfair Competition and Prohibited Marks

Prohibitions

7 No person shall

(a) make a false or misleading statement tending to discredit the business, goods or services of a competitor;

(b) direct public attention to his goods, services or business in such a way as to cause or be likely to cause confusion in Canada, at the time he commenced so to direct attention to them, between his goods, services or business and the goods, services or business of another;

(c) pass off other goods or services as and for those ordered or requested; or

(d) make use, in association with goods or services, of any description that is false in a material respect and likely to mislead the public as to

(i) the character, quality, quantity or composition,

(ii) the geographical origin, or

(iii) the mode of the manufacture, production or performance

of the goods or services.

(e) [Repealed, 2014, c. 32, s. 10]

R.S., 1985, c. T-13, s. 7; 2014, c. 32, ss. 10, 53, 56(F).

Warranty of lawful use

8 Every person who in the course of trade transfers the property in or the possession of any goods bearing, or in packages bearing, any trade-mark or trade-name shall, unless before the transfer he otherwise expressly states in writing, be deemed to warrant, to the person to whom the property or possession is transferred, that the trade-mark or trade-name has been and may be lawfully used in connection with the goods.

R.S., 1985, c. T-13, s. 8; 2014, c. 32, ss. 53, 54(F).

Prohibited marks

9 (1) No person shall adopt in connection with a business, as a trade-mark or otherwise, any mark consisting of, or so nearly resembling as to be likely to be mistaken for,

(a) the Royal Arms, Crest or Standard;

(b) the arms or crest of any member of the Royal Family;

(c) the standard, arms or crest of His Excellency the Governor General;

(d) any word or symbol likely to lead to the belief that the goods or services in association with which it is used have received, or are produced, sold or performed under, royal, vice-regal or governmental patronage, approval or authority;

(e) the arms, crest or flag adopted and used at any time by Canada or by any province or municipal corporation in Canada in respect of which the Registrar has, at the request of the Government of Canada or of the province or municipal corporation concerned, given public notice of its adoption and use;

(f) the emblem of the Red Cross on a white ground, formed by reversing the federal colours of Switzerland and retained by the Geneva Convention for the Protection of War Victims of 1949 as the emblem and distinctive sign of the Medical Service of armed forces and used by the Canadian Red Cross Society, or the expression "Red Cross" or "Geneva Cross";

(g) the emblem of the Red Crescent on a white ground adopted for the same purpose as specified in paragraph (f);

(g.1) the third Protocol emblem — commonly known as the "Red Crystal" — referred to in Article 2, paragraph 2 of Schedule VII to the *Geneva Conventions Act* and composed of a red frame in the shape of a square on edge on a white ground, adopted for the same purpose as specified in paragraph (f);

(h) the equivalent sign of the Red Lion and Sun used by Iran for the same purpose as specified in paragraph (f);

(h.1) the international distinctive sign of civil defence (equilateral blue triangle on an orange ground) referred to in Article 66, paragraph 4 of Schedule V to the *Geneva Conventions Act*;

(i) any territorial or civic flag or any national, territorial or civic arms, crest or emblem, of a country of the

Marques interdites

9 (1) Nul ne peut adopter à l'égard d'une entreprise, comme marque de commerce ou autrement, une marque composée de ce qui suit, ou dont la ressemblance est telle qu'on pourrait vraisemblablement la confondre avec ce qui suit :

a) les armoiries, l'écusson ou le drapeau de Sa Majesté;

b) les armoiries ou l'écusson d'un membre de la famille royale;

c) le drapeau, les armoiries ou l'écusson de Son Excellence le gouverneur général;

d) un mot ou symbole susceptible de porter à croire que les produits ou services en liaison avec lesquels il est employé ont reçu l'approbation royale, vice-royale ou gouvernementale, ou que leur production, leur vente ou leur exécution a lieu sous le patronage ou sur l'autorité royale, vice-royale ou gouvernementale;

e) les armoiries, l'écusson ou le drapeau adoptés et employés à toute époque par le Canada ou par une province ou municipalité au Canada, à l'égard desquels le registraire, sur la demande du gouvernement du Canada ou de la province ou municipalité intéressée, a notifié au public leur adoption et leur emploi;

f) l'emblème de la Croix-Rouge sur fond blanc, formé en transposant les couleurs fédérales de la Suisse et retenu par la Convention de Genève pour la protection des victimes de guerre de 1949 comme emblème et signe distinctif du service médical des forces armées, et employé par la Société de la Croix-Rouge Canadienne, ou l'expression « Croix-Rouge » ou « Croix de Genève »;

g) l'emblème du Croissant rouge sur fond blanc adopté aux mêmes fins que celles mentionnées à l'alinéa f);

g.1) l'emblème du troisième Protocole — communément appelé « cristal rouge » — visé au paragraphe 2 de l'article 2 de l'annexe VII de la *Loi sur les conventions de Genève*, composé d'un cadre rouge, ayant la forme d'un carré posé sur la pointe, sur fond blanc, adopté aux mêmes fins que celles mentionnées à l'alinéa f);

h) le signe équivalent des Lion et Soleil rouges employés par l'Iran aux mêmes fins que celles mentionnées à l'alinéa f);

h.1) le signe distinctif international de la protection civile — triangle équilatéral bleu sur fond orange —

Union, if the flag, arms, crest or emblem is on a list communicated under article 6ter of the Convention or pursuant to the obligations under the Agreement on Trade-related Aspects of Intellectual Property Rights set out in Annex 1C to the WTO Agreement stemming from that article, and the Registrar gives public notice of the communication;

(i.1) any official sign or hallmark indicating control or warranty adopted by a country of the Union, if the sign or hallmark is on a list communicated under article 6ter of the Convention or pursuant to the obligations under the Agreement on Trade-related Aspects of Intellectual Property Rights set out in Annex 1C to the WTO Agreement stemming from that article, and the Registrar gives public notice of the communication;

(i.2) any national flag of a country of the Union;

(i.3) any armorial bearing, flag or other emblem, or the name or any abbreviation of the name, of an international intergovernmental organization, if the armorial bearing, flag, emblem, name or abbreviation is on a list communicated under article 6ter of the Convention or pursuant to the obligations under the Agreement on Trade-related Aspects of Intellectual Property Rights set out in Annex 1C to the WTO Agreement stemming from that article, and the Registrar gives public notice of the communication;

(j) any scandalous, obscene or immoral word or device;

(k) any matter that may falsely suggest a connection with any living individual;

(l) the portrait or signature of any individual who is living or has died within the preceding thirty years;

(m) the words "United Nations" or the official seal or emblem of the United Nations;

(n) any badge, crest, emblem or mark

   (i) adopted or used by any of Her Majesty's Forces as defined in the *National Defence Act*,

   (ii) of any university, or

   (iii) adopted and used by any public authority, in Canada as an official mark for goods or services,

in respect of which the Registrar has, at the request of Her Majesty or of the university or public authority, as the case may be, given public notice of its adoption and use;

---

visé au paragraphe 4 de l'article 66 de l'annexe V de la *Loi sur les conventions de Genève*;

i) les drapeaux territoriaux ou civiques ou les armoiries, écussons ou emblèmes nationaux, territoriaux ou civiques, d'un pays de l'Union, qui figurent sur une liste communiquée conformément à l'article 6ter de la Convention ou en vertu des obligations prévues à l'Accord sur les aspects des droits de propriété intellectuelle qui touchent au commerce figurant à l'annexe 1C de l'Accord sur l'OMC et découlant de cet article, pourvu que la communication ait fait l'objet d'un avis public du registraire;

i.1) tout signe ou poinçon officiel de contrôle et garantie qui a été adopté par un pays de l'Union, qui figure sur une liste communiquée conformément à l'article 6ter de la Convention ou en vertu des obligations prévues à l'Accord sur les aspects des droits de propriété intellectuelle qui touchent au commerce figurant à l'annexe 1C de l'Accord sur l'OMC et découlant de cet article, pourvu que la communication ait fait l'objet d'un avis public du registraire;

i.2) tout drapeau national d'un pays de l'Union;

i.3) les armoiries, les drapeaux ou autres emblèmes d'une organisation intergouvernementale internationale ainsi que sa dénomination et son sigle, qui figurent sur une liste communiquée conformément à l'article 6ter de la Convention ou en vertu des obligations prévues à l'Accord sur les aspects des droits de propriété intellectuelle qui touchent au commerce figurant à l'annexe 1C de l'Accord sur l'OMC et découlant de cet article, pourvu que la communication ait fait l'objet d'un avis public du registraire;

j) une devise ou un mot scandaleux, obscène ou immoral;

k) toute matière qui peut faussement suggérer un rapport avec un particulier vivant;

l) le portrait ou la signature d'un particulier vivant ou qui est décédé dans les trente années précédentes;

m) les mots « Nations Unies », ou le sceau ou l'emblème officiel des Nations Unies;

n) tout insigne, écusson, marque ou emblème :

   (i) adopté ou employé par l'une des forces de Sa Majesté telles que les définit la *Loi sur la défense nationale*,

   (ii) d'une université,

(n.1) any armorial bearings granted, recorded or approved for use by a recipient pursuant to the prerogative powers of Her Majesty as exercised by the Governor General in respect of the granting of armorial bearings, if the Registrar has, at the request of the Governor General, given public notice of the grant, recording or approval; or

(o) the name "Royal Canadian Mounted Police" or "R.C.M.P." or any other combination of letters relating to the Royal Canadian Mounted Police, or any pictorial representation of a uniformed member thereof.

Excepted uses

(2) Nothing in this section prevents the adoption, use or registration as a trade-mark or otherwise, in connection with a business, of any mark

(a) described in subsection (1) with the consent of Her Majesty or such other person, society, authority or organization as may be considered to have been intended to be protected by this section; or

(b) consisting of, or so nearly resembling as to be likely to be mistaken for

(i) an official sign or hallmark mentioned in paragraph (1)(i.1), except in respect of goods that are the same or similar to the goods in respect of which the official sign or hallmark has been adopted, or

(ii) an armorial bearing, flag, emblem or abbreviation mentioned in paragraph (1)(i.3), unless the use of the mark is likely to mislead the public as to a connection between the user and the organization.

R.S., 1985, c. T-13, s. 9; 1990, c. 14, s. 8; 1993, c. 15, s. 58; 1994, c. 47, s. 191; 1999, c. 31, s. 209(F); 2007, c. 26, s. 6; 2014, c. 32, ss. 11, 53, 56(F).

Further prohibitions

10 Where any mark has by ordinary and *bona fide* commercial usage become recognized in Canada as designating the kind, quality, quantity, destination, value, place of origin or date of production of any goods or services, no person shall adopt it as a trade-mark in association with

(iii) adopté et employé par une autorité publique au Canada comme marque officielle pour des produits ou services,

à l'égard duquel le registraire, sur la demande de Sa Majesté ou de l'université ou autorité publique, selon le cas, a donné un avis public d'adoption et emploi;

n.1) les armoiries octroyées, enregistrées ou agréées pour l'emploi par un récipiendaire au titre des pouvoirs de prérogative de Sa Majesté exercés par le gouverneur général relativement à celles-ci, à la condition que le registraire ait, à la demande du gouverneur général, donné un avis public en ce sens;

o) le nom « Gendarmerie royale du Canada » ou « G.R.C. », ou toute autre combinaison de lettres se rattachant à la Gendarmerie royale du Canada, ou toute représentation illustrée d'un membre de ce corps en uniforme.

Exception

(2) Le présent article n'a pas pour effet d'empêcher l'adoption, l'emploi ou l'enregistrement, comme marque de commerce ou autrement, quant à une entreprise, d'une marque :

a) visée au paragraphe (1), à la condition qu'ait été obtenu, selon le cas, le consentement de Sa Majesté ou de telle autre personne, société, autorité ou organisation que le présent article est censé avoir voulu protéger;

b) composée de ce qui suit, ou dont la ressemblance est telle qu'on pourrait vraisemblablement la confondre avec ce qui suit :

(i) tout signe ou poinçon visé à l'alinéa (1)i.1), sauf à l'égard de produits identiques ou de produits semblables à ceux à l'égard desquels ce signe ou poinçon a été adopté,

(ii) les armoiries, drapeaux, emblèmes et sigles visés à l'alinéa (1)i.3), sauf si l'emploi de la marque est susceptible d'induire en erreur le public quant au lien qu'il y aurait entre l'utilisateur de la marque et l'organisation visée à cet alinéa.

L.R. (1985), ch. T-13, art. 9; 1990, ch. 14, art. 8; 1993, ch. 15, art. 58; 1994, ch. 47, art. 191; 1999, ch. 31, art. 209(F); 2007, ch. 26, art. 6; 2014, ch. 32, art. 11, 53 et 56(F).

Autres interdictions

10 Si une marque, en raison d'une pratique commerciale ordinaire et authentique, devient reconnue au Canada comme désignant le genre, la qualité, la quantité, la destination, la valeur, le lieu d'origine ou la date de production de produits ou services, nul ne peut l'adopter comme

such goods or services or others of the same general class or use it in a way likely to mislead, nor shall any person so adopt or so use any mark so nearly resembling that mark as to be likely to be mistaken therefor.

R.S., 1985, c. T-13, s. 10; 2014, c. 32, s. 53.

Further prohibitions

10.1 Where a denomination must, under the *Plant Breeders' Rights Act*, be used to designate a plant variety, no person shall adopt it as a trade-mark in association with the plant variety or another plant variety of the same species or use it in a way likely to mislead, nor shall any person so adopt or so use any mark so nearly resembling that denomination as to be likely to be mistaken therefor.

1990, c. 20, s. 79.

Further prohibitions

11 No person shall use in connection with a business, as a trade-mark or otherwise, any mark adopted contrary to section 9 or 10 of this Act or section 13 or 14 of the *Unfair Competition Act*, chapter 274 of the Revised Statutes of Canada, 1952.

R.S., c. T-10, s. 11.

Further prohibitions

11.1 No person shall use in connection with a business, as a trade-mark or otherwise, any denomination adopted contrary to section 10.1.

1990, c. 20, s. 80; 2014, c. 32, s. 56(F).

Definitions

11.11 In sections 11.12 to 11.2,

Minister means the member of the Queen's Privy Council for Canada designated as the Minister for the purposes of sections 11.12 to 11.2; (*ministre*)

responsible authority means, in relation to a wine or spirit, the person, firm or other entity that, in the opinion of the Minister, is, by reason of state or commercial interest, sufficiently connected with and knowledgeable of that wine or spirit to be a party to any proceedings in respect of an objection filed under subsection 11.13(1). (*autorité compétente*)

1994, c. 47, s. 192.

List

11.12 (1) There shall be kept under the supervision of the Registrar a list of geographical indications.

---

marque de commerce en liaison avec ces produits ou services ou autres de la même catégorie générale, ou l'employer d'une manière susceptible d'induire en erreur, et nul ne peut ainsi adopter ou employer une marque dont la ressemblance avec la marque en question est telle qu'on pourrait vraisemblablement les confondre.

L.R. (1985), ch. T-13, art. 10; 2014, ch. 32, art. 53.

Idem

10.1 Dans les cas où une dénomination est, au titre de la *Loi sur la protection des obtentions végétales*, à utiliser pour désigner une variété végétale, nul ne peut adopter la dénomination comme marque de commerce relativement à cette variété ou à une variété de la même espèce, ni l'utiliser d'une manière susceptible d'induire en erreur, ni adopter, ou utiliser ainsi, une marque dont la ressemblance avec la dénomination est telle qu'on pourrait vraisemblablement les confondre.

1990, ch. 20, art. 79.

Autres interdictions

11 Nul ne peut employer relativement à une entreprise, comme marque de commerce ou autrement, une marque adoptée contrairement à l'article 9 ou 10 de la présente loi ou contrairement à l'article 13 ou 14 de la *Loi sur la concurrence déloyale*, chapitre 274 des Statuts revisés du Canada de 1952.

S.R., ch. T-10, art. 11.

Idem

11.1 Nul ne peut employer en relation avec une entreprise une dénomination adoptée contrairement à l'article 10.1.

1990, ch. 20, art. 80; 2014, ch. 32, art. 56(F).

Définitions

11.11 Les définitions qui suivent s'appliquent aux articles 11.12 à 11.2.

autorité compétente Dans le cas d'un vin ou spiritueux, la personne, firme ou autre entité qui, de l'avis du ministre, a, du fait d'intérêts commerciaux ou de son statut étatique, des connaissances et des liens suffisants à leur égard pour être partie à la procédure d'opposition visée au paragraphe 11.13(1). (*responsible authority*)

ministre Le membre du Conseil privé de la Reine pour le Canada chargé par le gouverneur en conseil de l'application des articles 11.12 à 11.2. (*Minister*)

1994, ch. 47, art. 192.

Liste

11.12 (1) La liste des indications géographiques est tenue sous la surveillance du registraire.

Statement of Minister

(2) Where a statement by the Minister, setting out in respect of an indication the information mentioned in subsection (3), is published in the *Canada Gazette* and

(a) a statement of objection has not been filed and served on the responsible authority in accordance with subsection 11.13(1) and the time for the filing of the statement of objection has expired, or

(b) a statement of objection has been so filed and served, but it has been withdrawn or deemed under subsection 11.13(6) to have been withdrawn or it has been rejected pursuant to subsection 11.13(7) or, if an appeal is taken, it is rejected pursuant to the final judgment given in the appeal,

the Registrar shall enter the indication on the list of geographical indications kept pursuant to subsection (1).

Information

(3) For the purposes of subsection (2), the statement by the Minister must set out the following information in respect of an indication:

(a) that the Minister proposes that the indication be entered on the list of geographical indications kept pursuant to subsection (1);

(b) that the indication identifies a wine or that the indication identifies a spirit;

(c) the territory, or the region or locality of a territory, in which the wine or spirit is identified as originating;

(d) the name of the responsible authority in relation to the wine or spirit and the address of the responsible authority's principal office or place of business in Canada, if any, and if the responsible authority has no office or place of business in Canada, the name and address in Canada of a person or firm on whom service of any document or proceedings in respect of an objection may be given or served with the same effect as if they had been given to or served on the responsible authority itself; and

(e) the quality, reputation or other characteristic of the wine or spirit that, in the opinion of the Minister, qualifies that indication as a geographical indication.

Removal from list

(4) The Registrar shall remove an indication from the list of geographical indications kept pursuant to subsection

Énoncé d'intention du ministre

(2) Le registraire inscrit sur la liste les indications à l'égard desquelles, le ministre ayant fait publier dans la *Gazette du Canada* un énoncé d'intention donnant les renseignements visés au paragraphe (3) :

a) aucune déclaration d'opposition n'a été déposée ni signifiée à l'autorité compétente dans le délai imparti par le paragraphe 11.13(1);

b) la déclaration d'opposition, bien que présentée et signifiée, a été retirée — ou réputée l'avoir été en vertu du paragraphe 11.13(6) —, rejetée dans le cadre du paragraphe 11.13(7) ou, en cas d'appel, a été rejetée par un jugement définitif sur la question.

Renseignements

(3) Les renseignements suivants concernant l'indication doivent figurer dans l'énoncé d'intention visé au paragraphe (2) :

a) l'intention du ministre de faire inscrire l'indication sur la liste des indications géographiques;

b) la nature — vin ou spiritueux — du produit visé par l'indication;

c) le lieu d'origine — territoire, ou région ou localité de celui-ci — du vin ou spiritueux;

d) le nom de l'autorité compétente à l'égard du vin ou spiritueux et l'adresse de son siège ou de son établissement au Canada le cas échéant ou, à défaut, les nom et adresse au Canada d'une personne ou firme à qui des documents peuvent être remis ou des actes de procédure signifiés pour valoir remise ou signification à l'autorité compétente elle-même;

e) la réputation ou l'autre qualité ou caractéristique du vin ou spiritueux qui, de l'avis du ministre, justifie de faire de l'indication une indication géographique.

Suppression d'indications

(4) Le registraire supprime de la liste toute inscription relative à une indication sur publication par le ministre, dans la *Gazette du Canada*, d'un énoncé d'intention à cette fin.

1994, ch. 47, art. 192.

(1) on the publication in the *Canada Gazette* of a statement by the Minister that the indication is to be removed.

1994, c. 47, s. 192.

Statement of objection

11.13 (1) Within three months after the publication in the *Canada Gazette* of a statement referred to in subsection 11.12(2), any person interested may, on payment of the prescribed fee, file with the Registrar, and serve on the responsible authority in the prescribed manner, a statement of objection.

Ground

(2) A statement of objection may be based only on the ground that the indication is not a geographical indication.

Content

(3) A statement of objection shall set out

(a) the ground of objection in sufficient detail to enable the responsible authority to reply thereto; and

(b) the address of the objector's principal office or place of business in Canada, if any, and if the objector has no office or place of business in Canada, the address of the principal office or place of business abroad and the name and address in Canada of a person or firm on whom service of any document in respect of the objection may be made with the same effect as if it had been served on the objector.

Counter statement

(4) Within three months after a statement of objection has been served on the responsible authority, the responsible authority may file a counter statement with the Registrar and serve a copy on the objector in the prescribed manner, and if the responsible authority does not so file and serve a counter statement, the indication shall not be entered on the list of geographical indications.

Evidence and hearing

(5) Both the objector and the responsible authority shall be given an opportunity, in the manner prescribed, to submit evidence and to make representations to the Registrar unless

(a) the responsible authority does not file and serve a counter statement in accordance with subsection (4) or if, in the prescribed circumstances, the responsible authority does not submit evidence or a statement that the responsible authority does not wish to submit evidence; or

Déclaration d'opposition

11.13 (1) Toute personne intéressée peut, dans les trois mois suivant la publication dans la *Gazette du Canada* de l'énoncé prévu au paragraphe 11.12(2), et sur paiement du droit prescrit, produire au bureau du registraire et signifier à l'autorité compétente, de la manière prescrite, une déclaration d'opposition.

Motif

(2) Le seul motif qui peut être invoqué à l'appui de l'opposition est le fait que l'indication n'est pas une indication géographique.

Teneur

(3) La déclaration d'opposition indique :

a) le motif de l'opposition, avec détails suffisants pour permettre à l'autorité compétente d'y répondre;

b) l'adresse du siège ou de l'établissement de l'opposant au Canada, le cas échéant, ou, à défaut, l'adresse de son siège ou de son établissement à l'étranger et les nom et adresse, au Canada, d'une personne ou firme à qui tout document concernant l'opposition peut être signifié pour valoir signification à l'opposant lui-même.

Contre-déclaration

(4) L'autorité compétente peut, dans les trois mois suivant la date à laquelle la déclaration d'opposition lui a été signifiée, produire auprès du registraire et signifier à l'opposant, de la manière prescrite, une contre-déclaration; à défaut par elle de ce faire, l'indication n'est pas inscrite sur la liste.

Preuve et audition

(5) Il est fourni, de la manière prescrite, à l'opposant et à l'autorité compétente l'occasion de présenter la preuve sur laquelle ils s'appuient et de se faire entendre par le registraire, sauf dans les cas suivants :

a) l'autorité compétente ne produit ni ne signifie la contre-déclaration visée au paragraphe (4) ou, dans les circonstances prescrites, elle omet de présenter des éléments de preuve ou une déclaration énonçant son désir de ne pas le faire;

(b) the objection is withdrawn or deemed under subsection (6) to have been withdrawn.

Withdrawal of objection

(6) The objection shall be deemed to have been withdrawn if, in the prescribed circumstances, the objector does not submit evidence or a statement that the objector does not wish to submit evidence.

Decision

(7) After considering the evidence and representations of the objector and the responsible authority, the Registrar shall decide that the indication is not a geographical indication or reject the objection, and notify the parties of the decision and the reasons for the decision.

1994, c. 47, s. 192.

Prohibited adoption of indication for wines

11.14 (1) No person shall adopt in connection with a business, as a trade-mark or otherwise,

(a) a protected geographical indication identifying a wine in respect of a wine not originating in the territory indicated by the protected geographical indication; or

(b) a translation in any language of the geographical indication in respect of that wine.

Prohibited use

(2) No person shall use in connection with a business, as a trade-mark or otherwise,

(a) a protected geographical indication identifying a wine in respect of a wine not originating in the territory indicated by the protected geographical indication or adopted contrary to subsection (1); or

(b) a translation in any language of the geographical indication in respect of that wine.

1994, c. 47, s. 192; 2014, c. 32, s. 56(F).

Prohibited adoption of indication for spirits

11.15 (1) No person shall adopt in connection with a business, as a trade-mark or otherwise,

(a) a protected geographical indication identifying a spirit in respect of a spirit not originating in the territory indicated by the protected geographical indication; or

(b) a translation in any language of the geographical indication in respect of that spirit.

(b) l'opposition est retirée, ou réputée retirée, au titre du paragraphe (6).

Retrait de l'opposition

(6) Si, dans les circonstances prescrites, l'opposant omet de présenter des éléments de preuve ou une déclaration énonçant son désir de ne pas le faire, l'opposition est réputée retirée.

Décision

(7) Après avoir examiné la preuve et les observations des parties, le registraire décide que l'indication n'est pas une indication géographique ou rejette l'opposition et notifie aux parties sa décision motivée.

1994, ch. 47, art. 192.

Interdiction d'adoption : vins

11.14 (1) Nul ne peut adopter à l'égard d'une entreprise, comme marque de commerce ou autrement :

a) une indication géographique protégée désignant un vin pour un vin dont le lieu d'origine ne se trouve pas sur le territoire visé par l'indication géographique protégée;

b) la traduction, en quelque langue que ce soit, de l'indication géographique relative à ce vin.

Interdiction d'usage

(2) Nul ne peut employer à l'égard d'une entreprise, comme marque de commerce ou autrement :

a) une indication géographique protégée désignant un vin pour un vin dont le lieu d'origine ne se trouve pas sur le territoire visé par l'indication géographique protégée ou adoptée en contravention avec le paragraphe (1);

b) la traduction, en quelque langue que ce soit, de l'indication géographique relative à ce vin.

1994, ch. 47, art. 192; 2014, ch. 32, art. 56(F).

Interdiction d'adoption : spiritueux

11.15 (1) Nul ne peut adopter à l'égard d'une entreprise, comme marque de commerce ou autrement :

a) une indication géographique protégée désignant un spiritueux pour un spiritueux dont le lieu d'origine ne se trouve pas sur le territoire visé par l'indication géographique protégée;

b) la traduction, en quelque langue que ce soit, de l'indication géographique relative à ce spiritueux.

Prohibited use

(2) No person shall use in connection with a business, as a trade-mark or otherwise,

(a) a protected geographical indication identifying a spirit in respect of a spirit not originating in the territory indicated by the protected geographical indication or adopted contrary to subsection (1); or

(b) a translation in any language of the geographical indication in respect of that spirit.

1994, c. 47, s. 192; 2014, c. 32, s. 56(F).

Exception for personal names

11.16 (1) Sections 11.14 and 11.15 do not prevent a person from using, in the course of trade, that person's name or the name of the person's predecessor-in-title, except where the name is used in such a manner as to mislead the public.

Exception for comparative advertising

(2) Subject to subsection (3), sections 11.14 and 11.15 do not prevent a person from using a protected geographical indication in comparative advertising in respect of a wine or spirit.

Exception not applicable to packaging

(3) Subsection (2) does not apply to comparative advertising on labels or packaging associated with a wine or spirit.

1994, c. 47, s. 192; 2014, c. 32, s. 56(F).

Continued use

11.17 (1) Where a Canadian has used a protected geographical indication in a continuous manner in relation to any business or commercial activity in respect of goods or services

(a) in good faith before April 15, 1994, or

(b) for at least ten years before that date,

section 11.14 or 11.15, as the case may be, does not apply to any continued or similar use by that Canadian.

Definition of *Canadian*

(2) For the purposes of this section, **Canadian** includes

(a) a Canadian citizen;

(b) a permanent resident within the meaning of subsection 2(1) of the *Immigration and Refugee Protection Act* who has been ordinarily resident in Canada for not more than one year after the time at which the permanent resident first became eligible to apply for Canadian citizenship; and

(c) an entity that carries on business in Canada.

1994, c. 47, s. 192; 2001, c. 27, s. 271; 2014, c. 32, ss. 53(F), 56(F).

Exception for disuse

11.18 (1) Notwithstanding sections 11.14 and 11.15 and paragraphs 12(1)(g) and (h), nothing in any of those provisions prevents the adoption, use or registration as a trade-mark or otherwise, in connection with a business, of a protected geographical indication identifying a wine or spirit if the indication has ceased to be protected by the laws applicable to the WTO Member for which the indication is protected, or has fallen into disuse in that Member.

Exceptions for customary names

(2) Notwithstanding sections 11.14 and 11.15 and paragraphs 12(1)(g) and (h), nothing in any of those provisions prevents the adoption, use or registration as a trade-mark or otherwise, in connection with a business, of an indication in respect of a wine or spirit

(a) that is identical with a term customary in common language in Canada as the common name for the wine or spirit, as the case may be; or

(b) that is identical with a customary name of a grape variety existing in Canada on or before the day on which the Agreement comes into force.

Exception for generic names for wines

(3) Notwithstanding sections 11.14 and 11.15 and paragraphs 12(1)(g) and (h), nothing in any of those provisions prevents the adoption, use or registration as a trade-mark or otherwise, in connection with a business, of the following indications in respect of wines:

(a) to (e) [Repealed, SOR/2004-85]

(f) to (v) [Repealed, SOR/2004-85]

Exception for generic names for spirits

(4) Notwithstanding sections 11.14 and 11.15 and paragraphs 12(1)(g) and (h), nothing in any of those provisions prevents the adoption, use or registration as a trade-mark or otherwise, in connection with a business, of the following indications in respect of spirits:

(a) [Repealed, SOR/2004-85]

(b) Marc;

Canada pour plus d'un an après la date à laquelle ils sont devenus admissibles à la demande de citoyenneté canadienne;

c) les entités qui exploitent une entreprise au Canada.

1994, ch. 47, art. 192; 2001, ch. 27, art. 271; 2014, ch. 32, art. 53(F) et 56(F).

Exception — non-usage

11.18 (1) Les articles 11.14 et 11.15 et les alinéas 12(1)g) et h) n'ont pas pour effet d'empêcher l'adoption, l'emploi ou l'enregistrement à l'égard d'une entreprise, comme marque de commerce ou autrement, d'une indication géographique désignant un vin ou spiritueux et qui a cessé d'être protégée par le droit applicable au membre de l'OMC en faveur duquel l'indication est protégée, ou est tombée en désuétude chez ce membre.

Exception — nom usuel

(2) Les articles 11.14 et 11.15 et les alinéas 12(1)g) et h) n'ont pas pour effet d'empêcher l'adoption, l'emploi ou l'enregistrement à l'égard d'une entreprise, comme marque de commerce ou autrement, d'une indication géographique désignant un vin ou spiritueux et qui est identique :

a) soit au terme usuel employé dans le langage courant au Canada comme nom commun du vin ou spiritueux;

b) soit au nom usuel d'une variété de cépage existant au Canada à la date d'entrée en vigueur de l'Accord.

Exception — noms génériques de vins

(3) Les articles 11.14 et 11.15 et les alinéas 12(1)g) et h) n'ont pas pour effet d'empêcher l'adoption, l'emploi ou l'enregistrement à l'égard d'une entreprise, comme marque de commerce ou autrement, des indications suivantes, pour ce qui est des vins :

a) à e) [Abrogés, DORS/2004-85]

f) à v) [Abrogés, DORS/2004-85]

Exception — noms génériques de spiritueux

(4) Les articles 11.14 et 11.15 et les alinéas 12(1)g) et h) n'ont pas pour effet d'empêcher l'adoption, l'emploi ou l'enregistrement à l'égard d'une entreprise, comme marque de commerce ou autrement, des indications suivantes, pour ce qui est des spiritueux :

a) [Abrogé, DORS/2004-85]

b) Marc;

(c) [Repealed, SOR/2004-85]

(d) Sambuca;

(e) Geneva Gin;

(f) Genièvre;

(g) Hollands Gin;

(h) London Gin;

(i) Schnapps;

(j) Malt Whiskey;

(k) Eau-de-vie;

(l) Bitters;

(m) Anisette;

(n) Curacao; and

(o) Curaçao.

Governor in Council amendment

(5) The Governor in Council may, by order, amend subsection (3) or (4) by adding thereto or deleting therefrom an indication in respect of a wine or spirit, as the case may be.

1994, c. 47, s. 192; SOR/2004-85; 2014, c. 32, s. 56(F).

Exception for failure to take proceedings

11.19 (1) Sections 11.14 and 11.15 do not apply to the adoption or use of a trade-mark by a person if no proceedings are taken to enforce those sections in respect of that person's use or adoption of the trade-mark within five years after use of the trade-mark by that person or that person's predecessor-in-title has become generally known in Canada or the trade-mark has been registered by that person in Canada, unless it is established that that person or that person's predecessor-in-title first used or adopted the trade-mark with knowledge that such use or adoption was contrary to section 11.14 or 11.15, as the case may be.

Idem

(2) In proceedings respecting a registered trade-mark commenced after the expiration of five years from the earlier of the date of registration of the trade-mark in Canada and the date on which use of the trade-mark by the person who filed the application for registration of the trade-mark or that person's predecessor-in-title has become generally known in Canada, the registration shall not be expunged or amended or held invalid on the basis

c) [Abrogé, DORS/2004-85]

d) Sambuca;

e) Geneva Gin;

f) Genièvre;

g) Hollands Gin;

h) London Gin;

i) Schnapps;

j) Malt Whiskey;

k) Eau-de-vie;

l) Bitters;

m) Anisette;

n) Curacao;

o) Curaçao.

Pouvoirs du gouverneur en conseil

(5) Le gouverneur en conseil peut, par décret, modifier les paragraphes (3) ou (4) par l'adjonction ou la suppression d'indications désignant un vin ou un spiritueux, selon le cas.

1994, ch. 47, art. 192; DORS/2004-85; 2014, ch. 32, art. 56(F).

Exception — aucune procédure engagée

11.19 (1) Les articles 11.14 et 11.15 ne s'appliquent pas à l'adoption ou à l'emploi par une personne d'une marque de commerce si aucune procédure n'est engagée pour faire respecter ces dispositions à l'égard de cette adoption ou de cet emploi dans les cinq ans suivant la date à laquelle l'emploi de la marque de commerce par cette personne ou son prédécesseur en titre a été généralement connu au Canada ou la marque de commerce y a été enregistrée par cette personne, sauf s'il est établi que cette personne ou son prédécesseur en titre a adopté ou commencé à employer la marque tout en sachant que l'adoption ou l'emploi étaient contraires à ces articles.

Idem

(2) Dans le cas de procédures concernant une marque de commerce déposée et engagées après l'expiration des cinq ans suivant le premier en date du jour de l'enregistrement de la marque de commerce au Canada et du jour où l'usage de la marque de commerce par la personne qui a demandé l'enregistrement ou son prédécesseur en titre a été généralement connu au Canada, l'enregistrement ne peut être radié, modifié ou tenu pour invalide du fait des

of paragraph 12(1)(g) or (h) unless it is established that the person who filed the application for registration of the trade-mark did so with knowledge that the trade-mark was in whole or in part a protected geographical indication.

1994, c. 47, s. 192; 2014, c. 32, s. 14(F).

Transitional

11.2 Notwithstanding sections 11.14 and 11.15 and paragraphs 12(1)(g) and (h), where a person has in good faith

(a) filed an application in accordance with section 30 for, or secured the registration of, a trade-mark that is identical with or similar to the geographical indication in respect of a wine or spirit protected by the laws applicable to a WTO Member, or

(b) acquired rights to a trade-mark in respect of such a wine or spirit through use,

before the later of the date on which this section comes into force and the date on which protection in respect of the wine or spirit by the laws applicable to that Member commences, nothing in any of those provisions prevents the adoption, use or registration of that trade-mark by that person.

1994, c. 47, s. 192; 2014, c. 32, s. 56(F).

Registrable Trade-marks

When trade-mark registrable

12 (1) Subject to section 13, a trade-mark is registrable if it is not

(a) a word that is primarily merely the name or the surname of an individual who is living or has died within the preceding thirty years;

(b) whether depicted, written or sounded, either clearly descriptive or deceptively misdescriptive in the English or French language of the character or quality of the goods or services in association with which it is used or proposed to be used or of the conditions of or the persons employed in their production or of their place of origin;

(c) the name in any language of any of the goods or services in connection with which it is used or proposed to be used;

(d) confusing with a registered trade-mark;

alinéas 12(1)g) ou h) que s'il est établi que la personne qui a demandé l'enregistrement l'a fait tout en sachant que la marque était en tout ou en partie une indication géographique protégée.

1994, ch. 47, art. 192; 2014, ch. 32, art. 14(F).

Disposition transitoire

11.2 Les articles 11.14 et 11.15 et les alinéas 12(1)g) et h) n'ont pas pour effet d'empêcher l'adoption, l'emploi ou l'enregistrement, comme marque de commerce ou autrement, d'une indication géographique protégée par une personne qui, de bonne foi, avant la date d'entrée en vigueur du présent article :

a) soit a produit une demande conformément à l'article 30 en vue de l'enregistrement d'une marque de commerce qui est identique ou semblable à l'indication géographique relative à un vin ou spiritueux protégé par le droit applicable à un membre de l'OMC, ou a obtenu cet enregistrement;

b) soit a acquis le droit à une marque de commerce par l'usage.

Dans les cas où la protection est postérieure à cette date, c'est la date à laquelle commence la protection relative au vin ou spiritueux selon le droit applicable au membre qui est prise en compte.

1994, ch. 47, art. 192; 2014, ch. 32, art. 56(F).

Marques de commerce enregistrables

Marque de commerce enregistrable

12 (1) Sous réserve de l'article 13, une marque de commerce est enregistrable sauf dans l'un ou l'autre des cas suivants :

a) elle est constituée d'un mot n'étant principalement que le nom ou le nom de famille d'un particulier vivant ou qui est décédé dans les trente années précédentes;

b) qu'elle soit sous forme graphique, écrite ou sonore, elle donne une description claire ou donne une description fausse et trompeuse, en langue française ou anglaise, de la nature ou de la qualité des produits ou services en liaison avec lesquels elle est employée, ou en liaison avec lesquels on projette de l'employer, ou des conditions de leur production, ou des personnes qui les produisent, ou de leur lieu d'origine;

c) elle est constituée du nom, dans une langue, de l'un des produits ou de l'un des services à l'égard desquels

(e) a mark of which the adoption is prohibited by section 9 or 10;

(f) a denomination the adoption of which is prohibited by section 10.1;

(g) in whole or in part a protected geographical indication, where the trade-mark is to be registered in association with a wine not originating in a territory indicated by the geographical indication;

(h) in whole or in part a protected geographical indication, where the trade-mark is to be registered in association with a spirit not originating in a territory indicated by the geographical indication; and

(i) subject to subsection 3(3) and paragraph 3(4)(a) of the *Olympic and Paralympic Marks Act*, a mark the adoption of which is prohibited by subsection 3(1) of that Act.

Idem

(2) A trade-mark that is not registrable by reason of paragraph (1)(a) or (b) is registrable if it has been so used in Canada by the applicant or his predecessor in title as to have become distinctive at the date of filing an application for its registration.

R.S., 1985, c. T-13, s. 12; 1990, c. 20, s. 81; 1993, c. 15, s. 59(F); 1994, c. 47, s. 193; 2007, c. 25, s. 14; 2014, c. 32, ss. 15(F), 53.

When distinguishing guises registrable

13 (1) A distinguishing guise is registrable only if

(a) it has been so used in Canada by the applicant or his predecessor in title as to have become distinctive at the date of filing an application for its registration; and

(b) the exclusive use by the applicant of the distinguishing guise in association with the goods or services with which it has been used is not likely unreasonably to limit the development of any art or industry.

Effect of registration

(2) No registration of a distinguishing guise interferes with the use of any utilitarian feature embodied in the distinguishing guise.

Not to limit art or industry

(3) The registration of a distinguishing guise may be expunged by the Federal Court on the application of any interested person if the Court decides that the registration has become likely unreasonably to limit the development of any art or industry.

R.S., 1985, c. T-13, s. 13; 2014, c. 32, s. 53.

Registration of marks registered abroad

14 (1) Notwithstanding section 12, a trade-mark that the applicant or the applicant's predecessor in title has caused to be duly registered in or for the country of origin of the applicant is registrable if, in Canada,

    (a) it is not confusing with a registered trade-mark;

    (b) it is not without distinctive character, having regard to all the circumstances of the case including the length of time during which it has been used in any country;

    (c) it is not contrary to morality or public order or of such a nature as to deceive the public; or

    (d) it is not a trade-mark of which the adoption is prohibited by section 9 or 10.

Trade-marks regarded as registered abroad

(2) A trade-mark that differs from the trade-mark registered in the country of origin only by elements that do not alter its distinctive character or affect its identity in the form under which it is registered in the country of origin shall be regarded for the purpose of subsection (1) as the trade-mark so registered.

R.S., 1985, c. T-13, s. 14; 1994, c. 47, s. 194.

Registration of confusing marks

15 (1) Notwithstanding section 12 or 14, confusing trade-marks are registrable if the applicant is the owner of all such trade-marks, which shall be known as associated trade-marks.

Record

(2) On the registration of any trade-mark associated with any other registered trade-mark, a note of the registration of each trade-mark shall be made on the record of registration of the other trade-mark.

Amendment

(3) No amendment of the register recording any change in the ownership or in the name or address of the owner of any one of a group of associated trade-marks shall be made unless the Registrar is satisfied that the same change has occurred with respect to all the trade-marks in the group, and corresponding entries are made contemporaneously with respect to all those trade-marks.

R.S., c. T-10, s. 15.

Persons Entitled to Registration of Trade-marks

Registration of marks used or made known in Canada

16 (1) Any applicant who has filed an application in accordance with section 30 for registration of a trade-mark that is registrable and that he or his predecessor in title has used in Canada or made known in Canada in association with goods or services is entitled, subject to section 38, to secure its registration in respect of those goods or services, unless at the date on which he or his predecessor in title first so used it or made it known it was confusing with

(a) a trade-mark that had been previously used in Canada or made known in Canada by any other person;

(b) a trade-mark in respect of which an application for registration had been previously filed in Canada by any other person; or

(c) a trade-name that had been previously used in Canada by any other person.

Marks registered and used abroad

(2) Any applicant who has filed an application in accordance with section 30 for registration of a trade-mark that is registrable and that the applicant or the applicant's predecessor in title has duly registered in or for the country of origin of the applicant and has used in association with goods or services is entitled, subject to section 38, to secure its registration in respect of the goods or services in association with which it is registered in that country and has been used, unless at the date of filing of the application in accordance with section 30 it was confusing with

(a) a trade-mark that had been previously used in Canada or made known in Canada by any other person;

(b) a trade-mark in respect of which an application for registration had been previously filed in Canada by any other person; or

(c) a trade-name that had been previously used in Canada by any other person.

Proposed marks

(3) Any applicant who has filed an application in accordance with section 30 for registration of a proposed trade-mark that is registrable is entitled, subject to sections 38 and 40, to secure its registration in respect of the goods or services specified in the application, unless at the date of filing of the application it was confusing with

(a) a trade-mark that had been previously used in Canada or made known in Canada by any other person;

(b) a trade-mark in respect of which an application for registration had been previously filed in Canada by any other person; or

(c) a trade-name that had been previously used in Canada by any other person.

Where application for confusing mark pending

(4) The right of an applicant to secure registration of a registrable trade-mark is not affected by the previous filing of an application for registration of a confusing trade-mark by another person, unless the application for registration of the confusing trade-mark was pending at the date of advertisement of the applicant's application in accordance with section 37.

Previous use or making known

(5) The right of an applicant to secure registration of a registrable trade-mark is not affected by the previous use or making known of a confusing trade-mark or trade-name by another person, if the confusing trade-mark or trade-name was abandoned at the date of advertisement of the applicant's application in accordance with section 37.

R.S., 1985, c. T-13, s. 16; 1994, c. 47, s. 195; 2014, c. 32, s. 53.

Validity and Effect of Registration

Effect of registration in relation to previous use, etc.

17 (1) No application for registration of a trade-mark that has been advertised in accordance with section 37 shall be refused and no registration of a trade-mark shall be expunged or amended or held invalid on the ground of any previous use or making known of a confusing trade-mark or trade-name by a person other than the applicant for that registration or his predecessor in title, except at the instance of that other person or his successor in title, and the burden lies on that other person or his successor to establish that he had not abandoned the confusing trade-mark or trade-name at the date of advertisement of the applicant's application.

When registration incontestable

(2) In proceedings commenced after the expiration of five years from the date of registration of a trade-mark or from July 1, 1954, whichever is the later, no registration shall be expunged or amended or held invalid on the ground of the previous use or making known referred to in subsection (1), unless it is established that the person who adopted the registered trade-mark in Canada did so with knowledge of that previous use or making known.

R.S., 1985, c. T-13, s. 17; 2014, c. 32, s. 56(F).

When registration invalid

18 (1) The registration of a trade-mark is invalid if

(a) the trade-mark was not registrable at the date of registration;

(b) the trade-mark is not distinctive at the time proceedings bringing the validity of the registration into question are commenced;

(c) the trade-mark has been abandoned; or

(d) subject to section 17, the applicant for registration was not the person entitled to secure the registration.

Exception

(2) No registration of a trade-mark that had been so used in Canada by the registrant or his predecessor in title as to have become distinctive at the date of registration shall be held invalid merely on the ground that evidence of the distinctiveness was not submitted to the competent authority or tribunal before the grant of the registration.

R.S., 1985, c. T-13, s. 18; 2014, c. 32, s. 19.

Rights conferred by registration

19 Subject to sections 21, 32 and 67, the registration of a trade-mark in respect of any goods or services, unless shown to be invalid, gives to the owner of the trade-mark the exclusive right to the use throughout Canada of the trade-mark in respect of those goods or services.

R.S., 1985, c. T-13, s. 19; 1993, c. 15, s. 60; 2014, c. 32, s. 53.

Infringement

20 (1) The right of the owner of a registered trade-mark to its exclusive use is deemed to be infringed by any person who is not entitled to its use under this Act and who

(a) sells, distributes or advertises any goods or services in association with a confusing trade-mark or trade-name;

(b) manufactures, causes to be manufactured, possesses, imports, exports or attempts to export any goods in association with a confusing trade-mark or trade-name, for the purpose of their sale or distribution;

(c) sells, offers for sale or distributes any label or packaging, in any form, bearing a trade-mark or trade-name, if

(i) the person knows or ought to know that the label or packaging is intended to be associated with goods or services that are not those of the owner of the registered trade-mark, and

(ii) the sale, distribution or advertisement of the goods or services in association with the label or packaging would be a sale, distribution or advertisement in association with a confusing trade-mark or trade-name; or

(d) manufactures, causes to be manufactured, possesses, imports, exports or attempts to export any label or packaging, in any form, bearing a trade-mark or trade-name, for the purpose of its sale or distribution or for the purpose of the sale, distribution or advertisement of goods or services in association with it, if

(i) the person knows or ought to know that the label or packaging is intended to be associated with goods or services that are not those of the owner of the registered trade-mark, and

date d'enregistrement, ne peut être considéré comme invalide pour la seule raison que la preuve de ce caractère distinctif n'a pas été soumise à l'autorité ou au tribunal compétent avant l'octroi de cet enregistrement.

L.R. (1985), ch. T-13, art. 18; 2014, ch. 32, art. 19.

Droits conférés par l'enregistrement

19 Sous réserve des articles 21, 32 et 67, l'enregistrement d'une marque de commerce à l'égard de produits ou services, sauf si son invalidité est démontrée, donne au propriétaire le droit exclusif à l'emploi de celle-ci, dans tout le Canada, en ce qui concerne ces produits ou services.

L.R. (1985), ch. T-13, art. 19; 1993, ch. 15, art. 60; 2014, ch. 32, art. 53.

Violation

20 (1) Le droit du propriétaire d'une marque de commerce déposée à l'emploi exclusif de cette dernière est réputé être violé par une personne qui est non admise à l'employer selon la présente loi et qui :

a) soit vend, distribue ou annonce des produits ou services en liaison avec une marque de commerce ou un nom commercial créant de la confusion;

b) soit fabrique, fait fabriquer, a en sa possession, importe, exporte ou tente d'exporter des produits, en vue de leur vente ou de leur distribution et en liaison avec une marque de commerce ou un nom commercial créant de la confusion;

c) soit vend, offre en vente ou distribue des étiquettes ou des emballages, quelle qu'en soit la forme, portant une marque de commerce ou un nom commercial alors que :

(i) d'une part, elle sait ou devrait savoir que les étiquettes ou les emballages sont destinés à être associés à des produits ou services qui ne sont pas ceux du propriétaire de la marque de commerce déposée,

(ii) d'autre part, la vente, la distribution ou l'annonce des produits ou services en liaison avec les étiquettes ou les emballages constituerait une vente, une distribution ou une annonce en liaison avec une marque de commerce ou un nom commercial créant de la confusion;

d) soit fabrique, fait fabriquer, a en sa possession, importe, exporte ou tente d'exporter des étiquettes ou des emballages, quelle qu'en soit la forme, portant une marque de commerce ou un nom commercial, en vue de leur vente ou de leur distribution ou en vue de la vente, de la distribution ou de l'annonce de produits ou services en liaison avec ceux-ci, alors que :

(ii) the sale, distribution or advertisement of the goods or services in association with the label or packaging would be a sale, distribution or advertisement in association with a confusing trade-mark or trade-name.

Exception — *bona fide* use

(1.1) The registration of a trade-mark does not prevent a person from making, in a manner that is not likely to have the effect of depreciating the value of the goodwill attaching to the trade-mark,

(a) any *bona fide* use of his or her personal name as a trade-name; or

(b) any *bona fide* use, other than as a trade-mark, of the geographical name of his or her place of business or of any accurate description of the character or quality of his or her goods or services.

Exception — utilitarian feature

(1.2) The registration of a trade-mark does not prevent a person from using any utilitarian feature embodied in the trade-mark.

Exception

(2) No registration of a trade-mark prevents a person from making any use of any of the indications mentioned in subsection 11.18(3) in association with a wine or any of the indications mentioned in subsection 11.18(4) in association with a spirit.

R.S., 1985, c. T-13, s. 20; 1994, c. 47, s. 196; 2014, c. 32, ss. 22, 56(F).

Concurrent use of confusing marks

21 (1) Where, in any proceedings respecting a registered trade-mark the registration of which is entitled to the protection of subsection 17(2), it is made to appear to the Federal Court that one of the parties to the proceedings, other than the registered owner of the trade-mark, had in good faith used a confusing trade-mark or trade-name in Canada before the date of filing of the application for that registration, and the Court considers that it is not contrary to the public interest that the continued use of the confusing trade-mark or trade-name should be permitted in a defined territorial area concurrently with the use of the registered trade-mark, the Court may, subject to such terms as it deems just, order that the other party may continue to use the confusing trade-mark or trade-name within that area with an adequate specified distinction from the registered trade-mark.

Registration of order

(2) The rights conferred by an order made under subsection (1) take effect only if, within three months from its date, the other party makes application to the Registrar to enter it on the register in connection with the registration of the registered trade-mark.

R.S., c. T-10, s. 21; R.S., c. 10(2nd Supp.), s. 64.

Depreciation of goodwill

22 (1) No person shall use a trade-mark registered by another person in a manner that is likely to have the effect of depreciating the value of the goodwill attaching thereto.

Action in respect thereof

(2) In any action in respect of a use of a trade-mark contrary to subsection (1), the court may decline to order the recovery of damages or profits and may permit the defendant to continue to sell goods marked with the trade-mark that were in his possession or under his control at the time notice was given to him that the owner of the registered trade-mark complained of the use of the trade-mark.

R.S., 1985, c. T-13, s. 22; 2014, c. 32, s. 53.

Certification Marks

Registration of certification marks

23 (1) A certification mark may be adopted and registered only by a person who is not engaged in the manufacture, sale, leasing or hiring of goods or the performance of services such as those in association with which the certification mark is used.

Licence

(2) The owner of a certification mark may license others to use the mark in association with goods or services that meet the defined standard, and the use of the mark accordingly shall be deemed to be use thereof by the owner.

Unauthorized use

(3) The owner of a registered certification mark may prevent its use by unlicensed persons or in association with any goods or services in respect of which the mark is registered but to which the licence does not extend.

justes, ordonner que cette autre partie puisse continuer à employer la marque de commerce ou le nom commercial créant de la confusion, dans cette région, avec une distinction suffisante et spécifiée d'avec la marque de commerce déposée.

Inscription de l'ordonnance

(2) Les droits conférés par une ordonnance rendue aux termes du paragraphe (1) ne prennent effet que si, dans les trois mois qui suivent la date de l'ordonnance, cette autre partie demande au registraire de l'inscrire au registre, en ce qui regarde l'enregistrement de la marque de commerce déposée.

S.R., ch. T-10, art. 21; S.R., ch. 10(2ᵉ suppl.), art. 64.

Dépréciation de l'achalandage

22 (1) Nul ne peut employer une marque de commerce déposée par une autre personne d'une manière susceptible d'entraîner la diminution de la valeur de l'achalandage attaché à cette marque de commerce.

Action à cet égard

(2) Dans toute action concernant un emploi contraire au paragraphe (1), le tribunal peut refuser d'ordonner le recouvrement de dommages-intérêts ou de profits, et permettre au défendeur de continuer à vendre tous produits revêtus de cette marque de commerce qui étaient en sa possession ou sous son contrôle lorsque avis lui a été donné que le propriétaire de la marque de commerce déposée se plaignait de cet emploi.

L.R. (1985), ch. T-13, art. 22; 2014, ch. 32, art. 53.

Marques de certification

Enregistrement de marques de certification

23 (1) Une marque de certification ne peut être adoptée et déposée que par une personne qui ne se livre pas à la fabrication, la vente, la location à bail ou le louage de produits ou à l'exécution de services, tels que ceux pour lesquels la marque de certification est employée.

Autorisation

(2) Le propriétaire d'une marque de certification peut autoriser d'autres personnes à employer la marque en liaison avec des produits ou services qui se conforment à la norme définie, et l'emploi de la marque en conséquence est réputé en être l'emploi par le propriétaire.

Emploi non autorisé

(3) Le propriétaire d'une marque de certification déposée peut empêcher qu'elle soit employée par des personnes non autorisées ou en liaison avec des produits ou

Action by unincorporated body

(4) Where the owner of a registered certification mark is an unincorporated body, any action or proceeding to prevent unauthorized use of the mark may be brought by any member of that body on behalf of himself and all other members thereof.

R.S., 1985, c. T-13, s. 23; 2014, c. 32, s. 53.

Registration of trade-mark confusing with certification mark

24 With the consent of the owner of a certification mark, a trade-mark confusing with the certification mark may, if it exhibits an appropriate difference, be registered by some other person to indicate that the goods or services in association with which it is used have been manufactured, sold, leased, hired or performed by him as one of the persons entitled to use the certification mark, but the registration thereof shall be expunged by the Registrar on the withdrawal at any time of the consent of the owner of the certification mark or on the cancellation of the registration of the certification mark.

R.S., 1985, c. T-13, s. 24; 2014, c. 32, ss. 25(F), 53(E).

Descriptive certification mark

25 A certification mark that is descriptive of the place of origin of goods or services, and not confusing with any registered trade-mark, is registrable if the applicant is the administrative authority of a country, state, province or municipality that includes or forms part of the area indicated by the certification mark, or is a commercial association that has an office or representative in that area, but the owner of any certification mark registered under this section shall permit its use in association with any goods or services produced or performed in the area of which it is descriptive.

R.S., 1985, c. T-13, s. 25; 2014, c. 32, s. 26.

Register of Trade-marks

Register

26 (1) There shall be kept under the supervision of the Registrar

Un organisme non constitué en personne morale peut intenter une action

(4) Lorsque le propriétaire d'une marque de certification déposée est un organisme non constitué en personne morale, une action ou procédure en vue d'empêcher l'emploi non autorisé de cette marque peut être intentée par tout membre de cet organisme en son propre nom et pour le compte de tous les autres membres.

L.R. (1985), ch. T-13, art. 23; 2014, ch. 32, art. 53.

Enregistrement d'une marque de commerce créant de la confusion avec la marque de certification

24 Avec le consentement du propriétaire d'une marque de certification, une marque de commerce créant de la confusion avec la marque de certification peut, si elle présente une différence caractéristique, être déposée par toute autre personne en vue d'indiquer que les produits en liaison avec lesquels elle est employée ont été fabriqués, vendus, donnés à bail ou loués, et que les services en liaison avec lesquels elle est employée ont été exécutés par elle comme étant une des personnes ayant droit d'employer la marque de certification, mais l'enregistrement de cette marque de commerce est radié par le registraire sur le retrait du consentement du propriétaire de la marque de certification, ou sur annulation de l'enregistrement de la marque de certification.

L.R. (1985), ch. T-13, art. 24; 2014, ch. 32, art. 25(F) et 53(A).

Marque de certification descriptive

25 Une marque de certification descriptive du lieu d'origine des produits ou services et ne créant aucune confusion avec une marque de commerce déposée est enregistrable si le requérant est l'autorité administrative d'un pays, d'un État, d'une province ou d'une municipalité comprenant la région indiquée par la marque de certification ou en faisant partie, ou est une association commerciale ayant un bureau ou un représentant dans une telle région. Toutefois, le propriétaire d'une marque de certification déposée aux termes du présent article doit en permettre l'emploi en liaison avec tout produit ou service dont la région de production ou d'exécution est celle que désigne la marque de certification.

L.R. (1985), ch. T-13, art. 25; 2014, ch. 32, art. 26.

Registre des marques de commerce

Registre

26 (1) Sont tenus, sous la surveillance du registraire :

(a) a register of trade-marks and of transfers, disclaimers, amendments, judgments and orders relating to each registered trade-mark; and

(b) the register of registered users that was required to be kept under this subsection as it read immediately before section 61 of the *Intellectual Property Law Improvement Act* came into force.

Information to be shown

(2) The register referred to in paragraph (1)(a) shall show, with reference to each registered trade-mark, the following:

(a) the date of registration;

(b) a summary of the application for registration;

(c) a summary of all documents deposited with the application or subsequently thereto and affecting the rights to the trade-mark;

(d) particulars of each renewal;

(e) particulars of each change of name and address; and

(f) such other particulars as this Act or the regulations require to be entered thereon.

R.S., 1985, c. T-13, s. 26; 1993, c. 15, s. 61.

Register under *Unfair Competition Act*

27 (1) The register kept under the *Unfair Competition Act*, chapter 274 of the Revised Statutes of Canada, 1952, forms part of the register kept under this Act and, subject to subsection 44(2), no entry made therein, if properly made according to the law in force at the time it was made, is subject to be expunged or amended only because it might not properly have been made pursuant to this Act.

Trade-marks registered before *Unfair Competition Act*

(2) Trade-marks on the register on September 1, 1932 shall be treated as design marks or word marks as defined in the *Unfair Competition Act*, chapter 274 of the Revised Statutes of Canada, 1952, according to the following rules:

(a) any trade-mark consisting only of words or numerals or both without any indication of a special form or appearance shall be deemed to be a word mark;

(b) any other trade-mark consisting only of words or numerals or both shall be deemed to be a word mark if at the date of its registration the words or numerals or both would have been registrable independently of any defined special form or appearance and shall also be deemed to be a design mark for reading matter presenting the special form or appearance defined;

(c) any trade-mark including words or numerals or both in combination with other features shall be deemed

(i) to be a design mark having the features described in the application therefor but without any meaning being attributed to the words or numerals, and

(ii) to be a word mark if and so far as it would at the date of registration have been registrable independently of any defined form or appearance and without being combined with any other feature; and

(d) any other trade-mark shall be deemed to be a design mark having the features described in the application therefor.

Trade-marks registered under *Unfair Competition Act*

(3) Trade-marks registered under the *Unfair Competition Act*, chapter 274 of the Revised Statutes of Canada, 1952, shall, in accordance with their registration, continue to be treated as design marks or word marks as defined in that Act.

R.S., c. T-10, s. 26.

Indexes

28 (1) There shall be kept under the supervision of the Registrar

(a) an index of registered trade-marks;

(b) an index of trade-marks in respect of which applications for registration are pending;

(c) an index of applications that have been abandoned or refused;

(d) an index of the names of owners of registered trade-marks;

(e) an index of the names of applicants for the registration of trade-marks;

(f) a list of trade-mark agents; and

(g) the index of the names of registered users that was required to be kept under this subsection as it reads immediately before section 61 of the *Intellectual Property Law Improvement Act* comes into force.

List of trade-mark agents

(2) The list of trade-mark agents shall include the names of all persons and firms entitled to represent applicants in the presentation and prosecution of applications for the registration of a trade-mark or in other business before the Trade-marks Office.

R.S., 1985, c. T-13, s. 28; 1993, c. 15, s. 62.

Inspection

29 (1) Subject to subsection (2), the registers, the documents on which the entries therein are based, all applications, including those abandoned, the indexes, the list of trade-mark agents and the list of geographical indications kept pursuant to subsection 11.12(1) shall be open to public inspection during business hours, and the Registrar shall, on request and on payment of the prescribed fee, furnish a copy certified by the registrar of any entry in the registers, indexes or lists, or of any of those documents or applications.

Register of registered users

(2) The disclosure of documents on which entries in the register required to be kept under paragraph 26(1)(b) are based is subject to the provisions of subsection 50(6), as it reads immediately before section 61 of the *Intellectual Property Law Improvement Act* comes into force.

R.S., 1985, c. T-13, s. 29; 1993, c. 15, s. 63; 1994, c. 47, s. 197.

Applications for Registration of Trade-marks

Contents of application

30 An applicant for the registration of a trade-mark shall file with the Registrar an application containing

(a) a statement in ordinary commercial terms of the specific goods or services in association with which the mark has been or is proposed to be used;

(b) in the case of a trade-mark that has been used in Canada, the date from which the applicant or his named predecessors in title, if any, have so used the trade-mark in association with each of the general classes of goods or services described in the application;

(c) in the case of a trade-mark that has not been used in Canada but is made known in Canada, the name of a country of the Union in which it has been used by the applicant or his named predecessors in title, if any, and the date from and the manner in which the applicant or named predecessors in title have made it known in Canada in association with each of the general classes of goods or services described in the application;

(d) in the case of a trade-mark that is the subject in or for another country of the Union of a registration or an application for registration by the applicant or the applicant's named predecessor in title on which the applicant bases the applicant's right to registration, particulars of the application or registration and, if the trade-mark has neither been used in Canada nor made known in Canada, the name of a country in which the trade-mark has been used by the applicant or the applicant's named predecessor in title, if any, in association with each of the general classes of goods or services described in the application;

(e) in the case of a proposed trade-mark, a statement that the applicant, by itself or through a licensee, or by itself and through a licensee, intends to use the trade-mark in Canada;

(f) in the case of a certification mark, particulars of the defined standard that the use of the mark is intended to indicate and a statement that the applicant is not engaged in the manufacture, sale, leasing or hiring of goods or the performance of services such as those in association with which the certification mark is used;

(g) the address of the applicant's principal office or place of business in Canada, if any, and if the applicant has no office or place of business in Canada, the address of his principal office or place of business abroad and the name and address in Canada of a person or firm to whom any notice in respect of the application or registration may be sent, and on whom service of any proceedings in respect of the application or registration may be given or served with the same effect as if they had been given to or served on the applicant or registrant himself;

(h) unless the application is for the registration only of a word or words not depicted in a special form, a drawing of the trade-mark and such number of accurate representations of the trade-mark as may be prescribed; and

cas échéant, ont ainsi employé la marque de commerce en liaison avec chacune des catégories générales de produits ou services décrites dans la demande;

c) dans le cas d'une marque de commerce qui n'a pas été employée au Canada mais qui est révélée au Canada, le nom d'un pays de l'Union dans lequel elle a été employée par le requérant ou ses prédécesseurs en titre désignés, le cas échéant, et la date à compter de laquelle le requérant ou ses prédécesseurs l'ont fait connaître au Canada en liaison avec chacune des catégories générales de produits ou services décrites dans la demande, ainsi que la manière dont ils l'ont révélée;

d) dans le cas d'une marque de commerce qui est, dans un autre pays de l'Union, ou pour un autre pays de l'Union, l'objet, de la part du requérant ou de son prédécesseur en titre désigné, d'un enregistrement ou d'une demande d'enregistrement sur quoi le requérant fonde son droit à l'enregistrement, les détails de cette demande ou de cet enregistrement et, si la marque n'a été ni employée ni révélée au Canada, le nom d'un pays où le requérant ou son prédécesseur en titre désigné, le cas échéant, l'a employée en liaison avec chacune des catégories générales de produits ou services décrites dans la demande;

e) dans le cas d'une marque de commerce projetée, une déclaration portant que le requérant a l'intention de l'employer, au Canada, lui-même ou par l'entremise d'un licencié, ou lui-même et par l'entremise d'un licencié;

f) dans le cas d'une marque de certification, les détails de la norme définie que l'emploi de la marque est destiné à indiquer et une déclaration portant que le requérant ne pratique pas la fabrication, la vente, la location à bail ou le louage de produits ou ne se livre pas à l'exécution de services, tels que ceux pour lesquels la marque de certification est employée;

g) l'adresse du principal bureau ou siège d'affaires du requérant, au Canada, le cas échéant, et si le requérant n'a ni bureau ni siège d'affaires au Canada, l'adresse de son principal bureau ou siège d'affaires à l'étranger et les nom et adresse, au Canada, d'une personne ou firme à qui tout avis concernant la demande ou l'enregistrement peut être envoyé et à qui toute procédure à l'égard de la demande ou de l'enregistrement peut être signifiée avec le même effet que si elle avait été signifiée au requérant ou à l'inscrivant lui-même;

h) sauf si la demande ne vise que l'enregistrement d'un mot ou de mots non décrits en une forme spéciale, un dessin de la marque de commerce, ainsi que

(i) a statement that the applicant is satisfied that he is entitled to use the trade-mark in Canada in association with the goods or services described in the application.

R.S., 1985, c. T-13, s. 30; 1993, c. 15, s. 64; 1994, c. 47, s. 198; 2014, c. 32, s. 53.

Applications based on registration abroad

31 (1) An applicant whose right to registration of a trade-mark is based on a registration of the trade-mark in another country of the Union shall, before the date of advertisement of his application in accordance with section 37, furnish a copy of the registration certified by the office in which it was made, together with a translation thereof into English or French if it is in any other language, and such other evidence as the Registrar may require to establish fully his right to registration under this Act.

Evidence required in certain cases

(2) An applicant whose trade-mark has been duly registered in his country of origin and who claims that the trade-mark is registrable under paragraph 14(1)(b) shall furnish such evidence as the Registrar may require by way of affidavit or statutory declaration establishing the circumstances on which he relies, including the length of time during which the trade-mark has been used in any country.

R.S., c. T-10, s. 30.

Further information in certain cases

32 (1) An applicant who claims that his trade-mark is registrable under subsection 12(2) or section 13 shall furnish the Registrar with evidence by way of affidavit or statutory declaration establishing the extent to which and the time during which the trade-mark has been used in Canada and with any other evidence that the Registrar may require in support of the claim.

Registration to be restricted

(2) The Registrar shall, having regard to the evidence adduced, restrict the registration to the goods or services in association with which the trade-mark is shown to have been so used as to have become distinctive and to the defined territorial area in Canada in which the trade-mark is shown to have become distinctive.

R.S., 1985, c. T-13, s. 32; 2014, c. 32, ss. 53, 56(F).

Applications by trade unions, etc.

33 Every trade union or commercial association that applies for the registration of a trade-mark may be required to furnish satisfactory evidence that its existence is not contrary to the laws of the country in which its headquarters are situated.

R.S., c. T-10, s. 32.

Date of application abroad deemed date of application in Canada

34 (1) When an application for the registration of a trade-mark has been made in or for any country of the Union other than Canada and an application is subsequently made in Canada for the registration for use in association with the same kind of goods or services of the same or substantially the same trade-mark by the same applicant or the applicant's successor in title, the date of filing of the application in or for the other country is deemed to be the date of filing of the application in Canada, and the applicant is entitled to priority in Canada accordingly notwithstanding any intervening use in Canada or making known in Canada or any intervening application or registration if

(a) the application in Canada, including or accompanied by a declaration setting out the date on which and the country of the Union in or for which the earliest application was filed for the registration of the same or substantially the same trade-mark for use in association with the same kind of goods or services, is filed within a period of six months after that date, which period shall not be extended;

(b) the applicant or, if the applicant is a transferee, the applicant's predecessor in title by whom any earlier application was filed in or for any country of the Union was at the date of the application a citizen or national of or domiciled in that country or had therein a real and effective industrial or commercial establishment; and

(c) the applicant furnishes, in accordance with any request under subsections (2) and (3), evidence necessary to establish fully the applicant's right to priority.

Evidence requests

(2) The Registrar may request the evidence before the day on which the application is allowed pursuant to section 39.

How and when evidence must be furnished

(3) The Registrar may specify in the request the manner in which the evidence must be furnished and the period within which it must be furnished.

R.S., 1985, c. T-13, s. 34; 1992, c. 1, s. 133; 1993, c. 15, s. 65; 1994, c. 47, s. 199; 2014, c. 32, s. 53.

Disclaimer

35 The Registrar may require an applicant for registration of a trade-mark to disclaim the right to the exclusive use apart from the trade-mark of such portion of the trade-mark as is not independently registrable, but the disclaimer does not prejudice or affect the applicant's rights then existing or thereafter arising in the disclaimed matter, nor does the disclaimer prejudice or affect the applicant's right to registration on a subsequent application if the disclaimed matter has then become distinctive of the applicant's goods or services.

R.S., 1985, c. T-13, s. 35; 2014, c. 32, s. 53.

Abandonment

36 Where, in the opinion of the Registrar, an applicant is in default in the prosecution of an application filed under this Act or any Act relating to trade-marks in force prior to July 1, 1954, the Registrar may, after giving notice to the applicant of the default, treat the application as abandoned unless the default is remedied within the time specified in the notice.

R.S., c. T-10, s. 35.

When applications to be refused

37 (1) The Registrar shall refuse an application for the registration of a trade-mark if he is satisfied that

(a) the application does not conform to the requirements of section 30,

(b) the trade-mark is not registrable, or

(c) the applicant is not the person entitled to registration of the trade-mark because it is confusing with another trade-mark for the registration of which an application is pending,

and where the Registrar is not so satisfied, he shall cause the application to be advertised in the manner prescribed.

Notice to applicant

(2) The Registrar shall not refuse any application without first notifying the applicant of his objections thereto and his reasons for those objections, and giving the applicant adequate opportunity to answer those objections.

Doubtful cases

(3) Where the Registrar, by reason of a registered trade-mark, is in doubt whether the trade-mark claimed in the application is registrable, he shall, by registered letter, notify the owner of the registered trade-mark of the advertisement of the application.

R.S., c. T-10, s. 36.

Statement of opposition

38 (1) Within two months after the advertisement of an application for the registration of a trade-mark, any person may, on payment of the prescribed fee, file a statement of opposition with the Registrar.

Grounds

(2) A statement of opposition may be based on any of the following grounds:

(a) that the application does not conform to the requirements of section 30;

(b) that the trade-mark is not registrable;

(c) that the applicant is not the person entitled to registration of the trade-mark; or

(d) that the trade-mark is not distinctive.

Content

(3) A statement of opposition shall set out

(a) the grounds of opposition in sufficient detail to enable the applicant to reply thereto; and

(b) the address of the opponent's principal office or place of business in Canada, if any, and if the opponent has no office or place of business in Canada, the address of his principal office or place of business abroad and the name and address in Canada of a person or firm on whom service of any document in respect of the opposition may be made with the same effect as if it had been served on the opponent himself.

Frivolous opposition

(4) If the Registrar considers that the opposition does not raise a substantial issue for decision, he shall reject it and shall give notice of his decision to the opponent.

objections, avec les motifs pertinents, et lui avoir donné une occasion convenable d'y répondre.

Cas douteux

(3) Lorsque, en raison d'une marque de commerce déposée, le registraire a des doutes sur la question de savoir si la marque de commerce indiquée dans la demande est enregistrable, il notifie, par courrier recommandé, l'annonce de la demande au propriétaire de la marque de commerce déposée.

S.R., ch. T-10, art. 36.

Déclaration d'opposition

38 (1) Toute personne peut, dans le délai de deux mois à compter de l'annonce de la demande, et sur paiement du droit prescrit, produire au bureau du registraire une déclaration d'opposition.

Motifs

(2) Cette opposition peut être fondée sur l'un des motifs suivants :

a) la demande ne satisfait pas aux exigences de l'article 30;

b) la marque de commerce n'est pas enregistrable;

c) le requérant n'est pas la personne ayant droit à l'enregistrement;

d) la marque de commerce n'est pas distinctive.

Teneur

(3) La déclaration d'opposition indique :

a) les motifs de l'opposition, avec détails suffisants pour permettre au requérant d'y répondre;

b) l'adresse du principal bureau ou siège d'affaires de l'opposant au Canada, le cas échéant, et, si l'opposant n'a ni bureau ni siège d'affaires au Canada, l'adresse de son principal bureau ou siège d'affaires à l'étranger et les nom et adresse, au Canada, d'une personne ou firme à qui tout document concernant l'opposition peut être signifié avec le même effet que s'il était signifié à l'opposant lui-même.

Opposition futile

(4) Si le registraire estime que l'opposition ne soulève pas une question sérieuse pour décision, il la rejette et donne avis de sa décision à l'opposant.

Substantial issue

(5) If the Registrar considers that the opposition raises a substantial issue for decision, he shall forward a copy of the statement of opposition to the applicant.

Counter statement

(6) The applicant shall file a counter statement with the Registrar and serve a copy on the opponent in the prescribed manner and within the prescribed time after a copy of the statement of opposition has been served on the applicant.

Evidence and hearing

(7) Both the opponent and the applicant shall be given an opportunity, in the prescribed manner, to submit evidence and to make representations to the Registrar unless

  (a) the opposition is withdrawn or deemed under subsection (7.1) to have been withdrawn; or

  (b) the application is abandoned or deemed under subsection (7.2) to have been abandoned.

Withdrawal of opposition

(7.1) The opposition shall be deemed to have been withdrawn if, in the prescribed circumstances, the opponent does not submit either evidence under subsection (7) or a statement that the opponent does not wish to submit evidence.

Abandonment of application

(7.2) The application shall be deemed to have been abandoned if the applicant does not file and serve a counter statement within the time referred to in subsection (6) or if, in the prescribed circumstances, the applicant does not submit either evidence under subsection (7) or a statement that the applicant does not wish to submit evidence.

Decision

(8) After considering the evidence and representations of the opponent and the applicant, the Registrar shall refuse the application or reject the opposition and notify the parties of the decision and the reasons for the decision.

R.S., 1985, c. T-13, s. 38; 1992, c. 1, s. 134; 1993, c. 15, s. 66.

When application to be allowed

39 (1) When an application for the registration of a trade-mark either has not been opposed and the time for the filing of a statement of opposition has expired or it has been opposed and the opposition has been decided in favour of the applicant, the Registrar shall allow the application or, if an appeal is taken, shall act in accordance with the final judgment given in the appeal.

No extension of time

(2) Subject to subsection (3), the Registrar shall not extend the time for filing a statement of opposition with respect to any application that has been allowed.

Exception

(3) Where the Registrar has allowed an application without considering a previously filed request for an extension of time to file a statement of opposition, the Registrar may withdraw the application from allowance at any time before issuing a certificate of registration and, in accordance with section 47, extend the time for filing a statement of opposition.

R.S., 1985, c. T-13, s. 39; 1993, c. 15, s. 67.

Registration of Trade-marks

Registration of trade-marks

40 (1) When an application for registration of a trade-mark, other than a proposed trade-mark, is allowed, the Registrar shall register the trade-mark and issue a certificate of its registration.

Proposed trade-mark

(2) When an application for registration of a proposed trade-mark is allowed, the Registrar shall give notice to the applicant accordingly and shall register the trade-mark and issue a certificate of registration on receipt of a declaration that the use of the trade-mark in Canada, in association with the goods or services specified in the application, has been commenced by

(a) the applicant;

(b) the applicant's successor in title; or

(c) an entity that is licensed by or with the authority of the applicant to use the trade-mark, if the applicant has direct or indirect control of the character or quality of the goods or services.

Abandonment of application

(3) An application for registration of a proposed trade-mark shall be deemed to be abandoned if the Registrar has not received the declaration referred to in subsection (2) before the later of

(a) six months after the notice by the Registrar referred to in subsection (2), and

(b) three years after the date of filing of the application in Canada.

Form and effect

(4) Registration of a trade-mark shall be made in the name of the applicant therefor or his transferee, and the day on which registration is made shall be entered on the register, and the registration takes effect on that day.

Section 34 does not apply

(5) For the purposes of subsection (3), section 34 does not apply in determining when an application for registration is filed.

R.S., 1985, c. T-13, s. 40; 1993, c. 15, s. 68, c. 44, s. 231; 1999, c. 31, s. 210(F); 2014, c. 32, ss. 37(F), 53(E).

Amendment of the Register

Amendments to register

41 (1) The Registrar may, on application by the registered owner of a trade-mark made in the prescribed manner, make any of the following amendments to the register:

(a) correct any error or enter any change in the name, address or description of the registered owner or of his representative for service in Canada;

(b) cancel the registration of the trade-mark;

(c) amend the statement of the goods or services in respect of which the trade-mark is registered;

(d) amend the particulars of the defined standard that the use of a certification mark is intended to indicate; or

(e) enter a disclaimer that does not in any way extend the rights given by the existing registration of the trade-mark.

Conditions

(2) An application to extend the statement of goods or services in respect of which a trade-mark is registered has the effect of an application for registration of the trade-mark in respect of the goods or services specified in the application for amendment.

R.S., 1985, c. T-13, s. 41; 2014, c. 32, s. 53.

Representative for service

42 (1) The registered owner of a trade-mark who has no office or place of business in Canada shall name another representative for service in place of the latest recorded representative or supply a new and correct address of the latest recorded representative on notice from the Registrar that the latest recorded representative has died or that a letter addressed to him at the latest recorded address and sent by ordinary mail has been returned undelivered.

Change of address

(2) When, after the dispatch of the notice referred to in subsection (1) by the Registrar, no new nomination is made or no new and correct address is supplied by the registered owner within three months, the Registrar or the Federal Court may dispose of any proceedings under this Act without requiring service on the registered owner of any process therein.

R.S., c. T-10, s. 41; R.S., c. 10(2nd Supp.), s. 64.

Additional representations

43 The registered owner of any trade-mark shall furnish such additional representations thereof as the Registrar may by notice demand and, if he fails to comply with that notice, the Registrar may by a further notice, fix a reasonable time after which, if the representations are not furnished, he may expunge the registration of the trade-mark.

R.S., c. T-10, s. 42.

Notice for information

44 (1) The Registrar may at any time, and shall at the request of any person who pays the prescribed fee, by notice in writing require the registered owner of any trade-mark that was on the register on July 1, 1954 to furnish him within three months from the date of the notice with the information that would be required on an application for the registration of the trade-mark made at the date of the notice.

Amendments to register

(2) The Registrar may amend the registration of the trade-mark in accordance with the information furnished to him under subsection (1).

Failure to give information

(3) Where the information required by subsection (1) is not furnished, the Registrar shall by a further notice fix a reasonable time after which, if the information is not furnished, he may expunge the registration of the trade-mark.

R.S., c. T-10, s. 43.

Représentant pour signification

42 (1) Le propriétaire inscrit d'une marque de commerce qui n'a ni bureau ni siège d'affaires au Canada nomme un autre représentant pour signification en remplacement du dernier représentant inscrit ou fournit une adresse nouvelle et exacte du dernier représentant inscrit, sur avis du registraire que le dernier représentant inscrit est décédé ou qu'une lettre qui lui a été envoyée, par courrier ordinaire, à la dernière adresse inscrite a été retournée par suite de non-livraison.

Changement d'adresse

(2) Lorsque, après l'expédition de l'avis par le registraire, aucune nouvelle nomination n'est faite ou qu'aucune adresse nouvelle et exacte n'est fournie par le propriétaire inscrit dans les trois mois, le registraire ou la Cour fédérale peut statuer sur toutes procédures aux termes de la présente loi sans exiger la signification, au propriétaire inscrit, de toute pièce s'y rapportant.

S.R., ch. T-10, art. 41; S.R., ch. 10(2^e suppl.), art. 64.

Représentations supplémentaires

43 Le propriétaire inscrit d'une marque de commerce en fournit les représentations supplémentaires que le registraire peut exiger par avis et, s'il omet de se conformer à un tel avis, le registraire peut, par un autre avis, fixer un délai raisonnable après lequel, si les représentations ne sont pas fournies, il pourra radier l'inscription de la marque de commerce.

S.R., ch. T-10, art. 42.

Demande de renseignements

44 (1) Le registraire peut, et doit sur demande d'une personne qui verse le droit prescrit, enjoindre, par avis écrit, au propriétaire inscrit de toute marque de commerce figurant au registre le 1er juillet 1954 de lui fournir, dans les trois mois suivant la date de l'avis, les renseignements qui seraient requis à l'occasion d'une demande d'enregistrement d'une telle marque de commerce, faite à la date de cet avis.

Modification de l'inscription

(2) Le registraire peut modifier l'enregistrement en conformité avec les renseignements qui lui sont fournis selon le paragraphe (1).

Lorsque les renseignements ne sont pas fournis

(3) Lorsque les renseignements ne sont pas fournis, le registraire fixe, au moyen d'un nouvel avis, un délai raisonnable après lequel, si les renseignements ne sont pas fournis, il pourra radier l'enregistrement de la marque de commerce.

S.R., ch. T-10, art. 43.

Registrar may request evidence of user

45 (1) The Registrar may at any time and, at the written request made after three years from the date of the registration of a trade-mark by any person who pays the prescribed fee shall, unless the Registrar sees good reason to the contrary, give notice to the registered owner of the trade-mark requiring the registered owner to furnish within three months an affidavit or a statutory declaration showing, with respect to each of the goods or services specified in the registration, whether the trade-mark was in use in Canada at any time during the three year period immediately preceding the date of the notice and, if not, the date when it was last so in use and the reason for the absence of such use since that date.

Form of evidence

(2) The Registrar shall not receive any evidence other than the affidavit or statutory declaration, but may hear representations made by or on behalf of the registered owner of the trade-mark or by or on behalf of the person at whose request the notice was given.

Effect of non-use

(3) Where, by reason of the evidence furnished to the Registrar or the failure to furnish any evidence, it appears to the Registrar that a trade-mark, either with respect to all of the goods or services specified in the registration or with respect to any of those goods or services, was not used in Canada at any time during the three year period immediately preceding the date of the notice and that the absence of use has not been due to special circumstances that excuse the absence of use, the registration of the trade-mark is liable to be expunged or amended accordingly.

Notice to owner

(4) When the Registrar reaches a decision whether or not the registration of a trade-mark ought to be expunged or amended, he shall give notice of his decision with the reasons therefor to the registered owner of the trade-mark and to the person at whose request the notice referred to in subsection (1) was given.

Action by Registrar

(5) The Registrar shall act in accordance with his decision if no appeal therefrom is taken within the time limited by this Act or, if an appeal is taken, shall act in accordance with the final judgment given in the appeal.

R.S., 1985, c. T-13, s. 45; 1993, c. 44, s. 232; 1994, c. 47, s. 200; 2014, c. 32, s. 53.

Le registraire peut exiger une preuve d'emploi

45 (1) Le registraire peut, et doit sur demande écrite présentée après trois années à compter de la date de l'enregistrement d'une marque de commerce, par une personne qui verse les droits prescrits, à moins qu'il ne voie une raison valable à l'effet contraire, donner au propriétaire inscrit un avis lui enjoignant de fournir, dans les trois mois, un affidavit ou une déclaration solennelle indiquant, à l'égard de chacun des produits ou de chacun des services que spécifie l'enregistrement, si la marque de commerce a été employée au Canada à un moment quelconque au cours des trois ans précédant la date de l'avis et, dans la négative, la date où elle a été ainsi employée en dernier lieu et la raison de son défaut d'emploi depuis cette date.

Forme de la preuve

(2) Le registraire ne peut recevoir aucune preuve autre que cet affidavit ou cette déclaration solennelle, mais il peut entendre des représentations faites par le propriétaire inscrit de la marque de commerce ou pour celui-ci ou par la personne à la demande de qui l'avis a été donné ou pour celle-ci.

Effet du non-usage

(3) Lorsqu'il apparaît au registraire, en raison de la preuve qui lui est fournie ou du défaut de fournir une telle preuve, que la marque de commerce, soit à l'égard de la totalité des produits ou services spécifiés dans l'enregistrement, soit à l'égard de l'un de ces produits ou de l'un de ces services, n'a été employée au Canada à aucun moment au cours des trois ans précédant la date de l'avis et que le défaut d'emploi n'a pas été attribuable à des circonstances spéciales qui le justifient, l'enregistrement de cette marque de commerce est susceptible de radiation ou de modification en conséquence.

Avis au propriétaire

(4) Lorsque le registraire décide ou non de radier ou de modifier l'enregistrement de la marque de commerce, il notifie sa décision, avec les motifs pertinents, au propriétaire inscrit de la marque de commerce et à la personne à la demande de qui l'avis visé au paragraphe (1) a été donné.

Mesures à prendre par le registraire

(5) Le registraire agit en conformité avec sa décision si aucun appel n'en est interjeté dans le délai prévu par la présente loi ou, si un appel est interjeté, il agit en conformité avec le jugement définitif rendu dans cet appel.

L.R. (1985), ch. T-13, art. 45; 1993, ch. 44, art. 232; 1994, ch. 47, art. 200; 2014, ch. 32, art. 53.

Renewal of Registrations

Renewal

46 (1) The registration of a trade-mark that is on the register by virtue of this Act is subject to renewal within a period of fifteen years from the day of the registration or last renewal.

Notice to renew

(2) If the registration of a trade-mark has been on the register without renewal for the period specified in subsection (1), the Registrar shall send a notice to the registered owner and to the registered owner's representative for service, if any, stating that if within six months after the date of the notice the prescribed renewal fee is not paid, the registration will be expunged.

Failure to renew

(3) If within the period of six months specified in the notice, which period shall not be extended, the prescribed renewal fee is not paid, the Registrar shall expunge the registration.

Effective date of renewal

(4) When the prescribed fee for a renewal of any trade-mark registration under this section is paid within the time limited for the payment thereof, the renewal takes effect as of the day next following the expiration of the period specified in subsection (1).

R.S., 1985, c. T-13, s. 46; 1992, c. 1, s. 135.

Extensions of Time

Extensions of time

47 (1) If, in any case, the Registrar is satisfied that the circumstances justify an extension of the time fixed by this Act or prescribed by the regulations for the doing of any act, he may, except as in this Act otherwise provided, extend the time after such notice to other persons and on such terms as he may direct.

Conditions

(2) An extension applied for after the expiration of the time fixed for the doing of an act or the time extended by the Registrar under subsection (1) shall not be granted unless the prescribed fee is paid and the Registrar is satisfied that the failure to do the act or apply for the extension within that time or the extended time was not reasonably avoidable.

R.S., c. T-10, s. 46.

Transfer

Trade-mark transferable

48 (1) A trade-mark, whether registered or unregistered, is transferable, and deemed always to have been transferable, either in connection with or separately from the goodwill of the business and in respect of either all or some of the goods or services in association with which it has been used.

Where two or more persons interested

(2) Nothing in subsection (1) prevents a trade-mark from being held not to be distinctive if as a result of a transfer thereof there subsisted rights in two or more persons to the use of confusing trade-marks and the rights were exercised by those persons.

Registration of transfer

(3) The Registrar shall register the transfer of any registered trade-mark on being furnished with evidence satisfactory to him of the transfer and the information that would be required by paragraph 30(g) in an application by the transferee to register the trade-mark.

R.S., 1985, c. T-13, s. 48; 2014, c. 32, s. 53.

Change of Purpose in Use of Mark

Change of purpose

49 If a mark is used by a person as a trade-mark for any of the purposes or in any of the manners mentioned in the definition "certification mark" or "trade-mark" in section 2, it shall not be held invalid merely on the ground that the person or a predecessor in title uses it or has used it for any other of those purposes or in any other of those manners.

R.S., c. T-10, s. 48.

Licences

Licence to use trade-mark

50 (1) For the purposes of this Act, if an entity is licensed by or with the authority of the owner of a trade-mark to use the trade-mark in a country and the owner has, under the licence, direct or indirect control of the character or quality of the goods or services, then the use, advertisement or display of the trade-mark in that country as or in a trade-mark, trade-name or otherwise by that entity has, and is deemed always to have had, the same effect as such a use, advertisement or display of the trade-mark in that country by the owner.

Idem

(2) For the purposes of this Act, to the extent that public notice is given of the fact that the use of a trade-mark is a licensed use and of the identity of the owner, it shall be presumed, unless the contrary is proven, that the use is licensed by the owner of the trade-mark and the character or quality of the goods or services is under the control of the owner.

Owner may be required to take proceedings

(3) Subject to any agreement subsisting between an owner of a trade-mark and a licensee of the trade-mark, the licensee may call on the owner to take proceedings for infringement thereof, and, if the owner refuses or neglects to do so within two months after being so called on, the licensee may institute proceedings for infringement in the licensee's own name as if the licensee were the owner, making the owner a defendant.

R.S., 1985, c. T-13, s. 50; 1993, c. 15, s. 69; 1999, c. 31, s. 211(F); 2014, c. 32, s. 53.

Use of trade-mark by related companies

51 (1) Where a company and the owner of a trade-mark that is used in Canada by that owner in association with a pharmaceutical preparation are related companies, the use by the company of the trade-mark, or a trade-mark confusing therewith, in association with a pharmaceutical preparation that at the time of that use or at any time thereafter,

  (a) is acquired by a person directly or indirectly from the company, and

  (b) is sold, distributed or advertised for sale in Canada in a package bearing the name of the company and the name of that person as the distributor thereof, has the same effect, for all purposes of this Act, as a use of the trade-mark or the confusing trade-mark, as the case may be, by that owner.

Where difference in composition

(2) Subsection (1) does not apply to any use of a trade-mark or a confusing trade-mark by a company referred to in that subsection in association with a pharmaceutical preparation after such time, if any, as that pharmaceutical preparation is declared by the Minister of Health, by notice published in the *Canada Gazette*, to be sufficiently different in its composition from the pharmaceutical preparation in association with which the trade-mark is used in Canada by the owner referred to in subsection (1) as to be likely to result in a hazard to health.

Definition of *pharmaceutical preparation*

(3) In this section, ***pharmaceutical preparation*** includes

(a) any substance or mixture of substances manufactured, sold or represented for use in

(i) the diagnosis, treatment, mitigation or prevention of a disease, disorder or abnormal physical state, or the symptoms thereof, in humans or animals, or

(ii) restoring, correcting or modifying organic functions in humans or animals, and

(b) any substance to be used in the preparation or production of any substance or mixture of substances described in paragraph (a),

but does not include any such substance or mixture of substances that is the same or substantially the same as a substance or mixture of substances that is a proprietary medicine within the meaning from time to time assigned to that expression by regulations made pursuant to the *Food and Drugs Act*.

R.S., 1985, c. T-13, s. 51; 1996, c. 8, s. 32.

Offences and Punishment

Sale, etc., of goods

51.01 (1) Every person commits an offence who sells or offers for sale, or distributes on a commercial scale, any goods in association with a trade-mark, if that sale or

portant le nom de la compagnie ainsi que le nom de cette personne en tant que distributeur de cette préparation pharmaceutique,

a, pour l'application de la présente loi, le même effet que l'emploi, par le propriétaire, de cette marque de commerce ou de l'autre marque de commerce qui crée de la confusion avec cette marque de commerce, selon le cas.

Cas où la composition est différente

(2) Le paragraphe (1) ne s'applique pas à l'emploi d'une marque de commerce, ou d'une marque de commerce créant de la confusion, par une compagnie mentionnée à ce paragraphe, en liaison avec une préparation pharmaceutique, après le moment, le cas échéant, où le ministre de la Santé déclare, par avis publié dans la *Gazette du Canada*, que la composition de cette préparation pharmaceutique diffère suffisamment de celle de la préparation pharmaceutique en liaison avec laquelle la marque de commerce est employée au Canada par le propriétaire mentionné au paragraphe (1) pour qu'il soit probable qu'il en résulte un risque pour la santé.

Définition de *préparation pharmaceutique*

(3) Au présent article, ***préparation pharmaceutique*** s'entend notamment :

a) de toute substance ou de tout mélange de substances fabriqué, vendu ou représenté comme pouvant être employé :

(i) soit au diagnostic, au traitement, à l'atténuation ou à la prévention d'une maladie, d'un désordre, d'un état physique anormal, ou de leurs symptômes chez l'homme ou les animaux,

(ii) soit en vue de restaurer, corriger ou modifier les fonctions organiques chez l'homme ou les animaux;

b) de toute substance destinée à être employée dans la préparation ou la production d'une substance ou d'un mélange de substances décrits à l'alinéa a).

La présente définition exclut une substance ou un mélange de substances semblable ou identique à ceux que les règlements d'application de la *Loi sur les aliments et drogues* qualifient de spécialités pharmaceutiques.

L.R. (1985), ch. T-13, art. 51; 1996, ch. 8, art. 32.

Infractions et peines

Vente de produits

51.01 (1) Commet une infraction quiconque vend ou offre en vente — ou distribue à l'échelle commerciale — des produits en liaison avec une marque de commerce

distribution is or would be contrary to section 19 or 20 and the person knows that

(a) the trade-mark is identical to, or cannot be distinguished in its essential aspects from, a trade-mark registered for such goods; and

(b) the owner of that registered trade-mark has not consented to the sale, offering for sale, or distribution of the goods in association with the trade-mark.

(c) [*Deleted*]

Manufacture, etc., of goods

(2) Every person commits an offence who manufactures, causes to be manufactured, possesses, imports, exports or attempts to export any goods, for the purpose of their sale or of their distribution on a commercial scale, if that sale or distribution would be contrary to section 19 or 20 and the person knows that

(a) the goods bear a trade-mark that is identical to, or that cannot be distinguished in its essential aspects from, a trade-mark registered for such goods; and

(b) the owner of that registered trade-mark has not consented to having the goods bear the trade-mark.

(c) [*Deleted*]

Services

(3) Every person commits an offence who sells or advertises services in association with a trade-mark, if that sale or advertisement is contrary to section 19 or 20 and the person knows that

(a) the trade-mark is identical to, or cannot be distinguished in its essential aspects from, a registered trade-mark registered for such services; and

(b) the owner of the registered trade-mark has not consented to the sale or advertisement in association with the trade-mark.

(c) [*Deleted*]

Labels or packaging

(4) Every person commits an offence who manufactures, causes to be manufactured, possesses, imports, exports or attempts to export any label or packaging, in any form, for the purpose of its sale or of its distribution on a

alors que cette vente ou distribution est ou serait contraire aux articles 19 ou 20 et qu'il sait, à la fois :

a) que la marque de commerce est identique à une marque de commerce déposée à l'égard de tels produits ou impossible à distinguer d'une telle marque dans ses aspects essentiels;

b) que le propriétaire de la marque de commerce déposée n'a pas consenti à la vente, l'offre en vente ou la distribution des produits en liaison avec la marque de commerce.

c) [*Supprimé*]

Fabrication de produits, etc.

(2) Commet une infraction quiconque, en vue de leur vente — ou de leur distribution à l'échelle commerciale —, fabrique, fait fabriquer, a en sa possession, importe, exporte ou tente d'exporter des produits alors que cette vente ou distribution serait contraire aux articles 19 ou 20 et qu'il sait, à la fois :

a) que les produits portent une marque de commerce identique à une marque de commerce déposée à l'égard de tels produits ou impossible à distinguer d'une telle marque dans ses aspects essentiels;

b) que le propriétaire de la marque de commerce déposée n'a pas consenti à ce que les produits portent la marque de commerce.

c) [*Supprimé*]

Services

(3) Commet une infraction quiconque vend ou annonce des services en liaison avec une marque de commerce alors que cette vente ou annonce est contraire aux articles 19 ou 20 et qu'il sait, à la fois :

a) que la marque de commerce est identique à une marque de commerce déposée à l'égard de tels services ou impossible à distinguer d'une telle marque dans ses aspects essentiels;

b) que le propriétaire de la marque de commerce déposée n'a pas consenti à la vente ou l'annonce en liaison avec la marque de commerce.

c) [*Supprimé*]

Étiquettes ou emballages

(4) Commet une infraction quiconque fabrique, fait fabriquer, a en sa possession, importe, exporte ou tente d'exporter des étiquettes ou des emballages, quelle qu'en soit la forme, en vue de leur vente — ou de leur

commercial scale or for the purpose of the sale, distribution on a commercial scale or advertisement of goods or services in association with it, if that sale, distribution or advertisement would be contrary to section 19 or 20 and the person knows that

(a) the label or packaging bears a trade-mark that is identical to, or that cannot be distinguished in its essential aspects from, a registered trade-mark;

(b) the label or packaging is intended to be associated with goods or services for which that registered trade-mark is registered; and

(c) the owner of that registered trade-mark has not consented to having the label or packaging bear the trade-mark.

(d) [*Deleted*]

Trafficking in labels or packaging

(5) Every person commits an offence who sells or offers for sale, or distributes on a commercial scale, any label or packaging, in any form, if the sale, distribution or advertisement of goods or services in association with the label or packaging would be contrary to section 19 or 20 and the person knows that

(a) the label or packaging bears a trade-mark that is identical to, or that cannot be distinguished in its essential aspects from, a registered trade-mark;

(b) the label or packaging is intended to be associated with goods or services for which that registered trade-mark is registered;

(c) the owner of that registered trade-mark has not consented to having the label or packaging bear the trademark.

Registration of trade-mark

(5.1) In a prosecution for an offence under any of subsections (1) to (5), it is not necessary for the prosecutor to prove that the accused knew that the trade-mark was registered.

Punishment

(6) Every person who commits an offence under any of subsections (1) to (5) is liable

(a) on conviction on indictment, to a fine of not more than $1,000,000 or to imprisonment for a term of not more than five years or to both; or

(b) on summary conviction, to a fine of not more than $25,000 or to imprisonment for a term of not more than six months or to both.

Limitation Period

(7) Proceedings by way of summary conviction for an offence under this section may be instituted no later than two years after the day on which the subject-matter of the proceedings arose.

Disposition order

(8) The court before which any proceedings for an offence under this section are taken may, on a finding of guilt, order that any goods, labels, or packaging in respect of which the offence was committed, any advertising materials relating to those goods and any equipment used to manufacture those goods, labels or packaging be destroyed or otherwise disposed of.

Notice

(9) Before making an order for the destruction or other disposition of equipment under subsection (8), the court shall require that notice be given to the owner of the equipment and to any other person who, in the opinion of the court, appears to have a right or interest in the equipment, unless the court is of the opinion that the interests of justice do not require that the notice be given.

2014, c. 32, s. 42.

Importation and Exportation

Interpretation

Definitions

51.02 The following definitions apply in sections 51.03 to 51.12.

customs officer has the meaning assigned by the definition ***officer*** in subsection 2(1) of the *Customs Act*. (*agent des douanes*)

Minister means the Minister of Public Safety and Emergency Preparedness. (*ministre*)

relevant registered trade-mark means a trade-mark registered for goods that is identical to, or cannot be distinguished in its essential aspects from, a trade-mark on such goods, including their labels or packaging, that are detained by a customs officer. (*marque de commerce déposée en cause*)

working day means a day other than a Saturday or a holiday. (*jour ouvrable*)

2014, c. 32, s. 43.

Prohibition

No importation or exportation

51.03 (1) Goods shall not be imported or exported if the goods or their labels or packaging bear — without the consent of the owner of a registered trade-mark for such goods — a trade-mark that is identical to, or that cannot be distinguished in its essential aspects from, that registered trade-mark.

Exception

(2) Subsection (1) does not apply if

(a) the trade-mark was applied with the consent of the owner of the trade-mark in the country where it was applied;

(b) the sale or distribution of the goods or, in the case where the trade-mark is on the goods' labels or packaging, of the goods in association with the labels or packaging would not be contrary to this Act;

(c) the goods are imported or exported by an individual in their possession or baggage and the circumstances, including the number of goods, indicate that the goods are intended only for their personal use; or

(d) the goods, while being shipped from one place outside Canada to another, are in customs transit control or customs transhipment control in Canada.

Restriction

(3) The contravention of subsection (1) does not give rise to a remedy under section 53.2.

2014, c. 32, s. 43.

Request for Assistance

Request for assistance

51.04 (1) The owner of a registered trade-mark may file with the Minister, in the form and manner specified by the Minister, a request for assistance in pursuing remedies under this Act with respect to goods imported or exported in contravention of section 51.03.

Information in request

(2) The request for assistance shall include the trade-mark owner's name and address in Canada and any other information that is required by the Minister, including information about the registered trade-mark and the goods for which it is registered.

Validity period

(3) A request for assistance is valid for a period of two years beginning on the day on which it is accepted by the Minister. The Minister may, at the request of the trade-mark owner, extend the period for two years, and may do so more than once.

Security

(4) The Minister may, as a condition of accepting a request for assistance or of extending a request's period of validity, require that the trade-mark owner furnish security, in an amount and form fixed by the Minister, for the payment of an amount for which the trade-mark owner becomes liable under section 51.09.

Update

(5) The trade-mark owner shall inform the Minister in writing, as soon as practicable, of any changes to

  (a) the validity of the registered trade-mark that is the subject of the request for assistance;

  (b) the ownership of the trade-mark; or

  (c) the goods for which the trade-mark is registered.

2014, c. 32, s. 43.

Measures Relating to Detained Goods

Provision of information by customs officer

51.05 A customs officer who is detaining goods under section 101 of the *Customs Act* may, in the officer's discretion, to obtain information about whether the importation or exportation of the goods is prohibited under section 51.03, provide the owner of a relevant registered

trade-mark with a sample of the goods and with any information about the goods that the customs officer reasonably believes does not directly or indirectly identify any person.

2014, c. 32, s. 43.

Provision of information to pursue remedy

51.06 (1) A customs officer who is detaining goods under section 101 of the *Customs Act* and who has reasonable grounds to suspect that the importation or exportation of the goods is prohibited under section 51.03 may, in the officer's discretion, if the Minister has accepted a request for assistance with respect to a relevant registered trade-mark filed by its owner, provide that owner with a sample of the goods and with information about the goods that could assist them in pursuing a remedy under this Act, such as

(a) a description of the goods and their characteristics;

(b) the name and address of their owner, importer, exporter and consignee and of the person who made them;

(c) their quantity;

(d) the countries in which they were made and through which they passed in transit; and

(e) the day on which they were imported, if applicable.

Detention

(2) Subject to subsection (3), the customs officer shall not detain, for the purpose of enforcing section 51.03, the goods for more than 10 working days — or, if the goods are perishable, for more than five days — after the day on which the customs officer first sends or makes available a sample or information to the owner under subsection (1). At the request of the owner made while the goods are detained for the purpose of enforcing section 51.03, the customs officer may, having regard to the circumstances, detain non-perishable goods for one additional period of not more than 10 working days.

Notice of proceedings

(3) If, before the goods are no longer detained for the purpose of enforcing of section 51.03, the owner of a relevant registered trade-mark has provided the Minister, in

the manner specified by the Minister, with a copy of a document filed with a court commencing proceedings to obtain a remedy under this Act with respect to the detained goods, the customs officer shall continue to detain them until the Minister is informed in writing that

(a) the proceedings are finally disposed of, settled or abandoned;

(b) a court directs that the goods are no longer to be detained for the purpose of the proceedings; or

(c) the trade-mark owner consents to the goods no longer being so detained.

Continued detention

(4) The occurrence of any of the events referred to in paragraphs (3)(a) to (c) does not preclude a customs officer from continuing to detain the goods under the *Customs Act* for a purpose other than with respect to the proceedings.

2014, c. 32, s. 43.

Restriction on information use — section 51.05

51.07 (1) A person who receives a sample or information that is provided under section 51.05 shall not use the information, or information that is derived from the sample, for any purpose other than to give information to the customs officer about whether the importation or exportation of the goods is prohibited under section 51.03.

Restriction on information use — subsection 51.06(1)

(2) A person who receives a sample or information that is provided under subsection 51.06(1) shall not use the information, or information that is derived from the sample, for any purpose other than to pursue remedies under this Act.

For greater certainty

(3) For greater certainty, subsection (2) does not prevent the confidential communication of information about the goods for the purpose of reaching an out-of-court settlement.

2014, c. 32, s. 43.

Inspection

51.08 After a sample or information has been provided under subsection 51.06(1), a customs officer may, in the officer's discretion, give the owner, importer, exporter and consignee of the detained goods and the owner of the

au ministre, selon les modalités fixées par celui-ci, une copie de l'acte introductif d'instance déposé devant un tribunal dans le cadre d'un recours formé au titre de la présente loi à l'égard de ces produits, l'agent des douanes retient ceux-ci jusqu'à ce que le ministre soit informé par écrit, selon le cas :

a) du prononcé de la décision finale sur le recours, du règlement ou de l'abandon de celui-ci;

b) de la décision d'un tribunal ordonnant la fin de la rétention des produits pour l'exercice du recours;

c) du consentement du propriétaire de la marque à ce qu'il soit mis fin à cette rétention.

Poursuite de la rétention

(4) La survenance de l'un ou l'autre des faits visés aux alinéas (3)a) à c) n'empêche pas l'agent des douanes de continuer à retenir les produits en vertu de la *Loi sur les douanes* dans un but étranger au recours.

2014, ch. 32, art. 43.

Utilisation des renseignements fournis au titre de l'article 51.05

51.07 (1) La personne qui reçoit des échantillons ou des renseignements fournis au titre de l'article 51.05 ne peut utiliser ces renseignements et ceux obtenus au moyen des échantillons qu'en vue de fournir à l'agent des douanes des renseignements au sujet de l'éventuelle interdiction d'importation ou d'exportation des produits au titre de l'article 51.03.

Utilisation des renseignements fournis au titre du paragraphe 51.06(1)

(2) La personne qui reçoit des échantillons ou des renseignements fournis au titre du paragraphe 51.06(1) ne peut utiliser ces renseignements et ceux obtenus au moyen des échantillons qu'en vue d'exercer ses recours au titre de la présente loi.

Précision

(3) Il est entendu que le paragraphe (2) n'interdit pas la communication de renseignements au sujet des produits qui est faite confidentiellement afin de parvenir à un règlement à l'amiable.

2014, ch. 32, art. 43.

Inspection

51.08 L'agent des douanes qui a fourni des échantillons ou des renseignements en vertu du paragraphe 51.06(1)

relevant registered trade-mark an opportunity to inspect the goods.

2014, c. 32, s. 43.

Liability for charges

51.09 (1) The owner of a relevant registered trade-mark who has received a sample or information under subsection 51.06(1) is liable to Her Majesty in right of Canada for the storage and handling charges for the detained goods — and, if applicable, for the charges for destroying them — for the period beginning on the day after the day on which a customs officer first sends or makes available a sample or information to that owner under that subsection and ending on the first day on which one of the following occurs:

(a) the goods are no longer detained for the purpose of enforcing section 51.03 or, if subsection 51.06(3) applies, for the purpose of the proceedings referred to in that subsection;

(b) the Minister receives written notification in which the trade-mark owner states that the importation or exportation of the goods does not, with respect to the owner's relevant registered trade-mark, contravene section 51.03;

(c) the Minister receives written notification in which the trade-mark owner states that they will not, while the goods are detained for the purpose of enforcing section 51.03, commence proceedings to obtain a remedy under this Act with respect to them.

Exception — paragraph (1)(a)

(2) Despite paragraph (1)(a), if the goods are forfeited under subsection 39(1) of the *Customs Act* and the Minister did not, before the end of the detention of the goods for the purpose of enforcing section 51.03, receive a copy of a document filed with a court commencing proceedings to obtain a remedy under this Act with respect to the detained goods or the written notification referred to in paragraph (1)(b) or (c), the period ends on the day on which the goods are forfeited.

Exception — paragraph (1)(c)

(3) Despite paragraph (1)(c), if the goods are forfeited under subsection 39(1) of the *Customs Act* after the Minister has received the written notification referred to in that paragraph, the period ends on the day on which the goods are forfeited.

Joint and several or solidary liability

(4) The owner and the importer or exporter of goods that are forfeited in the circumstances set out in subsection (2) or (3) are jointly and severally, or solidarily, liable to the owner of the relevant registered trade-mark for all the charges under subsection (1) paid by the owner of the relevant registered trade-mark with respect to the period

(a) in the circumstances referred to in subsection (2), beginning on the day on which the goods are no longer detained for the purpose of enforcing section 51.03 and ending on the day on which the goods are forfeited; and

(b) in the circumstances referred to in subsection (3), beginning on the day on which the Minister receives the written notification referred to in paragraph (1)(c) and ending on the day on which the goods are forfeited.

Exception

(5) Subsections (1) to (3) do not apply if

(a) the detention of the goods for the purpose of enforcing section 51.03 ends before the expiry of 10 working days — or, if the goods are perishable, before the expiry of five days — after the day on which the customs officer first sends or makes available a sample or information to the trade-mark owner under subsection 51.06(1); and

(b) the Minister has not, by the end of the detention, received a copy of a document filed with a court commencing proceedings to obtain a remedy under this Act with respect to the detained goods or the written notification referred to in paragraph (1)(b) or (c).

2014, c. 32, s. 43.

No Liability

No liability

51.1 Neither Her Majesty nor a customs officer is liable for any loss or damage suffered in relation to the enforcement or application of sections 51.03 to 51.06 and 51.08 because of

(a) the detention of goods, except if the detention contravenes subsection 51.06(2);

(b) the failure to detain goods; or

(c) the release or cessation of detention of any detained goods, except if the release or cessation contravenes subsection 51.06(3).

2014, c. 32, s. 43.

Powers of Court Relating to Detained Goods

Application to court

51.11 (1) In the course of proceedings referred to in subsection 51.06(3), the court may, on the application of the Minister or a party to the proceedings,

(a) impose conditions on the storage or detention of the goods that are the subject of the proceedings; or

(b) direct that the goods are no longer to be detained for the purpose of the proceedings, on any conditions that the court may impose, if their owner, importer, exporter or consignee furnishes security in an amount fixed by the court.

Minister's consent

(2) If a party applies to have the detained goods stored in a place other than a bonded warehouse or a sufferance warehouse, as those terms are defined in subsection 2(1) of the *Customs Act*, the Minister must consent to the storage of the goods in that place before a condition to that effect is imposed under subsection (1).

Customs Act

(3) The court may impose a condition described in subsection (2) despite section 31 of the *Customs Act*.

Continued detention

(4) A direction under paragraph (1)(b) that the goods are no longer to be detained for the purpose of the proceedings does not preclude a customs officer from continuing to detain the goods under the *Customs Act* for another purpose.

Security

(5) In the course of proceedings referred to in subsection 51.06(3), the court may, on the application of the Minister or a party to the proceedings, require the owner of the relevant registered trade-mark to furnish security, in an amount fixed by the court,

(a) to cover duties, as defined in subsection 2(1) of the *Customs Act*, storage and handling charges, and any other amount that may become chargeable against the goods; and

c) du dédouanement ou de la fin de la rétention de produits, sauf si l'un ou l'autre est contraire au paragraphe 51.06(3).

2014, ch. 32, art. 43.

Pouvoirs du tribunal relativement aux produits retenus

Demande au tribunal

51.11 (1) Dans le cadre du recours mentionné au paragraphe 51.06(3), le tribunal peut, à la demande du ministre ou d'une partie :

a) assortir de conditions la rétention ou l'entreposage des produits visés;

b) ordonner qu'il soit mis fin, aux conditions qu'il peut préciser, à leur rétention pour l'exercice du recours, si une sûreté, dont il fixe le montant, est fournie par leur propriétaire, importateur, exportateur ou consignataire.

Consentement du ministre

(2) Si une partie demande que les produits retenus soient entreposés dans un établissement autre qu'un entrepôt d'attente ou un entrepôt de stockage au sens du paragraphe 2(1) de la *Loi sur les douanes*, le ministre doit approuver l'entreposage dans l'établissement avant que le tribunal ne fixe une condition à cet effet.

Loi sur les douanes

(3) Le tribunal peut fixer une condition visée au paragraphe (2) malgré l'article 31 de la *Loi sur les douanes*.

Poursuite de la rétention

(4) L'ordonnance rendue en vertu de l'alinéa (1)b) mettant fin à la rétention pour l'exercice du recours n'empêche pas l'agent des douanes de continuer à retenir les produits en vertu de la *Loi sur les douanes* dans un autre but.

Sûreté

(5) Dans le cadre du recours mentionné au paragraphe 51.06(3), le tribunal peut, à la demande du ministre ou d'une partie, obliger le propriétaire de la marque de commerce déposée en cause à fournir une sûreté, d'un montant fixé par le tribunal, en vue de couvrir les droits — au sens du paragraphe 2(1) de la *Loi sur les douanes* —, les frais de manutention et d'entreposage et les autres

(b) to answer any damages that may by reason of the detention be sustained by the owner, importer, exporter or consignee of the goods.

2014, c. 32, s. 43.

Damages against trade-mark owner

51.12 A court may award damages against the owner of a relevant registered trade-mark who commenced proceedings referred to in subsection 51.06(3) to the owner, importer, exporter or consignee of the goods who is a party to the proceedings for losses, costs or prejudice suffered as a result of the detention of goods if the proceedings are dismissed or discontinued.

2014, c. 32, s. 43.

Trade-mark Agents

Privileged communication

51.13 (1) A communication that meets the following conditions is privileged in the same way as a communication that is subject to solicitor-client privilege or, in civil law, to professional secrecy of advocates and notaries and no person shall be required to disclose, or give testimony on, the communication in a civil, criminal or administrative action or proceeding:

(a) it is between an individual whose name is included on the list of trade-mark agents and that individual's client;

(b) it is intended to be confidential; and

(c) it is made for the purpose of seeking or giving advice with respect to any matter relating to the protection of a trade-mark, geographical indication or mark referred to in paragraph 9(1)(e), (i), (i.1), (i.3), (n) or (n.1).

Waiver

(2) Subsection (1) does not apply if the client expressly or implicitly waives the privilege.

Exceptions

(3) Exceptions to solicitor-client privilege or, in civil law, to professional secrecy of advocates and notaries apply to a communication that meets the conditions set out in paragraphs (1)(a) to (c).

Trade-mark agents — country other than Canada

(4) A communication between an individual who is authorized to act as a trade-mark agent under the law of a country other than Canada and that individual's client that is privileged under the law of that other country and that would be privileged under subsection (1) had it been made between an individual whose name is included on the list of trade-mark agents and that individual's client is deemed to be a communication that meets the conditions set out in paragraphs (1)(a) to (c).

Individual acting on behalf of trade-mark agent or client

(5) For the purposes of this section, an individual whose name is included on the list of trade-mark agents or an individual who is authorized to act as a trade-mark agent under the law of a country other than Canada includes an individual acting on their behalf and a client includes an individual acting on the client's behalf.

Application

(6) This section applies to communications that are made before the day on which this section comes into force if they are still confidential on that day and to communications that are made after that day. However, this section does not apply in respect of an action or proceeding commenced before that day.
2015, c. 36, s. 66.

Legal Proceedings

Definitions

52 In sections 53 to 53.3,

court means the Federal Court or the superior court of a province; (*tribunal*)

duties has the same meaning as in the *Customs Act*; (*droits*)

Minister means the Minister of Public Safety and Emergency Preparedness; (*ministre*)

release [Repealed, 2014, c. 32, s. 44]
R.S., 1985, c. T-13, s. 52; 1993, c. 44, s. 234; 2005, c. 38, ss. 142, 145; 2014, c. 32, s. 44.

Proceedings for interim custody

53 (1) Where a court is satisfied, on application of any interested person, that any registered trade-mark or any trade-name has been applied to any goods that have been imported into Canada or are about to be distributed in Canada in such a manner that the distribution of the goods would be contrary to this Act, or that any indication of a place of origin has been unlawfully applied to any goods, the court may make an order for the interim custody of the goods, pending a final determination of the legality of their importation or distribution in an action commenced within such time as is prescribed by the order.

Security

(2) Before making an order under subsection (1), the court may require the applicant to furnish security, in an amount fixed by the court, to answer any damages that may by reason of the order be sustained by the owner, importer or consignee of the goods and for any amount that may become chargeable against the goods while they remain in custody under the order.

Lien for charges

(3) Where, by the judgment in any action under this section finally determining the legality of the importation or distribution of the goods, their importation or distribution is forbidden, either absolutely or on condition, any lien for charges against them that arose prior to the date of an order made under this section has effect only so far as may be consistent with the due execution of the judgment.

Prohibition of imports

(4) Where in any action under this section the court finds that the importation is or the distribution would be contrary to this Act, it may make an order prohibiting the future importation of goods to which the trade-mark, trade-name or indication of origin has been applied.

How application made

(5) An application referred to in subsection (1) may be made in an action or otherwise, and either on notice or *ex parte*.

Limitation

(6) No proceedings may be taken under subsection (1) for the interim custody of goods by the Minister if proceedings for the detention of the goods by the Minister may be taken under section 53.1.

R.S., 1985, c. T-13, s. 53; 1993, c. 44, s. 234; 2014, c. 32, s. 53.

Proceedings for detention by Minister

53.1 (1) Where a court is satisfied, on application by the owner of a registered trade-mark, that any goods to which the trade-mark has been applied are about to be imported into Canada or have been imported into Canada but have not yet been released, and that the distribution of the goods in Canada would be contrary to this Act, the court may make an order

(a) directing the Minister to take reasonable measures, on the basis of information reasonably required by the Minister and provided by the applicant, to detain the goods;

(b) directing the Minister to notify the applicant and the owner or importer of the goods, forthwith after detaining them, of the detention and the reasons therefor; and

(c) providing for such other matters as the court considers appropriate.

How application made

(2) An application referred to in subsection (1) may be made in an action or otherwise, and either on notice or *ex parte*, except that it must always be made on notice to the Minister.

Court may require security

(3) Before making an order under subsection (1), the court may require the applicant to furnish security, in an amount fixed by the court,

(a) to cover duties, storage and handling charges, and any other amount that may become chargeable against the goods; and

(b) to answer any damages that may by reason of the order be sustained by the owner, importer or consignee of the goods.

Application for directions

(4) The Minister may apply to the court for directions in implementing an order made under subsection (1).

Minister may allow inspection

(5) The Minister may give the applicant or the importer of the detained goods an opportunity to inspect them for the purpose of substantiating or refuting, as the case may be, the applicant's claim.

Where applicant fails to commence an action

(6) Unless an order made under subsection (1) provides otherwise, the Minister shall, subject to the *Customs Act* and to any other Act of Parliament that prohibits, controls or regulates the importation or exportation of goods, release the goods without further notice to the applicant if, two weeks after the applicant has been notified under paragraph (1)(b), the Minister has not been notified that an action has been commenced for a final determination by the court of the legality of the importation or distribution of the goods.

Where court finds in plaintiff's favour

(7) Where, in an action commenced under this section, the court finds that the importation is or the distribution would be contrary to this Act, the court may make any order that it considers appropriate in the circumstances, including an order that the goods be destroyed or exported, or that they be delivered up to the plaintiff as the plaintiff's property absolutely.

1993, c. 44, s. 234; 2014, c. 32, s. 53.

Power of court to grant relief

53.2 (1) If a court is satisfied, on application of any interested person, that any act has been done contrary to this Act, the court may make any order that it considers appropriate in the circumstances, including an order providing for relief by way of injunction and the recovery of damages or profits, for punitive damages and for the destruction or other disposition of any offending goods, packaging, labels and advertising material and of any equipment used to produce the goods, packaging, labels or advertising material.

Notice to interested persons

(2) Before making an order for destruction or other disposition, the court shall direct that notice be given to any person who has an interest or right in the item to be destroyed or otherwise disposed of, unless the court is of the opinion that the interests of justice do not require that notice be given.

1993, c. 44, s. 234; 2014, c. 32, s. 45.

Unaltered state — exportation, sale or distribution

53.3 (1) A court is not permitted, in any proceeding under section 53.1 or 53.2, to make an order under that section requiring or permitting the goods to be exported, sold or distributed in an unaltered state, except in a manner that does not affect the legitimate interests of the owner of the registered trade-mark or except in exceptional circumstances, if the court finds that

(a) goods bearing the registered trade-mark have been imported into Canada in such a manner that the distribution of the goods in Canada would be contrary to this Act; and

(b) the registered trade-mark has, without the consent of the owner, been applied to those goods with the intent of counterfeiting or imitating the trade-mark, or of deceiving the public and inducing them to believe that the goods were made with the consent of the owner.

Removal of trade-mark

(2) Subsection (1) also applies with respect to goods for which the only alteration is the removal of the trade-mark.

1993, c. 44, s. 234; 2014, c. 32, s. 45.

Evidence

54 (1) Evidence of any document in the official custody of the Registrar or of any extract therefrom may be given by the production of a copy thereof purporting to be certified to be true by the Registrar.

Idem

(2) A copy of any entry in the register purporting to be certified to be true by the Registrar is evidence of the facts set out therein.

Idem

(3) A copy of the record of the registration of a trade-mark purporting to be certified to be true by the Registrar is evidence of the facts set out therein and that the person named therein as owner is the registered owner of the trade-mark for the purposes and within the territorial area therein defined.

Idem

(4) A copy of any entry made or documents filed under the authority of any Act in force before July 1, 1954 relating to trade-marks, certified under the authority of that Act, is admissible in evidence and has the same probative force as a copy certified by the Registrar under this Act as provided in this section.

R.S., c. T-10, s. 54.

Jurisdiction of Federal Court

55 The Federal Court has jurisdiction to entertain any action or proceeding, other than a proceeding under section 51.01, for the enforcement of any of the provisions of

this Act or of any right or remedy conferred or defined by this Act.
R.S., 1985, c. T-13, s. 55; 2014, c. 32, s. 46.

Appeal

56 (1) An appeal lies to the Federal Court from any decision of the Registrar under this Act within two months from the date on which notice of the decision was dispatched by the Registrar or within such further time as the Court may allow, either before or after the expiration of the two months.

Procedure

(2) An appeal under subsection (1) shall be made by way of notice of appeal filed with the Registrar and in the Federal Court.

Notice to owner

(3) The appellant shall, within the time limited or allowed by subsection (1), send a copy of the notice by registered mail to the registered owner of any trade-mark that has been referred to by the Registrar in the decision complained of and to every other person who was entitled to notice of the decision.

Public notice

(4) The Federal Court may direct that public notice of the hearing of an appeal under subsection (1) and of the matters at issue therein be given in such manner as it deems proper.

Additional evidence

(5) On an appeal under subsection (1), evidence in addition to that adduced before the Registrar may be adduced and the Federal Court may exercise any discretion vested in the Registrar.
R.S., c. T-10, s. 56; R.S., c. 10(2nd Supp.), s. 64.

Exclusive jurisdiction of Federal Court

57 (1) The Federal Court has exclusive original jurisdiction, on the application of the Registrar or of any person interested, to order that any entry in the register be struck out or amended on the ground that at the date of the application the entry as it appears on the register does not accurately express or define the existing rights of the person appearing to be the registered owner of the mark.

Restriction

(2) No person is entitled to institute under this section any proceeding calling into question any decision given

by the Registrar of which that person had express notice and from which he had a right to appeal.

R.S., c. T-10, s. 57; R.S., c. 10(2nd Supp.), s. 64.

How proceedings instituted

58 An application under section 57 shall be made either by the filing of an originating notice of motion, by counter-claim in an action for the infringement of the trade-mark, or by statement of claim in an action claiming additional relief under this Act.

R.S., c. T-10, s. 58.

Notice to set out grounds

59 (1) Where an appeal is taken under section 56 by the filing of a notice of appeal, or an application is made under section 57 by the filing of an originating notice of motion, the notice shall set out full particulars of the grounds on which relief is sought.

Reply

(2) Any person on whom a copy of the notice described in subsection (1) has been served and who intends to contest the appeal or application, as the case may be, shall file and serve within the prescribed time or such further time as the court may allow a reply setting out full particulars of the grounds on which he relies.

Hearing

(3) The proceedings on an appeal or application shall be heard and determined summarily on evidence adduced by affidavit unless the court otherwise directs, in which event it may order that any procedure permitted by its rules and practice be made available to the parties, including the introduction of oral evidence generally or in respect of one or more issues specified in the order.

R.S., c. T-10, s. 59.

Registrar to transmit documents

60 (1) Subject to subsection (2), when any appeal or application has been made to the Federal Court under any of the provisions of this Act, the Registrar shall, at the request of any of the parties to the proceedings and on the payment of the prescribed fee, transmit to the Court all documents on file in the Registrar's office relating to the matters in question in those proceedings, or copies of those documents certified by the Registrar.

Register of registered users

(2) The transmission of documents on which entries in the register required to be kept under paragraph 26(1)(b) are based is subject to the provisions of subsection 50(6) of the *Trade-marks Act*, as it read immediately before

reçu un avis formel et dont elle avait le droit d'interjeter appel.

S.R., ch. T-10, art. 57; S.R., ch. 10(2ᵉ suppl.), art. 64.

Comment sont intentées les procédures

58 Une demande prévue à l'article 57 est faite par la production d'un avis de requête, par une demande reconventionnelle dans une action pour usurpation de la marque de commerce ou par un exposé de réclamation dans une action demandant un redressement additionnel en vertu de la présente loi.

S.R., ch. T-10, art. 58.

L'avis indique les motifs

59 (1) Lorsqu'un appel est porté sous le régime de l'article 56 par la production d'un avis d'appel, ou qu'une demande est faite selon l'article 57 par la production d'un avis de requête, l'avis indique tous les détails des motifs sur lesquels la demande de redressement est fondée.

Réplique

(2) Toute personne à qui a été signifiée une copie de cet avis, et qui entend contester l'appel ou la demande, selon le cas, produit et signifie, dans le délai prescrit ou tel nouveau délai accordé par le tribunal, une réplique indiquant tous les détails des motifs sur lesquels elle se fonde.

Audition

(3) Les procédures sont entendues et décidées par voie sommaire sur une preuve produite par affidavit, à moins que le tribunal n'en ordonne autrement, auquel cas il peut prescrire que toute procédure permise par ses règles et sa pratique soit rendue disponible aux parties, y compris l'introduction d'une preuve orale d'une façon générale ou à l'égard d'une ou de plusieurs questions spécifiées dans l'ordonnance.

S.R., ch. T-10, art. 59.

Le registraire transmet les documents

60 (1) Sous réserve du paragraphe (2), lorsqu'un appel ou une demande a été présenté à la Cour fédérale en vertu de l'une des dispositions de la présente loi, le registraire transmet à ce tribunal, à la requête de toute partie à ces procédures et sur paiement du droit prescrit, tous les documents versés aux archives de son bureau quant aux questions en jeu dans ces procédures ou des copies de ces documents par lui certifiées.

Registre des usagers inscrits

(2) La divulgation des documents sur lesquels s'appuient les inscriptions figurant dans le registre prévu à l'alinéa 26(1)b) est régie par le paragraphe 50(6) de la *Loi sur les marques de commerce*, dans sa version antérieure à

section 69 of the *Intellectual Property Law Improvement Act* came into force.

R.S., 1985, c. T-13, s. 60; 1993, c. 44, s. 238.

Judgments to be filed

61 An officer of the Registry of the Federal Court shall file with the Registrar a certified copy of every judgment or order made by the Federal Court, the Federal Court of Appeal or the Supreme Court of Canada relating to any trade-mark on the register.

R.S., 1985, c. T-13, s. 61; 2002, c. 8, s. 177.

General

Administration

62 This Act shall be administered by the Minister of Industry.

R.S., 1985, c. T-13, s. 62; 1992, c. 1, s. 145(F); 1995, c. 1, s. 62.

Registrar

63 (1) There shall be a Registrar of Trade-marks, who shall be the Commissioner of Patents appointed under subsection 4(1) of the *Patent Act*. The Registrar shall be responsible to the Deputy Minister of Industry.

Acting registrar

(2) When the Registrar is absent or unable to act or when the office of Registrar is vacant, his powers shall be exercised and his duties and functions performed in the capacity of acting registrar by such other officer as may be designated by the Minister of Industry.

Assistants

(3) The Registrar may, after consultation with the Minister, delegate to any person he deems qualified any of his powers, duties and functions under this Act, except the power to delegate under this subsection.

Appeal

(4) Any decision under this Act of a person authorized to make the decision pursuant to subsection (3) may be appealed in the like manner and subject to the like conditions as a decision of the Registrar under this Act.

R.S., 1985, c. T-13, s. 63; 1992, c. 1, s. 145(F); 1995, c. 1, s. 62; 2014, c. 20, s. 370.

Publication of registrations

64 The Registrar shall cause to be published periodically particulars of the registrations made and extended from time to time under this Act, and shall in such publication give particulars of any rulings made by him that are intended to serve as precedents for the determination of similar questions thereafter arising.

R.S., c. T-10, s. 64.

Regulations

65 The Governor in Council may make regulations for carrying into effect the purposes and provisions of this Act and, in particular, may make regulations with respect to the following matters:

(a) the form of the register and of the indexes to be maintained pursuant to this Act, and of the entries to be made therein;

(b) the form of applications to the Registrar;

(c) the registration of transfers, licences, disclaimers, judgments or other documents relating to any trade-mark;

(c.1) the maintenance of the list of trade-mark agents and the entry and removal of the names of persons and firms on the list, including the qualifications that must be met and the conditions that must be fulfilled to have a name entered on the list and to maintain the name on the list;

(d) the form and contents of certificates of registration;

(d.1) the procedure by and form in which an application may be made to the Minister, as defined in section 11.11, requesting the Minister to publish a statement referred to in subsection 11.12(2); and

(e) the payment of fees to the Registrar and the amount thereof.

R.S., 1985, c. T-13, s. 65; 1993, c. 15, s. 70; 1994, c. 47, s. 201.

Time limit deemed extended

66 (1) Where any time limit or period of limitation specified under or pursuant to this Act expires on a day when the Office of the Registrar of Trade-marks is closed for business, the time limit or period of limitation shall be deemed to be extended to the next day when the Office is open for business.

When Trade-marks Office closed for business

(2) The Office of the Registrar of Trade-marks shall be closed for business on Saturdays and holidays and on such other days as the Minister by order declares that it shall be closed for business.

Publication

(3) Every order made by the Minister under subsection (2) shall be published in the *Trade-marks Journal* as soon as possible after the making thereof.

R.S., c. T-10, s. 66.

Newfoundland

Registration of trade-mark before April 1, 1949

67 (1) The registration of a trade-mark under the laws of Newfoundland before April 1, 1949 has the same force and effect in the Province of Newfoundland as if Newfoundland had not become part of Canada, and all rights and privileges acquired under or by virtue of those laws may continue to be exercised or enjoyed in the Province of Newfoundland as if Newfoundland had not become part of Canada.

Applications for trade-marks pending April 1, 1949

(2) The laws of Newfoundland as they existed immediately before April 1, 1949 continue to apply in respect of applications for the registration of trade-marks under the laws of Newfoundland pending at that time and any trade-marks registered under those applications shall, for the purposes of this section, be deemed to have been registered under the laws of Newfoundland before April 1, 1949.

1993, c. 15, s. 71.

Use of trade-mark or trade-name before April 1, 1949

68 For the purposes of this Act, the use or making known of a trade-mark or the use of a trade-name in Newfoundland before April 1, 1949 shall not be deemed to be a use or making known of such trade-mark or a use of such trade-name in Canada before that date.

1993, c. 15, s. 71.

Transitional Provision

Prior applications for registration

69 An application for the registration of a trade-mark filed before this section comes into force shall not be refused by reason only that subsection 50(1) deems the use, advertisement or display of the trade-mark by a licensed entity always to have had the same effect as a use, advertisement or display of the trade-mark by the owner.

1993, c. 15, s. 71.

RELATED PROVISIONS

— 1992, c. 1, s. 135(2)

Transitional

135 (2) Where a notice was sent under subsection 46(2) of the said Act before the coming into force of subsection (1), the renewal of the registration of the trade-mark shall be dealt with and disposed of as if subsection (1) had not come into force.

AMENDMENTS NOT IN FORCE

— 2014, c. 20, s. 317

317 The long title of the English version of the *Trade-marks Act* is replaced by the following:

An Act relating to trademarks and unfair competition

— 2014, c. 20, s. 318

318 Section 1 of the English version of the Act is replaced by the following:

Short title

1 This Act may be cited as the *Trademarks Act*.

— 2014, c. 20, ss. 319(1), (2)

319 (1) The definition *distinguishing guise* in section 2 of the Act is repealed.

(2) The definitions *proposed trade-mark* and *representative for service* in section 2 of the Act are repealed.

— 2014, c. 20, s. 320

320 The Act is amended by adding the following after section 2:

Reference to *person*

2.1 Unless the context requires otherwise, a reference to **person** in this Act, in relation to a trademark, includes two or more persons who, by agreement, do not have the right to use the trademark in Canada except on behalf of both or all of them.

— 2014, c. 20, s. 321

321 (1) Subsections 6(2) to (4) of the Act are replaced by the following:

Confusion — trademark with other trademark

(2) The use of a trademark causes confusion with another trademark if the use of both trademarks in the same area would be likely to lead to the inference that the goods or services associated with those trademarks are manufactured, sold, leased, hired or performed by the same person, whether or not the goods or services are of the same general class or appear in the same class of the Nice Classification.

Confusion — trademark with trade name

(3) The use of a trademark causes confusion with a trade name if the use of both the trademark and trade name in the same area would be likely to lead to the inference that the goods or services associated with the trademark and those associated with the business carried on under the trade name are manufactured, sold, leased, hired or performed by the same person, whether or not the goods or services are of the same general class or appear in the same class of the Nice Classification.

Confusion — trade name with trademark

(4) The use of a trade name causes confusion with a trademark if the use of both the trade name and trademark in the same area would be likely to lead to the inference that the goods or services associated with the business carried on under the trade name and those associated with the trademark are manufactured, sold, leased, hired or performed by the same person, whether or not the goods or services are of the same general class or appear in the same class of the Nice Classification.

(2) Paragraph 6(5)(e) of the Act is replaced by the following:

(e) the degree of resemblance between the trademarks or trade names, including in appearance or sound or in the ideas suggested by them.

— 2014, c. 20, s. 322

322 The heading before section 7 of the Act is replaced by the following:

Unfair Competition and Prohibited Signs

— 2014, c. 20, s. 323

323 (1) Paragraph 9(1)(d) of the French version of the Act is replaced by the following:

d) un mot ou symbole susceptible de porter à croire que les produits ou services en liaison avec lesquels il est employé ont reçu l'approbation royale, vice-royale ou gouvernementale, ou que leur production, leur vente ou leur exécution a lieu sous le patronage ou sur l'autorité royale, vice-royale ou gouvernementale;

1994, c. 47, s. 191(2)

(2) Paragraph 9(1)(i.3) of the Act is replaced by the following:

Marque de commerce créant de la confusion avec un nom commercial

(3) L'emploi d'une marque de commerce crée de la confusion avec un nom commercial lorsque l'emploi des deux dans la même région serait susceptible de faire conclure que les produits liés à cette marque et les produits liés à l'entreprise poursuivie sous ce nom sont fabriqués, vendus, donnés à bail ou loués, ou que les services liés à cette marque et les services liés à l'entreprise poursuivie sous ce nom sont loués ou exécutés, par la même personne, que ces produits ou services soient ou non de la même catégorie générale ou figurent ou non dans la même classe de la classification de Nice.

Nom commercial créant de la confusion avec une marque de commerce

(4) L'emploi d'un nom commercial crée de la confusion avec une marque de commerce lorsque l'emploi des deux dans la même région serait susceptible de faire conclure que les produits liés à l'entreprise poursuivie sous ce nom et les produits liés à cette marque sont fabriqués, vendus, donnés à bail ou loués, ou que les services liés à l'entreprise poursuivie sous ce nom et les services liés à cette marque sont loués ou exécutés, par la même personne, que ces produits ou services soient ou non de la même catégorie générale ou figurent ou non dans la même classe de la classification de Nice.

(2) L'alinéa 6(5)e) de la même loi est remplacé par ce qui suit :

e) le degré de ressemblance entre les marques de commerce ou les noms commerciaux, notamment dans la présentation ou le son, ou dans les idées qu'ils suggèrent.

— 2014, ch. 20, art. 322

322 L'intertitre précédant l'article 7 de la même loi est remplacé par ce qui suit :

Concurrence déloyale et signes interdits

— 2014, ch. 20, art. 323

323 (1) L'alinéa 9(1)d) de la version française de la même loi est remplacé par ce qui suit :

d) un mot ou symbole susceptible de porter à croire que les produits ou services en liaison avec lesquels il est employé ont reçu l'approbation royale, vice-royale ou gouvernementale, ou que leur production, leur vente ou leur exécution a lieu sous le patronage ou sur l'autorité royale, vice-royale ou gouvernementale;

1994, ch. 47, par. 191(2)

(2) L'alinéa 9(1)i.3) de la même loi est remplacé par ce qui suit :

(i.3) any armorial bearing, flag or other emblem, or the name or any abbreviation of the name, of an international intergovernmental organization, if the armorial bearing, flag, emblem, name or abbreviation is on a list communicated under article 6ter of the Convention or pursuant to the obligations under the Agreement on Trade-related Aspects of Intellectual Property Rights set out in Annex 1C to the WTO Agreement stemming from that article, and the Registrar gives public notice of the communication;

1993, c. 15, s. 58(4)

(3) Paragraph 9(2)(b)(ii) is replaced by the following:

(ii) an armorial bearing, flag, emblem, name or abbreviation mentioned in paragraph (1)(i.3), unless the use of the mark is likely to mislead the public as to a connection between the user and the organization.

— 2014, c. 20, s. 324

324 Section 10 of the Act is replaced by the following:

Further prohibitions

10 If any sign or combination of signs has by ordinary and *bona fide* commercial usage become recognized in Canada as designating the kind, quality, quantity, destination, value, place of origin or date of production of any goods or services, no person shall adopt it as a trademark in association with the goods or services or others of the same general class or use it in a way likely to mislead, nor shall any person so adopt or so use any sign or combination of signs so nearly resembling that sign or combination as to be likely to be mistaken for it.

— 2014, c. 20, s. 325

325 Section 11 of the Act is replaced by the following:

Further prohibitions

11 No person shall use in connection with a business, as a trademark or otherwise, any sign or combination of signs adopted contrary to section 9 or 10.

— 2014, c. 20, s. 326

326 (1) The portion of subsection 12(1) of the Act before paragraph (a) is replaced by the following:

When trademark registrable

12 (1) Subject to subsection (2), a trademark is registrable if it is not

1993, c. 15, s. 59(F)

(2) Paragraph 12(1)(b) of the French version of the Act is replaced by the following:

b) qu'elle soit sous forme graphique, écrite ou sonore, elle donne une description claire ou donne une description fausse et trompeuse, en langue française ou anglaise, de la nature ou de la qualité des produits ou services en liaison avec lesquels elle est employée, ou en liaison avec lesquels on projette de l'employer, ou des conditions de leur production, ou des personnes qui les produisent, ou de leur lieu d'origine;

(3) Paragraph 12(1)(e) of the Act is replaced by the following:

(e) a sign or combination of signs whose adoption is prohibited by section 9 or 10;

(4) Subsection 12(2) of the Act is replaced by the following:

Utilitarian function

(2) A trademark is not registrable if, in relation to the goods or services in association with which it is used or proposed to be used, its features are dictated primarily by a utilitarian function.

Registrable if distinctive

(3) A trademark that is not registrable by reason of paragraph (1)(a) or (b) is registrable if it is distinctive at the filing date of an application for its registration, having regard to all the circumstances of the case including the length of time during which it has been used.

— 2014, c. 20, s. 327

327 Section 13 of the Act is repealed.

— 2014, c. 20, s. 328

1994, c. 47, s. 194

328 Sections 14 and 15 of the Act are replaced by the following:

Registration of confusing trademarks

15 Despite section 12, confusing trademarks are registrable if the applicant is the owner of all of the confusing trademarks.

— 2014, c. 20, s. 329

329 The heading before section 16 of the French version of the Act is replaced by the following:

Personnes ayant droit à l'enregistrement d'une marque de commerce

— 2014, c. 20, s. 330

330 (1) The portion of subsection 16(1) of the Act before paragraph (a) is replaced by the following:

Entitlement to registration

16 (1) Any applicant who has filed an application in accordance with subsection 30(2) for the registration of a registrable trademark is entitled, subject to section 38, to secure its registration in respect of the goods or services specified in the application, unless at the filing date of the application or the date of first use of the trademark in Canada, whichever is earlier, it was confusing with

1994, c. 47, s. 195

(2) Subsections 16(2) to (5) of the Act are replaced by the following:

Pending application

(2) The right of an applicant to secure registration of a registrable trademark is not affected by the previous filing of an application for registration of a confusing trademark by another person, unless the application for registration of the confusing trademark was pending on the day on which the applicant's application is advertised under subsection 37(1).

Previous use or making known

(3) The right of an applicant to secure registration of a registrable trademark is not affected by the previous use or making known of a confusing trademark or trade name by another person, if the confusing trademark or trade name was abandoned on the day on which the applicant's application is advertised under subsection 37(1).

— 2014, c. 20, s. 331

331 The Act is amended by adding the following after section 18:

Not to limit art or industry

18.1 The registration of a trademark may be expunged by the Federal Court on the application of any person interested if the Court decides that the registration is likely to unreasonably limit the development of any art or industry.

Personnes ayant droit à l'enregistrement d'une marque de commerce

— 2014, ch. 20, art. 330

330 (1) Le passage du paragraphe 16(1) de la même loi précédant l'alinéa a) est remplacé par ce qui suit :

Droit à l'enregistrement

16 (1) Tout requérant qui a produit une demande conforme au paragraphe 30(2) en vue de l'enregistrement d'une marque de commerce enregistrable a droit, sous réserve de l'article 38, d'obtenir cet enregistrement à l'égard des produits ou services spécifiés dans la demande, à moins que, à la date de production de la demande ou à la date à laquelle la marque a été employée pour la première fois au Canada, la première éventualité étant à retenir, la marque n'ait créé de la confusion :

1994, ch. 47, art. 195

(2) Les paragraphes 16(2) à (5) de la même loi sont remplacés par ce qui suit :

Demande pendante

(2) Le droit, pour un requérant, d'obtenir l'enregistrement d'une marque de commerce enregistrable n'est pas atteint par la production antérieure, par une autre personne, d'une demande d'enregistrement d'une marque de commerce créant de la confusion, à moins que la demande d'enregistrement de la marque de commerce créant de la confusion n'ait été pendante à la date de l'annonce de la demande du requérant en application du paragraphe 37(1).

Emploi antérieur ou révélation antérieure

(3) Le droit, pour un requérant, d'obtenir l'enregistrement d'une marque de commerce enregistrable n'est pas atteint par l'emploi antérieur, ou la révélation antérieure, par une autre personne, d'une marque de commerce ou d'un nom commercial créant de la confusion, si la marque de commerce ou le nom commercial créant de la confusion a été abandonné à la date de l'annonce de la demande du requérant en application du paragraphe 37(1).

— 2014, ch. 20, art. 331

331 La même loi est modifiée par adjonction, après l'article 18, de ce qui suit :

Aucune restriction à l'art ou à l'industrie

18.1 L'enregistrement d'une marque de commerce peut être radié par la Cour fédérale, sur demande de toute personne intéressée, si le tribunal décide que l'enregistrement est vraisemblablement de nature à restreindre d'une façon déraisonnable le développement d'un art ou d'une industrie.

— 2014, c. 20, s. 333

333 Subsection 21(1) of the English version of the Act is replaced by the following:

Concurrent use of confusing marks

21 (1) If, in any proceedings respecting a registered trademark the registration of which is entitled to the protection of subsection 17(2), it is made to appear to the Federal Court that one of the parties to the proceedings, other than the registered owner of the trademark, had in good faith used a confusing trademark or trade name in Canada before the filing date of the application for that registration, and the Court considers that it is not contrary to the public interest that the continued use of the confusing trademark or trade name should be permitted in a defined territorial area concurrently with the use of the registered trademark, the Court may, subject to any terms that it considers just, order that the other party may continue to use the confusing trademark or trade name within that area with an adequate specified distinction from the registered trademark.

— 2014, c. 20, s. 334

334 (1) Subsections 23(1) to (3) of the Act are replaced by the following:

Registration of certification marks

23 (1) A certification mark may be adopted and registered only by a person who is not engaged in the manufacture, sale, leasing or hiring of goods or the performance of services such as those in association with which the certification mark is used or proposed to be used.

Licence

(2) The owner of a certification mark may license others to use it in association with goods or services that meet the defined standard, and the use of the certification mark accordingly is deemed to be use by the owner.

Unauthorized use

(3) The owner of a registered certification mark may prevent its use by unlicensed persons or in association with any goods or services in respect of which it is registered but to which the licence does not extend.

(2) Subsection 23(4) of the English version of the Act is replaced by the following:

Action by unincorporated body

(4) If the owner of a registered certification mark is an unincorporated body, any action or proceeding to prevent unauthorized use of the certification mark may be brought by any member of that body on behalf of themselves and all other members.

— 2014, c. 20, s. 335

335 Section 24 of the French version of the Act is replaced by the following:

Enregistrement d'une marque de commerce créant de la confusion avec la marque de certification

24 Avec le consentement du propriétaire d'une marque de certification, une marque de commerce créant de la confusion avec la marque de certification peut, si elle présente une différence caractéristique, être déposée par toute autre personne en vue d'indiquer que les produits en liaison avec lesquels elle est employée ont été fabriqués, vendus, donnés à bail ou loués, et que les services en liaison avec lesquels elle est employée ont été exécutés par elle comme étant une des personnes ayant droit d'employer la marque de certification, mais l'enregistrement de cette marque de commerce est radié par le registraire sur le retrait du consentement du propriétaire de la marque de certification, ou sur annulation de l'enregistrement de la marque de certification.

— 2014, c. 20, s. 336

336 Section 25 of the Act is replaced by the following:

Descriptive certification mark

25 A certification mark that is descriptive of the place of origin of goods or services, and not confusing with any registered trademark, is registrable if the applicant is the administrative authority of a country, state, province or municipality that includes or forms part of the area indicated by the certification mark, or is a commercial association that has an office or representative in that area, but the owner of any certification mark registered under this section shall permit its use in association with any goods or services produced or performed in the area of which it is descriptive.

— 2014, c. 20, s. 337

337 Subsection 26(2) of the Act is amended by striking out "and" at the end of paragraph (e) and by adding the following after that paragraph:

(e.1) the names of the goods or services in respect of which the trademark is registered, grouped according to the classes of the Nice Classification, each group being preceded by the number of the class of the Nice Classification to which that group of goods or services belongs and presented in the order of the classes of the Nice Classification; and

— 2014, c. 20, s. 338

1993, c. 15, s. 62

338 Section 28 of the Act is replaced by the following:

— 2014, ch. 20, art. 335

335 L'article 24 de la version française de la même loi est remplacé par ce qui suit :

Enregistrement d'une marque de commerce créant de la confusion avec la marque de certification

24 Avec le consentement du propriétaire d'une marque de certification, une marque de commerce créant de la confusion avec la marque de certification peut, si elle présente une différence caractéristique, être déposée par toute autre personne en vue d'indiquer que les produits en liaison avec lesquels elle est employée ont été fabriqués, vendus, donnés à bail ou loués, et que les services en liaison avec lesquels elle est employée ont été exécutés par elle comme étant une des personnes ayant droit d'employer la marque de certification, mais l'enregistrement de cette marque de commerce est radié par le registraire sur le retrait du consentement du propriétaire de la marque de certification, ou sur annulation de l'enregistrement de la marque de certification.

— 2014, ch. 20, art. 336

336 L'article 25 de la même loi est remplacé par ce qui suit :

Marque de certification descriptive

25 Une marque de certification descriptive du lieu d'origine des produits ou services et ne créant aucune confusion avec une marque de commerce déposée est enregistrable si le requérant est l'autorité administrative d'un pays, d'un État, d'une province ou d'une municipalité comprenant la région indiquée par la marque de certification ou en faisant partie, ou est une association commerciale ayant un bureau ou un représentant dans une telle région. Toutefois, le propriétaire d'une marque de certification déposée aux termes du présent article doit en permettre l'emploi en liaison avec tout produit ou service dont la région de production ou d'exécution est celle que désigne la marque de certification.

— 2014, ch. 20, art. 337

337 Le paragraphe 26(2) de la même loi est modifié par adjonction, après l'alinéa e), de ce qui suit :

e.1) le nom des produits ou services à l'égard desquels cette marque est enregistrée, groupés selon les classes de la classification de Nice, chaque groupe étant précédé du numéro de la classe de cette classification à laquelle il appartient et étant présenté dans l'ordre des classes de cette classification;

— 2014, ch. 20, art. 338

1993, ch. 15, art. 62

338 L'article 28 de la même loi est remplacé par ce qui suit :

List of trademark agents

28 There shall be kept under the supervision of the Registrar a list of trademark agents, which shall include the names of all persons and firms entitled to represent applicants and others, including the registered owner of a trademark and parties to the proceedings under sections 38 and 45, in all business before the Office of the Registrar of Trademarks.

— 2014, c. 20, s. 339

1993, c. 15, s. 64; 1994, c. 47, s. 198

339 Sections 30 to 33 of the Act are replaced by the following:

Requirements for application

30 (1) A person may file with the Registrar an application for the registration of a trademark in respect of goods or services if they are using or propose to use, and are entitled to use, the trademark in Canada in association with those goods or services.

Contents of application

(2) The application shall contain

(a) a statement in ordinary commercial terms of the goods or services in association with which the trademark is used or proposed to be used;

(b) in the case of a certification mark, particulars of the defined standard that the use of the certification mark is intended to indicate and a statement that the applicant is not engaged in the manufacture, sale, leasing or hiring of goods or the performance of services such as those in association with which the certification mark is used or proposed to be used;

(c) a representation or description, or both, that permits the trademark to be clearly defined and that complies with any prescribed requirements; and

(d) any prescribed information or statement.

Nice Classification

(3) The goods or services referred to in paragraph (2)(a) are to be grouped according to the classes of the Nice Classification, each group being preceded by the number of the class of the Nice Classification to which that group of goods or services belongs and presented in the order of the classes of the Nice Classification.

Disagreement

(4) Any question arising as to the class within which any goods or services are to be grouped shall be determined by the Registrar, whose determination is not subject to appeal.

Standard characters

31 An applicant who seeks to register a trademark that consists only of letters, numerals, punctuation marks, diacritics or typographical symbols, or of any combination of them, without limiting the trademark to any particular font, size or colour shall

    (a) file a representation under paragraph 30(2)(c) that consists only of characters for which the Registrar has adopted standard characters;

    (b) include in their application a statement to the effect that they wish the trademark to be registered in standard characters; and

    (c) comply with any prescribed requirements.

Further evidence in certain cases

32 (1) An applicant shall furnish the Registrar with any evidence that the Registrar may require establishing that the trademark is distinctive at the filing date of the application for its registration if any of the following apply:

    (a) the applicant claims that their trademark is registrable under subsection 12(3);

    (b) the Registrar's preliminary view is that the trademark is not inherently distinctive;

    (c) the trademark consists exclusively of a single colour or of a combination of colours without delineated contours;

    (d) the trademark consists exclusively or primarily of one or more of the following signs:

        (i) the three-dimensional shape of any of the goods specified in the application, or of an integral part or the packaging of any of those goods,

        (ii) a mode of packaging goods,

        (iii) a sound,

        (iv) a scent,

        (v) a taste,

        (vi) a texture,

        (vii) any other prescribed sign.

Registration to be restricted

(2) The Registrar shall, having regard to the evidence adduced, restrict the registration to the goods or services in association with which, and to the defined territorial area in Canada in which, the trademark is shown to be distinctive.

Caractères standard

31 Le requérant, s'il veut enregistrer une marque de commerce qui consiste uniquement en des lettres, des chiffres, des signes de ponctuation, diacritiques ou typographiques ou en une combinaison de ces choses et qui n'est pas limitée à une police, une taille ou une couleur précises, est tenu :

    a) de fournir, en application de l'alinéa 30(2)c), une représentation qui consiste uniquement en des caractères pour lesquels le registraire a adopté des caractères standard;

    b) de fournir, dans sa demande, une déclaration portant qu'il souhaite que la marque de commerce soit enregistrée en caractères standard;

    c) de se conformer à toute exigence prescrite.

Autres preuves dans certains cas

32 (1) Le requérant fournit au registraire toute preuve que celui-ci peut exiger établissant que la marque de commerce est distinctive à la date de production de la demande d'enregistrement, si selon le cas :

    a) le requérant prétend qu'elle est enregistrable en vertu du paragraphe 12(3);

    b) elle n'a pas, selon l'avis préliminaire du registraire, de caractère distinctif inhérent;

    c) elle consiste exclusivement en une seule couleur ou en une combinaison de couleurs sans contour délimité;

    d) elle consiste exclusivement ou principalement en l'un ou plusieurs des signes suivants :

        (i) la forme tridimensionnelle de tout produit spécifié dans la demande ou d'une partie essentielle ou de l'emballage d'un tel produit,

        (ii) la façon d'emballer un produit,

        (iii) un son,

        (iv) une odeur,

        (v) un goût,

        (vi) une texture,

        (vii) tout autre signe prescrit.

L'enregistrement est restreint

(2) Le registraire restreint, eu égard à la preuve fournie, l'enregistrement aux produits ou services en liaison avec lesquels il est démontré que la marque de commerce est distinctive, et à la région territoriale définie au Canada où, d'après ce qui est démontré, la marque de commerce est distinctive.

Filing date

33 (1) The filing date of an application for the registration of a trademark in Canada is the day on which the Registrar has received all of the following:

(a) an explicit or implicit indication that the registration of the trademark is sought;

(b) information allowing the identity of the applicant to be established;

(c) information allowing the Registrar to contact the applicant;

(d) a representation or description of the trademark;

(e) a list of the goods or services for which registration of the trademark is sought;

(f) any prescribed fees.

Outstanding items

(2) The Registrar shall notify the applicant whose application does not contain all the items set out in subsection (1) of the items that are outstanding and require that the applicant submit them within two months of the date of the notice. Despite section 47, that period cannot be extended.

Application deemed never filed

(3) If the Registrar does not receive the outstanding items within those two months, the application is deemed never to have been filed. However, any fees paid in respect of the application shall not be refunded to the applicant.

— 2014, c. 20, s. 340

1994, c. 47, s. 199

340 (1) Subsection 34(1) of the Act is replaced by the following:

Date of application abroad deemed date of application in Canada

34 (1) Despite subsection 33(1), when an applicant files an application for the registration of a trademark in Canada after the applicant or the applicant's predecessor in title has applied, in or for any country of the Union other than Canada, for the registration of the same or substantially the same trademark in association with the same kind of goods or services, the filing date of the application in or for the other country is deemed to be the filing date of the application in Canada and the applicant is entitled to priority in Canada accordingly despite any intervening use in Canada or making known in Canada or any intervening application or registration, if

(a) the filing date of the application in Canada is within a period of six months after the date on which the earliest application was filed in or for any country of the Union for the registration of the same or substantially the same trademark in association with the same kind of goods or services;

(b) the applicant files a request for priority in the prescribed time and manner and informs the Registrar of the filing date and country or office of filing of the application on which the request is based;

(c) the applicant, at the filing date of the application in Canada, is a citizen or national of or domiciled in a country of the Union or has a real and effective industrial or commercial establishment in a country of the Union; and

(d) the applicant furnishes, in accordance with any request under subsections (2) and (3), evidence necessary to fully establish the applicant's right to priority.

(2) Subsection 34(2) is replaced by the following:

Evidence requests

(2) The Registrar may request the evidence before the day on which the trademark is registered under section 40.

(3) Section 34 of the Act is amended by adding the following after subsection (3):

Withdrawal of request

(4) An applicant may, in the prescribed time and manner, withdraw a request for priority.

Extension

(5) An applicant is not permitted to apply under section 47 for an extension of the six-month period referred to in paragraph (1)(a) until that period has ended, and the Registrar is not permitted to extend the period by more than seven days.

— 2014, c. 20, s. 341

341 Section 36 of the Act is replaced by the following:

Abandonment

36 If, in the opinion of the Registrar, an applicant is in default in the prosecution of an application filed under this Act, the Registrar may, after giving notice to the applicant of the default, treat the application as abandoned unless the default is remedied within the prescribed time.

— 2014, c. 20, s. 342

342 (1) Paragraph 37(1)(a) of the Act is replaced by the following:

(a) the application does not conform to the requirements of subsection 30(2);

(2) Subsection 37(1) of the Act is amended by striking out "or" at the end of paragraph (b), by adding "or" at the end of paragraph (c) and by replacing the portion after paragraph (c) with the following:

(d) the trademark is not distinctive.

If the Registrar is not so satisfied, the Registrar shall cause the application to be advertised in the prescribed manner.

(3) Section 37 of the Act is amended by adding the following after subsection (3):

Withdrawal of advertisement

(4) If, after the application has been advertised but before the trademark is registered, the Registrar is satisfied that the application should not have been advertised or was incorrectly advertised and the Registrar considers it reasonable to do so, the Registrar may withdraw the advertisement. If the Registrar withdraws the advertisement, the application is deemed never to have been advertised.

— 2014, c. 20, s. 343

343 (1) Paragraph 38(2)(a) of the Act is replaced by the following:

(a) that the application does not conform to the requirements of subsection 30(2), without taking into account if it meets the requirement in subsection 30(3);

(2) Subsection 38(2) of the Act is amended by striking out "or" at the end of paragraph (c) and by adding the following after paragraph (d):

(e) that, at the filing date of the application in Canada, the applicant was not using and did not propose to use the trademark in Canada in association with the goods or services specified in the application; or

(f) that, at the filing date of the application in Canada, the applicant was not entitled to use the trademark in Canada in association with those goods or services.

1993, c. 15, s. 66(2)

(3) Subsections 38(6) to (8) of the Act are replaced by the following:

Power to strike

(6) At the applicant's request, the Registrar may — at any time before the day on which the applicant files a counter statement — strike all or part of the statement of opposition if the statement or part of it

(a) is not based on any of the grounds set out in subsection (2); or

(b) does not set out a ground of opposition in sufficient detail to enable the applicant to reply to it.

Counter statement

(7) The applicant shall file a counter statement with the Registrar and serve a copy on the opponent in the prescribed manner and within the prescribed time after a copy of the statement of opposition has been forwarded to the applicant. The counter statement need only state that the applicant intends to respond to the opposition.

Evidence and hearing

(8) Both the opponent and the applicant shall be given an opportunity, in the prescribed manner and within the prescribed time, to submit evidence and to make representations to the Registrar unless

(a) the opposition is withdrawn or deemed under subsection (10) to have been withdrawn; or

(b) the application is abandoned or deemed under subsection (11) to have been abandoned.

Service

(9) The opponent and the applicant shall, in the prescribed manner and within the prescribed time, serve on each other any evidence and written representations that they submit to the Registrar.

Deemed withdrawal of opposition

(10) The opposition is deemed to have been withdrawn if, in the prescribed circumstances, the opponent does not submit and serve either evidence under subsection (8) or a statement that the opponent does not wish to submit evidence.

Deemed abandonment of application

(11) The application is deemed to have been abandoned if the applicant does not file and serve a counter statement within the time referred to in subsection (7) or if, in the prescribed circumstances, the applicant does not submit and serve either evidence under subsection (8) or a statement that the applicant does not wish to submit evidence.

Decision

(12) After considering the evidence and representations of the opponent and the applicant, the Registrar shall refuse the application, reject the opposition, or refuse the application with respect to one or more of the goods or services specified in it and reject the opposition with respect to the others. He or she shall notify the parties of the decision and the reasons for it.

— 2014, c. 20, s. 344

1993, c. 15, s. 67

344 Section 39 of the Act is replaced by the following:

Divisional application

39 (1) After having filed an application for the registration of a trademark, an applicant may limit the original application to one or more of the goods or services that were within its scope and file a divisional application for the registration of the same trademark in association with any other goods or services that were

(a) within the scope of the original application on its filing date; and

(b) within the scope of the original application as advertised, if the divisional application is filed on or after the day on which the application is advertised under subsection 37(1).

Identification

(2) A divisional application shall indicate that it is a divisional application and shall, in the prescribed manner, identify the corresponding original application.

Separate application

(3) A divisional application is a separate application, including with respect to the payment of any fees.

Filing date

(4) A divisional application's filing date is deemed to be the original application's filing date.

Division of divisional application

(5) A divisional application may itself be divided under subsection (1), in which case this section applies as if that divisional application were an original application.

— 2014, c. 20, s. 345

1993, c. 15, s. 68, c. 44, ss. 231(2) and (3); 1999, c. 31, s. 210(F)

345 Section 40 of the Act is replaced by the following:

Registration of trademarks

40 When an application for the registration of a trademark either has not been opposed and the time for the filing of a statement of opposition has expired, or has been opposed and the opposition has been decided in favour of the applicant, the Registrar shall register the trademark in the name of the applicant and issue a certificate of its registration or, if an appeal is taken, shall act in accordance with the final judgment given in the appeal.

— 2014, c. 20, s. 346

346 (1) The portion of subsection 41(1) of the Act before paragraph (b) is replaced by the following:

Amendments to register

41 (1) The Registrar may, on application by the registered owner of a trademark made in the prescribed manner and on payment of the prescribed fee, make any of the following amendments to the register:

(a) correct any error or enter any change in the name, address or description of the registered owner;

(2) Subsection 41(1) of the Act is amended by striking out "or" at the end of paragraph (d), by adding "or" at the end of paragraph (e) and by adding the following after paragraph (e):

(f) subject to the regulations, merge registrations of the trademark that stem, under section 39, from the same original application.

(3) Section 41 of the Act is amended by adding the following after subsection (2):

Obvious error

(3) The Registrar may, within six months after an entry in the register is made, correct any error in the entry that is obvious from the documents relating to the registered trademark in question that are, at the time that the entry is made, on file in the Registrar's office.

Removal of registration

(4) The Registrar may, within three months after the registration of a trademark, remove the registration from the register if the Registrar registered the trademark without considering a previously filed request for an extension of time to file a statement of opposition.

— 2014, c. 20, s. 347

347 Section 42 of the Act is repealed.

— 2014, c. 20, s. 348

348 The Act is amended by adding the following after section 44:

Registrar may require amendment

44.1 (1) The Registrar may give notice to the registered owner of a trademark requiring the owner to furnish the Registrar, in the prescribed time and manner, with a statement of the goods or services in respect of which the trademark is registered, in which those goods or services are grouped in the manner described in subsection 30(3).

Amendments to register

(2) The Registrar may amend the register in accordance with the statement furnished under subsection (1).

Failure to furnish statement

(3) If the statement required by subsection (1) is not furnished, the Registrar shall by a further notice fix a reasonable time after which, if the statement is not furnished, the Registrar may expunge the registration of the trademark or refuse to renew it.

Disagreement

(4) Any question arising as to the class within which any goods or services are to be grouped shall be determined by the Registrar, whose determination is not subject to appeal.

— 2014, c. 20, s. 349

1994, c. 47, s. 200(1)

349 Subsections 45(1) and (2) of the Act are replaced by the following:

Registrar may request evidence of use

45 (1) After three years beginning on the day on which a trademark is registered, unless the Registrar sees good reason to the contrary, the Registrar shall, at the written request of any person who pays the prescribed fee — or may, on his or her own initiative — give notice to the registered owner of the trademark requiring the registered owner to furnish within three months an affidavit or a statutory declaration showing, with respect to all the goods or services specified in the registration or to those that may be specified in the notice, whether the trademark was in use in Canada at any time during the three-year period immediately preceding the date of the notice and, if not, the date when it was last so in use and the reason for the absence of such use since that date.

Form of evidence

(2) The Registrar shall not receive any evidence other than the affidavit or statutory declaration, but may receive representations made in the prescribed manner and within the prescribed time by the registered owner of the trademark or by the person at whose request the notice was given.

Service

(2.1) The registered owner of the trademark shall, in the prescribed manner and within the prescribed time, serve on the person at whose request the notice was given any evidence that the registered owner submits to the Registrar. Those parties shall, in the prescribed manner and within the prescribed time, serve on each other any written representations that they submit to the Registrar.

Failure to serve

(2.2) The Registrar is not required to consider any evidence or written representations that was not served in accordance with subsection (2.1).

— 2014, c. 20, s. 350

1992, c. 1, s. 135(1)

350 Section 46 of the Act is replaced by the following:

Term

46 (1) Subject to any other provision of this Act, the registration of a trademark is on the register for an initial period of 10 years beginning on the day of the registration and for

Désaccord

(4) Toute question soulevée à propos de la classe dans laquelle un produit ou un service doit être groupé est tranchée par le registraire, dont la décision est sans appel.

— 2014, ch. 20, art. 349

1994, ch.47, par. 200(1)

349 Les paragraphes 45(1) et (2) de la même loi sont remplacés par ce qui suit :

Le registraire peut exiger une preuve d'emploi

45 (1) Après trois années à compter de la date d'enregistrement d'une marque de commerce, sur demande écrite présentée par une personne qui verse les droits prescrits, le registraire donne au propriétaire inscrit, à moins qu'il ne voie une raison valable à l'effet contraire, un avis lui enjoignant de fournir, dans les trois mois, un affidavit ou une déclaration solennelle indiquant, à l'égard de chacun des produits ou de chacun des services que spécifie l'enregistrement ou que l'avis peut spécifier, si la marque de commerce a été employée au Canada à un moment quelconque au cours des trois ans précédant la date de l'avis et, dans la négative, la date où elle a été ainsi employée en dernier et la raison pour laquelle elle ne l'a pas été depuis cette date. Il peut cependant, après trois années à compter de la date de l'enregistrement, donner l'avis de sa propre initiative.

Forme de la preuve

(2) Le registraire ne peut recevoir aucune preuve autre que cet affidavit ou cette déclaration solennelle, mais il peut recevoir des observations faites — selon les modalités prescrites — par le propriétaire inscrit de la marque de commerce ou par la personne à la demande de laquelle l'avis a été donné.

Signification

(2.1) Le propriétaire inscrit de la marque de commerce signifie, selon les modalités prescrites, à la personne à la demande de laquelle l'avis a été donné, la preuve qu'il présente au registraire, et chacune des parties signifie à l'autre, selon les modalités prescrites, les observations écrites qu'elle présente au registraire.

Absence de signification

(2.2) Le registraire n'est pas tenu d'examiner la preuve ou les observations écrites qui n'ont pas été signifiées conformément au paragraphe (2.1).

— 2014, ch. 20, art. 350

1992, ch. 1, par. 135(1)

350 L'article 46 de la même loi est remplacé par ce qui suit :

Durée

46 (1) Sous réserve de toute autre disposition de la présente loi, l'enregistrement d'une marque de commerce figure au registre pendant une période initiale de dix ans à compter de la

subsequent renewal periods of 10 years if, for each renewal, the prescribed renewal fee is paid within the prescribed period.

Notice to renew

(2) If the initial period or a renewal period expires and the prescribed renewal fee has not been paid, the Registrar shall send a notice to the registered owner stating that if the fee is not paid within the prescribed period, the registration will be expunged.

Failure to renew

(3) If the prescribed renewal fee is not paid within the prescribed period, the Registrar shall expunge the registration. The registration is deemed to have been expunged at the expiry of the initial period or the last renewal period.

Renewal

(4) If the prescribed renewal fee is paid within the prescribed period, the renewal period begins at the expiry of the initial period or the last renewal period.

Extension

(5) A registered owner is not permitted to apply under section 47 for an extension of the prescribed period until that period has expired, and the Registrar is not permitted to extend the period by more than seven days.

Prescribed period

(6) For the purposes of this section, the prescribed period begins at least six months before the expiry of the initial period or the renewal period and ends no earlier than six months after the expiry of that period.

— 2014, c. 20, s. 351

351 The Act is amended by adding the following after section 47:

Proceeding under section 45

47.1 (1) The Registrar shall grant an extension of any time limit fixed under this Act in the context of a proceeding commenced by the Registrar, on his or her own initiative, under section 45, if the extension is requested after the expiry of the time limit and within two months after its expiry.

One time extension

(2) No extension under subsection (1) shall be granted more than once.

— 2014, c. 20, s. 352

352 Subsection 48(3) of the Act is replaced by the following:

Transfer of application

(3) The Registrar shall, subject to the regulations, record the transfer of an application for the registration of a trademark on the request of the applicant or, on receipt of evidence satisfactory to the Registrar of the transfer, on the request of a transferee of the application.

Transfer of trademark

(4) The Registrar shall, subject to the regulations, register the transfer of any registered trademark on the request of the registered owner or, on receipt of evidence satisfactory to the Registrar of the transfer, on the request of a transferee of the trademark.

Removal of recording or registration

(5) The Registrar shall remove the recording or the registration of the transfer referred to in subsection (3) or (4) on receipt of evidence satisfactory to the Registrar that the transfer should not have been recorded or registered.

— 2014, c. 20, s. 353

353 Section 49 of the Act and the heading before it are replaced by the following:

Change of Purpose in Use of Trademark

Change of purpose

49 If a sign or combination of signs is used by a person as a trademark for any of the purposes or in any of the manners mentioned in the definition ***certification mark*** or ***trademark*** in section 2, no application for the registration of the trademark shall be refused and no registration of the trademark shall be expunged, amended or held invalid merely on the ground that the person or a predecessor in title uses the trademark or has used it for any other of those purposes or in any other of those manners.

— 2014, c. 20, s. 354

354 Subsection 57(1) of the Act is replaced by the following:

Exclusive jurisdiction of Federal Court

57 (1) The Federal Court has exclusive original jurisdiction, on the application of the Registrar or of any person interested, to order that any entry in the register be struck out or amended on the ground that at the date of the application the entry as it appears on the register does not accurately express or define the existing rights of the person appearing to be the registered owner of the trademark.

— 2014, c. 20, s. 355

355 Section 61 of the Act is renumbered as subsection 61(1) and is amended by adding the following:

Judgment sent by parties

(2) A person who makes a request to the Registrar relating to a judgment or order made by the Federal Court, the Federal Court of Appeal or the Supreme Court of Canada in a proceeding to which they were a party shall, at the request of the Registrar, send a copy of that judgment or order to the Registrar.

— 2014, c. 20, s. 356

356 Section 64 of the Act is replaced by the following:

Electronic form and means

64 (1) Subject to the regulations, any document, information or fee that is provided to the Registrar under this Act may be provided in any electronic form, and by any electronic means, that is specified by the Registrar.

Collection, storage, etc.

(2) Subject to the regulations, the Registrar may use electronic means to create, collect, receive, store, transfer, distribute, publish, certify or otherwise deal with documents or information.

Definition

(3) In this section, *electronic*, in reference to a form or means, includes optical, magnetic and other similar forms or means.

— 2014, c. 20, s. 357

357 Section 65 of the Act is replaced by the following:

Regulations

65 The Governor in Council may make regulations for carrying into effect the purposes and provisions of this Act and, in particular, may make regulations

  (a) respecting the form of the register to be kept under this Act, and of the entries to be made in it;

  (b) respecting applications to the Registrar and the processing of those applications;

  (c) respecting the manner in which the goods or services referred to in paragraph 30(2)(a) are to be described;

(d) respecting the merger of registrations under paragraph 41(1)(f), including, for the purpose of renewal under section 46, the deemed day of registration or last renewal;

(e) respecting the recording or registration of transfers, licences, disclaimers, judgments or other documents relating to any trademark;

(f) respecting the maintenance of the list of trademark agents and the entry and removal of the names of persons and firms on the list, including the qualifications that must be met and the conditions that must be fulfilled to have a name entered on the list and to maintain the name on the list;

(g) respecting certificates of registration;

(h) respecting the procedure by and form in which an application may be made to the Minister, as defined in section 11.11, requesting the Minister to publish a statement referred to in subsection 11.12(2);

(i) respecting proceedings under sections 38 and 45, including documents relating to those proceedings;

(j) respecting the payment of fees to the Registrar and the amount of those fees;

(k) respecting the provision of documents and information to the Registrar, including the time at which they are deemed to be received by the Registrar;

(l) respecting correspondence between the Registrar and any other person;

(m) respecting the grouping of goods or services according to the classes of the Nice Classification and the numbering of those classes; and

(n) prescribing anything that by this Act is to be prescribed.

— 2014, c. 20, s. 358

358 The Act is amended by adding the following after section 65:

Regulations — Madrid Protocol and Singapore Treaty

65.1 The Governor in Council may make regulations for carrying into effect

(a) despite anything in this Act, the Protocol Relating to the Madrid Agreement Concerning the International Registration of Marks, adopted at Madrid on June 27, 1989, including any amendments, modifications and revisions made from time to time to which Canada is a party; and

(b) the Singapore Treaty on the Law of Trademarks, done at Singapore on March 27, 2006, including any amendments and revisions made from time to time to which Canada is a party.

— 2014, c. 20, s. 358.1, as amended by 2014, c. 20, par. 367(88)(b)

358.1 Section 69 of the Act is replaced by the following:

Disclosure of documents

69 The disclosure of documents — on which entries in the register to be kept under paragraph 26(1)(b), as it read immediately before the day on which subsection 27(1) of the *Combating Counterfeit Products Act* comes into force, are based — is subject to subsection 50(6), as it read on June 8, 1993.

— 2014, c. 20, s. 358.2, as amended by 2014, c. 20, par. 367(88)(b)

358.2 Section 69 of the Act is repealed.

— 2014, c. 20, s. 358.3, as amended by 2014, c. 20, par. 367(88)(b)

358.3 The heading before section 69 of the Act is replaced by the following:

Transitional Provisions

— 2014, c. 20, s. 359, as amended by 2014, c. 20, par. 367(88)(c)

359 The Act is amended by adding the following after section 69:

Application not advertised

69.1 An application for registration in respect of which all of the items set out in subsection 33(1), as enacted by section 339 of the *Economic Action Plan 2014 Act, No. 1*, have been received by the Registrar before the day on which that section 339 comes into force, and that has not been advertised under subsection 37(1) before that day shall be dealt with and disposed of in accordance with

(a) the provisions of this Act other than section 31, subsection 33(1) and section 34, as enacted or amended by the *Economic Action Plan 2014 Act, No. 1*; and

(b) section 34, as it read immediately before the day on which section 339 of the *Economic Action Plan 2014 Act, No. 1* comes into force.

Application advertised

70 (1) An application for registration that has been advertised under subsection 37(1) before the day on which section

— 2014, ch. 20, art. 358.1, modifié par 2014, ch. 20, al. 367(88)b)

358.1 L'article 69 de la même loi est remplacé par ce qui suit :

Divulgation de documents

69 La divulgation des documents sur lesquels s'appuient les inscriptions figurant dans le registre prévu à l'alinéa 26(1)b), dans sa version à la veille de l'entrée en vigueur du paragraphe 27(1) de la *Loi visant à combattre la contrefaçon de produits*, est régie par le paragraphe 50(6), dans sa version au 8 juin 1993.

— 2014, ch. 20, art. 358.2, modifié par 2014, ch. 20, al. 367(88)b)

358.2 L'article 69 de la même loi est abrogé.

— 2014, ch. 20, art. 358.3, modifié par 2014, ch. 20, al. 367(88)b)

358.3 L'intertitre qui précède l'article 69 de la même loi est remplacé par ce qui suit :

Dispositions transitoires

— 2014, ch. 20, art. 359, modifié par 2014, ch. 20, al. 367(88)c)

359 La même loi est modifiée par adjonction, après l'article 69, de ce qui suit :

Demande non annoncée

69.1 La demande d'enregistrement à l'égard de laquelle le registraire a reçu, avant la date d'entrée en vigueur de l'article 339 de la *Loi n⁰ 1 sur le plan d'action économique de 2014*, tous les éléments énumérés au paragraphe 33(1), dans sa version édictée par cet article, et qui n'a pas été annoncée, au titre du paragraphe 37(1), avant cette date est régie, à la fois :

a) par les dispositions de la présente loi, à l'exception de l'article 31, du paragraphe 33(1) et de l'article 34, dans leur version édictée ou modifiée par la *Loi n⁰ 1 sur le plan d'action économique de 2014*;

b) par l'article 34 de la présente loi, dans sa version antérieure à cette date.

Demande annoncée

70 (1) La demande d'enregistrement qui a été annoncée, au titre du paragraphe 37(1), avant la date d'entrée en vigueur de

342 of the *Economic Action Plan 2014 Act, No. 1* comes into force shall be dealt with and disposed of in accordance with

(a) the provisions of this Act as they read immediately before the day on which section 342 of the *Economic Action Plan 2014 Act, No. 1* comes into force, other than subsections 6(2) to (4), sections 28 and 36, subsections 38(6) to (8) and sections 39 and 40; and

(b) the definition *Nice Classification* in section 2, subsections 6(2) to (4), sections 28 and 36, subsections 38(6) to (12), sections 39 and 40 and subsections 48(3) and (5), as enacted by the *Economic Action Plan 2014 Act, No. 1*.

Regulations

(2) For greater certainty, a regulation made under section 65, as enacted by section 357 of the *Economic Action Plan 2014 Act, No. 1*, applies to an application referred to in subsection (1), unless the regulation provides otherwise.

Nice Classification

(3) Despite subsection (1), the Registrar may require an applicant to amend the statement of goods or services contained in an application referred to in subsection (1) so that the goods or services are grouped in the manner described in subsection 30(3), as enacted by section 339 of the *Economic Action Plan 2014 Act, No. 1*.

Disagreement

(4) Any question arising as to the class within which any goods or services are to be grouped shall be determined by the Registrar, whose determination is not subject to appeal.

Declaration of use

71 For greater certainty, an applicant is not required to submit a declaration of use referred to in subsection 40(2), as that subsection read immediately before the day on which section 345 of the *Economic Action Plan 2014 Act, No. 1* comes into force, in order for the Registrar to register the trademark and issue a certificate of registration.

Registered trademarks — applications filed before coming into force

72 Any matter arising on or after the day on which section 345 of the *Economic Action Plan 2014 Act, No. 1* comes into force, in respect of a trademark registered on or after that day on the basis of an application filed before that day, shall be dealt with and disposed of in accordance with the provisions of this Act.

Registered trademarks

73 (1) Subject to subsections (2) to (4), any matter arising on or after the day on which section 345 of the *Economic Action Plan 2014 Act, No. 1* comes into force, in respect of a trademark registered before that day, shall be dealt with and disposed of in accordance with the provisions of this Act.

l'article 342 de la *Loi nº 1 sur le plan d'action économique de 2014* est régie, à la fois :

a) par les dispositions de la présente loi, dans leur version antérieure à cette date, à l'exception des paragraphes 6(2) à (4), des articles 28 et 36, des paragraphes 38(6) à (8) et des articles 39 et 40;

b) par la définition de *classification de Nice*, à l'article 2, les paragraphes 6(2) à (4), les articles 28 et 36, les paragraphes 38(6) à (12), les articles 39 et 40 et les paragraphes 48(3) et (5), édictés par la *Loi nº 1 sur le plan d'action économique de 2014*.

Règlements

(2) Il est entendu que tout règlement pris en vertu de l'article 65, édicté par l'article 357 de la *Loi nº 1 sur le plan d'action économique de 2014*, s'applique à la demande visée au paragraphe (1), sauf indication contraire prévue par ce règlement.

Classification de Nice

(3) Malgré le paragraphe (1), le registraire peut exiger du requérant la modification de l'état des produits ou services contenu dans la demande visée au paragraphe (1) pour rendre celui-ci conforme au paragraphe 30(3), édicté par l'article 339 de la *Loi nº 1 sur le plan d'action économique de 2014*.

Désaccord

(4) Toute question soulevée à propos de la classe dans laquelle un produit ou un service doit être groupé est tranchée par le registraire, dont la décision est sans appel.

Déclaration d'emploi

71 Il est entendu que le requérant n'a pas à fournir la déclaration visée au paragraphe 40(2), dans sa version antérieure à la date d'entrée en vigueur de l'article 345 de la *Loi nº 1 sur le plan d'action économique de 2014*, pour que le registraire enregistre la marque de commerce et délivre un certificat de son enregistrement.

Marque de commerce enregistrée — demande produite avant l'entrée en vigueur

72 Toute question soulevée à compter de la date d'entrée en vigueur de l'article 345 de la *Loi nº 1 sur le plan d'action économique de 2014* relativement à une marque de commerce enregistrée à compter de cette date au titre d'une demande produite avant cette date est régie par les dispositions de la présente loi.

Marque de commerce enregistrée

73 (1) Sous réserve des paragraphes (2) à (4), toute question soulevée à compter de la date d'entrée en vigueur de l'article 345 de la *Loi nº 1 sur le plan d'action économique de 2014* relativement à une marque de commerce enregistrée avant cette date est régie par les dispositions de la présente loi.

Application of paragraph 26(2)(e.1)

(2) Paragraph 26(2)(e.1) does not apply to a trademark referred to in subsection (1) unless the register is amended under section 44.1.

Amending register

(3) The Registrar may amend the register kept under section 26 to reflect the amendments to this Act that are made by the *Economic Action Plan 2014 Act, No. 1*.

Subsection 46(1)

(4) Subsection 46(1), as it read immediately before the day on which section 350 of the *Economic Action Plan 2014 Act, No. 1* comes into force, continues to apply to a registration that is on the register on the day before the day on which that section comes into force until the registration is renewed.

— 2014, c. 20, s. 360

Replacement of "wares"

360 The Act is amended by replacing "wares", wherever it occurs, with "goods".

— 2014, c. 20, s. 361

Replacement of "trade-mark"

361 The English version of the Act is amended by replacing "trade-mark", "trade-marks", "Trade-mark" and "Trade-marks" with "trademark", "trademarks", "Trademark" and "Trademarks", respectively.

— 2014, c. 20, s. 362

Replacement of "trade-name"

362 The English version of the Act is amended by replacing "trade-name", wherever it occurs, with "trade name".

— 2014, c. 20, s. 366(1)

Replacement of "trade-mark" in other Acts

366 (1) Unless the context requires otherwise, "trade-mark", "trade-marks", "Trade-mark", "Trade-marks", "trade mark" and "trade marks" are replaced by "trademark", "trademarks", "Trademark" or "Trademarks", as the case may be, in the English version of any Act of Parliament, other than this Act and the *Trademarks Act*.

— 2014, c. 20, ss. 367(1) to (4), (8), (9), (12) to (29), (33) to (63), (66) to (86), (99), (103)

Bill C-8

367 (1) Subsections (2) to (103) apply if Bill C-8, introduced in the 2nd session of the 41st Parliament and entitled the *Combating Counterfeit Products Act* (in this section referred to as the "other Act"), receives royal assent.

(2) If subsection 319(1) of this Act comes into force before subsection 7(2) of the other Act, then that subsection 7(2) is repealed.

(3) If subsection 7(2) of the other Act comes into force before subsection 319(1) of this Act, then that subsection 319(1) is repealed.

(4) If subsection 319(1) of this Act comes into force on the same day as subsection 7(2) of the other Act, then that subsection 319(1) is deemed to have come into force before that subsection 7(2) and subsection (2) applies as a consequence.

(8) If subsection 319(4) of this Act comes into force before subsection 7(3) of the other Act, then that subsection 7(3) is replaced by the following:

(3) The definition *distinctive* in section 2 of the Act is replaced by the following:

distinctive, in relation to a trademark, describes a trademark that actually distinguishes the goods or services in association with which it is used by its owner from the goods or services of others or that is adapted so to distinguish them; (*distinctive*)

(9) If subsection 319(4) of this Act comes into force on the same day as subsection 7(3) of the other Act, then that subsection 319(4) is deemed to have come into force before that subsection 7(3) and subsection (8) applies as a consequence.

(12) If subsection 319(5) of this Act comes into force before subsection 7(5) of the other Act, then that subsection 7(5) is repealed.

(13) If subsection 7(5) of the other Act comes into force before subsection 319(5) of this Act, then

(a) on the day on which that subsection 319(5) comes into force, the definition *proposed certification mark* in section 2 of the *Trademarks Act* is repealed; and

(b) that subsection 319(5) is replaced by the following:

(5) Section 2 of the Act is amended by adding the following in alphabetical order:

Nice Classification means the classification established by the Nice Agreement Concerning the International Classification of Goods and Services for the Purposes of the Registration of Marks, signed at Nice on June 15, 1957, including any amendments, modifications and revisions made from time to time to which Canada is a party; (*classification de Nice*)

(14) If subsection 319(5) of this Act comes into force on the same day as subsection 7(5) of the other Act, then that subsection 319(5) is deemed to have come into force before that subsection 7(5) and subsection (12) applies as a consequence.

(15) If subsection 326(4) of this Act comes into force before subsection 15(4) of the other Act, then that subsection 15(4) is repealed.

(16) If subsection 15(4) of the other Act comes into force before subsection 326(4) of this Act, then that subsection 326(4) is repealed.

(17) If subsection 326(4) of this Act comes into force on the same day as subsection 15(4) of the other Act, then that subsection 326(4) is deemed to have come into force before that subsection 15(4), and subsection (15) applies as a consequence.

(18) If section 327 of this Act comes into force before section 16 of the other Act, then that section 16 is repealed.

(19) If section 16 of the other Act comes into force before section 327 of this Act, then that section 327 is repealed.

(20) If section 327 of this Act comes into force on the same day as section 16 of the other Act, then that section 327 is deemed to have come into force before that section 16 and subsection (18) applies as a consequence.

(21) If section 328 of this Act comes into force before section 17 of the other Act, then that section 17 is repealed.

(22) If section 328 of this Act comes into force on the same day as section 17 of the other Act, then that section 17 is deemed to have come into force before that section 328.

(23) If subsection 330(2) of this Act comes into force before section 18 of the other Act, then that section 18 is repealed.

(24) If subsection 330(2) of this Act comes into force on the same day as section 18 of the other Act, then that section 18 is deemed to have come into force before that subsection 330(2).

(25) If subsection 330(2) of this Act comes into force before paragraph 55(a) of the other Act, then that paragraph 55(a) is repealed.

(26) If subsection 330(2) of this Act comes into force on the same day as paragraph 55(a) of the other Act, then that paragraph 55(a) is deemed to have come into force before that subsection 330(2).

(27) If section 331 of this Act comes into force before section 20 of the other Act, then that section 20 is repealed.

(28) If section 20 of the other Act comes into force before section 331 of this Act, then that section 331 is replaced by the following:

331 The English version of section 18.1 of the Act is replaced by the following:

Not to limit art or industry

18.1 The registration of a trademark may be expunged by the Federal Court on the application of any person interested if the Court decides that the registration is likely to unreasonably limit the development of any art or industry.

(29) If section 331 of this Act comes into force on the same day as section 20 of the other Act, then that section 331 is deemed to have come into force before that section 20 and subsection (27) applies as a consequence.

(33) If section 333 of this Act comes into force before paragraph 55(b) of the other Act, then that paragraph 55(b) is repealed.

(34) If paragraph 55(b) of the other Act comes into force before section 333 of this Act, then that section 333 is repealed.

(35) If section 333 of this Act comes into force on the same day as paragraph 55(b) of the other Act, then that paragraph 55(b) is deemed to have come into force before that section 333 and subsection (34) applies as a consequence.

(36) If section 338 of this Act comes into force before section 28 of the other Act, then that section 28 is replaced by the following:

28 Section 29 of the Act is replaced by the following:

Available to public

29 (1) The following shall be made available to the public at the times and in the manner established by the Registrar:

(a) the register;

(b) all applications for the registration of a trademark, including those abandoned;

(c) the list of trademark agents;

(d) the list of geographical indications kept under subsection 11.12(1);

(e) all requests made under paragraph 9(1)(n); and

(f) all documents filed with the Registrar relating to a registered trademark, an application for the registration of a trademark, a request under paragraph 9(1)(n) and objection proceedings under section 11.13.

Certified copies

(2) The Registrar shall, on request and on payment of the prescribed fee, furnish a copy certified by the Registrar of any entry in the register or lists, or of any of those applications, requests or documents.

Destruction of records

29.1 Despite subsection 29(1), the Registrar may destroy

(a) an application for the registration of a trademark that is refused and any document relating to the application, at any time after six years after the day on which the application is refused or, if an appeal is taken, on which final judgment in the appeal upholding the refusal is given;

(b) an application for the registration of a trademark that is abandoned and any document relating to the application, at any time after six years after the day on which the application is abandoned;

(c) a document relating to an expunged registration of a trademark, at any time after six years after the day on which the registration is expunged;

(d) a request under paragraph 9(1)(n) and any document relating to it, at any time after six years after

(i) the day on which the request is abandoned,

(ii) the day on which the request is refused or, if an appeal is taken, on which final judgment in the appeal upholding the refusal is given, or

(iii) the day on which a court declares that the badge, crest, emblem or mark in question is invalid or, if an appeal is taken, on which final judgment in the appeal upholding the declaration is given;

(e) a document relating to objection proceedings under section 11.13 with respect to a geographical indication that is removed from the list of geographical indications under subsection 11.12(4), at any time after six years after the day on which it is removed; and

(f) a document relating to objection proceedings under section 11.13 with respect to which a decision is made that the indication is not a geographical indication, at any time after six years after the day on which the decision is made or, if an appeal is taken, on which final judgment in the appeal upholding the decision is given.

e) les demandes présentées au titre de l'alinéa 9(1)n);

f) les documents produits auprès du registraire relativement à une marque de commerce déposée, à une demande d'enregistrement de marque de commerce, à une demande présentée au titre de l'alinéa 9(1)n) et à une procédure d'opposition visée à l'article 11.13.

Copies certifiées

(2) Le registraire fournit, sur demande et sur paiement du droit prescrit à cet égard, une copie, certifiée par lui, de toute inscription faite dans le registre ou sur les listes, ou de l'un de ces documents ou demandes.

Destruction de documents

29.1 Malgré le paragraphe 29(1), le registraire peut détruire :

a) la demande d'enregistrement d'une marque de commerce qui a été rejetée et tout document lié à celle-ci, six ans après la date du rejet ou, en cas d'appel, celle du jugement définitif confirmant le rejet;

b) la demande d'enregistrement d'une marque de commerce qui a été abandonnée et tout document lié à celle-ci, six ans après la date de l'abandon;

c) tout document lié à un enregistrement radié d'une marque de commerce, six ans après la date de la radiation;

d) la demande présentée au titre de l'alinéa 9(1)n) et tout document lié à celle-ci, six ans après :

(i) la date de l'abandon de la demande,

(ii) la date du rejet de celle-ci ou, en cas d'appel, celle du jugement définitif confirmant le rejet,

(iii) la date où un tribunal déclare invalide l'insigne, l'écusson, la marque ou l'emblème ou, en cas d'appel, celle du jugement définitif confirmant l'invalidité;

e) tout document lié à une procédure d'opposition visée à l'article 11.13 portant sur une indication géographique qui a été supprimée de la liste des indications géographiques en vertu du paragraphe 11.12(4), six ans après la date de cette suppression;

f) tout document lié à une procédure d'opposition visée à l'article 11.13 qui résulte en une décision qu'une indication n'est pas une indication géographique, six ans après la date de cette décision ou, en cas d'appel, celle du jugement définitif confirmant cette décision.

(37) If section 338 of this Act comes into force on the same day as section 28 of the other Act, then that section 28 is deemed to have come into force before that section 338.

(38) If section 339 of this Act comes into force before subsection 29(1) of the other Act, then that subsection 29(1) is repealed.

(39) If section 339 of this Act comes into force on the same day as subsection 29(1) of the other Act, then that subsection 29(1) is deemed to have come into force before that section 339.

(40) If section 339 of this Act comes into force before subsection 29(2) of the other Act, then that subsection 29(2) is repealed.

(41) If section 339 of this Act comes into force on the same day as subsection 29(2) of the other Act, then that subsection 29(2) is deemed to have come into force before that section 339.

(42) If section 339 of this Act comes into force before subsection 29(3) of the other Act, then that subsection 29(3) is repealed.

(43) If section 339 of this Act comes into force on the same day as subsection 29(3) of the other Act, then that subsection 29(3) is deemed to have come into force before that section 339.

(44) If section 339 of this Act comes into force before subsection 29(4) of the other Act, then that subsection 29(4) is repealed.

(45) If section 339 of this Act comes into force on the same day as subsection 29(4) of the other Act, then that subsection 29(4) is deemed to have come into force before that section 339.

(46) If section 339 of this Act comes into force before section 30 of the other Act, then that section 30 is repealed.

(47) If section 339 of this Act comes into force on the same day as section 30 of the other Act, then that section 339 is deemed to have come into force before that section 30, and subsection (46) applies as a consequence.

(48) If section 339 of this Act comes into force before section 31 of the other Act, then that section 31 is repealed.

(49) If section 339 of this Act comes into force on the same day as section 31 of the other Act, then that section 31 is deemed to have come into force before that section 339.

(50) If subsection 340(3) of this Act comes into force before subsection 33(2) of the other Act, then that subsection 33(2) is repealed.

(37) Si l'entrée en vigueur de l'article 338 de la présente loi et celle de l'article 28 de l'autre loi sont concomitantes, cet article 28 est réputé être entré en vigueur avant cet article 338.

(38) Si l'article 339 de la présente loi entre en vigueur avant le paragraphe 29(1) de l'autre loi, ce paragraphe 29(1) est abrogé.

(39) Si l'entrée en vigueur de l'article 339 de la présente loi et celle du paragraphe 29(1) de l'autre loi sont concomitantes, ce paragraphe 29(1) est réputé être entré en vigueur avant cet article 339.

(40) Si l'article 339 de la présente loi entre en vigueur avant le paragraphe 29(2) de l'autre loi, ce paragraphe 29(2) est abrogé.

(41) Si l'entrée en vigueur de l'article 339 de la présente loi et celle du paragraphe 29(2) de l'autre loi sont concomitantes, ce paragraphe 29(2) est réputé être entré en vigueur avant cet article 339.

(42) Si l'article 339 de la présente loi entre en vigueur avant le paragraphe 29(3) de l'autre loi, ce paragraphe 29(3) est abrogé.

(43) Si l'entrée en vigueur de l'article 339 de la présente loi et celle du paragraphe 29(3) de l'autre loi sont concomitantes, ce paragraphe 29(3) est réputé être entré en vigueur avant cet article 339.

(44) Si l'article 339 de la présente loi entre en vigueur avant le paragraphe 29(4) de l'autre loi, ce paragraphe 29(4) est abrogé.

(45) Si l'entrée en vigueur de l'article 339 de la présente loi et celle du paragraphe 29(4) de l'autre loi sont concomitantes, ce paragraphe 29(4) est réputé être entré en vigueur avant cet article 339.

(46) Si l'article 339 de la présente loi entre en vigueur avant l'article 30 de l'autre loi, cet article 30 est abrogé.

(47) Si l'entrée en vigueur de l'article 339 de la présente loi et celle de l'article 30 de l'autre loi sont concomitantes, cet article 339 est réputé être entré en vigueur avant cet article 30, le paragraphe (46) s'appliquant en conséquence.

(48) Si l'article 339 de la présente loi entre en vigueur avant l'article 31 de l'autre loi, cet article 31 est abrogé.

(49) Si l'entrée en vigueur de l'article 339 de la présente loi et celle de l'article 31 de l'autre loi sont concomitantes, cet article 31 est réputé être entré en vigueur avant cet article 339.

(50) Si le paragraphe 340(3) de la présente loi entre en vigueur avant le paragraphe 33(2) de l'autre loi, ce paragraphe 33(2) est abrogé.

(51) If subsection 33(2) of the other Act comes into force before subsection 340(3) of this Act, then that subsection 340(3) is replaced by the following:

(3) Subsection 34(5) of the French version of the Act is replaced by the following:

Prolongation

(5) Le requérant ne peut demander la prolongation, au titre de l'article 47, de la période de six mois prévue à l'alinéa (1)a) qu'après l'expiration de celle-ci. Le registraire ne peut la prolonger que d'au plus sept jours.

(52) If subsection 340(3) of this Act comes into force on the same day as subsection 33(2) of the other Act, than that subsection 340(3) is deemed to have come into force before that subsection 33(2), and subsection (50) applies as a consequence.

(53) If subsection 342(2) of this Act comes into force before section 34 of the other Act, then that section 34 is repealed.

(54) If section 34 of the other Act comes into force before subsection 342(2) of this Act, then that subsection 342(2) is repealed.

(55) If subsection 342(2) of this Act comes into force on the same day as section 34 of the other Act, then that subsection 342(2) is deemed to have come into force before that section 34, and subsection (53) applies as a consequence.

(56) If subsection 343(3) of this Act comes into force before section 35 of the other Act, then that section 35 is repealed.

(57) If section 35 of the other Act comes into force before subsection 343(3) of this Act, then that subsection 343(3) is repealed.

(58) If subsection 343(3) of this Act comes into force on the same day as section 35 of the other Act, then that subsection 343(3) is deemed to have come into force before that section 35 and subsection (56) applies as a consequence.

(59) If section 344 of this Act comes into force before section 36 of the other Act, then that section 36 is repealed.

(60) If section 36 of the other Act comes into force before section 344 of this Act, then that section 344 is replaced by the following:

344 Sections 39 and 39.1 of the Act are replaced by the following:

Divisional application

39 (1) After having filed an application for the registration of a trademark, an applicant may limit the original application to one or more of the goods or services that were within

(51) Si le paragraphe 33(2) de l'autre loi entre en vigueur avant le paragraphe 340(3) de la présente loi, ce paragraphe 340(3) est remplacé par ce qui suit :

(3) La version française du paragraphe 34(5) de la même loi est remplacée par ce qui suit :

Prolongation

(5) Le requérant ne peut demander la prolongation, au titre de l'article 47, de la période de six mois prévue à l'alinéa (1)a) qu'après l'expiration de celle-ci. Le registraire ne peut la prolonger que d'au plus sept jours.

(52) Si l'entrée en vigueur du paragraphe 340(3) de la présente loi et celle du paragraphe 33(2) de l'autre loi sont concomitantes, ce paragraphe 340(3) est réputé être entré en vigueur avant ce paragraphe 33(2), le paragraphe (50) s'appliquant en conséquence.

(53) Si le paragraphe 342(2) de la présente loi entre en vigueur avant l'article 34 de l'autre loi, cet article 34 est abrogé.

(54) Si l'article 34 de l'autre loi entre en vigueur avant le paragraphe 342(2) de la présente loi, ce paragraphe 342(2) est abrogé.

(55) Si l'entrée en vigueur du paragraphe 342(2) de la présente loi et celle de l'article 34 de l'autre loi sont concomitantes, ce paragraphe 342(2) est réputé être entré en vigueur avant cet article 34, le paragraphe (53) s'appliquant en conséquence.

(56) Si le paragraphe 343(3) de la présente loi entre en vigueur avant l'article 35 de l'autre loi, cet article 35 est abrogé.

(57) Si l'article 35 de l'autre loi entre en vigueur avant le paragraphe 343(3) de la présente loi, ce paragraphe 343(3) est abrogé.

(58) Si l'entrée en vigueur du paragraphe 343(3) de la présente loi et celle de l'article 35 de l'autre loi sont concomitantes, ce paragraphe 343(3) est réputé être entré en vigueur avant cet article 35, le paragraphe (56) s'appliquant en conséquence.

(59) Si l'article 344 de la présente loi entre en vigueur avant l'article 36 de l'autre loi, cet article 36 est abrogé.

(60) Si l'article 36 de l'autre loi entre en vigueur avant l'article 344 de la présente loi, cet article 344 est remplacé par ce qui suit :

344 Les articles 39 et 39.1 de la même loi sont remplacés par ce qui suit :

Demande divisionnaire

39 (1) Après avoir produit la demande d'enregistrement d'une marque de commerce, le requérant peut restreindre cette demande originale à l'un ou plusieurs des produits ou

its scope and file a divisional application for the registration of the same trademark in association with any other goods or services that were

(a) within the scope of the original application on its filing date; and

(b) within the scope of the original application as advertised, if the divisional application is filed on or after the day on which the application is advertised under subsection 37(1).

Identification

(2) A divisional application shall indicate that it is a divisional application and shall, in the prescribed manner, identify the corresponding original application.

Separate application

(3) A divisional application is a separate application, including with respect to the payment of any fees.

Filing date

(4) A divisional application's filing date is deemed to be the original application's filing date.

Division of divisional application

(5) A divisional application may itself be divided under subsection (1), in which case this section applies as if that divisional application were an original application.

(61) If section 344 of this Act comes into force on the same day as section 36 of the other Act, then that section 344 is deemed to have come into force before that section 36 and subsection (59) applies as a consequence.

(62) If section 345 of this Act comes into force before subsection 37(1) of the other Act, then that subsection 37(1) is repealed.

(63) If section 345 of this Act comes into force on the same day as subsection 37(1) of the other Act, then that subsection 37(1) is deemed to have come into force before that section 345.

(66) If section 345 of this Act comes into force before subsection 37(3) of the other Act, then that subsection 37(3) is repealed.

(67) If section 345 of this Act comes into force on the same day as subsection 37(3) of the other Act, then that subsection 37(3) is deemed to have come into force before that section 345.

(68) If subsection 346(1) of this Act comes into force before subsection 38(1) of the other Act, then that subsection 38(1) is repealed.

---

services visés par celle-ci et produire une demande divisionnaire pour l'enregistrement de la même marque de commerce en liaison avec d'autres produits ou services qui étaient visés par la demande originale à la date de sa production et, si la demande divisionnaire est produite le jour où la demande originale est annoncée en application du paragraphe 37(1) ou après ce jour, visés par celle-ci dans sa version annoncée.

Précisions

(2) La demande divisionnaire précise qu'il s'agit d'une demande divisionnaire et indique, de la façon prescrite, la demande originale correspondante.

Demande distincte

(3) La demande divisionnaire constitue une demande distincte, notamment pour le paiement des droits.

Date de la demande divisionnaire

(4) La date de production de la demande divisionnaire est réputée être celle de la demande originale.

Division d'une demande divisionnaire

(5) La demande divisionnaire peut elle-même être divisée en vertu du paragraphe (1), auquel cas, le présent article s'applique au même titre que si cette demande était la demande originale.

(61) Si l'entrée en vigueur de l'article 344 de la présente loi et celle de l'article 36 de l'autre loi sont concomitantes, cet article 344 est réputé être entré en vigueur avant cet article 36, le paragraphe (59) s'appliquant en conséquence.

(62) Si l'article 345 de la présente loi entre en vigueur avant le paragraphe 37(1) de l'autre loi, ce paragraphe 37(1) est abrogé.

(63) Si l'entrée en vigueur de l'article 345 de la présente loi et celle du paragraphe 37(1) de l'autre loi sont concomitantes, ce paragraphe 37(1) est réputé être entré en vigueur avant cet article 345.

(66) Si l'article 345 de la présente loi entre en vigueur avant le paragraphe 37(3) de l'autre loi, ce paragraphe 37(3) est abrogé.

(67) Si l'entrée en vigueur de l'article 345 de la présente loi et celle du paragraphe 37(3) de l'autre loi sont concomitantes, ce paragraphe 37(3) est réputé être entré en vigueur avant cet article 345.

(68) Si le paragraphe 346(1) de la présente loi entre en vigueur avant le paragraphe 38(1) de l'autre loi, ce paragraphe 38(1) est abrogé.

(69) If subsection 346(1) of this Act comes into force on the same day as subsection 38(1) of the other Act, then that subsection 38(1) is deemed to have come into force before that subsection 346(1).

(70) If subsection 346(2) of this Act comes into force before subsection 38(2) of the other Act, then that subsection 38(2) is repealed.

(71) If subsection 38(2) of the other Act comes into force before subsection 346(2) of this Act, then that subsection 346(2) is replaced by the following:

(2) Paragraph 41(1)(f) of the Act is replaced by the following:

> **(f)** subject to the regulations, merge registrations of the trademark that stem, under section 39, from the same original application.

(72) If subsection 346(2) of this Act comes into force on the same day as subsection 38(2) of the other Act, then that subsection 346(2) is deemed to have come into force before that subsection 38(2) and subsection (70) applies as a consequence.

(73) If subsection 346(3) of this Act comes into force before subsection 38(3) of the other Act, then that subsection 38(3) is repealed.

(74) If subsection 38(3) of the other Act comes into force before subsection 346(3) of this Act, then that subsection 346(3) is replaced by the following:

(3) Section 41 of the Act is amended by adding the following after subsection (3):

Removal of registration

(4) The Registrar may, within three months after the registration of a trademark, remove the registration from the register if the Registrar registered the trademark without considering a previously filed request for an extension of time to file a statement of opposition.

(75) If subsection 346(3) of this Act comes into force on the same day as subsection 38(3) of the other Act, then that subsection 346(3) is deemed to have come into force before that subsection 38(3) and subsection (73) applies as a consequence.

(76) If section 349 of this Act comes into force before section 39 of the other Act, then that section 39 is repealed.

(77) If section 349 of this Act comes into force on the same day as section 39 of the other Act, then that section 39 is deemed to have come into force before that section 349.

(78) If section 352 of this Act comes into force before section 40 of the other Act, then that section 40 is repealed.

---

(69) Si l'entrée en vigueur du paragraphe 346(1) de la présente loi et celle du paragraphe 38(1) de l'autre loi sont concomitantes, ce paragraphe 38(1) est réputé être entré en vigueur avant ce paragraphe 346(1).

(70) Si le paragraphe 346(2) de la présente loi entre en vigueur avant le paragraphe 38(2) de l'autre loi, ce paragraphe 38(2) est abrogé.

(71) Si le paragraphe 38(2) de l'autre loi entre en vigueur avant le paragraphe 346(2) de la présente loi, ce paragraphe 346(2) est remplacé par ce qui suit :

(2) L'alinéa 41(1)f) de la même loi est remplacé par ce qui suit :

> **f)** sous réserve des règlements, la fusion de tout enregistrement de la marque de commerce découlant d'une même demande originale divisée sous le régime de l'article 39.

(72) Si l'entrée en vigueur du paragraphe 346(2) de la présente loi et celle du paragraphe 38(2) de l'autre loi sont concomitantes, ce paragraphe 346(2) est réputé être entré en vigueur avant ce paragraphe 38(2), le paragraphe (70) s'appliquant en conséquence.

(73) Si le paragraphe 346(3) de la présente loi entre en vigueur avant le paragraphe 38(3) de l'autre loi, ce paragraphe 38(3) est abrogé.

(74) Si le paragraphe 38(3) de l'autre loi entre en vigueur avant le paragraphe 346(3) de la présente loi, ce paragraphe 346(3) est remplacé par ce qui suit :

(3) L'article 41 de la même loi est modifié par adjonction, après le paragraphe (3), de ce qui suit :

Suppression de l'enregistrement

(4) S'il a enregistré une marque de commerce sans tenir compte d'une demande de prolongation du délai préalablement déposée pour produire une déclaration d'opposition, le registraire peut, dans les trois mois qui suivent l'enregistrement, supprimer celui-ci du registre.

(75) Si l'entrée en vigueur du paragraphe 346(3) de la présente loi et celle du paragraphe 38(3) de l'autre loi sont concomitantes, ce paragraphe 346(3) est réputé être entré en vigueur avant ce paragraphe 38(3), le paragraphe (73) s'appliquant en conséquence.

(76) Si l'article 349 de la présente loi entre en vigueur avant l'article 39 de l'autre loi, cet article 39 est abrogé.

(77) Si l'entrée en vigueur de l'article 349 de la présente loi et celle de l'article 39 de l'autre loi sont concomitantes, cet article 39 est réputé être entré en vigueur avant cet article 349.

(78) Si l'article 352 de la présente loi entre en vigueur avant l'article 40 de l'autre loi, cet article 40 est abrogé.

(79) If section 40 of the other Act comes into force before section 352 of this Act, then that section 352 is replaced by the following:

352 Subsections 48(3) and (4) of the Act are replaced by the following:

Transfer of application

(3) The Registrar shall, subject to the regulations, record the transfer of an application for the registration of a trademark on the request of the applicant or, on receipt of evidence satisfactory to the Registrar of the transfer, on the request of a transferee of the application.

Transfer of trademark

(4) The Registrar shall, subject to the regulations, register the transfer of any registered trademark on the request of the registered owner or, on receipt of evidence satisfactory to the Registrar of the transfer, on the request of a transferee of the trademark.

Removal of recording or registration

(5) The Registrar shall remove the recording or the registration of the transfer referred to in subsection (3) or (4) on receipt of evidence satisfactory to the Registrar that the transfer should not have been recorded or registered.

(80) If section 352 of this Act comes into force on the same day as section 40 of the other Act, then that section 352 is deemed to have come into force before that section 40 and subsection (78) applies as a consequence.

(81) If section 357 of this Act comes into force before subsection 50(1) of the other Act, then that subsection 50(1) is repealed.

(82) If section 357 of this Act comes into force on the same day as subsection 50(1) of the other Act, then that subsection 50(1) is deemed to have come into force before that section 357.

(83) If section 357 of this Act comes into force before subsection 50(2) of the other Act, then that subsection 50(2) is repealed.

(84) If section 357 of this Act comes into force on the same day as subsection 50(2) of the other Act, then that subsection 50(2) is deemed to have come into force before that section 357.

(85) If section 357 of this Act comes into force before subsection 50(3) of the other Act, then that subsection 50(3) is repealed.

(86) If section 357 of this Act comes into force on the same day as subsection 50(3) of the other Act, then that subsection 50(3) is deemed to have come into force before that section 357.

(79) Si l'article 40 de l'autre loi entre en vigueur avant l'article 352 de la présente loi, cet article 352 est remplacé par ce qui suit :

352 Les paragraphes 48(3) et (4) de la même loi sont remplacés par ce qui suit :

Inscription du transfert — demande d'enregistrement

(3) Sous réserve des règlements, le registraire inscrit le transfert de toute demande d'enregistrement d'une marque de commerce sur demande du requérant ou, à la réception d'une preuve du transfert qu'il juge satisfaisante, d'un cessionnaire de la demande.

Inscription du transfert — marque de commerce

(4) Sous réserve des règlements, le registraire inscrit le transfert de toute marque de commerce déposée sur demande du propriétaire inscrit de la marque de commerce ou, à la réception d'une preuve du transfert qu'il juge satisfaisante, d'un cessionnaire de la marque.

Suppression de l'inscription du transfert

(5) Le registraire supprime l'inscription du transfert visé aux paragraphes (3) ou (4) à la réception d'une preuve qu'il juge satisfaisante que le transfert n'aurait pas dû être inscrit.

(80) Si l'entrée en vigueur de l'article 352 de la présente loi et celle de l'article 40 de l'autre loi sont concomitantes, cet article 352 est réputé être entré en vigueur avant cet article 40, le paragraphe (78) s'appliquant en conséquence.

(81) Si l'article 357 de la présente loi entre en vigueur avant le paragraphe 50(1) de l'autre loi, ce paragraphe 50(1) est abrogé.

(82) Si l'entrée en vigueur de l'article 357 de la présente loi et celle du paragraphe 50(1) de l'autre loi sont concomitantes, ce paragraphe 50(1) est réputé être entré en vigueur avant cet article 357.

(83) Si l'article 357 de la présente loi entre en vigueur avant le paragraphe 50(2) de l'autre loi, le paragraphe 50(2) est abrogé.

(84) Si l'entrée en vigueur de l'article 357 de la présente loi et celle du paragraphe 50(2) de l'autre loi sont concomitantes, ce paragraphe 50(2) est réputé être entré en vigueur avant cet article 357.

(85) Si l'article 357 de la présente loi entre en vigueur avant le paragraphe 50(3) de l'autre loi, ce paragraphe 50(3) est abrogé.

(86) Si l'entrée en vigueur de l'article 357 de la présente loi et celle du paragraphe 50(3) de l'autre loi sont concomitantes, ce paragraphe 50(3) est réputé être entré en vigueur avant cet article 357.

(99) On the first day on which both section 359 of this Act and section 28 of the other Act are in force, subsection 70(1) of the *Trademarks Act* is replaced by the following:

Application advertised

70 (1) An application for registration that has been advertised under subsection 37(1) before the day on which section 342 of the *Economic Action Plan 2014 Act, No. 1* comes into force shall be dealt with and disposed of in accordance with

(a) the provisions of this Act as they read immediately before the day on which section 342 of the *Economic Action Plan 2014 Act, No. 1* comes into force, other than subsections 6(2) to (4), sections 28, 29 and 36, subsections 38(6) to (8) and sections 39 and 40; and

(b) the definition **Nice Classification** in section 2, subsections 6(2) to (4), sections 28 to 29.1 and 36, subsections 38(6) to (12), sections 39 and 40 and subsections 48(3) and (5), as enacted by the *Economic Action Plan 2014 Act, No. 1*.

(103) If section 317 of this Act comes into force before any of the following provisions of the other Act, then any of the following provisions of the other Act that are not in force are repealed:

(a) section 8;

(b) section 9;

(c) section 12;

(d) section 13;

(e) subsection 15(1);

(f) subsection 15(3);

(g) subsection 24(1);

(h) subsection 24(2);

(i) section 32;

(j) subsection 33(1);

(k) section 41;

(l) section 47;

(m) section 49.

— 2014, c. 32, ss. 7(2), (3)

7 (2) The definition *distinguishing guise* in section 2 of the Act is repealed.

(3) The definitions *certification mark*, *distinctive*, *proposed trade-mark* and *trade-mark* in section 2 of the Act are replaced by the following:

certification mark means

(a) a sign or combination of signs that is used for the purpose of distinguishing or so as to distinguish goods or services that are of a defined standard from those that are not of that defined standard, with respect to

 (i) the character or quality of the goods or services,

 (ii) the working conditions under which the goods have been produced or the services performed,

 (iii) the class of persons by whom the goods have been produced or the services performed, or

 (iv) the area within which the goods have been produced or the services performed, or

(b) a proposed certification mark; (*marque de certification*)

distinctive, in relation to a trade-mark, describes a trade-mark that actually distinguishes the goods or services in association with which it is used by its owner from the goods or services of others or that is adapted so to distinguish them; (*distinctive*)

proposed trade-mark means a sign or combination of signs that is proposed to be used by a person for the purpose of distinguishing or so as to distinguish their goods or services from those of others; (*marque de commerce projetée*)

trade-mark means

(a) a sign or combination of signs that is used by a person for the purpose of distinguishing or so as to distinguish their goods or services from those of others,

(b) a proposed trade-mark, or

(c) a certification mark; (*marque de commerce*)

— 2014, c. 32, ss. 7(5)

7 (5) Section 2 of the Act is amended by adding the following in alphabetical order:

proposed certification mark means a sign or combination of signs that is proposed to be used for the purpose of distinguishing or so as to distinguish goods or services that are of a defined standard from those that are not of that defined standard, with respect to

(a) the character or quality of the goods or services,

(b) the working conditions under which the goods have been produced or the services performed,

(3) Les définitions de *distinctive*, *marque de certification*, *marque de commerce* et *marque de commerce projetée*, à l'article 2 de la même loi, sont respectivement remplacées par ce qui suit :

distinctive Se dit de la marque de commerce qui distingue véritablement les produits ou services en liaison avec lesquels elle est employée par son propriétaire de ceux d'autres personnes, ou qui est adaptée à les distinguer ainsi. (*distinctive*)

marque de certification Selon le cas :

a) signe ou combinaison de signes qui est employé pour distinguer, ou de façon à distinguer, les produits ou services qui sont d'une norme définie par rapport à ceux qui ne le sont pas, en ce qui concerne :

 (i) soit la nature ou la qualité des produits ou services,

 (ii) soit les conditions de travail dans lesquelles ont eu lieu leur production ou leur exécution,

 (iii) soit la catégorie de personnes qui les a produits ou exécutés,

 (iv) soit la région dans laquelle ont eu lieu leur production ou leur exécution;

b) marque de certification projetée. (*certification mark*)

marque de commerce Selon le cas :

a) signe ou combinaison de signes qui est employé par une personne pour distinguer, ou de façon à distinguer, ses produits ou services de ceux d'autres personnes;

b) marque de commerce projetée;

c) marque de certification. (*trade-mark*)

marque de commerce projetée Signe ou combinaison de signes qu'une personne projette d'employer pour distinguer, ou de façon à distinguer, ses produits ou services de ceux d'autres personnes. (*proposed trade-mark*)

— 2014, ch. 32, par. 7(5)

7 (5) L'article 2 de la même loi est modifié par adjonction, selon l'ordre alphabétique, de ce qui suit :

marque de certification projetée Signe ou combinaison de signes que l'on projette d'employer pour distinguer, ou de façon à distinguer, les produits ou services qui sont d'une norme définie par rapport à ceux qui ne le sont pas, en ce qui concerne :

a) soit la nature ou la qualité des produits ou services;

b) soit les conditions de travail dans lesquelles ont eu lieu leur production ou leur exécution;

(c) the class of persons by whom the goods have been produced or the services performed, or

(d) the area within which the goods have been produced or the services performed; (*marque de certification projetée*)

sign includes a word, a personal name, a design, a letter, a numeral, a colour, a figurative element, a three-dimensional shape, a hologram, a moving image, a mode of packaging goods, a sound, a scent, a taste, a texture and the positioning of a sign; (*signe*)

— 2014, c. 32, s. 8

8 Paragraph 6(5)(e) of the Act is replaced by the following:

(e) the degree of resemblance between the trade-marks or trade-names, including in appearance or sound or in the ideas suggested by them.

— 2014, c. 32, s. 9

9 The heading before section 7 of the Act is replaced by the following:

Unfair Competition and Prohibited Signs

— 2014, c. 32, s. 12

12 Section 10 of the Act is replaced by the following:

Further prohibitions

10 If any sign or combination of signs has by ordinary and *bona fide* commercial usage become recognized in Canada as designating the kind, quality, quantity, destination, value, place of origin or date of production of any goods or services, no person shall adopt it as a trade-mark in association with the goods or services or others of the same general class or use it in a way likely to mislead, nor shall any person so adopt or so use any sign or combination of signs so nearly resembling that sign or combination as to be likely to be mistaken for it.

— 2014, c. 32, s. 13

13 Section 11 of the Act is replaced by the following:

Further prohibitions

11 No person shall use in connection with a business, as a trade-mark or otherwise, any sign or combination of signs adopted contrary to section 9 or 10.

c) soit la catégorie de personnes qui les a produits ou exécutés;

d) soit la région dans laquelle ont eu lieu leur production ou leur exécution. (*proposed certification mark*)

signe Vise notamment les mots, les noms de personne, les dessins, les lettres, les chiffres, les couleurs, les éléments figuratifs, les formes tridimensionnelles, les hologrammes, les images en mouvement, les façons d'emballer les produits, les sons, les odeurs, les goûts et les textures ainsi que la position de tout signe. (*sign*)

— 2014, ch. 32, art. 8

8 L'alinéa 6(5)e) de la même loi est remplacé par ce qui suit :

e) le degré de ressemblance entre les marques de commerce ou les noms commerciaux, notamment dans la présentation ou le son, ou dans les idées qu'ils suggèrent.

— 2014, ch. 32, art. 9

9 L'intertitre précédant l'article 7 de la même loi est remplacé par ce qui suit :

Concurrence déloyale et signes interdits

— 2014, ch. 32, art. 12

12 L'article 10 de la même loi est remplacé par ce qui suit :

Autres interdictions

10 Si un signe ou une combinaison de signes, en raison d'une pratique commerciale ordinaire et authentique, devient reconnu au Canada comme désignant le genre, la qualité, la quantité, la destination, la valeur, la date de production ou le lieu d'origine de produits ou services, nul ne peut l'adopter comme marque de commerce en liaison avec ces produits ou services ou d'autres de la même catégorie générale, ou l'employer d'une manière susceptible d'induire en erreur, et nul ne peut ainsi adopter ou employer un signe ou une combinaison de signes dont la ressemblance avec le signe ou la combinaison de signes en question est telle qu'on pourrait vraisemblablement les confondre.

— 2014, ch. 32, art. 13

13 L'article 11 de la même loi est remplacé par ce qui suit :

Autres interdictions

11 Nul ne peut employer relativement à une entreprise, comme marque de commerce ou autrement, un signe ou une combinaison de signes adopté contrairement aux articles 9 ou 10.

— 2014, c. 32, s. 15(1)

15 (1) The portion of subsection 12(1) of the Act before paragraph (a) is replaced by the following:

When trademark registrable

12 (1) Subject to subsection (2), a trade-mark is registrable if it is not

— 2014, c. 32, ss. 15(3), (4)

15 (3) Paragraph 12(1)(e) of the Act is replaced by the following:

(e) a sign or combination of signs whose adoption is prohibited by section 9 or 10;

(4) Subsection 12(2) of the Act is replaced by the following:

Utilitarian function

(2) A trade-mark is not registrable if, in relation to the goods or services in association with which it is used or proposed to be used, its features are dictated primarily by a utilitarian function.

Registrable if distinctive

(3) A trade-mark that is not registrable by reason of paragraph (1)(a) or (b) is registrable if it is distinctive at the filing date of an application for its registration, having regard to all the circumstances of the case including the length of time during which it has been used.

— 2014, c. 32, s. 16

16 Section 13 of the Act is repealed.

— 2014, c. 32, s. 17

17 Section 15 of the Act is replaced by the following:

Registration of confusing trade-marks

15 Despite sections 12 and 14, confusing trade-marks are registrable if the applicant is the owner of all of the confusing trade-marks.

— 2014, c. 32, s. 18

18 The portion of subsection 16(3) of the Act before paragraph (a) is replaced by the following:

Proposed certification marks or trade-marks

(3) Any applicant who has filed an application in accordance with section 30 for registration of a proposed trade-mark or proposed certification mark that is registrable is entitled,

— 2014, ch. 32, par. 15(1)

15 (1) Le passage du paragraphe 12(1) de la même loi précédant l'alinéa a) est remplacé par ce qui suit :

Marque de commerce enregistrable

12 (1) Sous réserve du paragraphe (2), la marque de commerce est enregistrable sauf dans l'un ou l'autre des cas suivants :

— 2014, ch. 32, par. 15(3) et (4)

15 (3) L'alinéa 12(1)e) de la même loi est remplacé par ce qui suit :

e) elle est un signe ou une combinaison de signes dont les articles 9 ou 10 interdisent l'adoption;

(4) Le paragraphe 12(2) de la même loi est remplacé par ce qui suit :

Fonction utilitaire

(2) La marque de commerce n'est pas enregistrable si, à l'égard des produits ou services en liaison avec lesquels elle est employée, ou en liaison avec lesquels on projette de l'employer, ses caractéristiques résultent principalement d'une fonction utilitaire.

Marque de commerce distinctive

(3) La marque de commerce qui n'est pas enregistrable en raison des alinéas (1)a) ou b) peut être enregistrée si elle est distinctive à la date de production d'une demande d'enregistrement la concernant, eu égard aux circonstances, notamment la durée de l'emploi qui en a été fait.

— 2014, ch. 32, art. 16

16 L'article 13 de la même loi est abrogé.

— 2014, ch. 32, art. 17

17 L'article 15 de la même loi est remplacé par ce qui suit :

Enregistrement de marques de commerce créant de la confusion

15 Malgré les articles 12 et 14, les marques de commerce créant de la confusion sont enregistrables si le requérant est le propriétaire de toutes ces marques.

— 2014, ch. 32, art. 18

18 Le passage du paragraphe 16(3) de la même loi précédant l'alinéa a) est remplacé par ce qui suit :

Marques de commerce ou de certification projetées

(3) Tout requérant qui a produit une demande conformément à l'article 30 en vue de l'enregistrement d'une marque de commerce — ou de certification — projetée et enregistrable

subject to sections 38 and 40, to secure its registration in respect of the goods or services specified in the application, unless at the filing date of the application it was confusing with

— 2014, c. 32, s. 20

20 The Act is amended by adding the following after section 18:

Not to limit art or industry

18.1 The registration of a trade-mark may be expunged by the Federal Court on the application of any interested person if the Court decides that the registration is likely to unreasonably limit the development of any art or industry.

— 2014, c. 32, s. 23

23 Subsection 22(2) of the Act is replaced by the following:

Action

(2) In any action in respect of a use of a trade-mark contrary to subsection (1), the court may decline to order the recovery of damages or profits and may permit the defendant to continue to sell goods bearing the trade-mark that were in the defendant's possession or under their control at the time notice was given to them that the owner of the registered trade-mark complained of the use of the trade-mark.

— 2014, c. 32, s. 24

24 (1) Subsections 23(1) to (3) of the Act are replaced by the following:

Registration of certification marks

23 (1) A certification mark may be adopted and registered only by a person who is not engaged in the manufacture, sale, leasing or hiring of goods or the performance of services such as those in association with which the certification mark is used or proposed to be used.

Licence

(2) The owner of a certification mark may license others to use it in association with goods or services that meet the defined standard, and the use of the certification mark accordingly is deemed to be use by the owner.

Unauthorized use

(3) The owner of a registered certification mark may prevent its use by unlicensed persons or in association with any goods or services in respect of which it is registered but to which the licence does not extend.

(2) Subsection 23(4) of the English version of the Act is replaced by the following:

Action by unincorporated body

(4) If the owner of a registered certification mark is an unincorporated body, any action or proceeding to prevent unauthorized use of the certification mark may be brought by any member of that body on behalf of themselves and all other members.

— 2014, c. 32, s. 27

27 (1) Subsection 26(1) of the Act is replaced by the following:

Register

26 (1) There shall be kept under the supervision of the Registrar a register of trade-marks and of transfers, disclaimers, amendments, judgments and orders relating to each registered trade-mark.

(2) The portion of subsection 26(2) of the Act before paragraph (a) is replaced by the following:

Information to be shown

(2) The register shall show, with reference to each registered trade-mark, the following:

— 2014, c. 32, s. 28

28 Sections 28 and 29 of the Act are replaced by the following:

List of trade-mark agents

28 There shall be kept under the supervision of the Registrar a list of trade-mark agents, which shall include the names of all persons and firms entitled to represent applicants and others in the presentation and prosecution of applications for the registration of a trade-mark or in other business before the Office of the Registrar of Trade-marks.

Available to public

29 (1) The following shall be made available to the public at the times and in the manner established by the Registrar:

(a) the register;

(b) all applications for the registration of a trade-mark, including those abandoned;

(c) the list of trade-mark agents;

(d) the list of geographical indications kept under subsection 11.12(1);

(e) all requests made under paragraph 9(1)(n); and

(f) all documents filed with the Registrar relating to a registered trade-mark, an application for the registration of a trade-mark, a request under paragraph 9(1)(n) and objection proceedings under section 11.13.

Certified copies

(2) The Registrar shall, on request and on payment of the prescribed fee, furnish a copy certified by the Registrar of any entry in the register or lists, or of any of those applications, requests or documents.

Destruction of records

29.1 Despite subsection 29(1), the Registrar may destroy

(a) an application for the registration of a trade-mark that is refused and any document relating to the application, at any time after six years after the day on which the application is refused or, if an appeal is taken, on which final judgment in the appeal upholding the refusal is given;

(b) an application for the registration of a trade-mark that is abandoned and any document relating to the application, at any time after six years after the day on which the application is abandoned;

(c) a document relating to an expunged registration of a trade-mark, at any time after six years after the day on which the registration is expunged;

(d) a request under paragraph 9(1)(n) and any document relating to it, at any time after six years after

(i) the day on which the request is abandoned,

(ii) the day on which the request is refused or, if an appeal is taken, on which final judgment in the appeal upholding the refusal is given, or

(iii) the day on which a court declares that the badge, crest, emblem or mark in question is invalid or, if an appeal is taken, on which final judgment in the appeal upholding the declaration is given;

(e) a document relating to objection proceedings under section 11.13 with respect to a geographical indication that is removed from the list of geographical indications under subsection 11.12(4), at any time after six years after the day on which it is removed; and

(f) a document relating to objection proceedings under section 11.13 with respect to which a decision is made that the indication is not a geographical indication, at any time after six years after the day on which the decision is made or, if an appeal is taken, on which final judgment in the appeal upholding the decision is given.

— 2014, c. 32, s. 29

29 (1) Paragraph 30(a) of the Act is replaced by the following:

d'enregistrement de marque de commerce, à une demande présentée au titre de l'alinéa 9(1)n) et à une procédure d'opposition visée à l'article 11.13.

Copies certifiées

(2) Le registraire fournit, sur demande et sur paiement du droit prescrit à cet égard, une copie, certifiée par lui, de toute inscription faite dans le registre ou sur les listes, ou de l'un de ces documents ou demandes.

Destruction de documents

29.1 Malgré le paragraphe 29(1), le registraire peut détruire :

a) la demande d'enregistrement d'une marque de commerce qui a été rejetée et tout document lié à celle-ci, six ans après la date du rejet ou, en cas d'appel, celle du jugement définitif confirmant le rejet;

b) la demande d'enregistrement d'une marque de commerce qui a été abandonnée et tout document lié à celle-ci, six ans après la date de l'abandon;

c) tout document lié à un enregistrement radié d'une marque de commerce, six ans après la date de la radiation;

d) la demande présentée au titre de l'alinéa 9(1)n) et tout document lié à celle-ci, six ans après :

(i) la date de l'abandon de la demande,

(ii) la date du rejet de celle-ci ou, en cas d'appel, celle du jugement définitif confirmant le rejet,

(iii) la date où un tribunal déclare invalide l'insigne, l'écusson, la marque ou l'emblème ou, en cas d'appel, celle du jugement définitif confirmant l'invalidité;

e) tout document lié à une procédure d'opposition visée à l'article 11.13 portant sur une indication géographique qui a été supprimée de la liste des indications géographiques en vertu du paragraphe 11.12(4), six ans après la date de cette suppression;

f) tout document lié à une procédure d'opposition visée à l'article 11.13 qui résulte en une décision qu'une indication n'est pas une indication géographique, six ans après la date de cette décision ou, en cas d'appel, celle du jugement définitif confirmant cette décision.

— 2014, ch. 32, art. 29

29 (1) L'alinéa 30a) de la même loi est remplacé par ce qui suit :

(a) a statement in ordinary commercial terms of the specific goods or services in association with which the trade-mark has been or is proposed to be used;

(2) Paragraph 30(f) of the Act is replaced by the following:

(f) in the case of a certification mark, particulars of the defined standard that the use of the certification mark is intended to indicate and a statement that the applicant is not engaged in the manufacture, sale, leasing or hiring of goods or the performance of services such as those in association with which the certification mark is used or proposed to be used;

(f.1) in the case of a proposed certification mark, a statement that the applicant intends to license others to use the certification mark in Canada in association with goods or services that meet the defined standard;

(3) Paragraph 30(h) of the Act is replaced by the following:

(h) a representation or description, or both, that permits the trade-mark to be clearly defined and that complies with any prescribed requirements;

(4) Section 30 of the Act is amended by adding "and" at the end of paragraph (i) and by adding the following after that paragraph:

(j) any prescribed information or statement with respect to the trade-mark.

— 2014, c. 32, s. 30

30 The Act is amended by adding the following after section 30:

Standard characters

30.1 An applicant who seeks to register a trade-mark that consists only of letters, numerals, punctuation marks, diacritics or typographical symbols, or of any combination of them, without limiting the trade-mark to any particular font, size or colour shall

(a) file a representation under paragraph 30(h) that consists only of characters for which the Registrar has adopted standard characters;

(b) include in their application a statement to the effect that they wish the trade-mark to be registered in standard characters; and

(c) comply with any prescribed requirements.

— 2014, c. 32, s. 31

31 Sections 31 to 32 of the Act are replaced by the following:

Further evidence — registration abroad

31 An applicant whose trade-mark has been duly registered in their country of origin and who claims that the trade-mark is registrable under paragraph 14(1)(b) shall furnish any evidence that the Registrar may require establishing the circumstances on which they rely, including the length of time during which the trade-mark has been used in any country.

Further evidence in certain cases

32 (1) An applicant shall furnish the Registrar with any evidence that the Registrar may require establishing that the trade-mark is distinctive at the filing date of the application for its registration if any of the following apply:

(a) the applicant claims that their trade-mark is registrable under subsection 12(3);

(b) the Registrar's preliminary view is that the trade-mark is not inherently distinctive;

(c) the trade-mark consists exclusively of a single colour or of a combination of colours without delineated contours;

(d) the trade-mark consists exclusively or primarily of one or more of the following:

(i) the three-dimensional shape of any of the goods specified in the application, or of an integral part or the packaging of any of those goods,

(ii) a mode of packaging goods,

(iii) a sound,

(iv) a scent,

(v) a taste,

(vi) a texture,

(vii) any other prescribed sign.

Registration to be restricted

(2) The Registrar shall, having regard to the evidence adduced, restrict the registration to the goods or services in association with which, and to the defined territorial area in Canada in which, the trade-mark is shown to be distinctive.

— 2014, c. 32, s. 32

32 Section 33 of the Act is replaced by the following:

Filing date

33 (1) The filing date of an application for the registration of a trade-mark in Canada is the day on which the Registrar has received all of the following:

(a) an explicit or implicit indication that the registration of the trade-mark is sought;

(b) information allowing the identity of the applicant to be established;

(c) information allowing the Registrar to contact the applicant;

(d) a representation or description of the trade-mark;

(e) a list of the goods or services for which registration of the trade-mark is sought;

(f) any prescribed fees.

Outstanding items

(2) The Registrar shall notify the applicant whose application does not contain all the items set out in subsection (1) of the items that are outstanding and require that the applicant submit them within two months of the date of the notice. Despite section 47, that period cannot be extended.

Application deemed never filed

(3) If the Registrar does not receive the outstanding items within those two months, the application is deemed never to have been filed. However, any fees paid in respect of the application shall not be refunded to the applicant.

— 2014, c. 32, s. 33

33 (1) Subsection 34(1) of the Act is replaced by the following:

Date of application abroad deemed date of application in Canada

34 (1) Despite subsection 33(1), when an applicant files an application for the registration of a trade-mark in Canada after the applicant or the applicant's predecessor in title has applied, in or for any country of the Union other than Canada, for the registration of the same or substantially the same trade-mark in association with the same kind of goods or services, the filing date of the application in or for the other country is deemed to be the filing date of the application in Canada and the applicant is entitled to priority in Canada accordingly despite any intervening use in Canada or making known in Canada or any intervening application or registration, if

(a) the filing date of the application in Canada is within a period of six months after the date on which the earliest application was filed in or for any country of the Union for the registration of the same or substantially the same trade-mark in association with the same kind of goods or services;

Date de production de la demande

33 (1) La date de production de la demande d'enregistrement d'une marque de commerce au Canada est la date à laquelle le registraire a reçu :

a) l'indication, explicite ou implicite, que l'enregistrement de la marque de commerce est demandé;

b) des renseignements permettant d'établir l'identité du requérant;

c) des renseignements lui permettant de contacter le requérant;

d) une représentation ou une description de la marque de commerce;

e) la liste des produits ou services à l'égard desquels l'enregistrement est demandé;

f) les droits prescrits.

Éléments manquants

(2) Le registraire notifie le requérant dont la demande ne contient pas tous les éléments visés au paragraphe (1) des éléments manquants et exige que le requérant les soumette dans les deux mois suivant la date de la notification. Malgré l'article 47, ce délai ne peut être prolongé.

Demande réputée non produite

(3) Si le registraire ne reçoit pas les éléments manquants dans ce délai, la demande est réputée ne pas avoir été produite. Les droits payés dans le cadre de la demande ne sont toutefois pas remboursables.

— 2014, ch. 32, art. 33

33 (1) Le paragraphe 34(1) de la même loi est remplacé par ce qui suit :

La date de demande à l'étranger est réputée être la date de demande au Canada

34 (1) Malgré le paragraphe 33(1), lorsqu'un requérant produit une demande pour l'enregistrement d'une marque de commerce au Canada après que lui ou son prédécesseur en titre a produit une demande d'enregistrement, dans un autre pays de l'Union, ou pour un autre pays de l'Union, de la même marque de commerce, ou sensiblement la même, en liaison avec le même genre de produits ou services, la date de production de la demande dans l'autre pays, ou pour l'autre pays, est réputée être la date de production de la demande au Canada, et le requérant a droit, au Canada, à une priorité correspondante malgré tout emploi ou toute révélation faite au Canada, ou toute demande ou tout enregistrement survenu, dans l'intervalle, si les conditions suivantes sont réunies :

a) la date de production de la demande d'enregistrement au Canada ne dépasse pas de plus de six mois la production, dans un pays de l'Union, ou pour un pays de l'Union, de la plus ancienne demande d'enregistrement de la même

(b) the applicant files a request for priority in the prescribed time and manner and informs the Registrar of the filing date and country or office of filing of the application on which the request is based;

(c) the applicant, at the filing date of the application in Canada, is a citizen or national of or domiciled in a country of the Union or has a real and effective industrial or commercial establishment in a country of the Union; and

(d) the applicant furnishes, in accordance with any request under subsections (2) and (3), evidence necessary to fully establish the applicant's right to priority.

(2) Section 34 of the Act is amended by adding the following after subsection (3):

Withdrawal of request

(4) An applicant may, in the prescribed time and manner, withdraw a request for priority.

Extension

(5) An applicant is not permitted to apply under section 47 for an extension of the six-month period referred to in paragraph (1)(a) until that period has ended, and the Registrar is not permitted to extend the period by more than seven days.

— 2014, c. 32, s. 34

34 Subsection 37(1) of the Act is amended by striking out "or" at the end of paragraph (b), by adding "or" at the end of paragraph (c) and by replacing the portion after paragraph (c) with the following:

(d) the trade-mark is not distinctive.

If the Registrar is not so satisfied, the Registrar shall cause the application to be advertised in the prescribed manner.

— 2014, c. 32, s. 35

35 Subsections 38(6) to (8) of the Act are replaced by the following:

Power to strike

(6) At the applicant's request, the Registrar may — at any time before the day on which the applicant files a counter statement — strike all or part of the statement of opposition if the statement or part of it

(a) is not based on any of the grounds set out in subsection (2); or

(b) does not set out a ground of opposition in sufficient detail to enable the applicant to reply to it.

marque de commerce, ou sensiblement la même, en liaison avec le même genre de produits ou services;

b) le requérant produit une demande de priorité selon les modalités prescrites et informe le registraire du nom du pays ou du bureau où a été produite la demande d'enregistrement sur laquelle la demande de priorité est fondée, ainsi que de la date de production de cette demande d'enregistrement;

c) à la date de production de la demande d'enregistrement au Canada, le requérant est un citoyen ou ressortissant d'un pays de l'Union, ou y est domicilié, ou y a un établissement industriel ou commercial effectif et sérieux;

d) le requérant, sur demande faite en application des paragraphes (2) ou (3), fournit toute preuve nécessaire pour établir pleinement son droit à la priorité.

(2) L'article 34 de la même loi est modifié par adjonction, après le paragraphe (3), de ce qui suit :

Retrait

(4) Le requérant peut, selon les modalités prescrites, retirer sa demande de priorité.

Prolongation

(5) Le requérant ne peut demander la prolongation, sous le régime de l'article 47, de la période de six mois prévue à l'alinéa (1)a) qu'après l'expiration de celle-ci. Le registraire peut la prolonger d'au plus sept jours.

— 2014, ch. 32, art. 34

34 Le paragraphe 37(1) de la même loi est modifié par adjonction, après l'alinéa c), de ce qui suit :

d) la marque de commerce n'est pas distinctive.

— 2014, ch. 32, art. 35

35 Les paragraphes 38(6) à (8) de la même loi sont remplacés par ce qui suit :

Pouvoir du registraire

(6) Avant le jour où le requérant produit la contre-déclaration, le registraire peut, à la demande de celui-ci, radier tout ou partie de la déclaration d'opposition dans l'un ou l'autre des cas suivants :

a) la déclaration ou la partie en cause de celle-ci n'est pas fondée sur l'un des motifs énoncés au paragraphe (2);

b) la déclaration ou la partie en cause de celle-ci ne contient pas assez de détails au sujet de l'un ou l'autre des motifs pour permettre au requérant d'y répondre.

Counter statement

(7) The applicant shall file a counter statement with the Registrar and serve a copy on the opponent in the prescribed manner and within the prescribed time after a copy of the statement of opposition has been forwarded to the applicant. The counter statement need only state that the applicant intends to respond to the opposition.

Evidence and hearing

(8) Both the opponent and the applicant shall be given an opportunity, in the prescribed manner and within the prescribed time, to submit evidence and to make representations to the Registrar unless

(a) the opposition is withdrawn or deemed under subsection (10) to have been withdrawn; or

(b) the application is abandoned or deemed under subsection (11) to have been abandoned.

Service

(9) The opponent and the applicant shall, in the prescribed manner and within the prescribed time, serve on each other any evidence and written representations that they submit to the Registrar.

Deemed withdrawal of opposition

(10) The opposition is deemed to have been withdrawn if, in the prescribed circumstances, the opponent does not submit and serve either evidence under subsection (8) or a statement that the opponent does not wish to submit evidence.

Deemed abandonment of application

(11) The application is deemed to have been abandoned if the applicant does not file and serve a counter statement within the time referred to in subsection (7) or if, in the prescribed circumstances, the applicant does not submit and serve either evidence under subsection (8) or a statement that the applicant does not wish to submit evidence.

Decision

(12) After considering the evidence and representations of the opponent and the applicant, the Registrar shall refuse the application, reject the opposition, or refuse the application with respect to one or more of the goods or services specified in it and reject the opposition with respect to the others. He or she shall notify the parties of the decision and the reasons for it.

— 2014, c. 32, s. 36

36 The Act is amended by adding the following after section 39:

Divisional application

39.1 (1) After having filed an application for the registration of a trade-mark, an applicant may limit the original application to one or more of the goods or services that were within its scope and file a divisional application for the

Contre-déclaration

(7) Le requérant produit auprès du registraire une contre-déclaration et en signifie, dans le délai prescrit après qu'une déclaration d'opposition lui a été envoyée, copie à l'opposant de la manière prescrite. La contre-déclaration peut se limiter à énoncer l'intention du requérant de répondre à l'opposition.

Preuve et audition

(8) Il est fourni, selon les modalités prescrites, à l'opposant et au requérant l'occasion de soumettre la preuve sur laquelle ils s'appuient et de se faire entendre par le registraire, sauf dans les cas suivants :

a) l'opposition est retirée ou, au titre du paragraphe (10), réputée l'être;

b) la demande est abandonnée ou, au titre du paragraphe (11), réputée l'être.

Signification

(9) L'opposant et le requérant signifient à l'autre partie, selon les modalités prescrites, la preuve et les observations écrites qu'ils ont présentées au registraire.

Retrait de l'opposition

(10) Si, dans les circonstances prescrites, l'opposant omet de soumettre et de signifier la preuve visée au paragraphe (8) ou une déclaration énonçant son désir de ne pas soumettre de preuve, l'opposition est réputée retirée.

Abandon de la demande

(11) Si le requérant omet de produire et de signifier une contre-déclaration dans le délai visé au paragraphe (7) ou si, dans les circonstances prescrites, il omet de soumettre et de signifier la preuve visée au paragraphe (8) ou une déclaration énonçant son désir de ne pas soumettre de preuve, la demande est réputée abandonnée.

Décision

(12) Après avoir examiné la preuve et les observations des parties, le registraire rejette la demande, rejette l'opposition ou rejette la demande à l'égard de l'un ou plusieurs des produits ou services spécifiés dans celle-ci et rejette l'opposition à l'égard des autres. Il notifie aux parties sa décision motivée.

— 2014, ch. 32, art. 36

36 La même loi est modifiée par adjonction, après l'article 39, de ce qui suit :

Demande divisionnaire

39.1 (1) Après avoir produit la demande d'enregistrement d'une marque de commerce, le requérant peut restreindre cette demande originale à l'un ou plusieurs des produits ou services visés par celle-ci et produire une demande

registration of the same trade-mark in association with any other goods or services that were

(a) within the scope of the original application on its filing date; and

(b) within the scope of the original application as advertised, if the divisional application is filed on or after the day on which the application is advertised under subsection 37(1).

Identification

(2) A divisional application shall indicate that it is a divisional application and shall, in the prescribed manner, identify the corresponding original application.

Separate application

(3) A divisional application is a separate application, including with respect to the payment of any fees.

Filing date

(4) A divisional application's filing date is deemed to be the original application's filing date.

Division of divisional application

(5) A divisional application may itself be divided under subsection (1), in which case this section applies as if that divisional application were an original application.

— 2014, c. 32, s. 37(1)

37 (1) Subsection 40(1) of the Act is replaced by the following:

Registration of trade-marks

40 (1) When an application for the registration of a trade-mark, other than a proposed trade-mark or proposed certification mark, is allowed, the Registrar shall register the trade-mark and issue a certificate of its registration.

— 2014, c. 32, s. 37(3)

37 (3) Subsection 40(3) of the Act is replaced by the following:

Proposed certification mark

(2.1) When an application for the registration of a proposed certification mark is allowed, the Registrar shall give notice to the applicant accordingly and shall register the certification mark and issue a certificate of registration on receipt of a declaration that the use of the certification mark in Canada, in association with the goods or services specified in the application, has been commenced by an entity that is licensed by or with the authority of the applicant to use the certification mark.

divisionnaire pour l'enregistrement de la même marque de commerce en liaison avec d'autres produits ou services qui étaient visés par la demande originale à la date de sa production et, si la demande divisionnaire est produite le jour où la demande originale est annoncée en application du paragraphe 37(1) ou après ce jour, visés par celle-ci dans sa version annoncée.

Précisions

(2) La demande divisionnaire précise qu'il s'agit d'une demande divisionnaire et indique, de la façon prescrite, la demande originale correspondante.

Demande distincte

(3) La demande divisionnaire constitue une demande distincte, notamment pour le paiement des droits.

Date de la demande divisionnaire

(4) La date de production de la demande divisionnaire est réputée être celle de la demande originale.

Division d'une demande divisionnaire

(5) La demande divisionnaire peut elle-même être divisée en vertu du paragraphe (1), auquel cas, le présent article s'applique au même titre que si cette demande était la demande originale.

— 2014, ch. 32, par. 37(1)

37 (1) Le paragraphe 40(1) de la même loi est remplacé par ce qui suit :

Enregistrement des marques de commerce

40 (1) Lorsqu'une demande d'enregistrement d'une marque de commerce, autre qu'une marque de commerce ou de certification projetées, est admise, le registraire enregistre la marque de commerce et délivre un certificat de son enregistrement.

— 2014, ch. 32, par. 37(3)

37 (3) Le paragraphe 40(3) de la même loi est remplacé par ce qui suit :

Marque de certification projetée

(2.1) Lorsqu'une demande d'enregistrement d'une marque de certification projetée est admise, le registraire en donne avis au requérant. Il enregistre la marque de certification et délivre un certificat de son enregistrement après avoir reçu une déclaration portant qu'une entité à qui est octroyée, par le requérant ou avec son autorisation, une licence d'emploi de la marque de certification a commencé à employer la marque de certification au Canada, en liaison avec les produits ou services spécifiés dans la demande.

Abandonment of application

(3) An application for registration referred to in subsection (2) or (2.1) is deemed to be abandoned if the Registrar has not received the declaration before the later of

(a) six months after the date of the Registrar's notice, and

(b) three years after the filing date of the application in Canada.

— 2014, c. 32, s. 38

38 (1) The portion of subsection 41(1) of the Act before paragraph (a) is replaced by the following:

Amendments to register

41 (1) The Registrar may, on application by the registered owner of a trade-mark made in the prescribed manner and on payment of the prescribed fee, make any of the following amendments to the register:

(2) Subsection 41(1) of the Act is amended by striking out "or" at the end of paragraph (d), by adding "or" at the end of paragraph (e) and by adding the following after paragraph (e):

(f) subject to the regulations, merge registrations of the trade-mark that stem, under section 39.1, from the same original application.

(3) Section 41 of the Act is amended by adding the following after subsection (2):

Obvious error

(3) The Registrar may, within six months after an entry in the register is made, correct any error in the entry that is obvious from the documents relating to the registered trade-mark in question that are, at the time that the entry is made, on file in the Registrar's office.

— 2014, c. 32, s. 39

39 Subsection 45(1) of the Act is replaced by the following:

Registrar may request evidence of user

45 (1) The Registrar may at any time — and, at the written request made after three years from the date of the registration of a trade-mark by any person who pays the prescribed fee, the Registrar shall, unless he or she sees good reason to the contrary — give notice to the registered owner of the trade-mark requiring the registered owner to furnish within three months an affidavit or a statutory declaration showing, with respect to all the goods or services specified in the registration or to those that the Registrar may specify in the notice, whether the trade-mark was in use in Canada at any time during the three-year period immediately preceding the date of the notice and, if not, the date when it was last so in use and the reason for the absence of such use since that date.

— 2014, c. 32, s. 40

40 Section 48 of the Act is amended by adding the following after subsection (3):

Removal of registration

(4) The Registrar shall remove the registration of a transfer of a registered trade-mark on being furnished with evidence satisfactory to him or her that the transfer should not have been registered.

— 2014, c. 32, s. 41

41 Section 49 of the Act and the heading before it are replaced by the following:

Change of Purpose in Use of Trade-mark

Change of purpose

49 If a sign or combination of signs is used by a person as a trade-mark for any of the purposes or in any of the manners mentioned in the definition **certification mark** or **trade-mark** in section 2, no application for the registration of the trade-mark shall be refused and no registration of the trade-mark shall be expunged, amended or held invalid merely on the ground that the person or a predecessor in title uses the trade-mark or has used it for any other of those purposes or in any other of those manners.

— 2014, c. 32, s. 47

47 Subsection 57(1) of the Act is replaced by the following:

Exclusive jurisdiction of Federal Court

57 (1) The Federal Court has exclusive original jurisdiction, on the application of the Registrar or of any person interested, to order that any entry in the register be struck out or amended on the ground that at the date of the application the entry as it appears on the register does not accurately express or define the existing rights of the person appearing to be the registered owner of the trade-mark.

— 2014, c. 32, s. 48

48 Section 60 of the Act is replaced by the following:

Registrar to transmit documents

60 When any appeal or application has been made to the Federal Court under any of the provisions of this Act, the Registrar shall, at the request of any of the parties to the proceedings and on the payment of the prescribed fee, transmit to the Court all documents on file in the Registrar's office relating to the matters in question in those proceedings, or copies of those documents certified by the Registrar.

— 2014, c. 32, s. 49

49 Section 64 of the Act is replaced by the following:

Electronic form and means

64 (1) Subject to the regulations, any document, information or fee that is provided to the Registrar under this Act may be provided in any electronic form, and by any electronic means, that is specified by the Registrar.

Collection, storage, etc.

(2) Subject to the regulations, the Registrar may use electronic means to create, collect, receive, store, transfer, distribute, publish, certify or otherwise deal with documents or information.

Definition

(3) In this section, *electronic*, in reference to a form or means, includes optical, magnetic and other similar forms or means.

— 2014, c. 32, s. 50

50 (1) Paragraphs 65(a) and (b) of the Act are replaced by the following:

(a) the form of the register to be kept under this Act, and of the entries to be made in it;

(b) applications to the Registrar;

(b.1) the merger of registrations under paragraph 41(1)(f), including, for the purpose of renewal under section 46, the deemed day of registration or last renewal;

(2) Paragraph 65(d) of the Act is replaced by the following:

(d) certificates of registration;

(3) Section 65 of the Act is amended by striking out "and" at the end of paragraph (d.1), by adding "and" at the end of paragraph (e) and by adding the following after paragraph (e):

(f) the provision of documents, information or fees to the Registrar under this Act, including the time at which they are deemed to be received by the Registrar.

— 2014, c. 32, s. 55

Replacement of "date of filing"

55 The English version of the Act is amended by replacing "date of filing" with "filing date" in the following provisions:

— 2014, ch. 32, art. 49

49 L'article 64 de la même loi est remplacé par ce qui suit :

Moyens et forme électroniques

64 (1) Sous réserve des règlements, les documents, renseignements ou droits fournis au registraire sous le régime de la présente loi peuvent lui être fournis sous la forme électronique — ou en utilisant les moyens électroniques — qu'il précise.

Collecte, mise en mémoire, etc.

(2) Sous réserve des règlements, le registraire peut faire usage d'un moyen électronique pour créer, recueillir, recevoir, mettre en mémoire, transférer, diffuser, publier, certifier ou traiter de quelque autre façon des documents ou des renseignements.

Moyens et formes optiques ou magnétiques

(3) Au présent article, la mention de moyens électroniques ou de la forme électronique vise aussi, respectivement, les moyens ou formes optiques ou magnétiques ainsi que les autres moyens ou formes semblables.

— 2014, ch. 32, art. 50

50 (1) Les alinéas 65a) et b) de la même loi sont remplacés par ce qui suit :

a) sur la forme du registre à tenir en conformité avec la présente loi, et des inscriptions à y faire;

b) sur les demandes au registraire;

b.1) sur la fusion d'enregistrements sous le régime de l'alinéa 41(1)f), notamment sur la date réputée, pour les fins du renouvellement prévu à l'article 46, de l'enregistrement ou du dernier renouvellement;

(2) L'alinéa 65d) de la même loi est remplacé par ce qui suit :

d) sur les certificats d'enregistrement;

(3) L'article 65 de la même loi est modifié par adjonction, après l'alinéa e), de ce qui suit :

f) sur la fourniture de documents, de renseignements et de droits au registraire sous le régime de la présente loi, notamment sur le moment où il est réputé les avoir reçus.

— 2014, ch. 32, art. 55

Remplacement de « date of filing »

55 Dans les passages ci-après de la version anglaise de la même loi, « date of filing » est remplacé par « filing date » :

(a) the portion of subsection 16(2) before paragraph (a); and

(b) subsection 21(1).

— 2014, c. 32, s. 57

Amending the register

57 The Registrar of Trade-marks may amend the register kept under section 26 of the *Trade-marks Act* to reflect the amendments to that Act that are made by this Act.

— 2015, c. 36, s. 67

67 Paragraph 65(j) of the Act is replaced by the following:

(j) respecting the payment of fees to the Registrar, the amount of those fees and the circumstances in which any fees previously paid may be refunded in whole or in part;

(j.1) authorizing the Registrar to waive, subject to any prescribed terms and conditions, the payment of a fee if the Registrar is satisfied that the circumstances justify it;

— 2015, c. 36, s. 68

68 Section 66 of the Act is replaced by the following:

Time period extended

66 (1) If a time period fixed under this Act for doing anything ends on a prescribed day or a day that is designated by the Registrar, that time period is extended to the next day that is not a prescribed day or a designated day.

Power to designate day

(2) The Registrar may, on account of unforeseen circumstances and if the Registrar is satisfied that it is in the public interest to do so, designate any day for the purposes of subsection (1). If a day is designated, the Registrar shall inform the public of that fact on the website of the Canadian Intellectual Property Office.

— 2015, c. 36, s. 69

69 (1) Paragraphs 70(1)(a) and (b) of the Act are replaced by the following:

(a) the provisions of this Act as they read immediately before the day on which section 342 of the *Economic Action Plan 2014 Act, No. 1* comes into force, other than subsections 6(2) to (4), sections 28 and 36, subsections 38(6) to (8) and sections 39, 40 and 66;

(b) the definition ***Nice Classification*** in section 2, subsections 6(2) to (4), sections 28 and 36, subsections 38(6) to

(12), sections 39 and 40 and subsections 48(3) and (5), as enacted by the *Economic Action Plan 2014 Act, No. 1*; and

(c) section 66, as enacted by the *Economic Action Plan 2015 Act, No. 1*.

(2) Subsection 70(2) of the Act is replaced by the following:

Regulations

(2) For greater certainty, a regulation made under section 65 applies to an application referred to in subsection (1), unless the regulation provides otherwise.

— 2015, c. 36, ss. 70(1), (4) to (7)

2014, c. 20

70 (1) In this section, *other Act* means the *Economic Action Plan 2014 Act, No. 1*.

(4) If section 67 of this Act comes into force on the same day as section 357 of the other Act, then that section 357 is deemed to have come into force before that section 67.

(5) If subsection 367(99) of the other Act produces its effects before subsection 69(1) of this Act comes into force, then that subsection 69(1) is replaced by the following:

69 (1) Paragraphs 70(1)(a) and (b) of the Act are replaced by the following:

(a) the provisions of this Act as they read immediately before the day on which section 342 of the *Economic Action Plan 2014 Act, No. 1* comes into force, other than subsections 6(2) to (4), sections 28, 29 and 36, subsections 38(6) to (8) and sections 39, 40 and 66;

(b) the definition **Nice Classification** in section 2, subsections 6(2) to (4), sections 28 to 29.1 and 36, subsections 38(6) to (12), sections 39 and 40 and subsections 48(3) and (5), as enacted by the *Economic Action Plan 2014 Act, No. 1*; and

(c) section 66, as enacted by the *Economic Action Plan 2015 Act, No. 1*.

(6) If subsection 69(1) of this Act comes into force before subsection 367(99) of the other Act has produced its effects, then that subsection 367(99) is replaced by the following:

(99) On the first day on which both section 359 of this Act and section 28 of the other Act are in force, subsection 70(1) of the *Trademarks Act* is replaced by the following:

48(3) et (5), édictés par la *Loi nº 1 sur le plan d'action économique de 2014*;

c) par l'article 66, édicté par la *Loi nº 1 sur le plan d'action économique de 2015*.

(2) Le paragraphe 70(2) de la même loi est remplacé par ce qui suit :

Règlements

(2) Il est entendu que tout règlement pris en vertu de l'article 65 s'applique à la demande visée au paragraphe (1), sauf indication contraire prévue par ce règlement.

— 2015, ch. 36, par. 70(1) et (4) à (7)

2014, ch. 20

70 (1) Au présent article, *autre loi* s'entend de la *Loi nº 1 sur le plan d'action économique de 2014*.

(4) Si l'entrée en vigueur de l'article 67 de la présente loi et celle de l'article 357 de l'autre loi sont concomitantes, cet article 357 est réputé être entré en vigueur avant cet article 67.

(5) Si le paragraphe 367(99) de l'autre loi produit ses effets avant l'entrée en vigueur du paragraphe 69(1) de la présente loi, ce paragraphe 69(1) est remplacé par ce qui suit :

69 (1) Les alinéas 70(1)a) et b) de la même loi sont remplacés par ce qui suit :

a) par les dispositions de la présente loi, dans leur version antérieure à cette date, à l'exception des paragraphes 6(2) à (4), des articles 28, 29 et 36, des paragraphes 38(6) à (8) et des articles 39, 40 et 66;

b) par la définition de **classification de Nice** à l'article 2, les paragraphes 6(2) à (4), les articles 28 à 29.1 et 36, les paragraphes 38(6) à (12), les articles 39 et 40 et les paragraphes 48(3) et (5), édictés par la *Loi nº 1 sur le plan d'action économique de 2014*;

c) par l'article 66, édicté par la *Loi nº 1 sur le plan d'action économique de 2015*.

(6) Si le paragraphe 69(1) de la présente loi entre en vigueur avant que le paragraphe 367(99) de l'autre loi ne produise ses effets, ce paragraphe 367(99) est remplacé par ce qui suit :

(99) Dès le premier jour où l'article 359 de la présente loi et l'article 28 de l'autre loi sont tous deux en vigueur, le paragraphe 70(1) de la *Loi sur les marques de commerce* est remplacé par ce qui suit :

Trade-marks
AMENDMENTS NOT IN FORCE

Application advertised

70 (1) An application for registration that has been advertised under subsection 37(1) before the day on which section 342 of the *Economic Action Plan 2014 Act, No. 1* comes into force shall be dealt with and disposed of in accordance with

(a) the provisions of this Act as they read immediately before the day on which section 342 of the *Economic Action Plan 2014 Act, No. 1* comes into force, other than subsections 6(2) to (4), sections 28, 29 and 36, subsections 38(6) to (8) and sections 39, 40 and 66;

(b) the definition *Nice Classification* in section 2, subsections 6(2) to (4), sections 28 to 29.1 and 36, subsections 38(6) to (12), sections 39 and 40 and subsections 48(3) and (5), as enacted by the *Economic Action Plan 2014 Act, No. 1*; and

(c) section 66, as enacted by the *Economic Action Plan 2015 Act, No. 1*.

(7) If subsection 69(1) of this Act comes into force on the day on which subsection 367(99) of the other Act produces its effects, then

(a) that subsection 69(1) is deemed never to have come into force and is repealed; and

(b) paragraphs 70(1)(a) and (b) of the *Trademarks Act* are replaced by the following:

(a) the provisions of this Act as they read immediately before the day on which section 342 of the *Economic Action Plan 2014 Act, No. 1* comes into force, other than subsections 6(2) to (4), sections 28, 29 and 36, subsections 38(6) to (8) and sections 39, 40 and 66;

(b) the definition *Nice Classification* in section 2, subsections 6(2) to (4), sections 28 to 29.1 and 36, subsections 38(6) to (12), sections 39 and 40 and subsections 48(3) and (5), as enacted by the *Economic Action Plan 2014 Act, No. 1*; and

(c) section 66, as enacted by the *Economic Action Plan 2015 Act, No. 1*.

— 2017, c. 6, s. 60

1994, c. 47, s. 190(2)

60 The definitions *confusing* and *geographical indication* in section 2 of the *Trade-marks Act* are replaced by the following:

confusing, when applied as an adjective to a trade-mark or trade-name, means, except in sections 11.13 and 11.21, a trade-mark or trade-name the use of which would cause confusion in the manner and circumstances described in section 6; (*créant de la confusion*)

Demande annoncée

70 (1) La demande d'enregistrement qui a été annoncée, au titre du paragraphe 37(1), avant la date d'entrée en vigueur de l'article 342 de la *Loi n° 1 sur le plan d'action économique de 2014* est régie, à la fois :

a) par les dispositions de la présente loi, dans leur version antérieure à cette date, à l'exception des paragraphes 6(2) à (4), des articles 28, 29 et 36, des paragraphes 38(6) à (8) et des articles 39, 40 et 66;

b) par la définition de *classification de Nice* à l'article 2, les paragraphes 6(2) à (4), les articles 28 à 29.1 et 36, les paragraphes 38(6) à (12), les articles 39 et 40 et les paragraphes 48(3) et (5), édictés par la *Loi n° 1 sur le plan d'action économique de 2014*;

c) par l'article 66, édicté par la *Loi n° 1 sur le plan d'action économique de 2015*.

(7) Si le paragraphe 69(1) de la présente loi entre en vigueur le jour où le paragraphe 367(99) de l'autre loi produit ses effets :

a) ce paragraphe 69(1) est réputé ne pas être entré en vigueur et est abrogé;

b) les alinéas 70(1)a) et b) de la *Loi sur les marques de commerce* sont remplacés par ce qui suit :

a) par les dispositions de la présente loi, dans leur version antérieure à cette date, à l'exception des paragraphes 6(2) à (4), des articles 28, 29 et 36, des paragraphes 38(6) à (8) et des articles 39, 40 et 66;

b) par la définition de *classification de Nice* à l'article 2, les paragraphes 6(2) à (4), les articles 28 à 29.1 et 36, les paragraphes 38(6) à (12), les articles 39 et 40 et les paragraphes 48(3) et (5), édictés par la *Loi n° 1 sur le plan d'action économique de 2014*;

c) par l'article 66, édicté par la *Loi n° 1 sur le plan d'action économique de 2015*.

— 2017, ch. 6, art. 60

1994, ch. 47, par. 190(2)

60 Les définitions de *créant de la confusion* et *indication géographique*, à l'article 2 de la *Loi sur les marques de commerce*, sont respectivement remplacées par ce qui suit :

créant de la confusion Sauf aux articles 11.13 et 11.21, s'entend au sens de l'article 6 lorsque employé à l'égard d'une marque de commerce ou d'un nom commercial. (*confusing*)

indication géographique Indication désignant un vin ou spiritueux ou un produit agricole ou aliment d'une catégorie figurant à l'annexe comme étant originaire du territoire d'un

APPENDIX A

Certain Imperial Acts and Parts of Acts relating to Property and Civil Rights that were Consolidated in The Revised Statutes of Ontario, 1897, Volume III, pursuant to Chapter 13 of the Statutes of Ontario, 1902, that are not repealed by the Revised Statutes of Ontario, 1980 and are in force in Ontario subject thereto.

R.S.O. 1897, CHAPTER 322

An Act respecting Certain Rights and Liberties of the People

HIS MAJESTY, by and with the advice and consent of the Legislative Assembly of the Province of Ontario, enacts as follows:—

* * * * * * * * *

2. No man shall be taken or imprisoned nor prejudged of life or limb, nor be disseized or put out of his freehold, franchises, or liberties, or free customs, nor be outlawed, or exiled, or any otherwise destroyed, unless he be brought in to answer and prejudged of the same by due course of law; nor shall the King pass upon him, nor condemn him, but by lawful judgment of his peers, or by the law of the land; and the King shall sell to no man, nor deny or defer to any man, either justice or right. 25 Edw. I, (Magna Carta), c. 29; 5 Edw. III, c. 9; 25 Edw. III, st. 5, c. 4; and 28 Edw. III, c. 3. *Imprisonment, etc., contrary to law. Administration of justice.*

3. It is provided, agreed, and granted, that all persons, as well of high as of low estate, shall receive justice in the King's court; and none from henceforth shall take any revenge or distress of his own authority, without award of the King's court, though he have damage or injury, whereby he would have amends of his neighbour, either higher or lower. 52 Hen. III, (St. of Marlbridge), c. 1. *Of wrongful distresses, or defiances of the King's courts.*

R.S.O. 1897, CHAPTER 323

An Act concerning Monopolies, and Dispensation with penal laws, etc.

(Commonly called "THE STATUTE OF MONOPOLIES")

HIS MAJESTY, by and with the advice and consent of the Legislative Assembly of the Province of Ontario, enacts as follows:—

1. All monopolies, and all commissions, grants, licenses, charters, and letters patents, heretofore made or granted, or hereafter to be made or granted, to any person whatsoever, of or for the sole buying, selling, making, working, or using, of any thing within Ontario, or of any other monopolies, or of power, liberty, or faculty, to dispense with any others or to give license or toleration to do, use or exercise anything against the tenor or purport of any law or statute, or to give, or make, any warrant for any such dispensation, license, or toleration, to be had or made, or to agree or compound with any others for any penalty or forfeitures limited by any statute, or of any grant or promise of the benefit, profit or commodity of any forfeiture, penalty or sum of money that is, or shall be, due by any statute, before judgment thereupon had, and all proclamations, inhibitions, restraints, warrants of assistance, and all other matters and things whatsoever any way tending to the instituting, erecting, strengthening, furthering, or countenancing, of the same, or any of them, are altogether contrary to the laws of Ontario, and so are and shall be utterly void and of none effect, and in no wise to be put in use or execution. 21 Jac. I, c. 3, s. 1. *[All monopolies and grants, etc., thereof, or of dispensations and penalties declared void.]*

2. All monopolies and all such commissions, grants, licenses, charters, letters patents, proclamations, inhibitions, restraints, warrants of assistance, and all other matters and things tending as aforesaid, and the force and validity of them and every of them ought to be, and shall be forever hereafter examined, heard, tried and determined, by and according to the common law, and not otherwise. 21 Jac. I, c. 3, s. 2. *[Validity of all monopolies, and of all such grants, etc., shall be tried by the common law.]*

3. All persons whatsoever, shall stand and be disabled and incapable to have, use, exercise or put in use, any monopoly, or any such commission, grant, license, charters, letters patents, proclamation, inhibition, restraint, warrant of *[All persons disabled to use such grants, monopolies, etc.]*

APPENDIX A—MONOPOLIES

assistance, or other matter or thing tending as aforesaid, or any liberty, power or faculty, grounded, or pretended to be grounded, upon them, or any of them. 21 Jac. I, c. 3, s. 3.

Party aggrieved by any monopoly or grant, etc., shall recover treble damages by action in the Supreme Court with costs.

4. If any person shall be hindered, grieved, disturbed, or disquieted, or his goods or chattels any way seized, attached, distrained, taken, carried away, or detained, by occasion or pretext of any monopoly, or of any such commission, grant, license, power, liberty, faculty, letters patents, proclamation, inhibition, restraint, warrant of assistance, or other matter or thing tending as aforesaid, and will sue to be relieved in or for any of the premises, then and in every such case, the same person shall have his remedy for the same by action to be grounded upon this statute, the same action to be heard and determined in the Supreme Court against him by whom he shall be so hindered, grieved, disturbed, or disquieted, or against him by whom his goods or chattels shall be so seized, attached, distrained, taken, carried away, or detained, wherein, all and every such person which shall be so hindered, grieved, disturbed, or disquieted, or whose goods or chattels shall be so seized, attached, distrained, taken, or carried away, or detained, shall recover three times so much as the damages which he sustained by means or occasion of being so hindered, grieved, disturbed, or disquieted, or by means of having his goods or chattels seized, attached, distrained, taken, carried away, or detained; and

Action not to be unduly delayed.

in such suits, or for the staying or delaying thereof, no privilege, injunction or order of restraint, shall be in any wise prayed, granted, admitted, or allowed; and no person shall, after notice given that the action depending is grounded upon this statute, cause or procure any action grounded upon this statute to be stayed, or delayed, before judgment, by colour or means of any order, warrant, power or authority, save only of the court wherein such action as aforesaid shall be brought and depending, or after judgment had upon such action, shall cause or procure the execution of, or upon, any such judgment to be stayed or delayed by colour or means of any order, warrant, power or authority, save only by due process of law. 21 Jac. I, c. 3, s. 4.

Proviso for patents for new inventions.

5. Provided also, that any declaration before mentioned shall not extend to any letters patents, and grants of privilege, made, or hereafter to be made, of the sole working or making of any manner of new manufactures within Ontario, to the true and first inventor of such manufactures, which others at the time of making such letters patents and grants shall not use, so as also they be not contrary to the law, nor mischievous to the state, by raising prices of commodities at home, or hurt of trade, or generally inconvenient; but the

APPENDIX A—MONOPOLIES

same shall be of such force as they should be if this Act had never been made, and of none other. 21 Jac. I, c. 3, s. 6.

6. Provided also that this Act or anything therein contained shall not in any wise extend, or be prejudicial, to any grant, privilege, power, or authority whatsoever, heretofore made, granted, allowed, or confirmed, by any Act of Parliament now in force in Ontario, so long as the same shall so continue in force. 21 Jac. I, c. 3, s. 7.
<small>Proviso for existing grants by Act of Parliament.</small>

7. Provided also that this Act shall not extend to any warrant or Privy Seal made or directed, or to be made or directed by His Majesty, his heirs or successors, to the judges of the Supreme Court, justices of the peace, and other justices for the time being, having power to hear and determine offences done against any penal statute, to compound for the forfeitures of any penal statute depending in suit and question before them, or any of them, respectively, after plea pleaded by the party defendant. 21 Jac. I, c. 3, s. 8.
<small>Proviso for warrants to justices to compound penalties.</small>

456